Frank Schoonmaker's

ENCYCLOPEDIA OF WINE

Frank Schoonmaker's
ENCYCLOPEDIA
OF
WINE

HASTINGS HOUSE · PUBLISHERS

New York

Published simultaneously in Canada
by Saunders of Toronto, Ltd.
Don Mills, Ontario

SBN: 8038 - 1891-2

Library of Congress Catalog Card Number: 64-19083

Printed in the United States of America
Designed by Al Lichtenberg

Contents

Chapter Heading Vignettes Courtesy House Beautiful *Magazine*

ABBOCCATO — (Ah-bo-kah-toe) — Italian word which, when applied to wine, means sweet or semi-sweet. It is the equivalent of the French *moelleux*, and is used particularly in connection with the wines of Orvieto (*see*), which are customarily classified as either *secco* (dry) or *abboccato* (semi-sweet).

ACHAEA — (Ah-*key*-ya) — Greek province, forming the southern shore of the Gulf of Corinth in the Peloponnesus; produces a considerable quantity of red and white table wine, particularly in the neighborhood of Patras.

ACID — All wine, like lemonade, has a certain amount of acid — if too little, it is flat and insipid and unappetizing. But a wine that can be described as "acid" has too much. If this is the natural tartaric and malic acid of the grape (like lemonade in which one has put too much lemon juice) the wine is better described as "tart." If there is the taste or odor of vinegar (acetic acid) the wine is spoiled or sour. The two kinds of acidity are easy to tell apart — one sniff is enough. A tart wine may not be to one's taste; a spoiled or sour wine is not fit to drink.

ACID, ACETIC — The acid of vinegar, CH_3COOH. It is invariably and exclusively the result of a second, *acetic* fermentation in an already fermented and generally potable liquid such as beer, cider or wine. If these did not exist, neither would vinegar; the word comes directly from the French *vin aigre*, sharp or sour wine, and some purists have claimed that it should therefore never be used for cider or malt or even pineapple

1

vinegar. This, of course, is nonsense. Traces of acetic acid are present in all wines, especially old wines, but generally cannot be detected by taste or smell unless over one part per thousand, or .1%. White wines with over .12% and red wines with over .14% of acetic acid must be labeled "substandard" according to American law. This limit is arbitrary, possibly unfair in some instances, but on the whole, sound. Acetic fermentation can only take place in the presence of air, and is produced by a microorganism called the Acetobacter, or mycoderma aceti. The chemical formula is as follows:

Alcohol + Oxygen	Acetobacter	Acetic Acid		Water
$CH_3CH_2OH + O_2$	$\longrightarrow$	CH_3COOH	$+$	H_2O

An excess of acetic acid in a wine is almost always evidence of poor or careless cellar-work, and is completely inexcusable in a wine under five years old, providing, of course, that the wine has been properly stored since leaving the winery. Even wine with an excess of acetic acid will usually not become vinegar (*see*) unless "mother of vinegar" (a concentrate or culture of Acetobacter) is present. Wine experts and technicians generally (and accurately) call acetic acid, "volatile acid" (*see*); by laymen, a wine that has too much of it is often described as "spoiled" or "sour" or "gone."

ACIDITY, FIXED — The expert's term for the normal fruit acids which a wine contains — tartaric, malic, citric, lactic, etc.

ACIDITY, REAL — This is a layman's term for what a chemist would call the pH of a wine, the *intensity* of the acidity it contains. Without attempting to be at all technical, it is possible to say that some acids are more intense than others, so that wines may have the same fixed or same total acidity and yet a quite different pH. In general, liquids with a pH of 7 are neither acid nor alkaline, but neutral; those with a pH of 5 or less will turn litmus paper red (acid) and those with a pH of 8 or over will turn litmus paper blue (alkaline). The lower the pH of a wine, therefore, the more intense its acid. A Folle Blanche grown in a cool district in California may have a pH of 3.05, for example, and a Muscat from a warm district a pH of 3.95. These are extremes; the first will taste very tart, and the second extremely neutral and flat.

ACIDITY, TOTAL — Fixed acidity plus volatile acidity in a wine. A technician's term.

ACIDITY, VOLATILE — Acetic acid (*see*). The acid of spoiled wine. Easily detected, even by a beginner, if as much as ⅐ of 1% is present in a wine.

ADEGA — (Ah-*day*-gah) — A wine warehouse or cellar, though generally above ground, in Portugal. The equivalent of a *chai* in France or a *bodega* in Spain.

ADIGE — (*Odd*-dee-gee) — Important river of northern Italy, draining the picturesque and interesting vineyard district of the Italian Tyrol (*see*) as well as Valpolicella (*see*), running through Verona and empty-

2

ing into the Adriatic south of Venice. *See* also Alto Adige, Bolzano, Trentino.

AFFENTHALER — (*Ah*-fen-tah-lair) — German red wine from the Black Forest foothills near Baden-Baden. It is made mostly from the Spätburgunder or Pinot Noir grape, but is light in color, almost a *rosé,* and its quality is hardly more than passable. Its odd name has nevertheless given it a certain notoriety, like Zeller Schwarze Katz and Kröver Nacktarsch: *Affe,* in German, means "ape" or "monkey," and an Affenthaler is therefore a wine from "monkey valley." What is shipped to America often has a plastic gold-colored monkey wrapped around the bottle, but the wine, needless to say, is made no better by this gimmick.

ALSO, a red-wine grape widely grown in Württemberg, though generally interplanted with the Trollinger or other varieties. Its wine is undistinguished.

AFRICA — This vast continent produces wine only in its northern and southern extremities, in the Temperate Zones. *See* Algeria, Morocco, Tunisia, South Africa.

AGEING OF WINES — All wines, if properly stored, tend to improve somewhat with age, but, generally speaking, there has been too much emphasis placed on age, as if age itself were a virtue. It can be, but often is not. Every wine has its natural life span, its youth, its prime, its old age, and this pattern varies just as wines vary. Many wines are better when young, and all table wines (light, unfortified wines) lose their freshness and fruit and become "withered" and unattractive if kept too long in cask; all table wines and a few rare exceptions among fortified wines (Vintage Port, for example) improve in bottle even more than in wood, although some of them for only six or eight months, and some for 50 years. In general, 75% of the wine produced in the world is as good when a year old as it is ever likely to be, and will only deteriorate, not improve, after its third birthday. Wines that should generally be consumed by the time they are three years old, and certainly before the age of five, include:
All *vins rosés,* or pink wines, whether from California or France, or elsewhere.
All California white wines except a few made from the Chardonnay, the Pinot Blanc, the Sauvignon Blanc and the Johannisberg Riesling.
Most white Burgundies, the exceptions being those from the finest vineyards in unusually good years. Most of the dryer wines of the Loire and those of Alsace. Almost all Italian wines, the exceptions being a small, select company of reds made from the Nebbiolo grape (Barolo, Gattinara, Barbaresco, Valtellina), a few rare Chiantis, and a handful of others, as Aglianico del Vulture. All German wines except estatebottlings of good producers, superior vineyards and great years. Many dry Graves.
Most Beaujolais, and most of the lesser red wines of France. All California Zinfandels, most Gamays and even some Pinot Noirs.

3

AGLIANICO (Ahl-yan-*nee*-co) — Remarkable red wine, made from the Aglianico grape in the Italian province of Potenza, east of Naples. The better vineyards are planted entirely on the volcanic soil of Monte Vulture; in this isolated and rather backward district, well-equipped cellars are few, and genuine, well-made, unblended Aglianico del Vulture is not easy to come by. However, it is worth looking for — full-bodied, fine, with a notable bouquet. There are few red wines as good, and none better, in central or southern Italy.

AGLY, CÔTES D' — (Coat Dag-lee) — A district producing sweet, full-bodied, fortified wines, not far from the Spanish border, in southern France; as in nearby Rivesaltes and Banyuls (*see*), the principal grape varieties are the Grenache, Muscat and Malvoisie, and the wines must contain a minimum of 15% of alcohol by volume. Production is about 200,000 gallons a year. See Roussillon.

AHR — (Are) — Small river in Western Germany which joins the Rhine north of Coblenz. Its hillside vineyards are planted almost entirely to the Pinot Noir grape (here known as the Spätburgunder) and produce some of the best of Germany's not particularly distinguished red wines. These are rarely exported. The principal wine-producing towns are Ahrweiler, Neuenahr and Walporzheim.

AIGLE — (A-gl) — Swiss white wine of superior quality produced from the Fendant (Chasselas) grape in the Canton of Vaud east of Lake Geneva.

AISNE — (Aine) — French *département* north and east of the Marne, a portion of which is legally part of the Champagne Country and produces some Champagne (roughly 660,000 gallons a year), most of it of second-rate quality.

AIX — (Aches) — *See* Coteaux d'Aix.

ALAMBRADO — (Ahl-ahm-*bra*-doe) — Spanish term meaning a bottle enclosed in open wire netting (*alambre*); a form of packaging widely used in Spain for wines of better than ordinary quality.

ALAMEDA — (Al-ah-*me*-da) — County in northern California, on the east side of San Francisco Bay. One of the North Coast Counties (*see*), its principal vineyards are in the Livermore Valley, southeast of Oakland. These are planted with Sauvignon Blanc, Semillon, Pinot Blanc, Chardonnay and other superior varieties, almost all white; their white wines are among the most appreciated and best of California. Leading vineyards include Wente Bros., Concannon, Cresta Blanca, etc.
For Map, *see* CALIFORNIA.

ALBA — (*Ahl*-bah) — Important town south of Turin in the Italian region of Piedmont; famous for its white truffles; one of the principal centers of fine wine production in northern Italy. Barbaresco (*see*) is some four miles to the east, Barolo (*see*) about eight miles to the southwest.

ALBANA — (Ahl-*bahn*-ah) — Dry or semi-sweet white wine, rather high in alcohol, made from the grape of this name in the region of Emilia, Italy. The best of it comes from the village of Bertinoro, near Forli.

ALBANELLO — (Ahl-bahn-*nel*-lo) — White Sicilian wine made from the grape of this name in the province of Syracuse. High in alcohol, somewhat reminiscent of Marsala, it can be either dry or quite sweet.

ALBANO — (Ahl-*bahn*-no) — Dry, pleasant, inexpensive white wine from the Alban Hills, southeast of Rome. *See* Castelli Romani.

ALBARIZA — (Al-bar-*wreath*-ah) — The extraordinary and typical white chalky soil in the vineyards round Jerez in the Sherry Country of Spain, producing the highest grade Fino Sherries and Manzanillas. There is some similar soil in the Montilla district (*see*).

ALCOHOL — The colorless, volatile spirit, ethyl alcohol, C_2H_6O, is formed by the activity of enzymes secreted by living microorganisms known as yeast cells. These convert the sugar in grape juice into approximately equal parts of alcohol and carbon dioxide gas. This process is fermentation (*see*). Table wines contain from 8 to 14 or 15 per cent of alcohol by volume; fortified wines, i.e., wines to which more alcohol (in the form of brandy or high-proof neutral spirits) has been added, generally contain from 18 to 22 per cent.

ALEATICO — (Ahl-lay-*aht*-tee-co) — Italian grape and the wine, almost always red and generally sweet, made from it. The grape is of the Muscat family and the wine has an unmistakable and often pronounced Muscat flavor. The best of it comes from the island of Elba, and sometimes carries the name of Portoferraio, Elba's principal town.

ALELLA — (Ah-*lel*-ya) — An agreeable white wine from the village of Alella, just north of Barcelona in Spain. One of the most popular table wines of Catalonia, it is generally shipped in tall, slender brown bottles, like those in which Rhine wines go to market; is usually semi-sweet and rather heavily sulphured.

ALGERIA — (French, *Algérie*) — Former French colony, now an independent country on the Mediterranean coast of North Africa, bounded on the east by Tunisia and on the west by Morocco. Beginning about a hundred years ago, vast areas were planted in vineyard by French settlers, over 800,000 acres in all, and by 1959 the annual production was nearly three times that of the United States, roughly 400 million gallons a year. About two-thirds of this huge output was regularly shipped to France — some six times the total gallonage of all French wine exports put together — and nearly a third of the entire Algerian labor force (of course largely Mohammedan and therefore not wine-drinking), was engaged in grape-growing and wine-making. Most of the production was and still is rather common red table wine of 11-14% alcohol; blended with the wines of the Midi (*see*), it formed and still forms the base of France's *vin ordinaire*. Leading grape varieties are the Cinsault, Carignan and Alicante Bouschet.

The superior wines of Algeria are quite another matter, and some of them have been of surprising quality, particularly the reds and a few *rosés* from what the French called "delimited zones of superior quality" (*see* V.D.Q.S.) in the former *départements* of Oran, Alger, Mostaganem and Tlemcen. There are about a dozen such zones, with a total of some 65,000 acres under vineyard and an annual production of about 12 million gallons. The best vineyards are planted in mountainous country, generally from 30 to 50 miles back from the coast, at altitudes ranging from 1,500 to 2,500 feet. From east to west, the leading quality areas are as follows: Aïn-Bessem Bouira (s.e. of the city of Algiers); Medea and Côtes du Zaccar (s. and s.w. of Algiers); Haut-Dahra (near the coast, some hundred miles to the west); Mostaganem and Mostaganem-Kenenda (near the coast, e. of Oran); Aïn-el-Hadjar, Mascara and Coteaux de Mascara (s.e. of Oran); Monts du Tessalah, including Oued-Imbert, M'Silah, Crêtes des Berkèches, Parmentier (s. of Oran) and the Coteaux de Tlemcen (s.w. of Oran, not far from the Moroccan border). The red wine varieties most widely planted include the Carignan, Cinsault, Grenache, Cabernet, Morastel, Mourvèdre, Pinot, etc., with the Faranah, Clairette, Ugni Blanc and Aligoté dominating among the whites.

It is difficult to predict with any degree of confidence, let alone assurance, what will be the future of all this, at present so essential a part of Algeria's economy. A considerable proportion of French *colons* — land owners and technicians — have left the country; many large estates have been taken over and divided, and it is at least somewhat doubtful whether the new owners have the knowledge, organization and technical skills necessary for so major an enterprise. It is an unprecedented problem, to say the least, and if the Algerians succeed (as is to be hoped), it will surely be one of the few times in human history that a people manages to produce, in world competition and on an enormous scale, something that they are unwilling, on account of religious scruples, to consume.

ALICANTE — (Ah-lee-*kahn*-tay) — Wines from the province of this name, south of Valencia, on the Mediterranean coast of Spain. Most of these are sweet red wines, but there is a good deal of sound red Alicante produced which is a passable, inexpensive table wine, rather low in acid, made principally from the Grenache grape, (itself often called the Alicante in southern France).

ALICANTE-BOUSCHET — (Ah-lee-*kahn*-tay - Boo-shay) — One of a number of heavy-bearing, rather common red-wine grapes developed in the 19th century by L. & H. Bouschet, who were seeking a hybrid with deep color and high sugar content for the production of cheap bulk wine in the Midi district of southern France, and in Algeria. Unlike almost all other red wine varieties, it has red juice, being a cross of Teinturier du Cher x Aramon x Grenache. Widely planted in California during the Prohibition years as a "juice grape" for home wine-makers, it still ranks fourth in acreage among California wine grapes; it definitely has no place in any fine wine vineyard.

ALIGOTÉ — (Ah-lee-go-*tay*) — Productive white wine grape of secondary quality, widely grown in Burgundy, where it yields an undistinguished, very agreeable, short-lived white wine — an excellent *vin de carafe* if drunk when young. White Burgundies made from the Aligoté grape must be so labeled, as "Bourgogne-Aligoté"; they are rarely exported, but nearly a million gallons are produced in an average year.

ALMADÉN — (Al-ma-*den*) — California's largest producer of premium table wines, of Champagne, and of Sherry made by the Spanish *solera* process. The original or "home" vineyard is on the western rim of the Santa Clara Valley, some sixty miles south of San Francisco; first planted in 1852 by two Frenchmen, Théo Thée and his son-in-law, Charles Lefranc, it is the oldest producing vineyard in California, and takes its name from the famous quicksilver mine in the Santa Cruz Mountains nearby; this in turn was so called by early Spanish explorers after the greatest quicksilver mine in the world, at Almadén, southwest of Madrid, in Spain: the word is Moorish, and *al madén* means "the mine."

The Almadén vineyards (for what is left of the original plot is now hemmed in by housing developments and subdivisions) today include wide holdings in good districts less harassed by progress: 2,000 cool upland acres in San Benito County, directly south, vines in the Livermore Valley and in Sonoma.

Almadén was the first California winery to produce and market a *vin rosé*, and Almadén Grenache Rosé is the most widely sold premium table wine in this country, perhaps the best American *rosé*. Other pop-

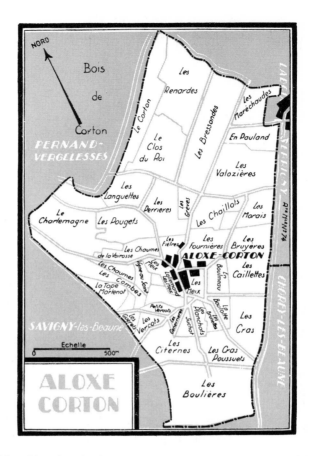

ular Almadén wines include Mountain Red and Mountain White, sound
and inexpensive; a good sparkling wine (California Champagne) made
in large part from the Pinot grape of France; California *solera* Sherries
made as Sherry is made in Spain; and a wide range of varietal wines that
take their names from the grape varieties of which they are made:
Cabernet Sauvignon, Pinot Noir (red), Pinot Chardonnay, Johannisberg
Riesling, Sauvignon Blanc, Pinot Blanc, Sylvaner, Semillon, etc. (white).

ALOXE-CORTON — (Ahl-ohss *Cor*-tawn) — Famous wine-producing
  commune of the Côte d'Or, Burgundy, and the northernmost important
  village of the Côte de Beaune. Unique in the fact that its red wines and
  white are almost equally celebrated, although the best of these do not
  carry the name Aloxe at all, and are sold as Corton (*see*), Corton-
  Charlemagne, Corton Clos du Roi, Corton Bressandes, etc. Certain
  wines from two nearby villages, Ladoix-Serrigny and Pernand Verge-

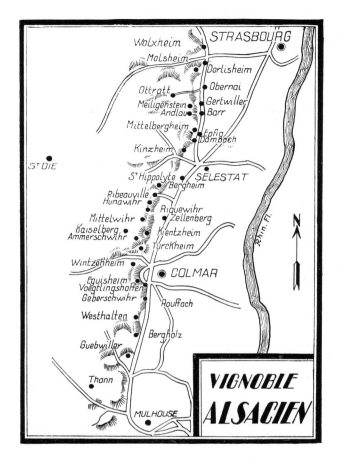

lesses, are also legally entitled to these names, and are produced on adjacent portions of the same impressive, steep, vineyard-covered hill. All of the above must come exclusively from the Pinot Noir or Chardonnay grape. The red Cortons of great years are probably the best, certainly the longest-lived wines of the Côte de Beaune, magnificent Burgundies of wonderful breed and texture: silky, well-balanced and fine. The white Cortons and Corton-Charlemagne are fully the equals of the best Meursaults, and in the opinion of many experts are even better. Wines marketed as Aloxe-Corton (with or without the name of a specific vineyard) are of a substantially lower class, lighter in body and alcohol, delicate and attractive but maturing early and comparatively short-lived.

ALSACE — (Al-sass) — Ancient French province (although most Alsatians speak a dialect of German among themselves) bordering the Rhine

9

north of Switzerland, and comprising the modern *départements* of Haut-Rhin and Bas-Rhin. The vineyards, which cover the lower slopes of the Vosges Mountains from near Mulhouse on the south to near Strasbourg on the north, are among the most beautiful in the world, and the small vineyard towns are exceedingly picturesque. White wines are produced almost exclusively (some 25 million gallons, in 1962, from 30,000 acres of vineyard), but there is a small amount of *vin rosé* and *vin gris*, the best of it made from the Pinot Noir grape plus, quite often, some Pinot Meunier, and sold as Pinot Rosé. The predominant white grape varieties, more or less in order of quality, are Riesling, Gewürztraminer — or Traminer (*see*), Pinot Gris (or "Tokay d'Alsace"), Pinot Blanc (Klevner), Muscat Ottonel, Sylvaner, Knipperlé, Chasselas.

The following, from north to south, are the more important vineyard towns, which have given their names to their surrounding districts: Marlenheim (largely *vin rosé*), Molsheim, Obernai, Goxwiller, Barr, Mittelbergheim, Dambach, Bergheim, Ribeauvillé, Hunawihr, Riquewihr, Beblenheim, Mittelwihr, Sigolsheim, Ammerschwihr, Kientzheim, Kaysersberg, Turckheim, Eguisheim, Husseren-les-Chateaux, Voegtlinshoffen, Guebwiller. However, there are many others, 92 in all, entitled to the name "Alsace" or "Vin d'Alsace," according to the new *Appellation Contrôlée* regulations, recently published. Specific vineyard names (as Kaeferkopf, Kanzlerberg, etc.) are sometimes, though on the whole rarely, used; these should not be confused with brand names which are much more common.

Alsatian wines are generally named after the grape or grapes from which they are made, principally those listed above, but often carry their village name as well; the word Zwicker means a blend (usually one with a Chasselas base), and Edelzwicker, a blend of superior, or "noble" varieties. The words "*Grand Vin*," "*Grand Cru*" and "*Grande Réserve*" may only be used on wines of superior varieties containing no less than 11% of natural alcohol by volume.

Shipped in slender *flutes* — tall, green bottles like those used in the German Moselle Valley nearby — not too high in alcohol (10-13%), exceedingly fragrant and on the average quite dry, Alsatian wines have achieved a great and merited popularity since World War I, not only throughout France, but in Great Britain and America.

ALSHEIM — (Ahls-heim) — German vineyard town between Oppenheim and Worms in Rheinhessen; some 600 acres of vineyard, largely planted to Sylvaner.

ALTAR WINES — Wines of whatever origin or type made to be used in the ceremony of the mass, and produced in accordance with the strict church regulations governing purity, naturalness and alcoholic content.

ALTO ADIGE — (*Ahl*-toe *Odd*-dee-gee) — The northern or upper portion of the Adige basin, in Italy, forming the modern province of Bolzano (*see*) and extending to the present Austrian frontier. The fertile valleys and hillsides of this mountainous Tyrol country have been fa-

10

mous for their wines since the days of Rome, and they produce today some 8 million gallons a year of light, fragrant, eminently agreeable, often excellent table wine, more than half of which is exported, in bulk, to Switzerland, Austria and Germany. The finer grades rank among Italy's best wines, and each of these will be found, with additional information concerning it, in its proper alphabetical place in this volume. *See*, therefore, Caldaro, Kuechelberger, Lagrein Rosato, Lago di Caldaro, Santa Giustina, Santa Maddalena, Terlano, etc. There are over 15,000 acres of vineyard in the province, the vines for the most part trained on superb, high "pergolas," which are a unique and charming feature of the lovely Tyrolean countryside. Grape varieties include such regional specialties as the Schiava, Lagrein and Blatterle, but there are plantings, as well, of Gewürztraminer, Sylvaner, Riesling, Pinot Blanc, Pinot Noir, Cabernet, Merlot, etc. Wines from these latter are usually marketed under their varietal name. Most of the Alto Adige wines mature early, and few improve greatly with age: the vines are cultivated and trained, and the wines are made with precisely this end in view; in the freshness of their youth they are among the most delightful table wines in the world.

ALTO DOURO — (*Ahl*-toe - *Du*-roe) — The classic zone of fine Port wine production. The mountainous area north and south of the Douro River upstream and east of Oporto, in Portugal.

AMABILE — (Ah-*ma*-beel-ay; Italian, "sweet or pleasing") — Used to describe a wine which, while sometimes or even usually dry, is in this special instance quite sweet. The term is used on one and only one American wine label, Louis M. Martini's *Moscato Amabile* from California's Napa Valley; this is a sweet, exceedingly fruity white Muscat wine, so low in alcohol (about 7%) that it has to be shipped and stored under refrigeration.

AMBOISE — (Awm-bwaz) — Picturesque little town and celebrated Renaissance chateau on the Loire River near Tours: also a number of fresh, fruity and engaging lesser wines produced nearby and entitled to the appellation "Touraine-Amboise." The whites, which resemble Vouvray, are made from the Chenin Blanc grape; the reds and *rosés* come from the Malbec, or Cot, the Gamay and occasionally the Cabernet Franc. Most of them are consumed locally, but there are some 250,000 gallons a year.

AMBONNAY — (*Awm*-bo-nay) — One of the best wine-producing villages of the Montagne de Reims in the French Champagne Country. Its vineyards are planted to the Pinot Noir.

AMELIORATION — Wine-maker's term, all too broadly used, to cover cellar practices some of which are entirely necessary and some of which are illegal; these include the adding of sugar to the juice or must before fermentation (chaptalization — *see*), the "correcting" of its acidity, etc., etc. Strict laws cover such matters in most wine-producing lands.

AMERICANO — (Ah-mair-ee-*kah*-no) — Name given by the peasant wine-producers of Italian Switzerland (round Locarno and Lugano in the Ticino, or Canton of Tessin) to the American vines which many of them planted when their original vineyards were destroyed by mildew and by the phylloxera (*see*). Unfortunately, most of these vines are of the variety called Isabella, an inferior, heavy-flavored cousin to the Concord, quite incapable of yielding good wine under any conditions. The other local wine, called Nostrano (literally, "ours"), comes from European vinifera vines and, while rarely distinguished, is a great deal better.

ALSO, a refreshing drink made of sweet Italian vermouth, Campari bitters, plus, usually, a dash of soda.

AMERICAN WINES — According to U.S. law and regulations, any and all wines produced in the United States. Prevailing trade usage is somewhat different; California wines may be called American but are rarely so labeled, nor are the unblended wines of New York or Ohio. The term is commonly employed only on blends of California and Eastern, as "American Sherry." In another and narrower sense, American Wines are those made entirely from native American grapes, such as Concord, Delaware, Catawba, Elvira and others, whether grown in California or in the East. *See* Grape, East, New York.

AMMERSCHWIHR — (*Ah*-mair-schveer) — Important wine-producing village in Alsace, almost totally destroyed in the last war, now largely rebuilt; its best vineyard, known for Riesings and Gewürztraminers of top quality, is the Kaeferkopf.

AMONTILLADO — (Ah-mone-tee-*yah*-doe) — A superior type of Spanish Sherry, generally fairly dry and paler than the average, although not as pale and light nor generally as dry as a Fino or Manzanilla. Its name comes originally from the place-name Montilla, a village and district south of Cordoba whose wines were legally sold as Sherry until quite recently. Literally it means a Sherry of the Montilla type, a "Montilla'd" wine; by usage a wine of finesse, breed and superior origin, that has acquired some color and increased body through age.

AMOROSO — (Ahm-o-*ro*-so) — A type of Spanish Sherry, generally a rather light-bodied Oloroso, considerably sweetened and brought to the color of dark amber by the addition of a sweetening agent or a much darker and sweeter wine. *See* Sherry, Arrope, Sancocho, Pedro Ximénez.

AMPUIS — (Ohm-pwee) — Small village on the right bank of the Rhône River, south of Lyon. Its vineyards, dating from Roman times, produce the celebrated red Côte Rôtie (*see*).

AÑADA — (Ahn-ya-da) — Used in Spain of wines that are of one specific vintage and at least a year old, as *vino de añada.*

ANDALUSIA — Famous, fertile and beautiful region, comprising most of the southernmost fourth of Spain; its best known wines are Sherry, Málaga, Montilla (*see*).

AÑEJO — (Ahn-*yea*-ho; Spanish, "aged") — Largely meaningless term except in its proper and original sense, which is, roughly, "at least a year older than the youngest wine in the cellar."

ANGELICA — One of the poorest and cheapest of American fortified wines, often little more than a blend of sweet, white grape juice and high-proof brandy. It is said to take its name from the city of Los Angeles; if so, it is something of which Los Angeles has no reason to feel proud.

ANGELUS — (Awn-shay-luhs) — One of the many 1st Growths of St. Emilion, sometimes listed as Clos de l'Angelus, sometimes as Château de l'Angelus. Its rather soft red wines (nearly 10,000 cases a year) are made by modern methods frowned on by some traditionalists. They are popular, early-maturing, agreeable, generally not too expensive, rarely great.

ANGLUDET, Château — (*Awn*-glu-day) — Important and good *bourgeois* vineyard of Cantenac-Margaux in the Haut-Médoc.

ANJOU — (Awn-shoe) — Historically, a province in west-central France. As far as wines are concerned, principally the *département* of Maine-et-Loire, on both sides of the Loire River, west and downstream from Touraine; the numerous and extremely diverse wines which this province produces. These include some of the best sweet white table wines of France, made from the Chenin Blanc grape (also called the Pineau de la Loire, although it is not a Pinot); dryer white wines that are fruity and good, though less distinguished, some from the Chenin and some from the Melon grape; a few excellent light reds from the Cabernet Franc, and some less good from the Cot, Groslot, etc.; a vast amount of *rosé*, generally not absolutely dry and ranging all the way from fine to poor in quality. A great deal of sparkling wine is also produced, most of it by the Champagne process, in and around Saumur.

The more important districts that produce, from late-picked grapes in good vintage years, the extremely fruity, rich, delicate dessert wines for which Anjou is above all famous, are the Coteaux du Layon (*see*), the Coteaux de la Loire (*see*), and the Coteaux de Saumur. These, like some of the lesser areas (the Coteaux du Loir, the Coteaux de l'Aubance, etc.), have their dry wines as well, and a little Muscadet is made along the western edge of Anjou.

By all odds the best red wines are those from around Saumur, Champigny (*see*) especially; and many of the finer *rosés*, also made from the Cabernet grape, are from this same area, although some from a little farther west, near Tigné and Brissac — they can be admirable. What is ordinarily shipped as "Anjou Rosé" is of a lesser class and made from the Groslot; it is really nothing more than a sound, inexpensive carafe wine, light, rather fruity, a bit on the sweet side.

For Map, *see* Loire.

APAGADO — (Ah-pa-*gah*-tho) — Literally, in Spanish, *apagar* is to put out, or extinguish, a light, or fire. Applied to wine, or more properly to

13

mosto (must) before fermentation, it means fresh grape juice to which some 16-18% of alcohol has been added, so that no fermentation can take place. The resulting, raw, alcoholic product is called *vin muté* or *mistelle* in French, and is used in Spain to sweeten the cheapest grades of Sherry; it is not far from what is sold as Angelica (*see*) in this country, but is hardly ever consumed unblended and at this stage of its development either in France or Spain.

APÉRITIF (French) — (Ah-*pair*-ee-teef) — A very broad term, meaning almost any drink taken before a meal as an "appetizer." A cocktail is an apéritif, so is Sherry, so is a glass of Champagne or white wine, if so consumed. The most popular apéritifs in France include Vermouth, both sweet and dry; Port; various fortified and flavored wines, prepared according to some special formula and often sold under proprietary names such as Byrrh, Dubonnet, St. Raphael, Cap Corse; stronger drinks, usually taken with water or soda, as Pernod, Pastis, Suze, Clacquesin, Amer Picon, etc. Almost all of these are more or less sweet and few of them, to the American palate, seem truly appetizing. In France they are drunk without food of any kind — food comes later. From the wine expert's perhaps biased point of view, the best apéritifs are Champagne, dry Sherry, and Sercial Madeira.

APPELLATION CONTRÔLÉE (French) — (Ah-pell-*ah*-see-awn Cawn-troll-*ay*) — Two words that now appear, often in small type, on the vast majority of French wine labels. They are the consumer's principal protection and his best friend, and of enormous value to all honest producers as well. All of the finer French wines except Champagne should carry this designation (*see*, however, V.D.Q.S.). Literally, it means that the name that the wine bears is one officially recognized and legally defined by governmental decree: the wine *must* come from the specific district, or township, or, in some instances, vineyard, from which it takes its name; from certain established varieties of grape and no others, and from grapes that have achieved a specified minimum of ripeness; it must have been made according to the traditional and proper usages of its district. It must, in other words, be genuine; this is not, of course, to say that it must be good. This admirable system of controls has largely been set up since 1935; standards have been established for over 200 different wines and the controls are rigidly enforced, violators being punished with extremely heavy fines, and in some instances, by imprisonment as well.

APPELLATION D'ORIGINE (French) — (Ah-pell-*ah*-see-awn *Dor*-re-gene) — A wine's name, in geographical terms — its place or origin, whether a whole district, as Burgundy; an American county, as Napa; a river valley, as Mosel or Moselle; a township, as Vosne-Romanée; an estate, as Château d'Yquem; or a single small parcel of vines, as Richebourg. Such names have been given wines since Biblical and Greek and Roman days, and most modern laws concerning labeling are based on this immemorial practice. There have of course been many abuses and there still are, but regulations on the whole are far more strict than they were a hundred or fifty or even twenty years ago.

In France, *Appellations d'Origine* are considered to fall into three categories, regulated officially by an admirable organization called the *Institut National des Appellations d'Origine des Vins et Eaux-de-Vie* (I.N.A.O., for short). The highest rank is the *Appellation Contrôlée* (*see*), often abbreviated to "A.O.C."; in this class are practically all of the famous wines of France.

In a highly honorable second category are what are known as the *Vins Délimités de Qualité Supérieure* (V.D.Q.S. — *see*), the Delimited Wines of Superior Quality. These, no less strictly regulated, make up what has been called a sort of "second team" of French wines; they carry a government seal on the label, and their number includes a good many dozens of excellent if less famous and less expensive local wines, produced throughout France and still, even now, in Algeria.

Below these are the wines that have only what is called an *Appellation Simple*, rather loosely protected by the general French statutes covering wine fraud and misrepresentation; these are not often exported.

Lastly, at the bottom of the ladder, are wines with no geographical appellation at all, sold simply, for example, as *Vin Rouge 12%*, or under a trade name, or brand. These of course may be blends of anything not found objectionable under the French pure food laws, and they need not be French wines at all unless they bear the words "Product of France" or the equivalent. There is nothing inherently objectionable about them (they are all cheap and some quite passable) providing the consumer knows exactly what he is getting. The address of the shipper on such wines has nothing whatsoever to do with the wine's origin: a bottle labeled "Vin Rosé, Durand-Dupont et Cie., Bordeaux, France," need not contain a single drop of Bordeaux wine.

APPETIZER — Anything taken in the way of food or drink to sharpen or whet the appetite; by contrast, the more exact French term, *apéritif* (*see*) means a pre-prandial drink, exclusively. It is common American usage to describe as "appetizer wines" the dryer fortified wines generally taken before a meal (most Sherry and Madeira, for example) and as "dessert wines" (*see*) the sweeter, fortified wines (Port, Muscatel, etc.) generally consumed afterwards.

APRE — (Ah-pr') — Harsh. French wine taster's term, most often used to describe rough young red wines of high tannin content.

APULIA — (Ap-*pew*-lee-ah) — Region in southeast Italy (Puglia), the "heel" of the Italian "boot." Generally first in total wine production among Italian "regions," with an average of some 130 million gallons a year, or nearly as much as the entire U.S. Most of this is very common *vino di taglio* (blending wine), with deep color, high alcohol and low acid. There are a few dessert wines of better than average quality.

ARAMON — (*Are*-ah-mawn) — A common and immensely productive grape, widely planted in the French Midi and to some extent in California. The red wine it yields is deficient in color and generally of poor quality.

ARBOIS — (Are-bwah) — Village and wine district in eastern France, near the Swiss border, forming part of the Côtes-du-Jura, in the ancient province of Franche-Comté. Red and *rosé* wines of superior quality are produced from the Poulsard, Trousseau and Pinot Noir; dry white wines from the Savagnin (Traminer) and Chardonnay (some of them made sparkling by the Champagne process) and two unusual and special wines, Vin Jaune and Vin de Paille (*see*) by special methods. Some *rosé* is exported.

ARCHE, Château de l' — (*Shat*-toe duh Larsh) — 2nd Classed Growth of Sauternes, now divided into two separate small properties, both entitled to the name. The best is chateau-bottled, and is an excellent sweet Sauternes.

ARCINS — (*Ar*-san) — Tiny wine-producing village in the Haut-Médoc, north of Margaux. Wines of secondary quality.

ARGENTINA — By a wide margin, the largest wine-producing and wine-consuming country of the Western Hemisphere. Exporting very little and importing even less, Argentina drinks her own wines, almost entirely table wines, at the rather astonishing rate of 200 million gallons a year, some eighty bottles per capita. Most of this is sound, inexpensive, quite ordinary, the red better than the *rosé* or white; it comes from the states of Mendoza and San Juan, and the vineyards are planted along the foothills of the Andes, not far from the Chilean border. There are some 400,000 acres under vines.

ARGOL — The crude tartar, or potassium bitartrate — cream of tartar being its refined form — which forms as a crystalline deposit in wine vats, during and after fermentation, and even sometimes, as a sediment, in bottled wine. In large wineries it is an important by-product, and is sold mostly to manufacturers of baking-powder.

AROMA — Very different from bouquet (*see*), the aroma of a wine is more pronounced and more distinctive when the wine is young, being directly related to the odor of fresh fruit. Certain varieties of grape (the Gewürztraminer, the Malvasia, the Muscat and the Concord, to cite a few extreme examples) can be identified, blindfolded, by their scent alone. Much of this aroma disappears during fermentation, and bone-dry wines rarely have as much aroma as those that have retained a certain amount of their natural grape sugar; aroma tends to diminish further as a wine is aged, and bouquet takes its place. The word is also used with a modifying adjective to describe a special, characteristic, fruity odor which certain wines possess, as "aroma of quince," or "apple," or "raspberries," or "blackberries." "Aromatic," on the other hand, is usually reserved for wines that have been deliberately flavored or "perfumed" with spices and herbs, such as many apéritifs, and vermouth.

ARRIÈRE-CÔTES — (Arry-air Coat) — Name given to a series of slopes in Burgundy, west of and roughly parallel to the Côte d'Or proper, producing wines, both red and white, of second quality, usually marketed as Bourgogne Rouge, Bourgogne Blanc, Passe-Tout-Grains, Aligoté, etc. *See* also Hautes Côtes.

ARROBA — (Ah-*ro*-ba) — Spanish measure, approximately 16 liters, or just over four U.S. gallons.

ARROPE — (Ahr-*ro*-pay) — Grape concentrate, used as a sweetening and coloring agent in less good Sherries. It is produced by boiling down unfermented grape juice to its "quintessence," or one-fifth of its volume, whereby it acquires a deep brown color and a burnt-sugar, or caramel, flavor. *See* Sherry.

ARSAC — (*Ar*-sack) — Wine-producing *commune* of the Haut-Médoc now entitled to the appellation Margaux: one 5th Growth vineyard, Château du Tertre *(see)* plus several *crus bourgeois.*

ARTISAN — (*Ar*-teas-zawn) — One of the minor classifications into which Bordeaux wines are traditionally divided. A *Cru Artisan* is a less good vineyard than a *Cru Bourgeois (see),* barely above a *Cru Paysan* in rank; such wines are the *ordinaires* of Bordeaux, almost always blended, rarely carrying a vineyard name, hardly every chateau-bottled.

ASCIUTTO — (Ah-*shoot*-toe) — Italian word which, when applied to wine, means dry, the opposite of sweet.

ASPRINIO — (Ahs-*sprin*-nee-o) — Dry, pale, rather agreeable, light white wine, produced just north of Naples, in Italy.

ASSMANNSHAUSEN — (Ahs-mans-how-zen) — Village on the Rhine immediately north of Rüdesheim, producing what is probably the best and certainly the most famous red wine of Germany. Made from the Pinot Noir grape (known in Germany as the Spätburgunder) this is, at its best, comparable to a light, mediocre Burgundy.

ASTI — (*Ass*-tea) — Important wine-producing town south of Turin, in the Piedmont region of Italy; famous particularly for its rather sweet sparkling wine, Asti Spumante, Italy's best known and most popular. It is also a major center of the Vermouth trade, and the hilly surrounding country produces a great deal of light white Muscat wine, largely from the Moscato di Canelli grape, and much red of good quality from the Barbera, Freisa, Grignolino and Nebbiolo. The total production of its little province is in excess of 20,000,000 gallons a year.

ALSO a town in the northern part of Sonoma County, California, home of the Italian-Swiss Colony, and also famous for its red table wines.

ASTRINGENT — Wine tasters' term, applied to wines that make the mouth pucker, generally because of an excess of tannin. Many excellent red wines are astringent when young; providing they are not bitter, this is not a serious flaw, for they will soften and mellow with age. In a young red wine, astringency is often, but not invariably, an indication that the wine will be long-lived.

ASZU — (Ahs-zoo) — A special, superior quality of sweet Tokay (*see*).

AUBE — (Ohb) — French *département*, e. of Paris, forming the southern and secondary part of the Champagne Country, with some 5,000 acres of vineyard.

AUBANCE — (Oh-bawnss) — Small river, tributary of the Loire, in the old French province of Anjou. The adjoining hillsides, "Les Coteaux de l'Aubance," produce good quality, semi-dry white wines from the Chenin Blanc grape, and very creditable *vins rosés,* the best of these made from the Cabernet Franc, around Brissac. The overall production of the delimited area is in the neighborhood of a half million gallons a year.

AUDE — (Ode) — French *département*, second only to Hérault (*see*) in total wine production, with some 300,000 acres of vineyard. Part of what is known as the Midi, its most important towns are Carcassonne and Narbonne; most of what it produces is simply *vin ordinaire* but two districts, Corbières (*see*) and the Minervois (partly in the Hérault) yield what are perhaps the best of the common table wines of France.

AUSLESE — (Ouse-lay-zeh; German, "Selection") — A German wine, whether from the Moselle, the Rhine, Franconia or elsewhere, of a very special and superior sort, considerably sweeter and a great deal more expensive than others made by the same producer in the same year. At the time of the *Lese,* or grape harvest, the especially ripe and perfect bunches, and those most affected by the Noble Mold, Botrytis (*see*), are put aside and pressed separately; the resulting wine is Auslese, and it rarely amounts to over 10-15% of a vineyard's production, even in favorable years. Auslese wines are often further graded, especially on the Moselle, and given such ratings as *feine* Auslese, *hochfeine* Auslese, and *feinste* Auslese; they are both dearer and sweeter than Spätlese (*see*), and an Auslese of a great year, especially from the Palatinate or Rhine, should properly be classified as a dessert wine. *See* also Beerenauslese, Pourriture Noble, Trockenbeerenauslese.

On at least two occasions (in 1953 and 1959) a wine more or less entitled to the name Auslese has been produced in the United States — by Widmer's Wine Cellars in the Finger Lakes district of New York State. Made from the "New York State Riesling" (which is really not a Riesling at all but an American grape, also called the "Missouri Riesling") it was pressed from selected bunches covered with the Noble Mold. Unlike its German counterpart, it was not sweet, but a dry, fruity *Naturwein* of exceptional quality.

AUSONE, Château — (Oh-zone) — Famous Great 1st Growth vineyard of St. Emilion, in the Bordeaux Country; with Château Cheval Blanc (*see*), it ranks officially as the best of the St. Emilions, and its wines bring as high prices as the most celebrated Médocs — Lafite, Latour, Margaux, etc.; many of them, especially prior to World War II, were of truly astonishing quality. The average production is some 2,500 cases a year. Ausone takes its name from the Latin poet and wine-lover,

CHÂTEAU AUSONE

St ÉMILION

✥ 1949 ✥

EDOUARD DUBOIS-CHALLON

Propriétaire
APPELLATION SAINT-ÉMILION CONTROLÉE
MIS EN BOUTEILLE AU CHÂTEAU.

ROUSSEAU FRERES. B.

Ausonius, who had an estate and vineyard somewhere in the neighborhood, though almost certainly not on the actual site of Château Ausone.

AUSONIUS — Roman man of letters, born in Bordeaux *circa* 310 A.D., eventually made consul by the Emperor Gratian, whose tutor he had been. He had a well-loved vineyard near what is now St. Emilion, though probably not on the site of Château Ausone which is nevertheless named after him; he also wrote a celebrated poem in praise of the Moselle River, its landscapes and its wines.

AUSTRALIA — Although there are no indigenous native vines in Australia, the history of viticulture and wine-making there rather closely parallels that of the United States, especially of California. The first grapes were planted near Sydney in 1788, and in 1830 a Mr. James Busby (the Australian prototype of California's Colonel Haraszthy) was sent to Europe to select and bring back superior grape varieties; he returned with 20,000 cuttings of over 600 sorts. As in California, the wines were given what the producers felt to be their appropriate European appellations — Sherry, Burgundy, Claret, Sauternes, etc. (although, on account of a British-Portuguese treaty, the Australian "Port" was called "Port type"); many of the early vineyards were devastated by the phylloxera, then replanted on American roots; again, as in California, great progress has been made in the way of quality and improved wine-making technique in the past two decades. Many Australian wines are surprisingly good today, the *flor* Sherries especially, and their increasing popularity in England is fully justified.

The vine was first introduced in New South Wales, but this state has long since been surpassed in viticultural importance by its neighbors, Victoria and especially South Australia. There are over 125,000 acres

19

of vineyard, and it is interesting to note that the best of these are about as far from the equator as San Francisco, between 34° and 38° south latitude.

AUSTRIA — To a far greater extent than Germany or even Switzerland, Austria is by tradition a wine-drinking country; it was of course even more so in the high old days of the Austro-Hungarian Empire, when the best vintages of what is now the Italian Tyrol, of Hungary, Czechoslovakia and Yugoslavia all found their way to Vienna. But even today the annual consumption is over seven gallons per capita, and far more wine is imported (largely from Italy) than exported.

Almost all of the better Austrian wines are white, and in character they tend to resemble those of the Italian Tyrol and of southern Germany, especially Baden (*see*); they are mostly shipped in tall, slender, green or brown bottles; many of them carry varietal grape names, as Riesling, Gewürztraminer, Sylvaner, Müller-Thurgau, plus such local favorites as Veltliner and Rotgipfler; some bear designations of superior quality, as *Spätlese* and *Auslese*, but are less sweet than their German counterparts. As a whole, they can be described as rather low in alcohol, fruity, refreshing, fairly dry, with good bouquet, and soon ready to drink.

Many of the most agreeable of all are produced practically in Vienna itself, and sold (as "open" wine, in the outdoor cafés of Grinzing and the Vienna suburbs) as Wiener, Nussberger, or Grinzinger, sometimes plus a vineyard name. Gumpoldskirchener (*see*), from vineyards some thirty miles south of Vienna, enjoys an even higher rating and is perhaps the best known Austrian wine today. A third district, also excellent, 40 miles west of Vienna on the steep Danube hillsides, yields Loibner, Kremser and Dürnsteiner.

The red wines, of little consequence and rarely seen outside Austria, are mostly made from the Pinot Noir, or Spätburgunder grape.

AUVERGNE — (Oh-vairn) — Famous old province in central France, near the headwaters of the Loire. Although of ancient reputation, its vineyards are of little consequence today, and names such as Chanturgues, Chateaugay and Corent are now hardly wine-names, in the real sense of the word, at all. These wines were largely made from the Gamay, or in rare instances from the Pinot Noir or Chardonnay; certainly they were and are much less remarkable than Auvergnats all over the world have led us to believe. Nevertheless, wines bearing the following appellations are entitled to the V.D.Q.S. seal: Côtes d'Auvergne, Côtes du Forez, Côtes Roannaises, Saint-Pourçain-sur-Sioule.

AUXEY-DURESSES — (*Oak*-say Deer-*ress*) — One of the good secondary wine-producing villages of the Côte de Beaune, in Burgundy, set down in a little side-valley northwest of Meursault. Both white wines and red of good quality are produced, from the Chardonnay, Pinot Blanc and Pinot Noir, the former comparable to the lesser Meursaults, the latter not unlike Volnays, albeit without as much body and class. Being little known, they are often excellent values.

AVELSBACH — (Ah-velz-bock) — Small but good Moselle wine district, south of Trier, Germany. Sometimes, not altogether correctly, classified as a Ruwer wine. Avelsbacher Herrenberg, Altenberg and Kupp are the best vineyards; the State Domain and the Cathedral of Trier are the principal vineyard owners — wine produced by the latter is sold as Dom Avelsbacher.

AVENSAN — (Ahv-on-sawn) — Wine-producing *commune,* just west of Margaux in the Haut-Médoc: one *cru exceptionnel,* Château Villegorge, plus several *crus bourgeois.*

AVIGNON — (*Ah*-veen-yawn) — Historic and interesting little city on the Rhône River, in southern France, seat of the Papacy from 1309 to 1377. An important center of the trade in the wines of the lower Rhône Valley — Châteauneuf-du-Pape, Tavel, Lirac, Gigondas, etc.

AVIZE — (Ah-veez) — Major wine-producing village in the Champagne Country of France, south of Épernay and the Marne; with Cramant, it is the most important *commune* of the Côte des Blancs, rated 100% in the official classification; its wines, produced entirely from the Chardonnay grape, have extraordinary finesse and class. *See* Champagne, Blanc de Blancs.

AY — (Eye) — Village in the Champagne Country, near Épernay, on the north or right bank of the Marne; its admirable hillside vineyards are planted almost entirely to Pinot Noir, and in the official rating, it is one of seven townships accorded the highest rating, 100%. *See* Champagne, Blanc de Noirs.

AYL — (I'll) — Important wine-producing village on the Saar, in Germany. Ayler Kupp and Herrenberg are the best vineyards.

AZAY-LE-RIDEAU — (*As*-zay-luh-*Re*-doe) — Charming little town and lovely Renaissance chateau west of Tours in the Chateau Country; also a pleasant, fruity white wine, somewhat like Vouvray, produced there from the Chenin Blanc grape, and legally entitled to the appellation "Touraine Azay-le-Rideau."

BACCHUS — Another name for Dionysus (*see*), the Greek and Roman god of wine.

BACHARACH — (*Bach*-ah-rach) — Small and picturesque town of the Mittel-Rhein (*see*), between Bingen and Coblenz. Once an important center of the German wine trade, still produces a certain number of Rhine wines of second quality, of which Bacharacher Posten and Bacharacher Wolfshöhle are perhaps the best known.

BACO — (Bah-co) — French hybridizer who has given his name plus a serial number to several of his successful hybrids (*see*). Baco No. 1 is a red wine grape now in production in several vineyards in the easttern United States. Baco No. 22A may now legally be used in the making of Armagnac, in France, though whether it is as good as the traditional Picpoul (*see*) certainly remains to be demonstrated.

BADACSONYI — (Bahd-ah-chony) — Celebrated Hungarian appellation of origin, used in conjunction with the name of a grape variety on a number of Hungary's finest table and dessert wines, as Badacsonyi Rizling (Riesling), B. Furmint (*see*), B. Muskotaly (Muscatel), etc.

BADEN — (Baad'n) — Large province in southwestern Germany, bounded on the south by Switzerland and on the west by Alsace. The Black Forest is its most important physical feature, and most of its extremely diverse and numerous vineyards are planted along the Black

Forest foothills and overlook the Rhine Valley. The wines, mostly white, in general very agreeable and in a few rare cases of high quality, are almost all consumed locally and are almost never exported. They include the Seeweine (*see*), produced along the northern shore of Lake Constance; Markgräfler (*see*), made from the Gutedel or Chasselas grape between Freiburg-im-Breisgau and the Swiss border; the good and interesting growths of the Kaiserstuhl (*see*), an odd sort of "island" of volcanic tufa in the middle of the Rhine Valley west of Freiburg; the various, occasionally distinguished wines of the Ortenau (*see*), directly across the Rhine from Strasbourg; the amusing Mauerweine (*see*), produced near Baden-Baden and shipped in Bocksbeutels, like the wines of Franconia; most of the wines of the Bergstrasse, north and south of Heidelberg.

For Map, *see* GERMANY.

BAD DÜRKHEIM — (Baad Dirk-heim) — Small resort town in the German Palatinate or Pfalz, important for its vineyards, of which it has the largest acreage of any township in Germany, and for its wines, both red (fair) and white (very good). *See* Dürkheim.

BAD KREUZNACH — (Baad Kroytz-nahch) — *See* Kreuznach.

BALANCE — Wine-taster's term, a little difficult to explain. Essentially, a well-balanced wine is one completely harmonious in its make-up, with nothing overly pronounced and no striking deficiency in its bouquet, flavor or aftertaste. If light, it will be delicate; if full-bodied, it will have a corresponding amount of flavor and character. A well-balanced wine may not be great; it is exactly what it should be in its type and class, and the term is high praise.

BALESTARD-LA-TONNELLE, Château — (Bahl-less-*tar* la Toe-*nell*) — One of the better 1st Growths of St. Emilion, sturdy, but with considerable class; there are some 3,000 cases a year. It is famous above all for a poem which François Villon wrote five hundred years ago in its praise, describing it as . . . "*ce divin nectar, Qui porte nom de Balestard.*" The complete poem now appears on the label.

BALLING — Hydrometer and scale generally used in the U.S. for measuring the sugar content of unfermented grape juice, and therefore the probable alcoholic content of the finished wine. Balling readings are in terms of grams of sugar per 100 grams of juice and roughly the Balling reading multiplied by .55 will give the wine's future alcoholic content by volume, e.g. juice of 22° Balling should give a 12% wine.

BANDOL — (Bahn-*dawl*) — Pleasant, lesser wines, white, red and above all *rosé*, produced on the Mediterranean Coast of France, round the twin resorts of Bandol and Sanary-sur-Mer, near Toulon. Although coming from the general region of the Côtes de Provence (*see*) these, like Cassis, but unlike most of the others, have been given an *appellation contrôlée* (*see*) although this is not by any means to say that they are better than Provence wines that carry instead the V.D.Q.S. seal (*see*). The reds and *rosés* are mostly from the Mourvèdre grape, plus Grenache and Cinsault; the whites from the Clairette and Ugni Blanc. There are about 60,000 gallons a year.

BANYULS — (Ban-*yulz*) — The most famous and perhaps the best of French dessert wines, somewhat comparable to a light Tawny Port; it is classified either as a *Vin Doux Naturel* (a sad misnomer since it is fortified) or, more correctly, as a *Vin de Liqueur.* By law, it must have at least 15% of alcohol by volume, but often runs much higher; it is russet-brown in color, quite sweet, and with age acquires a special bouquet and flavor known as *rancio* (*see*). Banyuls is made largely from the Grenache grape in a picturesque little district known as the *Côte Vermeille,* where the Pyrenees come down to the Mediterranean along the Spanish border. The tiny fishing port of Banyuls is the center of the trade, and the other villages of the zone, beloved of artists and summer tourists, are Collioure, Port-Vendres and Cerbère. The vineyards are terraced on steep, sun-drenched hillsides, and the grapes are picked late; even if unfortified, the wine would tend to be strong and sweet, but it receives the addition, before, during or after fermentation, of from 5% to 10% of high-proof brandy.

BARBACARLO — (Bar-ba-*car*-lo) — Italian red table wine of good quality, from southern Lombardy. Like two other oddly named wines, Buttafuoco and Sangue di Giuda (*see*), it is produced in the townships of Broni and Canneto Pavese, from various grape varieties including the Ughetto, Croatina, Moradella, etc.

BARBARESCO — (Bar-bar-*ess*-co) — Justly celebrated red wine of Piedmont, northwestern Italy, made from the Nebbiolo grape in two townships (Barbaresco itself, and Neive) within a few miles of the district which produces, from the same Nebbiolo grape, the very different and even more remarkable wine called Barolo. Unlike Barolo, Barbaresco is often shipped in what we have come to call "Bordeaux bottles," high-shouldered and straight-sided, whereas the sloping Burgundian form is used for Barolo. Lighter than Barolo, shorter lived, maturing more quickly and acquiring, after two or three years in bottle, the brownish, autumn-leaf color which the French call "pelure d'oignon" (*see*), it is a wine of true distinction and great class, certainly one of Italy's ten best.

BARBERA — (Bar-*bear*-ah) — A red wine grape grown principally in the region of Piedmont (northwestern Italy) and to some small extent in California; the wine made from this grape, deep-colored, full-bodied, full-flavored, somewhat lacking in distinction, very agreeable with Italian food and at its best when young.

BARBERONE — (Barr-bear-*own*-eh) — Literally, a "big Barbera" (*see*). Term rarely if ever used in Italy, sometimes applied to heavy red wines in California, usually without any justification or excuse, since few such wines are made, even in part, from the true Barbera grape.

24

BARDOLINO — (Bar-doe-*lean*-o) — Excellent light red wine produced round the village of the same name, on the eastern shore of Lake Garda, in northern Italy. Like Valpolicella, which is grown on a very different soil some ten miles further east, Bardolino is made mostly from Corvina, Negrara and Molinara grapes; hardly darker in color than a dark *rosé*, at its best when from one to three years old, rarely over 11% alcohol, fruity, charming, never great, it is one of the most delightful wines of the province of Verona, and a perennial favorite in Switzerland as well.

For Map, *see* ITALY.

BARET, Château — (Bah-ray) — Vineyard in the *commune* of Villenave-d'Ornon in the Graves district, near Bordeaux. Red (principally) and white wines of good quality, some 10,000 cases a year.

BAROLINO — (Barr-o-leeno) — Wine name without any standing or legal meaning formerly applied to lesser wines made in the environs of Barolo (*see*).

BAROLO — (Bar-oh-low) — Perhaps the best red wine of Italy, very full-bodied, slow-maturing, comparable to the great French wines of the Rhône Valley, such as Hermitage or Côte Rôtie. It is made from the Nebbiolo grape in Piedmont, south of Turin, in a small, strictly de-limited, hilly district of which the village of Barolo is the center and which includes as well the townships of Serralunga, Castiglione, Grinzane, Monforte, La Morra, Sommariva Perno, Verduno. Generally kept at least three years in wood before bottling (in "Burgundy" bottles), it deserves and almost requires additional ageing in bottle before being drunk, although it often throws considerable sediment. Powerful, deep-colored, long-lived, it is definitely a great wine and, at its best, a quite extraordinary one.

For Map, *see* ITALY.

BARR — (Bar) — Important wine-producing town in northern Alsace; its Rieslings and Gewürztraminers are among the best of the *département* of Bas-Rhin.

BARREL — As far as the wine trade is concerned, a wooden (preferably oak) container of any size in which wine is stored, aged and sometimes shipped. A barrel is readily movable; a cask, in many cases, is not.

BARRIQUE — (Bah-reek) — One of many French words meaning barrel, used particularly in the Bordeaux Country (*pièce* being the Burgundian equivalent) to designate the oak casks of 225 liters (roughly 60 U.S. gallons) in which Bordeaux wines are commonly stored and often shipped. A *barrique* is supposed to yield 24 cases of finished wine.

BARRO — (*Barr*-roe) — Spanish word meaning clay soil, used particularly in connection with the vineyards in the Sherry Country. The finest of these are planted on white, chalky soil, *albariza*; the less good (which give a heavier and coarser wine) on clay, *barro*; the poorest of all on sandy soil, *arena*.

25

BARSAC — (Bar-sack) — The northernmost and, after Sauternes itself, the most famous of the five townships of Sauternes. It is some twenty-five miles southeast of Bordeaux, and its vineyards are on low, rolling hills that overlook the Garonne River. All Barsacs, legally, are Sauternes, made by the same methods and from the same grape varieties. They are all rather sweet, though often somewhat less sweet than other Sauternes, and with a special delicacy and fruit. Château Climens and Château Coutet are the outstanding vineyards, but there are many smaller good ones; all the best of them chateau-bottle their production except in very poor vintage years.

For Map, *see* GRAVES-SAUTERNES.

BAS-MÉDOC — (Bah-*May*-dawk) — The northern, flatter, sandier and less fine portion of the Médoc (*see*). Its wines are entitled to the appellation "Médoc" (although of course not "Haut-Médoc") and most of the wine sold simply as "Médoc" comes from its vineyards. These are red Bordeaux of fairly good quality though no great distinction. There are no Classed Growths in the Bas-Médoc, but in general the best wines come from the villages of Bégadan, St. Christoly-de-Médoc, Valeyrac, etc.

BAS-RHIN — (Baa Ran) — The northern of the two *départements* into which Alsace (*see*) is divided. On the whole, its wines are of less distinction than those of Haut-Rhin, but a first rate *vin rosé* is made from the Pinot Noir grape at Marlenheim, and other vineyards, planted along the Vosges foothills, yield good Rieslings, Traminers, etc., at Obernai, Goxwiller, Barr, Mittelbergheim, Dambach, etc.

BASSERMANN-JORDAN — Distinguished wine-producing family, with a great estate [including Forster Jesuitengarten (*see*)] at Deidesheim, in the German Palatinate, or Pfalz. Among wine-lovers, the name is one of the most respected of Germany, and the label one of the most familiar as well as most beautiful. The late Dr. Friedrich von Bassermann-Jordan was considered the dean of German wine-producers; he was the author of a number of scholarly books on the history of the vine, and created in his home a sort of remarkable wine museum.

BASTARD — Sweet red or white wine from the Iberian Peninsula, popular in England in Elizabethan days, and mentioned by Shakespeare (*Measure for Measure, Henry IV*). It may be presumed to have got its name from the Bastardo grape, one of the principal varieties used in the making of Port (*see*) and also Madeira.

BASTO — (Baas-toe) — Spanish term meaning coarse or common, the opposite of *fino*. Applied to a Sherry of no breed and poor quality.

BATAILLEY, Château — (Bat-tie-yea) — 5th Classed Growth of Pauillac, in the Haut-Médoc, now divided into two separate properties, Château Batailley and Château Haut-Batailley (*see*). Produces some 8,000 cases of good quality Claret a year.

BATARD-MONTRACHET — (*Bat*-tarr Mon-rasch-*shay*) — One of the best and most celebrated white-wine vineyards of Burgundy, consisting of just twenty-eight acres, with an annual production of less than 5,000 cases. Generally ranked third (after Montrachet itself, and Chevalier Montrachet) among the Montrachet vineyards, it has consistently produced, at least since World War II, better wines than its reputed superiors. These, made exclusively from the Chardonnay grape, are pale gold in color, comparatively high in alcohol (13-14%), dry without being excessively so, and have a quite extraordinary wealth of bouquet and flavor. The best are estate-bottled. (*See* Montrachet.)

For Map, *see* PULIGNY, CHASSAGNE.

BÉARN — (Bay-arn) — Old French province, consisting of most of the modern *département* of Basses Pyrénées; its capital is Pau. Its best known wine is the rather sweet white Jurançon (*see*); but some more than passable *rosé* and dry white wines are also produced, are entitled to the V.D.Q.S. seal (*see*), and sold as Rosé de Béarn, Rousselet de Béarn (a white wine made at least in part from the grape of that name) or simply as Vin de Béarn.

BEAUJEU — (Bo-*shuh*) — Small town on the western edge of the Beaujolais Country, long considered the capital of the little district though today far overshadowed by Villefranche-sur-Saône. The Hospices de Beaujeu is a charity hospital, organized somewhat along the lines of the Hospices de Beaune (*see*) in that a large part of its endowment consists of vineyards; the wines from these (in Fleurie and other good *communes* of the Beaujolais) are usually labeled "Hospices de Beaujeu," but carry the name of their village of origin as well.

BEAUJOLAIS — (*Bo*-sho-lay) — One of the most popular and best-loved wines of France, nearly always red (an insignificant amount of *rosé* and white is produced and legally entitled to the name); also the district from which it comes, in southern Burgundy, just north of Lyon. The vineyards make up a rather small, compact area of vine-covered hills west of the main Paris-Lyon-Riviera railway line and road. Although traditionally part of Burgundy, its wines are very different from

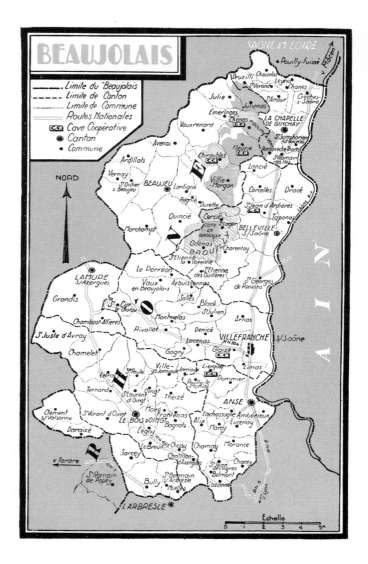

those of the great Côte d'Or, being made from a different grape, the Gamay, rather than the Pinot Noir; its prevailing soil, furthermore, is clay and granite rather than limestone. Only a few Beaujolais wines may legally be labeled "Bourgogne" (Burgundy) — these are admittedly the best; they come from nine specific villages or vineyard slopes: Brouilly, Côte-de-Brouilly, Chénas, Chiroubles, Fleurie, Juliénas, Morgon, Moulin-à-Vent, St. Amour. Any one of these names on a bottle of Beaujolais is

28

an indication, almost a guarantee, of superior quality; few such wines are ever sold as "Burgundy" or "Bourgogne," even though entitled to the name, being more saleable and worth more under the appellation of their village of origin. Ordinary Beaujolais is a light, agreeable, fruity, eminently drinkable red table wine; it is usually served at the temperature of the cellar rather than that of the dining room; it should be inexpensive, and is at its best when under two years old. Beaujolais Supérieur is a slightly better grade, with a somewhat higher minimum alcoholic content — 10%, rather than 9%, for the red; Beaujolais-Villages (or a wine labeled Beaujolais plus the name of a town) is of a higher class, and must come from one of 35 designated villages or *communes*, of which those listed above (Fleurie, etc.) are particularly outstanding. Even these wines should generally be served cool and drunk young — only exceptional bottles of great years improve appreciably after their third birthday, and many French gourmets prefer them when their age can still be counted in months, not years. Few wines go so wonderfully well with good food, and fine Beaujolais is unquestionably among the most agreeable red table wines in the world, fruity, full-bodied, with a special, almost spicy flavor and no trace of harshness.

BEAULIEU — (Bowl-yuh) — One of California's most famous vineyards, at Rutherford, in the Napa Valley. Founded by the late Georges de Latour in 1900, it has remained a family property, producing principally table wines (about 100,000 cases a year), plus a little Champagne and Sherry, etc. Most of these are sold under the BV (for Beaulieu Vineyards) brand, since the word "Beaulieu" is considered hard to pronounce, but many carry a special designation, as well as a varietal name, as *Beaumont* for a Pinot Noir, *Beauclair* for a Johannisberg Riesling, and Georges de Latour Private Reserve for a special and excellent Cabernet Sauvignon which bears a facsimile of the founder's signature on its label. Like almost all of the fine California vineyards, and in conformity with the well-established, perhaps unfortunate California pattern, Beaulieu produced a complete "line" of wines, including "Chablis," "Sauterne," "Burgundy," and most of the others. The best by far are the varietal wines noted above, plus Pinot Chardonnay, but BV is an honorable *marque*, and there are no bad wines sold under this label.

BEAUMES DE VENISE — (*Bome*-duh Ven-*ease*) — Sweet Muscat wine (*see*) made in the French *département* of Vaucluse.

BEAUMONT — (Bo-mont or Bo-mawn) — Red wine, made from the Pinot Noir grape, by Beaulieu Vinyards (*see*) in California's Napa Valley.
    ALSO, BEAUMONT-SUR-VESLE, one of the less important wine-producing villages of the Montagne de Reims, in the French Champagne Country.

BEAUNE — (Bone) — The principal center of the Burgundy wine trade, a picturesque little city of some 12,000, famous both for its wines and for its ancient buildings, among them the Hospices de Beaune (*see*), an extraordinary charity hospital dating from 1443. Beaune has given its

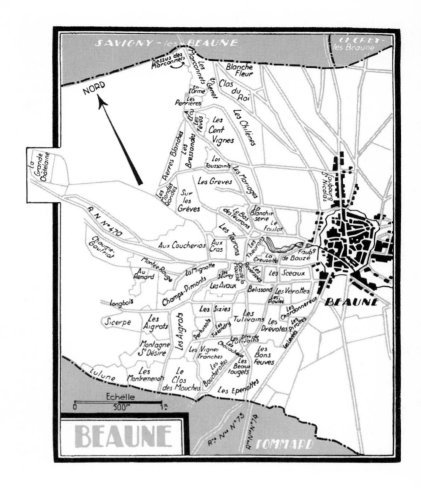

name to the southern half of the Côte d'Or (Côte de Beaune) as well as to the wines, almost all red, produced by its own 1,350 acres of hillside vineyard, west of the town. The best of these are of extremely high quality, remarkable for their distinction, balance and grace, comparable to the better wines of Pommard, the township which directly adjoins Beaune on the south. Leading vineyards include Les Grèves, Les Fèves, Les Cent Vignes, Les Marconnets, Bressandes, Cras, Champs-Pimont, Clos de la Mousse, Clos des Mouches, Clos du Roi, Teurons, Avaux, Aigrots, etc. The best known white, not unlike a Meursault in character, is Clos des Mouches. (*See* also Côte de Beaune.)

30

BEAUREGARD, Château (*Bo*-ray-gaar) — 1st Growth vineyard of Pomerol, one of the fifteen or twenty best of this little district. A number of other Bordeaux chateaux also bear this name, but their wines are of little interest or consequence.

BEAUSÉJOUR, Château — (*Bo*-say-sure) — Excellent 1st Growth of St. Emilion, presently divided into two properties with different owners, both entitled to the name. Together they produce some 4,000 cases a year. There are other chateaux of the same name in Montagne-St. Emilion, Puisseguin-St. Emilion, St. Estèphe in the Médoc, etc., but their wines are by no means of the same class.

BEERENAUSLESE — (Bearen-ouse-lay-zeh; German, "Berry-selection") — A German wine of an exceedingly rare, special and expensive sort, made from individual grape berries selected for their over-ripeness at the time of the *Lese,* or picking. In the production of Auslese (*see*) the most perfect and ripest bunches are set aside and pressed separately; here the selection is in terms, not of bunches, but of chosen, single grapes, cut from the bunches with tiny scissors. Beerenauslesen are produced by leading growers in all of the more important German wine districts only, with rare exceptions, in years ranked as good or great, and, with no exceptions at all, more as a matter of prestige than profit. Quite sweet though not at all cloying, with an almost indescribable wealth of bouquet and fruit and flavor, properly served only with dessert or after dinner, they are among the most remarkable white wines in the world, fully worth the fabulously high prices they bring.

BELAIR, Château — (Bel-air) — One of the very best 1st Growths of St. Emilion, directly adjoining Château Ausone (*see*) and owned by the same family. Annual production is just under 4,000 cases. Incidentally, there exist, in the Bordeaux Country, some fifteen properties, all producing wine, called Château Bel-Air (so spelled), and at least one vineyard called "Bélair," though without mention of a chateau. These should not be confused with the original, which is, by a long way, the best, although one Château *de* Bel Air in Lalande-de-Pomerol (*see*) and another Château Bel-Air in Pomerol both produce good red wine.

BEL-AIR-MARQUIS-D'ALIGRE, Château—(Bel-Air-Mar-kee-Dal-leegr) — *Cru Exceptionnel* of Soussans-Margaux. One of the best of the non-classified Haut-Médoc vineyards, producing better wine than many 4th and 5th Growths today.

BELGRAVE, Château — (Bel-grahv) — 5th Classed Growth of St. Laurent, Haut-Médoc. Annual production, some 14,000 cases. Should not be confused with many less good vineyards called "Château Bellegrave."

BELLET — (Bel-lay) — Popular and agreeable *vin rosé* (also occasionally a white wine) produced near Nice, on the French Riviera. There are only about fifty acres of vineyard entitled to the name, and the annual production amounts to some 50,000 bottles, promptly and happily consumed by the Niçois themselves and by thirsty tourists.

BELLEVUE, Château — (Bel-vuu) — 1st Growth of St. Emilion. Best known of literally dozens of chateaux so named, both in the Bordeaux Country and elsewhere.

BENICARLÓ — (Ben-nee-car-*lo*) — Town on the Mediterranean Coast of Spain, south of Valencia, known for its heavy, deep-colored blending wines.

BENTONITE — *See* Fining.

BERCY — (Bair-see) — Section along the Seine in Paris where a large part of the city's common table wine is received, handled and distributed.

BERGERAC — (*Bear*-shair-rack) — Town of 17,000 on the Dordogne River, east of Bordeaux, center of a large wine-producing area, with an annual yield of over 3 million gallons. Most of this is white and of only fair quality at best. (*See* Monbazillac.)

BERGHEIM — (Bairg-heim) — One of the best wine-producing villages of Alsace, in the *département* of Haut-Rhin. Renowned for its Rieslings, Gewürztraminers, etc.; its leading vineyard is called the Kanzlerberg.

BERGSTRASSE — (*Bairg-strah*-suh) — German wine district of secondary importance, paralleling the Rhine from Wiesloch to Weinheim, near Heidelberg.

BERINGER BROTHERS — Important producers of California wine, with cellars at St. Helena, in the Napa Valley. The winery has over 1,000 feet of impressive tunnels, cut back into the hills and used for ageing. The Beringer wines are widely sold in California and can occasionally be found in the East; they include one special red wine called "Barenblut," a few varietal wines, plus the inevitable generics — Burgundy, Claret, Sauterne, Chablis and all the rest. The quality is well above the California average. Beringer also produces a superior California brandy.

BERLIQUET, Château — (*Bear*-lee-kay) — One of the better 1st Growth vineyards of St. Emilion.

BERNKASTEL — (Bairn-cat'l) — Picturesque and world-famous little town in the heart of the Moselle wine country; its best wines are among the most expensive and most highly regarded of Germany. All of these are estate-bottled and carry the name of a specific vineyard, since wines sold simply as "Bernkasteler" or "Bernkasteler Riesling" are of a much inferior grade, and generally prepared with the addition of sugar. By all odds the most famous vineyard is Bernkasteler Doktor (or Doktor-und-Graben); others producing wines of almost equal quality include B. Lay, B. Badstube, B. Schwanen, B. Schlossberg, etc. Among the leading growers and estate-bottlers are Dr. Thanisch, the St. Nikolaus Hospital, the Pfarrkirche St. Michael, Geller, Melsheimer, Prüm, etc.

BESTES FASS — (Bestess Fahss) — Literally, "the best barrel." Term sparingly used by the estate-bottlers of Rhine wines to designate the

very best cask of a given vintage, usually a Beerenauslese (*see*) or Trockenbeerenauslese (*see*). The equivalent on the Moselle is *Bestes Fuder*. Neither term is ever abused, and wines so labeled are great rarities and invariably expensive.

BÉZIERS — (Behz-yea) — City of some 60,000 in the *département* of Hérault, southern France, in the heart of what is known as the Midi wine district, and an important center of the trade in *vin ordinaire*.

BEYCHEVELLE, Château — (Baysh-vell) — Well-known vineyard, and the fine red Bordeaux wine which it produces, at St. Julien, in the Haut-Médoc. Officially classified in 1855 as a 4th Growth, Château Beychevelle now brings a higher price than many 2nds, and is notable for its texture, delicacy and breed. The present elaborate chateau, dating from 1757, overlooks the estuary of the Gironde; its name is said to be derived from the French, "baisse-voile," or "lower sail" — a gesture of respect which all passing ships paid to the Duke of Épernon, one-time owner of the estate and Grand Admiral of the French Fleet.

BIANCO — (Bee-*onk*-ko; Italian, "white") — The common word for white in Italian; a *vino bianco* is any white wine. *See*, however, *Vino Rosso*.

BIARNEZ — (*Be*-ar-nes) — 19th century French poet and wine-lover who published, in 1849, a remarkable description and eulogy, in verse, of the wines of Bordeaux.

BIENNE — (Be-*en*) — Lake in the Canton of Berne, Switzerland. Its steep northern shore is one long terraced vineyard and gives (largely from the Fendant grape) a number of light, good-quality white wines — Twanner, Schafiser, Daucher, Inser, etc.

33

BIENVENUE-BÂTARD-MONTRACHET — (Be-*an*-vay-noo *Bat*-tarr Mon-rasch-*shay*) — Small northern portion of the already small Bâtard-Montrachet vineyard, in Burgundy, whose admirable, golden, fairly dry, full-bodied wines, among the best of France, must henceforth carry this rather clumsy name. Until quite recently they were sold as Bâtard-Montrachet, and there are few experts, if indeed any, who could distinguish between them. (*See* Montrachet.)

BIG — A wine with more than the average amount of body, alcohol and flavor; not necessarily either fine or great, quite possibly a wine without much distinction. A too "big" wine has a tendency to be heavy and coarse.

BIKAVER — (Beek-ah-vair) — Deep-colored, full-bodied Hungarian red wine, made in and around the village of Eger, from the Kadarka grape, plus several French varieties including the Cabernet and Gamay.

BINGEN — (*Bing*-en) — Important wine town (720 acres of vineyard) of Hessia, in Germany, overlooking the confluence of the Rhine and Nahe, and directly across the Rhine from Rüdesheim. Back of it rises the celebrated Scharlachberg, or "scarlet hill," one of the most famous vineyard sites of Hessia, although the color of its soil is much more dark brick-red than scarlet. The township of Bingen now includes the adjacent vineyards of Büdesheim and Kempten, and all of these produce, from the Riesling, Sylvaner and Müller-Thurgau grape, white wines of excellent quality, surpassed in Hessia only by those of Nierstein, Nackenheim, and perhaps Oppenheim. The best vineyards are Scharlachberg, Hausling, Steinkautsweg, Rheinberg, Pfarrgarten, Ohligberg, Mainzerweg, etc.; the leading producers include the State Domain, the Villa Sachsen (Curt Burger's Erben), Ohlig, etc. Corkscrews, in German, are sometimes jokingly referred to as "Bingen pencils," the idea being that citizens of Bingen are more likely to have corkscrews than pencils in their pockets.

BINNING — The laying away of bottled wine for ageing (*see*). In the case of table wines and sparkling wines, the bottles should invariably be stored on their side, lying down, so that the wine is in contact with the cork. Temperature and other factors are important. (*See* Cellar.)

BISCHÖFLICHES KONVIKT — (Bish-*huff*-lish-ess Kaun-vikt) — A Catholic refectory for students at Trier, on the Moselle; a large part of its endowment is in the form of vineyards in Piesport, Ayl, Eitelsbach, Kasel, etc. The wines that carry its label are much sought after.

BISCHÖFLICHES PRIESTERSEMINAR — (Bish-*huff*-lish-ess *Priest*-ter-sem-me-*narr*) — A Catholic seminary at Trier, on the Moselle, with imporant holdings in many of the better vineyards of the Moselle, Saar and Ruwer. The wines are estate-bottled and carry the seminary's name and label.

BISHOP — One of the many versions of Mulled Wine (*see*), and not the best. Most recipes call for a bottle of Port (not a good one, let us hope), an unpeeled orange, stuck with cloves and halved, and a few spoonfuls of sugar, heated together in an enamel saucepan.

BITTER — A wine-taster's term. Bitterness is generally perceptible only in the aftertaste of a wine. It is a fault sometimes due to the variety of grape (the Sauvignon Vert in California, for example), sometimes to climate (an overly dry year, in most cases), and sometimes to unskillful cellar work. Occasionally in red wines but hardly ever in white, it is a flaw that will disappear with age.

BLACK FOREST — *See* Baden.

BLACK ROT — A fungus disease to which grape vines are subject, particularly in moist areas and in periods of exceptional humidity. It attacks both the leaves and the grapes themselves, and copper sulphate is commonly used as a preventive.

BLACK VELVET — Famous tipple of Victorian days, half Champagne, half stout. There is practically nothing that can be said in its favor except that it is obviously better than BROWN VELVET, which is half Champagne, half Port.

BLAGNY — (*Blan*-ye) — Tiny hilltop village of the Côte de Beaune, Burgundy. Classified as a *hameau* (hamlet) rather than a *commune* (township), it sits astride the line dividing Meursault (*see*) from Puligny-Montrachet and has vines in both. Its excellent red wines and even better whites are therefore sold under a confusing multiplicity of names — the reds, which are delicate, fine, comparable to the lighter Volnays, as "Blagny-Côte de Beaune"; the whites most often as "Meursault-Blagny" or, more rarely, "Puligny-Montrachet, Hameau de Blagny."

BLANC DE BLANCS — (Blawn duh Blawn) — A white wine made from white grapes. A term originally and properly used in the Champagne district of France to describe wines made entirely from the white Chardonnay grape, as distinguished from other white wines made from the Pinot Noir (Blanc de Noirs, *see*) or blends of the two. Blanc de Blancs Champagnes are made mostly in the villages of Cramant, Le Mesnil and Avize; they are remarkable for their delicacy, pale green-gold color, lightness and bouquet. Of late years the term has become widely used in other districts (Provence, the Loire Valley, etc.) where it is entirely meaningless, since, in these districts, *all* white wines are made from white grapes, *none* from black.

BLANC DE NOIRS — (Blawn duh Nwar) — A white wine made from black grapes; especially a Champagne produced entirely from black grapes of the Pinot Noir variety. A few such are made, largely by small producers or *manipulants*, in the villages of Ay, Bouzy, Verzenay, Mailly, Hautvillers, etc.; they are rather full-bodied, soft, darker in color than Blanc de Blancs.

BLANC-FUMÉ — (Blawn-Foo-may) — Name given locally to the Sauvignon Blanc grape in and around the town of Pouilly-sur Loire (*see*). A Pouilly-Fumé, or Pouilly-Blanc-Fumé, is therefore a wine made from the Sauvignon Blanc grape in this district, and thus distinguished from the common wines of the same district, made from the Chasselas grape, which are sold as "Pouilly-sur-Loire." The origin of the term "fumé" (literally, "smoked") is uncertain.

BLANCHOTS — (Blawn-show) — One of the seven Grand Cru vineyards of Chablis (*see*).

BLANQUEFORT — (Blawnk-for) — Southernmost *commune* of the Médoc; its little tidal stream, the Jalle de Blanquefort, forms the official boundary between the Médoc district and that of Graves. Few wines of any consequence.

BLANQUETTE DE LIMOUX — (Blawn-*kett* duh Lee-*moo*) — Sparkling white wine, generally decidedly on the sweet side, produced round the town of Limoux, near Carcassonne, in southern France.

BLAYE — (Bly) — Town and large wine-producing area in the Bordeaux Country, north of Bourg and opposite the Médoc, on the right bank of the Gironde estuary. Its annual production is in the neighborhood of 4 million gallons, about nine-tenths of it white and, on the whole, of mediocre quality. The red — fruity, soft and rather full-bodied — is somewhat better. The superior grades, both red and white, are entitled to the appellation "Premières Côtes de Blaye"; the commoner sorts are sold as "Blaye" or "Blayais," or, perhaps more frequently, as just Bordeaux Blanc or Bordeaux Rouge, although not all of the whites are entitled even to this modest name.

BLENDING — Practice of mixing or "marrying" wines of somewhat different characteristics, or origin, or age, for any one of many diverse reasons, some wholly proper and honorable and some much less so. Virtually all Sherries, including the best, are blends; so are most but not all of the best Champagnes. On the other hand, the finest table wines of the world are emphatically not blends, and they would be much less interesting and less good if they were. The legitimate reasons for blending are largely these: (1) to produce a wine of consistent quality and character, year after year, which a consumer may buy with confidence under a familiar name or label; (2) to produce something better in the way of a wine than any of its component parts; (3) to render a wine acceptable which would otherwise be much less so, or not acceptable at all. Not even a purist could object to such blends, *providing, of course*, that the final product is honestly labeled, does not pretend to a vintage which is not its own, nor to be a wine of specific origin when it contains an admixture of others, and, finally, that it has not wholly lost its individuality and character in becoming something acceptable, perhaps, but basically uninteresting, and "standard." Unfortunately, not all blends, by any means, fulfill these conditions.

BLUE FINING — *See* Fining.

BÖCKELHEIM — (*Bick*-el-heim) — *See* Schloss Böckelheim.

BOCKSBEUTEL — (Bawks-boy-tel) — The squat, flat-sided, green flagon in which the German wines of Franconia (Würzburger, Steinwein, etc.) are traditionally shipped, as are also the Mauerweine of Baden. A somewhat similar bottle is widely used in Chile. It presumably gets its name from its fancied resemblance to a goat's scrotum.

BOCKSTEIN — (*Bawk*-stein) — One of the best vineyards of Ockfen, on the Saar, in Germany. Its light white wine, of admirable quality in good vintage years, is sometimes sold as Bocksteiner, more often as Ockfener Bockstein. Like all Saar wines, it is classified, in general, as a Moselle.

BODEGA — (Bo-day-ga) — A wine storage room or "cellar" in Spain, usually above ground. Also a winery, with its installations.

BODENHEIM — (*Bo*-den-heim) — Wine-producing town in the German province of Rheinhessen, south of Mainz. Its wines (Bodenheimer) are generally made from the Sylvaner grape unless specifically labeled "Riesling"; while less distinguished than the neighboring Niersteiners, for example, they are among the better Hessian wines, soft, well-balanced and attractive. Best vineyards include B. Kahlenberg, B. Hoch, B. St. Alban, etc. Leading producers are Oberstleutnant Liebrecht and the German State Domain.

BODENTON — (Beau-den-tohn) — A special, unique, unmistakable and disagreeable flavor, called *goût de terroir* in French, and often *Bodengeschmack* in German, which certain wines possess, due to the fact that they were produced on heavy clay or alluvial soil.

BODY — A wine-taster's term, often misused. Body means substance. A full-bodied wine is not necessarily high in alcohol, but it is the opposite of watery or thin; it gives an impression of weight, rather than lightness. Full body is not always a virtue — in many white wines and in some red it can be a fault, for only in rare instances and in very great wines does it go hand in hand with delicacy and finesse and distinction. A very full-bodied Moselle or Riesling or Chablis or Champagne or even Zinfandel is a wine that lacks balance, and probably lacks fruit and charm. On the other hand, a great Burgundy or a fine Cabernet, let alone a superior Barolo or Châteauneuf-du-Pape, must have body and plenty of it.

BOLZANO — (Ball-*zahn*-no) — Capital of the Italian Tyrol, an attractive little city on the Adige River, not far from the Brenner Pass, and Austria. The province of Bolzano (like that of Trento, immediately to the south) was part of Austria until 1918, and Bolzano was known as Bozen. It is an important center of the wine trade; the hills to the northeast and northwest are covered with pergola-vineyards, and a number of admirable and well-known wines (Santa Maddalena, Santa Giustina, etc.) are produced just outside the city limits. For additional information concerning these and other wines of the Tyrol, *see* Tyrol and Alto-Adige.

BOMMES — (Bawm) — One of the five townships, or *communes,* which constitute the Sauternes district of France, the others being Barsac (*see*), Preignac, Fargues and Sauternes itself. Bommes numbers, within its boundaries, such great estates as Château La Tour-Blanche, Ch. Lafaurie-Peyraguey, Ch. Rayne-Vigneau, Ch. Rabaud-Promis and Ch. Rabaud-Sigalas, all of them officially ranked as 1st Growth vineyards.

BONARDA — (Bo-*nar*-da) — Italian red wine grape widely grown in Piedmont, especially in the provinces of Alessandria and Asti.

BONNES MARES — (Bonn *Mar*) — Celebrated Burgundian vineyard, producing what is unquestionably one of the dozen finest red wines of the Côte d'Or. It consists of 37 acres of vines, of which some 32 are in the *commune* of Chambolle-Musigny, the remaining 5 in Morey-St. Denis. Its maximum legal yield (hardly ever attained) is approximately 5,000 cases. Situated about half way between Chambertin and Musigny, its wine has some of the characteristics of both of its illustrious neighbors — the power and great class of Chambertin, somewhat attenuated; the incomparable finesse of Musigny, though to a less remarkable degree.

For Map, *see* MOREY, CHAMBOLLE.

BONNEZEAUX — (Bonn-zo) — One of the best small vineyard areas in the French province of Anjou, part of the Coteaux du Layon (*see*). Some 250 acres of the Chenin Blanc (Pineau de la Loire) variety yield white wines that are quite sweet, distinguished by their fruitiness and bouquet.

BONTEMPS — (Bonn-tawn) — Small wooden utensil, in the form either of a scoop or pail, used in cellars in the Bordeaux Country. As such it has become the emblem of a well-known confraternity of wine-lovers, that of the Médoc.

BOORDY — Interesting and unusual small vineyard at Riderwood, Maryland, near Baltimore. It was founded and developed by Philip and

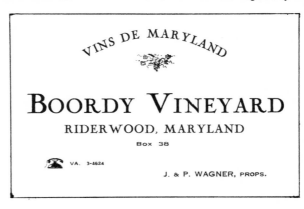

38

Jocelyn Wagner, first more or less as a hobby, then as an experimental nursery of Franco-American hybrid vines, and more recently as a commercial winery with an annual output of some 3,000 cases, approximately one-third red, one-third white and one-third *rosé*. Mr. Wagner, until his retirement, was editor of the Baltimore Sun, and has written a number of books on viticulture and wine-making. He was one of the first to introduce the superior, modern hybrids (*see*) and has done more, perhaps, than any one individual to popularize them in the Eastern states, where they have acquired greatly increased importance.

The Boordy wines are American *vins de pays* in the truest sense of the word, and it is to be regretted that the pattern set by their production has not been more widely followed, as it well could be, in scores of other areas all the way from New York to Nebraska and from Michigan to Texas. Made from carefully chosen varieties, well-vinified, with definite character but not much of the pronounced "Eastern grape" taste and aroma, the Boordy wines have grown steadily in popularity, and the entire production is now sold and consumed locally, in Baltimore, Washington, etc.

BORDEAUX — (Bor-*doe*) — Seaport and city of 240,000 on the Garonne River in southwestern France. A few miles north of the city, the Garonne is joined by the Dordogne to form the broad estuary of the Gironde; this has given its name to the *département* which comprises the entire Bordeaux wine country; its 110,000 acres of vineyard produce some 70 million gallons of wine a year, substantially more table wine than the United States.

Practically all of this wine is entitled to the name "Bordeaux," and this appellation is a sort of catch-all, or lowest common denominator. "Bordeaux Supérieur" is very little better — the wine must have slightly more alcohol (10½% as against 9¾%) and its maximum legal production per acre is somewhat lower. Both wines may and generally do come from inferior portions of the Bordeaux Country — if they came from the Médoc or St. Emilion or Graves or Sauternes they would be so labeled. In general, they are mass-produced and blended.

The better districts in the Bordeaux Country have been defined and delimited with characteristic French precision: each one produces wine of a somewhat different character or class. Thus, north of the city, forming the left or west bank of the Gironde estuary, are the low, gravelly hills of the incomparable Médoc, producing red wines almost exclusively, and many of the greatest red wines of the world. West and south of Bordeaux is the wide district of Graves, with white wines ranging from dry to semi-sweet, and many excellent reds. Along the southern edge of Graves, in turn, are the five little villages (including Barsac) which alone are entitled to the famous name Sauternes. Across the Garonne, beyond the intervening hills and the Dordogne, are the vineyards of St. Emilion and Pomerol — this is red wine country, second only to the Médoc in quality. Lesser wine districts include Côtes de Bourg, Fronsac, Lalande-de-Pomerol, Montagne-St. Emilion, Néac, etc.; white wine districts of less importance and less fame are Entre-

Deux-Mers, Côtes-de-Blaye, Ste. Croix-du-Mont, Loupiac, Cadillac, Premières-Côtes-de-Bordeaux, Cérons (actually part of Graves), Graves-de-Vayres (not part of Graves), etc.

The red wines of Bordeaux have been known as "Claret" in English-speaking countries ever since the three-hundred-year occupation of the region by the English (1154-1453); the French term *Clairet* has an altogether different meaning and is used to designate a sort of *vin rosé*. Ordinary Claret is simply a pleasant table wine, but the very best Claret is second to no other red wine in the world, fine Burgundy being its only real rival; it is made principally from the Cabernet Sauvignon grape,

plus a good deal of Cabernet Franc and Merlot, often a little Malbec, Petit Verdot and Carmenère; while lighter in alcohol than Burgundy, it is generally deeper in color and even longer-lived — certain Médocs of great vintages have been known to hold up, and even to improve, for fifty, sixty and even eighty years.

White Bordeaux is a whole family of wines, some quite dry, some extremely sweet, though all made from grapes of the Semillon and Sauvignon Blanc varieties, plus an occasional minor admixture of Muscadelle. Graves, Sauternes and Barsac are known, like Claret, the world over.

What goes to market as "Bordeaux Blanc" is a rather common wine, golden, ranging from dry to semi-sweet. The superior grades have, of course, their superior, and more limiting, appellations.

The finer Bordeaux wines, both red and white, invariably carry either (a) the name of one of the better districts (as Médoc, Graves, St. Emilion, Sauternes) or, more specifically, (b) the name of a village in one of these districts (as St. Julien, Margaux, Pauillac), or, most specifically of all, (c) the name of the actual vineyard or chateau, where the wine was made. As a general rule it may be said that the more specific the name, the better the wine. The finest Bordeaux, both red and white, carry, without exception, the name and label of a particular chateau, plus the statement that they were bottled at the chateau where grown, as *mise du château*, or *mis en bouteilles au chateau*.

BORDEAUX MIXTURE — Our name for what the French call *bouillie bordelaise,* a fungicide spray made of copper sulphate and slaked lime, widely used in Europe against oidium and mildew. It is this (or some quite similar, related product) that so often gives the French and German vineyards their characteristic blue-green tinge in summertime.

BOTA — (Bo-ta) — Spanish for Butt (*see*).

BOTRYTIS CINEREA — (Bo-treat-iss Sin-air-eh-ah) — The "noble mold," called *Edelfäule* in German and *pourriture noble* in French. A highly beneficient mold which in certain districts (notably the Rhine Valley and the Sauternes Country) forms on the skins of the ripening grapes, bringing about a concentration of sugar and flavor and a vast improvement in the quality of the resulting wine. In the case of white wines, at least, it imparts no moldy taste whatsoever.

BOTTLE — The ordinary European wine bottle, whatever its form, generally contains ¾ U.S. quart, or a little less; the precise reason for this size is unknown, but some have declared it to be the proper ration of wine for a good trencherman at one sitting. American wine bottles, those used for California and N.Y. State wines, are a little larger, of ⅘ quart capacity; half bottles, in all cases, generally contain one-half as much. On the other hand there are many exceptions, and fortunately American law requires that the actual net contents be stated on the label, or blown into the glass. A bottle's shape and its color are useful but by no means infallible clues to a wine's origin and type:

the straight-sided, high-shouldered "Bordeaux bottle" is used, in green glass, for all red Bordeaux, and in clear glass for nearly all white, but the same or a very similar bottle is used in almost all other wine-producing countries, and sometimes for very dissimilar wines. The slope-shouldered "Burgundy bottle" is also that of the Rhône Valley, of many Italian and Spanish wines, and, in a somewhat heavier version, that of Champagne. The slender, tapering "Rhine bottle" is brown on the Rhine, but green in Alsace and on the Moselle, and a colorless *"flute"* of nearly the same form serves for many *rosés*. Italy provides us with all sorts of straw-covered bottles, of various shapes and sizes, and both Germany and Chile have their stumpy flagons. Actually, the form of the bottle makes no difference at all, providing, of course, that it can be easily binned. All wines, however, age more quickly in small bottles than in large, and a half-bottle of a given vintage will always be readier than a full bottle, and both than a magnum of the same wine. Champagne is occasionally an exception, since most Champagne is normally fermented and stored in regular size bottles and loses something by being decanted into jeroboams, splits, half-bottles, Nebuchadnezzars, and all the rest. All wines are somewhat affected by light, and all last longer, except under absolutely ideal cellar conditions, when in green or brown bottles, and the possibly less attractive brown bottle, in the author's experience, seems to be the best.

The best known oversize bottles of France are these: Magnum - 2 bottles; Double-Magnum (sometimes called Jeroboam) - 4 bottles; Jeroboam or Rehoboam - 6 bottles; Imperial or Methuselah - 8; Salmanazar - 12; Balthazar - 16; Nebuchadnezzar - 20.

BOTTLE SICK — Unhappy condition in which a wine generally finds itself immediately after bottling. All wines are badly shaken and "numbed" by passing through the filtration which normally precedes bottling, the bottling-machine, etc. If sound, they invariably recover from this bottle-sickness, but sometimes only after ninety days or more. Somewhat the same effect is produced, especially in old or delicate wines, by rough handling, even long after bottling — it is for this reason that fine wines should be "rested," at least for a week or two, before they are opened.

BOUCHES-DU-RHÔNE — (Boosh-dew-Rone) — French *département,* that of Marseille, Aix-en-Provence, Arles and the Rhône delta. Its best wines are the white Cassis (*see*), a perennial favorite with bouillabaisse; the white and *rosé* wines of Palette, some of the Côtes de Provence, the Coteaux d'Aix, etc., none of them, to be truthful, very distinguished.

BOUCHET — (*Boo*-shay) — Local name given to the Cabernet grape in the St. Emilion district of Bordeaux, where the Cabernet-Sauvignon is called the Bouchet or Petit Bouchet, and the Cabernet Franc, the Gros Bouchet. Under no circumstances should these be confused with the Bouschet hybrids, so called after their creator, Henri Bouschet, mostly mass-production grapes of high yield and low quality, grown in the French Midi district and to some extent in Algeria and California.

BOUCHONNÉ — (Boo-shon-*nay*) — French for corky (*see*), from *bou-chon*, cork.

BOUGROS — (*Boo*-gro) — One of the seven Grand Cru vineyards of Chablis (*see*).

BOUQUET — The complex of diverse, interesting and pleasing odors which a good, mature wine gives off once it is opened; everything that such a wine says to the nose (as distinguished from the palate); one of a fine wine's greatest attractions and greatest charms. On the basis of bouquet alone, many experts can determine a fine wine's origin, its grape variety, its approximate age, its condition, its class and value. Young wines may have aroma or odor or perfume or "fruit" or "flower"; bouquet is distinct from all these, may include all of them, but comes mainly from esters developed by the slow oxidation of certain elements in the wine, including alcohol but above all fruit acids. Wines with high acid, coming from northern vineyards, almost invariably have more bouquet than those with lower acid, from sunnier zones; similarly, wines from chalky, stony and, on the whole, less fertile soil, have more bouquet than others, as do wines made from grapes that have matured slowly, in a temperate climate, without excessive heat. One does not have to be any sort of expert to like and appreciate the bouquet of a fine wine.

BOURG — (Bourg) — Name shared (in most instances with some suffix) by at least twenty towns and villages in France. The one of interest to wine-drinkers, neither the largest nor the most beautiful of the lot, has no suffix and is in the Bordeaux Country, on the Gironde estuary, directly across from the Médoc. The area of which it is the center produces some 2 million gallons of wine annually, a little over a third of it white wine of mediocre quality, the rest red, and much of it far from bad. Apart from the general appellation, "Bordeaux Rouge" (under which most of it is sold), it is entitled, when red, to the names "Bourg," "Bourgeais," and "Côtes de Bourg," but these are rarely seen on wine labels outside France. Full-bodied, well-balanced, made largely from the Cabernet grape, it is a red wine that deserves to be better known than it is.

BOURGEOIS — One of the main categories of Bordeaux wine, qualitative rather than geographical, however, as in the expressions *"cru bourgeois,"* or "bourgeois growth." In the whole Bordeaux Country there are well over 5,000 separate vineyards; less than 200 of these constitute what might be called the aristocracy, the "classed growths" (*see*) of the Médoc, Sauternes, St. Emilion, etc. In highly honorable second place comes a whole collection of others, smaller and less famous chateaux, some but not all of which practice chateau-bottling; known as the *"crus bourgeois"* and *"crus bourgeois supérieurs,"* these often produce wines as good as those of their reputed superiors, and their labels are worth looking for. A partial list of such chateaux has been included in the appendix. It is important to note that a bourgeois growth of a good vintage is not by any means an ordinary wine, and may be a truly excellent one.

BOURGOGNE — (Boor-*gon*-yuh) — French for the province of Burgundy *(see)* and its wine.

BOURGOGNE MOUSSEUX — (Boor-*gon*-yuh Moo-*suh*) — French for Sparkling Burgundy *(see)*.

BOURGUEIL — (Boor-guhy) — Village in the old French province of Touraine, in the Loire Valley, long famous for its red wines, made entirely from the Cabernet Franc grape, although the best of these generally carry the appellation St. Nicolas-de-Bourgueil *(see)*, and come from an adjacent township, higher up on the Loire hillsides. One of the most agreeable lesser red wines of France, Bourgueil should be drunk fairly young, preferably at cellar temperature. It is rather light (rarely over 11½%), delicate, fruity, fresh, of a brilliant light ruby color. Total production amounts to something over a half million gallons a year. Students of French literature will recall that it was at Bourgueil that Rabelais situated his "Abbaye de Thelème" and that it was here that Ronsard met his *"belle Angevine,* Marie," whose charms he celebrated in some of the greatest lyrics of the French Renaissance.

BOUSCAUT, Château — (Boose-ko) — One of the most important and best-tended vineyards of the Graves District, south of Bordeaux. It is in the township of Cadaujac, and produces some 10,000 cases of good quality Claret and about half as much good dry white Graves, per year. Invariably chateau-bottled.

BOUZY — (Booz-ee) — Major wine-producing village in the Champagne Country of France, rated as one of the best. *See* Champagne.
   ALSO an extremely pleasant red still wine made in the same village from the Pinot Noir grape and, for the most part, consumed locally.

BOYD-CANTENAC, Château — (Boyd-Cawnt-nack) — 3rd Classed Growth of Cantenac-Margaux, Haut-Médoc.

BRACCHETO — (Bra-*kay*-toe) — Red Piedmontese wine, generally *frizzante (see),* made from the grape of this name.

BRANAIRE-DUCRU, Château — (Bran-air Dew-crew) — 4th Classed Growth of St. Julien, Haut-Médoc, directly adjoining Beychevelle and accorded the same rank in 1855. Its wine (some 6,000 cases a year) by no means deserves such rating today, although there has been some recent improvement, thanks to a change in ownership.

BRANE-CANTENAC, Château — (Brawn Cawnt-nack) — 2nd Classed Growth of Cantenac-Margaux, Haut-Médoc, with an annual production of about 7,000 cases of good quality Claret. While hardly one of the best of the 2nds today, its wine is dependable, generally not too expensive, and almost always a good value, well-balanced and sound.

BRAUNEBERG — (Brown-uh-bairg) — Famous wine-producing village on the Moselle, in Germany; long considered, even by such discerning tasters as Thomas Jefferson, the Moselle's best; formerly known as

Dusemond (from the Latin *mons dulcis,* "sweet mountain" — supposedly because of the excellence and sweetness of its wines). Today these wines, less fashionable, are no less admirable, quite comparable to those of Wehlen and Zeltingen, full-bodied, fine and rich. The best vineyards are Brauneberger Juffer, Falkenberg, Hasenlaufer, Kammer, Sonnenuhr, Lay, and the leading producers include Haag, Von Schorlemer, the St. Nikolaus Hospital, the Brauneberger Winzerverein, etc.

BRAZIL — Only the very southernmost corner of Brazil, the state of Rio Grande do Sul, is sufficiently far from the equator and temperate enough in climate to provide proper growing conditions for the vine. There are some 90,000 acres of vineyard, a good part of them producing table grapes; the wine is undistinguished.

BRILLANTE — (Bree-yantay) — White, slightly sweet, Spanish table wine. This, like Diamante, is a trade name.

BRILLIANT — Term applied to a wine impeccably clear, as all good wines should be.

BRISTOL — City and major seaport in the west of England, long famous for its trade with France, Spain, the West Indies, etc. Several important British wine merchants (Avery, Harvey) have their home offices in Bristol; the latter now markets in the United States two popular Spanish Sherries under the names "Bristol Milk" and "Bristol Cream."

BROCHON — (*Broh*-shawn) — Village directly north of Gevrey-Chambertin, on the Côte d'Or, in Burgundy. All of its better vineyards, about 125 acres, produce red wines legally entitled to the name Gevrey-Chambertin, and one rarely, if ever, sees a bottle labeled "Brochon."

BROLIO — (Brole-yo) — Perhaps the most celebrated castle and wine-estate of the Chianti Country: a famous fortress in the Medieval wars between Siena and Florence. There was an old saying that "when Brolio growls, all Siena trembles," and one of the battles around its walls was so bloody that Dante said that it "colored the Arbia red" (the Arbia being a small river nearby). For over 800 years, Brolio has been the property of the Ricasoli family; Bettino Ricasoli, in the 19th century, was the first Premier of reunited Italy after Cavour.

Brolio Chianti is properly regarded as one of the four or five best Chiantis, and is among the sturdiest and longest-lived red wines of Italy. As is often the case with fine *classico* Chianti, the younger wine is shipped in straw covered *fiaschi,* and the older, finer *riserva* in ordinary wine bottles like Bordeaux.

BROUILLY — (*Brew*-ye) — One of the best and most famous wine-producing districts of the Beaujolais (*see*). Like Moulin-à-Vent, it is not a township, but a strictly delimited zone, and consists of portions of the *communes* of Odenas, St. Lager, Cercié, Quincié and Charentay, all surrounding the celebrated Côte de Brouilly (*see*), a hill crowned by a chapel which is the site of an annual pilgrimage. As a wine, Brouilly,

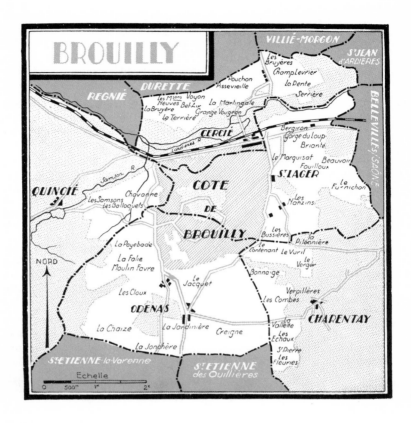

or Beaujolais-Brouilly, is one of the most typical and most attractive of the Beaujolais, especially when young; fruity, full-bodied, full-flavored, sturdy, yet soon ready and, as compared with other Beaujolais (Moulin-à-Vent, Morgon, etc.) relatively short-lived, it is among the most agreeable red table wines in the world.

BROUSTET, Château — (Brew-stay) — 2nd Classed Growth of Barsac, producing some 3,000 cases a year of white wine, a little less sweet than most Barsac but of considerable distinction and breed.

BRUT — (Brute) — French term applied to the dryest Champagnes and other sparkling wines, dryer than "Extra Dry." Properly it means, in this instance, "unmodified" — a Champagne to which no *dosage,* or sweetening, has been added. Actually, all *brut* Champagnes, or practically all, do contain some *dosage;* this is not supposed to exceed 2% at most, but in many instances does. Most Champagne houses ship their best wines, both vintage and non-vintage, as *brut,* but the term alone is no guarantee of quality. *See* Champagne.

BUAL — (Also BOAL) — Name of one of the leading grape varieties of Madeira (*see*) and the sweet, fine, golden wine made from it.

BUCELLAS — (Boo-sailas) — White Portuguese table wine, produced near Lisbon.

BÜDESHEIM — (Bew-des-heim) — *See* Bingen.

BUENA VISTA — (Bway-na Vee-sta) — Historic California vineyard, at Sonoma, north of San Francisco. It was founded, not long after the Gold Rush, by an extraordinary Hungarian nobleman, Count (a title which he later abandoned in favor of the more democratic one of "Colonel") Agoston Haraszthy *(see),* who has not incorrectly been called "the father of modern California viticulture." Famous from Civil War days until its cellars were largely destroyed by the San Francisco earthquake, it got off to a fresh start when purchased by Frank Bartholomew (now president of United Press-International) in 1943, and is today once more a producer of premium wines. Most of the wines that now carry the Buena Vista label are varietals, sold under the name of the grape from which they are made, but there are a few special designations, as Vine Brook, Rose Brook, etc.

BUGEY — (Byew-shay) — Little district in the *département* of Ain, northeast of Lyon, producing a variety of very light but often agreeable and refreshing wines, red, white and *rosé,* entitled to the V.D.Q.S. seal *(see).* Most of these are sold as *Vins du Bugey* or *Roussette du Bugey,* plus, in some cases, one of the village names as Montagnieu or Virieu.

BUHL, Reichsrat von — (Buel) — Largest vineyard owner and estate-bottler of the Pfalz, or Palatinate, in Germany. Major holdings in Forst, Deidesheim, Ruppertsberg, etc.

BUHLERTAL — (Buel-ler-tahl) — Small vineyard district near Baden-Baden, in southwestern Germany. Pleasant red and white wines of little more than local interest. *See* Baden.

BULGARIA — Balkan country with some 400,000 acres of vineyard and an annual production of some 50 million gallons of wine, about two-thirds of it red. A substantial amount is exported, mainly to the Soviet Union, Czechoslovakia and Eastern Germany.

BULK PROCESS — Method of making sparkling wine, considerably less expensive and less slow than the true Champagne process, never as good. The wines are not fermented in bottle but in large sealed tanks, and drawn off into bottle under pressure. No wine so made may be called Champagne *(see)* in France; in the United States such wines must carry the words "Bulk Process" or the equivalent, on their labels.

BURDIN — (Buhr-dan) — One of the better known French Hybridizers. (*See* Hybrids.)

BURGER — Productive white wine grape of poor quality, known in Germany and Alsace as the Elbling *(see)* or Eisling. Widely planted in California, it gives a dull wine, common, low in acid, much used in the cheaper grades of California "Chablis" and "Sauterne."

BURGUNDY (French, Bourgogne) — Old French province southeast of Paris, long an independent Duchy; the world famous wines, red, white, and in rare instances *rosé,* from this region, which is generally considered to comprise the *départements* of Yonne (the Chablis district), Côte d'Or (area of the greatest Burgundies, both red and white), Saône-et-Loire (Macon, Pouilly-Fuissé, etc.) and part of Rhône (Beaujolais).

However, by no means all of the wines produced in these four *départements* are entitled to the name "Burgundy" (or "Bourgogne"); French law reserves this name for wines made from certain superior grape varieties, grown in certain specific townships, and all true Burgundies are therefore better-than-average wines of some well-defined type and some known, established origin. The total production is only about one-third that of Bordeaux — it amounts to less than 2% of the wine produced in France. This percentage has declined sharply in the last hundred years — vineyard acreage in Burgundy is now less than half of what it was in 1870.

Truly fine Burgundy is therefore something of a rarity and always will be; it is produced only on a few narrow, especially favored hillsides, in a country of generally unfavorable climate, principally from two grape varieties which yield very little to the acre. A few additional figures may serve to make this even clearer:

In a typical, fairly copious year of good quality, 1962, the wine production of Burgundy amounted to 1½% of that of France, or to some 30 million gallons. Now 48% (of this 1½%) was Beaujolais; 17% was Macon or Macon *Supérieur;* nearly 4% was what is called "Bourgogne *grand ordinaire"* (the lowest legal grade, and what most Sparkling Burgundy is made of); 6% was Bourgogne Aligoté *(see)*, a white carafe wine made from a second-rate grape; 2% was Passe-tout-grains (an inexpensive blend of Gamay and Pinot, rarely exported), and about 5% was simply called Bourgogne, honest wine, no doubt, but of no special quality.

Out of the remaining 18% (less than one-third of 1% of the total wine production of France) came the world's supply of all those wines beloved of gourmets in all countries: Chablis, Pouilly-Fuissé, Meursault, Montrachet, Chambertin, Clos Vougeot, Nuits-Saint-Georges, Corton, Beaune, Pommard, and all the others. For these, *see* each, in its proper alphabetical place, in this volume. *See,* also, Beaujolais, Passe-tout-grains, Gamay, Pinot, Chardonnay, Macon, Côte d'Or, Sparkling Burgundy, etc., as well as the listing of Burgundian towns and vineyards in the Appendix.

With a handful of exceptions — Chablis, perhaps Pouilly-Fuissé, and a few rare, outstanding Beaujolais — all of the wines that have made

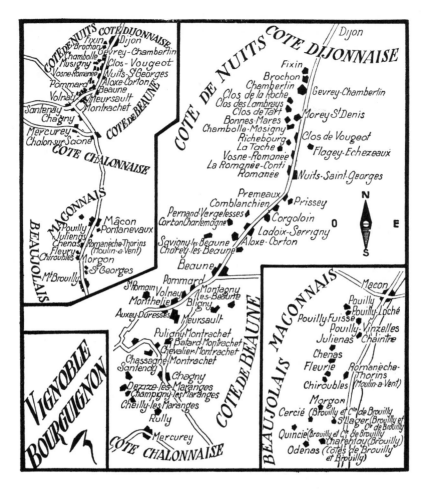

Burgundy's international and enduring fame come from one extraordinary strip of hillside vines. This, the "Côte d'Or," or "Golden Slope," extends from near Dijon to well south of Beaune and faces south of east over the wide plain of the Saône, beyond which the Alps are occasionally visible in clear weather. All of these wines are made either from the Pinot Noir or from the Chardonnay grape, and all of them carry either the name of the *commune,* or township, from which they come (as Pommard, Beaune, Nuits-Saint-Georges, Chambolle-Musigny), or the name of some specific vineyard plot, or *climat,* which produced them (as Richebourg, Musigny, Bonnes Mares); often they carry both (as Pommard Épenots, Beaune Grèves, Meursault Perrières, etc.). These vineyard plots are very small, rarely over forty acres in extent

49

and often much smaller, usually divided among many different owners, some of whom estate-bottle their production, while others sell their wine soon after the vintage to a shipper, or *négociant*. Such wines, when both genuine and good (and unfortunately, despite all the controls, there are some which are neither) are unsurpassed in the world: the reds have a warmth and fruit and vigor and bouquet, a combination of power and finesse, matched by no other wines; and of all the white wines in the world, the white Burgundies are those that most true gourmets would prefer to drink with their meals.

The word BURGUNDY, alas, in a great many countries, including the United States, is considered a generic term applicable to red wine, however and wherever produced, even to sweet red wines made from Concord grapes in New York State or in Michigan or Ohio. There is possibly a little more justification for the use of the name in California, where wines so labeled are at least made from European grape varieties, but as contrasted with the very strict French controls, which even govern pruning methods and maximum yield per acre, there are almost none, and it is common practice to bottle "Burgundy" and "Claret" out of the same tank. The name, so used, has become meaningless, and those interested in finding an honorable American counterpart of a French Burgundy will do better to look for bottles labeled Pinot Noir, Chardonnay, Pinot Blanc and Gamay-Beaujolais — these are true cousins, and in some cases quite distinguished cousins, to the real Burgundies of France.

BÜRKLIN-WOLF — (Beerk-lin-Wolf) — Celebrated wine producer and estate-bottler of the German Palatinate, or Pfalz, with large vineyards in Wachenheim, Deidesheim, Forst, etc.

BUTT — Large barrel or cask, especially of the sort and size in which Sherry is traditionally aged and shipped. It holds just over 150 U.S. gallons.

BUTTAFUOCO — (Boot-ta-Fwo-co) — One of the three oddly named and rather agreeable red wines [the others being Barbacarlo and Sangue di Giuda (*see*)] produced near Pavia, in northern Italy. The vineyards are in the township of Broni and Canneto Pavese.

BYRRH — (Beer) — Well-known French apéritif, with a red wine base, made in the town of Thuir, Pyrénées Orientales.

C

CABERNET — (Cab-air-nay) — Superb red wine grape, responsible in large part for the great Clarets of Bordeaux, and, in the North Coast Counties of California, for what are rightly considered America's best red wines. The name Cabernet, or Cabernet Sauvignon, on a California wine label, is therefore an indication, almost a guarantee, of superior quality, and it is under this name that America's finest "Clarets" are sold. Actually, there exist two Cabernet grapes, distinct but closely related: the smaller and less productive Cabernet Sauvignon predominates in the Médoc and in California, and gives a longer-lived, slower-maturing wine, with more tannin; the Cabernet Franc is the leading variety in the St. Emilion district, produces Chinon, Bourgeuil, Champigny, and many excellent *rosés* in the Loire Valley. Both Cabernets are planted in Chile and the best red wines of South America generally carry this name. The so-called "Ruby-Cabernet," rather widely planted in California during the past decade, is not a true Cabernet but a very productive, recently developed cross of Carignan x Cabernet Sauvignon — it is not, on the basis of present evidence, a really superior wine grape, and, in any case, has no established right to this name.

CABERNET ROSÉ D'ANJOU — (Cab-air-nay *Rose*-A *Dawn*-shoe) — Legally a *rosé* wine made from the Cabernet Franc grape in a clearly defined area in the Loire Valley in western France, an area more or less comprising the old province of Anjou *(see)*. Several *appellations contrôlées* are involved, since Rosé de Cabernet is made almost everywhere in Anjou — round Saumur and on the Coteaux de l'Aubance (perhaps the best), the Coteaux du Layon, the Coteaux de la Loire, etc., etc. The variations in quality are nevertheless not as great as all this complicated terminology would lead one to believe: the wine, while much better than the ordinary Rosé d'Anjou, made from the Groslot, is pleasant, inexpensive, usually a little sweet, by no means extraordinary.

CABINET — (Cab-ee-*net*) — Often written Kabinett. A term employed in Germany, especially in the Rheingau district, to designate a superior grade or special reserve of Natural (i.e. unsugared) wine, usually estate-bottled. Originally *Kabinettweine* were those which the vineyard owner put aside for his own use, but the term has come to be more and more loosely used, and today many proprietors designate as Cabinet wines any lots which bring more than a certain minimum price, per bottle or per cask, when sold. This minimum may vary considerably from one producer to another, and even from one vintage to the next. In general, all wines labeled Auslese *(see)* or Spätlese *(see)* are ranked as Cabinet wines, but so, in many cases, are others of less distinguished class. The term is somewhat differently used at Schloss Johannisberg *(see)*.

CABRIÈRES — (Cab-ree-*air*) — *Vin Rosé,* made from Carignan and Cinsault grapes, near Lodève, in southern France. It is one of the better wines of the Midi, and entitled to the V.D.Q.S. seal.

CADILLAC — (Cad-dee-yak) — Picturesque little town in the French Bordeaux Country, facing Graves and Sauternes across the Garonne river and forming part of the district called "Premières Côtes de Bordeaux." Its rather sweet white wines are not unlike Sauternes, but of lower quality and less class.

CAHORS — (Kah-*or*) — Interesting, excellent, almost legendary red wine, produced round the old city of this name, north of Toulouse in central France. It is made principally from the Malbec grape, but vinified in the ancient, traditional way, and it is perhaps the most deeply colored of fine French red wines, its dark crimson tinged, one might almost say, with black, like certain of the best wines of Valtellina, in northern Italy. Slow-maturing, remarkably long-lived, firm but not harsh, it has unmistakable distinction and a special cachet of its own, some affinity to a good, full-bodied red Graves. Those interested in wine "discoveries" will do well to seek it out, although the best is not easy to come by, and it is greatly to be regretted that under French law it is entitled only to the V.D.Q.S. seal, rather than the *Appellation Contrôlée* which it obviously deserves.

CAILLOU, Château — (Ky-you) — 2nd Classed Growth of Barsac, and definitely one of the best of these. Not to be confused with many other Bordeaux chateaux bearing quite similar names.

CAIRANNE — (Kay-*rahn*) — One of the better wine-producing villages of the lower Rhône Valley, in France, some twenty-five miles northeast of Avignon. Its red, white and *rosé* wines are among the best of those sold as Côtes-du-Rhône, and carry the special appellation Côtes-du-Rhône-Cairanne.

CALDARO — (Kahl-*dar*-o) — Picturesque little vineyard town some ten miles southwest of Bolzano, in the Italian Tyrol. The surrounding hillsides are covered with vines trained on their characteristic pergolas, and produce a remarkably diverse collection of fresh, light, eminently agreeable table wines, both red and white. Many of these, notably those made from the Traminer *aromatico* (Gewürztraminer), the Riesling, Silvaner (Sylvaner), Pinot *bianco* (Pinot Blanc), Moscato Giallo and Pinot *nero* (Pinot Noir) are marketed under these varietal names. What is sold as Caldaro or Caldaro Collina is a rather tart red wine, light in body and color but fruity and appetizing, made from a grape known as the Schiava (*see*). A somewhat finer but very similar wine is called Lago di Caldaro (*see*) and comes from the steep shores of a little lake three miles to the south. In Austrian days Caldaro was called Kaltern, and the lake wine was known as Kaltererseewein; in Switzerland and Austria, where both wines are still great favorites, they are often still so listed and so sold.

CALIFORNIA — America's one major vineyard country, producing over 80% of the wine consumed in the United States, as against about 6% of imports and some 14% from the other states, much of the latter being made of grapes grown in California, but crushed and fermented elsewhere. There are some 400,000 acres under vines and the crop varies between 2.3 and 3.2 million tons of grapes a year; a little less than half of this is made into wine, most of the rest being marketed as table grapes or raisins. In 1961 the state's 241 bonded wineries (there were over 500 in 1940) produced a total of 159 million gallons, as compared with an average of 68 million gallons in the years 1936-1940.

At present, and for that matter ever since the repeal of Prohibition, two-thirds of California's output is and has been fortified wine (Sherry, Port, Angelica, Muscatel) rather than table wine, which predominates in almost all other wine-producing lands, Australia being an odd exception. Thus California produces only one-eighth as much table wine as Spain, but over three times as much Sherry, and only one-fourth as much table wine as Portugal, but nearly ten times as much Port. With a few rare and notable exceptions, most of this is mass-produced for a mass market, sold and consumed when less than a year old; it is poor stuff, drunk because it contains 20% of alcohol by volume, and is cheap.

In the past twenty years, and particularly in the past ten, however, the producers of superior wine in California have made extraordinary progress, especially in the field of table wines. The cheaper California

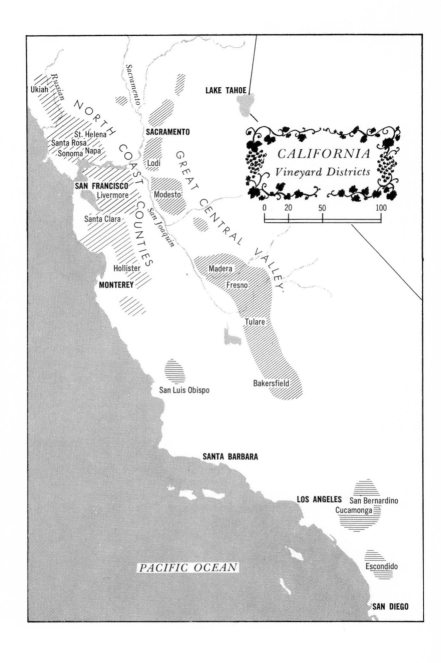

Ukiah

Russian

NORTH

Sacramento

LAKE TAHOE

St. Helena
Santa Rosa
Sonoma Napa

SACRAMENTO

COAST

Lodi

SAN FRANCISCO
Livermore

Modesto

Santa Clara

San Joaquin

COUNTIES

Hollister

Madera

Fresno

MONTEREY

Tulare

GREAT CENTRAL VALLEY

San Luis Obispo

Bakersfield

SANTA BARBARA

LOS ANGELES San Bernardino
Cucamonga

Escondido

PACIFIC OCEAN

SAN DIEGO

CALIFORNIA
Vineyard Districts

0   20   50   100

reds and whites are, on the average, quite as good as the *vin ordinaire* of France or Italy or Spain, and the finer ones, the varietal wines (*see*), can stand comparison with all but the rare, truly great wines from European vineyards. The plantings of fine European grape varieties (Cabernet, Pinot, Riesling, Semillon, etc.) have greatly increased; in equipment and technique, California's best wineries are now on a par with those of Germany and France.

Grapes are grown in most of California's 58 counties (there are bonded wineries in 28), but the major wine districts are two: the cool North Coast area, centered round San Francisco, producing principally table wines; and the much warmer interior valleys, where most of the fortified wines are made. The North Coast area includes the counties, from north to south, of Mendocino, SONOMA, NAPA, Contra Costa, Alameda (the LIVERMORE Valley), SANTA CLARA, Santa Cruz and SAN BENITO (those in caps being the more important). In the interior valleys there are vast irrigated areas where raisin and table grapes predominate and where cheap fortified wines are made, often from culls — over 60% of the grapes used for wine in California are not "wine grapes" but what the California Wine Institute itself calls "raisin or table grapes." The counties where these are grown, in the San Joaquin and Great Central valleys, are, from north to south, Sacramento, San Joaquin, Stanislaus, Madera, Fresno, Tulare, Kings and Kern. Fresno County alone produces three times as much wine as the entire fine wine district round San Francisco.

A third district, directly east of Los Angeles, in San Bernardino County (the largest county in the United States) has some 25,000 acres of wine grapes, and produces wines comparable to, and in general superior to, those of the French Midi.

Several species of grape vine grow wild west of the Rockies, including *Vitis californica* and *Vitis arizonica*, but *Vitis vinifera*, the "wine-bearing" grape of Europe, was brought to California by Franciscan monks, who established a chain of missions from what is now the Mexican border all the way to Sonoma, north of San Francisco, before 1840. The original grape introduced, now known as the Mission, is a hardy variety giving on the whole poor wine; it has been largely replaced, and now ranks only sixth among red wine grapes, in acreage. What was planted in its stead, especially during Prohibition, hardly represented an improvement and the leading red wine varieties in acreage are, today: Zinfandel (of uncertain origin, productive, giving a rather common but agreeable wine, fruity, not too heavy, fair — and in superior mountain vineyards, quite good); Carignan (the "old dependable" of the French Midi and of Algeria — rather coarse, full-bodied wines, no real quality but not too bad); the Alicante Bouschet (an inferior hybrid, which has no possible virtue except the deep color of the wine it yields); the Grenache (in the proper location, and *only* there, an admirable grape for *rosé*; elsewhere, a passable variety for Port-type wine); the Mission; the Mataro (a common, coarse, productive grape from Spain); the Petit Syrah (an aristocrat in France, the grape of red Hermitage; very probably *not* the same variety in California, possibly the Duriff, yielding very full-bodied wines without any trace of distinction or breed).

The roster of mass-production white "wine grapes" is much shorter, since by far the largest part of inexpensive California white wine is made from the Sultanina, or Thompson Seedless, a vastly productive raisin grape which gives a neutral, almost flavorless, pale white wine. The leading true wine grape is the Palomino (excellent for Sherry, almost worthless for table wine); the next, the Sauvignon Vert, is definitely no better; the third, the Burger, is so poorly thought of in its native Alsace that it will not even be "tolerated" in the better Alsatian vineyards after 1965.

Nevertheless, on the whole, the cheap, ordinary table wines of California are at least as good as the *vins ordinaires* of Italy and France. If they were sold under honest American names, and presented with less fanfare, the reds would be quite acceptable; the whites (as is very often the case with *ordinaires*) somewhat less so.

When it comes to better table wines, California has little to be ashamed of and in fact much of which we can be proud. These increasingly tend to go to market under their "varietal" names — the name of the variety of grape from which they are made — and no one could devise a more honest system of labeling. This, plus the name of a respectable vineyard and a good district, is about all that a wine-buyer can ask in the way of a guarantee, and those who know California wines ask for Cabernet Sauvignon and Pinot Noir when they want fine red wine, and Chardonnay, Johannisberg Riesling, Pinot Blanc, Sauvignon Blanc, etc. when they want fine white. These are still produced in limited quantity, but their quality is at least as good as European wines in the same price bracket, and their production will increase as more people come to appreciate this fact.

The following list of California varietal wines is complete, except for a few oddities which are of no great interest and not widely available:

WHITE WINES

Variety	Quality	Nearest European Equivalent
Chardonnay (or Pinot Chardonnay)	Excellent	Pouilly-Fuissé or Chablis
Johannisberg Riesling (or White Riesling)	Excellent	Dry Rhine Wines
Sauvignon Blanc	Very good	Superior Dry Graves
Pinot Blanc	Very good	Lesser White Burgundy-Macon Blanc
Chenin Blanc (or White Pinot)	Very good	Vouvray or Saumur
Traminer (or Gewürztraminer)	Very good	Alsatian
Sylvaner	Good	Lesser Rhine Wines
Veltliner	Good	White Austrian Wines
Semillon	Good	Dry Graves
Folle Blanche	Fair	Vin Blanc Sec
Grey Riesling	Fair	Vin Blanc

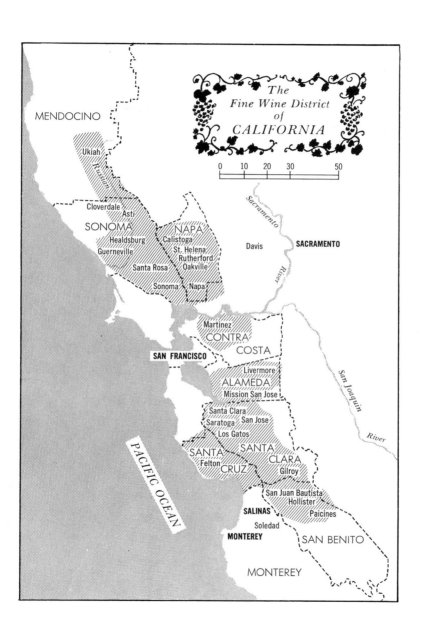

The
Fine Wine District
of
CALIFORNIA

| 0 | 10 | 20 | 30 | | 50 |

MENDOCINO

PACIFIC OCEAN

Russian

Ukiah

Cloverdale
Asti
SONOMA
Healdsburg
Guerneville
Santa Rosa
Sonoma

NAPA
Calistoga
St. Helena
Rutherford
Oakville
Napa

Sacramento

Davis

SACRAMENTO

Sacramento River

Martinez
CONTRA
COSTA

SAN FRANCISCO

Livermore
ALAMEDA
Mission San Jose

San Joaquin

Santa Clara
Saratoga
Los Gatos
San Jose
SANTA
CLARA

SANTA
Felton
CRUZ
Gilroy

San Joaquin River

San Juan Bautista
Hollister
SALINAS
Paicines

Soledad
MONTEREY
SAN BENITO

MONTEREY

RED WINES

Cabernet Sauvignon	Excellent	Red Bordeaux
Pinot Noir	Very good	Lesser Burgundy
Gamay Beaujolais	Very good	Beaujolais
Barbera	Good	Italian Barbera
Gamay	Fair	Lesser Red Macon
Zinfandel	Fair	Vin Rouge

ROSÉ WINES

Grenache	Excellent	Tavel
Grignolino	Fair	Italian Grignolino
Gamay	Fair	Vin Rosé

All of these grape varieties and wines will be found, described in much greater detail, in their proper alphabetical place in this volume; and additional details concerning them in the Appendix.

The California producers who have undertaken the difficult and often unprofitable and thankless job of turning out this country's best wines and marketing them under honest but relatively unknown varietal names, deserve well of all wine drinkers and of their country. They are of course not very numerous, but they are the elite of California, and most of them are in the North Coast counties. It is to be regretted that they cannot all be listed here, but at least, below, are those that have some national distribution, whose wines are not just locally available. Most of them, and their plant managers and wine makers as well, have a genuine love of good wine and an inextinguishable enthusiasm for it, and rarely willingly deviate from the path that leads toward better quality. This is by no means a blanket endorsement of everything they make, but in general they are people of good taste and good will.

Leading Producers of Varietal Wines

Vineyard	*County* or District
Almadén Vineyards	Santa Clara-San Benito, etc.
Beaulieu Vineyard	Napa
Beringer Bros.	Napa
Buena Vista	Sonoma
Christian Brothers	Napa, etc.
Concannon	Livermore
Cresta Blanca	Livermore
Inglenook	Napa
F. Korbel & Bros.	Sonoma
Charles Krug	Napa
Louis M. Martini	Napa, Sonoma
Paul Masson Vineyards	Santa Clara
Sebastiani	Sonoma
Souverain Cellars	Napa
Weibel	Alameda
Wente Bros.	Livermore

California also produces a substantial amount of sparkling wine, most of it made by the authentic Champagne process and therefore legally entitled to the appellations California Champagne and Sparkling Burgundy. However, in our laws there are no restrictions (like those that exist in France) as to the grape varieties that can be used and only a few, especially honorable, top producers conform voluntarily to what are the legal minimum standards abroad. The best California Champagnes are made, and well made, largely from the Chardonnay and Pinot Blanc, and they are extremely good sparkling wines, better, in the opinion of most experts, than those of New York State, and among the best produced in the world outside the Champagne Country of France. But there is a large amount of California sparkling wine, most of it labeled Champagne, which is a long way from fine. The best and most dependable producers, in alphabetical order, are Almadén, Beaulieu, Korbel and Paul Masson; also Christian Brothers, Cresta Blanca and Weibel.

In the field of California Sherry and Port, the situation is even worse: hardly a half-dozen producers follow the classic and costly solera method which is normal practice in Spain and Portugal, but what these producers make is remarkably good. Almadén has been the principal pioneer in this field but Louis M. Martini also produces a good Sherry and Ficklin Vineyards an outstanding Port. But most California Sherry and Port is a sort of by-product of the raisin and table-grape industry, and the average age of California Sherry and Port, when it reaches the consumer, is under ten months.

A more discriminating public of wine-drinkers (and their numbers are increasing daily) can certainly help make of California one of the very good, possibly great, wine districts of the world. But there is a long road ahead and the good producers need, meanwhile, all the encouragement they can get.

CALON-SÉGUR, Château — (Cal-awn Say-gour) — 3rd Classed Growth of St. Estèphe, Haut-Médoc. Produces some 15,000 cases a year of outstandingly good Claret, full-bodied, yet soft and fine. One of the best 3rd Growths today.

CALUSO — (Cahl-loos-o) — Town north of Turin, in the Piedmont region of Italy, and the unusual, rather sweet white wine which is its specialty. This is made from grapes of the Erbaluce variety, left to partially raisin (*see Passito*) indoors over the winter, and pressed and fermented in the spring.

CAMENSAC, Château — (Cam-on-sack) — 5th Classed Growth of. St. Laurent, Haut-Médoc.

CAMPANIA — (Cam-pan-ee-ah) — Italian district south of Rome, including Naples, Capri, Vesuvius, etc.; source, in Roman days, of what were then considered the world's best wines, as Falerno (*see*). Now produces some 60 million gallons of table wine, of varying quality, a year. The finer wines of Campania include Lachryma Christi, Capri, Gragnano (*see*).

CAMPARI — (Cam-*par*-ree) — Pink, bitter-sweet, Italian apéritif, used in the Americano cocktail, and the Negroni, more often drunk unmixed with a twist of lemon peel and a dash of soda. There is also a sweet Campari, much less good.

CAMPIDANO DI CAGLIARI — (Comp-pi-*don*-no dee *Cal*-yar-ee) — Important wine-producing district near the city of Cagliari, on the island of Sardinia. Pale white and red wines, rather high in alcohol.

CAÑA — (*Cahn*-ya) — Small, slender tumbler with a heavy bottom out of which Manzanilla is usually drunk in southern Spain. The *venencias*, or long-handled little dippers, used for taking samples of Manzanilla from the cask in Sanlúcar de Barrameda, are generally made of *caña*, or bamboo (instead of whalebone and silver, as in Jerez), and these probably gave the glass both its unusual shape, and its name.

CANADA — Apart from a few scattered plantings in British Columbia, Canada's one vineyard district is the Niagara peninsula, between lakes Erie and Ontario. The wines much resemble those of New York State, being made from the same varieties of grape — Concord, Catawba, Niagara, Delaware, etc. Experiments with some of the new French hybrids (*see*) since World War II have been very encouraging and seem to give promise of far better quality in the not too distant future. The annual production of the Dominion, of all types of wine, is in the neighborhood of 6 million gallons.

CANARY ISLANDS — Canary wines, celebrated in England in Elizabethan times, have almost ceased to exist commercially, the vineyards having been repeatedly devastated by insects and fungus diseases brought in from overseas. A good deal of red and white wine is made (some 1½ million gallons a year), a little exported — mainly to South America — but the once-famed "Canary Sack" is a thing of the past.

CANELLI — (Kahn-*nell*-lee) — Important vineyard town not far from Asti, in Italian Piedmont. Famous above all for a special variety of Muscat grape to which it has given its name, Moscato di Canelli, and for the light, often sweet, very fragrant wine made from it, widely used in Asti Spumante (*see*) and also in Italian Vermouth.

CANON, Château — (Can-awn) — One of the best 1st Growth vineyards of St. Emilion, producing about 7,000 cases a year of sturdy, full-bodied, generally long-lived red wine.

CANON-FRONSAC — *See* Côtes-Canon-Fronsac.

CANTEMERLE, Château — (Cawnt-mairl) — 5th Classed Growth of Macau, Haut-Médoc. Produces some 10,000 cases a year of very good Claret, notable for its admirable balance and bouquet. One of the best of the 5th Growths today, and not far, in character, from the finer red Graves.

CANTENAC — (Cawnt-nack) — Major wine-producing *commune* in the Médoc, adjoining Margaux on the south. Its Clarets, very similar to those of Margaux and of substantially equal quality, have been, since 1954, officially entitled to this name which was traditionally theirs. Leading vineyards include Château Brane-Cantenac, Palmer, Kirwan, d'Issan, Cantenac-Brown, Boyd-Cantenac, Prieuré-Lichine, etc.

CANTENAC-BROWN, Château — (Cawnt-nack Brown) — 3rd Classed Growth of Cantenac-Margaux, Médoc, which, unlike some others, still deserves its 1855 rating. Produces about 4,000 cases a year of honorable red wine which has the typical breed and finesse of its district.

CANTENAC-PRIEURÉ, Château — (Cawnt-nack Pre-oo-ray) — One of the 4th Classed Growths of Cantenac, in the Haut-Médoc, now known as Prieuré-Lichine (see).

CANZEM — (Kahnt-zem) — See Kanzem.

CAPRI — (Cop-pree) — Dry white wine, one of the best of southern Italy, produced on the island of Capri, near Naples, but also, legally, on the neighboring island of Ischia and on the mainland nearby, the "Capri district" being considered to include these, both of which produce wine often superior to that of Capri itself. The quality of Capri varies considerably from one shipper to another and much of what is exported is by no means first rate.

CARAFE — Clear glass bottle or decanter for holding wine and serving it at table. Young, inexpensive, "open" wines are generally served *en carafe* in France, and a *vin de carafe* is any wine of this sort, so served. Carafes are also used for decanting (see) old red wines that have thrown sediment in bottle. A small carafe or decanter is sometimes called a *carafon*.

CARBONATED — As far as wine is concerned, one made sparkling, like "club soda" and most popular soft drinks, not by the ancient and costly *méthode champenoise*, nor even by the faster, cheaper, but passably good "bulk process" (see), but simply by the addition, under pressure, of CO_2 (carbon dioxide). Such wines tend to lose their sparkle rapidly, and have large bubbles very unlike the creamy *mousse* of good Champagne. According to American law they have to be labeled "carbonated" and according to French law "gazéifié": there are no good ones, certainly none worth what they cost, considering the high tax they pay.

CARBONNIEUX, Château — (*Car*-bawn-*yuh*) — Important vineyard of Léognan, in the Graves district of Bordeaux, producing some 5,000 cases of good red wine a year, and about 8,000 cases of even better white; it is the latter wine, pale, racy, dry, one of the half dozen best Graves, which has made the name famous. According to a possibly apocryphal story, it was once consumed in vast quantities at the teetotal court of the Sultan of Turkey and known there, on account of the Koran's strict prohibition of wine, as *Eau Minérale de Carbonnieux* or "Carbonnieux mineral water."

CAREMA — (Car-*eh*-ma) — Superior red wine made from the Nebbiolo grape (see) north of Turin, in northwestern Italy. Rarely exported.

CARIGNAN — (Car-reen-*yan*) — Productive red wine grape, widely planted in southern France, Spain, Algeria and California (where it is second in acreage only to the Zinfandel). While by no means of the highest quality, it yields a quite satisfactory, ordinary table wine in many areas.

CARMENÈRE — (Car-men-*air*) — Secondary grape variety of the Bordeaux Country, probably related to the Cabernet.

CARMIGNANO — (Car-mean-*ya*-no) — Important wine-producing town in the Monte Albano district northwest of Florence; once famous in its own right, its wine now usually goes to market as Chianti; it ranks with Pomino and Rufina as one of the best of the non-*classico* kind. *See* Tuscany, Chianti.

CARPANO — (*Car*-pan-o) — The oldest and one of the best manufacturers of Italian vermouth, producing two kinds, the regular, and a rather bitter-sweet one called "*Punt e Mes*"; both are excellent, but better straight or with soda, than in a cocktail.

CARRASCAL — (Car-rahs-*cahl*) — One of the largest and best vineyards of the Sherry Country and after Macharnudo perhaps the most famous. It is planted on white, chalky, *albariza* soil northwest of the town of Jerez, and produces some three or four thousand butts a year of fine, rather full-bodied wine.

CARRUADES — (Car-roo-*odd*) — Name given to the secondary wine of Château Lafite (*see*) in the Haut-Médoc, generally those cuvées (usually from younger vines) considered not quite worthy of the famous Lafite label, being lighter, with less depth and less class; chateau-bottled, the wine is nevertheless very good, the equal of many third and fourth classed growths, and of some seconds. It is sold as Carruades de Château Lafite, is less expensive, and sooner ready to drink.

CASEL — (Kah-zl) — Often spelled Kasel. The most important vineyard town of the Ruwer, a tributary of the Moselle, producing pale, light, delicate white wines, of great bouquet and charm. Leading vineyards include Niesgen, Taubenberg, Steiniger, Kohlenberg, Kernagel, Hitzlay, etc.

CASK — Wooden container, generally with round or oval heads, in which wine is matured and stored; oak is by all odds the best wood, chestnut (in Europe) and redwood (in California) being barely passable substitutes. Casks of widely varying shapes and sizes are used for different wines. The following list includes the most important:

District	Name	Liters	U.S. Gallons	Cases
Chablis	Feuillette	136	36	15
Tokay	Gönez	144		
Champagne	Pièce	200	53	21
Beaujolais	Pièce	212	56	23
Bordeaux	Barrique*	225	57	24

District	Name	Liters	U.S. Gallons	Cases
Burgundy	Pièce	228	58	25
Sherry	Butt		151	63
Port	Pipe		151	63
Rhine	Halbstück	600	153	68
California	Puncheon		160	70
Alsace	Foudre	1000	264	108
Moselle	Fuder	1000	264	108

* A *Tonneau*, in Bordeaux, is the equivalent of 4 Barriques, but there is no cask of this size.

CASSE — (Cass) — Disease to which wines are subject, the symptoms of which are a persistent cloudiness and an off taste. The cause is usually an excess of metallic salts, and even brief contact with copper or iron can bring about *casse* in an otherwise sound wine. There are a number of remedies, but none effective once the wine is bottled.

CASSIS — (Cas-seece) — Picturesque little fishing village on the Mediterranean east of Marseille; its dry white wine, pleasant, made principally from the Ugni Blanc grape, pale gold, traditionally the wine to drink with bouillabaisse. Some 20,000 cases a year are produced, plus a certain amount of less good red and quite good *rosé* also entitled to the name.

ALSO, a syrup made from black currants, (*cassis,* in French), as deep purple in color and as sweet as blackberry jam, though generally with 10-16% of alcohol. Widely used to sweeten and flavor mixed apéritifs, including dry vermouth and white wine, it is a Burgundian specialty and the best of it is produced in Dijon. Only the deplorable but now diminishing French preference for sweet apéritifs (Port, Pineau des Charentes, and all the others) can conceivably explain its popularity.

CASTEGGIO — (Cahs-*tedg*-jo) — Italian wine-producing town, in southern Lombardy, center of a small, hilly district overlooking the Po Valley, in which the Pinot Noir and Pinot Blanc, transplanted from France, have been successfully cultivated for many decades. Much of the wine from these (and a good deal of the pale, light, local Moscato wine as well) is shipped to Piedmont and made into *Spumante* (*see*), or sparkling wine. A little of it, surprisingly good, is bottled as still wine in Casteggio, and some of this is even exported, notably under the brand name "Frecciarossa," which means "Red Arrow" in Italian.

CASTELL — (Cahz-tell) — Wine-producing town on the Main River near Würzburg, in Franconia. Its wine is of course shipped in the traditional *Bocksbeutel*, and its best vineyard is the Schlossberg.

CASTELLI DI JESI — (Cahs-*stel*-lee dee *Yay*-zee) — Wine district in east-central Italy, in the foothills of the Apennines some twenty miles from the Adriatic port of Ancona, which produces one of the lightest, most popular and best white table wines of Italy. This is made from the Verdicchio grape (*see*) in some half-dozen villages of which Cupramontana is the most important; it is usually exported in a special, slender, amphora-like bottle, and often sold simply as "Verdicchio." Dry, pale, with a freshness and breed rare in white wines from so far south, it deserves its international acceptance and increasing fame.

CASTELLI ROMANI — (Cahs-*stel*-lee Ro-*mahn*-nee) — The popular, common, inexpensive, and often quite agreeable table wine of Rome, produced round the villages of the Alban Hills, southeast of the city, and not far from Anzio. The best of this (for there are many sorts) is a dry white wine with an almost amber tinge, usually served in carafe and drunk young, rather coarse and lacking in distinction but by no means unpleasant with good Roman food. It comes principally from the villages of Frascati (*see*), Marino, Grottaferrata, Genzano, Albano, Ariccia, Rocca di Papa, Velletri, etc.

CATALONIA — (Spanish, Cataluña — Cat-ah-*loon*-ya) — Large region of northeastern Spain, bounded on the north by France and on the east by the Mediterranean, generally considered to comprise the provinces in which Catalan is spoken: Barcelona, Gerona, Lerida, Tarragona. These produce a remarkably diverse collection of wines, ranging all the way from the sweet, heavy Priorato (which was formerly known as "Tarragona Port") to the light, pale, white wines of the Panadés (which, when made to sparkle by the Champagne process, were formerly known as "Spanish Champagne"). There are many good, though never great, table wines as well, all relatively inexpensive. *See* Tarragona, Priorato, Panadés, Alella.

CATAWBA — (Ca-*taw*-ba) — Native American grape of somewhat uncertain origin, believed to be an accidental hybrid of wild, indigenous varieties (it is of the species *labrusca*) probably first found growing in the woods along the Catawba River, in the Carolinas. In any case, in the 1820s, it was being cultivated in Montgomery County, Maryland, and in the District of Columbia, where it found a champion in the person of a Major John Adlum, who once hopefully stated that, "in bringing this grape into public notice, I have rendered my country a greater service than I could have done had I paid off the national debt" (then $84,000,000). Time has perhaps proved him wrong, but for the better part of a century the Catawba was the leading wine grape of America; it was the basis of Nicholas Longworth's famous sparkling wine, produced along the banks of the Ohio, near Cincinnati; it is still one of the most widely grown of native grapes, both in Ohio and in the Finger Lakes district of New York State. It is a light red grape, highly productive, giving a white wine with a pronounced native or "foxy" flavor. Much of this is used in New York State Champagne, and is found good by those who do not object to its assertive taste; some passable non-sparkling Catawbas have been made, generally quite tart but with the same basic fault. There also exists an amber horror, a 16% or 18% fortified Catawba, foxy and sweet, of which it would be impossible to say anything favorable. Few people, in any case, today, would agree with what Longfellow wrote when he received a gift of Sparkling Catawba from Nicholas Longworth:

Very good in its way
Is the Verzenay,
Or the Sillery, soft and creamy;
But Catawba wine
Has a taste more divine,
More dulcet, delicious, and dreamy.

CAVE — (Cah-v) — The French word for cellar. This can mean, as in English, a storage space underground, or simply a collection of bottles. Commercially, it is just as meaningless as in English — a term to be regarded as suspect on a wine label unless a good deal of sound information follows it directly. Thus *"mis en bouteille dans nos caves"* does NOT mean estate-bottled; *"Les Caves de Chablis"* can be just a brand; a *caviste*, however, is unequivocally a "cellar-man."

CELLAR — Storage space for wine and, by inference, the wine it contains; traditionally, but by no means necessarily, below ground. There are few underground cellars in the Bordeaux Country, few in California, almost none in Spain. Whether underground or no, a wine cellar should be cool, with as even a temperature as possible throughout the year, free from vibration, and dark. A somewhat damp cellar is likely to be cooler than one absolutely dry; some ventilation is essential. The ideal cellar temperature is between 55° and 60°, with 45° and 70° as perhaps permissible extremes; within these limits, the cooler the cellar, the more slowly wines will develop and the longer they will live.

Apart from one's current requirements, the wines that should be laid away in a cellar (the bottles horizontal, of course, so that the wine covers the cork) are those most likely to increase in value and improve with age; many wines (*see* Ageing) do neither. A carefully kept record, or cellar-book, will be found a most useful and helpful guide: it should show at least, for each wine, where purchased, when purchased, price, when served, to whom, with what food, and tasting notes.

CÉPAGE — (Say-*pahj*) — Variety of grape vine. Thus one may say that the Pinot Noir and Chardonnay are the leading *cépages* of Burgundy. *Cep* means an individual vine or vine-stock.

CÉRONS — (*Say*-rawn) — Village in the Bordeaux Country, officially part of Graves, adjoining Barsac and the Sauternes district. Its golden, rather sweet wines, fairly high in alcohol but with a good deal of fruit, bouquet and breed, are more like Sauternes than Graves. The official Cérons district includes as well the townships of Illats and Podensac; total production is some 400,000 gallons a year.

CERTAN, Château — (Sair-tawn) — One of the very best vineyards and wines of Pomerol, in the Bordeaux Country. Vieux-Château-Certan (*see*) is just next door and at least equally distinguished.

CHABLAIS — (Shab-lay) — Wine-producing district in the Canton of Vaud, in southern Switzerland. The vineyards, planted to the Fendant or Chasselas grape, extend from Villeneuve, at the eastern tip of Lake Geneva, southeast along the upper Rhône Valley. The wines are all white, fairly full-bodied, and some of them, as Yvorne and Aigle, rank among the best Swiss wines.

CHABLIS — (Shab-lee) — Little town southeast of Paris, in the *département* of Yonne, and the surrounding district, which produces some of the most famous of all white Burgundies (*see* also the Appendix, Page 395). Chablis may be made only from the Chardonnay grape, and the zone entitled to the name is strictly delimited, comprising only certain areas of chalky soil in a total of 20 small *communes*. The average annual production, including Chablis Grand Cru and Chablis Premier Cru, is roughly 350,000 gallons; in addition, some 90,000 gallons of "Petit Chablis" are made, also from the Chardonnay, from less fine vineyards in the same 20 *communes*. Petit Chablis is a lighter wine, of less distinction and class, shorter lived and soon ready — much of it is drunk up as carafe wine in Paris restaurants when less than a year old. The finest Chablis, that called Grand Cru, must come from a single slope consisting of seven tiny vineyards: Vaudésir, Les Clos, Grenouilles, Valmur, Blanchots, Preuses, Bougros (*see*, however, Moutonne); such wine generally carries the vineyard name in addition to the words "Grand Cru"; a good deal of it is estate-bottled, and only some 6,000 cases are produced in favorable years; crop failures on account of frost are frequent. Chablis Premier Cru, too, quite often carries a vineyard name, and in good years is a wine of almost equal quality; the 1st Growth vineyards (*Climats Classés Premiers Crus*) include: Montée de Tonnerre, Monts-de-Milieu, Vaulorent, Vaucoupin, Fourchaume, Côte-de-Léchet, Vaillon, Beugnon, Butteaux, Les Forêts, Montmain, and some dozen others. Wines labeled simply Chablis, without vineyard name or designation as to growth (*cru*), may be assumed to be from less good vineyards, although they are of a higher class than Petit Chablis. The quality of Chablis varies enormously from one vintage to another, that of poor years being often disagreeably thin and tart. At its best, it is a dry, almost austere wine, pale straw in color, remarkably clean on the palate, with a delicate, fleeting bouquet, and a characteristic flavor often described as "flinty." In other countries the name is loosely used and is largely meaningless; in the United States (as formerly in Spain, Chile, etc.) any white table wine, wherever made and of whatever grapes, may call itself "Chablis." Those interested in finding a California counterpart of this fine French wine should look for bottles labeled "Chardonnay," or "Pinot Chardonnay."

CHAI — (Shay) — Building used for wine storage in France, generally above ground, as distinguished from a *cave*, or true cellar. Commercially, the two terms are largely interchangeable.

CHAINTRÉ — (*Shan*-tray) — One of four townships in Burgundy producing white wines entitled to the name Pouilly-Fuissé (*see*).

CHALON — (*Sha*-lawn) — *See* Côte Chalonnaise.

CHAMBERTIN — (*Shawm*-bair-tan) — Remarkable and famous vineyard of the Burgundian Côte d'Or, consisting of 32 acres of Pinot Noir vines, and producing one of the very greatest red wines of the world. One directly adjoining vineyard, the 37-acre Clos de Bèze (*see*), is also entitled to the name, although its wines are more often sold as Chambertin-Clos de Bèze. The total production of both *climats* together rarely exceeds 6,000 cases, and an authentic Chambertin of a good vintage is invariably expensive. It may be added that it is worth what it costs, for there is no better red Burgundy and few as good — powerful, long-lived, with astonishing class and breed, it is a "noble" wine, in the true sense of the word. The vineyard has been celebrated since about the year 600 A.D., and its reputation has never waned: its wine was the favorite of Napoleon, and of it Alexandre Dumas wrote that "nothing makes the future look so rosy as to contemplate it through a glass of Chambertin." Today the 69 acres are divided among numerous growers, a majority of whom estate-bottle. Many other nearby vineyards, of excellent but somewhat less exalted class, produce wines that carry the name Chambertin, in various specific combined forms, rigidly controlled by the French government. Thus the entire *commune* is now known as Gevrey-Chambertin (*see*), and the less good wines of the *commune* are marketed under this regional name; of a higher grade are those that

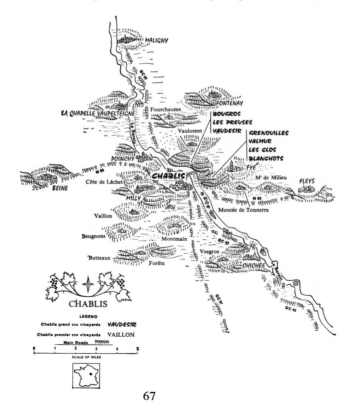

67

CHAMBERTIN
CLOS DE BĒZE
APPELLATION CONTROLÉE

PIERRE GELIN
PROPRIÉTAIRE A FIXIN ET GEVREY-CHAMBERTIN (COTE-D'OR)

carry the appellation Gevrey-Chambertin, plus a vineyard name; while the plots closest to Chambertin itself, both geographically and in quality, are classified as Grands Crus (great growths) and each has a special name of its own: Latricières-Chambertin, Mazoyères-Chambertin, Charmes-Chambertin, Mazis-Chambertin, Griotte-Chambertin, Ruchottes-Chambertin and Chapelle-Chambertin (*see* each of these, in its proper alphabetical place, in this encyclopedia).

For Map, *see* GEVREY.

CHAMBÉRY — (*Shawn*-bay-ree) — Small city in the French *département* of Savoie, east of Lyon, known especially for its pale, light, dry vermouth, which many wine experts consider one of the best apéritifs. Dolin and Boissière are the leading brands.

CHAMBOLLE-MUSIGNY — (*Shawm*-boll *Moos*-een-ye) — Celebrated wine-producing township of the Côte d'Or which, like many another Burgundian village, has added the name of its finest vineyard (Musigny) to its own original village name (Chambolle). There are some 420 acres under vines, all, except for a tiny portion of Musigny (*see*) producing red wines exclusively, and some of the most charming, delicate and fragrant of all Burgundy. Musigny and Bonnes Mares (*see*), the two best, are sold under these names without mention of Chambolle; the next highest in quality, ranked as Premiers Crus and often truly admirable, go to market as Chambolle-Musigny plus a vineyard name, as Les Amoureuses, Les Charmes, etc.; what is labeled simply Chambolle-Musigny comes last of all, is often rather light, but generally makes up in finesse for what it lacks in body.

CHAMBRER — (French; *Shawm*-bray) — To warm a red wine, from the temperature of the cellar to that of the dining-room. The only proper way to do this is to bring the bottle to the dining room an hour or more ahead of time, and let it stand. No wine worth drinking should be set near an open fire or plunged into hot water — common practices, alas, both of them. *See* Serving, Temperature.

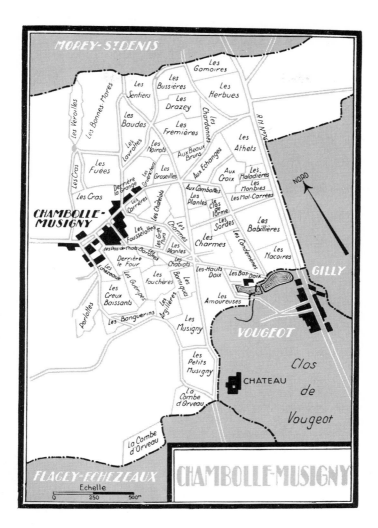

CHAMPAGNE — (Sham-pain) — Strictly speaking, Champagne means French Champagne: a specific wine made by a specific process, from only certain varieties of grape, in a legally delimited part of France. The Champagne Country lies east of Paris, and consists principally of the *département* of the Marne (plus portions of the Aube, Haute Marne and Aisne); the total area under vines (some 25,000 acres) is less than 1% of the vineyard land of France, and far less than 1% of French wine is therefore Champagne. The better vineyards are planted along a series of chalky hillsides south of the old cathedral city of Reims, and

69

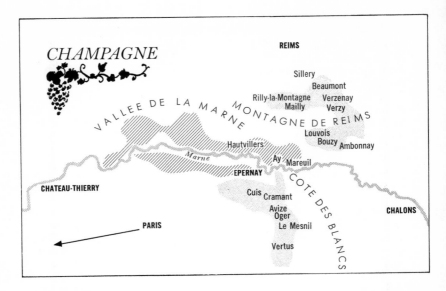

on slopes overlooking the Marne Valley nearby, north and south of
Épernay. There are three main districts that produce superior wine:
(1) the *Montagne de Reims*, yielding, from the Pinot Noir grape, its
"wines of the Mountain," notable for their body and power; (2) the
Vallée de la Marne, just north of Épernay, producing, also from the
Pinot Noir, its "wines of the River," particularly soft and round; and
(3) the *Côte des Blancs*, which gives, almost entirely from the Chardonnay grape, its *blanc de blancs*, outstanding in delicacy and finesse.
Within these three districts, the various *communes* have been officially
ranked and rated according to the average of excellence of the wines
they yield. Thus Verzenay, Mailly, Bouzy, Ambonnay (all on the
Montagne de Reims), Ay (in the *Vallée de la Marne*) and Avize and
Cramant (on the *Côte des Blancs*) are rated 100%, or "*hors classe.*"
But many other *communes* (Mareuil-sur-Ay, Dizy-Magenta, Hautvillers, Le Mesnil, etc., etc.) are very nearly as good and rate 90-98% or
80-89%. Most commercial Champagnes are blends of wines from various *communes* in all three districts, and the proportions often vary
according to the individual character of each vintage.

The Champagne vineyards are the northernmost of France and, as
might be expected, there is a wide variation, from one year to another,
in the quality of the wine they yield. The more expensive and best
French Champagnes carry a vintage, which means that they were made
in large part from wines produced in a single, particularly favorable
year. Non-vintage Champagnes are almost invariably blends of less
good *plus* good years, for alone, the former would hardly be salable.

However, the matter of vintage years on labels is notoriously one
difficult to regulate and control. The method set up for Champagne is

both practical and effective, allowing the producer some latitude and discretion while protecting the public against large-scale fraud. Briefly, no producer may sell, as the wine of a given vintage, over 80 per cent of his actual production for that year: in other words, what is sold as 1959 Champagne cannot exceed four-fifths of what was produced in that particular year.

At the same time, a producer who finds that his 1959, unblended, is too heavy and too alcoholic (as was often the case), may, if he sees fit, blend in some 1958 or 1960 and still call his wine "1959." But by doing so he will not increase, by as much as a single bottle, what he can legally sell as 1959.

In addition, Vintage Champagnes must be submitted to an inter-professional committee of experts, for tasting and approval, before they are shipped, and no Champagne may be shipped, carrying a vintage, until it is three years old.

Since virtually all Champagnes are blends, Champagne is one of the very few wines (perhaps the *only* French wine) on which a brand is more important than a vineyard or district name. The larger and better-known French producers are listed below. However, a small amount of interesting and often excellent Champagne is sold under the name of its *commune* of origin, as Cramant, Avize, Le Mesnil, Ay, Mailly, etc. This is made, generally, by small producers and vineyard owners and is unblended.

The shippers below are listed in the approximate order of their annual total sales, but of course this is no index to quality, since price, inevitably, plays a major role. All experts would agree, for example, that Krug, Bollinger and Roederer belong in the topmost class, although their output is far below that of many of their competitors. Most major Champagne houses are also large vineyard owners, and the extent of their vineyard holdings is, in some degree, an indication of consistent quality. Their rank, in total acreage of vines, is therefore given in parentheses for the top twelve.

Moët et Chandon (1)	Bollinger (9)
Mercier	Taittinger (7)
Pommery-Greno (2)	Irroy
Mumm (8)	Pol Roger
Veuve Clicquot (3)	Henriot (6)
Heidsieck Monopole (11)	Philipponnat
Charles Heidsieck	Krug
Lanson (5)	Delbeck
Ayala-Montebello-Duminy (12)	Deutz et Geldermann
Piper-Heidsieck	Billecart-Salmon
De Castellane	Veuve Laurent-Perrier
Gauthier	Georges Goulet
S.A.M.E.	Delamotte
Perrier-Jouet (10)	Salon
Roederer (4)	

The Pinot Noir (and to a much lesser extent the Pinot Meunier) and the Chardonnay are the grape varieties cultivated to the virtual exclusion of all others; the first two of these, of course, are black grapes, but pressed as soon as picked they give white wine (or, in rare instances, a pink or *rosé*).

The still wines of the Champagne Country (*see Champagne Nature*) are made sparkling by a special, laborious and expensive process, imitated the world over but known the world over as the *méthode champenoise*, or Champagne Process. A carefully predetermined amount of sugar is added (about 3⅓ oz. per gallon to produce a pressure of six atmospheres), plus yeast, to the still wine, to bring about a second fermentation; the wine is then bottled and corked or sealed immediately, and the bottles are stacked away. The second fermentation takes place *in bottle*, over a period of months or years, and gives of course a small amount of additional alcohol, plus CO_2, or carbon dioxide; this, unable to escape, remains dissolved, under pressure, in the wine. But sediment is also formed in the wine during fermentation, and this must be got rid of; in order to accomplish this, without sacrificing the wine's sparkle, the bottles are placed individually, neck down, in inclined perforated racks, or "pulpits," then shaken and turned daily, by hand, over a period of months. The sediment finally slides down against the cork, and is then ejected, by a process known as "disgorging." At this point, all Champagnes (and all sparkling wines made by the Champagne process) are absolutely bone dry; before the bottle is finally recorked, therefore, it receives what is known as its *dosage* — generally a sugar syrup with an old wine base, sometimes plus a little brandy. It is this *dosage* and only this which determines the dryness or sweetness of the finished wine. In theory, but rarely in practice, the various designations of dryness are supposed to indicate the precise degree of *dosage,* as *Brut,* up to 1½ %; *Extra Dry,* up to 3%; *Dry,* or *Sec,* up to 4% or more. *Nature* is supposed to mean, but rarely does, a Champagne that has received no *dosage* at all. Once "dosed" and given its final, wired-down cork, Champagne is ready to market; despite much nonsense that has been written to the contrary, Champagne improves in bottle, *after* disgorging, hardly at all; most very old Champagnes found to be in good condition — and they can be superb — have been aged in the original cellars *before* disgorging, with the sediment still in the bottle.

A great many countries have finally recognized, by treaty or trade agreement, that Champagne is an appellation of origin, and belongs to its French originators; they have adopted other names for their own sparkling wines, as *Sekt,* in Germany, *Spumante,* in Italy, and even *Xampán,* in Catalonia. However, in the United States, any sparkling wine, even red wine, may be called Champagne provided, (1) it is made by the same bottle-fermented process as French Champagne, and, (2) that it bears on its label in easy-to-read type its geographical origin, as "California," "American," "New York State," etc. There are no legal restrictions as to the grape varieties that may be used, nor the areas of production, and the less expensive domestic Champagnes are perhaps comparable to French *vins mousseux* (*see*) but certainly not to French Champagne. On the other hand, a number of reputable producers in

California and in the Finger Lakes district of New York State are attempting to produce and indeed producing Champagnes that are comparable in quality to all but the best French. Such producers, especially in California, are tending to use a large proportion of Chardonnay or other superior grapes, and the increasing popularity of their wines is the best proof of this improved quality.

Sparkling wines can, of course, be made in a variety of other, less expensive ways. *See* Bulk Process, Carbonated Wine, etc.

CHAMPAGNE NATURE — (Shahm-pahn Nat-*tewer*) — In general usage, the still white or red wine of the Champagne Country: the white, formerly a favorite carafe wine in Paris restaurants, is not unlike an especially fresh, light Chablis, the red, like an extremely delicate Burgundy. Their official name is now *"Vin Originaire de la Champagne Viticole"* (quite a mouthful for a small wine!). None is exported.

CHAMPIGNY — (*Shahm*-peen-ye) — Village southeast of Saumur in the Loire Valley; its light, tender, fragrant red wine, somewhat resembling Chinon, made from the Cabernet Franc grape, and properly considered the best red wine of Anjou.

CHANTEPLEURE — (Shawnt-plurr) — Rather fanciful name given to the spigot of a wine-barrel, generally made of box-wood, and inclined to squeak ("sing") when opened; thus it "sings" *(chante)* and "weeps" *(pleure)* as the wine runs out. The wine confraternity of Vouvray, one of the many in France, is known as the Confrerie de la Chantepleure. In other parts of France the same word is often used to designate a glass pipette, or "thief," used to take a sample of wine out of the bung hole of a barrel.

CHANTURGUES — (Shawn-teerg) — Almost mythical red wine, produced (in infinitesimal quantities) not far from Clermont-Ferrand, near the headwaters of the Loire, in what was once the old province of Auvergne. Although loyally described by Auvergnats the world over as the world's best, it is in truth a small, pleasant Gamay, a hard-to-find *vin de pays*.

CHAPELLE-CHAMBERTIN — (Sha-*pell Shawm*-bair-tan) — Excellent Burgundian vineyard comprising 13 acres directly adjoining the Clos de Bèze *(see),* and producing less than a thousand cases a year of red wine of admirable quality. *See* Chambertin.

CHAPITRE — (Shap-*peet*-truh) — French for chapter-house; name often given in France to a vineyard adjoining, and presumably or formerly connected with, an important church. *See* Clos du Chapitre.

CHAPTALIZATION (French) — (Shap-tally-zah-see-on) — The process, widely decried but often helpful and in some instances necessary in wine-making, of adding sugar to the must, or grape juice, before fermentation. It takes its name from, and was presumably invented by, Chaptal, Napoleon's Minister of Agriculture (although honey, for precisely the same reason, has been used in wine-making for centuries). It is properly resorted to in cooler countries and in poor years when the grapes do not have enough sugar of their own to produce an acceptable wine; it can be, and often is, abused. Its purpose is not to make a sweet wine, but one with a proper minimum alcoholic content; *nor does it involve adding water as well as sugar to the must.* It is authorized rarely, and only in very poor years, in Bordeaux; always, but within very strict limits, in Burgundy; not at all in California, where it is unnecessary. The cheaper German wines (never those marked *"Natur,"* or those estate-bottled) and many in New York State and Ohio are made with the addition of sugar *and* water; this not only brings the alcoholic content up to par, but also reduces the wine's final total acidity, which might otherwise be excessive. It also, of course, (as the producers are quite aware) greatly increases the amount of wine that can be made from a given tonnage of grapes. Truly superior wines are never so made.

CHARACTER — Wine tasters' term. A wine with character is one, whether passable or good or outstanding, that has definite and unmistakable qualities, whether due to its geographical origin, its grape variety, or something else. A wine without character is dull and uninteresting.

CHARBONO — (*Shar*-bo-no) — Wine grape, probably of Italian origin, which produces a rather agreeable, somewhat rough, full-bodied red wine in California, especially in the Napa Valley.

CHARDONNAY — (*Shar*-doe-nay) — One of the very finest of all white wine grapes, rivaled only by the true Riesling. In France it produces all of the great white Burgundies, including Chablis, Montrachet, Pouilly-Fuissé, etc., and it is the white grape of the Champagne Country. In California, due to its extremely small yield per acre, it is not widely planted; its wine, almost always marketed as "Pinot Chardonnay," is perhaps the best white table wine made in the United States, and comes generally from the North Coast Counties (*see*). Although often called the "Pinot Chardonnay," not only in America but in French statutes, it is not, in the opinion of the most competent botanists and ampelographers, a true Pinot at all, nor related to the Pinot Noir, Pinot Blanc, etc.

ALSO, a small village in the Maconnais district of France.

CHARLEMAGNE — (In French, Sharl-*mahn*) — King of the Franks, and Emperor (742-814 A.D.). Said to have been responsible for the planting of the first vines at Schloss Johannisberg (after observing, from his palace at Ingelheim, across the Rhine, that snow melted on this slope earlier than elsewhere); he seems also to have had a vineyard at Aloxe-Corton (*see*) in Burgundy, with which his name is still associated — Corton-Charlemagne; in the year 775 he conveyed a portion of this domain to the Abbey of Saulieu.

Until quite recently there existed a white Burgundy wine called simply "Charlemagne," made partly from the inferior Aligoté grape (*see*), as distinguished from Corton-Charlemagne, made exclusively from the Chardonnay. These Aligoté vines have now been pulled out, and the difference between the two appellations has ceased to exist; a wine labeled "Charlemagne" is now a Corton-Charlemagne.

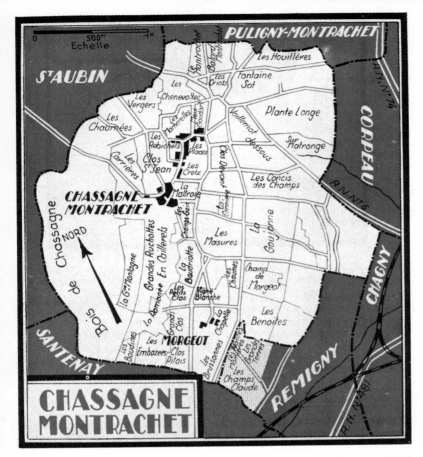

CHASSAGNE
MONTRACHET

CHARMAT PROCESS — (*Shar*-mah) — Another name for the Bulk Process (*see*), used in the making of sparkling wines.

CHARMES — (Sharm) — Burgundian vineyard name, designating certain specific plots in the *communes* of Meursault (*see*), Chambolle-Musigny (*see*) and Gevrey-Chambertin. This last, known as CHARMES-CHAMBERTIN, consists of 31 acres, separated from Chambertin itself only by a narrow vineyard road; it produces admirable red wines, only slightly inferior in body and distinction to those of its incomparable neighbor.

CHASSAGNE-MONTRACHET — (Shass-*anya* Mon-rasch-*shay*) — Important wine-producing township, near the southern end of the Côte d'Or, in Burgundy. There are some 750 acres of vineyard, and the average annual production is in the neighborhood of 100,000 gallons, 40% of it white wine of extremely high quality, the balance red, often very good but rarely of absolutely top class. Within the communal limits of Chassagne lie major portions of Montrachet and Bâtard-Montrachet, as well as Criots-Bâtard-Montrachet (*see*) in its entirety — three of the greatest dry white-wine vineyards of France; wines from these, however, do not carry mention of Chassagne-Montrachet on their labels, and are sold simply under the vineyard name alone. However, of almost equal excellence, and magnificent white wines by any standards, are Chassagne-Montrachet Les Ruchottes, Caillerets, Chenevottes, Morgeot, and a few others, while white wines labeled simply Chassagne-Montrachet are almost always good and sometimes quite remarkable. Many of the lesser red Chassagnes have a rather pronounced earthy taste, or *goût de terroir*; the finer ones are marketed as Chassagne-Montrachet plus a vineyard name, as Clos St. Jean, La Boudriotte, La Maltroie, Morgeot, etc., and there are few better values on the market, in the way of red Burgundies, than these. *See* Montrachet.

CHASSELAS — (Shahss-la) — Productive and hardy white grape (occasionally pink) of which many sub-varieties exist. Several of these are justly famous as table grapes; none can be considered a truly superior wine grape, since, except in extremely cool regions, their wines have a tendency to be low in acid, flat, very short-lived. Nevertheless, in Switzerland, where it is known as the Fendant, the Chasselas is by all odds the leading wine grape, as it is in Markgräflerland, in southern Baden (*see*), where it is known as the Gutedel. It is also widely cultivated round Pouilly-sur-Loire (*see*) and, as a mass production grape, in Alsace. In California it has never yielded any wine of consequence or interest, but has sometimes been confused with the Palomino.

CHASSE-SPLEEN, Château — (Chass-spleen) — Superior vineyard and its red wine, of Moulis, in the Haut-Médoc. Originally rated as a *Cru Bourgeois Supérieur*, it has enjoyed the rather rare rank of *Cru Exceptionnel* since 1932, and its wine is better than many of the lesser classed growths.

CHATEAU — (Shot-toe) — As far as this wine encyclopedia is concerned, and properly, as in France, a house attached, both by proximity and ownership, to a specific vineyard. Many "chateaux," especially in the less renowned sections of the Bordeaux Country, are simply country homes or small farmhouses, whose owners cultivate their own vines and make their own wine. According to French law, the word "chateau" may not appear on a label, as part of the name of a wine, unless a *bona fide* vineyard exists and has produced it and has some traditional right to the name.

Of several hundred such chateaux, or vineyard properties, listed in this volume, almost all will be found alphabetically listed under their own name (as Château Lafite under "L," Château d'Yquem under "Y," etc.). The exceptions, below, are those where the word "chateau" forms an integral part of the name and does not refer to an individual vineyard property.

CHATEAU-BOTTLED — A wine bottled on the property which produced it, by the vineyard owner, especially in the Bordeaux Country (the equivalent in most other areas is "estate-bottled"). Chateau-bottling is practiced by the vast majority of the owners of better vineyards in Bordeaux, in all except the poorest years, and often even then. It is a definite guarantee of authenticity, to a much lesser extent of quality. Wines chateau-bottled are invariably so marked, usually on a branded cork but in any case on the label. *"Mise du Château"* and *"Mis en bouteilles au Château"* are the customary terms used.

CHÂTEAU-CHALON — (*Shot*-toe *Shal*-lawn) — Unusual and rare white wine of the Jura, not the product of a chateau, but of a tiny, hilltop village that bears this name. Among French wines it is an exception to all rules, much closer in character to an unfortified Sherry or Montilla from southern Spain than to any other wine from French vineyards. Its grape variety is the Savagnin, said to be a sort of Traminer, although Château-Chalon has no resemblance to any other Traminer in bouquet or flavor, even when young. It is the only French wine (except Fitou — *see*) which, legally, has to be stored in cask for a specified period (in this instance, six years) before bottling, and it has its own special bottle, the *clavelin* (*see*). Actually, it is a sort of unique, accidental French version of Sherry, and it matures in casks that are not kept full, under a layer of *flor* yeast, just as Fino Sherry and Montilla do in Spain. Higher in acid than these and lower in alcohol (the legal minimum is 12%), it is much less good, and its fame is based more on its uniqueness than on its quality.

CHÂTEAU GRILLET — (*Shot*-toe *Gree*-yay) — Remarkable tiny vineyard (its production is the smallest of any French wine having its own *Appellation Contrôlée*) on the west bank of the Rhône River south of Lyon. It is the property of the Gachet family, and like Condrieu nearby, its grape is the Vionnier or Viognier. The total output is generally under 2,000 bottles a year, and the wine is as extraordinary as it is rare: golden, dry, full-bodied, rather high in alcohol, with a unique, spicy bouquet and flavor.

CHÂTEAUNEUF-DU-PAPE — (Shot-toe-*nuff* dew *Pop*) — Celebrated sturdy red wine of the Rhône Valley, from the village of this name, some dozen miles north of the old papal city of Avignon, in southern France. The *"château neuf"* (new castle), now a ruin, was the summer home of the Avignon Popes in the 14th century; the vineyards are planted on an extraordinary, high, stony tableland, dominating the Rhône and the surrounding fertile plain; the soil consists of the coarsest sort of gravel and small boulders on which it seems impossible that vines should grow. As a district, Châteauneuf-du-Pape is the most important of the Rhône, some four miles by five in extent, and its annual production (99% red, about 1% white) is in the neighborhood of a million gallons. About a dozen different grape varieties are grown and most of the wine contains some admixture of most if not all of these; more or less in the order of their importance, they are: Syrah, Grenache, Cin-

MISE AU DOMAINE

Chateauneuf-du-Pape

S. C. A. PROP. PLANTIN

APPELLATION CHATEAUNEUF-DU-PAPE CONTROLÉE

DOMAINE de MONT-REDON

HENRI PLANTIN, PROPRIÉTAIRE - RÉCOLTANT A CHATEAUNEUF - DU - PAPE (Vse)

Product of France
Contents : 3/4 Pint   *Table Wine*

sault, Mourvèdre, Clairette, Picpoul, Terret Noir, Counoise, Roussanne, Bourboulenc, etc. The wine is deep crimson in color, full-bodied, generous, fairly high in alcohol (usually 13-14%); it is softer and matures more quickly than Hermitage and Côte-Rôtie, being quite drinkable when about three years old and at its best between the ages of five and ten years. The best of it is estate-bottled, and the finer vineyards include the Domaine de Mont-Redon, Cabrières-les-Silex, La Solitude, Château Fortia, Château de la Nerthe, Château des Fines Roches, Château Rayas, Château de Vaudieu, etc.; the district produces as well, as might be expected, a great deal of sound but more ordinary wine.

For Map, *see* RHONE.

CHATILLON-EN-DIOIS — (*Shat*-tee-yawn on *Dee*-wah) — Red, *rosé* and white wines produced along the eastern edge of the Rhône Valley, near the little town of Die (*see*). Unlike Clairette de Die (*see*) they are not sparkling. This is a new *Appellation Contrôlée*; the amount produced is very small, and little if any is likely to be exported.

CHAVIGNOL — (Shahv-enn-yawl) — One of the better *communes* of the district of Sancerre (*see*) in the upper Loire Valley of France. Also famous for its small, round cheeses, made of goat's milk, and known as *crottins de Chavignol*.

CHEILLY-LES-MARANGES — (*Shay*-ye lay Mar-*ronj*) — Village south of Santenay, at the extreme southern end of the Côte d'Or in Burgundy. Produces a little red wine of only passable quality.

CHENAS — (Shay-nass) — Township in the very heart of the Beaujolais Country of France, bounded on the north by Julienas and on the south by Fleurie. About half of the vineyards entitled to the name "Moulin-à-Vent" lie within its communal limits (the others in Romanèche-Thorins, to the east). The finer wines of Chenas are therefore almost invariably marketed as Moulin-à-Vent, but what remains and is called simply Chenas, should not by any means be disprized — somewhat lighter than Moulin-à-Vent and maturing more quickly, it is a typical Beaujolais and an extremely good one.

CHENIN BLANC — (Shay-nan Blawn) — White wine grape of excellent quality, sometimes known as the Pineau de la Loire, though it is not one of the true Pinots, nor related to them. In the French provinces of Touraine and Anjou it is the predominant white variety, almost to the exclusion of all others, and is solely responsible for Vouvray, Saumur, Coteaux du Layon, Savennières and other ancient and famous wines. In northern California — Sonoma, Napa and Santa Clara counties, especially — it is being successfully and more and more widely grown, for it is highly productive and yields a fresh, pale, early-maturing wine of considerable finesse and breed. Unfortunately it is sometimes confused with the Pinot Blanc and even more frequently referred to as the White Pinot; it is neither, and deserves to be known by its own proper and proud name.

CHERIBITA — (Chair-ee-*be*-ta) — Pidgin Spanish-English for Sherry-and-bitters, an old English morning favorite that has managed to make itself known, through Jerez and Gibraltar, in southern Spain.

CHEVAL BLANC, Château — (Shev-al Blawn) — Celebrated and remarkable vineyard of the St. Emilion district, generally rated at least on a par with Ausone, as St. Emilion's best. In great years its wines have extraordinary distinction, softness and bouquet and are among the finest of all Clarets; they bring as high prices as those of Lafite and Margaux, perhaps mature more quickly. The vineyard normally produces some 10,000 cases a year but was gravely damaged early in 1956 by a cold wave of unprecedented severity; its yield will be affected for some years to come.

79

NET CONTENTS 1 PINT & 8 FL.OZ.   PRODVCT OF ITALY   ALCOHOL BY VOLUME 12½%

CHIANTI
RED WINE
DELL'ANTICA FATTORIA DI NICCOLO MACHIAVELLI
S. ANDREA IN PERCVSSINA
S. CASCIANO VAL DI PESA (FIRENZE)
PROPRIETA
C.ti SERRISTORI

CHEVALIER, Domaine de — (Shev-al-yea) — Excellent vineyard in the Graves district, *commune* of Léognan. Its white wine, something of a rarity, is outstanding, perhaps the finest of dry white Graves; its red is comparable to the 2nd classed growths of the Médoc. There are some 3,000 cases a year, mostly red.

CHEVALIER-MONTRACHET—(Shev-*val*-yea Mon-rasch-shay)—Tiny Burgundian vineyard, consisting of only 17 acres of sloping and stony soil, which produces from 500 to 1,000 cases a year of one of the very best dry white wines of France. It lies directly west of, and uphill from, Montrachet (*see*), entirely within the communal limits of Puligny (*see*), and its wine, as might be expected, is a great rarity, expensive but of memorable quality.

CHIANTI — (Key-*ant*-tee) — A wonderfully agreeable, and in some cases quite distinguished, Italian table wine, sprightly and appetizing, which has acquired some, at least, of its world-wide fame thanks to the attractive straw-covered bottle (*fiasco*) in which it is customarily shipped. In Italy, it is the common red wine (occasionally but rarely white) of Tuscany, usually and properly drunk young, often as a carafe wine, in the restaurants of Florence. Inexpensive, refreshing, almost a little piquant (as the result of a special method of fermentation — *see Governo*) it goes admirably with Italian food. The annual wine production of Tuscany is in the neighborhood of 100 million gallons, and it is safe to say that well over half of this calls itself Chianti.

Much of this, of course, is rather poor stuff, with little except its name, its price, and its straw-covered bottle to recommend it. Actually, however, this fancy straw-wrapped *fiasco* (*see*) generally costs less, in Italy, than an ordinary new wine bottle: hand labor is cheap and the glass is much thinner and weighs less. The Italian Government exercises little or no control over the "vintage" that such cheap wines carry when exported, and certainly most of the very cheap Chianti shipped abroad since World War II has been much less good than the common red wine of California, and anything but a credit to the ancient and honorable name it bore.

The finer, "classic" Chianti is a wine of an altogether different and much superior sort — well-balanced, firm, improving considerably with age in bottle, one of Italy's best. This is made from the San Gioveto and Cannaiolo grapes, plus a small amount of white Trebbiano and white Malvasia, in a delimited area between Florence and Siena comprising four townships (Greve, Radda, Castellina and Gaiole) plus portions of six others; the total yield is about 6 million gallons a year. *Chianti Classico,* unless bottled outside its zone of production, carries on the neck of the bottle the seal of the producers' association, the *Marca Gallo* — a black target with a cock in the center; it often carries the name of a specific estate or vineyard owner, as Barone Ricasoli (Brolio, Meleto), Conte Serristori (Machiavelli), Marchese Antinori; the very finest grades are aged in bottle, bear an authentic vintage, and are shipped in ordinary, straight-sided wine bottles, like Bordeaux.

However, a good deal of excellent Chianti is produced in Tuscany outside this classic zone. There are six other legally defined areas, of which Rufina (*see*) and Montalbano rank as very good, the Colli Fiorentini and Colli Pisani as good, but with small production; most of the very cheap Chiantis shipped abroad come from the Colli Senesi and Colli Arentini, both of them mediocre, and are often stretched with blending wines from other parts of Italy. A number of the better producers outside the classic zone have formed a separate association and taken as their "seal" a white *Putto,* which resembles a Della Robbia angel; this, too, is a mark of better than average quality.

White Chianti, made mostly from the Trebbiano grape (*see*), is a dry, golden, rather full-bodied wine, agreeable but of no great distinction.

Counterparts and imitations of Chianti have been produced outside Italy in most countries where Italians have settled, including Argentina and California. Rarely made from the same grape varieties, these rarely resemble Chianti, although some of them are very good, even excellent, red table wines.

For Map, *see* ITALY.

CHIARELLO — (Key-are-el-lo) — *See* Chiaretto.

CHIARETTO — (Key-are-et-toe) — *Rosé* wine, certainly one of Italy's best, produced round the southern end of Lake Garda, between Milan and Verona. Light, fresh, pale, low in alcohol (10-11%), it is never as good as when drunk young, as *vino aperto,* or "open" wine, on the lakeside terraces of the villages where it is made. However, some is now being bottled for export and, if properly handled and *not too old,* this can be very pleasant. The best Chiarettos come from the village of Padenghe, Moniga, Manerba, and the Polpenazze, all in the province of Brescia, and are made from the local red wine grapes, the Gropello, Schiava, Marzemino. Equally good, but somewhat different in character, are the *rosés* from the eastern shore of Garda, in the province of Verona; these are generally sold as Chiarello rather than Chiaretto, although the terms are virtually interchangeable; their producing grape varieties are basically those of Bardolino (*see*) and in distinction and flavor they are very close to the lightest Bardolino reds.

CHICLANA — (Chee-*clah*-nah) — Small town at the southern end of the Sherry Country, near Cadiz. Its wines are of second quality.

CHILE — The oldest and by far the most important wine-producing country of Latin America. Wine was being made in Chile before 1600; now, with a population of less than 5½ million, Chile produces and indeed consumes more table wine than the United States. Much of this is of surprisingly good quality, from superior grape varieties and well made, but it is only fair to add that most of the Chilean wines shipped to the United States since World War II have been bought by our importers only because they were cheap, and were far from outstanding and far from their country's best.

As might be expected, the vine flourishes in Chile only in the central, temperate zone of this 2,600-mile-long country, and on account of the cold Humboldt current in the Pacific, somewhat closer to the equator than in Europe or in California — generally between 30° and 40° south latitude. Most of the best vineyards are in the fertile central valley, not far from Santiago, and the majority of them are irrigated.

The modern history of wine in Chile dates from about 1850, when for the first time expert French vintners and cuttings of the finer French vines were brought over from Europe; since then, Chilean viticulture and wine-making has largely followed French methods and tradition, though of course in a vastly different climate and on very different, largely volcanic soil.

By all odds the best Chilean wines, those truly fit for export, are made from the "noble" grape varieties and quite often carry a varietal name, as Cabernet, Semillon, Riesling (the last usually shipped in a squat, local version of the German *Bocksbeutel*); others, like their California compeers, are sold as Sauternes (in this case with a final "s"), Chablis, Borgoña (Burgundy), Rhin (Rhine wine), etc. These may or may not come from the original European varieties, but are rarely made from heavy-bearing, mass-production grapes, and Chile has a surprisingly large acreage of Pinot, Sauvignon, Folle Blanche (here called *Loca Blanca*), Merlot, Malbec, etc. Some quite good sparkling wine is made, much of it sweeter than it should be. Superior grades of still wines are usually labeled *Reservado* or *Gran Vino* and these designations are subject to government control.

CHINON — (She-nawn) — Birthplace of the immortal Rabelais; picturesque and historic little town in the old French province of Touraine, famous for its red wine, the *"bon vin breton"* of Rabelais' chronicles, and for the fact that it was here that Joan of Arc first met the Dauphin, later crowned King of France at Reims. The wine, made entirely from the Cabernet Franc grape, is *"bon et frais"* as it was in Rabelais' time — fresh, light, best when young and served at cellar temperature, one of the most delightful of the lesser red wines of France. The annual production rarely exceeds 200,000 gallons, most of it consumed locally; it is not often exported.

CHIPIONA — (Chip-pee-*o*-nah) — Little summer resort and wine-producing town, on the Atlantic Coast of Spain, near Jerez. It is in the Manzanilla zone, just west of Sanlúcar de Barrameda, but the Moscatel from its sandy vineyards is better known than its dry wine.

CHIROUBLES — (Sheer-roubl) — Village in the Beaujolais Country and its excellent red wine, fruity, racy and charming. Most of the annual production (roughly 140,000 gallons) goes early to market and is soon consumed, gains less by ageing than other Beaujolais from nearby villages such as Chenas, Morgon, etc.

CHOREY-LES-BEAUNE — (*Shor*-ray lay Bone) — Wine-producing village in Burgundy, directly north of Beaune. There are some 400 acres of vineyard, mostly planted on flat land and giving no wine of any real consequence. The legal appellation, Chorey-Côte de Beaune, is rarely used, and most of the wine is blended.

CHRISTIAN BROTHERS — Catholic Order, originally founded shortly after 1700 by St. Jean Baptiste de La Salle, in France. Its official name in English is "Brothers of the Christian Schools" and it is primarily a teaching Order. In the United States, the Christian Brothers are now one of the largest wine producers in the North Coast County area of California, with important vineyards at Mont La Salle on the edge of the Napa Valley, and a large ageing cellar, formerly known as the Greystone Winery, in St. Helena. Their annual production is in the neighborhood of a million cases, plus a substantial amount of California brandy. Christian Brothers' Port, Sherry and Champagne have acquired wide acceptance, as have a number of the table wines produced, some of which carry varietal names.

CHUSCLAN — (Shuss-clawn) — Pleasant and palatable *rosé* wine of the Côtes-du-Rhône; the zone of production consists of five townships on the right bank of the Rhône, north of Tavel and west of Orange, Chusclan itself being the most important of the five.

CINQUETERRE — (*Chink*-way-ter-ray) — Italian white wine produced in five villages (whence, presumably, its name), on the Ligurian coast between Genoa and Spezia; of these Riomaggiore is the most important. Rather high in alcohol, golden in color, occasionally dry but more often somewhat sweet, with a pronounced and unusual bouquet, it is an interesting wine but one that will hardly appeal to all palates.

CINSAULT — (San-so) — Superior red-wine grape, giving a firm, full-bodied, deep-colored wine of definite character and good class. Although rarely vinified alone, it plays an important albeit minor role in Châteauneuf-du-Pape, in Tavel, and in many of the better red and *rosé* wines of the French Midi.

CIRÓ — (Chee-ro) — Italian red wine, high in alcohol and usually somewhat sweet, from the region of Calabria. Should not be confused with Giró, a somewhat similar wine made in Sardinia.

CISSAC — (*See*-sack) — Wine-producing *commune* of the Haut-Médoc, adjoining St. Estèphe: many good *bourgeois* growths.

CLAIRET — (Clair-ray) — Old French term (whence the English word Claret) applied centuries ago to the then rather light red wines of Bordeaux; revived since World War II, it is now the name given to certain specially vinified red Bordeaux wines, soon ready to drink and without much color or tannin. These resemble full-bodied *vins rosés*, although deeper in color than most such wines; they are usually served at cellar-temperature or chilled, and may be passably agreeable or quite good, depending on where they were made, by whom, and on the grape varieties used.

CLAIRETTE — (Clair-*rette*) — Productive, good quality, white wine grape, widely grown in southern France and to some extent in California. Although white, it is used to some small extent in the making of red Châteauneuf-du-Pape and the *rosé* of Tavel. Alone, it gives a pleasant, well-balanced, rather neutral wine without much bouquet or fruit; one produced near Montpellier in the Midi, has, astonishingly and absurdly enough, been granted an *Appellation Contrôlée* — Clairette du Languedoc, and another from near Nimes, Clairette de Bellegarde, shares the same honor. Neither remotely merits it.

CLAIRETTE DE DIE — (Clair-*rette* duh Dee) — French sparkling wine, generally rather sweet and with a pronounced Muscat flavor, produced round the town of Die, in the *département* of the Drôme, along the eastern edge of the Rhône Valley. It is made principally from the Clairette grape, from which it takes its name, but with enough Muscat to give it its special character and bouquet.

CLAPE, La — (La Clop) — Red, white and *rosé* wines produced just east of Narbonne, in southern France. Made from the commoner varieties of grape (Carignan, etc.), they are hardly outstanding but carry nevertheless the V.D.Q.S. seal.

CLARET — Loosely and widely used term, meaning, in most countries other than England, a light red wine. Thus, in the U.S., any and all red table wines may be labeled "claret," whatever their origin, character or type; it is a catch-all term, and hardly one that inspires confidence on a wine label. The name has no meaning and no legal status in France, nor has Clarete (*see*) in Spain or Chile. Traditionally (although not legally) in England, the word means red Bordeaux, but red Bordeaux wines are almost never so labeled.

CLARETE (Spanish) — (Clar-*ate*-tay) — Term used in Spain, especially in the Rioja district, to describe any red wine which is rather light both in body and color.

CLASSED GROWTH — Used in this encyclopedia to designate wines of a specific vineyard or estate or "growth" (particularly those of Bordeaux) that have been officially classed, or classified. The first such official grading was the famous Classification of 1855 (*see*), and almost all mentions of "Classed Growth" in this volume, have direct reference to, and are based on, this.

CLASSIFICATION OF 1855 — In preparation for the *Exposition Universelle*, held in Paris in 1855, a committee of experts and wine brokers officially classified the leading wines of two great Bordeaux districts, the Médoc and Sauternes. Their ratings were largely based on the opinions and prices then prevailing, and despite many changes in ownership, etc., the classification remains surprisingly accurate, after over a hundred years. However, only 60 wines of the Médoc, 22 of Sauternes and 1 of Graves, were ranked; it is greatly to be regretted that St. Emilion, Pomerol, and most of Graves, plus all of the lesser districts, were not included in the committee's assignment. The 60 "Classed Growths" of the Médoc, it should be clearly understood, represent only the extreme elite of nearly a thousand estates, all producing wine of above average quality. The 1855 Classification is given in the appendix, and all of the chateaux will be found, in their alphabetical place, in this volume; it is essential to remember that a 3rd Growth or 4th Growth wine is by no means a third- or fourth-rate wine, but a noble wine indeed — a duke, if you wish, compared to the kingly Firsts. All of the Classed Growths may fairly be considered as great vineyards; many others, called *Crus Bourgeois* or *Crus Bourgeois Supérieurs*, also produce admirable wine.

CLAVELIN — (Clahv-lan) — Special sort of stumpy bottle, holding 62 centiliters or about 20½ ounces, used in the Jura district of France for Château-Chalon and for certain *vins jaunes*.

CLEAN — Essentially, a clean wine is a sound wine, one without any "off" aroma or taste, palatable, agreeable, refreshing. It is a term that can quite properly be applied to a young wine as well as an old one, to an inexpensive wine as well as a very great one. A wine that is not clean is bad, generally not fit to drink.

CLERC-MILON-MONDON, Château — (Clair-*Me*-lawn-*Mawn* dawn) — 5th Classed Growth of Pauillac, Haut-Médoc. Some 3,000 cases a year.

CLIMAT (French) — (Clee-ma) — Used in connection with wine, means, especially in Burgundy, a specific, named vineyard, whether owned outright by a single proprietor, or split up among many.

CLIMENS, Château — (Clee-mense) — One of the two best vineyards and perhaps the greatest wine of Barsac, generally regarded as second only to Yquem in the hierarchy of Sauternes (Barsac being of course part of the Sauternes district). Sweet, luscious, golden, with extraordinary fruit and breed, it more than merits its rank as a 1st Classed Growth, and is one of the truly incomparable dessert wines of the world. There are some 4,500 cases a year.

CLINET, Château — (*Clee*-nay) — One of the better 1st Growths of Pomerol.

CLOS — (Clo) — Originally, in France, a walled or otherwise enclosed vineyard, as Clos de Vougeot. The term today is much more loosely used, but may not appear on a French wine label, as part of the name of a wine, unless such a Clos, or vineyard, genuinely exists, and actually produces the wine in question.

CLOS, Les — (Clo) — Celebrated *Grand Cru* vineyard of Chablis (*see*), one of the best of the seven so classified.

CLOS DE BÈZE — (*Clo*-duh Bezz) — Celebrated Burgundian vineyard, consisting of 37 acres directly adjoining Chambertin (*see*) on the north; its magnificent red wines are legally entitled to the name Chambertin, but more often sold as Chambertin-Clos de Bèze. They are fully the equals of other Chambertins, and some experts consider them even better.
For Map, *see* GEVREY.

CLOS BLANC — (Clo Blawn) — One of the better vineyards of Pommard, in Burgundy, rated as a Première Cuvée, and giving a red wine, despite its name.

CLOS DU CHAPITRE — (*Clo* dew Shap-*peet*-truh) — Name given to several French vineyards, notably two: one in the village of Fixin (*see*), at the northern end of the Côte de Nuits, which produces a red Burgundy of outstanding quality and breed; the other in the village of Viré (*see*) north of Macon, which yields an excellent dry white wine, made from the Chardonnay grape, and one of the best of the Maconnais.

CLOS DES CORVÉES — (Clo day Cor-vay) — Perhaps the best vineyard of Prémeaux, near the southern end of the Côte de Nuits, in Burgundy. Its excellent red wine, full-bodied, round, with a rather agreeable trace of earthiness, is entitled to the appellation Nuits-Saint-Georges and is invariably estate-bottled. The adjoining and hardly inferior Clos des Argillières is part of the same domain.

CLOS FOURTET — (Clo Foor-tay) — Superior 1st Growth vineyard of St. Emilion; its red wine, sturdy, full-bodied and long-lived. Its production amounts to some 5,000 cases a year.

CLOS DES GOISSES — (Clo day Gwass) — Extraordinary and unique vineyard at Mareuil-sur-Ay in the Champagne district of France. It consists of one extremely steep hillside overlooking the Marne, and is planted to both Pinot Noir and Chardonnay grapes. The resulting wine is fairly full-bodied, but with outstanding quality and class. It is about the only French Champagne which carries a specific vineyard name, and in good years is usually shipped as "nature," completely unsweetened.

CLOS DES LAMBRAYS — (*Clo* day *Lawm*-bray) — Superior vineyard, 14 acres in extent and classified as a *Premier Cru* (1st growth), in the township of Morey-Saint-Denis (*see*), in Burgundy. Its red wine is one of the heaviest, fullest-bodied and longest lived of the Côte d'Or.

CLOS DES MOUCHES — (Clo day Moosh) — Well-known vineyard of Beaune, in Burgundy, producing an attractive, fine-textured red wine and, curiously enough, a perhaps even better white. This latter, Beaune's only white wine of any consequence, is comparable to a Meursault.

CLOS DE LA MOUSSE — (Clo duh la Moose) — One of the good vineyards of Beaune, in Burgundy. Not to be confused with the preceding, it gives only red wine.

CLOS DE LA PERRIÈRE — (*Clo* duh la Per-ry-*air*) — Burgundian vineyard, and its excellent red wine. *See* Fixin, Perrière. The CLOS DES PERRIÈRES is one small, especially renowned portion of the Perrières vineyard in Meursault (*see*), giving a white wine of remarkable balance and breed.

CLOS DE LA ROCHE — (Clo duh la *Rawsh*) — Distinguished Burgundy vineyard, officially classified as a *Grand Cru* (great growth) in the *commune* of Morey-Saint-Denis. It produces, from 37 acres of vines, approximately 3,000 cases of red wine a year — wine which, at its best, is one of the truly great Burgundies, quite the equal in power and depth, if not always in class and breed, of Chambertin.

CLOS DU ROI — (Clo dew Rwah) — Two quite distinct vineyards in Burgundy, both producing red wines of excellent quality. The finer and more famous of the two is in the township of Aloxe-Corton, and its wines are sold as Corton-Clos du Roi (*see* Corton); the other is in Beaune (*see*) and produces Beaune Clos du Roi.

CLOS ST. JEAN — (Clo San Shawn) — Excellent vineyard in Chassagne-Montrachet (*see*). With Les Boudriottes and La Maltroie, it produces about the best red wines of this celebrated little Burgundian town.

CLOS SAINT-DENIS — (Clo San Den-nee) — Leading Burgundy vineyard, one of the best of the *commune* of Morey, or Morey-Saint Denis, and officially ranked as one of the 23 *Grand Crus* (great growths) of the Côte de Nuits. Its 16 acres yield some 1,500 cases a year of a particularly sturdy, well-knit red wine, long-lived and slow to mature.

CLOS SAINT-JACQUES — (Clo San Shock) — Excellent vineyard in the township of Gevrey-Chambertin (*see*), in Burgundy, officially ranked as a *Premier Cru*, and perhaps the best of those so ranked. Its red wine is outstanding, full-bodied, fine, and brings nearly as high a price as Chambertin itself.

CLOS DE TART — (Clo duh *Tarr*) — One of the great vineyards of Morey-Saint-Denis, in Burgundy, officially classified as a *Grand Cru*. Its 17 acres make up a single property, and yield annually about a thousand cases of very full-bodied, long-lived red wine.

For Map, *see* MOREY.

CLOS DE VOUGEOT — (Clo duh *Voo*-sho) — World-famous Burgundian vineyard, the largest (124 acres) of the Côte d'Or, created on what had been, until then, waste land, by Cistercian monks in the 12th century. Its average annual production is now in the neighborhood of 10,000 cases, but 65 producers own portions, some obviously much larger than others, of the Clos, and a Clos de Vougeot of a given year is thereafter not one, but 65 different wines, some estate-bottled, some not, some fuller-bodied than others and some better. The finest wines are traditionally those that come from the upper part of the vineyard, which here is bounded by Musigny (*see*) and Grands Échézeaux (*see*), but the entire Clos produces red Burgundy of classic quality, distinguished perhaps more for its breed and bouquet than for its body and power. The picturesque and venerable Château de Vougeot, with its massive, ancient wine-presses, is now the property of the Burgundian wine confraternity, the Chevaliers du Tastevin. A little red wine is produced called simply Vougeot, but not Clos de Vougeot, and a white wine of first-rate quality, the Clos Blanc de Vougeot. *See* also Vougeot.

CLOUDY — A wine that is not clear or brilliant. No sound and good wine is ever cloudy, but the term should NOT be applied to a clear wine which has thrown sediment (*see*) in bottle.

COARSE — A wine lacking in finesse, common, heavy, with plenty of body and not much else. Cheap California Burgundies are usually coarse, and so is most of the red *vin ordinaire* that the average Frenchman drinks every day.

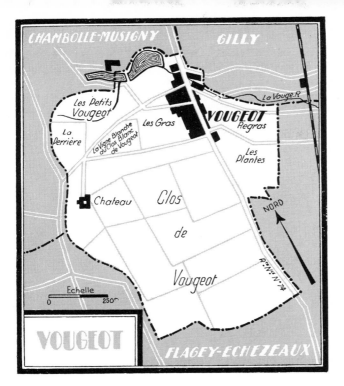

COBBLER — Old-fashioned American mixed drink, really a sort of julep, although generally made with wine. There are dozens of recipes, but always involving shaved ice in a tall glass, sliced fruit and/or a sprig of mint and sugar. Over this one pours three or four ounces of red or white table wine, or even Sherry or Port.

COLLAGE — (Col-*lajh*) — French term for fining (*see*), or clarifying wine, through the addition of any one of many different substances or products to the wine before bottling. An essential step in wine-making.

COLARES (also COLLARES) — (Co-*lar*-rays) — Interesting Portuguese red wine, produced north of Estoril and west of Cintra along the dunes and sandy foothills of the Atlantic Coast. The predominating vine is the Ramisco, planted in ditches or pits in the clay subsoil which underlies ten feet or more of sand. Rather full-bodied and "fleshy," somewhat lacking in subtlety but improving with age, Colares has definite character, but not all wine-drinkers will find it deserving of the extremely high regard in which it is held in England.

COLLI EUGANEI — (*Call*-lee Oo-gahn-*nay*-ee) — Chain of vineyard-covered hills near Padua, some thirty miles southwest of Venice; the diverse, rarely outstanding wines (the Venetians' *vin ordinaire*) from this district, both red and white.

89

COLMAR — (Call-mar) — City in the *département* of Haut-Rhin, France; an important center of the Alsatian wine trade.

COLOMBARD — (Co-lawm-bar) — Productive, good quality white wine grape, grown principally in the Cognac district of France, but to some extent in the northern fine table wine district of California. It is sometimes called the *Colombar* or *Colombier* in France, and often the "French Colombard" in California, where there are some 1,500 acres in all. In France, it gives an agreeable, not very distinguished, dry white wine, fuller-bodied and higher in alcohol than the *Folle Blanche,* but also rather high in acid and therefore suitable for distillation. In California, its wine is well-balanced, pale, fresh, rather tart, and widely used in California "Chablis" and in the lesser grades of California Champagne.

COLOR — An expert can tell a great deal about a wine, particularly a white wine, by looking at it in a clear glass, tilted either against a white tablecloth or against the light, or in a silver *tastevin,* in the Burgundian fashion. A good wine in any case should be clear and brilliant. Dry white table wines from cooler districts should be somewhere between the color of pale straw and that of gold, with a distinct greenish cast; white table wines from Bordeaux, and Italy, and some (though rarely the best) from California, may be as gold as ripe corn with almost no green at all; in practically all white table wines a trace of amber or brown is either a tell-tale sign of age, or, in a younger wine, an indication that the wine is sightly "maderized" (*see*) and will probably be short-lived. Sweeter white wines should be gold, never at all brown unless very old. Red wines have their own range from purple (generally a very young wine, almost always a poor one) to a sort of autumnal crimson-brown, like oak-leaves in the fall. This last, which the French call *pelure d'oignon,* or onion skin, comes invariably to fine red wines as they grow older — it can best be noted along the edge of the wine in a tilted glass. *Rosé* wines, too, have their variations — from the color of a strawberry almost to that of an orange; both extremes are bad, and a *rosé* too orange is generally too old, one too pink generally no good to begin with. All of these graduations of color are very subtle and it is hard to remember and recognize and judge them except after long experience. They are more for the wine expert than for the novice.

COMBLANCHIEN — (Caum-*blawn*-she-ann) — Tiny village far more famous for its marble quarries (which supplied much of the stone for the Opéra in Paris) than for its wine; it lies south of Nuits-Saint-Georges and Premeaux, near the southern end of the Côte de Nuits, and was the only town of the Côte to be badly damaged in World War II.

COMMANDARIA — *See* Cyprus.

COMMON — Applied to a wine, means about what it does when applied to a person. Perhaps not disagreeable, perhaps sound and clean, perhaps an ordinary table wine adequate for everyday use. Nothing that can be called fine.

COMMUNE (French) — (Cawm-mune) — A township; a small administrative unit in France, consisting of a village and its surrounding land. Often used in this encyclopedia, and always in this sense.

CONCORD — Blue-black, slip-skin American grape of the *labrusca* species, by far the most widely planted of the "native," Eastern varieties. It takes its name from Concord, Massachusetts, where it appeared as a seedling in the garden of Mr. Ephriam Bull, in 1843. It is doubtless a cross of two *labrusca* varieties, perhaps one of them the Catawba; hardy and productive, a good table grape, and a wholly satisfactory variety for jelly and unfermented grape juice, it rapidly became both popular and famous. It is responsible today for most of the sweet, so-called "Kosher" wine, where its pronounced "foxy" flavor is apparently not considered objectionable. As a true wine grape, however, it has almost nothing to recommend it: it can hardly be made into wine at all unless heavily sugared, and a dry Concord table wine is assertive in flavor and extremely common. It is nevertheless the dominant variety in a good deal of New York State "Burgundy" and most New York State "Port."

CONDRIEU — (*Cawn*-dree-uh) — Interesting and unusual white wine of the Rhône Valley, produced some thirty miles south of Lyon, in the three communes of Condrieu, Vérin and St. Michel. Its terraced vineyards, planted to the Viognier or Vionnier grape, are as steep as those of Côte Rôtie nearby, and their output is absurdly small, amounting to a mere 6-700 cases a year. Almost all of this is consumed locally, and in the famous Restaurant de la Pyramide (Point) at Vienne, where it is a favorite specialty. Condrieu is something of a changeling of a wine: it can be fairly dry or moderately sweet, depending on the vintage and the producer; it is often faintly *pétillant* or sparkling when young; golden in color, fruity, it has a special and distinctive bouquet.

CONEGLIANO — (Cawn-ell-*ya*-no) — Small city north of Venice, known for its important wine school and viticultural station, but even more for its white wines, made from the Verdiso grape, and among the best of northern Italy. These are of several types, of which the most engaging is perhaps the extremely light, dry, pale green-gold wine sold as Verdiso; the somewhat sweeter Prosecco is also of superior quality, however, and there are some good sparkling and semi-sparkling sorts as well.

CONSEILLANTE, Château La — (Cawn-say-yawnt) — Excellent vineyard of Pomerol, in the Bordeaux Country, separated from Château Cheval Blanc (this, of course, a St. Emilion) only by a winding country road. Its red wine is outstanding, velvety, rich and full; there are some 4,000 cases a year.

CONSTANCE — One of the largest lakes of Western Europe, bounded on the south by Switzerland, on the east by Austria and on the north by Germany. The Rhine, rising in Switzerland, empties into and runs out of Lake Constance, just as the Rhône into and out of Lake Geneva. Lake Constance is known in German as the Bodensee, and a few wines, almost all of them consumed locally, are produced along its northern shore, and known as *Seeweine*; of these the Ruländer or Pinot Gris is perhaps the best, but there is an interesting oddity known as *Weissherbst*, an exceedingly pale *rosé* made from the Pinot Noir.

CONSTANTIA — South African wine from near Cape Town which, during most of the 19th century, enjoyed a fame and vogue in England and the Low Countries and even France such as no other non-European wine has even approached. It came from a vineyard called Groot Constantia (now State-owned), originally planted by the Dutch governor, Simon van der Stel, before 1700, and named after his wife, Constance. Huguenot refugees from France played a large role in the establishment of the vineyards, and the predominating vine seems to have been the Muscadelle du Bordelais. The estate is still producing wine today, as are also Klein Constantia and High Constantia, which adjoin it. Their wines, while often of good and even superior quality, are far indeed from deserving the international rank of our great-grandfathers' days. Future students of the history of wine may explain this; like the decline of Falerno (*see*), it is for the moment a mystery.

COOKING WINE — Inexcusable term, since it would lead one to believe that something not good enough to drink could be good enough to eat. The truth is that the only two major elements which bad wines and good have in common — water and alcohol — are largely dissipated in cooking by evaporation (the alcohol, being more volatile, almost completely) and what remains is the flavor — quality is no less important in the saucepan than in the wine glass. There are a few reservations, none the less. What is left in the bottom of a wine bottle (if there is no sediment), can certainly be kept overnight and used for cooking the next day, or even, if kept in the refrigerator, two or three days later. A wine loses its bouquet, so kept, and picks up a little of what experts call "volatile acidity"; in cooking, this is no disadvantage since the bouquet is evanescent anyway and volatile acidity, within reason, is an asset in the kitchen. Let skeptics prepare the same dish using Madeira, Sherry and Marsala, for example — Madeira will be found the best, nine times out of ten, simply because it is far higher in volatile acid. The French have known this for a long time, which is why they have so many distinguished dishes *à Madère*, and ordinarily leave Sherry to the Spaniards, and Marsala to the Italians.

COOPERAGE — General term applied to a totality of wooden casks or vats or barrels (i.e. those made by a cooper) used for storage in a given cellar or winery. Thus "100,000 gallons of cooperage" means a storage capacity of 100,000 gallons, whether used or not; "new cooperage" means unused casks or barrels, etc. By a long margin the best wood for wine storage is oak; redwood (in California) and chestnut (in Europe) are acceptable substitutes, although wines stored in these do not develop in the same way, or as rapidly. The use of glass-lined concrete or metal tanks, especially for white and *rosé* wines, is increasing both in Europe and in America.

92

COOPERATIVE — (Co-oh-pair-ah-teev) — A winery or cellar owned and operated jointly by a number of small producers; there are hundreds of such in Europe and a good many in California, some of quite modest size and others that rank among the largest wineries and cellars in the world. They have come into being primarily because the small grower, except in districts of famous and expensive wine, cannot afford alone the machinery and cellar equipment he needs to make and bottle properly and market profitably his own wine.

CORBIÈRES — (Cor-be-*air*) — District of vineyard-covered, rolling hills, southeast of Carcassonne, in what is known as the Midi of France. This, in general, is the homeland of *vin ordinaire*, but Corbières, while inexpensive and produced on a large scale, belongs in a somewhat higher category — it is recognized as an *appellation d'origine* and has been accorded the V.D.Q.S. seal. Legally, it can be red, *rosé* or white; the sturdy red is by all odds the best, and is made mostly from the Grenache, Carignan, Terret and Cinsault varieties of grape. Corbières Supérieur is a superior grade, and Corbières du Roussillon comes from a zone a little farther south, in the *département* of Pyrénées Orientales.

CORBIN, Château — (Cor-ban) — 1st Growth vineyard of St. Emilion, one of a number of chateaux that bear, in various combined forms, this ancient name; all of them produce good wine and all were part of a single feudal domain. Thus we have, in addition to Château Corbin, Château Corbin-Michotte, Château Grand-Corbin, Château Corbin-Despagne, Château Grand-Corbin-David, and several others, all in the section known as Graves-St. Emilion — the gravelly plateau which adjoins the *commune* of Pomerol, and boasts, as its most famous wine, Château Cheval Blanc.

CORGOLOIN — (*Cor*-go-lwan) — Southernmost village of the Côte de Nuits, in Burgundy. Its wines are of secondary quality, and hardly ever exported.

CORKAGE — Fee paid to a restaurant for the privilege of having one's own wine, purchased elsewhere, served there with a dinner or for a party. If not too high, this is a legitimate charge, and anything up to 40% of the value of the wine (unless it is an expensive rarity) is fair. If Corkage is not charged, one has been done a favor, and the wine waiter should be very liberally tipped.

CORKS — Plastic "corks" are more and more tending to replace those made of the bark of *Quercus suber* (the cork oak) in sparkling wine, not only in America but in Europe; most of the Sherry and Port produced in this country is now shipped with a screw-cap or some such "closure," and even many inexpensive table wines in both France and Italy are sent to market with some simple, ingenious cap which does not require a corkscrew. All this greatly alarms the traditionalists, but they are wrong. Common wine (at least 95% of the world's production) is made to be consumed almost as soon as bottled, and providing its container is sanitary, cheap, and gives no bad taste to the wine, there can be no legitimate objection to it, and it is certainly better than the goatskins, leather flasks, re-used bottles, and all the picturesque paraphernalia of the wine business of a century ago. The same thing, precisely, is true of the "closures."

On the other hand, precisely the opposite is true of wines capable of ageing and improvement in bottle. For these, the elite, corks are still irreplaceable and indispensable. They permit the slow evaporation and eventual slight oxidation of the wine which give it bouquet and distinction.

A cork's length, and even its quality, should be in relation to the expected life span of the wine it is supposed to protect, for longer corks last longer. Thus, a Beaujolais may legitimately have a much shorter cork than a great Burgundy, and a Rhine wine a shorter cork than a great red Bordeaux.

Normally, even the best corks have a life of not much over twenty years, even in the best cellars, and have to be replaced after about two decades.

The fact that a cork is "loose" rather than "tight" in its bottle, is usually an indication that the wine has been poorly stored, upright rather than on its side. A cork that is dry and hard to pull means usually that the wine has been kept in too dry a cellar, but has nothing to do with its quality. That the top of a cork, beneath its capsule, should be moist or even black with mould, means nothing at all. Unless a wine is frankly corky, it is impossible, even for an expert, to say more of a cork until he tastes the wine.

CORKSCREW — Device for pulling corks: in its simplest, traditional form, a wire spiral attached to some sort of handle. But there are literally hundreds of diverse and ingenious modifications today, some admirably efficient, some wholly worthless.

A wine-drinker, in choosing a corkscrew, should keep in mind that the screw itself, or worm or *mèche,* is far more important than all the elaborate, silver-plated or wooden levers or double-levers, or reverse helixes, which are supposed to bring out the cork with a minimum of effort. All are pretentious and ridiculous unless the screw itself is properly designed. A good one is easy to recognize: it is not a gimlet, but an open spiral, in which one can easily insert an old-fashioned kitchen match, and of which the outside diameter is between $\frac{5}{16}$ and $\frac{3}{8}$ of an inch. The screw itself should be thin and tapered, (few are) with a sharp point, which follows the spiral and is not centered. Those of drawn steel, somewhat rectangular in cross section rather than round, are the best, but hard to come by. Under no circumstances should a good corkscrew have a sharp cutting edge on the outer side of its spiral. It is *essential,* if it is to be used for fine wine, that the screw be from 2¼ to 2¾ inches long.

This said, a wine lover may suit his fancy, but it is certainly a fact that a corkscrew with some sort of lever or double screw arrangement is vastly to be preferred when one is dealing with long corks, old bottles, and, above all, with wines that one wishes to open in a pouring basket, or cradle.

94

Another type of cork-puller, with nothing much to recommend it, consists of two parallel, thin, flexible blades, attached to a handle and separated by about the diameter of a wine cork. Inserted on each side of the cork, these blades permit one, after a good deal of maneuvering and twisting and pulling, to bring out the cork unpierced, and presumably reusable. This may be of some interest in a commercial cellar, but is hardly of importance in the home.

In recent years, an entirely new type of cork extractor has come on the market, of which the essential elements are a hollow needle and a cartridge of compressed air or CO^2 or freon gas, which is injected into the space between the lower end of the cork and the wine itself, so that the cork is actually pushed, rather than pulled out of the bottle. This ingenious idea offers many advantages, and such devices, when perfected, may well replace the corkscrews commonly used. They are particularly effective when one is dealing with an old, friable cork, likely to crumble or break; the air or gas injected has no effect whatsoever on the wine. Unfortunately, in most cases, the needles of these instruments are too short to transpierce the long corks used in the finest wines.

CORKY — Many people say "corked" when they mean "corky." All bottled wines (except those with screw-caps or other such "closures") are corked; a corky wine is one that has the definite and disagreeable odor and flavor of a bad cork. Such bottles come along occasionally, even from the best of cellars; the odor and off-flavor are due to some invisible flaw in what appears a perfect cork; generally the cork, when pulled, has the same scent of rotten wood to a pronounced degree. There is nothing to do with such wines except pour them down the drain; fortunately, they arrive only about one time in a thousand, or less.

CORNAS — (Cor-nahss) — Sturdy but not particularly distinguished red wine of the Rhône Valley, made from the same Syrah grape as Hermitage (*see*) a dozen miles further south and on the opposite (or west) bank of the Rhône. Total production amounts to some 25,000 gallons a year; the wine often has a rather marked *goût de terroir*, especially when young, but ages well.

CORONATA — (Cor-o-*na*-ta) — Good white wine produced on the hills back of Genoa, Italy.

CORPS — (Cor) — French for "body." *See* Corsé.

CORSÉ (French) — (Cor-say) — Full-bodied. The noun is *corps*.

CORSICA — (In French, *Corse*) — Large Mediterranean island, one of the *départements* of France. As far as wine is concerned, it produces hardly enough for its own requirements and exports little to the mainland, except to a few Corsican restaurants in Paris, Marseille, Nice, etc. There exists a rather sweet apéritif known as "Cap Corse"; the best table wines (full-bodied table reds and pleasant but heady *rosés*) are produced near St. Florent, on the north coast, and what is sold as Patrimonio is generally the most dependable of these.

CORTAILLOD — (Cor-tie-yo) — Pale red wine, fruity and agreeable, but often almost *rosé* or *oeil de perdrix* in color, produced round the village of this name, on Lake Neuchâtel, in Switzerland. Its grape is the Pinot Noir of Burgundy.

CORTESE — (Cor-*tay*-zay) — Italian white wine grape of superior quality, grown mostly in Piedmont, where it yields a fresh, light, pale, short-lived wine, eminently agreeable, usually sold as Cortese though sometimes under a town name such as Gavi. The principal zone of production is some thirty miles north of Genoa. The word *cortese*, incidentally, means "courteous" in Italian, just as *soave* (*see*) means "suave."

CORTON — (Cor-tawn) — Generally and rightly regarded as the greatest red wine of the Côte de Beaune (*see*); also a white wine of the very highest class. Both are produced in the Burgundian village of Aloxe-Corton (*see*), plus small portions of two adjoining *communes*, Ladoix-Serrigny and Pernand-Vergelesses. The lighter and less distinguished (although very good) wines of these *communes* are marketed simply as Aloxe-Corton or Pernand-Vergelesses; the finer as Corton, or as Corton plus the name of a vineyard — e.g., Corton Bressandes, Corton Clos du Roi (both red) or Corton-Charlemagne (white). The vineyards entitled to these proud names have been most carefully delimited; they produce, in an average year, some 20,000 cases of red wine and some 7,000 cases of white (the latter, except for a small fraction, all Corton-Charlemagne). Several of the best *cuvées* of the Hospices de Beaune (*see*) are in fact Cortons. Corton Château Grancey is not a vineyard, but a none-the-less excellent and authentic Corton, bottled at Château Grancey, in Aloxe-Corton, by the vineyard owner, Louis Latour.
For Map, *see* ALOXE.

CORVINO — (Cor-*vee*-no) — Red wine grape widely grown in northern Italy, especially in the districts that produce Bardolino (*see*) and Valpolicella (*see*). Unknown or at least unidentified in most other wine countries.

CORVO DI CASTELDACCIA — (Cor-vo dee Cas-tel-*datch*-cha) — One of the better known table wines of Sicily, usually white although some red is produced. The vineyards are just east of Palermo and form part of the estate of the Dukes of Salaparuta.

COSECHERO — (Co-say-*chay*-ro) — Literally, in Spanish, a harvester (*cosecha*, harvest); in wine parlance, a vineyard-owner.

COS D'ESTOURNEL, Château — (*Cawss* Dess-tour-*nell*) — Outstanding vineyard of St. Estèphe, in the Haut-Médoc, one of the best of the 2nd Classed Growths. The chateau is a sort of ridiculous, Victorian version of a pagoda, but the vines face, across a little tidal stream and its salt meadows, those of Château Lafite. The wine is consistently excellent, full and sturdy, yet soft and fine. There are some 15,000 cases a year.

96

1960

Corton-Charlemagne

APPELLATION CONTROLÉE

Ancien Domaine des Comtes de Grancey

Mis en bouteilles à la propriété

LOUIS LATOUR, à Beaune (Côte-d'Or) Bourgogne

COS LABORY, Château — (*Cawss* La-bo-*ree*) — 5th Classed Growth of St. Estèphe, Haut-Médoc. Directly adjoins Cos d'Estournel, but produces a lighter and less distinguished red wine. A very respectable 5th Growth, none the less.

COSTIÈRES-DU-GARD — (Caws-tee-*yare* dew Gahr) — Red, *rosé*, and white wines produced on the hills along the River Gard, or Gardon, in the *départements* of Gard and Hérault, in southern France. Although entitled to the seal of V.D.Q.S. (*see*), they may legally come from any one of 18 varieties of grape, few of them of any real quality; the wine is common, at best a superior sort of *vin ordinaire*.

CÔTE, La — (Coat) — Large wine-producing district in Switzerland, the steep northern shore of Lake Geneva (or Lac Léman) between Geneva and Lausanne, in the Canton of Vaud. The wines, all white and made from the Fendant or Chasselas grape, are light, fresh, reasonably pleasant carafe wines, nothing more.

COTEAUX D'AIX — (Coat-toe *Dakes*) — Pleasant and popular wines, red, white and *rosé*, produced round the fine old university city of Aix-en-Provence, in southern France. They are classified as *Vins Delimités de Qualité Supérieure*, or V.D.Q.S. (*see*) and the better of them carry the V.D.Q.S. seal.

COTEAUX DE L'AUBANCE — *See* Aubance.

COTEAUX DU LAYON — (Co-toe due Lay-ohn) — The banks of a small river, tributary of the Loire, in western France; in both quantity and quality by far the most important wine-producing district of the province of Anjou, with over 10,000 acres of vines (Chenin Blanc) and an annual production of some two million gallons of white wine entitled to this name. The district also produces a very substantial quantity of white wine from less good vineyards, this sold simply as Anjou, and a great deal of *rosé* (from the Cabernet Franc and Groslot) marketed either as Rosé de Cabernet or Anjou Rosé. The fine white wines of the Coteaux du Layon range from fairly dry to very sweet, depending on the vineyard and the year; at their best they are rich, golden wines of astonishing texture and breed, quite comparable to the finer Sauternes and Barsacs and the great Ausleses of the Rhine. The two most famous vineyard areas are Bonnezeaux and Quarts de Chaume and from a quality standpoint the leading wine-producing villages are Rochefort-sur-Loire, Beaulieu-sur-Layon, St. Aubin-de-Luigne, Rablay, Faye, Chavagnes, etc.

For Map, *see* LOIRE.

COTEAUX DU LOIR — (Co-toe-due Lwahr) — Minor wine-producing district north of Tours, in France. Not to be confused with the Loire, of which it is a tributary, the Loir runs westward along the extreme northern limit of the cultivation of the vine; there are some 1,500 acres of vineyard (largely Pinot Noir and Chenin Blanc) which yield red and white wines of quite remarkable quality, though only in exceptionally good years. The most celebrated vineyard is that of Jasnières (*see*).

COTEAUX DE LA LOIRE — (Co-toe duh la Lwahr) — Literally, the Loire hillsides, and, in general, the wines produced along the Loire River, in France; legally and specifically, however, two delimited districts, one directly south of the city of Angers, capital of the old province of Anjou, the second farther west, round the town of Ancenis, near Nantes. Wines from the latter zone are made from the Melon grape and are sold as Muscadet (*see*) des Coteaux de la Loire. Wines from the former are labeled Anjou-Coteaux-de-la-Loire; made from the Chenin Blanc, here harvested very late, they are rather sweet white wines of outstanding quality, fruit and bouquet. Savennières (*see*) is the most important wine-producing village.

COTEAUX DE SAUMUR — (Co-toe duh *So*-muhr) — *See* Saumur.

COTEAUX DE TOURAINE — (Co-toe duh Tour-rain) — General name given to a vast variety of pleasant local wines, still and sparkling, red, white and *rosé*, produced along the Loire River, and its tributaries, the Cher and Indre, in the old French province of Touraine, round Tours. The finer of these have their own, more restrictive appellations, as Vouvray, Montlouis, Chinon, etc.

CÔTE DE BEAUNE — (*Coat* duh *Bone*) — The southern half of the celebrated Burgundian Côte d'Or (*see*), that long, narrow belt of hillside vineyards which is responsible for almost all of the greatest Burgundies. Unlike the northern half, known as the Côte de Nuits (*see*), the Côte de Beaune produces white wine (Montrachet, Meursault, Corton) fully as famous as its red (Pommard, Volnay, Beaune, Corton, etc.). These latter, for all their wonderful refinement and softness and charm, are less great, less extraordinary than those of the Côte de Nuits; they mature more quickly and are shorter lived.

A wine labeled "Côte de Beaune" without any mention of town or vineyard, is a regional wine, often of secondary quality, from the township of Beaune itself; it is less good than a wine labeled simply "Beaune." A wine labeled "Côte de Beaune-Villages" is a wine or a

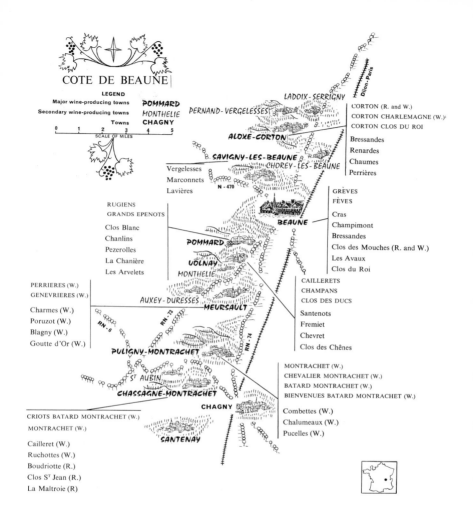

COTE DE BEAUNE

LEGEND

Major wine-producing towns **POMMARD**

Secondary wine-producing towns *MONTHELIE*

Towns CHAGNY

0 1 2 3 4 5
SCALE OF MILES

LADOIX-SERRIGNY

CORTON (R. and W.)
CORTON CHARLEMAGNE (W.)
CORTON CLOS DU ROI

PERNAND-VERGELESSES

Bressandes
Renardes
Chaumes
Perrières

ALOXE-CORTON

SAVIGNY-LES-BEAUNE
CHOREY-LES-BEAUNE

Vergelesses
Marconnets
Lavières

N - 470

GRÈVES
FÈVES

RUGIENS
GRANDS EPENOTS

Clos Blanc
Chanlins
Pezerolles
La Chanière
Les Arvelets

BEAUNE

Cras
Champimont
Bressandes
Clos des Mouches (R. and W.)
Les Avaux
Clos du Roi

POMMARD

VOLNAY

MONTHELIE

CAILLERETS
CHAMPANS
CLOS DES DUCS

PERRIERES (W.)
GENEVRIERES (W.)

AUXEY-DURESSES

MEURSAULT

Santenots
Fremiet
Chevret
Clos des Chênes

Charmes (W.)
Poruzot (W.)
Blagny (W.)
Goutte d'Or (W.)

RN - 6
RN - 73
RN - 74

PULIGNY-MONTRACHET

MONTRACHET (W.)
CHEVALIER MONTRACHET (W.)
BATARD MONTRACHET (W.)
BIENVENUES BATARD MONTRACHET (W.)

ST AUBIN

CHASSAGNE-MONTRACHET

CHAGNY

Combettes (W.)
Chalumeaux (W.)
Pucelles (W.)

CRIOTS BATARD MONTRACHET (W.)
MONTRACHET (W.)

Cailleret (W.)
Ruchottes (W.)
Boudriotte (R.)
Clos St Jean (R.)
La Maltroie (R)

SANTENAY

blend of wines from a township or townships of the Côte de Beaune
other than Beaune; it, too, is a regional, rarely of top class. A wine,
however, that carries the appellation "Côte de Beaune" *preceded by
the name of a village* (as Monthélie-Côte de Beaune, Saint-Aubin-Côte
de Beaune, Santenay-Côte de Beaune, etc.) must come from that specific village; such wines, although generally inexpensive, are in many
cases excellent.

CÔTE DE BROUILLY — (Coat duh *Brew*-ye) — Excellent vineyard district in the Beaujolais Country of France, consisting of portions of four

99

communes (Odenas, St. Lager, Cercié and Quincié), and producing some 125,000 gallons a year of fruity, full-bodied red wine, rather high in alcohol (13-14%) and, surprisingly, best drunk young. It is a heavier and bigger wine than Brouilly *(see)* but not always a more agreeable one. The vineyards are on the steep slopes of an extraordinary round hill called Mont de Brouilly; the name comes from a tiny village, the Hameau (hamlet) de Brouilly.

For Map, *see* BROUILLY.

CÔTE CHALONNAISE — (Coat Shall-lone-*nays*) — Vineyard district in Burgundy, south of the Côte d'Or but north of Macon; produces a number of good red and white wines from Pinot Noir and Chardonnay grapes, of which the best known are Mercurey, Rully, Givry and Montagny *(see)*. It takes its name from the town of Chalon-sur-Saône, near its southern end.

CÔTE DE NUITS — (*Coat* duh *Nwee*) — The more northerly of the two main sections of the Burgundian Côte d'Or *(see)*; perhaps the greatest red wine district in the world, the Médoc of the Bordeaux Country being its only real rival. An insignificant amount of white wine is produced *(see* Musigny, Clos de Vougeot, Nuits-Saint-Georges) but the reds include most of those responsible for Burgundy's world-wide reputation. The area takes its name from Nuits-Saint-Georges, its principal town, and extends from Fixin on the north to Corgoloin, where the Côte de Beaune *(see)* begins, on the south; its narrow hillside vineyards are hardly a mile wide, but they produce Chambertin, Bonnes Mares, Musigny, Clos de Vougeot, Échézeaux, Richebourg, Romanée-Conti, Nuits-Saint-Georges and many others almost equally illustrious. Such wines, however, never carry the appellation Côte de Nuits, but are sold under the far more specific *commune* or vineyard names. A wine labeled Vin Fin de la Côte de Nuits, or one that carries the new appellation Côte de Nuits-Villages, is a regional Burgundy, perhaps good but not outstanding in quality, quite possibly a blend.

CÔTE D'OR — (Coat Dor) — Literally, in French, "golden slope"; *département* in the heart of the old province of Burgundy *(see)*, southeast of Paris, taking its name from this same "golden," vineyard-covered hillside, on which most of the great Burgundy wines are grown. The slope in question extends from near Dijon, to Santenay, south of Beaune, faces southeast over the wide, flat, fertile valley of the Saône, and parallels for some thirty-five miles the main railway line and one of the main roads from Paris to Lyon, Marseille and the Riviera; the vineyards form a sort of mile-wide band along the hillside, between the rocky outcroppings and trees near the crest, and the fertile farmland below. There are a few other vineyards, of vastly less interest and fame, on parallel slopes farther west, the Arrière-Côtes *(see)*, but this single hillside is the true kernel of the Burgundy wine country. It consists of three well-defined sections, each one of which is named after its principal town — the Côte de Dijon, the Côte de Nuits *(see)* and the Côte de Beaune *(see)*. The Côte de Dijon has no vineyards of importance: its best wine is an agreeable *vin rosé*, made from Pinot Noir grapes in the village of Marsannay-la-Côte; all of the great wines come from the other two sections. Côte d'Or, incidentally, is *not* a wine name — no wine may legally be sold under this appellation.

For Map, *see* BURGUNDY, CÔTE DE BEAUNE.

CÔTE RÔTIE — (Coat Ro-tee) — Celebrated red wine of the Rhône Valley, produced near Vienne, and some twenty miles south of Lyon. The vineyards, which overlook a great bend in the river and face almost due south, are incredibly steep, and consist really of a series of narrow terraces, held up by retaining walls, or *murgeys*, and of necessity worked by hand. Their cultivation is therefore expensive and their production small, rarely over a total of 12,000 cases a year. There are 52 officially listed *quartiers*, or vineyard areas, but the two main divisions are the Côte Brune and Côte Blonde, the former with somewhat darker soil and producing a somewhat sturdier, longer-lived wine. According to legend, a noble lord of the district, one Maugiron, once bequeathed the Côte Blonde to his blonde daughter and the Côte Brune to her dark-haired sister. The main grape is the Syrah, here interplanted with from 10% to 20% of white grapes of the Viognier variety, which produces Château Grillet and Condrieu *(see)* nearby. A fine Côte Rôtie of a great year is truly admirable wine, deep-colored, full-bodied, long-lived, yet with great distinction and class; certain experts claim to detect in it the scent of violets and raspberries. It has been famous since the days of Rome.

CÔTES DE BERGERAC — (Coat duh *Bair*-shair-rack) — Rather common red and white wines produced round the town of this name, east of Bordeaux, in southwestern France.

CÔTES DE BLAYE — (Coat duh *Bly*) — *See* Blaye.

CÔTES DE BORDEAUX — (Coat duh Bor-*doe*) — Name given to two adjoining vineyard districts in the Bordeaux Country, both on the rather steep right bank of the Garonne river, southeast of Bordeaux itself. Correctly, the northern and more important of the two is called the Premières Côtes de Bordeaux; it produces some rather ordinary red wine, plus a great deal of good, fairly sweet and sometimes very sweet white wine, recalling that of the Sauternes district (directly across the river) but with less distinction and class. Cadillac *(see)* is the best know of the various village names. The southern area is called Côtes de Bordeaux-Saint Macaire, and only white wines may be so labeled; most of these, too, are sweet, but a few dryer ones are now being made, some of them of good quality.

CÔTES DE BUZET — (Coat duh Boo zay) — Red and white wines entitled to the V.D.Q.S. seal but of not much interest except locally, produced southeast of Bordeaux, in France.

CÔTES-CANON-FRONSAC — (Coat-*Can*-nawn-*Frawn*-sack) — One of the best of the less-known red wines of Bordeaux, coming from a small, strictly delimited area just west of St. Emilion.

CÔTES DE DURAS — (Coat duh *Dew*-rahs) — Red and semi-sweet white wine (the latter somewhat like Monbazillac) produced east of Bordeaux, in France.

CÔTES DE FRONSAC — (Coat duh *Frawn*-sack) — Good red wine produced on hillside vineyards near the town of this name, west of St. Emilion in the Bordeaux Country. Less fine than Côtes-Canon-Fronsac (*see*).

CÔTES DU JURA — (Coat do *Shu*-ra) — Literally, the Jura hillsides; the general, regional name under which most Jura wines (other than Château-Chalon, Arbois and L'Étoile) are sold. The vineyards are due east of the Burgundian Côte d'Or, more or less parallel to the Franco-Swiss frontier, and they are planted along the foothills and lower slopes of the Jura Mountains. Red, white and *rosé* wines, and some sparkling wines, too, are entitled to the appellation. They are rarely much above the level of good *vins de pays*, and are rarely exported.

CÔTES DU LUBERON — (*Coat* dew *Loo*-bay-rawn) — Red, white and *rosé* wines, of which the last are by a wide margin the best, produced in the hilly district east of Avignon and north of the Durance River, in southern France.

CÔTES DU MARMANDAIS — (*Coat* dew *Mar*-mawn-day) — Red and white wines entitled to the V.D.Q.S. seal but of purely local interest, produced round the town of Marmande, on the Garonne River, in southwestern France.

CÔTES DE MONTRAVEL — (*Coat* duh Mawn-tra-*vel*) — *See* Montravel.

CÔTES DE PROVENCE — (Coat duh Pro-*vawnce*) — The red, *rosé* and white wines coming from the hilly country along the Mediterranean coast between Marseille and Nice. Early-maturing, fairly light, pleasant, and on the whole inexpensive, these have long been popular among visitors to the Riviera; they are now being shipped, in increasing quantity, to other parts of France, and even exported. The *rosés*, fresh, rather light in color, generally sold in special amphora-like bottles, are perhaps the best of them; the whites (predominantly made from the Ugni Blanc and Clairette) are often marketed as *Blanc de Blancs* (*see*), are pale gold, dry, agreeable, not especially distinguished; the reds (from the Grenache, Cinsault, Mourvèdre, Carignan, and two locally known varieties, the Pecoui-Touar and the Oeillade) are soft, garnet rather than crimson, low in tannin, although quite high in alcohol, soon ready. The heart of the production zone is the *département* of the Var, and the better known vineyards include: Domaine des Moulières, Château de Selle, Château Ste. Roseline, Château St. Martin, Coteau du Ferrage, Domaine de l'Aumérade, Domaine du Noyer, Domaine de St. Maur, Domaine de Minuty, Clos de la Bastide Verte, Domaine du Jas d'Esclans, Domaine de Rimauresq, Domaine de Castel Roubine, Clos

LYON

CÔTE ROTIE
CONDRIEU
CHATEAU GRILLET
VIENNE

CROZES-HERMITAGE
SAINT JOSEPH
TAIN
TOURNON
HERMITAGE
Isère

CORNAS
SAINT PÉRAY
VALENCE

N

CÔTES DU RHÔNE

LEGEND

Towns · AVIGNON
Rivers · *Rhône*
Major Vine yards · **HERMITAGE**
Lesser Vine yards · CORNAS · VIOLES

Drôme

Rhône

CAIRANNE
RASTEAU
ORANGE
VIOLES
GIGONDAS
VACQUEYRAS
Mt Ventoux
CHUSCLAN
LAUDUN
CHATEAUNEUF DU PAPE
LIRAC
TAVEL
AVIGNON
BEAUMES DE VENISE
Luberon
NIMES
Durance
ARLES
CAMARGUE

E. B. Stevens

MEDITERRANEAN SEA

MARSEILLE

SCALE OF MILES
0 5 10 15 20 25 30

de Rolars, Domaine de la Croix, Clos Mireille, Domaine du Galoupet, Domaine de la Source Ste. Marguerite, Clos Cibonne, Domaine de Mauvannes.

CÔTES-DU-RHÔNE — (Coat dew Rone) — General name given to the wines produced in the Rhône Valley between Vienne, south of Lyon, and Avignon, a distance of 120 miles. The finer of these, of course, are

103

all sold under more specific village or district names, from north to south, as follows: Côte Rôtie and Condrieu (part) in the *département* of the Rhône; Château Grillet and the rest of Condrieu in the *département* of the Loire; Hermitage and Crozes-Hermitage in the Drôme; Cornas, St. Péray and St. Joseph in the Ardèche; Tavel and Lirac in the Gard; Châteauneuf-du-Pape, Rasteau and Muscat de Beaumes-de-Venise in the Vaucluse (*see* all of these). The remainder, amounting to over 10 million gallons in favorable years, less than 1% of it white, is called Côtes-du-Rhône. This, however, is further subdivided and classified by law, and the superior grades generally carry a village or *département* name as well — Côtes-du-Rhône-Gigondas or Côtes-du-Rhône-Ardèche, for example; the village names used most frequently are Cairanne, Chusclan, Gigondas, Laudun and Vacqueras (*see*). Twenty different grape varieties are authorized, the more important being the Syrah, Grenache, Mourvèdre, Cinsault, Clairette, Roussanne, Marsanne, Viognier. Côtes-du-Rhône *Rouge* is a pleasant, soft, rather inexpensive table wine, sound and good but without any claim to greatness; Côtes-du-Rhône *Rosé* resembles a rather light and somewhat common *rosé* of Tavel; the white, often lacking in finesse and fruit, is generally the least good of the three.

CÔTES DE TOUL — (Coat duh Tool) — Red, white and *rosé* wines (the last usually called *vin gris*), light, agreeable, extremely low in alcohol, produced near Toul in the old French province of Lorraine. Although made mostly from Pinot and Gamay grapes, they are really nothing more than good *vins de pays*, and are rarely exported, if indeed ever. They nevertheless carry the V.D.Q.S. seal.

CÔTES DU VENTOUX — (Coat dew Vawn-too) — *See* Ventoux.

COUDERC — (Coo-dairk) — French grape hybridizer, several of whose crosses, carrying his name plus a serial number, are now being grown with some success in the eastern United States. *See* Hybrids.

COUHINS, Château — (Coo-*anse*) — Well-known vineyard in the township of Villenave d'Ornon, Graves district. Produces a little red wine but a considerably larger amount of good quality, dry white Graves.

COULANT — (*Coo*-lawn) — Literally, in French, "running," as of a stream of water. As a wine taster's term it means easy to drink, and is applied to light, fresh, tender wines, low in tannin and alcohol.

COULÉE DE SERRANT — (*Cool*-lay duh *Sair*-ran) — *See* Savennières.

COULURE — (Coo-lare) — One of the many afflictions of the vineyard owner, the disastrous result of persistent rain or very cold weather during the flowering season of the vine — some blossoms are never properly pollinated; the embryo grapes never develop and eventually fall off. This has no effect on quality but may reduce the crop by as much as half, and occasionally even more. A less severe version of the same thing is called, in French, *millerandage* — a few flowers in each bunch are only partially pollinated and result in tiny, seedless grapes, called *millerands*, or "shot berries." Since these are generally very sweet, they can bring about an actual improvement in the quality of the resulting wine, though of course at the sacrifice of volume.

COUPÉ — (*Coo*-pay) — French word which, when applied to wine, means "cut," or blended. A *vin de coupage* is a blending wine.

COUR-CHEVERNY — (Coor-*Shev*-air-nee) — Pleasant white *vin de pays* produced near Blois, in the French Chateau Country. It is entitled to the V.D.Q.S. seal.

COUTET, Château — (*Coo*-tay) — One of the two great vineyards of Barsac (Climens being the other), officially and correctly ranked as a 1st Growth; some 6,000 cases a year. Its wine is the prototype of classic Barsac; golden, rich, but not cloyingly sweet, racy, fruity, with a fine bouquet, great distinction and breed.
   ALSO, a 1st Growth vineyard of St. Emilion which produces, of course, red wine exclusively.

CRADLE — Wire, wicker or straw basket (French, *panier*) made to hold a bottle of wine in nearly the same horizontal position it occupied in the cellar, thus permitting it to be brought to the table and served without disturbing the sediment. Cradles are useful and almost necessary for the proper service of many old red wines, but to use a cradle for a wine that has no sediment at all, is sheer pretentiousness and snobbery.

CRAMANT — (*Cram*-maun) — Important wine-producing village in the Champagne Country, south of Épernay, rated as one of the very best. Its wines, all made from the white Chardonnay grape, are remarkable for their delicacy, bouquet and breed, and are among the rare Champagnes quite often sold unblended and under the village name (i.e., as Cramant), rather than a brand. *See* Champagne, Blanc de Blancs.

CRÉMANT — (Cray-maun) — French term, literally "creaming," applied to wines which are mildly sparkling — between *pétillant* and *mousseux*. Should not be confused with Cramant (*see*), which is a place name. A *Crémant de Cramant* actually exists — it is a light, most agreeable Champagne from the town of Cramant, with less pressure and less sparkle than most Champagnes.

CRÉPY — (Cray-pee) — Pleasant little white wine produced in the Haute-Savoie, France, not far from the southern shore of Lake Geneva. It is marketed in tall, slender bottles, like Alsatian wines, but made from the Chasselas (or Fendant) grape, and much resembles the light white wines of Switzerland. Annual production amounts to some 12,000 cases.

CRESZENZ — (Cress-zenz) — German wine-term meaning growth, or "Production of," properly followed by the name of the vineyard owner. May only be used on natural (i.e. unsugared) wines, but does *not* necessarily mean estate-bottled.

CRIADERA — (Cree-ah-*dair*-ah) — Literally, in Spanish, a nursery. As applied to wines (rather than children or plants) its use is confined to the Sherry Country, where wines are aged and blended in *soleras* (*see*). The *criadera*, in Jerez, is the section in which young wines are cared for, selected and graded before being admitted to what might be called their university, the *solera* proper. The word may, however, be correctly used to include all of the stages of the *solera* itself, except of course the lowest and final one.

CRIOTS-BÂTARD-MONTRACHET — (*Cree*-oh *Bat*-tarr Mon-rasch-*shay*) — New appellation, created since the last world war, under which some four or five hundred cases a year of superlative white Burgundy are now sold. The vineyard, in the township of Chassagne-Montrachet (*see*), consists of a small prolongation, to the south, of Bâtard-Montrachet (*see*). The wines from the two plots are both of very high quality and can hardly be told apart, even by an expert.

CROIZET-BAGES, Château — (Crwah-zay-*Baj*) — One of the less distinguished of the 5th Classed Growths of Pauillac, Haut-Médoc.

CROZES-HERMITAGE — (Crows *Air*-me-*taj*) — Comparatively new appellation, used since 1952 to designate the red and white Rhône wines produced in 11 townships north, east and south of the one extraordinary hillside which alone yields Hermitage (*see*). Until then many of the better red wines of this district had been sold as "Crozes" and some excellent whites as "Mercurol," village names both, and both now part of the Crozes-Hermitage zone. The reds are made exclusively from the Syrah grape and the whites from the Roussanne and Marsanne; they are not unlike Hermitage but rather more common, with less distinction and less bouquet. About four-fifths of the production is red, one-fifth white, and the total is about double that of Hermitage itself, not far from 150,000 gallons a year.

CRÖV — (Kruhv) — Also spelled Kröv (*see*).

CRU — (Crew) — French word meaning "growth." When applied to wine, a specific vineyard and the wine it produces; by implication, one of superior quality, as *vin de cru*. The word is not, as some writers in English have supposed, the past participle, *crû*, of the verb *croître*, to grow, but a quite separate noun, written without the circumflex. Most classifications of French wines divide the various wines and vineyards into *crus*, as *Grand Cru, Premier Cru, Deuxième Cru, Cru Classé*, etc.

CRU CLASSÉ — (Crew Class-A) — *See* Classed Growth.

CRUSTED — Term applied to an old red wine, usually a vintage Port, which has thrown a heavy sediment, in the form of a film, or "crust," over the inner face of the bottle. Such wines should generally be carefully decanted before serving.

CUIS — (Quee) — Wine-producing village of secondary importance in the Champagne Country of France. South of Épernay and part of the Côte des Blancs, it is nevertheless one of the villages in which both white grapes (Chardonnay) and black (Pinot Noir) are grown.

106

CUSSAC — (*Coo*-sack) — Small wine-producing town of the Haut-Médoc, between Margaux and St. Julien. Secondary red wines.

CUVAISON — (Coo-vay-zawn) — Practice, essential in the making of red wine, of allowing the juice and skins to ferment together, thereby giving color and additional tannin to the wine. CUVAGE is the length of time this process lasts, a mere matter of hours in the case of *vins rosés*, generally from two days to a week for red wines.

CUVÉE — (Coo-vay) — From the French *cuve*, vat, tank or cask, especially a large one, in which wines are fermented or blended. Therefore a specific lot or "batch" or blend of a given wine, possibly different from others that may carry the same or a quite similar label. The term is loosely and not always accurately used. Thus the "English cuvée" of a given Champagne house will be a blend presumably made for the English market, but quite possibly on a vast scale, far more than any vat or *cuve* could contain; the "Tête de Cuvée" of a chateau or domain will be its best lot of that vintage, whether from one cask or ten; a "Première Cuvée" (a term once widely used in Burgundy but now fortunately tending to disappear) simply means one of the best wines of a given *commune*.

CYNAR — (*See*-nar) — Odd Italian apéritif made from artichokes. It has no legitimate place in a wine dictionary, but some people have thought it a flavored wine, and the truth may as well be told.

CYPRUS — Large island of the eastern Mediterranean, with over 150,000 acres of producing vineyard, and a wine tradition dating back to the Crusades. Richard Coeur de Lion celebrated his marriage to Queen Berengaria (in the year 1191) in Cyprus wine, and the golden Commandaria, first produced round Limassol by the Knights of the Order of the Templars and St. John, was famous throughout Western Europe. Most of the Cyprus wine now exported is sweet, fortified, somewhat comparable to Madeira, and it has enjoyed a recent vogue in England. The best is still usually sold as Commandaria.

CZECHOSLOVAKIA — Has some 50,000 acres of vineyard, mostly round Melnik, in the Elbe Valley north of Prague, and in the vicinity of Brno (Brunn) in the province of Moravia. The wines, almost all consumed locally, are not outstanding.

D-E

DALMATIA — The mountainous, picturesque and charming eastern shore of the Adriatic Sea, a province of Jugo-Slavia, between Trieste and the Albanian border. A great deal of wine is produced, although little of outstanding quality. Those generally considered the best include a full-bodied, rather dry white from near Mostar, called Žilavka; a red, labeled Dingać and pronounced "Dingatch"; and a somewhat sweet red, high in alcohol, called Prošek; lastly, and almost everywhere, a pleasant *rosé* called Ružica, "little rose."

DAMBACH — (Dahm-bach) — One of the better small, wine-producing villages of Alsace, not far from Sélestat, in the *département* of Bas-Rhin.

DAME BLANCHE, Château La — (Dam Blawnch) — One of the rare Médoc vineyards producing white wine exclusively; it is situated only a few hundred yards north of the legal boundary of Graves, at Le Taillan, near Blanquefort. Its wine, being white, is not entitled to the appellation Médoc, and is rated a Bordeaux Supérieur.

DAME JEANNE — (Dam Shahn) — This is the French term from which the English *demijohn* is derived; literally "Lady Joan," it means about the same thing as in English, an oversize bottle of no fixed capacity, which may or may not be covered with straw or wicker, or set in a wood frame. Much *vin ordinaire* is so shipped in France, but very large Bordeaux bottles (jeroboams, impériales, etc.) are often called *Dames Jeannes*, as well.

DÃO — (Dawn) — One of the best Portuguese table wines, produced round the town of Viseu in a hilly country half-way between Lisbon and

108

Oporto. The reds, deep colored, rather full-bodied, extremely fruity, somewhat lacking in breed, are made primarily from the same grape varieties as Port — the Tourigo, the Tinta, the Alvarelhão, the Bastardo. The whites are rather high in alcohol, golden, full-bodied, and these, too, are made mostly from white Port varieties — the Arinto, etc. Rarely shipped to the United States, Dão is beginning to acquire considerable acceptance in England.

DAUZAC, Château — (Doe-zack) — 5th Classed Growth of Labarde-Margaux, Haut-Médoc. Some 4,000 cases a year of good quality, rather delicate red wine.

DAVID — Author of the Psalms (circa 150 B.C.) in the 104th of which is written: "Wine maketh glad the heart of man."

DEBOURBAGE — (Day-boor-baj) — Practice, highly beneficial in the making of white wine, of delaying the fermentation of the newly pressed juice for some twenty-four hours, until it has had a chance to clear and can be drawn off its gross lees, or original coarse sediment. To accomplish this worthy end, the juice must either be held at a very low temperature or treated with metabisulphite and then (usually) set to ferment with a culture of selected yeast. These processes are all accepted parts of modern wine technique, but there are still more than a few famous European cellars which would greatly benefit by their introduction.

DEBRÖI HÁRSLEVELÜ — (Da-brewie Hahrsh-lav-a-loo) — Dry white Hungarian table wine, officially ranked as a *grand cru.*

DECANT — To transfer a wine from its original bottle to another vessel — carafe, bottle or decanter — usually for serving. The purpose of decanting is to separate the clear wine from any sediment which it may have thrown: this is almost never necessary in dealing with white wines, or red wines that have been less than five years in bottle, but old Rhône wines, many old Clarets and even some old Burgundies are better when decanted than when served, no matter how carefully, in a cradle. Preferably, wines should be decanted two hours or more before they are served, if possible in the cellar; the bottle is first placed as gently as possible in a cradle, the cork drawn, and the wine poured slowly into the carafe against a lighted candle until the first sign of sediment appears.

DECANTER — Glass carafe into which old wines are decanted, and in which young, inexpensive wines are often served. Also, the rather more elaborate vessels, usually of cut crystal, in which Sherry, Madeira and even Port are sometimes kept, greatly to their detriment, on the sideboard. No good wine, not even a brown Sherry or heavy Madeira, liberally fortified with brandy, can stand more than a few days of such treatment without deteriorating, and sideboard decanters are no less decorative and far more useful in their original and proper role — for spirits.

DECIZE-LES-MARANGES — (Day-zeez lay Mar-ronj) — Tiny village

1947er Deidesheimer Kieselberg
Riesling Auslese

ORIGINALABFÜLLUNG

near the southern end of the Côte d'Or, in Burgundy. Its passable red wine is usually sold as Côte-de-Beaune-Villages (*see*).

DEIDESHEIM — (*Die*-dess-heim) — Famous and picturesque little town in the German Palatinate, or Pfalz: with the adjoining villages of Forst, Ruppertsberg and Wachenheim, it produces the best of the Palatinate's white wines. There are nearly a thousand hillside acres under vines, over 60% Rieslings, and the finer Deidesheimers invariably carry the word "Riesling," as well as a specific vineyard name, on their label, as Deidesheimer Hohenmorgen Riesling, etc. The leading vineyard sites, or *Lagen,* include: Hohenmorgen, Grainhübel, Kieselberg, Kränzler, Leinhöhle, Geheu, Grain, Rennpfad, Kalkhofen, Reiss, Mühle, Herrgottsacker, Langenmorgen, Hofstück, plus many others, and among the producers whose names and labels are known the world over, are Basserman-Jordan, Bürklin-Wolf, Reichsrat von Buhl, Koch-Herzog Erben, etc. The village is quaint and charming, with fine old patrician houses in red sandstone, a venerable Rathaus, or Town-Hall, and dozens of winding narrow streets and walled gardens green in summer with apricots and figs. The wines are full-bodied, with great bouquet, and range all the way from dry to very sweet; they have remarkable distinction, the Rieslings especially, and fully deserve their international reputation.

DEKELEIA — (Day-kel-lay-ah) — Red and white table wines, of no special distinction, from near Marathon, in Greece. The name has somehow found its way into almost all existing wine dictionaries and is included here for tradition's sake, and for no other reason.

DELAWARE — One of the best and most widely planted of our native American varieties, almost unique in that it yields excellent table grapes which are also excellent for wine. Its precise ancestry and origin are unknown; some botanists feel that it is an accidental cross of the wild

110

Labrusca vine of our Northern woods and the wild Southern Aestivalis or Bourquiniana of the Carolinas; others believe it has some European Vinifera blood. It first was noted in 1850 in a vineyard at Frenchtown, New Jersey, whence it was transplanted to Delaware, Ohio, and it therefore takes its name from this small town, rather than from the river or the state.

A pink grape, it has white juice and yields white wine, fresh, pale, well-balanced but rather high in acid, with the definite but not too oppressive native-grape or "foxy" flavor and aroma of its Labrusca ancestors. It is widely used in Eastern Champagnes and until the arrival of the new French hybrids (*see*) was consistently responsible for the best white table wines of New York State and Ohio.

DELICATE — Wine tasters' term, properly applicable to wines that are light, rather than full or big; subtle, rather than coarse or sturdy; fine and elegant, rather than great.

DELICATESSEN — This familiar word which, in its original German, means "delicate viands" or "fancy foods," is also the name of a grape, an American hybrid developed by the late T. V. Munson, of Denison, Texas. It is said to give a deep-colored red wine of good quality, but it is no longer grown on any commercial scale.

DEMI, DEMIE — (Dem-me) — These, in French, are the masculine and feminine forms of the same word, and both mean "half"; oddly enough, beer (*bière*), which is feminine, takes the masculine form, and wine (*vin*), which is masculine, takes the feminine. This is less illogical than it seems: *une demie* means a half-bottle of wine (half of *une bouteille*); *un demi* means, or should and used to, a half-liter (half of *un litre*, roughly a pint) of beer, but French beer glasses have grown smaller year by year, and today when you order *un demi* you get about seven ounces.

DEMIJOHN — A large, squat, round bottle or jug, generally wicker-covered, holding anywhere from one to ten gallons. In French it is called a *bonbonne* or *Dame Jeanne*.

DEMI-SEC — (Dem-me-seck) — Literally, in French, "half-dry"; actually, when applied to Champagne or other sparkling wines, it means sweet, and now that it is no longer fashionable to label Champagnes, even the sweetest of them, "*doux*," the demi-secs are about the most heavily dosed, or sweetest, on the market, containing anywhere from 6% to 8% of sugar syrup or liqueur, as against about half as much for wines marked "*sec*." The term is rarely used of still wines, and has no precise meaning in this connection, other than vaguely "on the sweet side."

DÉPARTEMENT — (Day-*part*-te-mawn) — Administrative unit in France, more or less the equivalent of an American county. There are 90 of them. Term often used in this volume, in giving the location of certain villages and vineyards.

111

DEPOSIT — (French, *dépôt*) — Sediment which many red wines and some white tend to throw in the course of their normal evolution in bottle. In the case of white wines this generally takes the form of colorless crystals of tartaric acid, harmless and tasteless; but red wine sediment, containing tannin and pigment, is usually bitter and always disagreeable — it should be left behind in the bottle when the wine is poured.

DESMIRAIL, Château — (Day-me-*rye*) — Classed in 1855 as a 3rd Growth of Margaux, Haut-Médoc. No longer exists as an independent vineyard. The name now belongs to the owners of Château Palmer (*see*) and is used on the lesser red wines of that chateau.

DESSERT WINE — Rather confusing term, since it is used, on the whole correctly, in two widely different senses. In California it means a fortified wine, generally, but by no means always, a sweet one; it is perhaps worth noting that the word "sweet" has also come to have precisely this same special meaning, and a "sweet wine producer," in California, may be a person with a sour disposition who manufactures nothing but the dryest of dry Sherry. A dessert wine, in perhaps more sensible and better usage, is a wine that one might properly serve with dessert, whatever its alcoholic content: for most tastes, Sauternes would fall into this category, together with sweet Sherry, Port, Banyuls, and even the Beerenauslesen and Trockenbeerenauslesen of the Rhine.

DETZEM — (*Dets*-em) — Ancient little wine-producing village on the Moselle, in Germany. Ten Roman miles from Trier, on the old Roman road to Mainz, it took its name from the tenth milestone (*ad decimum lapidem*); its wines are of no real quality or importance.

DÉZALEY — (Day-za-lay) — One of the best dry white wines of Switzerland, produced on steep, terraced vineyards overlooking Lake Geneva, east of Lausanne in the Canton of Vaud. Although made from the Fendant or Chasselas grape, it has considerable distinction and its reputation on the whole is deserved. *See* Lavaux.

DHRON — (Drone) — Vineyard town on the Moselle, between Trittenheim and Piesport. Its wines are of good, not extraordinary quality, but with fine bouquet — the best is Dhroner Hofberg (sometimes labeled Dhronhofberger), and other superior vineyards include Sängerei, Grosswingert, Roterde, Kandel, Hengelberg.

DIE — (Dee) — Town east of the Rhône Valley, known for its sparkling wine, Clairette de Die (*see*).

DIENHEIM — (*Dean*-heim) — Wine-producing town in Rheinhessia, on the Rhine south of Nierstein and Oppenheim, where the escarpment of the *Rheinfront* falls away to the alluvial plain toward Worms. The Dienheimer wines are soft and pleasant but a bit common, with some *Bodenton*, the coarse taste of heavy soil. Best vineyards include Dienheimer Goldberg, Krottenbrunnen, Guldenmorgen, Tafelstein, and the leading producer is the Staatsweingut, the German Government.

DIJON — (Dee-jawn) — Principal city (Pop. 112,000) of Burgundy, in the French *département* of Côte d'Or, although less important in the wine trade than Nuits-Saint-Georges and Beaune. There is a saying to the effect that Dijon is the capital of La Bourgogne (the province) and Beaune (*see*) the capital of Le Bourgogne (the wine). The Côte de Dijon begins at the city's southern edge; it is the northernmost and by far the least important of the three vineyard slopes that make up the celebrated Côte d'Or (*see*). A major tourist center, Dijon is also known for its mustard, made with a white wine base, and for its great annual Gastronomic Fair.

DIONYSUS — In Greek mythology, a nature god, especially of the vine and of wine, the son of Zeus and Semele, the earth goddess. He was also called Bacchus and his symbol was the thyrsus, a staff wreathed with ivy and grape leaves and surmounted by a pine cone.

DISGORGING — From the French *dégorgement*, one of the essential, final steps in the making of Champagne (*see*), by which the sediment is removed from the bottled wine before it receives its *dosage,* or sweetening, and its final cork.

DISTINGUISHED — Used by a wine expert, this is the highest sort of praise, almost the equivalent of the German word *edel*, and reserved for wines of truly extraordinary balance and class. The quality of such wines is immediately obvious, even to a beginner.

DIZY — (Dee-zee) — One of the better wine-producing towns of the French Champagne Country, directly across the Marne from Épernay. Its vineyards are almost entirely planted to Pinot Noir, and are officially rated 95%, which means its grapes bring 5% less, per kilo or per ton, than those from the adjoining town of Ay, rated 100%.

DOISY-DAËNE, Château — (Dway-zee Day-ayne) — 2nd Classed Growth of Barsac, Sauternes, properly considered one of the best of these, lying, as it does, between Coutet and Climens; very small output. Recently the owners have been pioneers in the production of a dry white wine from this district, sold, not as Barsac, but as "Bordeaux Sec de Doisy-Daëne"; of excellent quality, racy, light and fine, this is already acquiring the acceptance it deserves.

DOISY-DUBROCA, Château — (Dwazy-Do-bro-ca) — One of the very good classified 2nd Growths of Barsac, in France. Its wine is notable for its elegance, breed and fine bouquet.

DOISY-VEDRINES, Château — (Dwah-zee Vay-dreen) — 2nd Classed Growth of Barsac, Sauternes, originally part of the same vineyard as Doisy-Daëne. Some 3,000 cases a year.

DOLCETTO — (Dawl-*chet*-toe) — Italian red wine grape of good quality, widely grown in Piedmont, especially on the higher slopes in the provinces of Alessandria and Cuneo. Precocious and productive, it gives a rather soft red wine, short-lived, soon ready to drink, usually sold under the varietal name.

DOLE — (Doe-ll) — The best red wine of Switzerland, produced in the high, rocky, upper valley of the Rhône, in the Canton of Valais. It is made from the Pinot Noir grape plus, quite often, a good deal of Gamay, is full-bodied, deep-colored, quite high in alcohol, long-lived. In character it perhaps is closer to Côte Rôtie than to the Burgundies of the Côte d'Or.

DOM — (Dawm) — In German, the word for Cathedral: as far as wine is concerned, especially the Hohe Domkirche, or Cathedral of Trier, on the Moselle, which has a few important vineyards as part of its endowment. The finest include part of the Scharzhofberg, at Wiltingen on the Saar, and vines at Avelsbach, south of Trier. The Cathedral's wines are estate-bottled but by no means better than wines made by laymen in adjacent vineyards. See also Dom Perignon.

DOMAENE — (Doe-may-nuh) — German for the French word *domaine* or English "domain" — as far as wine is concerned, a vineyard property. In Germany it is often and almost exclusively applied to the state-owned vineyards, or Stáatsweingüter, which are numerous and justly famous, in the Rheingau, in Hessen, and on the Nahe, Moselle and Saar.

DOMAINE — (Doe-*main*) — Vineyard holdings or vineyards making up a single property or estate, although these vineyards may or may not be widely separated in different *communes* or townships, and bear entirely different names. A single Burgundian *Domaine* may, for example, comprise vines in Chambertin, Clos de Vougeot, Corton and Montrachet; the wines from these will of course be kept scrupulously separate, and will be marketed under the various vineyard appellations, with the name of the *Domaine* appearing only as the producer, not as the name of the wine. Many Domaine wines are estate-bottled (*see*) although by no means all; those that are, carry on their labels the words *Mise du Domaine* or *Mis en Bouteilles au Domaine*.

The word is quite differently used in the Bordeaux Country and in Provence where it is practically synonymous with Château, e.g., Domaine de Chevalier, Domaine des Moulières, etc.

DOM PERIGNON — (Dawm *Pay*-reen-yawn) — Cellar-master at the Abbey of Hautvillers, in the Champagne Country, from 1670 to 1715; this is a singularly gracious old building and commands an incomparable view of the vineyards and of Épernay and the Marne Valley. It was here, according to well-publicized tradition, that Dom Perignon "invented" Champagne, and made his celebrated remark, on first tasting it, "I am drinking stars." Actually, of course, no one "invented" Champagne, and the old monk never claimed to have done so. He was, like his contemporary, Dom Oudard, one of the most competent and imaginative wine technicians of his day, and there is no doubt that he was one of the first to experiment with cork closures, then rare in France, and to make what is now known as a *cuvée* by blending wines of different origins and of both black grapes and white. But modern Champagne owes fully as much to half a hundred nameless and forgotten experts as to him.

The Abbey of Hautvillers is now the property of the great Champagne house of Moët et Chandon, and a statue of Dom Perignon has been set up in the courtyard. The name "Dom Perignon" has been given to Moët's best and most expensive wine, shipped in the sort of slender-necked, low-shouldered bottle used for all Champagnes a hundred years ago. However, it was found necessary to discontinue the use of corks tied down with string instead of wire, and sealed with wax instead of foil (all Champagnes came this way, and in wicker hampers, in our great-grandfathers' days) for there is, after all, a limit to archaism. The wine does not always merit its great present reputation, but is generally of outstanding quality.

DOMTAL — (Dawm-tahl) — Originally the name of a vineyard in Nierstein, on the Rhine, literally "cathedral-valley"; this has now become a generic appellation, and includes not only a diocese but all of Rheinhessen. Practically any wine that may be labeled Liebfraumilch may also be called Niersteiner Domtal. This is certainly a shocking violation, in spirit at least, of German law concerning appellations of origin, but the consumer surely has a right to know what the name means — in this case, practically nothing.

DORDOGNE — (Dor-dawn) — Important river of southwestern France, joining the Garonne just north of Bordeaux, to form the tidal estuary of the Gironde; also a *département* farther east, bordering the Bordeaux Country and producing a good deal of rather common wine, mostly white and somewhat sweet, sold as Monbazillac (*see*), Montravel, etc.

DOSAGE — (Doe-saj) — All Champagne is absolutely bone dry up to the moment when it is "disgorged" and receives what is known as its *dosage*. This consists of anywhere from a teaspoonful to two ounces of syrup, or *liqueur d'expédition*, and the amount determines whether the wine is Brut, or Extra Dry, or Sec, or Demi-sec. There exist various formulas for the syrup, but generally there are three parts of cane sugar or rock candy to two of old wine, plus in some cases a little special brandy known as *esprit de Cognac*, double distilled, 140 proof.

DOURO — (Due-ro) — One of Portugal's three great rivers, all of which rise in Spain and change their spelling and their nationality before they empty into the Atlantic: the Tajo becomes the Tejo, the Duero, the Douro, and the northernmost is the Spanish Miño on its northern bank and the Portuguese Minho on its southern. For wine lovers, all three are relatively undistinguisned in Spain, but the Douro, once it crosses the border, becomes the spinal column and even the principal highway of one of the world's great wine countries. *See* Port.

DOUX — (Doo) — Simply means "sweet" in its ordinary French sense, but applied to wine it becomes much more complicated. The good, natural, not-quite-dry table wines are more properly described as *moelleux* — the best Graves for example; another adjective, *liquoreux*, is applied to the naturally sweet wines, such as the great Sauternes and the finer white wines of Anjou; a *vin doux* is generally a wine possessing a sweetness not entirely normal — one only partially fermented and heavily sulphured, as the *vin doux de Gaillac*; or a sweet fortified wine, as the so-called *vins doux naturels* of the eastern Pyrenees; or the very sweetest and on the whole the poorest of Champagnes. The term, in brief, is one rarely applied to good, let alone outstanding, wines.

DRACHENBLUT — (Drak-en-bloot) — Literally, in German, "dragon's blood." So-called, usually with a wink, it is a pale, watery red wine, of poor quality at best, produced on a hill known as the Drachenfels, on the east bank of the Rhine, near Bonn.

DRÔME — (Droam) — French *département* on the left bank of the Rhône south of Lyon; that of Hermitage, Crozes, Mercurol (*see* all of these).

DRUNKARDS' LINE — An affectionate name given to the single track railway which follows the winding Moselle Valley from Trier to Piesport in Germany; the *Saufbähnchen.*. Its timetable reads like a wine-list but there is no club car and no dining car, nor hardly a wine produced along its route which runs as high as 11% alcohol; its average of passenger sobriety is certainly higher than that on the Super-Chief.

DRY — As far as wine is concerned, the opposite of sweet is not sour, but dry; and even an extremely dry wine is no more necessarily sour than unsugared coffee is sour. Practically all of the widely used table wines of the world are dry rather than sweet, as are many apéritif wines such as Fino and Amontillado Sherry, Verdelho and Rainwater Madeira, and some Marsalas.

In California, the word has acquired a somewhat different connotation and, colloquially at least, is synonymous with unfortified. Thus, in California — in wine parlance — wines under 14%, even if sweet, are "dry wines." Similarly, dry Sherry is often referred to as "sweet" (i.e., fortified).

DUBONNET — (Due-bawn-nay) — Excellent, popular, widely-advertised French apéritif made, according to a proprietary formula, of sweet, red, fortified wine, quinine and various herbs. It is used as an ingredient in many cocktails but more often, in France at least, served straight or with ice and soda. Dubonnet is also manufactured under license in California, and theoretically according to the same formula, but the basic wine is of course not the same and the end product is vastly different and much less good.

DUCRU-BEAUCAILLOU, Château — (*Dew*-crew *Bo*-ky-you) — 2nd Classed Growth of St. Julien, Haut-Médoc; some 12,000 cases a year. *"Caillou"* in French means pebble, and *"beau,"* of course, means beautiful; the vineyard is just north of Beychevelle and extends down to the river on gravelly soil, as its name indicates. The wines in the past were rather hard, slow to mature, and brought prices below some of the other 2nd Growths; there has been a striking improvement in the last decade.

116

DUHART-MILON, Château — (*Dew*-harr *Mee*-lawn) — 4th Classed Growth of Pauillac, Haut-Médoc, adjoining Lafite and Mouton-Rothschild, producing some 12,000 cases a year of good Claret, full-bodied, slow-maturing, better than some chateaux that have a higher official rank.

DULCE — (Dool-they) — Literally, in Spanish, means "sweet." Applied to wine, in a special sense, it means a sweetening agent, any one of many, added to the dry wines of the Sherry Country to make them more acceptable abroad. Most of these are very sweet wines from sun-dried grapes, others are concentrates — *see* Pedro Ximénez, Arrope, Apagado, Sancocho, Vino de Color.

DULL — A dull wine is like a dull person — perhaps honorable and sound, but not very interesting and certainly not much fun. Such a wine may be dry, full-bodied and have other qualities; it should certainly be cheap.

DUR — (Dewr) — Literally, "hard," in French. As a wine-tasters' term it has almost exactly the same meaning and connotation as its English equivalent. *See* Hard.

DURAS — *See* Côtes de Duras.

DURBACH — (Door-bak) — German wine-producing town in Baden, almost directly across the Rhine from Strasbourg. Many of the wines, Rieslings, Traminers and Ruländers (Pinot Gris), are far from bad and some of them occasionally quite remarkable, but most of them are drunk up by the local gentry and by thirsty tourists before they are two years old.

DURFORT-VIVENS, Château — (*Dear*-for *Vee*-venns) — Classed in 1855 as a 2nd Growth of Margaux, Médoc. No longer exists as an inpendent property.

DURIFF — (Dew-reef) — Rather common red wine grape, grown to some small extent in the Rhône Valley. It bears a superficial resemblance to the Petit Syrah of Hermitage, but does not have the Syrah's unfortunate tendency to drop its fruit before maturity (*see* Coulure); for this reason, it used to be known to the peasant *vignerons* of the district as the "Syrah-*que-ten*," which could perhaps be translated as the "Holdfast-Syrah"; it is nevertheless not a Syrah at all and its wine is of poor quality. It seems very probable that the so-called "Petit Syrah" of California, which is one of the most widely planted of red wine grapes there, is in fact the Duriff, rather than the illustrious vine whose name it has assumed.

DÜRKHEIM — (*Deark*-heim) — Usually called, except of course on wine labels, Bad Dürkheim (on account of its mineral springs) this happens to be the largest wine-producing township in all Germany, with nearly 2,000 acres of vineyard. It is an agreeable small town, with the wooded hills of the Mittel-Haardt sheltering it on the west, and its many hotels overlook a mile or so of sloping vineyards, and then the flat and fertile Rhine Valley. There is a good deal of red wine, mostly quite poor and made from the Portugieser grape, a large amount of fair, and a little very good white wine: the best is Riesling, and is so labeled, plus a vineyard name, as Dürkheimer Michelsberg Riesling. Spielberg, Hochbenn, Schenkenböhl, Fuchsmantel, Feuerberg, are other well-known *Lagen*.

EARTHY — This is perhaps the best English translation of what the French call a *goût de terroir* and the Germans a *Bodengeschmack*, a rather odd, special flavor which certain soils tend to give to the wines they yield. If too pronounced, this can be highly disagreeable, and is usually the mark of a coarse wine produced, often from the best of grape varieties, on heavy, alluvial soil. It is easy to recognize, almost impossible to describe.

EAST INDIA — Old term, less used now than formerly, to designate Oloroso Sherries of a particular brown, sweet, full-bodied sort. Originally such wines were supposed to have received additional ageing in the holds of sailing vessels, in the course of a voyage to the East Indies and back.

EBERBACH — (Eh-bear-bach) — *See* Kloster Eberbach.

ECCLESIASTICUS — A book of the Apocrypha (about 180 B.C.) in which is written: "Wine drunk with moderation is the joy of the soul and the heart."

ÉCHÉZEAUX — (*Esh*-shay-zo) — Important Burgundian vineyard of the Côte de Nuits, between the Clos de Vougeot and Vosne-Romanée, 79 acres in all, with an average production of some 6,000 cases a year. Lying mostly on the gently-sloping, lower half of the *Côte,* it gives a wine more remarkable for its subtlety than its power, rather light in color and body, but racy and fine.

ECHT — (Ekt) — German adjective meaning "real" or "genuine"; applied to wine, it may only be used in connection with wines which are unsugared and is thus substantially synonymous with *natur, rein,* etc.

EDEL — (Eh-dell) — German word meaning "noble," or, in a wider sense, "superior" or "fine." Thus *Edelfäule* means the "Noble Mold" or *pourriture noble; Edeltraube* a superior variety of grape; *Edelbeerenauslese* a particularly good wine of this exalted class; and *Edelzwicker,* in Alsace, a wine made from a blend of superior grapes. The Alsatians sometimes treat the word *Gentil* (as in *gentilhomme,* or gentleman) as another French equivalent of *Edel,* and this word is sometimes used on Alsatian wine labels, although rather loosely.

EDELFÄULE — (Eh-del-foy-luh) — *See* Pourriture Noble.

EDELGEWÄCHS — *See* Gewächs, Edel.

EDELZWICKER — (*A*-del-zvick-er) — Alsatian wine term, meaning a blended wine made from superior grape varieties. *Edel* is the German word for "noble," although in Alsace usually translated as *Gentil* (*see*), and the *Edeltrauben* or *plants nobles* are considered to include the Riesling, Gewürztraminer, Traminer, Pinot Gris, Pinot Blanc, Muscat and Sylvaner. An Edelzwicker may be a blend of any or all of these, often grown in the same vineyard and picked together. *See* Zwicker.

EGER — (A-gair) — Important Hungarian wine-producing town, set in mountainous country some 120 miles northeast of Budapest, and especially famous for two red wines, Egri Bikavér ("bull's blood") and Egri Kadarka (which is the name of a grape). These are grown in Eger and some dozen surrounding villages, and were much appreciated in Austria, Germany and even the United States in happier and more tranquil days. Both are full-bodied, deep-colored, long-lived, the Kadarka made from the grape of that name, the Bikavér from a number of different varieties including the Kadarka but also the Gamay, the Cabernet Franc, and others.

ÉGLISE — (A-gleeze) — Means church in French. The Clos l'Église, Clos l'Église-Clinet and Domaine de l'Église are well-known vineyards of Pomerol, each producing some 2,000 cases a year of very full-bodied, good quality Claret.

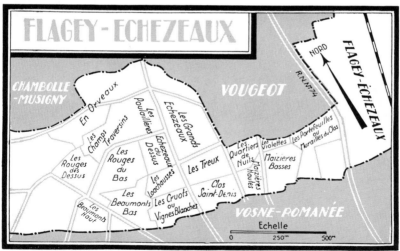

NOTE: All of the wines of Flagey-Échézeaux (there are 179 acres of vineyard) are entitled to the village appellation "Vosne-Romanée." *Grands Échézéaux,* as shown, is a single 22½-acre *climat,* and only wines from this plot have a right to this distinguished name. Wines from *Les Beaumonts* (also, and no less correctly, written *Les Beaux Monts*) are usually sold as "Vosne-Romanée Les Beaumonts." Those from the following vineyards (84 acres in all) may legally be labeled *"Échézeaux"*: Les Treux, Clos St. Denis, Les Cruots ou Vignes Blanches, Les Rouges du Bas, Champs Traversins, Les Poulaillères, Les Loachaussés, plus parts of En Orveaux, Les Quartiers de Nuits, and Les Échézeaux du Dessus.

EGRAPPAGE — (Eh-grah-*pahj*) — Process, essential in the making of all good wine, of removing the grapes from their stems prior to pressing and/or fermentation. In the old days this procedure was less strictly observed for red wines, some stems being left to ferment with the skins; the resulting wines were harsher, higher in tannin, slower to develop, but unquestionably longer-lived.

EGUISHEIM — (*Aig*-wiss-heim) — Good wine producing village in Alsace, just south of Colmar in the *département* of Haut-Rhin.

EITELSBACH — (I-tells-bach) — Tiny town on the Ruwer, a tributary of the Moselle, in Germany; most of its renowned, steep, splendid vineyards once belonged to a Carthusian monastery, but have been, for over a century, the property of the Rautenstrauch family, although still called Eitelsbacher Karthäuserhofberg, or "Carthusians' Hill." This, some seventy acres in all, is divided into a number of vineyard-plots, or *Lagen* — Kronenberg, Sang, Burgberg, etc. — and one of these names, too, appears on the crowded little label, which is almost in the nature of a pretty collar around the bottle's neck; there is a joke to the effect that the German wine with the longest name has the smallest label. The wine is nevertheless worth looking for and remembering, for it is one of the very best of the Mosel-Saar-Ruwer, especially in good vintage years — very light, rather austere, with a bouquet of incredible floweriness and distinction. Authentic Eitelsbachers are made by a few other producers, but Rautenstrauch's is, by a wide margin, the best.

EISWEIN — (Ice-vine) — Rare oddity in the way of German wine — it could almost be called an accidental Auslese — made from the first pressing of frozen grapes. The vintage, or grape harvest, comes very late on the Moselle and Rhine, and severe night frosts are not uncommon: perhaps once in a decade temperatures as low as 20° Fahrenheit are recorded, and when the pickers go back in the vineyards the next morning they find the less ripe grapes, with lower sugar content, frozen solid, but the over-ripe grapes with sweeter juice only partially frozen. They must nevertheless be harvested, and are brought to the *Kelterhaus*, put in a hydraulic press and subjected to pressure, sometimes after but often without a preliminary effort to break or crush

120

the individual berries. The first run of juice therefore comes almost entirely from the ripest berries, and this, if fermented separately, is Eiswein. The result is interesting but usually a long way below true Auslese quality — more of a freak than a fine wine. With the increasingly wide adoption of the pneumatic Willmes press, it seems unlikely that much Eiswein will be made in the future, although a number of celebrated vineyards produced such wine in 1961.

ELBA — (*El*-ba) — Island in the Tyrrhenian Sea, a dozen miles off the west coast of Italy. Produces a substantial amount of red and white table wine, most of it rather common and high in alcohol, and (especially around Portoferraio) one red dessert wine that is internationally famous. This, made from the Aleatico grape (*see*), is somewhat on the order of a light Port, with a pronounced, unmistakable Muscat bouquet and flavor.

ELBLING — (L-bling) — Productive German wine grape of poor quality, known in California as the Burger and in Alsace sometimes as the Eisling. Giving a flat, dull wine low in acid, it is planted in the less good German districts and its wine, in Germany, generally goes into cheap sparkling wine, or *Sekt*. In Alsace and in Lorraine, it is temporarily "tolerated," but will no longer be legally a wine-grape after 1965. In California it is no better.

ELDERBERRY — Shrub of the genus *Sambucus* which grows wild in many parts of Europe and the United States. Its cream-colored flowers have a rather pronounced odor, and in the bad old days, were often used (or so they say) to give additional bouquet to Moselles and Rhine wines; the dark purple berries have undoubtedly yielded wine of a sort in Europe and America for centuries, but require a great deal of added sugar to produce anything at all potable. Elderberry juice has often been used (illegally, and, let us hope, no longer) to give added color to light red wines, especially Port.

ELEGANT — Wine taster's term, a good bit less flattering than "distinguished" but often meaning almost the same thing. It can be applied to small, light wines of great vineyards in off years, which have finesse and breed but not much else to recommend them, as the adjective "distinguished" could not; wines of comparatively common origin are in rare instances distinguished, but they are almost never elegant.

ELTVILLE — (Elt-veel) — Major wine-producing town of the Rheingau, the easternmost except Hochheim of those that are well-known, with nearly 500 acres of vines, giving wines which are rarely remarkable but consistently sound and good. The best vineyards are Sonnenberg, Langenstück, Klumbchen, Mönchhanach, Kalbspflicht, Taubenberg, Sandgrub, etc. A number of famous producers have their cellars in Eltville, including Graf Eltz and Freiherr Langwerth von Simmern and the Verwaltung der Staatsweingüter, or German State Domain. Eltville is also an important center for sparkling wines, Matheus Müller and many others.

ELTZ — (Eltz) — One of the great vineyard-owning families of Germany, with extensive holdings in the best *Lagen*, or sites, of Rauenthal, Eltville and Kiedrich in the Rheingau. Count Eltz is also the owner of Schloss Eltz, a lovely old Renaissance manor-house on the Rhine in Eltville, and his irreproachable estate-bottled wines carry the words Schloss Eltz, as well as a vineyard name, on their label, plus the family coat-of-arms, and the words Gräflich Eltz'sche Gutsverwaltung.

ELVIRA — One of the better and better-known native white Eastern grapes, closely resembling and perhaps identical with what is called the "Missouri Riesling." It is of course not a Riesling at all, but a seedling of a Labrusca X Riparia cross. It was first noted and popularized by Jacob Rommel in Missouri in 1869; it is a cousin to the Noah, but better in quality. Its wine, especially from the Finger Lakes district, is fresh and attractive, with a rather pronounced native-grape or "foxy" aroma, but considerable distinction nonetheless.

EMERSON, Ralph Waldo (1803-1882) — American essayist, who wrote, "Give me wine to wash me clean of the weather-stains of cares."

EMILIA — (A-meal-ee-ah) — North Italian province. Bologna, Ferrara and Ravenna are its principal cities, and it is justly celebrated for its food, less for its wines. Few of these are of much distinction. The best known is probably Lambrusco *(see)*, especially that produced round the town of Sorbara, west of Bologna.

ENFER — (En-fair) — One of a number of rather unusual and interesting dessert wines, made from grapes that have been partially dried or raisined *(see Passito)* in the Valle d'Aosta, in the extreme northwestern corner of Italy. These, produced in very small quantity, are almost without commercial interest; they include, as well as the Enfer of the village of Arvié, and the somewhat better known *Caluso (see)*, a Malvasia from Nus, a Moscato from Ciambave, etc.

ENKIRCH — (*En*-keersh) — Little vineyard town at the northern or downstream end of the Mittel-Mosel, in Germany. Steffensberg, Herrenberg, Battereiberg and Montenubel are the best *Lagen*.

ENOLOGY (Also OENOLOGY) — The whole science of wine — its production, its care and handling.

ENTRE-DEUX-MERS — (Awn-truh Duh Mair) — Literally, "Between-Two Seas." One of the major divisions of the Bordeaux wine country, comprising almost one-fifth of the whole Gironde *département*. Geographically, it consists of a triangle of rather lovely, rolling hills between the two confluent rivers, Garonne and Dordogne, and should perhaps more logically be called Entre-Deux-Fleuves. Portions of it (Côtes de Bordeaux, Loupiac, Ste. Croix-du-Mont, Graves de Vayres and Ste. Foy-Bordeaux) are considered separate districts under French wine law; what remains produces a vast amount (not far from 10 million gallons a year) of rather common and inexpensive white wine. Red wines are not entitled to the appellation, and are sold as Bordeaux or Bordeaux Supérieur.

Until quite recently, Entre-Deux-Mers wines were generally some-what on the sweet side; faced with a declining demand, the growers made a courageous and intelligent decision, and set out to produce dry wines exclusively. They adopted the amusing slogan, *"Entre deux huîtres* (between two oysters) — *Entre-Deux-Mers"*; the quality of the wines has improved and is still improving; they are today good values in their price class, though hardly distinguished.

For Map, *see* BORDEAUX.

EPERNAY — (*A*-pear-nay) — One of the two main centers of the French Champagne trade, Reims being the other; a rather pedestrian modern town on the Marne River east of Paris, under which extends a veritable rabbit-warren of cellars and tunnels, doubtless 200 miles and more of them in all, those of Moët et Chandon, Pol Roger, Mercier, de Castel-lane and many others. South of the town and sometimes called the Côte d'Epernay, is what is more properly known as the Côte des Blancs, with Cramant, Avize and other famous *crus*; across the Marne are Ay, Hautvillers and the equally celebrated villages of the Côte des Noirs. *See* Champagne.

EPLUCHAGE — (Eh-ploosh-shaj) — Operation of picking over, by hand, the newly harvested grapes before they are crushed or pressed, so as to eliminate defective bunches and berries. This is normal procedure in wineries interested in superior quality.

ERBACH — (Air-bach) — Justly famous little vineyard town on the Rhine, producing some of the Rheingau's most distinguished wines. The incomparable Marcobrunn (*see*) is mostly in Erbach, and the other celebrated plots include Steinmorgen, Honigberg, Siegelsberg, Brühl, Hohenrain, Rheinhell, Kahlig, Seelgass, etc., all yielding rather hard, firm wines, long-lived and obviously of great class.

123

ERBALUCE — (Air-ba-*loo*-chay) — White wine grape cultivated in northern Italy, especially used in the making of the *passito* of Caluso (*see*).

ERDEN — (*Air*-den) — Tiny, wine-producing village on the Moselle near Zeltingen. Its vineyards are among the steepest of Germany, as the name of one of them, Treppchen ("little stairway") would indeed indicate, and the spicy, delicate wines they produce are among the best of the Moselle. The better plots include, in addition to Treppchen, Busslay, Prälat, Herrenberg, Kranklay, etc.

ERMITAGE — (*Air*-me-taj) — Variant spelling of Hermitage (*see*), no less correct but less widely used. Also a white wine from the Canton of Valais, in Switzerland, made from the Marsanne grape.

ESCHERNDORF — (*Esh*-shern-dorf) — Important wine town in Franconia, after Würzburg one of the very best. Its wines, made from the Sylvaner or Riesling (the label generally tells which) are of course shipped in the traditional stumpy flagon, or Bocksbeutel. The best vineyards — there are some 200 acres in all — include Lump, Eulengrube, Hengstberg and Kirchberg.

ESTATE-BOTTLING — Praiseworthy practice, which wine-lovers the world over should do all in their power to encourage, whereby vineyard owners bottle the unblended product of their own vines. Like Chateau-Bottling and *Original-Abfüllung*, which are virtually the same thing, Estate-Bottling is almost a guarantee of authenticity and to some extent an indication of superior quality; it has been standard procedure in the finer Bordeaux and German vineyards for many decades and has become increasingly general in Burgundy, the Côtes-du-Rhône, the Loire Valley, etc., since World War I. Many wines, unfortunately, appear to be estate-bottled when they are not, and carry statements on their labels, calculated to deceive the unwary, yet basically meaningless. Some such statements are quite factual, yet mean only that the wine was bottled by the shipper (by no means the same thing as the producer) rather than by the restaurant where served or the retail store where sold. The following terms, for example, have nothing to do with Estate-Bottling:

Mis en bouteilles dans nos caves	*Mis en bouteille dans nos chais*
Mise de l'origine	*Produced and bottled by* (in English, on a French wine)
Mis en bouteille au vignoble	*Mis en bouteilles à Beaune* (etc.)

Those who are interested in getting the real thing will be well advised to give their preference to wines and labels which conform with the following generalizations:

1. Statements having to do with Estate-Bottling should be on the main label, not the strip. If in English (as "Estate-Bottled"), the statement should also appear on the main label in one of the various forms (see below) in French.

2. The label should state that the wine comes from someone who is a vineyard owner, not just a shipper, although a person may be and is

often both. Thus *négociant* means "shipper," *éleveur* more or less the same thing; but *propriétaire* means "vineyard owner," *récoltant* a grower who harvests his own crop, *viticulteur* and *vigneron* mean "wine grower."

3. It should be stated unequivocally that the wine was bottled by the person who made it, or at least on his premises. The following terms are those generally used to indicate this fact:

Mise du Domaine	*Mise au Domaine*
Mis en bouteilles au Domaine	*Mise du Propriétaire*
Mis en bouteilles par le Propriétaire	*Mise à la Propriété*

In the United States, too, the term "Estate-bottling" has come to have a specific new meaning, and can only be used on California and other wines made *exclusively* from grapes grown by the producer himself. On the other hand, the phrase "Produced and bottled by . . ." means only that 75% of the wine need come from the vineyard named on the label; and if the words "Made by . . ." appear, only 10% of the wine need be of the shipper's own production.

EST EST EST — Light, semi-sweet white wine, made from the Moscatello grape round the villages of Montefiascone and Bolsena, north of Rome. It owes its curious name (which of course in Latin means, "It is, It is, It is") to the often-told story of the wine-loving German bishop who, on his way to Rome, sent his servant ahead as a scout and taster. The latter was instructed to write the word "Est" on the walls of every tavern where he found the wine especially good. On reaching Montefiascone he wrote, not "Est", but "Est! Est!! Est!!!," and the bishop, on his arrival, proceeded to drink himself to death. His tomb, with an inscription in Latin which tells the story, has been piously preserved.

ESTOURNEL — *See* Cos d'Estournel.

ESTUFA — (Ess-*too*-fa) — Portuguese term meaning either a hot-house for the cultivation of plants and flowers, or, in the special case of wine, a room in which Madeira, for example, is held when first made, at a high temperature, thanks to which it acquires its special "Madeira" flavor.

ETAMPÉ — French wine shipper's term, largely meaningless, sometimes used to describe Bordeaux or other wines which are not Chateau- or Estate-Bottled, but which nevertheless carry a vineyard name. It has no precise legal meaning under French law, but indicates, more or less, that the shipper guarantees its authenticity and quality.

ETOILE — (A-twahl) — Still or occasionally sparkling white wine produced round the village of this name in the French Jura — there are some 10,000 cases a year.

ETNA — (*Et*-na) — Famous active volcano in Sicily, sometimes spelled Aetna in English, rising to 10,758 feet from the sea south of the Straits of Messina. A large portion of its eastern slope is planted to vines. The higher of these, round the villages of Nicolosi, Trecastagni, Zafferana, etc., at over 2,000 feet, produce red and white wines of exceptional quality and breed, with good acidity and not too much alcohol. They are the best table wines of Sicily and are sold as Etna.

EVANGILE, Château de l' — (*A*-vawn-geel) — One of the best vineyards of Pomerol. In a normal year some 4,000 cases of excellent red wine.

EYQUEM — (A-kem) — The Château d'Eyquem is a rather large vineyard near Bourg (*see*) in the Bordeaux Country, produces ordinary red wine, plus a little dry white of second quality. The Clos d'Eyquem, at La Brède, Graves district, is a small property giving a rather undistinguished dry white wine. Neither should be confused with Château d'Yquem (*see*), greatest of Sauternes and one of the most celebrated white wines of the world.

F-G-H

FALERNO — (Fal-*lair*-no) — The most celebrated wine (Falernian) of ancient Rome, praised in the most extravagant fashion by Pliny and Horace, and considered "immortal," certain vintages having been opened and found good after over a century. It was produced near Formia, on the coast north of Naples, and the identical hillsides are planted in vines today. What they now yield is rather good but by no means extraordinary, sound red and dry white wines that are pleasant but a long way from immortal. They have nothing in common with the Falerno of antiquity except their geographical origin and their name.

FARGUES — (Farg) — Least important of the five townships of the French Sauternes Country. Its best known vineyards are Château Rieussec (*see*) Château Romer, and Château de Fargues, the last owned by the Marquis de Lur-Saluces. White wines exclusively.

FASS — (Fahss) — German word for barrel, especially the 600-liter *Halbstück* used in the Rheingau. The plural is Fässer, pronounced *Fesser. See* also Bestes Fass.

FAUGÈRES — (Fo-share) — Passably good red and white wine produced north of Béziers, in the French Midi. A surprisingly agreeable brandy comes from the same production zone and is distilled in Bédarieux.

FAVERGES — (Fa-vairj) — Pale, dry white wine from the district known as Lavaux, on the north shore of Lake Geneva, in Switzerland. It is made from the Fendant or Chasselas grape and the vineyard is owned by the Canton of Fribourg. Pleasant, hardly remarkable.

FAYE — (Fie) — Important wine-producing town on the Coteaux du Layon (*see*), in Anjou. Sweet white wines of top quality and a few good *rosés*.

FENDANT — (*Fawn*-dawn) — Name given in Switzerland to the Chasselas grape, which is by a wide margin the leading variety in this happy and thirsty small country. It is, on the whole, a far from remarkable grape for wine, but in the Cantons of Vaud, Valais and Neuchâtel it yields a great many fresh, often fine and almost invariably agreeable white wines.

FERMENTATION — Process by which sugar is transformed into alcohol (*see*) plus carbon dioxide, and by which grape juice becomes wine. Although fermentation had been observed since the dawn of history, it was thought to be a wholly spontaneous phenomenon until Pasteur, in 1857, showed it to be work of living organisms — more specifically, of zymase, the enzyme of yeast. Modern technical knowledge goes much farther, and in most good cellars and wineries today fermentation is no longer left to chance but is carefully controlled, above all as regards the temperature of the fermenting must: the fermenting-rooms are often warmed in Champagne and Burgundy, and the must itself generally cooled in California. Other practices go much farther, and involve the sterilization of the juice with sulphur dioxide and the introduction of special strains of yeast; in some instances white wines are now fermented under pressure, in glass-lined steel tanks. Red wines are fermented with their skins, white wines without (*see* Cuvaison). Fermentation normally continues until all, or practically all, of the grape sugar has been converted; it can be stopped at any time, as in the making of Port, by the addition of brandy or high-proof spirits (*see* Fortified Wine), and even without such addition, it will tend to slow down and stop as soon as 14% or 15% of alcohol by volume has been attained.

FERMENTATION, MALO-LACTIC — Secondary fermentation which takes place in many table wines, either shortly after the original fermentation or, more normally, in the spring following the vintage. Through its action, much of the malic acid which wine normally contains, and which is the acid of unripe fruit, is transformed into milder lactic acid, rendering the wine, to the palate, less green, less harsh and less tart. Chemically speaking, malic acid is $COOH . CH_2 . CHOH . COOH$ whereas lactic acid is $CH_3 . CHOH . COOH$: the wine therefore releases a certain amount of CO_2, or carbon dioxide gas, in this conversion.

Most European producers welcome this Malo-lactic Fermentation, and do everything possible to encourage it; however, due to different climatic conditions in California, and the lower average acidity of the wines, it is not considered beneficial there, and is by no means regarded as a blessing.

FERRAN, Château — (*Fair*-rawn) — Good secondary vineyard of Martillac in the Graves district. Some 3,000 cases a year of red wine, plus a lesser amount of dry white.

FERRAND, Château de — (*Fair*-rawn) — Large 2nd Growth St. Emilion vineyard, producing some 10,000 cases a year of sound, agreeable Claret.

FERRIÈRE, Château — (Ferr-ry-*air*) — 3rd Classed Growth of Margaux, Haut-Médoc. Very small production.

FEUILLETTE — (Foo-*yet*) — Small oak barrel, of 136-liter or about 36-gallon capacity, in which the wines of Chablis were traditionally stored. Such barrels have largely been replaced by the conventional Burgundian *pièces*, holding 228 liters, and the change is all for the better.

FIASCO — (Fee-*ask*-ko) — This word simply means "flask" in Italian; the plural is *fiaschi* (fee-*ask*-key). The *fiasco* used for wine, especially but not exclusively for Chianti, is round-bottomed, often hand-blown; thin and light, it would be extremely fragile without its straw-covering, and of course would not stand up on a table. The straw is woven on before the *fiaschi* are filled. Properly speaking, a true *fiasco* traditionally holds two liters, but they come today in all sorts of sizes and shapes.

FIEUZAL, Château — (*Fee*-oo-zahl) — One of the best vineyards of Léognan, in the Graves district, now ranked as a *Cru Classé*. Some 8,000 cases a year of superior red wine, and a lesser quantity of less good white.

FIGEAC, Château — (*Fee*-jack) — One of the largest and best vineyards of the St. Emilion district, adjoining Cheval Blanc. Its soft, sturdy wines (some 10,000 cases a year when in full production) are not far inferior to those of its illustrious neighbor, and fully merit their 1st Growth rank. A half dozen other nearby vineyards, all good but somewhat less famous, also carry the name Figeac but in a combined form: Châteaux La Tour-du-Pin-Figeac, La Tour-du-Pin-Figeac-Moueix, La Tour-Figeac, Grand Barrail-Lamarzelle-Figeac, Yon-Figeac, Cormey-Figeac, etc.

FILHOT, Château — (*Fee*-yo) — Justly famous Sauternes vineyard, owned by the Countess de Lacarelle, née Lur-Saluces, and sister of the owner of Yquem. Although officially ranked as a 2nd Classed Growth, its wine, a shade dryer than most Sauternes but of great distinction and breed, generally sells for a higher price than many 1sts. There are some 5,000 cases a year.

FILLETTE — (Fee-yet) — Literally, in French, a young girl. The word is used in the Loire Valley, especially in Touraine, to mean a half-bottle of wine.

FILTERING — The clarifying of a wine, prior to bottling, by passing it through any one of many different types of filter. Too heavy or severe a filtration can "numb" a wine and destroy many of its finer qualities, and many of the very best wines of the world are never filtered at all. It is by no means, however, a practice that should be condemned, for, if not carried to extremes, it is usually helpful and often necessary, par-

129

ticularly these days, now that the public is reluctant to accept wines that are not absolutely brilliant and have a minimum of sediment, or none. Many German and Swiss wines are now "sterile-filtered," all bacteria thus being removed; this process permits earlier bottling and has many other advantages, but it unquestionably tends to shorten a wine's life.

FINE — Wine taster's term, rather loosely used. It is properly applied to any wine that has an inherent, unmistakable superiority, whether due to its origin, its grape variety, or other factors.

FINESSE — Breed or class or distinction, rendering a wine out of the ordinary. A full-bodied wine that has finesse can often be described as great; without finesse it would be simply heavy or common.

FINGER LAKES — The principal wine-producing district of New York State; after California, the most important of the U.S. The long, narrow lakes, southeast of Rochester, are four in number, roughly parallel, and, on a map at least, they look rather like imprints left by four enormous fingers, whence their name. Only two of them, Keuka and Canandaigua, are known for their vineyards, (Seneca and Cayuga having other claims to fame); the first grapes were planted here in 1829, and wine has been produced on a commercial scale since Civil War days. Until recently, almost all of the grapes were of the native, Eastern varieties (Delaware, Catawba, Elvira, Niagara, Isabella, Iona, Concord, etc.) but many of the newer hybrids have been planted since Prohibition, and the results seem very promising. There are four major wineries — Pleasant Valley (Great Western), Urbana (Gold Seal), and Taylor's, on Lake Keuka; and Widmer's, at Naples on Lake Canandaigua. A great deal of Champagne, or sparkling wine, is produced, nearly half of our national output, as well as fortified wines and table wines; most of these carry, in addition to the required words, "New York State," the common European appellations, as Sherry, Port, Burgundy, Sauterne, etc.; many of them are blended with California wines brought in by tank car. A few, and generally the best, bear varietal names, especially Delaware, Elvira, Riesling (*see*), or that of one of the French hybrids — Baco, Couderc or Seibel, plus a number.

FINING — Traditional method of clarifying wine (*collage*, in French) known since Roman days, whereby certain substances are added to the wine in barrel and gradually settle, carrying down, in the form of sediment or lees, the suspended particles and leaving the wine clear. White of egg, isinglass (from the bladders of sturgeon), gelatine, casein and fresh blood have all been used in this way, as have many types of clay including Bentonite (aluminum silicate) from Wyoming and *tierra de Lebrija* from southern Spain. Various chemical products are also employed when specific problems arise, as potassium ferrocyanide ("blue fining") when the wine contains an excess of iron or copper; this last has the odd and disturbing property of turning the wine bright blue, but this is only temporary and almost all German wines and many from California are so treated.

FINO — (Fee-no) — Type of Sherry: the palest, lightest, most delicate, generally the dryest and, in the opinion of many experts, the best. It has a wholly distinctive and memorable bouquet, the result of the *flor* (*see*) under which it passes a good deal of its life in cask, and of course partially derives its quality from its blending and ageing in *soleras* (*see*). Served chilled, it is one of the best of apéritifs.

FITOU — (Fee-too) — One of the best red wines of the French Midi, produced (largely from Grenache and Carignan grapes) just south of Narbonne, in the district known as Hautes-Corbières. Full-bodied if somewhat common, it is inexpensive, often a good value. According to law it has to be aged two years in wood before bottling; it carries an *Appellation Contrôlée*.

FIXIN — (*Feex*-an) — Northernmost village of the Côte de Nuits, in Burgundy; its red wines, too little known, are often among the best values in the way of fine Burgundy that can be found, comparable, in character and quality, to the better Gevrey-Chambertins. There are five outstanding vineyards; the Clos des Hervelets, the Clos de la Perrière (*see*), the Clos du Chapitre, Les Arvelets, and the recently created Clos Napoléon.

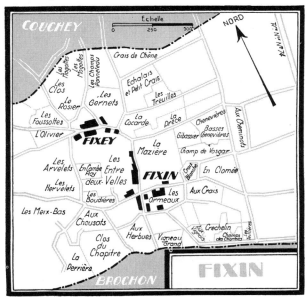

NOTE: The *Clos Napoléon,* a fairly recent appellation, was formerly called "Aux Cheusots" and is so shown on this old map. It was granted this new name in honor of a remarkable and famous Memorial, "Napoléon's Awakening," the work of the sculptor, Rude (who was also responsible for the Arc de Triomphe, in Paris), in the pine woods directly above and behind the vineyard.

FLAGEY — (*Flaj*-jay) — Village north of Vosne-Romanée on the Côte de Nuits, in Burgundy. Its official name is Flagey-Échézeaux; both Échézeaux and Grands Échézeaux (*see*) lie within its communal limits, but both wines are invariably sold under their vineyard name, usually without any mention of Flagey. The lesser wines of Flagey are entitled to the appellation Vosne-Romanée.

For Map, see ÉCHÉZEAUX.

FLAT — Applied to Champagne or other sparkling wines, one that has lost its sparkle; to still wines, one too low in acid, unattractive, neutral, dull.

FLÉTRI — (Flay-tree) — Swiss wine term. A *vin flétri*, in the Canton of Valais, is a sweet wine made from grapes either picked late, when almost raisins, or left on straw mats in the sun, like a *vin de paille*, or *passito* (*see*). There is no *pourriture noble* in this dry, mountain country and a *vin flétri* is very different from a Rheingau Auslese or a French Sauternes. The grape, although here known as the Malvoisie, seems actually to be the Ruländer, or Pinot Gris.

FLEURIE — (Flur-ree) — Little town in the very heart of the Beaujolais Country; its attractive, fruity, fragrant red wine, one of the Beaujolais' most typical and best.

FLEUR-PETRUS, Château La — (Fluhr-Pet-ruhss) — Small but good Pomerol vineyard, producing about 2,000 cases a year.

FLINTY — Used to describe a dry, clean, hard, almost austere white wine (such as Chablis) which has a special bouquet recalling the smell of flint struck with steel. The French call it *pierre-à-fusil*, which is the same thing.

FLIP — Mixed drink made either with spirits or with wine, or both, having as its ingredients shaved ice, sugar, bitters, plus an egg and wine, or wine and brandy.

FLOR — (Floor) — The Spanish word for "flower"; in connection with wine, it means an unusual and special yeast, native to the Sherry Country. This is also called "film yeast" in California, where it has recently been introduced (as in South Africa and Australia), and is known to technicians as *mycoderma vini*. Naturally in Spain and through inoculation in other lands, it forms a white film or "flower" on the surface of certain wines soon after fermentation, the casks being only three-quarters full and the wine exposed to the air. It lives and multiplies there, gradually forming a layer as much as half an inch thick, looking not unlike cottage cheese, and it radically affects the bouquet and flavor of the wine. Oddly enough it only forms and prospers on the lighter wines and these, thanks to its working, become Finos and Amontillados (*see*); those with little or no *flor* turn into Olorosos. (*See* Sherry.) The *flor* is also native to the Manzanilla and Montilla districts (*see*) and to Château Chalon (*see*) in France. It has greatly improved the quality of the better dry California Sherries of late and done equally good service in South Africa and Australia.

FLOWER — Like all fruit-bearers, grape vines have their flowers; these are a good deal less spectacular than those of the cherry, the peach, the orange and the apple, to mention but four, but they are no less necessary antecedents to the fruit, and either a succession of rainy days or a period of cold weather during the blossoming season can and often does bring about a disaster, especially in the form of *coulure* (*see*). The critical flowering period is called *floraison* in French, and to the French wine-grower it is often a week or fortnight of sleepless worry.

FLOWERY — Special term of high praise applied to the bouquet of certain wines, more particularly white wines, which to the nose recall the scent of flowers. The finer Moselles have this quality to a pronounced degree, but a few other wines, particularly those produced on stony soil from the Riesling grape and in cool districts, share this special excellence.

FLUTE — Name given, in French, to a special form of bottle, like that used in Alsace and on the Rhine, but generally of clear glass. Many *rosé* wines are now shipped in flutes. Also a rather attractive, traditional glass, often used in France for Champagne, in the shape of a slender V, sometimes with a stem.

FOGARINA — (Fo-gar-*een*-na) — Red wine of rather low alcohol and high acid, produced in the province of Reggio Emilia, northern Italy.

FOLLE BLANCHE — (Fall Blawnch) — Variety of white grape, widely grown in France under a confusing multiplicity of names, and to some small extent in northern California. Fairly productive, it gives a pale, light wine, not distinguished but fresh, clean and very high in acid; unfortunately, its tightly packed bunches are fatally vulnerable to mildew and mold, and in many districts it is being replaced for this reason. It is unquestionably the best of all grapes for brandy, but, unhappily, in the calcareous soil of the Cognac Country, it has not done well since the phylloxera, when grafted on American root stocks, and is gradually being supplanted by the less good if hardier Ugni Blanc (*see*); in Armagnac, too, where it is known as the Piquepoule or Picpoul, various other mediocre grapes are being planted, including even one of the Baco hybrids. Round Nantes, at the mouth of the Loire, it is called the Gros Plant and gives a tart but otherwise rather neutral white carafe wine, which has lost out in popular favor to the Muscadet. As Picpoul, it is extensively planted in the French Midi, but yields nothing of any real consequence. In California, its wine is occasionally but rarely bottled under the varietal name, more often used in California "Chablis," to which its higher acid brings a welcome and refreshing tartness, and, for this same reason, in many of the better California Champagnes.

FOREZ — (For-ez) — Red and *rosé* wines of no great interest, made from the Gamay grape in Auvergne, near the headwaters of the Loire.

FORST — (Forst) — Justly celebrated little town, of well under a thousand inhabitants and some 500 acres of vines, which produces what are certainly among the best and perhaps, all things considered, the best

white wines of the German Pfalz, or Palatinate. The vinyards are 70% planted to the Riesling grape and the wines, while quite full-bodied, have extraordinary elegance and bouquet, said to be due to outcroppings of a special sort of black basalt in the vineyards. All of the leading Palatinate producers have vineyard holdings in Forst, and the better, named vineyard sites, or *Lagen*, of which there must be in all nearly a hundred, are: Kirchenstück, Jesuitengarten, Ungeheuer, Ziegler, Kranich, Pechstein, Elster, Mühlweg, etc., etc.

FORTIFIED — Old British euphemism for wines that have been "spiked," or liberally laced with brandy or other spirits somewhere between the vineyard and the bottle, as Port, Sherry, Muscatel (in almost all cases), Madeira, Marsala, etc. Our Federal authorities have seen fit to forbid the use of the term on labels and in advertising, no doubt for good and sufficient reason, since it is an obvious truism that people should not be induced to drink certain wines on account of their higher alcoholic content; the simultaneous suppression of the term "unfortified" is a good deal harder to explain. American vintners seem to have accepted these restrictions without complaint, and they now apply to precisely the same wines, the perhaps more genteel terms "apéritif wines" and "dessert wines." The French are as bad as we are — *see* Banyuls.

FOUDRE — (Food'r) — French term for a large cask of indefinite size.

FOURCHAUME — (Foor-showm) — One of the largest and best first-growth vineyards of Chablis.

FOURTET, Clos — (Foor-tay) — Picturesque and famous vineyard of St. Emilion, lying practically in the town itself. Its wine (some 5,000 cases a year) is exceptionally sturdy, long-lived, slow to mature.

FOXINESS — Foxes have had to do with vineyards since Biblical days, generally as consumers, but many of the early settlers in America called the wild, native grape the "Fox grape" and in many Eastern states it is still so called (to "fox," of course, means to intoxicate as well as to trick); its pronounced special aroma is unmistakable, whether as a grape or its juice or the wine made from it, and all native varieties share the characteristic, especially the red or black ones, as Concord Isabella, Ives, etc., but to a definite degree the whites as well — Delaware, Catawba, Elvira. The French, who began to import American grape cuttings at the time of the phylloxera (*see*), and who were the first hybridizers of American and European varieties, called this special aroma or taste "*queue de renard*" or "fox's tail," for no well established reason, and it is still so called. Wines having this wholly American tang are usually found either delicious or undrinkable by those who taste them for the first time, but this is wholly a matter of personal preference, and no field for an expert.

FRAGRANT — Of a wine, one that has an especially pronounced and agreeable bouquet, or aroma.

FRAIS — (Fray) — French word for "fresh." It also means cool, however, and *servir très frais* on a French wine label means "serve well chilled."

FRANCE — France has been called the world's vineyard. Nearly a third of all the wine of the world is produced in France, and French wine is the universal standard by which wine is judged. Yet, out of an annual production of some seven billion bottles a year, less than 10% has any real claim to superior quality, and at least four-fifths is nameless — called *vin rouge, vin blanc, vin rosé, vin ordinaire*, and is simply a staple, like potatoes or milk. Frenchmen drink it with their meals not because the water in France is bad (it isn't — they have less typhoid than we do) but because this sort of wine is cheap, goes well with food, is cheering and pleasant and (drunk thus) hardly more intoxicating than beer; they like it better than coffee or tea or sweet carbonated drinks, and, in the opinion of many doctors (including, of course, Pasteur, who said so) it is a healthier mealtime beverage for adults than milk. They like it, so much that France imports far more wine than she exports, consumes more than her own three million acres* of vineyard can provide.

All of France, including the Riviera, is farther north than Buffalo or Boston, and nearly a third of France lies beyond the northern limit of commercial viticulture, its climate too sunless and cold, or too rainy and undependable for wine-growing. The line has been clearly drawn by a dozen centuries of trial and error; it begins on the Atlantic Coast near Nantes, in southern Brittany, parallels the Loire some fifty miles to the north, sweeps up to include the Champagne Country east of Paris,

---

* It is interesting to note that there were nearly five million acres under vines a century ago. The average annual production, however, has hardly declined at all; this is of course due to increased regional specialization and more efficient agricultural methods, as with wheat, corn, etc., in the U.S.

and runs on east to the border of Luxembourg on the Moselle. South of this line, except in a few mountainous districts, it is safe to say that there is hardly a French farm on which the vine has not been planted at one time or another and where wine has not been made. About two-thirds of the 90 *départements* of France have commercial vineyards, and there are at least 5 or 6 which regularly produce more table wine than California.

Yet France is a country of small vineyards rather than large: there are few, if indeed any, that comprise as much as 500 acres under one ownership. Modern cooperatives, increasingly well run, in some districts permit operations on a larger scale, but most French wine is produced by artisans and peasant farmers, who are quite content to be so called and who take a true artisan's pride in what they make. Most of them now send their young wines, for analysis and constructive criticism, to their local, well-staffed government stations, and willingly accept the technical advice they receive.

For in no other country is wine produced according to such strict rules as in France, and the rules have been established, it is important to remember, by the growers themselves, and simply ratified by the State. The whole precise, immensely complicated classification of districts and townships and *crus* comes from the producers, and no better proof could exist of their deep interest in the quality of what they make. Clear lines of demarcation have been drawn, with the accord of all concerned, between the great wines and the good wines and the *vins ordinaires*.

Most of the very best French wines have been given a special legal designation, *"Appellation Contrôlée"* (*see*), and these words appear on the label except in the case of Champagne (where they are considered unnecessary). They mean that the French Government guarantees the origin of such wines, and their right to the name they bear; violations are considered fraud, and are severely punished. These words are also, to some degree, an assurance of quality, since they may only appear on wines made from specified, superior varieties of grape, in delimited districts, and according to rules which forbid over-production, improper blending, and everything else which is not in keeping with local tradition and good cellar practice.

In all, there are nearly three hundred of these *Appellations Contrôlées* (all listed in this encyclopedia), plus scores of variant and combined forms (as "Beaujolais," "Beaujolais Supérieur," "Beaujolais Villages," for example): some, such as "Bordeaux," cover a whole district producing millions of gallons annually, while others, such as "Château-Grillet" or "Montrachet," are restricted to the output of a tiny vineyard or a single farm. Sixteen *vins mousseux*, or sparkling wines, plus Champagne, have been accorded this rank, and about the same number of fortified wines, most of these from the Mediterranean Coast and the eastern Pyrenees; the rest are table wines, and they include all of the best and practically all of the well-known wines of France — the Burgundies, the Bordeaux, the wines of the Rhône Valley and of the Loire, and a scattering of others from the Jura, Provence, etc., etc.

136

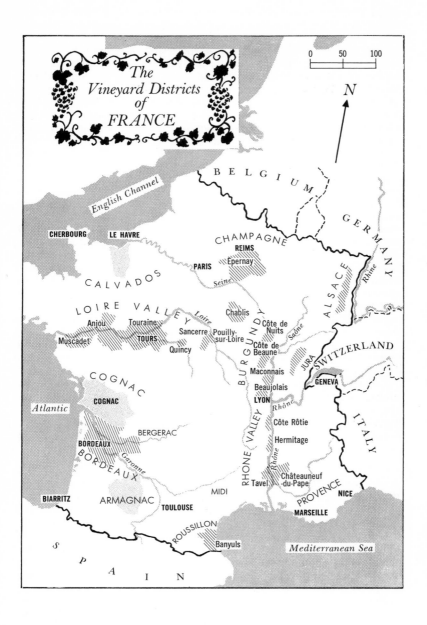

The Vineyard Districts of FRANCE

0   50   100

N

BELGIUM

GERMANY

English Channel

CHERBOURG   LE HAVRE

CHAMPAGNE

REIMS

PARIS   Épernay

Seine

CALVADOS

LOIRE VALLEY

Loire

Chablis

Anjou   Touraine

Côte de
Nuits

BURGUNDY

ALSACE

Rhine

Muscadet   TOURS   Sancerre Pouilly-
sur-Loire

Quincy

Côte de
Beaune

Saône

SWITZERLAND

JURA

Maconnais

Beaujolais

COGNAC

LYON

GENEVA

Atlantic

COGNAC

Rhône

ITALY

Côte Rôtie

BERGERAC

RHONE VALLEY

Hermitage

BORDEAUX

BORDEAUX

Garonne

Châteauneuf
-du-Pape

Rhône

BIARRITZ

ARMAGNAC

MIDI

Tavel

TOULOUSE

PROVENCE

NICE

MARSEILLE

ROUSSILLON

S   P   A   I   N

Banyuls

Mediterranean Sea

Below these in rank, forming what might be called a sort of "second team," or "junior varsity," come some fifty others, officially known as V.D.Q.S., *"Vins Délimités de Qualité Supérieure."* These (all listed in their alphabetical place in this volume) are also controlled, though less stringently, by the French Government, and carry the V.D.Q.S. seal, which looks rather like a postage stamp, on their label. Few of these are exported, although some are of good, even excellent quality, and may well become increasingly interesting in this period of rising wine prices; the best known, perhaps, are the Côtes de Provence, Rosé de Bearn, Corbières, Minervois, Cahors. The better Algerian wines were also classified in this way, though what will be the future of wine-growing in that troubled country it is, of course, too early to say.

In a still lower, less official category come the *vins de pays*, the little "country" wines, usually consumed locally, often interesting and charming, often sold under the name of their village or *département* in the local inns and taverns.

The lowest grade of all, of course, is *vin ordinaire:* this, in France, must be marked with its alcoholic content, (as 12°, or 12%), but carries no designation of origin; it may be and usually is blended, but may not be watered; it is strictly covered by the French equivalents of our pure food regulations, but by not much else in the way of controls. When sold under a brand name, as Vin du Postillon, Vin des Rochers, Pampre d'Or, Prefontaine, etc., it is called a *Vin de Marque*, the word *marque* meaning "brand" in French.

Not far from one-third of the space in this whole encyclopedia is devoted to French wine, properly and appropriately, for if most French wine is admittedly common or mediocre, the best is simply incomparable: there are no red wines and no sparkling wines on earth as good as the best French, and few white wines better — none, surely, except perhaps the rarest and finest estate-bottlings of the Moselle and Rhine.

Of all of the fruits of nature and man's skill that have, over the centuries, given delight and comfort to people of good taste in all countries, the wines of France are easily first, and by a wide margin. Our whole literature is full of their praise, and a roster of the enthusiastic lovers of French wine in the past five hundred years would read like a Who's Who of the Western World.

FRANCONIA — Our name for one of the important if secondary German wine districts, the upper valley of the Main, east and west of Würzburg, called Franken in German. Traditionally, all of the Franconian wines are shipped in flagons called Bocksbeutel (*see*); they are made from the Sylvaner (here, oddly enough, often the best); the Riesling; and from crosses of the two, the Müller-Thurgau and so-called Mainriesling. The name of the grape variety usually appears on the label, plus of course the name of the town and the producing vineyard. The leading vineyard towns are Würzburg, Escherndorf, Iphofen, Randersacker, Rödelsee, etc. Sometimes wines from all of these are shipped as Steinwein (*see*), but this is certainly improper and possibly, we all may hope, illegal. The leading producers include properties of the

German State, several charitable endowments, and a half dozen noble families; a few grower-cooperatives, or Winzergenossenschaften, are making good progress.

For Map, *see* GERMANY.

FRANKEN RIESLING — (Frank-N Reece-ling) — Name sometimes given to the Sylvaner grape (*see*), although it is emphatically not a true Riesling. As a result of this misnomer, wine made from the Sylvaner may legally be labeled Riesling in the United States. *See* Franconia.

FRAPPÉ — (Frap-*pay*) — Used of a wine, means very, very cold. A liqueur served *frappé* is poured over shaved ice.

FRASCATI — (Frahs-*scot*-tee) — An attractive little town in the Alban Hills, southeast of Rome. Its white wine is one of the best of the Castelli Romani (*see*), a great favorite in Rome, and more often bottled for export than most of the others. Dry, golden, full-bodied, generally about 12% alcohol, it is an agreeable table wine, though hardly a distinguished one.

FRECCIAROSSA — (*Fraitch*-cha-*roas*-sa) — Brand name (it means "red arrow") of a popular and good table wine from Lombardy, Italy. *See* Casteggio.

FREISA — (*Fray*-sa) — Superior Italian red wine grape, and the wine made from it, notably in that hilly part of Piedmont lying between Turin and Casale Monferrato; the Freisa of Chieri is particularly famous. Two quite different wines, however, are made: the one more likely to appeal to the average wine drinker is a dry red wine, fruity, often a little tart and rough when young, but quite ready to drink and possessing a special and remarkable bouquet by the age of three; even more popular in Italy, but rarely exported, is the Freisa that is both *abboccato* (*see*) and *frizzante* (*see*) — bottled early, slightly sweet and slightly sparkling, it is not a wine that will please all palates, despite its bouquet and fruit. A few plantings of the Freisa grape exist in California, but it is not possible, as yet, to give any sort of judgment as to what they are capable of producing. The name is often misspelled Fresia in California, and pronounced "*free*-si-a," like the flower.

FRIEDRICH WILHELM GYMNASIUM — (*Free*-drich *Vil*-helm Gim-*nah*-zee-um) — Famous secondary school in Trier, on the Moselle, in Germany. Thanks to gifts and bequests over the years, its endowment now includes extensive vineyards in many of the best townships of the Moselle and Saar, including Trittenheim, Graach, Zeltingen, Mehring, Oberemmel and Ockfen. The wines, generally estate-bottled, carry the Gymnasium's label and name.

FRESH — Despite the fact that many people have been led to believe that an old wine is necessarily better than a younger one, this is by no means the case — the majority of wines are at their best when young. Most white wines, all *rosés*, and a good many lighter reds have an engaging freshness in their youth which they tend to lose after their third or fourth birthday, if not sooner. A fresh wine is one which has not lost this early charm.

FRIBOURG — (Free-boorg) — Canton in western Switzerland, producing a few red and white wines of no great value. *See* Faverges.

FRIULARO — (Free-oo-*lahr*-ro) — Red wine grape and the wine made from it in the province of Padua, near Venice, Italy. Undistinguished, but popular in Venice as ordinary table wine.

FRIZZANTE — (Freez-*zahn*-tay) — Italian wine term meaning slightly sparkling, or *pétillant*, or crackling, usually as the result of a minor secondary fermentation in bottle. Many Italian wines, even red wines, are deliberately bottled before their original fermentation is entirely complete, while they still contain some sugar from the grape. Eventually such wines become a little "prickly" or "fizzy" and even foam up briefly when poured; most of them remain a little sweet. *Frizzante* wines of this sort are much prized in northern Italy, though to an educated palate they appear merely oddities, and hardly wine at all. They are rarely if ever shipped to the United States since, according to existing regulations, they would be classified as "sparkling wine" and pay the sparkling wine tax.

FRONSAC (*Frawn*-sack) — Small red-wine district in the Bordeaux Country, which deserves to be better known than it is. The little town of Fronsac, from which it takes its name, is on the Dordogne just west (downstream) from St. Emilion and Libourne, and the vineyards are on steep hills overlooking the verdant and singularly beautiful river valley. The best are in a zone entitled to the name Côtes-Canon-Fronsac, but Côtes-de-Fronsac is an appellation of only slightly lower class. Both produce extremely robust, deep-colored wines, what the French call "fleshy," and soft, somewhat recalling the Pomerols but with less breed. They have long been popular in northern Europe and are good values. Total production amounts to some 400,000 gallons a year.

FRONTIGNAN — (*Frawn*-teen-yawn) — Town on the Mediterranean Coast of France, near Sète, and its sweet, golden Muscat wine; this is the best French wine of its type, a *vin de liqueur* of considerable distinction and real class. These qualities, rare in Muscatels, it owes to the fact that it is made from a special, much superior variety of grape, the Muscat-doré-de-Frontignan. Usually fortified, it must legally contain a minimum of 15% alcohol by volume. The same grape has been transplanted to other countries, and is grown to some small extent in California's Napa Valley, where it gives a much dryer and quite different wine.

FRONTON — (*Frawn*-tawn) — Red and *rosé* wines of purely local interest, produced round the town of this name, some twenty miles north of Toulouse, in southern France. They are sometimes sold as Côtes de Fronton, and are entitled to the V.D.Q.S. seal (*see*).

140

FROST — Of the many anxieties that beset the vintner and cause him sleepless nights, none is as bad as frost. And since most of the best table wines and sparkling wines of the world are produced fairly close to the northern limit of the vine, frost is a worry shared by most good wine growers. Even California is not exempt, and the Napa Valley vineyards were grievously damaged in April, 1964. Theoretically, the danger exists in French and German vineyards for about six weeks — roughly from the first of April until the days of the Ice Saints (*see*) are past, on May 15th — yet the vines of Pouilly-Fumé, on the Loire, were severely hurt on May 28, 1961, by the latest damaging frost in the history of the French Weather Bureau. Similarly, vines are supposed to be safely dormant during the winter, but St. Emilion and certain other sections of Bordeaux suffered a veritable disaster in February, 1956, when sub-zero weather arrived after a period of warm days, and many thousands of vines were killed outright.

Even three or four degrees of frost, during the critical weeks, can mean the partial or total loss of the year's crop, and in some cases the damage is more lasting, and the following year's vintage, as well, is impaired. A few progressive growers in some of the northern districts, notably Chablis, the Moselle, the Loire, now set out smudge-pots or little fuel-oil stoves in their vineyards, and these, while not 100% effective and yet very expensive, have proven enormously helpful — in Chablis, in 1960, *only* the growers with stoves in their vineyards produced wine worth harvesting.

FRUITY — Said of a wine which has the definite and attractive aroma and flavor of fresh fruit, though not necessarily and certainly not to a pronounced degree, that of grapes (*see* Grapey). Almost all fine young wines are fruity, few poor ones are, and almost no old wines, however good. California Zinfandels have this charming quality when young; so have all better *vins rosés*, which is why they are so popular in America; so has Beaujolais; so have the Alsatian wines, almost all German wines, and to a lesser degree the best Rieslings, Sylvaners and Pinots of California.

FUDER — (Foo-der) — Oak cask in which Moselle wines are stored, in Germany. Its standard capacity is 1,000 liters (264 U.S. gallons), or 108 cases of finished wine.

FUISSÉ — (*Fwee*-say) — One of the four townships in which Pouilly-Fuissé (*see*) is made, west of Macon, in southern Burgundy.

FULL — Wine-taster's term, related to Body (*see*), and no less often wrongly defined and wrongly used. Its proper place is in the tasting-room, not the laboratory, and it has only the vaguest connection with alcoholic content or specific gravity. Heavy cream weighs less than light cream and both weigh much less per quart than skimmed milk; a wine expert, if induced to taste them, would describe heavy cream as full-bodied, and skimmed milk as thin and light. Alcohol weighs less than water, and a quart of 20% dry Sherry less than a quart of 9% Moselle; gallon for gallon, the Moselle may well weigh more than the sturdiest Châteauneuf-du-Pape, with 14% of alcohol by volume. Yet no competent taster would ever describe the Moselle as the "fuller" wine of the two. On the other hand, he would almost certainly say that the Châteauneuf-du-Pape was "fuller" than the dry Sherry.

FUNCHAL — (Foon-shal) — Port and principal town of the island of Madeira, in which most Madeira wines are stored and aged and whence they are shipped.

FURMINT — (Foor-mint) — Celebrated white wine grape of Hungary, the principal and informing variety of Tokay. Many other Hungarian wines, however, are made from the Furmint, and these are generally so labeled, so Somloi Furmint, Badacsonyi Furmint, Pécsi Furmint, etc., the first word in each case indicating their district or town of origin.

GAILLAC — (Guy-yack) — White wine produced round the town of this name, on the River Tarn, some thirty miles northeast of Toulouse, in southern France. Sometimes dry but usually a little on the sweet side, it is widely drunk in France as a *vin de comptoir,* or "bar wine," by the glass. Pale, low in acid, often heavily sulphured, rather bland and without much distinction or class, made from a grape known locally as the Mauzac, it is rather ordinary at best. Much of it is converted into a fairy sweet, inexpensive *Mousseux,* or sparkling wine. Total production of Gaillac, Premières Côtes de Gaillac and Gaillac Mousseux is in the neighborhood of 2½ million gallons a year.

GAILLAT, Domaine de — (Guy-yat) — Small vineyard in the Graves district near Langon, yielding a pleasant, pale, dry white wine.

GALLISATION — The adding of water and sugar to grape juice before fermentation in order to reduce the acidity and increase the alcoholic content of the finished wine — and of course, incidentally, to increase its volume. This practice is outlawed in many wine countries, including most of France, Portugal and California. It is permitted within strict limits in the eastern United States, in Germany and in certain other of the colder wine producing countries of the world.

GALLON — The old American saying, "a pint's a pound the world around," leaves out of consideration the British Empire, where a pint is 20 ounces, and there are 20 shillings but only 16 ounces, in a pound. The British, or Imperial Gallon is of 160 ounces, or 1⅕ times the U.S. Gallon of 128 ounces (our ounces being slightly larger). The same proportions hold, of course, for pints and quarts. There are 3.785 liters to the U.S. gallon, and a liter is 1.057 U.S. quart.

GAMAY — (Gam-may) — Excellent red wine grape, grown to the virtual exclusion of all other varieties in the Beaujolais Country of France; here, on prevailingly clay and granitic soil, it yields a better wine than even the Pinot Noir. Farther north in Burgundy, where the soil is predominantly calcareous (as on the Côte d'Or) the Gamay does much less well, is ranked as an inferior grape, and cannot legally be planted in the better vineyards, where the Pinot Noir's supremacy remains unchallenged. Wines (*see* Passe-tout-Grains) are occasionally made from the two varieties crushed and fermented together.

The true Gamay, or Gamay du Beaujolais, is planted to a small extent in California, especially in Santa Clara, San Benito, Contra Costa and Napa counties, and yields a remarkable wine, often superior to any Pinot Noir from the same vineyard. Usually this is sold as Gamay du Beaujolais, and it should by no means be confused with the ordinary California wine called simply "Gamay," made from a much inferior and far more productive grape which is possibly not a Gamay at all.

GARD — (Gahr) — French *département* extending from the lower Rhône Valley well into what is called the Midi, third among French *départements* (after the Hérault and the Aude) in total wine production, its output of table wine being substantially more than that of the United States. Most of this, of course, is nothing but *vin ordinaire (see)*. Some of the best *vins rosés* of France, however, are produced in the Gard, along or near the Rhône, notably Tavel, which is internationally famous, and Lirac *(see)*.

GARDA — (*Gar*-da) — The largest and one of the most beautiful of the Italian Lakes, noted for its mild climate (lemons are grown even commercially in certain sheltered corners); its northern tip extends into what was, prior to 1918, Austrian territory, and the low hills round its wide southern end are largely covered with vineyards. These produce quite a collection of different wines, red, white and *rosé*, all of which, oddly enough, seem to have a certain family resemblance: they are all low in alcohol, rarely reaching 12%, and therefore easy to drink; they are delightfully fresh and fruity when young, and improve practically not at all with age; they are, in other words, wonderfully good carafe wines, among the best such wines in the world. Most of them are drunk up, gratefully and promptly, by the North Italians themselves and their Swiss neighbors, with the enthusiastic help of a good many thirsty tourists. Of recent years a certain number of well-equipped wineries have begun to bottle these wines for export, in many cases with considerable success; if the wines are bottled and sold early enough, or well before their third birthday, they stand travel well and can be as delightful, or nearly so, as they are at home. Unquestionably, the best of the reds is Bardolino *(see)* — and incidentally the village called Garda adjoins Bardolino, and its wines are entitled to this name; the best white is probably Lugana *(see)*, made at the southern end of the lake from the Trebbiano grape *(see);* the *rosés* are called Chiarello or Chiaretto *(see)*. However, there are many others, from Moniga, Padenghe, Polpenazze, and other villages, and they are worth investigating.

GARGANEGA — (Gar-*gahn*-eh-ga) — White Italian grape, largely responsible for the excellent white wine of Soave *(see)*.

GARONNE — (Gar-*rawn*) — Largest river of southwestern France, rising in the Spanish Pyrenees near Luchon, flowing by way of Toulouse to Bordeaux, just north of which it is joined by the Dordogne, to form the wide estuary of the Gironde *(see)*. It is navigable as far up as Bordeaux, and the vineyards of Sauternes, Graves, Cadillac, Ste.-Croix-du-Mont, etc., overlook its valley.

GATTINARA — (Got-tee-*nah*-ra) — Splendid Italian red wine, easily one of Italy's half dozen best, made from the same distinguished Nebbiolo grape as Barolo *(see)* and Barbaresco, but in an altogether different part of Piedmont, round the village of this name, northeast of Turin and southwest of Lake Maggiore. Full-bodied, slow-maturing, long-lived, with a fine bouquet and great depth of flavor, it is a great wine by any standards and can readily hold its own against the best reds of the French Rhône Valley. Unfortunately, its production is small, and it is hard to come by outside Italy.

GAU ALGESHEIM, GAU BICKELHEIM, GAU ODERNHEIM — Three little wine towns in Rheinhessen, Germany, all three important in the production of rather ordinary Liebfraumilch.

GAUDICHOTS, Les — (Lay Go-dee-show) — Famous old Burgundian vineyard in the heart of the best portion of Vosne-Romanée: some twenty years ago practically its entire acreage was officially reclassified and made part of La Tâche *(see)*, thereby tripling the extent and production of that even more prestigious parcel of vines. Although Les Gaudichots has therefore practically ceased to exist as a separate entity, its name still often appears in current articles on Burgundy and books on wine. Formerly it bounded La Tâche on the north and west, and was separated from Romanée-Conti only by another narrow, celebrated vineyard plot, La Grande Rue.

GAVI — (*Gah*-vee) — Dry white wine, one of Italy's best, made from the Cortese grape *(see)* round the little town of Gavi in Piedmont. It is generally shipped in tall, slender, green bottles like the wines of Alsace; pale, fresh, light, it should be consumed when still young.

GAZIN, Château — (*Gaz*-zan) — One of the fine large vineyards of Pomerol, ranked as a 1st Growth. Some 8,000 cases a year of full-bodied, good quality red wine. There is also a Château Gazin of considerably less importance at Léognan, in the Graves district.

GEISENHEIM — (Guy-zen-heim) — Important wine-producing town in the Rheingau, with nearly 500 acres of vineyard, almost entirely Rieslings. In great years (as 1893, 1945 and 1959) the Geisenheimers are of top quality, with great fruit and breed, and the better *Lagen* include Rothenberg, Mäuerchen, Katzenloch, Lickerstein, Klauserweg, Mönchpfad, Altbaum, Morschberg, etc. The town is even more famous for its school of viticulture, the Lehr-und-Forschungsanstalt für Wein-, Obst- und Gartenbau, one of the great wine schools of the world.

GÉNÉREUX — (Shay-nay-ruh) — French wine-tasters' term, applied to a big, hearty, warming wine, as Châteauneuf-du-Pape or Chambertin.

GENERIC — Wine name or designation of class unrelated to the wine's origin, as *vin rosé,* sparkling wine, apéritif wine, *pelure d'oignon,* etc. The question of what are known in the United States as "semi-generic" names is much more thorny. Most of these are old, traditional, geographical place names that now have been declared, at least to some extent, in the public domain. They are names that were in wide general use before today's strict rules regarding appellations went into effect, and it is an unquestioned fact that wines from New York State and Ohio and California (not to mention Australia, South Africa and Chile) were being sold as "Sherry," "Port," "Rhine wine," "Burgundy" and the like, well over a hundred years ago. In most cases no fraud was intended, and the wine was simply given the existing wine name that seemed best to fit it. All this is of course now highly displeasing to the Spaniards who regard the name "Sherry," to the Portuguese who regard the name "Port," and to the French, who consider "Burgundy," "Sauternes," "Chablis" and "Champagne," as part of their national patrimony. There is much to be said on both sides, but a majority of countries have come to accept the French-Spanish-Portuguese-German point of view, and have renounced the use of these place names by international accord. The U.S. Government has so far refused, and has considered that it would work a grave injustice on California vintners, for example, to deprive them of appellations which have come to have substantial trade value and which their grandfathers were allowed freely to use. A not too unfair compromise seems to have been worked out; the number of such "semi-generic" appellations is limited and will not be extended (an American wine may be labeled Sauterne but not Barsac, Chablis but not Pouilly, Rhine Wine but not Rüdesheimer); such wines, furthermore, must show their origin, (as California, New York State, or American) in type substantially as large and readable as the foreign appellations they have assumed.

GENEVA — (French, *Genève*) — Largest city of French-speaking Switzerland; there are a few small vineyards in the canton of this name, yielding a white wine on the order of a light Neuchâtel.

GENTIL — (Shawn-tee) — Alsatian wine-grower's term, meaning a superior grape variety, or *plant noble.* Wines so labeled are generally blends of several such varieties, often grown and picked together. *See* Edelzwicker.

GERMANY — Despite the wholly merited and centuries-old fame of its Rhine wines and Moselles, Germany can hardly be called either a major wine-producing or a true wine-drinking country. As in America, wine is treated there more as an occasional and festive beverage than as a daily necessary. Germany's vineyard acreage is less than one-fifth that of Portugal, and the average German drinks less than one-tenth as much wine as the sober average Swiss.

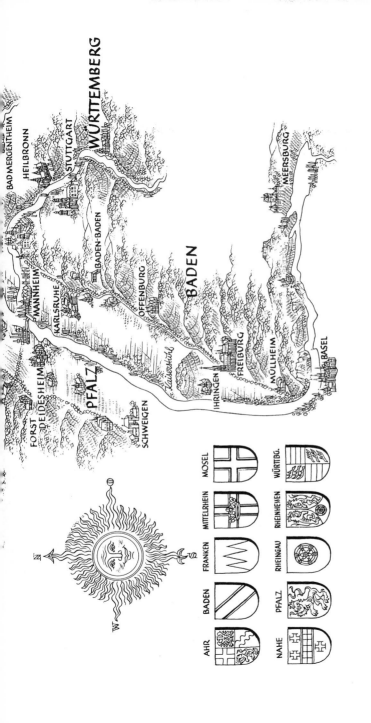

WÜRTTEMBERG

BAD MERGENTHEIM
HEILBRONN
STUTTGART

MEERSBURG

MANNHEIM
KARLSRUHE
BADEN-BADEN
OFFENBURG

BADEN

FREIBURG
MÜLLHEIM
BASEL

FORST
DEIDESHEIM

PFALZ

SCHWEIGEN

Kaiserstuhl

IHRINGEN

W

N

S

AHR   BADEN   FRANKEN   MITTELRHEIN   MOSEL

NAHE   PFALZ   RHEINGAU   RHEINHESSEN   WÜRTTBG.

Nevertheless, Germany manages to export more white wine to the United States than even France, and at least three times as much as any other country; all experts agree that the finest German wines are of astonishing quality, quite possibly the best in the world, and even the sound less expensive ones have their special character and charm: they are light, refreshing, easy to drink, fruity, fragrant, unfailingly agreeable, and their popularity is not at all surprising. Of course, it must be kept in mind that in Germany, as in all other wine-producing lands, there is more, much more, mediocre and common wine than good, but Germany's average of quality is perhaps the highest of all.

All German wines of any real consequence are white; with rare exceptions they are low in alcohol (8% to 11% is the normal range), fairly high in acid (which makes them fresh and occasionally tart), usually with a trace or more of pleasing sweetness as well. Those ranked as the best and, in any case, the most expensive, are very sweet indeed. They are shipped for the most part in tall, slender bottles (brown for Rhine wines, green for Moselles) but some in stumpy, flat-sided flagons called *Bocksbeutel.*

The very southernmost German vineyards are as far north as Newfoundland, and many of them at the latitude of Labrador. Grapes can only be grown commercially on south-facing hillsides along river valleys (the Rhine and most of its tributaries) and only a few, hardy varieties of grape can be successfully cultivated; fortunately, almost all of these yield superior white wine. In order of quality they are; the Riesling, the Gewürztraminer (rare), the Sylvaner, the Ruländer (rare), the Müller-Thurgau plus a few others. These names often appear on German wine labels; if they do not, it may be assumed that Moselle and Rheingau wines are made from the Riesling, but Rheinhessen, Pfalz and Franconian wines from the more productive Sylvaner.

The vineyards of the Rhine Valley proper are divided into two minor and three major districts. That called the Rheingau is acknowledged the best, faces due south over the Rhine between Wiesbaden and Rüdesheim, and includes such celebrated wine towns as Hochheim, Johannisberg, Rüdesheim, etc. Rheinhessen is on the west or left bank of the Rhine south of the Rheingau and of Mainz: it produces, in addition to the world's supply of Liebfraumilch, such perennial favorites as Niersteiner, Oppenheimer, etc. Rheinpfalz, or the Palatinate, still further south, is also on the left, west bank of the Rhine and borders Alsace; its best vineyard towns are Forst, Deidesheim, Wachenheim, Ruppertsberg. The two minor districts are, first, the so-called Mittel-Rhein, in the Rhine gorge between Rüdesheim and Coblenz; then, on the Black Forest foothills, facing Alsace, the scattered and not-too-important vineyards of Baden.

The Rhine's most important tributary, in terms of water but even far more in terms of wine, is the Moselle. Here wines are produced fully equal to the Rhine's best in quality, although very different, and the Moselle, in turn, has its tributaries, the Saar and Ruwer, hardly less distinguished.

Two other river valleys, tributaries of the Rhine, also deserve to be

148

considered independent districts, not only on account of their considerable acreage of vineyard but because of the distinctive character of the wines they grow. The river Nahe (*see*) joins the Rhine at Bingen, directly opposite Rüdesheim; it produces many wines of high quality some fifteen miles upstream, to the southwest, round Bad Kreuznach and Schloss Böckelheim. Lastly the Main, before joining the Rhine near Mainz, cuts its winding way through the vine-covered hills of Franconia, or Franken (*see*); the most famous of its *Frankenweine* come from Würzburg and a half dozen other villages nearby, and are shipped in a special sort of stumpy flagon called *Bocksbeutel* (*see*).

German wines have a nomenclature entirely their own. As far as better wines are concerned, the pattern is not too far from that prevailing in France: the wines carry the name of the town from which they come (as Johannisberg, Rüdesheim, Piesport, Nierstein) plus, if they are of superior grade, the name of the specific vineyard that produced them, Johannisberger Klaus, Rüdesheimer Berg Bronnen, Piesporter Lay, Niersteiner Rehbach. There are a few exceptions — wines of extraordinary fame that bear only a vineyard name: Schloss Vollrads, (from the town of Winkel), Steinberger (from the town of Hattenheim), Scharzhofberger (from the town of Wiltingen), etc.

German wines, furthermore, carry on their labels a good deal of rather esoteric information very important to the buyer. Many German wines, especially in poor years, have to have sugar added to them during fermentation; there is nothing wrong or illegal about this, but superior wines are not so made. Unsugared wines bear such designations as the following, whereas "sugared" wines may not: *Natur, Rein, Naturwein* (meaning genuine and natural); *Wachstum, Creszenz, Gewächs* (meaning "Growth," and followed by the vineyard owner's name); *Original-Abfüllung, Kellerabfüllung, Schlossabzug* (meaning estate-bottled); *Cabinet* or *Kabinett* (meaning superior reserve); *Spätlese* (meaning late picking); *Auslese* (special selection), etc.

As might be expected, wines labeled *Spätlese* and *Auslese* are sweeter and more expensive, those labeled *Beerenauslese* and *Trockenbeerenauslese* even more so. Estate-bottling is a complete guarantee of authenticity; an indication, but not a guarantee, of superior quality. The vintage year is extremely important, perhaps even more so than in France: oddly enough, the less expensive, sugared wines are often better in poor years than in good, although this is of course not true of wines that are natural and unsugared.

Wine names that are *non*-geographic, as Liebfraumilch and Moselblümchen, are legally meaningless, and any wine, from the best to the poorest, may be so labeled. The same thing is true of a number of names that appear geographical but are not, as Zeller Schwarze Katz and Kröver Nacktarsch, and most wines so labeled are of dubious quality, to say the least.

The cost of producing wine in Germany's basically unfavorable northern climate is higher than in any other country in the world: it follows that very cheap German wines are almost always poor (far less good than comparably priced wines from California); the medium priced ones, if carefully selected, are both good wines and good values; the best are extraordinary, always expensive and sometimes fabulously so — rare bottles often bring as much as twenty dollars and sometimes twice that. To the true wine lover they are worth it, for they are incomparable and unique.

GEROPIGA — (Jair-o-pea-ga) — Fresh grape juice reduced by evaporation to a concentrate or syrup, used to give added sweetness and body to the less fine grades of Port.

GERS — (Jair) — *Département* of southwestern France producing, in the way of wine, little of interest except what is distilled into Armagnac. There are a few agreeable white and *rosé vins de pays* but none really worth exporting.

GEVREY-CHAMBERTIN — (Jev-ray *Shawm*-bair-tan) — World-famous wine-producing town, eight miles south of Dijon, in Burgundy; red wines exclusively. Like many other villages of the Côte d'Or (*see*) Gevrey has added to its name the appellation of its most famous vineyard, Chambertin (*see*). The finest wines of this extraordinary *commune* do not, however, carry the town name: what is sold as Gevrey-Chambertin is a sound, secondary, almost a regional Burgundy, from the less good vineyards; of a distinctly higher grade are those that are labeled Gevrey-Chambertin 1er Cru, or Gevrey-Chambertin plus the name of a vineyard, as Gevrey-Chambertin, La Combe aux Moines. Still better, and very great wines by any standards, are the Grands Crus: Latricières-Chambertin, Mazoyères-Chambertin, Charmes-Chambertin, Mazis-Chambertin, Griotte-Chambertin, Ruchottes-Chambertin and Chapelle-Chambertin. It is perhaps worth noting that Gevrey-Chambertin, Clos St. Jacques, although not officially a Grand Cru, is rated at least on a par with these. Of course, what is called simply Chambertin, or Chambertin-Clos de Bèze, is the best of all.

GEWÄCHS — (Ge-*vex*) — Means "growth" in German, and on a wine label or wine list is usually followed by the producer's name. It is usually but not invariably an indication of estate-bottling. See Wachstum, Original-Abfüllung.

GEWÜRZTRAMINER — (Ge-*vertz*-tram-me-ner or Ge-voors-tram-me-*nair*) — Excellent and unusual wine grape, though actually merely a selection of the Traminer (*see*). It is widely planted in Alsace, and to some extent in Germany and in the Tyrol; a shy bearer, it is pinkish in color and gives a highly special, extremely spicy, rather soft white wine, which some wine-drinkers find almost too heavily perfumed; it nevertheless brings a higher price than even the Riesling in its native Alsace. There are some important new plantings in California, and the wine runs true to type, although its spiciness (the name, in German, means "spicy Traminer") is on the whole less pronounced.

GHEMME — (*Ghem*-may) — Very good red wine, made from the Nebbiolo grape (*see*) round the village of this name, south of Lake Maggiore in Italian Piedmont.

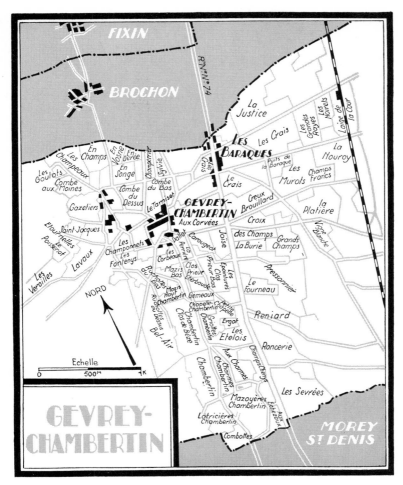

GIEN — (Shan) — Little town on the Loire, upstream from Orléans and directly south of Paris; it is more famous for its pottery and faïence than for its wine, but some agreeable, light *vins de pays*, red, white and *rosé*, are produced on the nearby hillsides called the Côtes de Gien, and carry, when bottled, the V.D.Q.S. seal.

GIGONDAS — (*She*-gone-das) — Red and *rosé* wine of the Rhône Valley, produced round the village of this name at the foot of the Mont-Ventoux (*see*) northeast of Avignon. The red on the whole is better than the *rosé* — full-bodied, rather high in alcohol (often 13%), yet surprisingly soft, not unlike a lesser Châteauneuf-du-Pape; the *rosé* is pleasant enough when young but has a marked tendency to maderise

151

(*see*). The proper name of both is Côtes-du-Rhone-Gigondas, and both are sometimes sold in a stubby, long-necked, square-shouldered bottle, recalling the bottles sometimes used for Port.

GIRÓ — (Gee-*ro*) — Red dessert wine, on the order of a light Port, produced near Cagliari, on the Italian island of Sardinia.

GIRONDE — (She-rawnd) — The *département* of Bordeaux (*see*), as such the most important of France in the field of fine wine, since practically the entire Bordeaux wine district lies within its borders.

ALSO, the river, or tidal estuary, formed by the Garonne and Dordogne rivers which meet north of the city, and thanks to which Bordeaux is a seaport. Most of the better Médoc vineyards overlook the Gironde, as do those of Bourg and Blaye.

GISCOURS, Château — (Shees-coor) — 3rd Classed Growth of Labarde-Margaux, Haut-Médoc, producing some 20,000 cases a year of fine, rather delicate Claret. Somewhat neglected for a period of years, Giscours is rapidly regaining its former high place.

GIVRY — (*She*-vree) — One of the good, less known wine-producing *communes* of the Côte Chalonnaise (*see*). More red wine than white.

GLACIER — (*Glah*-see-A) — An odd, rather agreeable but almost bitter white wine produced in a high Alpine valley near Sierre, in the Swiss Canton of Valais.

GLASSES — Proper wine glasses play an extremely important role in the tasting and appreciation of fine wine. From a taster's standpoint, the best glasses are stemmed, made of thin, clear crystal, more-or-less tulip-shaped, very large; 6 ounces should be considered minimum capacity, 8 or 10 ounces greatly to be preferred; of course they are never filled much over one-third full. This is not a matter of mere fancy nor of fashion, for fine wines taste better in such glasses: the wine's color can be seen and judged, and the tulip-shaped glass serves as a sort of chimney, concentrating the wine's bouquet and channeling it upwards to the nose.

A number of wine districts — the Moselle, Champagne, Vouvray, Anjou, and even Manzanilla, for example — have their special regional

Typical and conventional wine glasses

glass, and still other shapes are traditional in other regions. All such glasses can and often do provide amusement and interest to the hobbyist and specialist, though whether any of them is as good or better than the basic, simple tulip-shape, is doubtful, to say the least.

GLÖGG — (Glug) — A traditional Swedish cold-weather drink, a special type of hot spiced wine. It is usually made with aquavit or brandy just before serving in cups or glasses containing a few almonds and raisins.

GOÛT — (Goo) — In French, simply means taste. In connection with wine, when applied to Champagne, it is a rather undependable indication of sweetness, as *Goût Américain* (fairly sweet) or *Goût Anglais* (quite dry); of other wines it is used, plus an adjective or descriptive phrase, of wines that have a special or unusual flavor, either agreeable or (more frequently) disagreeable. Thus *Faux Goût* means an "off" (literally "false") taste; *Goût de Bois* means Woody; *Goût de Bouchon* means Corky; *Goût de Cuit* that a wine tastes sugared or "cooked"; *Goût de Ferment* or *de Lie* means Yeasty; *Goût de Terroir* (*see*), the rather special taste of wines grown on heavy soil. On the other side of the ledger, there are *Goût de Noisette*, which means Nutty; *Goût de Violette, de Framboise*, etc., applied to wines which, to some enthusiastic tasters, appear to have the scent of violets, the flavor of raspberries, and so on.

GOVERNO — (Go-*vair*-no) — Name given, in Italian (sometimes *Governo alla Toscana*), to a special method of vinification widely used in the Chianti Country, and which often plays a major part in giving Chianti its special flavor and character. Some 10% of the grapes harvested — usually of the rarer varieties, Cannaiolo, Mammolo, Colorino, etc. — are not pressed, but put aside to raisin on straw trays. They are then crushed and set to ferment in late November and, once fermentation is under way, they are added to the already fermented Chianti wine; the vats are then sealed, with a bubble-valve to allow CO_2 to escape, and so left until spring. A slow, slight, secondary fermentation of course takes place, and the final result is a wine that is faintly, almost imperceptibly sparkling, with an attractive freshness and a bit of "prickle" on the tongue.

GOXWILLER — (*Gawks*-vee-lehr) — Village in northern Alsace, producing good wines and some altogether remarkable fruit brandies — Kirsch, Mirabelle, Framboise, etc. Alfred Hess is the leading distiller.

GRAACH — (Gr-ach) — Famous little town of the Mittel-Mosel, it is on the right bank of the river between Bernkastel and Wehlen, and its 240 acres of vineyard form part of the same incomparable steep hillside as those of its even more illustrious neighbors. The Graacher wines are admirable — sprightly and fragrant, perhaps a bit lighter and less overpowering than the Wehleners, but of equal distinction. The best plots include Himmelreich, Domprobst, Stablay, Abstberg, Goldwingert, Münzlay, plus the Josephshof, a single property adjoining Wehlen and belonging to the Kesselstatt family: the wines from this are sold as Josephshöfer, not Graacher.

153

GRACE DE DIEU, Château La — (*Grahss* duh *D'yuh*) — Good small vineyard of the St. Emilion district, deserving to be better known.

GRAGNANO — (Gran-*yah*-no) — A soft, light, red wine, fruity and pleasing, not absolutely dry, produced not far from Pompeii, southeast of Naples, in Italy.

GRAND PONTET, Château — (Grawn *Pawn*-tay) — One of the many 1st Growth St. Emilion vineyards; about 2,500 cases a year.

GRAND-PUY-DUCASSE, Château — (Grawn-*Pwee*-Dew-*cass*) — 5th Classed Growth of Pauillac, Médoc. Some 3,500 cases a year of very sound, pleasant red wine.

GRAND-PUY-LACOSTE, Château — (Grawn-*Pwee*-La-*cost*) — 5th Classed Growth of Pauillac, Médoc. One of the most dependable and consistent of the 5th Growths, 7,000 cases a year.

GRAND ORDINAIRE — (Grawnd Or-dee-nair) — A superior grade of *vin ordinaire* entitled to some sort of geographical appellation protected by French law; the wine, while better than average, need not be in any way exceptional. Examples are "Bourgogne Grand Ordinaire" (the cheapest legal Burgundy), Corbières in the French Midi, etc.

GRAND ROUSSILLON — (Grawn *Roo*-see-yawn) — One of a number of appellations (Côtes d'Agly, Côtes de Haut-Roussillon, Maury, Rive-saltes — but Grand Roussillon is the broadest term of all) given to the sweet, fortified wines produced in the *département* of Pyrénées Orien-tales, near Perpignan. These must contain a minimum of 15% alcohol by volume, but generally run higher; they are made principally from the Grenache, Muscat and Malvoisie grapes and somewhat resemble a rather light Port. Under all of these appellations, there are about 8 mil-lion gallons sold a year. *See* also Banyuls, Rancio.

GRAND VIN — (Grawn Van) — Literally, in French, "great wine," al-though the term has not legally been defined and is rather freely used. Not a reliable indication of superior quality.

GRANDE RESERVE — (Grawnd Ray-zairv) — Only in Alsace does this term have any official or legal standing; elsewhere it is used by many producers, bottlers and shippers, supposedly to designate a superior grade of what they sell, but how much it means depends on the pro-ducer's commercial policy, or his whim. However, Alsatian wines may not carry this designation unless they are made from grapes of one of the "noble" varieties that have attained a fixed minimum of ripeness; the result is a rough equivalent of a German *Spätlese*.

GRANDE RUE, La — (Grawnd Roo) — Extraordinary little vineyard forming what is almost a three-acre corridor (or street, as its name would indicate) from east to west through the very kernel of the best vineyard-land of Vosne-Romanée. Its wine is altogether astonishing; produced by old vines and in extremely small quantity, it is unsurpassed, perhaps even unequalled, by Romanée-Conti, Richebourg and La Tâche. It would be impossible to give higher praise.

GRANDS ÉCHÉZEAUX — (Grawnz *Zesh*-shay-zo) — Great Burgundian vineyard and its splendid red wine. Lying just above the Clos de Vougeot, bounded by Musigny on the north, its 22 acres could hardly be more superbly placed, and what they yield is a classic Burgundy, far fuller, richer and more distinguished than what is called simply Échézeaux (*see*), and certainly one of the 20 best red wines of the Côte d'Or. For Map, *see* ÉCHÉZEAUX.

GRAPE — In all probability (leaving out of consideration the original apple of the Garden of Eden) the first fruit cultivated by man. Grape seeds, resembling those of our present-day wine grapes, have been found in Egyptian tombs and in the remains of lake dwellings dating from the Age of Bronze. Noah is said to have planted the first vineyard, but the arts of vine-dressing and wine-making are far older than the beginnings of recorded history.

All grapes belong to the genus *Vitis*; there are some forty species, all native to the temperate zone. The most important of these, by an immense margin, is *Vitis Vinifera*, the *"wine-bearer,"* which, apart from some native American sorts and recent hybrids, is the only species grown commercially to any real extent in the world. There are of course an almost limitless number of varieties of *Vinifera* — botanists and ampelographers have recognized and classified several thousand, and at least several hundred have recognizable characteristics and are cultivated. These are propagated by planting cuttings, or by grafting, for they do not remain true to type if grown from seed. Grapes grown from seed are called seedlings and it is usually impossible to determine their precise ancestry, except in experimental vineyards, under controlled conditions.

Different varieties have their special uses and advantages: some give particularly good table grapes, others produce the best raisins; some are extremely productive and give common wine, others, shy-bearers, yield the best; some will do well under almost any conditions, others require a specific sort of soil and climate. There are apparently only about twenty, and certainly less than forty, capable of yielding outstanding wine.

GRAPEY — A wine should taste like wine, not like fresh grapes. But certain grapes always seem to impart their special flavor to wines made from them — the Muscat is one such grape and the Concord another (to a lesser degree, so are many of the other Eastern varieties). Lacking in subtlety, too pronounced in flavor, such wines are never highly regarded by an expert. One soon tires of them.

GRAVES — (Grahv) — The word in French simply means gravel, or gravelly soil, and is used in a combined form in connection with several districts of the Bordeaux Country (*see* below). Alone, it means a specific, defined area on the left bank of the Garonne River, largely west and south of the city of Bordeaux. Total production in a normal year is in the neighborhood of 2 million U.S. gallons, of which about one-fourth is red wine, the rest white. The appellation Graves Supérieures is restricted to *white* wines of at least average quality or better, despite the

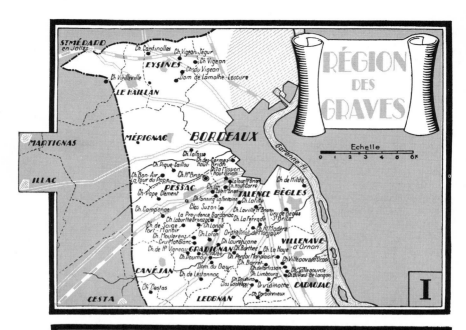

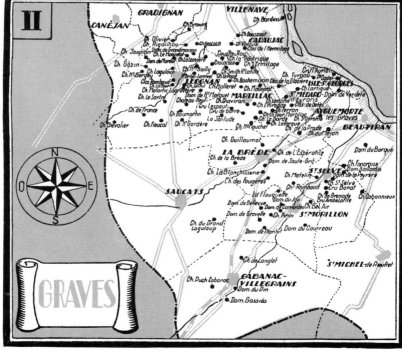

fact that the finest red Graves consistently bring higher prices than the finest white; most of these reds, however, do not carry the name Graves but are sold under the label of a specific chateau. Ignored, with the single and notable exception of Château Haut-Brion, by those responsible for the Classification of 1855, the Graves chateaux have now been officially classified, at least in part, though how competently is perhaps open to question: the official classification will be found in the Appendix.

The best red Graves come from the *communes* of Pessac, Léognan, Martillac, and include Châteaux Haut-Brion, La Mission-Haut-Brion, Pape-Clément, Haut-Bailly, Chevalier, Malartic-Lagravière, Smith-Haut-Lafitte, etc. In character they are closer to the Médocs than to the St. Emilions, Pomerols, etc.; they age well, but with rare exceptions have a little less distinction, are a little less "classic" than their Médoc compeers, and someone has quite properly said that they are like soft, as compared with glossy, prints from the same negative, less distinct and less clean.

The finest white Graves come principally from the *commune* of Léognan, plus a few exceptions from Talence, Pessac, Martillac, Cadaujac, etc.; these are dry wines, although with a trace of *moelleux*, or softness — they are often better, being lighter and dryer, in years rated fair or poor than in years rated great, although this is by no means true of the reds. The best are: Domaine de Chevalier, Laville-Haut-Brion, Pontac-Montplaisir, Carbonnieux, Olivier, Bouscaut, etc., but many others of less fame produce good wines too, including several near Langon, at the extreme southern end of the Graves district. The rare white wine of Château Haut-Brion, at least in the author's opinion, is often too high in alcohol and often surpassed in quality by several of those listed above.

Officially the Graves district includes three townships (Cérons, Podensac and Illats) which adjoin Barsac and produce rather sweet, golden wines, of excellent class but far nearer Sauternes than what one expects from a wine labeled Graves. These wines are usually marketed as Cérons (*see*).

The white Graves are made largely from Sauvignon Blanc and Semillon grapes, and where the former predominates the quality is better. Red Graves comes from the Cabernets (*see*), plus some Merlot, Malbec, Petit Verdot, etc.

Further information may be found under the names of the *communes* and chateaux listed above, the grape varieties, etc.

GRAVES-ST. EMILION — (Grahv Sant A-*me*-lee-on) — Not an appellation according to French law, but a term widely and properly used in connection with a large part of the official St. Emilion district, to designate the gravelly upland plain, behind and north of the steep hills that look down on the Dordogne Valley. The wines of Graves-St. Emilion are at least as good: they include Châteaux Cheval Blanc, Figeac, Grand Corbin, etc.

GRAVES DE VAYRES — (Grahv duh Vair) — Secondary Bordeaux district, geographically part of Entre-Deux-Mers, on the left bank of the

Dordogne River, not far from St. Emilion. The dry white wines are passable, the reds less good. Some of the whites are now shipped in tall, green Alsace bottles, but they resemble neither Alsatian wines nor the truly fine wines of Graves proper.

GRAY RIESLING — *See* GREY.

GREAT — Great wines, like great novels and great men, do not come along every day, and the term should be reserved for those extraordinary ones that are head and shoulders above their fellows — certainly less than 1% of the world's production. A great wine should have no flaws, perfect balance, real distinction. Such bottles are never cheap, but they are worth whatever one pays for them.

GRECO DI GERACE — (*Gray*-co dee Jer-*ratch*-chay) — Famous white wine, not always up to advance billing as far as quality is concerned, produced at the extreme Calabrian "toe" of Italy, not far from the Straits of Messina.

GREECE — In no ancient civilization, so far as we can judge, did wine play such a major role as in that of Greece; in the Greek art and Greek literature that have come down to us, the vine, the grape and wine are omnipresent, perhaps even more so than in the Bible. Clearly, they were a familiar part of everyday common living; they were even the basis of a religious cult, that of Dionysus.

It is hard therefore not to come to the conclusion that the Greek wines of antiquity were better than what Greece produces today. Greece is an important wine-growing country, with twice the production of Germany; she exports a vast tonnage of excellent raisins (mostly what are known to the trade as "currants" — actually the sun-dried berries of the Black Corinth grape) and a good deal of sweet fortified wine, principally in barrel to Switzerland, Malta and Northern Europe. Some of these — the Muscat of Samos, and those made from the Mavrodaphne grape in various districts — are of fairly good quality; there are no outstanding wines at all.

Many, perhaps even most, Greek table wines are flavored with resin (*retsina*) which renders them wholly unacceptable to a wine-drinker not yet accustomed to this highly special, turpentine taste. Tourists can nevertheless find some quite passable wines these days, the best (this is not intended as praise) from the Peloponnesus (Achaia, Arcadia, Messenia) and from the islands — Cephalonia, Leukas, Corfu, Zante, Santorin, etc. As might be expected in this southern latitude and warm climate, most of them are rather high in alcohol, lacking in finesse and breed.

GREEN — Wine taster's term meaning raw, harsh, with a disagreeable acidity; lacking softness, roundness and maturity. This is not necessarily a matter of age, though young wines are more often green than older ones.

GREEN HUNGARIAN — Productive white grape of uncertain origin, grown to a limited extent in some of the better California districts. It gives a pale, fairly agreeable but rather neutral wine, which is more often used in blends than sold under this name.

GRÊLE — (Grell) — French word for hail: like frost, one of the major natural hazards of a wine-grower's life. Hail storms are by no means infrequent in most vineyard countries, and if heavy they can be nothing short of catastrophic; an entire crop is often destroyed in a matter of minutes and the vines so gravely damaged that even the following year's vintage is affected. Even light hail can take its toll during the ripening season, for the bruised berries give a wine (red wine, especially) that has what the French call a *goût de grêle*, or "hail taste," readily recognizable by an expert, as a faint overtone of rot in an otherwise sound wine.

GRENACHE — (Gren-*nahsh*) — Very productive but good quality wine grape, widely planted in southern France, in the Rioja district of northern Spain (where it is known as the Garnacha) and in California. It is one of the varieties used in Châteauneuf-du-Pape, and, differently vinified, gives the sweet, heavy dessert wine of Banyuls, as well as a superior grade of California Port. On the whole its best wines, however, are *vins rosés*, notably Tavel (*see*), and others in the Rhône Valley, and the excellent Grenache Rosé of California. A white variety of Grenache also exists, but is less widely grown.

GREY RIESLING — Misnamed and mediocre white grape (since it is not a Riesling and has none of the characteristics of one) rather widely planted in California, especially in the Livermore Valley. It has also been called the Grey Duchess (another misnomer, since it is unrelated to the Duchess grape of New York State); its true name is the Chauché Gris and in its native France — it comes from the district round Poitiers — it is so poorly thought of that it is not used in any French wine having an appellation. In California it gives a mild, soft wine, not disagreeable but without much character; it is hard to explain its present vogue, for it is much less good than the much less popular Sylvaner.

GRIGNOLINO — (Grin-yo-*lean*-no) — Excellent Italian red wine grape; also the wine made from it, notably in a hilly district known as the Monferrato (*see*), north of the town of Asti, in Italian Piedmont. When genuine and of good quality, Grignolino is an interesting and unusual wine, with a quite special character and flavor; in color it tends to be what the French call *tuilé*, with a hint of orange in its crimson; it gives an impression of lightness, although it is often high in alcohol (13-14%); its bouquet is almost unmistakable.

There are some plantings of Grignolino in California, in Sonoma and especially in Cucamonga near Los Angeles, where it is often made into a very passable *vin rosé*.

GRILLET — *See* Château Grillet.

GRINZING — (*Grint*-zing) — Suburb of Vienna, producing some of the most pleasant of the pale, dry, fruity white wines of Austria. The principal grape varieties are the Veltliner, the Riesling and Sylvaner, and although some superior Grinzingers are bottled and even exported, far more is consumed as open wine in the little local taverns when under a year old.

GRIOTTE-CHAMBERTIN — (Gree-*aut Shawm*-bair-tan) — One of the Grand Cru vineyards adjoining Chambertin (*see*), 14 acres in all; a great red Burgundy wine.

GROPELLO — (Gro-*pel*-lo) — Italian wine grape, used in making some of the lesser red wines of Garda (*see*) as well as in Chiaretto (*see*).

GROSLOT — (Gro-lo) — Productive red wine grape of fair quality widely grown in the Loire Valley of France, where it yields most of the rather common, less expensive, semi-sweet *Rosé d'Anjou* (when made from the far superior Cabernet, this is invariably labeled *"Cabernet Rosé d'Anjou"*). Farther east, in Touraine, the Groslot gives some rather more than passable carafe wines.

GROS PLANT — (Gro Plawn) — Name given to the Folle Blanche grape and the fresh, light, tart white wine made from it round Nantes, near the mouth of the Loire. It is entitled to the V.D.Q.S. seal.

GRUAUD LAROSE, Château — (*Grew*-oh La-*rose*) — 2nd Classed Growth of St. Julien, Haut-Médoc. One of the very largest Bordeaux vineyards, with an average annual production of nearly 20,000 cases. Gruaud Larose for many years (in fact until just before World War II) consisted of two separate domains, Gruaud-Larose-Sarget and Gruaud-Larose-Faure. Reunited at last, their wine is one of the most popular and best of the St. Juliens.

GRUMELLO — (Groom-*mel*-lo) — One of the best red wines of Valtellina (*see*) made from the Nebbiolo grape near Sondrio, Italy, not far from the Swiss Border.

GUEBWILLER — (*Gub*-vill-*lehr*) — One of the better wine-producing towns of southern Alsace.

GUIRAUD, Château — (*Ghee*-roe) — 1st Classed Growth of Sauternes: about 8,000 cases a year. Major vineyard, not far from Yquem, and producing a very comparable although somewhat less distinguished wine.

GUMPOLDSKIRCHEN — (*Goom*-poldz-keerk-en) — Certainly the best known wine-producing town of Austria and, with those of the Wachau district (Loiben, Krems, Dürnstein), doubtless the best. Its light, pale, fragrant, fruity white wines have been Viennese favorites for generations, and the vineyards are less than an hour's drive from Vienna, to the south. Most Gumpoldskirchners sold in bottle carry a grape name, as Veltliner, Riesling, Gewürztraminer, Rotgipfler, etc.; some of them a designation such as Spätlese or Auslese, and occasionally a specific vineyard name as well. Few of them could be described as extraordinary, but almost all of them are fresh and clean and attractive, and good values.

GUNTERSBLUM — (*Goon*-terz-bloom) — Major vineyard town in Rhein-hessen, with nearly a thousand acres under vines. Most of these are Sylvaners and the resulting wine, of good but not distinguished quality, is for the most part sold as Liebfraumilch.

GUTEDEL — (Goot-*eh*-del) — German name for the productive but mediocre Chasselas (or Fendant or Sweetwater) grape — an exaggeration if there ever was one, since the white wine it yields is a long way from *edel* (noble) and by no means always *gut* (good). It is the principal variety of Markgräflerland (*see*) in southern Baden, where it gives a quite passable, mild *Schoppenwein*, and is also sometimes called by this name in California, where it is responsible for something equally innocuous and uninteresting.

HAARDT — (Hart) — Chain of hills in the German Rheinpfalz or Palatinate, their lower slopes covered with the vineyards that have made this district's fame. Overlooking the wide, fertile Rhine Valley, like a northern prolongation of the French Vosges, these extend from Schweigen, on the French frontier, northward for nearly fifty miles. All of the finer Pfalz wines come from the central portion, the so-called Mittel-Haardt, which embraces such famous wine towns as Deidesheim, Forst, Ruppertsberg, Wachenheim, Dürkheim, etc.; the Ober-Haardt, to the south, and the Unter-Haardt, the northern section, are districts of large production and relatively common quality.

HAIL — *See* Grêle.

HALBSTÜCK — (*Hahlb*-shtick) — Six hundred-liter cask in which Rhein-gau wines are generally stored and aged. The word *Stück* means "piece," and 1,200-liter casks of this sort do exist, but are rare. When Rhine wines are sold in barrel, a Halbstück is assumed to yield 800 bottles or 68 cases of finished wine.

HALLCREST — One of the better small California vineyards at Felton, in Santa Cruz County. The owner is a San Francisco attorney, Mr. Chaffee Hall; only two wines are produced and sold under the Hall-crest label, a Cabernet Sauvignon and a Johannisberg Riesling.

HALLGARTEN — (*Hahl*-gar-ten) — Important wine-producing town of the Rheingau, with some 370 acres of vines. Like Rauenthal and Kied-rich, this is an upland village, set well back from the river, and its best vineyards (Schönhell, Mehrhölzchen, Deutelsberg, Hendelberg, Jungfer) are only about a stone's throw from the famous Steinberg. The Hall-gartener wines, especially in good years, are fine and forthright and sturdy — often the fullest-bodied of the whole Rheingau. Leading producers are Prince Löwenstein, Engelmann, and three co-operative cellars.

HANZELL VINEYARDS — Small vineyard estate near Sonoma, in California, created and owned by the late James D. Zellerbach, former

United States Ambassador to Italy. Mr. Zellerbach was a Burgundy enthusiast and Hanzell is planted in Pinot Noir and Chardonnay. The first vintage was that of 1956, and the wine is generally of high quality; the quantity very limited.

HARASZTHY, Agoston — (Har-*ras*-the) — Often and quite fairly called the "father of California viticulture," a talented, impetuous Hungarian count who changed his title into the more democratic one of "Colonel" when he immigrated to this country. He founded a town in Wisconsin and gave it his name (later changed to Sauk City), moved west, was the first sheriff of San Diego, a member of the State Assembly, planted vineyards. The most famous and successful of these was Buena Vista, in Sonoma County. In 1861 he was officially sent to Europe by California's Governor Downey and returned with cuttings of some 300 different grape varieties, thereby laying the foundation of California's wine industry: the report of this trip, which he wrote on his return to Buena Vista, is a minor masterpiece, readable, informative, overflowing with the Colonel's unquenchable optimism and enthusiasm. Soon thereafter he was struck by a series of misfortunes — financial difficulties, problems brought on by the Civil War, phylloxera in his vineyard, a disastrous fire — and went to Nicaragua in an effort to recoup his fortunes through the distillation of rum. There, in 1869, he disappeared; it is believed he fell into a river infested with alligators.

HARD — Wine taster's term, meaning austere, without much charm or suppleness. Many excellent wines, however, are hard in their youth and come round splendidly with time. Hardness, unless accompanied by greenness, is not necessarily a fault, but can be an indication of probable long life. The wines of Chablis and those of the Saar are almost always a little hard; so, in their youth, are the great Clarets of Pauillac.

HARO — (Ha-ro) — Brown little city on the upper Ebro River, in Spain, principal center of the Rioja wine trade. During the final decades of the last century, when the phylloxera had devastated Bordeaux but had not yet crossed the Pyrenees into Spain, over a hundred French families settled in Haro: many of the town's *bodegas*, much of its viticultural tradition and its wine-making methods date from those briefly prosperous days.

HARSH — In a wine, harshness is hardness carried to an extreme, generally accompanied by astringency. Occasionally, particularly in red wines and providing other qualities are present, this will disappear in time.

HARSLEVELU — (Hahrsh-lava-loo) — White Hungarian wine grape, used with the Furmint and some Muscat, in Tokay.

HATTENHEIM — (*Hot*-ten-heim) — Charming old village in the Rheingau, producing outstanding wines. Its 475 acres of vineyard include a portion of the Marcobrunn (*see*) and the celebrated Steinberg in its entirety, although the wines from these two plots are not sold as Hatten-

162

heimer, but under the vineyard name alone. The other distinguished sites, or *Lagen,* giving somewhat lighter wines, almost equally remarkable but more delicate, include: Nussbrunnen, Wisselbrunnen, Mannberg, Engelmannsberg, Willborn, Hassel, Weiher, etc., and the leading producers are Graf von Schönborn, Freiherr Langwerth von Simmern, Schloss Reinhartshausen, and the Staatsweingut, or German State Domain.

HAUT — (Oh) — French word meaning "high," or, in certain combinations, "upper" or "higher" or "top." There is rarely any implication of superior quality, only of altitude: Bas-Armagnac, for example, produces far better brandy than Haut-Armagnac. The confusion arises only because, usually, in France and the world over, hillsides and upland districts yield better wines than lowlands and plains. However this is a broad generalization, not a rule.

HAUT-BAGES-LIBERAL, Château — (Oh-Baj-Leeb-bear-ahl) — 5th Classed Growth of Pauillac, Haut-Médoc. Some 4,000 cases a year.

HAUT-BAILLY, Château — (Oh-Bye-ye) — One of the best vineyards of Léognan, in the Graves district. Produces red wine exclusively, some 3,000 cases a year of very long-lived, generally rather slow-maturing Claret. Ranked deservedly as a 1st Growth of Graves.

HAUT-BATAILLEY, Château — (Oh-*Bat*-tie-yay) — 5th Classed Growth of Pauillac, Haut-Médoc. The 1855 Classification gives only Batailley, but the vineyard has since been divided and both portions are legally entitled to the name and 5th Growth rank. About 4,000 cases a year of sound, good Claret.

HAUT-BENAUGE — (Oh-Ben-ohj) — Agreeable dry white wine, produced on the right bank of the Garonne, near the southern boundary of the Entre-Deux-Mers district. One of the better inexpensive white Bordeaux.

HAUT-BRION, Château — (Oh-*Bree*-awn) — One of the very greatest red wines of Bordeaux, the only wine of Graves officially ranked in 1855, when it was quite properly placed on a par with Lafite, Latour and Margaux as one of the four 1st Classed Growths of Bordeaux. The vineyard, just outside of the city limits of Bordeaux on the west, is now almost surrounded by suburban villas; its extent is approximately 100 acres and its production averages 10,000 cases a year. In good vintages its wine is altogether remarkable and even in poor years far from bad. There is a little white Haut-Brion produced, which carries the chateau label, printed in silver rather than gold: unquestionably a great wine, this is often almost too full-bodied and too high in alcohol and there are other more distinguished white Graves. *See* illustration on following page.

HAUT COMTAT — (Oh *Cawn*-ta) — Red or *rosé* wine produced in six *communes* north of Avignon, in the Rhône Valley. A V.D.Q.S. wine (*see*) of better than average quality, rarely exported.

PRODUCE OF FRANCE

1947

SPÉCIMEN

CHATEAU HAUT·BRION

PREMIER GRAND CRU CLASSÉ

APPELLATION GRAVES CONTRÔLÉE

MIS EN BOUTEILLES AU CHATEAU

S.A. DU CHÂTEAU HAUT·BRION, PROPRIÉTAIRE A PESSAC (GIRONDE)

DÉPOSÉ

HAUT-GARDÈRE, Château — (Oh-Gar-*dair*) — One of the good vineyards of Léognan in the Graves district, producing mostly red wines.

HAUT-MÉDOC — (Oh-May-dawk) — The higher, southern and far better part of the Médoc, extending from the northern edge of the city of Bordeaux to beyond St. Estèphe; all of the Classed Growths and all of the wines which have made the Médoc's fame are in this area. Most of the wines commonly sold as Médoc come from the sandy, lowland country farther north, and are much less good. Haut-Médoc is therefore a superior appellation, strictly defined by French law, and a wine so labeled will almost always be better than something called simply "Médoc."

HAUT MONTRAVEL — *See* Montravel.

HAUT NOUCHET, Château — (Oh New-shay) — Good, lesser vineyard in the Graves district. Sound red wines.

HAUT-PEYRAGUEY, Clos — (Oh-Pay-rah-gay) — 1st Classed Growth of Sauternes. One of the very best vineyards of Bommes (*see*); excellent, golden, sweet wine, typical Sauternes. Small production.

HAUT-RHIN — (Oh-ran) — French *département* comprising the southern and, as far as wine is concerned, the superior half of Alsace. The vineyards are planted along the lower foothills of the forest-covered Vosges Mountains and are strikingly beautiful, with dozens of picturesque little villages, some of them with their medieval walls intact.

HAUT-SAUTERNES — (Oh Saw-tairn) — Wine name widely used but without any legal standing. Commercially, a very sweet Sauternes of superior quality which may (but need not) come from a higher and better vineyard. When a shipper offers Sauternes and Haut-Sauternes, the latter may be presumed to be sweeter, better and more expensive,

164

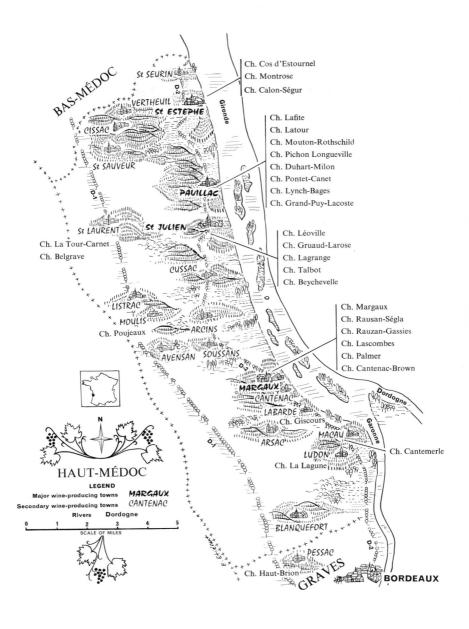

Ch. Cos d'Estournel
Ch. Montrose
Ch. Calon-Ségur

Ch. Lafite
Ch. Latour
Ch. Mouton-Rothschild
Ch. Pichon Longueville
Ch. Duhart-Milon
Ch. Pontet-Canet
Ch. Lynch-Bages
Ch. Grand-Puy-Lacoste

Ch. Léoville
Ch. Gruaud-Larose
Ch. Lagrange
Ch. Talbot
Ch. Beychevelle

Ch. Margaux
Ch. Rausan-Ségla
Ch. Rauzan-Gassies
Ch. Lascombes
Ch. Palmer
Ch. Cantenac-Brown

BAS-MÉDOC

St SEURIN
VERTHEUIL
St ESTEPHE
CISSAC

Gironde

St SAUVEUR

PAUILLAC

St LAURENT   St JULIEN

Ch. La Tour-Carnet
Ch. Belgrave

CUSSAC

LISTRAC
MOULIS
Ch. Poujeaux   ARCINS

AVENSAN SOUSSANS

MARGAUX
CANTENAC
LABARDE
Ch. Giscours
ARSAC   MACAU

Ch. Cantemerle

LUDON
Ch. La Lagune

Dordogne

Garonne

N

HAUT-MÉDOC

LEGEND
Major wine-producing towns   **MARGAUX**
Secondary wine-producing towns   *CANTENAC*
Rivers   Dordogne

0   1   2   3   4   5
SCALE OF MILES

BLANQUEFORT

PESSAC

Ch. Haut-Brion   GRAVES   BORDEAUX

but the term, basically, is meaningless. It is no less so in California where, without the final "s," it is sometimes similarly used on a sweeter version of a producer's "California Sauterne."

HAUTVILLERS — (Oh-vee-lay) — Village in the Champagne Country, a Premier Cru rated 90%, which means that its grapes bring 10% less per kilogram, or per ton, than those for example, of Ay, next door, rated 100%. Black grapes are grown exclusively. It was in the Abbey of Hautvillers that Dom Perignon (*see*) conducted his celebrated experiments, and the Abbey has been called, perhaps with partial justification, "the birthplace of Champagne."

HAZY — Said of a wine that is possibly clear but certainly not brilliant; this is usually the first step on the road to cloudiness. A hazy wine is almost certainly "off," may be "sick." *See*, however, Sediment.

HEAVY — Full-bodied, without delicacy or much distinction. An unfavorable term, but less severe than "coarse" (*see*).

HECTARE — (Hec-tar) — Metric measure of area containing 10,000 square meters — 2.471 acres. Vineyard area in France is commonly expressed in hectares, and yield figured in hectoliters per hectare. Superior vineyards often have, as their maximum legal yield, 30 or 35 "hectos" per hectare — roughly 320 to 375 gallons per acre.

HECTOLITER — Metric system term for 100 liters, the equivalent of 26.42 U.S. gallons, or 22.03 British imperial gallons. Wine production figures in France are usually given in hectoliters (or, colloquially, "hectos").

HÉRAULT — (A-ro) — French *département* on the Mediterranean, half way, more or less, between Marseille and the Spanish border. It is the heart of that vast *vin ordinaire* country known as the Midi, and although not much larger than a large American county, has more acres of vineyard (460,000) than California, and produces nearly twice as much wine as the United States. Most of this is common, cheap red table wine, coarse, made from the most productive varieties, usually light in color and low in alcohol and often blended with the stronger and darker wines of Algeria. The vines stretch in an immense green band along the gently rolling coastal plain for nearly a hundred miles: Béziers, Sète and Montpellier are the main centers of the wine trade. A few wines of superior quality are grown, notably the sweet white Muscats of Frontignan and Lunel, and some more than passable red table wines in a district known as the Minervois, in the hills back of Béziers.

HERMITAGE — (*Air*-me-taj) — Deservedly famous wine of the Rhône Valley, produced on a single steep, spectacular, terraced hillside some 50 miles south of Lyon. It is sometimes and not incorrectly spelled Ermitage or L'Hermitage, and the town where it is made is called Tain l'Hermitage. The vineyards are rock and face due south; they cover an area a half-mile wide and less than two miles long, and their total yield is approximately 50,000 cases a year. About one-third of this is white, made from Roussanne and Marsanne grapes; two-thirds red, made from the Syrah. An insignificant amount of *Vin de Paille* (*see*) is also produced, from white grapes left to semi-raisin on straw mats, and this of course is quite sweet, golden, high in alcohol (often 15%). White Hermitage is a dry, full-bodied, pale gold wine, with definite character and pronounced bouquet; the red is decidedly better — deep colored, very long-lived, forthright and fine. The late George Saintsbury described one red Hermitage as "the manliest wine" he had ever drunk, and the adjective was well chosen. Many legends exist (most with little or no foundation) having to do with the origin of the vineyards, their name, and the Syrah grape, which some believe to have been brought from Shiraz, in Persia, by a returning crusader, who became a hermit and built a chapel on the hill; others have pointed out that the "crusader" in question, Gaspard de Sterimberg, arrived in 1225, had been fighting in the religious wars in southern France and had never been within a thousand miles of Persia. It is probable that the vineyards existed in Roman days; no one can surely say why they are called Hermitage; and the origin of the Syrah grape is unknown. Officially there are 18 *quartiers*, or vineyard areas, in the Hermitage hillside, all named, but few if any Hermitage labels carry such names, and most of what appear to be vineyard appellations on Hermitage labels are really nothing of the sort, but simply brands. The *quartiers* are as follows: Beaumes, Les Bessards, La Croix, La Croix de Jamanot, Les Diognières, Les Diognières et Torras, Les Greffieux, Les Gros des Vignes, L'Hermite, L'Homme, Maison Blanche, Le Méal, Les Murets, Péléat, La Pierrelle, Les Roucoules, Les Signaux, Varogne.

HESSIA — Perhaps more properly called Rheinhessen, a German state; as far as wine is concerned, a district in Western Germany, bounded on the east and north by the Rhine, on the south by the Pfalz, and on the west by the Valley of the Nahe. Mainz is its principal city, and Rhine Wine is its occupation: there are over 30,000 acres of vineyard, and the average annual production is about 14 million gallons, nearly 90% of it white. The Sylvaner is by all odds the leading grape, although the best Hessian wines are made from the Riesling and almost invariably so labeled. Wine is produced in 155 different villages (amusingly enough, 120 of these have names that end in "-heim") but all of the truly superior wines come from about ten towns, all strung along the Rhine, rather than from the fertile, rolling country back from the river. These ten, more or less in order of quality, are: Nierstein, Nackenheim, Oppenheim, Bingen, Dienheim, Bodenheim, Laubenheim, Guntersblum, Alsheim and Worms — all of them will be found listed, in their proper alphabetical place, in this encyclopedia; together, they have about 6,000 acres of vines. Practically all the rest of the wine grown in Rheinhessen (and much produced in these ten towns as well) is either sold as "open" wine or labeled Liebfraumilch (*see*); this is a general catch-all name, and quite meaningless: *see* also Domtal.

These cheaper Hessian wines have not much except their price to recommend them; mild, soft, often heavily sulphured, without any real character, they reflect credit neither on the Germans who make and sell them, nor on American consumers who seem to buy them in preference to far better Rieslings and Sylvaners from California.

The fine wines of Hessia are another story: made from the Riesling (occasionally the Sylvaner) in the first six of the ten towns listed above, they often have real distinction and many of them can fairly be called great. Less "classic" perhaps than the finest Rheingaus, they have great fruit and fragrance, elegance and ripeness and great charm. It goes without saying that the best of them carry a town and vineyard name, and are estate-bottled.

HEURIGE — (*Hoy*-rig-guh) — Name generally given to the fresh young wine served in carafe or by the glass in the many cafés round Vienna.

HIGH TOR — One of the very few remaining Hudson Valley vineyards engaged in wine production, near New City in Rockland County. Red, white and *rosé* wines are made in comparatively small quantity, and from French hybrid vines like those of Boordy Vineyard (*see*) in Maryland. Mr. Everett Crosby is the owner.

HOCHHEIM — (Hawch-heim) — Important wine-producing town in Germany, properly considered part of the Rheingau, although it over-looks the Main rather than the Rhine, and is separated from the other vineyards by at least ten miles of farm and orchard land. There are nearly 500 acres under vines, and the better plots (as Domdechaney, Kirchenstück, Stein, Daubhaus, Hölle, etc.) give wines that have the unmistakable Rheingau stamp of character and breed, though perhaps somewhat gentled and softened. Leading producers are Aschrott, Dom-dechant Werner, Graf von Schönborn, the City of Frankfurt (Weingut der Stadt Frankfurt), and the German State Domain.

HOCK — The Englishman's general term for Rhine wine, as Claret for Red Bordeaux. It is supposed to be derived from Hochheimer, and in any case has replaced the older "Rhenish" in current British usage; no very good reasons have ever been advanced to explain why Hochheim, almost outside the Rheingau proper, was selected for this honor, in-stead of, more logically, "Jo," "Hat," or "Rue," for Johannisberger, Hattenheimer and Ruedesheimer. But who are we to carp? It is still legally possible, under American regulations, to manufacture some-thing called California Hock, and indeed New York Hock and Ohio Hock, in the United States.

HOLMES, Oliver Wendell (1809-1894) — American author and physi-cian, who, in addressing the Massachusetts Medical Society in Boston, May 30, 1860, said: "Wine is a food."

HOMER — Greek epic poet of antiquity, who said: "Wine gives strength to weary men."

HORACE — (65-8 B.C.) — Roman poet, who wrote: "Who prates of war or want after taking wine?"

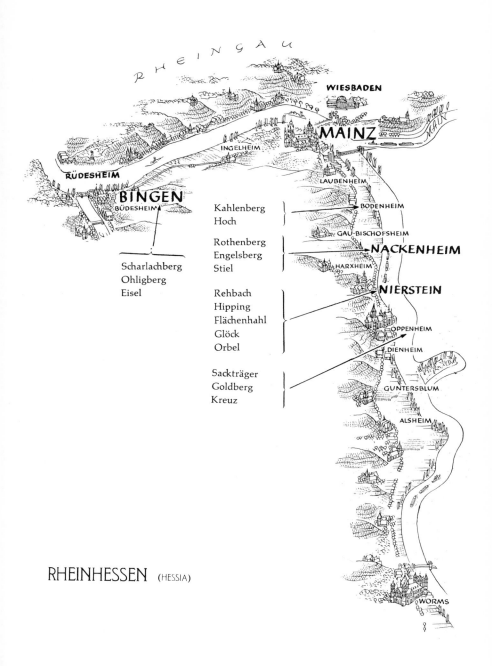

R H E I N G A U

WIESBADEN

MAINZ

INGELHEIM

RÜDESHEIM

LAUBENHEIM

BINGEN

BÜDESHEIM

Kahlenberg
Hoch

BODENHEIM

GAU-BISCHOFSHEIM

Rothenberg
Engelsberg
Stiel

NACKENHEIM

Scharlachberg
Ohligberg
Eisel

HARXHEIM

NIERSTEIN

Rehbach
Hipping
Flächenhahl
Glöck
Orbel

OPPENHEIM

DIENHEIM

Sackträger
Goldberg
Kreuz

GUNTERSBLUM

ALSHEIM

RHEINHESSEN (HESSIA)

WORMS

HOSPICES DE BEAUNE — (Awss-peace duh Bone) — One of the most beautiful buildings of Europe, a charity hospital (often referred to as the "Hôtel Dieu") in the Burgundian town of Beaune; scene annually, on the third Sunday of November, of what is perhaps the most famous wine auction in the world. Since its foundation in 1443 it has been bequeathed holdings in many of the best vineyards of the Côte de Beaune: these constitute its principal endowment and the wines from these provide most of its revenue. The prices brought at the auction, a most picturesque affair, tend to establish the level of Burgundy wine prices for the vintage in question. Although the wines are sold when still new, and delivered in barrel, the Hospices name is almost never abused; the wines are of superior quality and generally worth the high prices they bring.

The Hospices vineyards consist of over 40 different plots, 127 acres in all, and produce some 500 *pièces* (barrels of 228 liters) or 7,500 cases a year (although only 27 *pièces* in 1940 and 753 *pièces* in 1966). The product of each vineyard is auctioned separately, under the name of its *cuvée,* which in most cases is that of its donor, and prices vary widely according to the origin, reputation and quality of each wine. Listed below are the various *cuvées,* more or less in the order of the prices they regularly bring, together with the origin of each, and (merely as an indication) the number of cases of each produced in 1966, the most copious and perhaps the most successful year in the 100-year history of this sale.

There is no one standard label for the Hospices wines, but the consumer has the right to expect that the name of the *cuvée* and its *appellation contrôlée* should appear, as well as the name of the bottler; in some instances, each bottle is numbered.

It should perhaps be added that a little *Eau-de-Vie de Marc,* distilled from the grape skins or hulls, is also sold at the same auction, though this of course is of the preceding vintage.

170

THE HOSPICES DE BEAUNE Cuvées

Name	Appellation Contrôlée	Cases in 1959
(Red Wine)		
Nicolas Rolin	Beaune	975
Guigone de Salins	Beaune	1,100
Charlotte Dumay	Corton	725
Docteur Peste	Corton	750
Dames Hospitalières	Beaune	700
Dames de la Charité	Pommard	800
Blondeau	Volnay	675
Brunet	Beaune	525
Jehan de Massol	Volnay-Santenots	350
Clos des Avaux	Beaune	900
Estienne	Beaune	700
Billardet	Pommard	775
Pierre Virely	Beaune	850
Gauvain	Volnay-Santenots	750
Betault	Beaune	800
Rousseau-Deslandes	Beaune	825
General Muteau	Volnay	825
Maurice Drouhin[4]	Beaune	——
Boillot	Auxey-Duresses	150
Arthur Girard[1]	Savigny-les-Beaune	750
Fouquerand	Savigny Vergelesses	925
J. Lebelin[2]	Monthelie	400
Forneret	Savigny Vergelesses	625
Rameau-Lamarasse[5]	Pernand Vergelesses	—
(White Wine)		
François de Salins	Corton-Charlemagne	75
de Bahèzre de Lanlay	Meursault-Charmes	400
Albert Grivault	Meursault-Charmes	175
Baudot	Meursault-Genevrières	425
Philippe le Bon[3]	Meursault-Genevrières	275
Jehan Humblot	Meursault	325
Goureau	Meursault	325
Loppin	Meursault	350

[1] This originally consisted of two separate *cuvées,* one called Du Bay Peste and the other Cyrot; both will generally be found listed in books published prior to 1937. From 1937 through 1943 their wines were made as a single *cuvée,* called Du Bay Peste et Cyrot. In order to avoid confusion with the *Cuvée Docteur Peste,* the name was then changed to Arthur Girard, a recent and major benefactor of the Hospices, who, in 1936, had bequeathed a large part of his fortune to the Hotel-Dieu.
[2] Prior to 1937 consisted of two separate *cuvées,* J. Lebelin and Henri Gélicot. They were then combined, and the *Cuvée Henri Gélicot* has ceased to exist.
[3] Until 1955 formed part of the *Cuvée Jehan Humblot.* The two were then separated, since the wine of Jehan Humblot is entitled only to the appellation Meursault, whereas that of Philippe Le Bon may be called Meursault-Genevrières.
[4] A new *cuvée,* first sold in 1960, resulting from the bequest of a vineyard in the township of Beaune by the late Maurice Drouhin, long a director of the Hospices.
[5] A new *cuvée,* sold for the first time in 1966.

HOSPICES DE NUITS — (Awss-peace duh Nwee) — Hospital in Nuits-Saint-Georges, in Burgundy, which, like the far more famous Hospices de Beaune, has an endowment in the form of vineyards and sells wines which carry its name. Many of these come from the best *climats* of Nuits, and are of high quality.

HUDSON RIVER — Table grapes of native American varieties have long been grown in the Hudson Valley, especially on the right or west bank between Newburgh and Kingston, and a few rather half-hearted and not very successful efforts have been made to produce wine. The one interesting, surviving vineyard is a fairly new one — Mr. Everett Crosby's High Tor *(see)*.

HUNAWIHR — (*Hoo*-nav-veer) — Exceedingly picturesque village in Alsace, perched on a vineyard-covered hill northwest of Colmar. Very good wines.

HUNGARY — Traditionally, the greatest wine country of Eastern Europe, although now surpassed in total output by Roumania and by the Soviet Union. Roughly the size of Georgia, Hungary annually produces about three times as much wine as Germany and has more acres planted to wine grapes than the United States.

Hungarian wines have been famous for centuries, Tokay especially, and were well-known and appreciated in America even in pre-Civil War days. Those now being exported are of fair and occasionally good quality, but they are certainly more standardized and less remarkable than in the past — apparently the inevitable fate of wines grown under a Socialist economy. Most of the labels carry a geographic designation — a town or district name, used as an adjective and ending in "i," as *Badacsonyi, Egri, Szekszárdi, Debröi, Soproni, Mori, Somlyöi, Pécsi, Gyöngyosi, Balatonfüredi, Villányi,* and of course *Tokaji.* Generally, this is followed by a second name, which is usually but not always that of a grape; the leading white wine grapes, more or less in order of quality, are *Furmint, Hárslevelü, Rizling* (or *Olaszrizling*), *Veltelini, Kéknyelü, Muskotály, Ezerjó* and *Leányka;* for red wine, *Kadarka,* above all, and *Vörös.*

Bikavér, which means "bull's blood," is an exception and Egri Bikavér (from Eger), generally regarded as the best Hungarian red, is a blend of varieties including the *Kadarka* but also a few others of French origin. Similarly, when it comes to Tokay, made from the *Furmint* and *Hárslevelü,* terms such as *szamorodni, aszu, essentia* and *puttonyos* have to do with methods of vinification, and for these, *see* Tokay.

HUNTER RIVER — One of the oldest and best vineyard districts of Australia *(see),* which produces some highly creditable red and white table wines.

HUSSEREN-LES-CHÂTEAUX — (*Hess*-ser-en-lay-Shat-toe) — Attractive little wine-producing town in southern Alsace, remarkable for the three ruined castles on top of its steep, vineyard-covered hill — these constitute a famous landmark and are visible for miles. The wines of Husseren are of outstanding quality.

HYBRID — In viticulture, the result of a cross of two grape varieties. Botanically, the idea is a fairly new one, less than two centuries old; applied to the grape, it is wholly revolutionary, since the wine-bearing vine has been almost entirely propagated by cuttings rather than seeds since the dawn of human history. Most hybrids are an attempt to combine the best qualities of two quite different parent vines, or to produce an offspring able to contend with some special problem, such as the phylloxera, without compromising its superiority. Considering the fact that there is hardly such a thing as a pure strain of grape, or one surely able to transmit its specific qualities to its seedlings, this is a monumental problem, and it is surprising that so much definite progress has been made. There is no doubt, for example, that a number of the newer hybrids are capable of giving better wine in our Eastern states than any of the original "native" varieties; hybrids also provide quite passable wine for home use in many parts of France. These crosses usually bear the name of the hybridizer, often plus a serial number, in France — as Seibel 5279, Couderc 4401, Baco No. 1, Bouschet, and Müller-Thurgau; in other countries they have a bad tendency, like illegitimate children, to claim the name of their more illustrious parent, however few of his or her characteristics they may possess; as a result, wines are often presented to a somewhat confused public under names that sound familiar but to which the wines have no well authenticated right. Thus we have Goldriesling and Mainriesling in Germany, Emerald Riesling (*see* Riesling) and Ruby Cabernet in the United States.

Mr. Philip Wagner of *The Baltimore Sun* and of Boordy Vineyard *(see)* has done much to popularize the better hybrids in America. Extensive experiments in hybridizing are being carried on by the University of California's College of Agriculture, at Davis, California, and by similar establishments in several continents and at least a dozen countries. It seems certain that much of benefit to the wine-drinker will eventually come out of all this, though how soon is perhaps another question.

I-J

ICE — While an acceptable companion to almost all spirits (since it merely replaces the water lost in distillation) ice, like water, is a confirmed enemy of fine wine, and should never be put in fine wine — there is enough mediocre stuff produced to quench the world's thirst for wine-and-soda, sangría, and all the rest.

ICE BUCKET — Except in restaurants, ice buckets seem to be used less and less generally in this day of electric refrigeration; this is to be regretted, for white wines and *rosés* and Champagnes are far better served in a bucket. Pre-chilling, however useful, does not accomplish the same end; chilled wines lose their freshness and sprightliness and charm as they warm up during a meal, and the last glass rarely tastes as good as the first. Of red wines, particularly if brought to table at slightly below room temperature, the opposite is of course true; they improve as they warm up and taste better and better, as they should.

Many ice buckets are poorly designed, and the wine in the neck of a Rhine or Moselle bottle, for example, never gets chilled at all. In such cases it is perfectly correct procedure to put the bottle in the bucket neck down for ten minutes or so, before the capsule is cut away and the cork drawn.

ICE SAINTS — In German, *Eis Heiligen,* the patron saints of four days in May, the 12th through the 15th, during which danger of spring frost is still considered to exist in German vineyards, especially those of the Moselle and Saar. Their names are St. Pancratius, St. Servatius, St.

Bonifacius, and finally *die kalte Sophie,* or cold St. Sophia. Once they are past, the growers breathe easier, and in fact killing frosts after May 15th are almost unknown. *See,* however, Frost.

IHRINGEN — (*Ear*-ring-en) — One of the best wine-producing villages of the Kaiserstuhl, near Freiburg, in southwestern Germany. It is particularly noted for its Ruländer, or Pinot Gris, much like a top-grade Alsatian and perhaps the finest white wine of Baden.

IMPÉRIALE — (M-pay-ray-ahl) — Oversize bottle, in which Clarets of great years are occasionally laid away, for slower development and longer life. Holds as much as eight ordinary bottles.

INDRE — (An-dr) — Tributary of the Loire, in the French Chateau Country. Most of the red, white and *rosé* wines produced along its banks are entitled to the appellation "Touraine"; they are really nothing more than sound *vins de pays,* but light and fresh and very agreeable.

INFERNO — (In-*fair*-no) — Perhaps the most famous of the five classic red wines of Valtellina *(see),* produced along the northern edge of the Lombardy region of Italy, not far from the Swiss border.

INGELHEIM — (*Ing*-el-heim) — Picturesque and historic little town in Hessia, facing Johannisberg across the Rhine. Today it produces some rather common red wine, never exported, and a certain amount of even less distinguished white. Its fame comes from the fact that Charlemagne spent a good deal of time in his castle there and, according to tradition, once observed that the snow melted earlier than elsewhere on one especially favored opposite hillside. He therefore ordered that vines be planted in what is still regarded as one of the world's great vineyards, Schloss Johannisberg.

INGHILTERRA — (Ing-gil-*terr*-ra) — *See* Marsala.

INGLENOOK — Famous old California vineyard, at Rutherford, in the Napa Valley. The first vines were planted in 1879 by Gustave Niebaum (or Nybom), a retired Finnish sea captain and one of the first directors of the Alaska Commercial Company, and the impressive stone winery was constructed a decade later. Until very recently the property still belonged to Captain Niebaum's collateral descendants including John Daniel, Jr., who directed it and has been an important figure in California viticulture since the end of Prohibition. The production is not large; the entire emphasis is on varietal wines, and on quality. Particularly noteworthy are Inglenook's Cabernet Sauvignon, Pinot Noir, Pinot Chardonnay and Traminer, but a few others are produced including a Charbono (from the grape of that name), a Red Pinot (from the Pinot St. Georges) and sound, less expensive wines sold under the name Navalle. The sale of the vineyard and cellars to United Vintners (Petri) was announced in the early summer of 1964.

IONA — Native, Eastern, red-purple grape, but giving white wine, rather widely planted in the Finger Lakes district. It takes its name from Iona Island, in the Hudson not far from Peekskill, where it was first grown.

IPHOFEN — (*Eep*-ho-fen) — One of the better wine-producing towns of Franconia, in Germany. Its white wines are shipped in Bocksbeutels, and the top vineyards are Julius-Echter-Berg, Kronsberg, Kammer, Kalb, etc.

IRANCY — (*E*-rawn-see) — Pleasant, inconsequential red and *rosé* wine, produced round the village of this name, some ten miles southwest of Chablis, in northern Burgundy. It is entitled only to the appellation "Bourgogne"; when made from the Pinot Noir, it is a fresh and delightful *vin de pays,* but all too often it comes, as it may legally, from two far less distinguished grapes, the César and the Tressot, and is wholly ordinary.

IROULÉGUY — (Ee-roo-lay-ghee) — Full-bodied, golden, dry white wine, also a less fine red, produced round St. Jean-Pied-de-Port, not far from Biarritz in the western Pyrenees. Of purely local fame, it is often quite good and, in local cellars, surprisingly long-lived. It is entitled to the V.D.Q.S. seal.

ISABELLA — An old, heavy-flavored Eastern grape, an inferior predecessor of the Concord, now fortunately little used for wine. Through sheer stupidity or bad luck, it was planted rather widely in certain parts of southern Switzerland and northern Italy at the time of the phylloxera *(see)* to which it is of course immune. Its almost undrinkable deep-colored wine is there, particularly in the Swiss Canton of Tessin, or the Ticino, known as "Americano" *(see),* hardly the best possible propaganda for the United States.

ISCHIA — (Isk-*key*-ah) — Island facing Capri across the Bay of Naples. Produces a considerable amount of very good, pale, dry, white wine, most of it marketed, quite legally, as "Capri" *(see),* it being considered that the Capri production zone includes both Ischia and the adjoining island of Procida.

ISERA — (Ee-*sair*-ah) — Small town in the Italian Trentino *(see),* not far from Lake Garda. Known for its excellent light red wine and its even better *rosé,* both made from the Marzemino grape, and both sold as Marzemino d'Isera.

ISLAND BELLE — Native red grape of poor quality, also called Campbell's Early, which has unfortunately been widely planted along the Pacific Coast in the State of Washington, and on the islands northwest of Seattle. Its wine has a pronounced "foxy" flavor and is mediocre at best.

ISRAEL — Wine has been made in what is now Israel since the beginning of recorded history — certainly almost everywhere in Biblical days — and then, after a thousand "dry" years (which makes our own American Prohibition seem really no longer than a school recess) again since 1890. With the help of Baron Edmond de Rothschild, vines were planted and a winery constructed in 1886 at Richon Le Zion, southeast of Tel Aviv.

Most of the real progress in modern wine production dates, however, as might be expected, from 1948, when Israel became an independent state; this small land is therefore perhaps the oldest and yet the youngest wine-producing country in the world. Much has been accomplished: there are over 30,000 acres under vines; production in 1961 was in excess of 6 million gallons and had tripled in six years. Some 6% of this is exported and the U.S. is by all odds the largest customer.

The vineyard districts are scattered, the major ones are round Richon Le Zion, near Tel Aviv, and Zichron Jacob, southeast of Haifa; there are small, recent plantings in the Jerusalem corridor, and in the Lachish, Ashkelon and Beersheva areas further south. The grape varieties, selected for this latitude and its generally warm, arid climate, are principally, for red wine, the Alicante, Carignan, Grenache, Alicante Bouschet, and for white wines, the Muscat of Alexandria, the Muscat of Frontignan, and the Clairette; there are, however, plantings of Malbec, Cabernet Sauvignon, Semillon, Ugni Blanc and even Concord.

Since Israel has adhered to the Madrid Convention (unlike the United States), European names such as Champagne, Sauternes, Burgundy, Port, Sherry, etc., no longer appear on Israeli wine labels. There are some twenty wineries, mostly cooperatives, of which a number export; the Carmel Wine Co., or more correctly, the Société Coopérative Vigneronne des Grandes Caves, is the most important.

The wines are increasingly well-made, by competent technicians and with good equipment. Most of them are consumed in Israel, where they are inexpensive, and a large proportion of those shipped to the U.S. are consumed by observant Jews for ritualistic purposes, for which, for obvious reasons, they are often preferred.

While never of exceptional quality, they are honest, good, not overpriced.

ISSAN, Château d' — (*Dee*-sawn) — 3rd Classed Growth of Cantenac-Margaux. One of the better vineyards of Cantenac; some 3,000 cases a year of Claret distinguished for its finesse and breed. The old-fashioned gold label carries the proud devise, *Regum mensis arisque Deorum,* "For the Tables of Kings and the Altars of the Gods."

ITALIA — (Ee-*tal*-ee-ah) — Special type of Marsala *(see).*

ITALY — *Oenotria tellus,* immemorial "Land of Wine," Italy deserves her ancient name as does no other country, perhaps not even France. Every province of Italy produces wine; one acre out of every eight of Italian soil is either given over to vineyard or has, at least, its small quota of vines. Far smaller than California, Italy produces seven times as much wine as the United States, 20 per cent of all the wine of the world — a billion gallons a year.

Most of this, of course, is the most ordinary sort of wine — undistinguished, inexpensive, made to be drunk within a year. On the other hand, between the Alps and Sicily, Italy possesses an extraordinary diversity of climates, soils, grape varieties and viticultural traditions, and

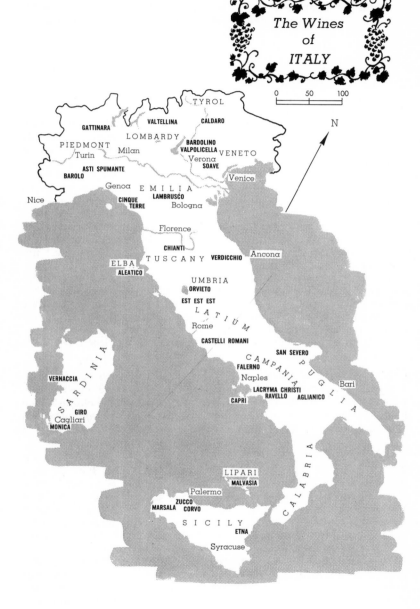

The Wines
of
ITALY

0   50   100

N

TYROL

GATTINARA
VALTELLINA   CALDARO
LOMBARDY
PIEDMONT   BARDOLINO
Turin   Milan   VALPOLICELLA   VENETO
Verona   SOAVE
ASTI SPUMANTE
BAROLO
Venice

Genoa   EMILIA
CINQUE   LAMBRUSCO
TERRE   Bologna
Nice

Florence
CHIANTI
ELBA   TUSCANY   VERDICCHIO   Ancona
ALEATICO

UMBRIA
ORVIETO

EST EST EST

LATIUM
Rome

CASTELLI ROMANI

SAN SEVERO
CAMPANIA
FALERNO
Naples
VERNACCIA   LACRYMA CHRISTI   Bari
RAVELLO   AGLIANICO
SARDINIA   CAPRI

GIRO
Cagliari
MONICA   CALABRIA

LIPARI
MALVASIA

Palermo
ZUCCO
MARSALA   CORVO

SICILY
ETNA
Syracuse

The Wines
of
NORTHERN ITALY

0   50   100

SANTA MADDALENA
TERLANO
LAGREIN
CALDARO

Lake
Maggiore

Lake
Como VALTELLINA

CONEGLIANO

GATTINARA   LOMBARDY

Lake
Garda VALPOLICELLA VENETO
BARDOLINO

PIEDMONT

Milan

LUGANA
CHIARETTO

Verona
SOAVE

Venice

Turin   FREISA

Po River

Adige River

BARBERA
BARBARESCO GRIGNOLINO
ASTI SPUMANTE CORTESE
BAROLO

LAMBRUSCO

EMILIA

Genoa   CINQUE TERRE

Bologna

VERMENTINO

Nice

Florence RUFINA

Arno River

CHIANTI CLASSICO

VERDICCHIO

TUSCANY

almost every province has at least some specialties fit for export. In
recent years, Italy has often shipped more wine to the United States
than even France; but even little Switzerland buys eight times as much
Italian wine as the United States does.

Few Italian wines, if indeed any, can equal in quality the best German and French. However, there are literally dozens of Italian wines
that are quite remarkable — interesting, distinctive, and of outstanding
excellence, their price considered. Nearly all of these are classed as
"Vini Tipici" (see), are under strict government control as to authenticity, and carry the red seal of the *Instituto Nazionale per l'Esportazione*
(INE). They are all listed in their proper alphabetical place in this
encyclopedia.

It would hardly be possible for anyone except a professional or a
specialist to be familiar, even superficially, with all the wines of Italy.
But there are at least thirty or forty or fifty worth cultivating and any
catalogue of this elite would include at least the following:

Several of the red wines of Piedmont, magisterial BAROLO, full-bodied GATTINARA, and somewhat lighter BARBARESCO, all three made from the Nebbiolo grape, plus a few of their sturdy cousins, BARBERA, FREISA, GRIGNOLINO; the classic VALTELLINA of Lombardy; BARDOLINO and VALPOLICELLA from the province of Verona; two or three red wines from the Italian Tyrol, SANTA MADDALENA, LAGO DI CALDARO, perhaps SANTA GIUSTINA; the characteristic LAMBRUSCO of Emilia (although it will not please everyone); *Classico* CHIANTI, preferably that shipped in ordinary wine bottles rather than in *fiaschi;* GRAGNANO from near Naples, possibly AGLIANICO DEL VULTURE, though this is hard to find.

In the way of dry wines, or semi-dry: the CORTESE of Piedmont, especially that sold as Gavi; the LUGANA of Lake Garda and, of course, SOAVE from near Verona; the pale TERLANO and TRAMINER *aromatico* from the Alto Adige; the VERDISO of Conegliano, near Venice, and the VERDICCHIO from the Castelli di Jesi; ORVIETO, perhaps EST EST EST, and the Castelli Romani wines, such as FRASCATI; CAPRI and LACHRYMA CHRISTI from near Naples; and the white ETNA from Sicily.

As *vins rosés,* the CHIARETTO (Chiarello) of Garda, LAGREIN ROSATO from the Italian Tyrol.

Among dessert wines, MARSALA, of course; the ALEATICO of Elba; the VINO SANTO produced both in Tuscany and the Trentino, half a dozen different sorts of MOSCATO, and many others. And, as sparkling wines, ASTI SPUMANTE, and, for those who like a dryer wine, the GRAN SPUMANTE made out of the French Pinot grapes of Casteggio.

With hardly any exceptions (Est Est Est being one and Chiaretto another) Italian wines take their names either from their town or district of origin, or from a variety of grape. The labels as a whole are dependable, and the wines honest. It must be admitted, however, that as far as vintages are concerned, this is not altogether the case; Italian wines *do* vary in quality from year to year, but much less than those of Germany and France, and Italians themselves rarely pay any attention to the vintage when ordering wine, and cheerfully accept whatever vintage is currently available. Many Italian wines would not even carry a vintage if it were not for the exigencies of foreign buyers; often such buyers prefer an old vintage, even on wines that are vastly better when drunk young, and many Italian shippers are quite willing to cooperate, feeling that the matter is of little or no importance. Vintage years on Italian wines are therefore largely to be distrusted. As a matter of fact, with at most a dozen exceptions, all Italian wines are as good when three years old as they are ever likely to be. Those worth ageing are Barolo, Barbaresco, Gattinara, Ghemme, Valtellina (all made from the Nebbiolo grape), Freisa and possibly Grignolino, the better grades of Chianti and a few other Tuscan wines; perhaps Aglianico del Vulture. All of these are red. Dessert wines such as Marsala are aged in wood and are ready to drink when bottled.

IVES — Red, native, Eastern grape, believed to be a seedling, or accidental cross of other varieties, first grown along the Ohio River near Cincinnati in the 1850's. It gives a heavy, deep-colored, coarse wine with a pronounced "foxy" flavor, which few except the most confirmed devotees of Eastern wines find acceptable, let alone good; it is used, but hardly ever straight, in many New York State Burgundies, both still and sparkling.

JAMES — Native American black grape, of the Southern Muscadine family, and therefore related to the Scuppernong, sometimes used for wine in the Carolinas.

JASNIÈRES — (Shan-yare) — Small district producing interesting (although generally not commercial) wines along the northern edge of the French province of Touraine. Principal grape varieties are the Chenin Blanc for white wine and the Cabernet Franc and Pinot Noir for red.

JEFFERSON, Thomas (1743-1826) — Author of the Declaration of Independence, sometime Ambassador to France, and third President of the United States, who wrote: "No nation is drunken where wine is cheap and none sober where the dearness of wine substitutes ardent spirits as the common beverage."

JEREZ — (Hair-eth) — Attractive and prosperous little city in southern Spain, on the main road and main railway line from Seville to Cadiz; the birthplace of Sherry, which is called *Jerez* or *Vino de Jerez* in Spanish. The vineyards that have made the city's fame and its wealth lie mostly to the west and southwest of the town, out of sight of the highway; many of the streets run between the high, white, windowless walls of the bodegas in which Sherry (*see*) is stored and aged.

JEROBOAM — Oversize wine bottle, holding as much as six ordinary bottles, in which Clarets of great years are sometimes laid away. The jeroboam is also used for Champagne, but here the wine is fermented in regular bottles and then "transfused" just prior to shipment; this of course has a tendency to shorten its life.

JEROPIGA — *See* Geropiga.

JESI or IESI — (Yay-zee) — Town in central Italy, not far from Ancona. The surrounding villages produce, from the Verdicchio grape, one of the best Italian dry white wines. *See* Castelli di Jesi.

JESUITENGARTEN — (Yez-you-*eat*-en-gar-ten) — Name (literally, "Jesuits' Garden") given to three different and widely separated vineyards in Germany; alone, i.e. without a village name, to one at Oberemmel on the Saar, property of the Friedrich Wilhelm Gymnasium; Winkeler Jesuitengarten, which adjoins Schloss Vollrads in the Rheingau, is even better known; and Forster Jesuitengarten is by far the most famous of all, one of the Palatinate's best *Lagen*, and owned by the Bassermann-Jordan family.

JOHANNISBERG — World-famous little village, and its even more celebrated castle (*see* Johannisberg, Schloss, below) overlooking the Rhine in the heart of the German Rheingau. Its production figures are hardly impressive — there are only 66 acres in the Schloss or castle vineyard (part of these usually non-productive through the rotation of replanting) and only about 200 more under vines in the whole township. These would be hard pressed to supply the whole world's demand for Johannisberger, and commercial wines so labeled, with no indication of specific vineyard site, or producer's name, or estate-bottling, may legitimately be looked on with skepticism. The name Dorf Johannisberger is no better, since *Dorf*, in German, simply means village. On the other hand, the true Johannisbergers, with vineyard name and Original-Abfüllung, are of a quality hardly surpassed and not often equaled in the Rheingau, wines of extraordinary grace and breed and bouquet. The more dependable *Lagen*, or vineyard names, are these: Klaus, Hölle, Vogelsang, Kläuserpfad, Kläuserberg, Kläusergarten, Kahlenberg, Goldatzel, etc. Leading producers include Graf von Schönborn, Geromont, Landgraf von Hessen (formerly Krayer Erben), Anton Eser, etc.

JOHANNISBERG RIESLING — Name usually given to the true Riesling grape in California to differentiate it from other varieties which, in fact, are not Rieslings at all — the so-called Franken Riesling (really the Sylvaner), the Grey Riesling (really the Chauché Gris), the Emerald Riesling, the Goldriesling and the Mainriesling, all of which are crosses, giving wine of lower quality.

JOHANNISBERG, Schloss — Germany's most famous vineyard, spectacularly situated on one of the steepest of the Rheingau's hillsides, commanding an incomparable view over the fertile and busy Rhine Valley. According to tradition, it was the Emperor Charlemagne who first ordered vines planted on its slope (having observed, from his palace at Ingelheim across the river, that snow melted sooner there than elsewhere); by 1100 a Benedictine abbey had been constructed on the site, and when church properties were secularized in 1801, this became the property of Prince William of Orange. The Congress of Vienna ceded it to the Emperor of Austria, and he bestowed it on Prince Metternich; it is still the property of the Metternich family, and their home. The present castle, however, is new, the old *Schloss* having been bombed during the last war, and almost entirely destroyed.

Experts are somewhat of two opinions regarding the present quality of the Schloss Johannisberg wines, and it can hardly be denied that, since 1953, they have consistently been surpassed by other Rheingau wines of less prestigious reputation, and even by others from nearby plots in the village of Johannisberg itself. Doubtless the eclipse, if such it may be called, is only temporary, for it would be impossible to over-praise the excellence of the Schloss Johannisbergers of the great pre-war years.

The wines are now sold under two quite different labels, with differently colored capsules indicating the various gradations of quality. The more familiar label carries the Metternich *Wappen*, or coat-of-arms,

and three wines are so marketed: the *Rotlack*, or red capsule, is the cheapest, generally a dry wine of decided breed but not outstanding quality; the *Grünlack*, green capsule, is a step higher, and is generally but not always a Spätlese; the best, the *Rosalack*, pink capsule, is not produced every year, and is in most cases an Auslese. The alternate label carries a drawing in color of the *Schloss* and vineyard, and is reserved for Cabinet wines; these, here at Schloss Johannisberg, are not necessarily of better grade than the others, but are marketed through other channels. It should perhaps be added that, in poor years, only a small portion of the wine is estate-bottled, the rest being made into sparkling wine, or Sekt.

JOHNSON, Samuel (1709-1784) — British author and lexicographer, quoted by his biographer, James Boswell, as saying, "Wine gives great pleasure and every pleasure is of itself a good." He also described Claret as drink "for boys," assigning Port to men and brandy to heroes.

JOSEPHSHOF — (*Yo*-zefs-hof) — Excellent vineyard at Graach on the Moselle, owned in its entirety and for over a century by the Kesselstatt family; both the steeply terraced vines and the picturesque buildings at their foot belonged to the Monastery of St. Martin until 1802, when they were secularized and given their present name. Although in the township of Graach, the Josephshof directly adjoins Wehlen, and its wine, sold as Josephshöfer, is generally more like a Wehlener than a Graacher, rich and full-bodied rather than sprightly, big and fine rather than delicate and charming.

JOURNAL — (Shoor-nahl) — Old Burgundian measure of area, about five-sixths of an acre.

JULIÉNAS — (Jule-*yea*-nahss) — One of the most important *communes* and one of the best wines of the Beaujolais — perhaps less fruity than Brouilly and less engaging than Fleurie — but a firm wine of unusual distinction, balance and fine texture. Total production is between one-fourth and one-half million gallons a year.

JURA — (Shu-ra) — Mountain range, *département*, and wine-growing district in eastern France, not far from the Swiss border. The vineyards are strung along the Jura foothills, which run roughly parallel to the Burgundian Côte d'Or, from the town of Arbois southward for some fifty miles, in the old French province of Franche-Comté. Neither in quality nor in quantity are the wines of much consequence — total production, about half of it white, is generally well under a half million gallons a year — but the very diversity of the Jura wines makes them rather interesting. The *rosé* wine of Arbois (*see*) is probably the best as well as the best-known, and the only one likely to be found outside of France; the others include a rather more than passable sparkling wine called L'Étoile; a distinct oddity, Château-Chalon (*see*), which might be called a French version of unfortified Sherry; a small quantity of *vin de paille* (*see*); finally, some fairly good reds and whites, the best marketed under the appellation Arbois.

JURANÇON — (Shoor-awn-sawn) — Rather sweet, golden wine, celebrated in history and legend, produced on the Pyrenees foothills south and west of Pau, in southwestern France. It is made from grape varieties unknown in other districts, the Petit Manseng, the Gros Manseng and the Courbu; it has a special, spicy bouquet and flavor which some local enthusiasts have compared to the scent of carnations and the taste of cinnamon or cloves. The individual vineyard holdings are small, and the vines trained high, almost pergola-fashion; surprisingly, the average production is not far from 200,000 gallons a year. Rarely found on wine-lists, even in France, yet well-balanced, interesting and long-lived, Jurançon was of course a favorite wine of King Henry IV (who was born in Pau), and on the whole deserves its reputation.

MIS EN BOUTEILLES AU CHATEAU

CHÂTEAU LAFITE-ROTHSCHILD
1947
APPELLATION PAUILLAC CONTRÔLÉE

DÉPOSÉ

FRANCE

184

K-L

KABINETT — *See* Cabinet.

KADARKA — (*Ka*-dar-ka) — Hungarian red wine grape, widely planted in that once happy country, and responsible for the vast majority of red wines ranked officially there as *Premiers Grands Crus*. These carry the name Kadarka plus a regional appellation of origin on their labels, as Szekszárdi Kadarka, Pécsi Kadarka, Villányi Kadarka, Gyöngyosi Kadarka and Egri Kadarka. It was once thought to be identical with the Zinfandel of California, although the wine it yields is of a far different character; this comforting theory has now gone pretty well by the board.

KAEFERKOPF — (Kay-fer-Kopf) — One of the rare wines of Alsace to carry a specific vineyard name. The Kaeferkopf is in the *commune* of Ammerschwihr, and yields admirable Rieslings and Gewürztraminers.

KAISERSTUHL — (Kai-ser-shtool) — Interesting little wine-producing district in Baden, southwest Germany. This consists of an extraordinary "island" of volcanic tufa, rising out of the fertile Rhine Valley between Colmar (in Alsace) and Freiburg-im-Breisgau; its wines are not unlike those of Alsace, and most of the Alsatian grape varieties are grown, but perhaps the best here are made from the Ruländer, or Pinot Gris, and come from the villages of Ihringen, Endingen, Achkarren and Bötzingen.

KALLSTADT — (Kahl-Shtat) — One of the better wine-producing villages of the Pfalz, north of Dürkheim, with over 700 acres of vines, including a fairly high percentage of Rieslings. Good vineyards include Kobnert, Kreuz, Steinacker, Annaberg, and one with the extraordinary name of Saumagen, or "sow-belly."

KANZEM — (Kahnt-zem) — Celebrated wine-producing village on the Saar, in Germany, with some hundred precious acres of Riesling vines. In great years its wines are close in quality to those of Wiltingen and Ockfen (there can hardly be higher praise) and its best vineyard sites or *Lagen* include Sonnenberg, Berg, Altenberg, Unterberg.

KANZLERBERG — (*Kahnz*-lehr-bairg) — Remarkable vineyard in the town of Bergheim, Haut-Rhin, producing some of the very finest wines of Alsace, Gewürztraminers especially.

KARTHÄUSERHOFBERG — Celebrated vineyard on the Ruwer, in Germany. *See* Eitelsbach.

KAYSERSBERG — (*Kayz*-zerz-bairg) — Picturesque and justly famous little wine town in Alsace. Its Rieslings and Gewürztraminers are of top quality and it is the birthplace of Dr. Albert Schweitzer.

KELLER — (Kel-ler) — Simply means cellar, in German; thus *Kellerarbeit* means cellar-work, *Kellermeister* means cellar-master. However, see below.

KELLERABFÜLLUNG — (Kel-ler-*ahb*-fil-lung); also KELLERABZUG (Kel-ler-*ahb*-zook) — Literally, the first of these means "cellar-filling," and the second, "cellar-drawing-off"; for all practical purposes they mean the same thing, Estate-Bottled, and one or the other, or *Original-Abfüllung* (the commonest forms of all) will almost always be found on the label of a fine German wine, followed by the name of the producer. KELLEREIABFÜLLUNG (Kel-ler-*rye*-ahb-fil-lung) is not at all the same thing, is not at all an indication of estate-bottling, and means simply "bottled in the cellars of —"; the name that follows is usually *not* the producer's.

KESSELSTATT — (*Kes*-sel-shtat) — Old titled family with extensive vineyard holdings on the Moselle, Saar and Ruwer, in Germany. These include, in addition to a central cellar in Trier, the entire Josephshof (*see*) in Graach, considerable acreage in the best *Lagen* of Piesport, vines at Casel on the Ruwer and at Oberemmel and Niedermennig on the Saar.

KEUKA, Lake — (Q-ka) — One of New York State's Finger Lakes, and perhaps the most important of all, as far as wine is concerned; the little town of Hammondsport is at its southern end, and the three wineries where Taylor wines, Great Western and Gold Seal are produced, are all nearby.

KIEDRICH — (Key-drich) — Little vineyard town of the Rheingau, set back in the hills between Rauenthal and Hallgarten, producing excellent wines which, like the Rauenthalers, deserve to be as well-known abroad as they are in Germany; fruity, racy, spicy, they are truly admirable in good years. There are some 320 acres of vines, and the best plots are: Gräfenberg, Wasserrose, Sandgrub and Turmberg; the leading producers: Graf Eltz, Dr. Weil, Freiherr von Ritter zu Groensteyn and the State Domain.

KINHEIM — (Kin-heim) — Small, secondary vineyard town on the Moselle near Traben-Trarbach.

KIRWAN, Château — (Keer-wan) — 3rd Classed Growth of Cantenac-Margaux, one of the larger vineyards of this township, of old reputation; some 10,000 cases a year.

KLEVNER — (*Klev*-ner) — Name given in Alsace and in Germany to the Pinot Blanc grape, less widely grown along the Rhine than the Pinot Gris, or Ruländer, and giving less good wine, but ranked nonetheless as a *plant noble*, or superior variety.

KLOSTER EBERBACH — (Klaws-ter-Eh-ber-bach) — Ancient Gothic monastery in the Rheingau, founded by Augustinian monks in 1116 but almost immediately taken over by the Cistercians, under the direction of the same remarkable man who created the Clos de Vougeot on a bare, Burgundian hillside, the wine-loving St. Bernard-de-Clairvaux. Here, as in Burgundy, the Cistercians constructed a wall that still stands around their superb vineyard, the Steinberg, and within a century after its foundation, Kloster Eberbach had become the principal center of German viticulture and the German wine trade, with a branch in Cologne and a fleet of wine ships on the Rhine. Fortunately, although the monastery was secularized in 1801 and is now the property of the German State, most of what the Cistercians created has been preserved; the old buildings, with their great vaulted rooms and venerable wine-presses, are intact and were actually in service until quite recently. Wine auctions are still occasionally held here, and the whole establishment, hidden in a narrow, wooded valley back of Hattenheim and Erbach, is of the greatest possible interest to anyone who likes wine and has a taste for history, or vice versa.

KNIPPERLÉ — (*Nip*-per-lay) — Mediocre Alsatian grape, known in Germany and Switzerland as the Räuschling (by no means to be confused with the Riesling); its white wine is of fair quality, better on the whole than that from the Gutedel or Chasselas, and most of it is consumed locally.

KÖNIGSBACH — (Ker-nigs-bach) — One of the best wine-producing villages of the Pfalz, lying well up on the Mittel-Haardt hillsides, just south of Deidesheim. There are some 325 acres of vineyard, a good deal of it in Rieslings; von Buhl is the largest producer but there is an important *Winzerverein*; the best plots are Idig, Satz, Rolandsberg, Harle, Reiterpfad.

KORBEL — Famous old winery in Sonoma County, California, especially known for its Champagne, one of America's best. Founded in 1881 by four brothers of this name, who had emigrated from Czecho-Slovakia and made a considerable fortune in lumber, it remained a family enterprise until quite recently; the first vines were planted round enormous redwood stumps near Guerneville, in the Russian River Valley, and the stone winery there dates from 1886. Czech wine-makers were brought over from the Viticultural School of Melnik, near Prague, and imposed their high old-world standards, planting only the better varieties of vine and adhering rigidly to French methods of Champagne making. A few table wines and fortified wines were produced in the past and it has recently been announced that this production will shortly be resumed.

KREUZNACH — (Kroytz-nach) — Also called Bad Kreuznach (it has mineral springs and some modest local fame as a watering-place), this is the center of the Nahe wine country, and lies some ten miles up this lesser stream from Bingen, where the Nahe joins the Rhine. A number of good vineyards (Hinkelstein, Kröttenpfuhl, Kahlenberg, Narrenkappe, etc.) are actually within the town limits, and the Kreuznacher wines rank with those of Schloss Böckelheim as the best of the Nahe. There is also an important wine school in Kreuznach, and the filters manufactured in its celebrated *Seitz-Werke* are gratefully used by vintners all over the world.

KRÖV — (Kruhv) — Sometimes written Cröv, a pretty little town on the Moselle near Traben-Trarbach. Its 250 acres of vines yield a fairly ordinary wine which has nevertheless achieved fame and popularity on account of the odd name and comic label under which it is sold. Kröver Nacktarsch literally means "naked behind," and the label shows a small boy being spanked, with his trousers down.

KRUG, Charles — Oldest of the important Napa Valley vineyards, just north of St. Helena, in California. It was planted in 1858 by Charles Krug, who had learned wine-making in his native Germany, and the original stone winery was constructed in 1861. Since 1943, it has been the property of the Mondavi family, and has achieved an important place in the premium wine field. Varietal table wines, sold under the Charles Krug name, include Cabernet Sauvignon, Pinot Noir, Chardonnay, Johannisberg Riesling, Traminer, Chenin Blanc, etc. A number of sound, pleasant, lesser wines are sold under the Napa Vista label, and some inexpensive, agreeable reds and whites under the "CK" brand.

KUECHELBERGER — (*Cue*-kell-bairg-er) — Light and fragrant red wine of the Italian Tyrol, produced just outside the attractive resort town of Merano, and a great favorite there. It is made from the Schiava Meranese grape (*see*).

LABRUSCA — One of the principal species of native North American grape, *Vitis Labrusca*, of which the Concord is a typical example.

LACHRYMA CHRISTI — (*La*-cree-ma *Kris*-tee) — Celebrated white wine (a little red, less good, is also produced) grown on the slopes of Mt. Vesuvius, near Naples. Made from the Greco della Torre grape, pale gold in color, it is a bit softer and less austerely dry than the wine of Capri, produced nearby, and in character and flavor not too far from a fairly dry Graves. The name, of course, means "Tears of Christ" and there are many stories to explain its origin. The lovely Bay of Naples country has been called a "fragment of Paradise," and, according to one account, the Lord, returning to earth, found this heavenly corner of the world "inhabited by demons" (presumably the Neapolitans); touched and distressed. He wept, and where His tears fell there sprung up green vines — the vines of the Lachryma Christi vineyards.

Unembellished by such pious legend, a sparkling Lachryma Christi is made in many parts of Italy, including Piedmont; it may not, of course, carry the words "del Vesuvio" on its label unless it comes from the original, delimited vineyard zone.

LADOIX-SERRIGNY — (La-dwa *Say*-reen-ye) — Village in Burgundy on the Côte de Beaune. *See* Aloxe-Corton.

LAFAURIE-PEYRAGUEY, Château — (La-fo-*ree*-Pay-rah-gay) — 1st Classed Growth of Sauternes. One of the best vineyards of Bommes (*see*) and one of the most impressive chateaux of the Sauternes district. Full-bodied, golden, very sweet wine, typical Sauternes.

LAFITE, Château — (La-feet) — In the opinion of most impartial experts, and perhaps in the mind of the general public as well, the *ne plus ultra* of Claret and the greatest red wine vineyard in the world. Lafite, or Lafite-Rothschild (both names are correct and both have been used at various times on the chateau label) was ranked first among the 1st Growths in the Bordeaux Classification of 1855, and has maintained its place with surprising consistency over the decades. Its special fame dates from the 17th century, when it was the property of M. de Ségur, and it was purchased in 1868 by Baron James de Rothschild for 5 million gold francs.

There are something less than 150 acres under vines (Cabernet, Merlot, Petit Verdot) and the annual yield is not far from 15,000 cases, plus perhaps half as much of a second, lesser wine sold as Carruades (*see*) de Château Lafite. The fermenting rooms, the *chais* and cellars are models of what such installations should be, and the "Library" of bottles extends back, great vintage by great vintage, to before 1800.

The wine of Lafite varies, as all Bordeaux wines vary, from one year to another, although Lafite less than most, but of its best vintages it is hard to speak except in terms of the highest praise. Rarely over 12½% alcohol, they have an astonishing authority, impeccable breed, fruit and fragrance and depth of flavor, all the qualities with which a great Claret should be endowed. For Label, *see* Page 184.

LAFLEUR, Château — (La-*Flerr*) — One of the *Premiers Grands Crus* of Pomerol. An admirable small vineyard, some 1,200 cases a year of excellent Claret.

LAGE — (La-guh) — In German, a specific, named vineyard, or plot of vines; what the Burgundians would call a *climat*, and the Bordelais a *cru*. The plural is *Lagen*.

LAGO DI CALDARO — (*La*-go dee Kahl-dar-o) — Small lake not far from Bolzano, in the Italian Tyrol; the excellent, light red wine produced on the steep, lake-side vineyards to its west and north. Made from the Schiava *gentile* grape (*see*), fragrant, well-balanced, it is superior to the neighboring Caldaro (*see*), and one of north Italy's best.

LAGRANGE, Château — (La-Grawnj) — 3rd Classed Growth of St. Julien, Haut-Médoc. One of the less distinguished of the 3rd Growths. Approximately 10,000 cases a year.

LAGREIN ROSATO — (La-*grain* Roas-*sa*-toe) — Delightful *rosé* wine of the Italian Tyrol, produced practically in the suburbs of Bolzano (*see*), and known as Lagreiner Kaetzer when this district was part of Austria, before 1918. It is made from the Lagrein grape.

LAGRIMA — (*La*-gree-ma) — An especially sweet and heavy type of Malaga wine, produced around the city of this name, in southern Spain.

LAGUNE, Château La — (La-Lag-*guhn*) — 3rd Classed Growth of Ludon, Haut-Médoc. Southernmost of the classed vineyards of the Médoc, only some seven miles from the northern limit of Graves, La-Lagune produces a fine, firm, slow maturing Claret which, in character, is perhaps closer to the better red Graves of Pessac than to the Médoc wines as a whole. The chateau has recently changed hands: a most ambitious program of replanting has been undertaken, and the new cellar installations are among the handsomest and best of the whole Bordeaux Country. The quality of the wine is certain to improve.

LALANDE-DE-POMEROL — (La-*lawnd*-duh-*Paum*-may-rawl) — Secondary Bordeaux district, adjoining Pomerol on the north. Its wines, all red, resemble those of Pomerol but are less fine. Château Bel-Air and Château de la Commanderie are considered the best vineyards.

LAMBRAYS — (*Lawm*-bray). Burgundian vineyard. *See* Clos des Lambrays.

LAMBRUSCO — (Lom-*bruce*-co) — Unusual red wine, almost always slightly sparkling or *frizzante* (*see*), produced just west of Bologna in northern Italy, especially around the village of Sorbara. Made principally from the grape of the same name, extremely fruity, somewhat sweet, with an intense and extraordinary bouquet, it is a great favorite throughout the region of Emilia and perhaps Italy's best wine of this class. It is not a class likely to appeal to a real wine lover, let alone an expert.

LAMOTHE, Château — (La mote) — 2nd Classed Growth of Sauternes. Good quality, sweet white wine. There are four other minor chateaux in the Bordeaux Country with this identical name.

LANDES — (Lawnd) — French *département* directly south of Bordeaux; flat, sandy, sparsely populated and largely covered with pine forests, it produces little wine of any consequence, but some Armagnac of fine quality along its eastern edge near Villeneuve-de-Marsan.

LANGOA-BARTON, Château — (*Lawn*-go-ah-*Bar*-tawn) — 3rd Classed Growth of St. Julien. One of the best of the 3rd Growths; some 7,500 cases a year of fine Claret, a typical St. Julien.

LANGUEDOC — (Long-guh-dawk) — Ancient French province, extending along the Mediterranean from the Rhône River to beyond Narbonne; as far as wine is concerned, this is known as the Midi, and produces most of the *vin ordinaire* of France; the three *départements* of Hérault, Aude and Gard rank 1, 2, and 3 in total vineyard acreage and total production among the ninety French *départements*. The vast bulk of this is common stuff, and goes to market simply as *vin rouge*, but there are some excellent sweet Muscat wines produced at Frontignan (*see*) and Lunel, a well-known sparkling wine at Limoux (*see*), and table wines of rather more than passable quality in a number of specific, delimited zones. A few of these have been granted an *Appellation Contrôlée*, and a number of others may carry the V.D.Q.S. seal. *See* the following: Clairette, Fitou, Corbières, Minervois, Cabrieres, Saint-Georges-d'Orgues, etc.

LARCIS-DUCASSE, Château — (*Lar*-see-Do-*cass*) — 1st Growth of St. Emilion. Some 4,000 cases a year. High quality red wine.

LAROSE, Château — (La-Rose) — *See* Gruaud-Larose. There are however two very minor Bordeaux chateaux called Château Larose, two others called Château Laroze, and, finally, the Co-operative Cellar of Pauillac puts out a good, fairly inexpensive, agreeable red wine called La Rose de Pauillac.

LARRIVET-HAUT-BRION, Château — (*La*-ree-vay-Oh-*Bree*-awn) — Good small vineyard of Léognan, Graves. Some 2,000 cases of red wine a year.

LASCOMBES, Château — (Lahs-Caumb) — 2nd Classed Growth of Margaux. Now one of the better 2nds, giving some 5,000 cases of Claret a year.

LA TÂCHE — (La Tasch) — Celebrated Burgundian vineyard and its great red wine. *See* Tâche.

LATIUM — *See* Lazio.

LATOUR, Château — (La-tour) — 1st Classed Growth of Pauillac. Admirable and world famous vineyard, legally and properly ranked as one of the three best of the Médoc, a worthy rival of Margaux and Lafite. Its 110 acres are planted on thin, poor, unfertile, gravelly soil, and the yield per acre is extremely low: the resulting wine, some 10,000 cases a year, is one of the most robust and sturdy of Clarets, deep-colored, long-lived, astringent when young but obviously of great class, developing a splendid bouquet as it grows older.

There are literally scores of chateaux in the Bordeaux Country having the words Tour or La Tour as part of their name. The most important of these are listed elsewhere, in their proper alphabetical place, in this encyclopedia. They should not, of course, be confused with the one great original Château Latour, which has a stylized tower, surmounted by a lion, on its familiar, old-fashioned label.

LATOUR-POMEROL, Château — (La-*tour*-*Paum*-may-rawl) — Good 1st Growth vineyard of Pomerol, owned by the owner of Château Pétrus. About 4,000 cases a year of fine, soft Claret.

LATRICIÈRES-CHAMBERTIN — (Lat-tree-*see*-air *Shawm*-bair-tan) — Distinguished Burgundy vineyard and its red wine, officially a *Grand Cru* and, after Chambertin and Clos de Bèze, one of the best of this extraordinary little district. Seventeen acres in extent, it directly adjoins Chambertin on the south, shares the same exposure and practically the same soil.

LAUBENHEIM — (Lau-ben-heim) — Small wine-producing town on the Rhine south of Mainz, in Hessia. Its 300 acres of vineyard produce rather soft and common wines of mediocre quality.

LAUDUN — (Lo-*duhn*) — Village of the lower Rhône Valley, in France, west of the river and north of Tavel and Lirac. Its red, *rosé* and white wines, of which the last are regarded as the best, are marketed as Côtes-du-Rhône-Laudun.

LAUSANNE — (Lo-*zahn*) — Attractive city on the northern shore of Lake Geneva, itself the owner of two celebrated vineyards nearby, the Clos des Abbayes and the Clos des Moines. Both produce good quality, dry white wines from the Fendant grape.

LAVAUX — (La-vo) — District of extremely impressive terraced vine-yards on the northern shore of Lake Geneva, between Vevey and Lausanne, in the Canton of Vaud. It produces some of the best white wines of Switzerland.

LAVILLEDIEU — (La-*veal*-dee-uh) — Red and white wines of some small local fame, produced northwest of Toulouse in southern France. They are entitled to the V.D.Q.S. seal.

LAVILLE-HAUT-BRION, Château — (La-*veel*-Oh-*Bree*-awn) — Excellent small vineyard at Talence, on the outskirts of Bordeaux. It produces some 1,500 cases a year of what is certainly one of the very finest dry white Graves.

LAYON — (Lay-ohn) — Little river in Anjou, tributary of the Loire, famous for its white wines. *See* Coteaux du Layon.

LAZIO — (*Lotes*-ee-o) — The region of Rome, in Italy. Produces over 50 million gallons of table wine a year, almost all of it consumed locally, more white wine than red. Perhaps a third of this total comes from the Castelli Romani (*see*) and is sold as such, or as Frascati, Albano, etc.

LEES — Heavy, coarse sediment which young wines throw in barrel before they are ready for bottling. These are left behind when the wine is "racked" or transferred from one barrel to another, and this process is generally repeated two or three times before the wine is bottled.

LÉOGNAN — (Lay-own-yawn) — One of the very best wine-producing villages of the Graves district, some seven miles southwest of Bordeaux. Its red wines and its white are equally distinguished and its best vineyards include Domaine de Chevalier, Châteaux Carbonnieux, Haut-Bailly, Malartic-Lagravière, Fieuzal, Olivier, etc.

LÉOVILLE-BARTON, Château — (*Lay*-oh-veel-*Bar*-tawn) — 2nd Classed Growth of St. Julien, Haut-Médoc. A very good 2nd Growth, giving approximately 7,500 cases a year.

LÉOVILLE-LAS-CASES, Château — (*Lay*-oh-veel-*Lahss*-Kahz) — 2nd Classed Growth of St. Julien, Haut-Médoc. Justly celebrated vineyard and its consistently good, well-balanced, fine-textured Claret. Usually over 12,000 cases a year.

LÉOVILLE-POYFERRÉ, Château — (*Lay*-oh-veel-*Pwah*-fair-ray) — On the whole the best vineyard of St. Julien, fully meriting its rank as a 2nd Classed Growth. Its excellent red wine (about 12,000 cases a year) is perhaps a little fuller-bodied than the other Léovilles, and generally brings a slightly higher price.

LEISTADT — (*Ly*-shtat) — Vineyard town in the German Palatinate north of Dürkheim; white wines of fair quality and a few mediocre reds.

LÉMAN, Lac — (*Lay*-mawn) — What the French and Swiss call what *we* call Lake Geneva; a good part of its northern or Swiss shore is covered with vineyards.

LESSONA — (Less-*sone*-ah) — Superior red wine from the Piedmont region of Italy, made from the Nebbiolo grape in the province of Vercelli.

L'EVANGILE, Château — *See* Evangile.

LIBOURNE — (Lee-*Boorn*) — Town on the Dordogne River, some twenty miles east of Bordeaux; an important center of the wine trade, especially the wines of St. Emilion, Pomerol, Fronsac, etc., all produced nearby.

LIEBFRAUENSTIFT — (Leeb-frau-en-shtift) — Twenty-six-acre vineyard surrounding the Gothic Liebfraunenkirche, or Church of Our Lady, in the city of Worms, on the Rhine. There are of course hundreds of churches called Liebfraunenkirche in Germany; this one happens to be, in all probability, the orginal source of Liebfraumilch. The vines are planted on heavy alluvial soil well inside the city and not far from the river, and the wines they produce, while unquestionably authentic, are rather common and a long way from the best of Rheinhessen; they are sold as Liebfrauenstiftswein, not as Liebfraumilch.

LIEBFRAUMILCH — (Leeb-frau-milsh) — In German, this word, which is certainly one of the most universally known of wine names, simply means, "Milk of the Blessed Mother." It was probably originally given to the wine produced by a few acres of vines round the Liebfrauenkirche in Worms, on the Rhine (the Liebfrauenstift — *see* — and by no means an outstanding vineyard); but it has long since turned into a meaningless passepartout of a name, vaguely synonymous with Rhine Wine. The cheapest and poorest wines of Rheinhessen may be and usually are shipped as Liebfraumilch, and a number of producers in the Palatinate have now entered the lists, with Liebfraumilchs of their own. On the other hand, a few shippers have found it advantageous to offer some excellent wines as Liebfraumilch — wines from Nierstein, Nackenheim, Oppenheim, etc., which are properly entitled to these more precise and honorable names. The consumer's only guide to quality (other than such rarely used terms as Spätlese and Auslese) is the name of the shipper. This may or may not be the producer's name, and in most instances is not.

LIESER — (*Leez*-zer) — Little wine town near Bernkastel, on the Moselle; its wines are of good but not top quality, being somewhat heavier than the Bernkastelers, Graachers, etc., with less bouquet and breed. Schlossberg and Niederberg are the best vineyards.

LIEU-DIT — (Lee-uh-dee) — In French, a place name that has no precise official meaning, other than one based purely on tradition and local usage.

LIGHT — According to American law, a light wine is one that contains less than 14% alcohol by volume. It is not in this sense, however, that the word is used by experts — it is the opposite of Full-Bodied but also the opposite of Heavy, and as such can be complimentary. Light wines may have finesse and fruit and charm; only in rare instances can they be called Great.

LILLET — (*Lee*-lay) — Fairly dry French apéritif, made with a white wine base, plus herbs and brandy.

LIMOUX — (Lee-*moo*) — Town in southern France, not far from Carcassonne, which produces some white wines of quite considerable local fame. The best known of these is the sparkling Blanquette de Limoux, made by the Champagne process, generally rather sweet; Limoux Nature is a still, dry white wine, pleasant enough but hardly remarkable.

LIPARI — (*Lee*-par-ree) — Largest of a group of small islands off the north coast of Sicily; according to Greek mythology, home of Aeolus, god of the west wind. Several of the islands, especially Salina, produce a famous golden, dessert wine, made from the Malvasia grape and usually sold as Malvasia di Lipari.

LIQUEUR — (Lee-*kerr*) — In common, conventional usage, a sweet after-dinner drink, high in alcohol. Applied to whiskey or brandy, it means, rather vaguely, one of sufficiently fine quality to be consumed straight in this way, although of course not sweet. But the word has other and specific meanings as far as wine is concerned, notably two, with respect to Champagne: the solution of sugar, or rock-candy, in wine, which is added (usually plus a yeast culture) to the young wine before bottling, to bring about a second fermentation in bottle, is called *liqueur de tirage;* the quite similar syrup, added in the form of *dosage* *(see),* to sweeten the bone-dry, already sparkling wine at the time of disgorging, to make it *brut,* or extra dry or *demi-sec,* is called *liqueur d'expédition.*

In addition, liqueur, when applied to the great, naturally sweet dessert wines — those of Sauternes and Anjou, for example — means the sweetness, or unfermented grape sugar, left in the finished wine: thus one can say, of a Château d'Yquem, that it contains 14% alcohol, plus perhaps 4% of liqueur.

However, what is called a *vin de liqueur* is almost always a fortified wine (it would be called a *vin liquoreux — see —* if its sweetness were wholly natural and involved no addition of brandy); the term is generally applied in this sense to wines from the eastern Pyrenees, such as Banyuls, Grand Roussillon, etc.; prepared in a slightly different way, these are called *vins doux (see).*

LIQUOREUX — (Lee-cor-ruh) — Used in French to describe a sweet, luscious white wine that has retained, without fortification, a good deal of natural grape sugar, or liqueur *(see).*

LIRAC — (*Lee*-rack) — Village immediately north of Tavel, in the lower Rhône Valley; its *rosé* wine, very like Tavel, although sometimes lighter and with less character. The predominant grape is the Grenache.

LISBON — Capital and chief city of Portugal. Also a general term used by the British wine trade to designate the sweet, fortified and table wines, red and perhaps more often white, produced near Lisbon. Carcavelos is the best known of these.

LISTRAC — (*Leece*-trac) — Village in the Haut-Médoc, producing no wines of great class but a good deal of sturdy, well-balanced, agreeable and inexpensive Claret. Most of this is entitled to the appellation Moulis *(see),* the rest, usually labeled Listrac, carries the designation "Appellation Haut-Médoc Contrôlée." Listrac has long been a favorite wine on French dining-cars. There is a large co-operative cellar, and the better vineyards *(crus bourgeois supérieurs)* include: Châteaux Fourcas-Hostein, Fonreaux, Lestage, Sémeillan, Clarke, etc.

LITER — Metric measure of volume: 1.057 U.S. quart; .88 British quart. A liter contains 1000 cubic centimeters, and a liter of distilled water weighs one kilogram, or 2.2 pounds.

LIVERMORE — Town in Alameda County, California, some forty miles southeast of San Francisco. The surrounding Livermore Valley has been recognized since the 1880's as one of the best table wine districts of the United States; its rolling, gravelly soil seems particularly well adapted to the production of white wines, and such famous European varieties as the Sauvignon Blanc, Semillon, Pinot Blanc and Chardonnay are widely planted, as are also the Grey Riesling and Ugni Blanc. The leading producers are Wente Bros., Concannon and Cresta Blanca.

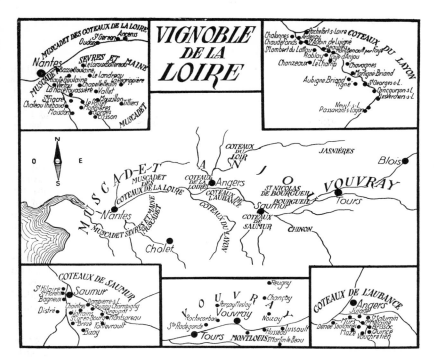

LOCHÉ — (*Lo*-shay) — Wine-producing village south of Macon, in southern Burgundy; it adjoins Vinzelles, Fuissé, Pouilly, etc., and its fresh, agreeable white wine, made from the Chardonnay grape, is sold under the appellation Pouilly-Loché.

LOGROÑO — (Lo-groan-yo) — Little city and province on the Ebro River in northern Spain; as a center of the wine trade, the town is less important than Haro *(see),* but most of the celebrated Rioja district is in the province of Logroño and this, of course, produces by far the best table wines of Spain.

LOIR, Le — (Luh Lwahr) — Tributary of the Loire, west of Paris. Its best wine is Jasnières *(see).*

LOIRE, La — (La Lwahr) — The longest and one of the most beautiful rivers of France, traversing, in the course of its 600-mile journey from its source, west of Lyon, to the Atlantic, near Nantes, a whole series of different provinces and viticultural areas. Its wines, sometimes collectively called *Vins de la Loire,* include a most diverse and interesting collection of reds, whites, and *rosés,* ranging all the way in quality from poor to great. All of the more important ones will be found listed, in their alphabetical place, in this volume. *See* Pouilly-Fumé Sancerre, Quincy, Touraine, Vouvray, Bourgueil, Chinon, Saumur, Anjou, Muscadet, etc., etc.

LOMBARDY — Important region of northern Italy; its capital is Milan. Produces between 50 and 60 million gallons of table wine a year, the best of it from three widely separated districts: that of Valtellina *(see),* around Sondrio, east of Lake Como and not far from the Swiss border; second, a hilly area south of Pavia and the Po River, including Casteggio *(see)* and the vineyards of Barbacarlo, etc.; finally, the western and southern shores of Lake Garda *(see).*

For Map, *see* ITALY.

LORCH — (Lork) — Town on the Rhine, considered by courtesy as belonging to the Rheingau, although it is actually in the Rhine gorge, north of Assmannshausen; its wines are made in large part from the Sylvaner grape, and, in character and quality, are more like those of the Mittel-Rhein than those of the Rheingau proper. Pfaffenweis, Bodenthal and Krone are considered the better *Lagen,* and Graf von Kanitz is an outstanding producer.

LORRAINE — (Lor-raine) — Ancient French province which produces nothing worth exporting in the way of wine, but a few amusing and agreeable *vins de pays*; most of these come from the upper Moselle Valley between Metz and Toul, and the best of them are the so-called *vins gris* (see), small, light, fresh *rosés,* produced around Bruley, Liverdun and on the Côtes de Toul.

LOULOUMET, Clos — (Clo *Lu*-lu-may) — Small vineyard at Toulenne, near the southern edge of the Graves district, producing a pleasant, soft, fairly dry white wine.

LOUPIAC — Village on the right bank of the Garonne, directly opposite Barsac, in the Bordeaux Country. Although geographically part of the Premières Côtes de Bordeaux *(see),* it forms a distinct district and has its own appellation. Its white wines, decidedly sweet, are heavier and more common than Sauternes, but similarly made and of the same general type.

LOUVIÈRE, Château La — (La-*Loo*-vee-air) — Important vineyard at Léognan, in the Graves district. Both red wines and white.

LÖWENSTEIN, Prince — Major German wine producer, with important holdings at Hallgarten in the Rheingau and also in Franconia. The official name of the domain, which appears on the label, is the *Fürstlich Löwenstein-Wertheim-Rosenberg'sches Weingut.*

LUBERON — (Lou-bay-rawn) — Chain of hills along the northern bank of the Durance River, east of Avignon. Some very good *rosé* wines are produced, and some quite passable reds. *See* Côtes du Luberon.

LUDON — (*Lou*-dawn) — *Commune* near the southern end of the Haut-Médoc. By all odds its best vineyard is Château La-Lagune *(see),* a 3rd Classed Growth, but there are one or two *crus bourgeois supérieurs,* Château Pomiès-Agassac, etc.

LUGANA — (Loo-*gahn*-na) — Very agreeable dry white wine produced around the tiny village of this name, at the southern end of Lake Garda, in northern Italy. It is made from the Trebbiano grape *(see),* and is generally the best of the white Garda wines.

LUGNY — (*Loon*-ye) — One of the more important wine-producing villages of the Maconnais *(see);* white wines of good quality from the Chardonnay grape.

LUNEL — (Lew-nel) — One of three towns on the Mediterranean Coast of France (Rivesaltes and Frontignan being the others) producing a sweet Muscat wine of justified reputation and high quality. Lunel's vineyard area lies west of Nîmes, is much the smallest of the three, and the total production of Muscat de Lunel is well under 10,000 cases a year. The informing grape is the Muscat de Frontignan.

LUSSAC-SAINT-EMILION — (Lou-sac-Sant-A-*me*-lee-awn) — Secondary wine district, northeast of St. Emilion, and entitled to the name only in this combined form. Its red wines are full, often a bit common, not too expensive. A good deal of white wine is also made but this, not entitled to the appellation, is sold as Bordeaux Blanc.

LUXEMBOURG — (*Lukes*-em-boorg) — The Moselle River, after leaving France, skirts the Grand Duchy of Luxembourg for some twenty miles, and along its northern bank there are over 2,000 acres of vineyard. These produce, mostly from the Riesling grape, fresh, light, rather tart white wines, not unlike small German Moselles. The town of origin and the grape variety appear on the labels, and the leading wine producing villages are Wormeldingen, Remich, Wintringen, Ehnen, Grevenmacher and Wasserbillig. A little sparkling wine is also made.

LYNCH-BAGES, Château — (Lansh-Baaj) — 5th Classed Growth of Pauillac. Now one of the better and more popular of the 5th Growth Clarets, a deep-colored, powerful, robust wine that brings a higher price than many 3rd and 4th Growths and even than some 2nds.

LYNCH-MOUSSAS, Château — (Lansh-*Moo*-sah) — 5th Classed Growth of Pauillac. Less well known and less good than the preceding.

LYON — (*Lee*-awn) — Third city of France (pop. 470,000), situated at the junction of the Saône and Rhône rivers, famous for the excellence of its food, and for the fondness which its citizens demonstrate daily for the wines of the Beaujolais district, nearby. It has often been said (first said, it would appear, by Léon Daudet) that there are not two rivers in Lyon, but three: the Rhône, the Saône . . . and the Beaujolais.

LYONNAIS — Name given to a few, small, rather nondescript wines produced round Lyon in the *département* of the Rhône. The best of them are like poor Beaujolais, but they are entitled to the V.D.Q.S. seal.

M

MACAU — (Mac-co) — One of the southernmost villages of the Haut-Médoc, but not a wine name or appellation. By all odds its best wine is Château Cantemerle *(see)*.

MACHIAVELLI — Illustrious Italian statesman and political commentator, whose books, *The Prince* and *The History of Florence*, have come to be regarded as classics. Long attached to the Court of the Medici, he wrote these books at his family estate at Sant 'Andrea in Percussina, south of Florence. His home — a "national monument" today — is now part of one of the most celebrated estates of the Chianti Country, that of the Conti Serristori, whose best wine is called *Chianti Machiavelli,* and is regarded as one of Italy's most distinguished. This is shipped in ordinary wine bottles rather than *fiaschi;* a second wine of somewhat less remarkable quality is shipped both in *fiaschi* and in bottles, under the name *St. Andrea;* it, too, carries the Serristori name.

MACON — (*Mac*-cawn) — Important town (Pop. 22,000) on the River Saône in southern Burgundy; a major center of the wine trade. As a wine, Macon may be red, *rosé,* or white; if red or *rosé,* it must be made exclusively from Gamay, Pinot Noir or Pinot Gris grapes, or a blend of these; if white, from the Chardonnay alone, being legally sold either as Macon Blanc or Pinot-Chardonnay-Macon. The average annual production is over 2 million gallons, about 60% of it red. Red Macon is a pleasant, sound, generally inexpensive wine, less fruity and attractive than good Beaujolais, though somewhat firmer and coarser. In the field of white wines, Pouilly-Fuissé, Pouilly-Loché, and Pouilly-Vinzelles are

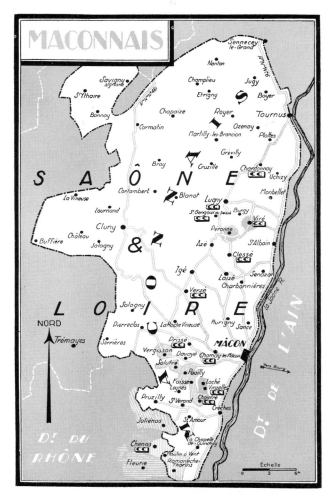

entitled to the appellation Macon, but almost never so sold; most of what is marketed as Macon Blanc comes from the less known *communes* of the Maconnais farther north and is a somewhat similar but less expensive wine, dry, fresh, palatable, but with less notable finesse and breed.

MACONNAIS — (*Mac*-cawn-nay) — Large district in southern Burgundy, consisting of much of the *département* of Saône-et-Loire, centered around the town of Macon *(see)*. Pouilly-Fuissé, Pouilly-Vinzelles and Pouilly-Loché are all in the Maconnais, as are Viré *(see)*, Lugny and Clessé, all three producing superior white wines from the Chardonnay grape. Most of the lesser wines of the Maconnais, however, are sold simply as Macon and Macon Blanc.

MADEIRA — Portuguese island, far out in the Atlantic, which has been famous for its wines for nearly four hundred years. Oddly enough, these first achieved what might be called international reputation and standing because of the favor they enjoyed in America in colonial days: clipper ships, following the prevailing trade winds, made Madeira a regular port-of-call, taking on water and supplies plus a few casks of wine on their return voyage from Europe to Charleston or Philadelphia, Baltimore or New York or Boston. The sea voyage reputedly improved the wine, and a good many 18th and 19th century Madeiras, bottled in this country, carried on their label the name of the vessel that transported them, and the year of the voyage.

It has often been stated and quite possibly is true that the British taste for Madeira dates from our War of Independence, when returning British officers spoke enthusiastically of the quality of bottles they had tasted in American cellars. In any case, a few decades later, the Madeira trade had followed the pattern set by Port, Sherry and Marsala and was largely in English hands. Like almost all European wine lands, but more severely than most, Madeira was invaded and its vineyards devastated in the late 1800's by two plagues of New World origin — the oidium (a sort of mildew) and the phylloxera. The island's economy never entirely recovered, and it is safe to say that Madeiras of as high quality have never since been made. Nor is America today the principal market for Madeira: France (where it is used principally in cooking), Sweden and Denmark each import three or four times our modest annual total of under 15,000 gallons.

All Madeiras, of course, are fortified wines, brought up to their strength of 18-20% by the addition of high-proof brandy. Although aged and blended in *soleras*, like Sherry (true vintage Madeira hardly exists, if indeed at all), they are made by a quite different process, much like that used for Marsala, and owe their characteristic flavor to the fact that they are kept, for a period of months, in special rooms called *estufas* at a high temperature.

Madeira, it should be kept in mind, is not by any means just one wine but a whole company of wines, ranging from very dry to very sweet, from pale straw (Rainwater) to deep gold (Malmsey) in color, from cheap to very expensive, from mediocre to extraordinary in quality. As cooking wines, even the lesser grades are remarkable and no Sherry or Marsala can replace them. As apéritif or dessert wines, those of exceptional class are quite properly high-priced, and are increasingly hard to find. The nomenclature has become more and more standardized, and most of the old, once-famous export houses have come together and tend, increasingly, to draw their wines from jointly held stocks. The old system of individual vineyard names has pretty much disappeared, like true vintage wines, in Madeira, and is not likely soon to return.

The finest Madeiras, with a few exceptions, take their name from the grape from which they are made. The dryest, called Sercial, is somewhat comparable to a Fino Sherry, but with an altogether special and often extraordinary bouquet and character. One called Verdelho could be described as its cousin, but is now rarely available. Boal or Bual is a good deal sweeter and more golden, almost a dessert wine by modern standards, although our grandfathers drank it with terrapin and shad. Malmsey, deep gold, very sweet, can be entirely remarkable, and it seems too bad that wines such as this, however magnificent, are a little out of fashion today.

Rainwater Madeira, the palest of all, was, it seems, created by an American wine-lover called "Rainwater Habisham," who developed a special system of fining and clarifying to render his family wine the lightest and the most like rainwater, of all. It has become a name in general and unrestricted usage.

MADERISÉ — (Mad-*dare*-ee-zay) — French term applied to wine, especially a white or *rosé* wine, which is past its prime, has become somewhat oxidized, has acquired a brownish tinge, plus an aroma and flavor reminiscent of Madeira. Anything but a favorable term; a *maderisé* wine is one that is well on its way to becoming spoiled.

In English, the terms "maderized" and "oxidized" are often used interchangeably, but strictly speaking a maderized wine is one which has acquired this different and special character through a combination of heat, plus contact with the air or with oxygen, whereas when the term "oxidized" is used, there is no implication that the wine has (either accidentally or otherwise) been stored in a warm place, or been "baked."

MADIRAN — (Mad-dee-rawn) — Sturdy red wine produced north of Pau and Tarbes, between Bordeaux and the Pyrenees, in southwestern France.

MAGDELAINE, Château — (Mag-duh-lain) — One of the 1st Growth vineyards of St. Emilion, directly adjoining Ausone and Belair on the escarpments overlooking the Dordogne Valley. Some 2,000 cases a year of wine that is generally full, soft and fine.

MAGENCE, Château — (Ma-shawnse) — One of the best of the less-known vineyards of the Graves district of Bordeaux, in the *commune* of Saint-Pierre-de-Mons. Dry white wines of considerable bouquet and breed.

MAGNUM — Bottle of double normal capacity. Since wines, red wines especially, tend to develop and age more slowly in large bottles than in small, Clarets and Burgundies of great years are often put up in magnums for laying away. Champagne is occasionally fermented in magnums (*never* in bottles of over magnum size) but, more often, transfused from standard bottles into magnums when disgorged — a process tending to shorten rather than lengthen the wine's life: that Champagne is better in magnums is a harmless myth. The use of magnums for lesser wines is in some cases a convenience, more often an affectation.

MÁLAGA — (*Ma*-la-ga) — City and province on the Mediterranean, in southern Spain: the sweet, brown, fortified wine produced by hillside vineyards in this district, mostly from Pedro Ximénez and Muscat grapes. The cheaper grades are usually sweetened with *arrope* (a grape concentrate, *see*), the better ones through the addition of a special, so-called PX wine, made from sun-dried Pedro Ximénez grapes. Normally both are aged and blended in *soleras*.

The Malaga grape of California is a table grape and has no connection whatsoever with Málaga wine, except that California "Malaga" may legally be made from it.

MALBEC — (Mal-beck) — Excellent red wine grape, also known as the Cot or Pressac, and widely cultivated in the Bordeaux Country, as well as round Cahors in south-central France. It gives a well-balanced wine of considerable finesse, which matures more rapidly than the Cabernets.

MALCONSORTS — (Mal-cawn-sor) — Outstanding small vineyard in the *commune* of Vosne-Romanée, in the heart of Burgundy. It is bounded on the north by La Tâche and on the south by Nuits-Saint-Georges, Les-Boudots. Its 15 acres of vines produce a remarkable red wine, well balanced, distinguished, but often with a faint earthy taste or *goût de terroir*.

MALESCOT-SAINT-EXUPÉRY, Château — (*Mal*-less-co-Sant-Ex-*oo*-pay-ree) — One of the better 3rd Classed Growths of Margaux. Some 5,000 cases a year of Claret known for its finesse and bouquet.

MALLE, Château de — (Shat-toe duh Mal) — 2nd Classed Growth of Preignac, Sauternes. Some 4,000 cases a year of ripe, fine, typical Sauternes. The vineyard and its charming chateau have belonged to the Lur-Saluces family (owners of Yquem and Filhot) for over two centuries. A dry wine, not entitled to the *appellation* Sauternes, is now also being produced.

MALMSEY — English for Malvasia (*see*), the sweet, fortified amber wine made from the grape of this name, wherever grown; now principally the island of Madeira, but also Cyprus, Sardinia, Sicily, Lipari and other Mediterranean lands. George, Duke of Clarence (1449-1478), a younger brother of Edward IV, is said to have been drowned in a butt of Malmsey wine.

MALVASIA — (Mal-va-*zee*-ah) — Ancient and famous white wine grape (a red variant exists but is far less important) originally from Greece and the Aegean Islands, transplanted to most other Mediterranean countries, to the island of Madeira, South Africa and California. Its wine, usually called Malmsey in English, is, when fortified in the traditional way, extremely sweet and luscious, heavy in body, golden in color but turning deep amber with age, long-lived, with great bouquet. That of Madeira (*see*) is perhaps the most famous, but another of at least equal quality is produced on a little archipelago of islands off the north coast of Sicily, and sold as Malvasia di Lipari, the most important island of this group. A few wines are made from the Malvasia grape in California — some table wines of undistinguished quality, even a sparkling wine, and a few dessert wines which are hardly remarkable, but better than the rest.

MALVOISIE — (Mal-vwah-zee) — French for Malvasia (*see*), a superior dessert wine grape, widely planted in the *département* of Pyrénées Orientales, where, in conjunction with the Grenache and other varieties, it yields the sweet, amber fortified wines for which this district is known — Banyuls, Rivesaltes, Maury, Grand Roussillon, etc. It is sometimes known by this name, rather than as Malvasia, in California.

MANCHA, La — (La *Mahn*-cha) — Wide, treeless, rolling, upland country, south of Madrid, in Spain; scene of Don Quixote's exploits. Its vast vineyards, including those of Valdepeñas (*see*) produce much of the better, common table wine of Spain.

MANZANILLA — (Mahn-thahn-*neel*-ya) — Legally, a Spanish Sherry; in fact, a quite different wine, although made on the edge of the Sherry Country, by similar methods, and from the identical varieties of grape. Unless specifically prepared for export, it is a very pale, almost painfully dry wine (although neither fruity nor tart), with between 15% and 17% alcohol by volume, a fine, highly special bouquet, and a flavor which is appetizing, faintly bitter, almost salty: some authorities have claimed, rather fancifully, that this is due to the sea wind which blows off the Atlantic over the vines and through the *bodegas*, for the Manzanilla vineyards are some ten miles west of Jerez, around the little white town of Sanlúcar de Barrameda, on the ocean and not far from the mouth of the Guadalquivir River, whence Columbus sailed for America and Magellan for the Pacific.

The word Manzanilla is the diminutive of *manzana*, apple, and means crab-apple in Spanish; it also means camomile, but despite some efforts by wine-loving etymologists, it is hard to see any connection between these and the wine, which is very unlike cider and even more unlike camomile tea. Traditionally, it is the wine of bullfighters, and the favorite wine of Seville, where it is drunk out of small, stumpy, cylindrical glasses called *cañas*. Perhaps on account of its almost excessive dryness, it has never been as popular abroad as in Spain. Two of the best and best-known brands are La Gitana (which is pronounced La He-*tah*-na, and means "the Gypsy Girl") and La Guita (which is pronounced La *Gui*-ta and means "the String," on account of the string sewn through its cork, which forms a sort of seal).

It should be added that Manzanilla, like Sherry, becomes darker in color and higher in alcohol as it grows old in barrel; there exist, although rarely for sale, deep brown Manzanillas that have 21% of natural alcohol by volume, and these, remarkable and interesting but not for all palates, are perhaps the dryest wines on earth.

MARC — (Mar) — Grape pressings; the mass of skins and seeds left in the press after the wine (red wine) or juice (white wine) has been extracted. Also the brandy distilled from this, *Eau-de-Vie-de-Marc*. In the

205

Champagne Country, the word has a different, special meaning: 4,000 kilograms (8,800 lbs.) of grapes, the load that one of the presses generally used there can handle at one time; normally these four metric, or long, tons yield twelve 200-liter barrels of usable wine, some 635 gallons in all, plus some 50 gallons of poorer quality, this last rarely used by the better Champagne producers.

MARCOBRUNN — (Mar-co-bruhn) — Celebrated German vineyard, one of the Rheingau's best. It takes its name from the *Marcobrunnen,* an attractive little fountain in red sandstone which, on the old river road, marks the village boundary of Erbach and of Hattenheim. About half the vines are in each village, although the fountain is in Erbach, and a local poet has written, "Let Erbach keep the water. Give Hattenheim the wine." Wines from the Erbach portion (produced by Schloss Reinhartshausen, the State Domain, or *Staatsweingüter,* etc.) are generally marketed as Erbacher Markobrunn, and those from over the border of Hattenheim (from Freiherr Langwerth von Simmern, Graf von Schönborn, etc.) simply as Marcobrunner.

Although particularly outstanding in dry years, the Marcobrunners on the whole are unsurpassed by the wines of any other German vineyard — fruity, racy, well-balanced, they have truly astonishing bouquet and breed.

MAREUIL-SUR-AY — (Ma-ruy-soor-eye) — Wine-producing village in the Champagne Country of France, rated 98% as against 100% for Ay (*see*), next door. The vineyards are planted almost entirely to Pinot Noir, but there is a little Chardonnay, as in the Clos des Goisses (*see*).

MARGAUX — (Mar-go) — One of the best sections of the Haut-Médoc, producing Clarets remarkable for their bouquet, silky texture and great breed. The appellation now covers, in addition to the small township of Margaux proper, most of the neighboring *communes* — Cantenac, Soussans, Arsac and Labarde. The finest Margaux wines of course carry a chateau label: Château Margaux, a *grand seigneur*, and its scarcely less illustrious cousins, Rausan-Ségla, Rauzan-Gassies, Brane-Cantenac, Palmer, Kirwan, etc.

MARGAUX, Château — (Mar-go) — 1st Classed Growth of Margaux. One of the very greatest of the Bordeaux vineyards, producing a Claret of truly incomparable distinction and class — delicate, velvety, suave, well-balanced and astonishingly long-lived, with a bouquet unsurpassed by any other red wine on earth. The chateau itself is extremely impressive and the great high *chai* with its round stone columns is hardly less so. The vineyards produce some 15,000 cases of red wine a year, all chateau-bottled, plus a small quantity of dry white wine, sold as "Pavillon Blanc de Château Margaux"; this last, while pleasant enough, is by no means remarkable. For Label, *see* Page 230.

MARKGRÄFLER — (Mark-*gray*-flur) — Mild, undistinguished, fairly agreeable white wine produced south of Freiburg, in Baden, Germany.

It is made from the Chasselas grape, here called the Gutedel, and its production zone is called Markgräflerland; most of it is consumed young, as *Schoppenwein*, for it is short-lived and hardly deserves bottling.

MARLENHEIM — (*Mar*-len-heim) — Wine producing village in northern Alsace, due west of Strasbourg, on the Paris road; it is perhaps the only Alsatian *commune* in which black grapes predominate. From these, mostly Pinot Noir, the growers make the best *rosé* of Alsace and one of the best of France — racy, fruity and delicate. This is sometimes given the local name of *Vorlauf.*

MARMANDAIS — (*Mar*-mawn-day) — District of mediocre, nondescript wines southeast of Bordeaux, round the town of Marmande. For no very good reason its reds and whites have been accorded the V.D.Q.S. seal, and the name Côtes du Marmandais.

MARQUE — (Mark) — Simply means brand, in French; *marque deposée* means registered trademark. A *vin de marque* is a wine sold under a trade name rather than a regional or vineyard name; it can be anything and come from anywhere. No such wine is entitled to an *Appellation Contrôlée,* nor to the V.D.Q.S. seal.

MARQUÉS DE MURRIETA — (Mar-*case* day Moo-ree-*A*-ta) — One of the better-known Spanish Riojas, produced by the family of this name on their estate at Ygay, just east of Logroño. As is usually the case in this part of the world, the red wine is distinctly better than the dry white, though both are long-lived.

MARQUÉS DE RISCAL — (Mar-*case* day *Reece*-cahl) — One of the best red wines of the Rioja and of Spain, produced on family estates in an oddly named village, Elciego, "The Blind Man," not far from Haro, but in the Province of Álava rather than Logroño. It can stand comparison with many far more famous wines of France.

MARQUIS-D'ALESME-BECKER, Château — (Mar-*kee*-Dal-*lem*-*Beck*-kair) — 3rd Classed Growth of Margaux. About 2,000 cases a year.

MARQUIS-DE-TERME, Château — (Mar-kee-duh-Tairm) — 4th Classed Growth of Margaux, Médoc. Today one of the best of the 4th Growths, producing about 7,500 cases a year of light, "tender," fine-textured Claret.

MARSALA — (Mar-sahl-la) — The best known of Italian fortified wines, 17% to 19% alcohol by volume, amber in color, occasionally dry but more often somewhat sweet, roughly comparable to Sherry. It takes its name from the city of Marsala in western Sicily, around which it is produced, and was originally made during the latter half of the 18th century by a few English families (Woodhouse, Ingham, etc.) in an attempt to create a less expensive substitute for the Spanish and Portuguese wines which were then at the height of their popularity in England. The zone of production is today strictly delimited, and only certain grape varieties (the Grillo, Catarratto and Inzolia) may be used. Like Sherry, Marsala in its original state (*Marsala vergini*) is a dry wine, brought up to 17% or 18% by fortification with high-proof grape brandy, and then to the desired degree of sweetness by the addition of an extremely sweet, concentrated grape juice, called either *sifone* or *mosto cotto*, depending on how it was made.

Marsalas are divided into a number of specific categories, each legally defined, as follows: 1. "*Italia*" (also called *Marsala fini*, or *Italia particolare*, or I.P.), which must contain 17% alcohol and 5% grape sugar — these are the lightest and least expensive; 2. *Marsala superiori* (also S.O.M. or L.P., and formerly "*Inghilterra*") which must contain 18% alcohol — these may be either sweet or dry, must contain 10% grape sugar if sweet, but little sugar or none if classified as dry; most of the Marsala that is exported falls in this class; finally, 3. *Marsala vergini* (also called "*Solera*"), bone dry, 18% wines, aged and blended in *soleras,* like the Sherries of Spain, and entirely unsweetened. In addition, various apéritifs and "tonic" wines are produced with a Marsala base, *Marsala all' uovo* (with egg), *Marsala chinato* (with quinine), etc.

MARSANNAY or MARSANNAY-LA-CÔTE — (*Mar*-san-nay) — Village on the Côte de Dijon, in Burgundy; its wine, Rosé de Marsannay, made from the Pinot Noir grape, is one of the lightest, freshest and most delightful *vins rosés* of France. A small quantity of interesting white wine is also produced, and sold under its euphonious varietal name, as Chardonnay-de-Marsannay, and a most agreeable red wine, often labeled Pinot Noir de Marsannay.

MARTIGNY — (Mar-teen-ye) — Swiss town southeast of Lake Geneva; with Sion, the principal center of the wine trade in the district known as the Valais (*see*).

MARTILLAC — (Mar-tee-yack) — Important wine-producing village in the French Graves district, its red wines on the whole better than its white. These, firm sturdy wines that mature rather slowly, include Châteaux Smith-Haut-Lafitte, Haut-Nouchet, Latour-Martillac, Lagarde, Ferran, etc.

MARTINI, Louis M. — One of the leading producers of premium wine in California. The large, modern winery is at St. Helena, in the Napa Valley, and was constructed in 1933: there are three vineyards, one just south of St. Helena, adjoining Beaulieu; another, south of Napa, was known as La Loma in pre-Prohibition days; the third and most remarkable, now called Monte Rosso and planted in the 1880's, is high up in the Mayacamas hills, in Sonoma County. In addition to the usual collection of California "generics" (Chablis, Dry Sauterne, Rhine Wine, Burgundy, Claret, Chianti, etc.) Louis Martini produces a number of varietal wines that rank with California's best: Cabernet Sauvignon, Pinot Noir, a Barbera which is perhaps superior to any made in Italy, a first-rate Johannisberg Riesling, an interesting Folle Blanche, White Pinot, Sylvaner, Dry Semillon, etc. There is also an extremely good dry Sherry.

MARYLAND — The state has one interesting winery. *See* Boordy Vineyard.

MARZEMINO — (Mar-zay-*me*-no) — Superior wine grape, used in northern Italy in the production of red and *rosé* wines. *See* Isera, Chiaretto.

MASCARA — (*Mosk*-ka-ra) — Extremely full-bodied, deep-colored red wine (legally, but rarely, *rosé* and white as well) produced in a delimited district near Oran, in Algeria. On account of its high alcohol (13-15½%), its body, color and softness, it is in great demand as a blending wine, and despite all the regulations forbidding such practices, some of it unquestionably finds its way into the cheaper, commercial Bordeaux and Burgundies.

MASSON, Paul — Colorful Frenchman, born in Burgundy, who immigrated to California, married the daughter of Charles Lefranc, the owner and co-founder (1852) of Almadén Vineyards. He later created his own brand of California Champagne, made largely from grapes on his father-in-law's vineyard, planted additional vineyards, built what he termed his "chateau" at Saratoga nearby, and after, by all accounts, a merry and fruitful life, died in 1940. His most recently planted vineyard, high up on the hills back of Saratoga, was purchased in 1936, together with the brand name, by a San José stockbroker, Martin Ray; then resold, not long after America's entry in World War II, to the Seagram Company, and finally transferred to its present owners, the Paul Masson Company, now one of the largest premium wine producers of California.

Perhaps the most extraordinary feature of all this is that the owners of three distinct and competing wineries now claim 1852 as their founding date: Almadén, since they now own the acres where Charles Lefranc planted his first grapes in 1852 plus the farmhouse (now one of the most charming country homes in California) where he lived; Martin Ray, since he bought the Paul Masson Champagne Company and a vineyard planted in the 1880's, and despite the fact that he later resold both; the Paul Masson Company, since they own the name and label, and since the old labels used to carry the words: "Vineyards Established 1852."

MATARÓ — (Mah-tar-*ro*) — Productive, rather common red wine grape of Spanish or French origin (it is called the Mourvèdre in France, and permitted in Châteauneuf-du-Pape, although not widely grown there). Extensively planted in California, it generally gives a rather coarse wine and ranks hardly on a par with the Carignan. There is also a town of this name just north of Barcelona, but if this is indeed the original home of the vine in question, the good people of Mataró, let it be noted to their credit, have never said so.

MATEUS — Popular brand of Portuguese table wine which has acquired wide acceptance in America. It is shipped in flagons and is, in fact, a somewhat sweet *rosé*.

MAUPERTUIS — (Mo-pair-twee) — Name formerly given to one particular portion of the Clos de Vougeot, now quite without any legal meaning although the name still occasionally appears on Clos de Vougeot labels.

MAURY — (Mo-ree) — Subdivision of Grand Roussillon (*see*), a vineyard district northwest of Perpignan, in the French eastern Pyrenees; it produces over a half million gallons a year of sweet, fortified *vin de liqueur*, made mostly from the Grenache grape.

MAVRODAPHNE — Greek name for one of the best-known red wine grapes of the Balkans and the Eastern Mediterranean, known in other countries by its more common name of Mavroud. The best Greek table wines shipped to the United States and some sweet, Port-type wines as well often carry this varietal name.

MAXIMIN GRÜNHAUS — (Max-ee-mean Grune-haus) — Tiny village and famous vineyard on the Ruwer, in the Moselle district of Germany, which produces, though only in good years, white wines of the very highest class. There are 120 acres under vines, most of them forming a single domain, that of the Von Schubert family; the labels usually carry an additional indication of vineyard plot, as Maximin Grünhäuser Herrenberg, Bruderberg, etc. In 1921 and again in 1959, the estate produced a collection of *hochfeine* Auslese, *hochfeinste* Auslese, Beerenauslese, and the like, unsurpassed in Germany.

MAYACAMAS — Range of wooded hills, of volcanic origin, running from north to south and separating the Napa and Sonoma valleys, in California. There are many vineyards along the lower slopes, on both sides, and a few high up in the hills — Mont La Salle (*see*), one called Monte Rosso, planted in the 1880's and belonging to Louis M. Martini (*see*), and finally the Mayacamas Vineyards, a small, family affair, established in 1941 by Mr. and Mrs. Jack Taylor, which produces an excellent white wine from the Chardonnay grape.

210

MAY WINE — Originally a German specialty: a sweetened, light white wine flavored with the aromatic leaves of the herb *Waldmeister*, or woodruff. It is served well-chilled, in a bowl, with spring fruits, traditionally strawberries, floating in it. Very passable May Wine is now made in the United States.

MAZIS-CHAMBERTIN — (*Mahz*-zi *Shawm*-bair-tan) — Admirable red Burgundy, and the 31-acre vineyard from which it comes, directly adjoining Chambertin-Clos de Bèze (*see*) on the north; a firm, big wine, slow-maturing but of unmistakable class, not far from Chambertin itself in quality.

MAZOYÈRES-CHAMBERTIN — (Mahz-zoy-*yare Shawm*-bair-tan) — Largest vineyard (47 acres) of Gevrey-Chambertin, ranked as a *Grand Cru*; its excellent red wine, an outstandingly fine red Burgundy.

MÉDOC — (*May*-dawk) — Triangle of land, world-famous for its red wines, extending some fifty miles north from Bordeaux, bounded on the west by the dunes and pine forests along the Atlantic, and on the east by the Gironde estuary. The good vineyards overlook or are near the estuary; they cover a strip of gently rolling, gravelly hills from six to ten miles wide, and their average production is not far from 2 million cases a year. This is a red wine district exclusively, and the few whites are entitled only to the appellations Bordeaux and Bordeaux Supérieur.

Wines labeled simply "Médoc" almost invariably come from the lower, sandier, less fine, northern third of the district (called the Bas-Médoc, although this is *not* a wine name); while never great, they are generally well-balanced Clarets of good quality and some breed. The Haut-Médoc (and this *is* an appellation — *see*) produces wines of a far higher class: they are sometimes sold under this name, but more often under one of the celebrated village or *commune* names — Margaux, Moulis, St. Julien, Pauillac, St. Estèphe — but most often of all under the label of a chateau. Well over half of the great Bordeaux chateaux (Lafite, Latour, Margaux, Mouton-Rothschild, the three Léovilles, the two Pichon-Longuevilles, Cos d'Estournel, Brane-Catnenac, Palmer, etc.) come from the Haut-Médoc, and even the lesser wines are outstanding.

To sum up, Médoc is a red wine appellation well above Bordeaux Rouge or Bordeaux Supérieur in quality, less good, since less limiting, than Haut-Médoc. However, even the least expensive Médoc must, according to French law, come from what is recognized as one of the best red wine districts of France, and be made from grape varieties (the Cabernets, Merlot, Malbec, etc.) second to none. It is or should be, therefore, very definitely a superior wine.

See map on following page.

MELETO — (May-lay-to) — One of the more famous estates in the Chianti Country; also part of the traditional holdings of the Ricasoli family. Its wine is somewhat lighter and earlier-maturing than that of Brolio (*see*).

211

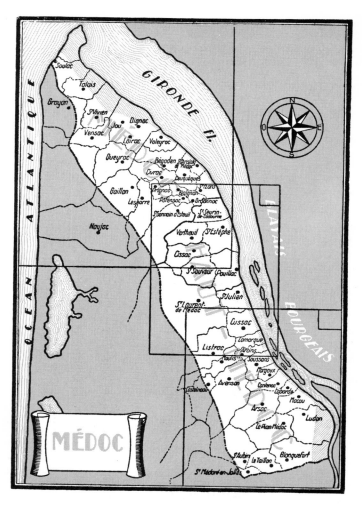

MELLOW — Mature, soft, ripe; without greenness or harshness. In many instances, somewhat sweet.

MELNIK — (Mel-nik) — Red, white and sparkling wines produced round the town of this name, in Czechoslovakia; hardly ever exported, but considered that country's best.

MELON — (Muh-lawn) — A white wine grape with a faint muscat flavor, known as the Muscadet (*see*) in the lower Loire Valley of France, where it produces the popular wine of that name. Also cultivated to a certain extent in Burgundy where its wine is of mediocre quality.

212

MENDOCINO — The northernmost of the so-called North Coast Counties of California. Its vineyards, mostly around Ukiah in the upper part of the Russian River Valley, produce very good red wines, Zinfandels especially. The whites, made principally from the Colombard and Sauvignon Vert, are of lesser quality.

MENDOZA — (Men-dos-sa) — Largest wine-producing province in Argentina, along the foothills of the Andes, west of Buenos Aires, and not far from the Chilean border.

MÉNETOU-SALON — (*Men*-A-too-*Sal*-lawn) — Interesting and attractive *vins de pays,* red, white and *rosé,* produced round the village of this name not far from Bourges, in central France. The red and *rosé* are made from the Pinot Noir, the white from the Sauvignon Blanc; there are only about 4,000 cases a year, but the name is now an *Appellation Contrôlée.*

MERANO — (May-rahn-no) — Resort town in the Italian Tyrol, known for its excellent local wines, such as *Küchelberger* (*see*).

MERCUREY — (*Mair*-coo-ray) — Best known and best red wine (a little less good white is made) of the Côte Chalonnaise, from the village of this name, northwest of the Chalon-sur-Saône, in Burgundy. It is made entirely from the Pinot Noir (or the Chardonnay, when white) and comparable to a rather light, secondary Burgundy of the Côte de Beaune.

MERCUROL — (*Mair*-coo-rawl) — Village in the central Rhône Valley and its fine, dry, white wine, formerly sold under the village name, now as Crozes-Hermitage (*see*).

MERLOT — (Mair-lo) — Distinguished red wine grape, nearly as important as the two Cabernets (*see*) in the Bordeaux Country, where it gives softness, fruit, grace and charm to many famous wines that would be less attractive without it. Early ripe and quite productive, yielding wines that are less astringent and sooner ready (if shorter lived) than the Cabernets, it is a variety that presents obvious temptations to the grower, and there are certainly vineyards and indeed districts in which it has been too widely planted. On the other hand, a judicious admixture of Merlot would certainly improve most, if indeed not all, Cabernet Sauvignons in California; one major planting exists, at Almadén's Paicines vineyard, but it is still too early to give a considered opinion as to its quality.

   The Merlot is planted and vinified alone in several of the better districts of northern Italy, especially the Alto Adige (*see*). There it yields a soft, round, eminently agreeable red wine, without much body or depth, but with a great deal of bouquet and fruit.

MESLAND — (May-lawn) — Fresh, fruity and attractive *vin rosé* made from the Gamay grape in the Loire Valley of France, between Blois and Tours. Its full and proper name is "Touraine-Mesland," the latter being the *commune* from which it comes.

MESNIL, Le — (Luh May-neel) — One of the best wine-producing villages of the Côte des Blancs, in the French Champagne Country, rated 99% (as against 100% for its two superiors, Cramant and Avize). White Chardonnay grapes are grown exclusively and the wine has great delicacy and breed.

METALLIC — Having a particular, acrid, unpleasant taste, not unlike greenness, which white wines sometimes acquire and red wines more rarely, possibly through contact with metal.

METHUSALEM — Variously spelled, an oversize Champagne bottle, holding as much as eight ordinary bottles.

MEUNIER — (*Munn*-yea) — Sub-variety of the Pinot Noir, a superior wine grape although far less remarkable than its distinguished cousin; it may no longer legally be cultivated in the better Burgundian vineyards but is still rather widely planted in the Champagne Country, in Alsace, and in California, where it is often confused with the Pinot Noir. The word *Meunier* in French means "miller," and this grape is called Pinot Meunier because the under-side of its leaf is whitish, as if it had been sprinkled with white dust, or flour.

MEURSAULT — (*Mere*-so) — Ancient wine-producing village of the Côte d'Or, in Burgundy (its name is supposed to derive from the Latin *Muris Saltus*, meaning Leap of the Mouse, though for no very plausible reason). After Pommard, two miles to the north, its annual production is the largest of any *commune* of the Côte, averaging about 150,000 gallons, practically all of it white. The vastly greater part of this is made from the Chardonnay grape, although the Pinot Blanc is also authorized, and the best of it, of course, carries a vineyard name as well as the general appellation Meursault. Leading vineyards, in about this order of quality, include: Perrières (42 acres), Genevrières (42 acres), Charmes (69 acres), Blagny (5 acres), La Pièce-sous-le-Bois (28 acres), Dos d'Ane (7 acres), Poruzot (24 acres), Jennelotte (12 acres), Bouchères (10 acres), Goutte d'Or (14 acres). Even the lesser Meursaults are white Burgundies of high quality and real distinction; the finer ones are surpassed by only a few great rarities among the dry white wines of France. Green-gold in color, full-bodied but racy, rather high in alcohol but well-balanced, dry but not at all austerely so, they are remarkable, and fully merit their fame.

MEXICO — As might be expected, our southern neighbor, Mexico, has a climate poorly suited to wine-growing, since a good part of its area is actually in the Tropic Zone, and even its northernmost corner, near San Diego, is as far south as Egypt. Vines are nevertheless grown, more for table grapes than for wine, in many provinces of Mexico, particularly in Lower California and in some of the higher central states where the prevailing weather is somewhat cooler on account of the altitude. By international, or even California standards, Mexican wines, however, are rarely of even passable quality; probably the best are those produced round the old Spanish Mission of Santo Tomás at

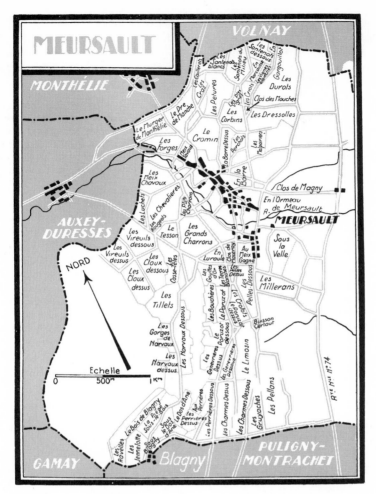

Ensenada on the Pacific, just south of the U.S. border. These, today, are well-made, sound, ordinary wines with no real distinction — the reds generally better than the whites. Other grape-growing districts of some importance are in the states of Durango, Coahuila and Chihuahua. Total production amounts to less than a million gallons a year.

MIDI — (Me-dee) — In French, means both 12 M., Noon, and, in a general sense, the South — an *accent du Midi* is a French Southern accent. It is a rather more specific term when applied to wine: the Rhône Valley is excluded, so are both Provence and the Côte d'Azur. A *vin du Midi* is commonly understood to mean an ordinary table wine produced along the Mediterranean Coast of France, between Nîmes, Carcassonne and the Spanish border. *See* also Languedoc.

MILAZZO — (Me-*lotz*-zo) — One of the better red wines of Sicily, made round the town of this name, west of Messina, from the Nocera grape.

MILDE — (*Mil*-duh) — German wine taster's term, meaning pleasantly soft, possibly a bit sweet, rather lacking in character.

MILDEW — A grave malady of the vine caused by a virus or fungus; also called the *peronospora* or *mosaic,* and related to the *oidium.* Of American origin, this was introduced into Europe accidentally about the middle of the 19th century and produced almost as serious damage as the *phylloxera* which arrived a few years later. Within limits, it can now be controlled through the use of copper sulphate sprays or flowers of sulphur in powder form.

MILLÉSIME — (*Meal*-lay-*seem*) — French for date or year; vintage, when applied to wine. A wine that is *millésimé* (meal-*lay*-see-*may*) is one marked with its vintage.

MINERVOIS — (Me-nair-vwah) — With Corbières, about the best of the not particularly distinguished wines of the French Midi — often an agreeable, full-bodied, well-balanced red table wine, far from bad, deserving the V.D.Q.S. seal which it is entitled to bear. The delimited production zone is the hilly country west and northwest of Narbonne; the authorized grape varieties are the ordinary ones of Languedoc — Grenache, Cinsault, Carignan, etc.; white and *rosé* wines may also be called Minervois, but these are much less good.

MISE — (Meeze) — Literally, "putting"; but into bottles, or "bottling," when applied to wine. Thus *Mise du Château* means Chateau-Bottling, etc.

MISE DU CHÂTEAU — (Meeze due Shat-toe) — *See* Chateau-Bottled.

MISSION — First of the European vinifera vines to reach California, this is a red wine grape of only fair quality at best, brought in during the early years of the 19th century by Franciscan monks and planted around their missions — whence, presumably, its name. Although unquestionably of European origin, it has never been further identified and some have believed it to be a seedling, or inadvertent cross. It gives a poor table wine and, when used for Port, a wine often deficient in color; its main use is for Angelica (*see*), which is hardly a recommendation, but it nevertheless ranks sixth in total acreage among wine grapes in California.

MISSION-HAUT-BRION, Château La — (Shat-toe La *Me*-see-awn-O-*Bree*-awn) — 1st Growth of Pessac, Graves. Directly opposite Haut-Brion, on the Bordeaux-Arcachon road, La Mission-Haut-Brion is second only to its illustrious neighbor among the vineyards and red wines of Graves. It was created in the 17th century by a religious order, the "Prêcheurs de la Mission" (whence its name); its 40 acres annually produce some 4,500 cases of wine. This, which generally brings a somewhat higher price than the 2nd Classed Growths of the Médoc, is a truly admirable Claret, velvety, generous and fine; lighter and earlier maturing than Haut-Brion, it is in the same noble class.

MITTELBERGHEIM — (Mit-tel-*bairg*-heim) — Important wine-producing village in Alsace, not far from Barr, in the *département* of Bas-Rhin. Fairly good wines which should not be confused with the decidedly better ones of Bergheim, in the Haut-Rhin some twenty miles further south.

MITTELHAARDT — *See* Haardt.

MITTEL-MOSEL — *See* Moselle.

MITTELWIHR — (Mit-tel-veer) — Little Alsatian vineyard town, almost totally destroyed in World War II; completely rebuilt, it is again producing wines of better than average quality.

MOELLEUX — (Mwah-luh) — French wine tasters' term applied usually to white wines which, while not sweet, are emphatically not bone dry; "mellow" is a poor, imprecise English equivalent — a wine may "mellow" but does not become *moelleux* with time; essentially, the sweetness of a *moelleux* wine is the sort of sweetness we mean when we say, "sweet as a nut." Literally, the French word means "marrowy."

MOLDY — Having the unpleasant odor and flavor which mold usually (but by no means always) imparts to grapes and the wines made from them. This is far more likely to be present in red wines than in white, since mold attacks the skins first of all and since, in the making of red wine, the skins are fermented with the juice; it can be the result of hail just prior to the vintage, but more often it is brought on by warm, humid weather during the ripening season: in this case it is practically identical with rot. *See Pourriture Noble.*

MOLINARA — (Mo-lee-*nar*-ra) — Superior Italian red wine grape, used especially in Valpolicella (*see*) and Bardolino.

MOLSHEIM — (Maulz-heim) — Busy, small town near Strasbourg in northern Alsace; wines of superior but not exceptional quality.

MONBAZILLAC — (Mawn-*baz*-zee-yak) — Soft, rather common, sweet white wine, produced east of Bordeaux in the *département* of the Dordogne. It is made mostly from the Semillon grape, plus a little Muscadelle, and is usually between 13% and 14% in alcohol. The vineyards are on rolling hills south of Bergerac; their total production is not far from 1½ million gallons a year.

MONDEUSE — (Mawn-duhz) — Superior if not outstanding French red wine grape, widely grown in the Savoie and the upper Rhône Valley east of Lyon, to some small extent in California. It gives a rather fruity wine of definite character, and makes a superior *rosé* (*see* Montagnieu). A less interesting white variety also exists.

MONFERRATO — (Mawn-fair-*rot*-toe) — Perhaps the finest wine district of Italy, and certainly one of the great wine regions of the world, although few bottles, if any, ever carry the name. It consists of a country of rather steep, rolling hills, some sixty miles by forty, directly south of the wide, fertile Po River valley, in Italian Piedmont: the provinces of Alessandria and Asti, plus part of Cuneo and part of Turin. Its statistics are impressive — the little province of Alessandria produces more table wine than California, Asti more sparkling wine than the United States. Almost all of the wines for which Piedmont is famous (Barolo, Barbaresco, Freisa, Grignolino, Gavi, Cortese) come from its hillside vineyards, and its Moscato di Canelli (*see*) is the base of most Asti Spumante and most Italian Vermouth.

MONICA — (Mo-*nee*-ca) — Sweet, red wine, made from the grape of the same name, near Cagliari, on the Italian island of Sardinia. Somewhat on the order of a light Port, generally about 17% alcohol.

MONIGA — (Mo-*nee*-ga) — Village on the southwestern shore of Lake Garda (*see*), producing an excellent fresh *rosé* wine, only occasionally marketed under the village name, usually as Chiaretto (*see*).

MONOPOLE — (*Mawn*-o-pole) — Entirely meaningless term sometimes used on wine labels in connection with a brand name. It is in no sense related to the wine's origin or its quality.

MONT — (Mawn) — Pleasant, fresh dry white *vin de pays,* produced not far from the Château de Chambord, in the Loire Valley; sometimes called Mont-près-Chambord, and sometimes Cour-Cheverney, it may carry the V.D.Q.S. seal.

MONTAGNE-SAINT-EMILION — (Mawn-*tan*ya-Sant-A-*me*-lee-awn) — Important wine-producing *commune* adjoining St. Emilion (*see*) on the northeast. Its sturdy red wines are of good quality, and if they lack the distinction and the velvety softness of the St. Emilions proper, they are correspondingly less expensive, and often excellent values. The better known Châteaux include: Roudier, Montaiguillon, des Tours, Negrit, Plaisance, La Bastienne, Moulin-Blanc, etc.

MONTAGNIEU — (Mawn-tan-yuh) — *Rosé*, white and (rarely) red wine produced in a district known as the Bugey, in the upper Rhône Valley between Lyon and Geneva. Fresh, light and attractive, often *pétillant,* or slightly sparkling, it has made many friends, especially at the Ostellerie du Vieux Pérouges, near Lyon, where it is featured. As a commercial wine, it hardly exists, but is entitled to the V.D.Q.S. seal.

MONTAGNY — (*Mawn*-tan-ye) — In general, with Rully (*see*), the best white wine of the Côte Chalonnaise, in Burgundy. Made from the Chardonnay grape, dry, fresh, light and clean-tasting, it deserves to be better known.

MONTS-DE-MILIEU — (*Mawn*-duh-*Meel*-yuh) — One of the very best *Premier Cru* vineyards of Chablis, in the *communes* of Fyé and Fleys; like Montée de Tonnerre (*see*), it is almost deserving of *Grand Cru* rank.

MONTÉE DE TONNERRE — (*Mawn*-tay du Taw-*nair*) — Perhaps the very best of the *Premier Cru* vineyards of Chablis, giving a wine of great distinction and bouquet which possibly deserves *Grand Cru* rank. The name comes from the road that climbs up and over the hill to the nearby town of Tonnerre, and has nothing to do with thunder.

MONTEFIASCONE — (Mawn-tay-fee-ass-*co*-nay) — Small town north of Rome, near Lake Bolsena, where the celebrated Moscatello wine called Est Est Est (*see*) is produced.

MONTEPULCIANO — (Mawn-tay-pul-*chon*-no) — Red wine from southern Tuscany, in Italy, produced round the picturesque old hill town of this name. Of only passable quality today, it was extravagantly praised by the English poet, Leigh Hunt, in the early 19th century, as "the king of wines," echoing the earlier opinion of the wine-loving author-physician Dr. Francesco Redi, in his *Bacco in Toscana*. It is not, oddly enough, made from the Montepulciano grape (which is a good red wine variety of southern Italy) but from the Mammolo and San Gioveto (*see* Chianti).

MONTHÉLIE — (*Mawn*-tay-lee) — Tiny village back of Volnay, on the Côte de Beaune, in Burgundy. Its red wines, usually labeled Monthélie or Monthélie-Côte de Beaune, are among the best of the less known Burgundies, certainly superior to many Pommards, and are worth looking for, since they are generally inexpensive.

MONTILLA — (Mawn-tee-ya) — Excellent, unusual, and all too little known wine, produced in a district of arid, chalky hills, round the villages of Montilla and Los Moriles, south of Cordoba, in Spain. Until recently a large part of the production was shipped to Jerez and sold as Sherry, and the term Amontillado basically means a Sherry of the Montilla type, a "Montilla'd" wine; this operation is no longer legal, and Montilla-Los Moriles is now the proud possessor of an appellation of its own. Its main difference from Sherry lies in the fact that it is rarely if ever fortified; made from the Pedro Ximénez grape grown on upland vineyards under a relentless sun, it has 15-16% of natural alcohol by volume, and even more when old. Like Sherry, it is made with flor yeasts, stored in ventilated *bodegas,* blended in *soleras.* During its youth, however, it is kept not in wood, but in huge earthenware jars, or *tinajas,* shaped like Roman amphoras, higher than a man. Like Sherry, it has its Finos and its Olorosos, though few of the latter and these rarely sweetened; what is ordinarily sold is a very pale, clean, dry wine, possibly with less breed and bouquet than a first-class Fino Sherry or a Manzanilla, but perhaps pleasanter and easier to drink since it has not been fortified. It is served chilled both as an apéritif and as a table wine, especially with *mariscos,* or shellfish; there are those, including the author of these pages, who think it better with clams or oysters than any other wine, including Chablis.

MONT LA SALLE — Principal California vineyard of The Christian Brothers (*see*), high up in the hills northwest of Napa. It takes its name from the founder of the Order, Jean Baptiste de La Salle.

MONTLOUIS — (Mawn-lou-we) — Village almost directly across the Loire from Vouvray, in France. Its white wines made, like Vouvray, from the Chenin Blanc grape, were legally sold as Vouvray until 1938 and are of substantially the same quality today; they are usually somewhat cheaper, given equal quality, being less known. Total production amounts to some 350,000 gallons a year.

MONTPEYROUX — (Mawn-*pay*-roo) — Red and *rosé* wine of better than average quality, produced in the hilly country north of Béziers, in the French Midi. It carries the V.D.Q.S. seal.

MONTRACHET — (Mawn-rasch-*shay*) — Extraordinary 18½-acre vineyard of the Côte d'Or, in Burgundy, producing the most celebrated and expensive dry white wine of France. Just over half of its area lies within the communal limits of Puligny-Montrachet (*see*), the rest in Chassagne-Montrachet: it has given its name to both villages, as well as to a few specific, small plots of vines which directly adjoin it, notably Chevalier-Montrachet and Batard-Montrachet (*see*). Its wine, like all of the finest white Burgundies, is made entirely from the Chardonnay grape, and the total production amounts to hardly over a thousand cases a year. The name is said to come from the Latin *Mons rachicensis*, which became *Mont-Rachat,* or "Bald-Hill"; the first "t" is still silent (as well as the last), and the barren hilltop behind the stony vineyards is covered with thin scrub and almost "bald," even today. The vineyard itself is nevertheless probably the most valuable agricultural land in France, despite its small yield per acre, and its wine, rivaled in Burgundy only by that of its immediate neighbors, is wholly remarkable. Pale gold in color, with a hint of green, high in alcohol (rarely under 13%), with tremendous bouquet, flavor and class, dry but with an underlying trace of luscious softness, especially in good years, it is, as someone has said, "not so much a wine as an experience."
For Map, *see* PULIGNY, CHASSAGNE.

MONTRAVEL — (Mawn-ra-*vel*) — Vineyard district in southeastern France and its rather undistinguished, semi-sweet, golden wine. The vineyards are on the north bank of the Dordogne, upstream (east) from St. Emilion, and although the production zone is bounded on three sides by the Bordeaux Country, Montravel is *not* entitled to the name "Bordeaux," and is marketed as Côtes de Montravel, Haut-Montravel, or simply Montravel. Made mostly from the Semillon grape, it is properly classified as a Vin de Bergerac (*see*), like Monbazillac, Côtes de Duras etc., which it much resembles.

MONTROSE, Château — (Mawn-rose) — 2nd Classed Growth of St. Estèphe, Haut-Médoc. One of the firmest and sturdiest of the great Médoc Clarets, deep-colored, slow-maturing, long-lived; its quality has improved considerably in the last few years. Production amounts to some 10,000 cases a year.

MOORE'S DIAMOND — Native, Eastern white grape, giving a rather spicy, tart, pale wine, developed in the 1860's near Lake Keuka by

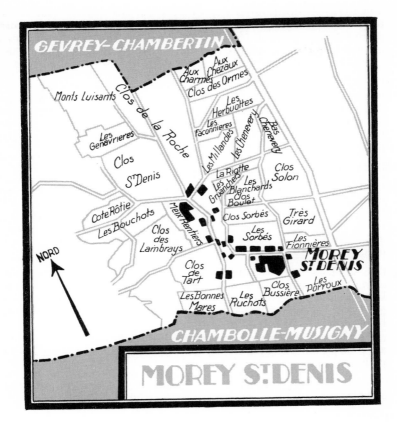

Jacob Moore, and still planted to some extent in the Finger Lakes vine-yards.

MÓR — (Mor) — Town and district in Hungary, not far from Budapest, producing a full-bodied, golden wine from the Ezerjo grape, called Mori Ezerjo.

MOREY-SAINT-DENIS — (*Mor*-ray San Day-*nee*) — Burgundian village on the Côte de Nuits, producing a number of red wines of the very highest class, firm, sturdy and long-lived. Its best vineyards include a portion of Bonnes Mares, the Clos de la Roche, the Clos St. Denis, the Clos de Tart and the Clos des Lambrays; the wines from these, however, are generally sold under the vineyard, rather than the village, name. What is labeled Morey-St. Denis is of a somewhat less exalted class, often equally full-bodied with less distinction. A little white wine of second quality is also produced in the *climat* known as Monts-Luisants.

MORGEOT — (Mor-jo) — Vineyard or district name, traditionally given to certain excellent red and white Burgundies produced in the southern part of the *commune* of Chassagne-Montrachet (*see*). The precise area entitled to the appellation is now in dispute and awaiting a final decision by the French courts.

MORGON — (*Mor*-gawn) — One of the best and yet least typical red wines of the Beaujolais, and the village from which it comes. It is less fruity than other wines of its district, matures less quickly and takes on, with time, an odd, marked resemblance to the Burgundies of the Côte d'Or. Local experts say of any Beaujolais which evolves this way, that "*il morgonne*," or it is developing like the wine of Morgon.

MORILES, Los — (Loze Mo-ree-lace) — *See* Montilla.

MOROCCO — Former French Protectorate in North Africa, now an independent country, producing largely for its European population some ten million gallons of wine a year. The best of this comes from round Meknes and is a pleasant, ordinary red wine, surprisingly light and good for one grown at this southern latitude. It is rarely, if ever, exported.

MOSCATEL — (Maws-cah-tel) — Portuguese version of Muscat or Muscatel. That produced at Setubal, southeast of Lisbon, ranks among the very finest wines of its type in the world — very sweet, deep amber in color, with an overwhelming fruit and bouquet and flavor. It is of course fortified.

This is also the Spanish spelling, and Moscatels of varying quality are produced in many parts of Spain, those of Sitges and Málaga being perhaps the best.

MOSCATELLO — (Mos-cot-*tel*-lo) — Sub-variety of the Muscat grape. *See* Moscato.

MOSCATO — (Mos-*cot*-toe) — Italian word for Muscat, a variety of grape, or family of grapes (for there are literally dozens of subvarieties); also, the widely different wines made from these, in all parts of Italy. One of them, the Aleatico (*see*) is red; the others white. They include sparkling wines — Asti Spumante (*see*), for example, many dessert wines, and even a few dry or semi-dry white table wines. They all have, to a greater or lesser degree, a characteristic and unmistakable bouquet and flavor. The better known are as follows: the MOSCATO DI CANELLI, or Moscatello, which takes its name from the village of Canelli, near Asti, where it gives an extremely aromatic, pale, sweet white wine, low in alcohol, used in Asti Spumante and Italian Vermouth; the same or a very similar subvariety produces the Est Est Est (*see*) of Montefiascone. The MOSCATO GIALLO of the Trentino and Alto Adige (*see*) is a distinguished, natural white wine, about as sweet as Sauternes, with 13% to 15% alcohol. The true dessert wines (15% to 17% alcohol, extremely sweet) are the MOSCATO DI CAGLIARI (from Sardinia), the MOSCATO DI PANTELLERIA (from a small island between

MOSEL-SAAR-RUWER

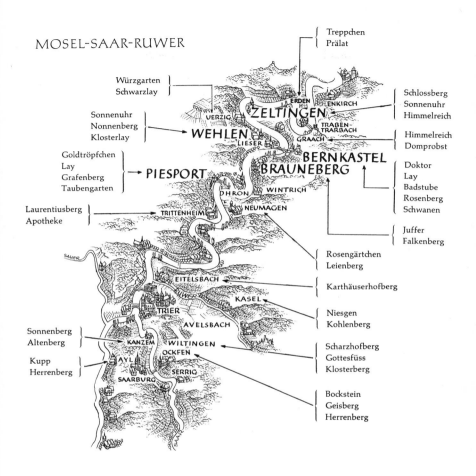

Treppchen
Prälat

Würzgarten
Schwarzlay

Schlossberg
Sonnenuhr
Himmelreich

Sonnenuhr
Nonnenberg
Klosterlay

Himmelreich
Domprobst

Goldtröpfchen
Lay
Grafenberg
Taubengarten

Doktor
Lay
Badstube
Rosenberg
Schwanen

Laurentiusberg
Apotheke

Juffer
Falkenberg

Rosengärtchen
Leienberg

Karthäuserhofberg

Niesgen
Kohlenberg

Sonnenberg
Altenberg

Scharzhofberg
Gottesfüss
Klosterberg

Kupp
Herrenberg

Bockstein
Geisberg
Herrenberg

Sicily and Tunisia), the MOSCATO DI SIRACUSA (from Syracuse, in Sicily), the MOSCATO DI TRANI (from near Bari, in southern Italy), etc. There are many others.

MOSEL — (Mo-z'l) — German version of Moselle (*see*). The wine district is officially called Mosel-Saar-Ruwer, and this is the designation that appears on wine labels.

MOSELBLÜMCHEN — (*Mo*-z'l-*blim*-shen) — What the Germans, who are the only ones to use it, called a *Fantasie-Name*, a quite meaningless wine name — in English, "Little-Moselle-Flower." Usually a blend of the very cheapest wines of the Moselle Valley, almost always "sugared," never estate-bottled.

MOSELLE — (Mo-*zell*) — (In German, MOSEL, pronounced *Mo*-z'l) — The Moselle River rises in France, skirts the little Grand Duchy of Luxembourg, and then winds for nearly a hundred miles down one of the most beautiful valleys of western Germany, from Trier to where it joins the Rhine at Coblenz. Even in France there are a few vineyards along its banks (*see* Lorraine), and others of greater extent in Luxembourg (*see*), but those of real consequence and international fame are all in Germany. Officially, the wine district is called Mosel-Saar-Ruwer (the latter being two of the Moselle's small tributaries); there are some 20,000 acres under vines, of which perhaps one quarter yield superior wine, and the average annual production is not far from 10 million gallons.

Approximately at the latitude of Winnipeg, these are the northernmost commercial vineyards in the world; they are planted on unimaginably steep hillsides, on unfertile, slate soil, and the Riesling grape is grown almost exclusively. Apart from the wines of the two tributary valleys, the Saar and Ruwer (and these can be admirable), all of the best Moselles come from one central section of the main valley, the Mittel-Mosel, extending from Trittenheim some forty miles to Traben-Trarbach. Thin, tart, even acid in poor vintage years, Moselle wines at their best are perhaps the most delicate, the most fragrant and most distinguished of all white wines. They rarely exceed 11% of alcohol by volume, and often have substantially less; pale, flowery, spicy, with great breed, they are like no other wines on earth.

The finer Moselles carry on their labels, with a few rare exceptions, the name of a village, plus that of a specific vineyard, as Wehlener Sonnenuhr, from the town of Wehlen; Bernkasteler Doktor, from the town of Bernkastel; Ockfener Bockstein, from the Bockstein vineyard in the town of Ockfen. Most of them are estate-bottled, and their labels so state. The higher grades often carry an indication of late-picking (*Spätlese* — *see*), or of having been made from selected grapes (*Auslese, feine Auslese*, etc.— *see*).

What follows is a list of the best vineyard towns, with asterisks indicating their respective quality. Each of these towns will be found, together with the names of its best vineyards, in its alphabetical place in this encyclopedia.

Mittel-Mosel: *Trittenheim, *Neumagen, *Dhron, ***Piesport, *Wintrich, **Brauneberg, *Lieser, ***Bernkastel, ***Graach, ***Wehlen, ***Zeltingen, **Erden, **Uerzig, *Traben-Trarbach.

Saar: *Wawern, **Kanzem, ***Wiltingen, **Oberemmel, *Niedermennig, **Ayl, **Ockfen.

Ruwer: **Maximin Grunhaus, **Eitelsbach, *Casel, *Avelsbach.

Under American wine law, Moselle is considered a semi-generic name, and a California Moselle may legally be marketed, even if made from raisin grapes or table grapes. Fortunately, there seems to be little demand for such wines, which of course bear no resemblance to the German original, and the designation is now rarely used in the United States.

MOU — (Moo) — French wine taster's term meaning soft, flat, wholly lacking in character.

MOÛT — (Moo) — Must (*see*) in French — unfermented or fermenting grape juice up to the moment it becomes wine.

MOULIÈRES, Domaine des — (Mool-*yare*) — One of the better vineyards of Provence, northeast of Toulon, producing a *rosé* wine of excellent quality, shipped, like many others from this region, in a rather attractive, special, amphora-like bottle.

MOULIN-À-VENT — (*Moo*-lahn-ah-*Vawn*) — Generally ranked as the finest wine of the Beaujolais, and almost always the most expensive; certainly, by a considerable margin, the longest-lived. The vineyards are partly in the *commune* of Romanèche-Thorins and partly in Chenas (*see*); they cover the slopes of a round hill, crowned with the ancient *moulin-à-vent* or windmill, which gave the vineyard and the wine its name. A good Moulin-à-Vent of a good year can almost be classified as a great wine; deep-colored, sturdy, rather high in alcohol (usually over 13%), it "fills the mouth," as the French say, and, at the same time, has considerable breed and class.

MOULINET, Château — (*Moo*-lee-nay) — Small vineyard in the Pomerol district, little known, but producing an exceptionally good and typical red wine, velvety, round and fine. Some 4,000 cases a year.

MOULIS — (Moo-lee) — Sub-division of the Haut-Médoc (like Margaux, St. Julien, St. Estèphe, etc.) although the least famous and least important of these. It produces hardly any great wine at all, but, on the other hand, much that is good, dependable, well-balanced and not too expensive. The delimited zone comprises the township of Moulis and most of that of Listrac, plus portions of five others nearby, and the better Châteaux include: Chasse-Spleen and Poujeaux-Theil (both ranked as Crus Exceptionnels — *see*), and such good Bourgeois Growths as Poujeaux-Marly, Lestage-Darquier, Dutruch-Grand-Poujeaux, etc.

MOUNTAIN — Old English name for Malaga wine.
ALSO, in California, term used to designate wines from upland or hillside vineyards, rather than from irrigated, overly productive vines planted on the flat valley floor. Even if blended, non-varietal, and inexpensive, as "Mountain Red" and "Mountain White," these are on the whole better wines and better values than the common run. Although the word has not yet been strictly defined by law or regulation, an effort is being made by Federal and State authorities to limit its use to wines with some right to this description.

MOURASTEL — (Moor-ras-tel) — Undistinguished red wine grape, probably of French origin, grown to some extent in California, notably in

225

the Livermore Valley, where it yields a pleasant enough, soft but rather common wine. Also spelled Morrastel in the French Midi.

MOURVÈDRE — (Moor-vedr) — Red wine grape. *See* Mataró.

MOUSSEUX — (Moo-*suh*) — French word meaning foaming or effervescent; sparkling, when applied to wine. All French sparkling wines, no matter how produced, whether by the Champagne method, the Charmat process of fermentation in bulk, or even if simply carbonated (*gazéifié*) belong in this category of *Vins Mousseux*; Champagne, despite its obvious *mousse*, or foam, is never so listed or so described, it being considered in a class apart. The following French *mousseux*, and only these, carry an *Appellation Contrôlée* and are therefore certified, as to origin, by the French Government (all other names are brands): Anjou Mousseux, Arbois Mousseux, Blanquette de Limoux, Bordeaux Mousseux, Bourgogne Mousseux (Sparkling Burgundy), Clairette de Die, Côtes du Jura Mousseux, L'Étoile Mousseux, Gaillac Mousseux, Montlouis Mousseux, St. Péray Mousseux, Saumur Mousseux, Seyssel Mousseux, Touraine Mousseux and Vouvray Mousseux (Sparkling Vouvray).

MOUTON BARON PHILIPPE, Château — New name, since 1956, for what was previously Château Mouton-d'Armailhacq (see below); so called after its owner, Baron Philippe de Rothschild. Its production has been deliberately restricted and its wine today is certainly outstanding in its category. One of the very finest of the 5th Classed Growths.

MOUTON-D'ARMAILHACQ — (Moo-tawn-*Dar*-my-yock) — 5th Classed Growth of Pauillac, Haut-Médoc. One of the best of the 5th Growth Clarets, probably deserving a somewhat higher rank. It directly adjoins and forms part of the same property as Mouton-Rothschild. It took its name from a celebrated Monsieur d'Armailhacq, one of the great viticulturalists and wine experts of the 19th century, its then owner; its name has just recently been changed to Château Mouton-Baron-Philippe, after its present proprietor, Baron Philippe de Rothschild. It produces something less than 10,000 cases a year.

MOUTON-ROTHSCHILD, Château — (*Moo*-tawn-Rawt-sheeld) — World-famous Bordeaux vineyard and its magnificent red wine. Classified in 1855 as a 2nd Growth (albeit 1st of the 2nds), Mouton never fully accepted this lesser status, and its proud devise reads, "*Premier ne puis. Second ne daigne. Mouton suis.*" ("I cannot be a First. I do not deign to be a Second. I am Mouton.") Today its wines bring fully as high prices as the 1st Growths, and it is a First in all except official rank.

Its wine, perhaps the biggest, most powerful and most robust of the great Clarets, is made almost entirely from the Cabernet Sauvignon grape. Often a little astringent and harsh in its youth, it is slow-maturing, exceedingly long-lived, and develops with time an almost unmistakable special character of its own, great depth of flavor, fine balance and a splendid bouquet. It has been called, with Latour, the "manliest" of the red Bordeaux, and it is a superb wine by any standards.

MOUTONNE — (Moo-*tawnn*) — Formerly the commercial name under which a popular Chablis, produced by the Long-Depaquit family, was sold; since 1950 a specific *Grand Cru* Chablis coming from that family's 5¾ acre vineyard, most of it forming part of Chablis Vaudésir and a lesser portion part of Chablis Preuses.

MUID — (Mwee) — Old and far from specific French term for a small cask or large barrel, varying in meaning from one district to another — in fact, from 250 to 685 liters. Actually, the term *"demi-muid"* is often used in the Cognac Country for the 5-600 liter barrels in which Cognac is traditionally aged.

MULLED WINE — Red wine to which sugar, lemon peel, nutmeg, cloves and occasionally cinnamon have been added; heated and served hot.

MÜLLER-THURGAU — *(Mew*-lair-*Tour*-gau) — Widely-grown, productive German grape variety, one of many Riesling x Sylvaner crosses, yielding wines that tend to be short-lived, low in total acid, pleasing, soft, often a bit flat and dull.

MÜNSTER — (Min-ster) — One of the better wine-producing towns of the Nahe Valley, in Germany. Pittersberg, Dautenpflänzer and Langenberg are considered superior *Lagen*.

227

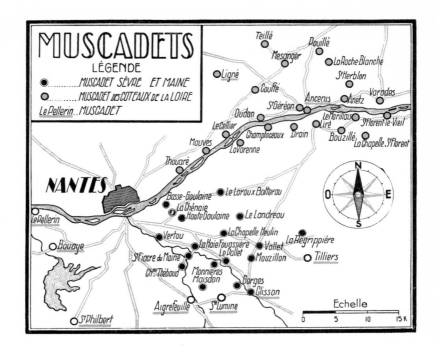

MUSCADETS

LÉGENDE

● ....*MUSCADET SÈVRE ET MAINE*

○ ....*MUSCADET DES COTEAUX DE LA LOIRE*

Le Pellerin..*MUSCADET*

Teillé · Pouillé · Mesanger · La Roche-Blanche · Ligné · St Herblon · Couffé · Varades · Ancenis · Anetz · St Géréon · Oudon · Le Marillais · St Florent-le-Vieil · Le Cellier · Liré · Champtoceaux · Drain · Bouzillé · La Chapelle St Florent · Mauves · La Varenne

Thouaré

NANTES

Basse-Goulaine · Le Loroux-Bottereau · La Chênaie · Haute Goulaine · Le Landreau · Le Pellerin · Vertou · La Chapelle Heulin · La Haie Fouassière · La Regrippière · St Fiacre du Maine · Le Pallet · Vallet · Tilliers · Chne Thébaud · Mouzillon · Monnières · Maisdon · Gorges · Clisson · Bouaye · Aigrefeuille · Ste Lumine · St Philbert

Echelle

0   5   10   15 K

MUSCADELLE — (*Mus*-cad-*del*) — White wine grape of the Bordeaux Country, where, however, it is never cultivated or vinified alone. Interplanted with the Semillon and Sauvignon Blanc, in a proportion never exceeding 5% or 10%, it gives a faint hint of agreeable Muscat flavor to most of the sweeter Bordeaux white wines, the Sauternes and Barsacs especially.

MUSCADET — (Muhs-cad-day) — Light white wine produced round the old Breton capital, Nantes, in the lower Loire Valley of France. The grape from which it comes is also known locally as the Muscadet, although its true name is the Melon, and as such it was brought from Burgundy to the Loire Valley some three centuries ago; a grape of little consequence or quality elsewhere, it yields, in this particular zone, a small, fresh, pale, agreeable, early-maturing wine, dry but generally not green or acid, with good fruit and a faint trace of almost muscat flavor. Up to twenty or thirty years ago it was regarded as little more than a *vin de pays*, a good, inexpensive, local wine; however, particularly since the last war, it has begun to enjoy an extraordinary vogue in Paris, throughout northern France, and even in the export trade. There are two principal producing areas: the so-called "Région de Sèvre-et-Maine," southeast of Nantes and including the important vineyard towns of

228

Vallet, Clisson, Vertou, St. Fiacre, Gorges and Louroux-Bottereau; and the Coteaux de la Loire (*see*), up the river to the northeast. The total production of Muscadet is in excess of 5 million gallons a year, almost all of it made by small peasant growers — although there are some 20,000 acres of vineyard, no single holding amounts to as much as fifty acres.

MUSCADINE — Native American family of vines, considered by most botanists a sub-genus of *vitis*. The Muscadines cannot be successfully crossed with, nor grafted on, other grape varieties, and there have been those who have gone so far as to say that they are not truly grapes at all, but a somewhat similar and related fruit. Nevertheless, wine from the Muscadine, especially from the Scuppernong, its best-known variety, has been made in the Carolinas, Florida and the Gulf States for several centuries, and at one time a single vine on Roanoke Island covered two acres of pergola and yielded 2,000 gallons of wine a year. The two main sorts of Muscadine are technically classified as *Rotundifolia* (on account of its round leaves) and *Munsoniana* (after T. V. Munson, one of the early American writers on grapes and wine). Muscadine wine has a pronounced and special flavor. Its juice requires the addition of considerable sugar to become wine at all and what it has yielded in the past could more properly be described as a sort of sweet, light cordial, with a pronounced special flavor, than as a proper, normal wine.

MUSCAT — Table, raisin and wine grape, of which literally scores of subvarieties exist, ranging all the way in color from pale yellow to blue-black, in quality from excellent to poor, in yield from prolific to shy-bearing; all, to a varying degree, have the special, characteristic, unmistakable Muscat odor and flavor, both as fresh grapes and as wine. Muscats of one sort or another are widely planted in Italy, southern France, Spain, Portugal, Greece, Tunisia, and on almost all of the Mediterranean islands, notably Sardinia, Sicily, Elba, Pantelleria, Cyprus, and the whole Aegean archipelago; also in Alsace, the Tyrol and Hungary; and, of course, very widely, in California.

A catalogue of the various sorts of Muscat would be of more interest to a botanist than to a wine drinker: of those that produce sweet, fortified wine, perhaps the worst is the productive Muscat of Alexandria (and of California); perhaps the best is the Muscat *doré* de Frontignan (*see*). Then there is the Aleatico (*see*), which gives a red dessert wine; the Muscadelle, used in Sauternes; the Muscat Ottonel of Alsace; the Moscatello responsible for Italy's Est Est Est, etc. — but the list is endless. *See* also, in this volume, Moscato, Moscatello, Moscatel, and Muscadelle, as well as under the names of the districts and countries mentioned above.

MUSIGNY — (*Moos*-een-ye) — One of the very greatest of red Burgundies, and the 25-acre vineyard from which it comes, directly above and behind the Clos de Vougeot, in the *commune* of Chambolle-Musigny (*see*), to which it has given its name. The total production is well under

2,000 cases a year (plus from 50 to 100 cases of an excellent dry white wine known as Musigny Blanc). In delicacy, distinction, and that indefinable combination of qualities often called "breed," Musigny is unsurpassed by any other red wine of the Côte d'Or, or indeed of the world, and equaled by few. Lighter and sometimes called "more feminine" than Chambertin, it belongs in the same noble and incomparable class and, especially since World War II, can easily hold its own against even Romanée-Conti.

MUST — Grape juice in the process of becoming wine.

MUSTY — Disagreeable odor and flavor which wines sometimes possess, generally due to the fact that the casks and the cellar itself have not been kept immaculately clean. It is related to moldy, but comes from a quite different cause, and experts can usually tell the two apart by tasting.

MUTÉ — (Mew-tay) — Unfermented or partially fermented wine, in which fermentation has been arrested, usually through the addition of high proof brandy. Widely used in the making of apéritifs and also for blending, in order to give sweetness and body to wines that need both.

N-O

NACKENHEIM — (*Nock*-en-heim) — One of the very best wine-producing towns of Rheinhessen, second in quality perhaps only to Nierstein. Its vineyards directly overlook the Rhine south of Mainz; the hillside soil is the color of brick and gives wines, both from the Riesling and Sylvaner, of exceptional fruit and bouquet and breed. Best *Lagen* include Rothenberg, Stiel, Engelsberg, Fenchelberg, Kapelle, Fritzenhöll.

NAHE — (Nah) — German river, tributary of the Rhine, which it joins at Bingen, opposite Rüdesheim. Further upstream, round Bad Kreuznach and beyond, the steep red sandstone hills are covered with vineyards, and the Nahe Valley is quite properly considered a major, separate, viticultural district; it has over 4,000 acres of vineyard and an annual production of about 2 million gallons. Much of this, made from the Riesling and the Sylvaner, is a long way from bad, and the Nahe wines on the whole deserve to be better known. In character they are like the good Niersteiners and Nackenheimers of Rheinhessen, with perhaps greater sprightliness. The most celebrated single vineyard, property of the German State, is Schloss Böckelheim (*see*), but there are others equally good round the valley's principal town, Kreuznach (or Bad Kreuznach) and in the villages of Niederhäuser, Norheim, Roxheim, Münster, Bretzenheim, Winzerheim and even one called, rather confusingly, Rüdesheim, which has no connection with its more famous namesake on the Rhine.

For Map, *see* GERMANY.

NAIRAC, Château — (Nay-rack) — 2nd Classed Growth of Barsac.

NANTES — (Nawnt) — Chief city of lower Brittany, on the Loire River near its mouth. A wide area of rolling hills nearby, especially to the southeast, produces the increasingly popular dry, white Muscadet (*see*), and another very pleasant, less famous dry white wine called Gros Plant (*see*).

NAPA — Celebrated California wine district, the valley and county of this name, northeast of San Francisco. The valley's lower end, south of the town of Napa, is on tidewater, and touches San Francisco Bay; the 1,800-foot summit of Mt. St. Helena, at its northern end, is often covered with snow as late as March — this, a famous landmark, was so named by a Russian princess after her patron saint, in pre-American days; it is an extinct or at least inactive volcano, and geysers and hot springs in the village of Calistoga at its foot, attest to the fact. The famous Silverado Trail, of which Robert Louis Stevenson wrote, runs up the east side of the valley, and vineyards have been planted on the gravelly valley floor and the adjoining foothills since before 1860.

Thus rich in history and tradition, Napa is also a strikingly beautiful bit of country, its vineyards running back into wooded hills, especially on the west, and a number of California's most renowned wineries are strung along or near the main road. These include Inglenook, Beaulieu, Louis M. Martini, Beringer Bros., Charles Krug, the so-called Greystone Winery of the Christian Brothers, and many smaller ones of considerable local fame — Mayacamas, Souverain, Schramsberg, Stony Hill — set back in the hills.

Essentially a district of table wines, Napa produces some of California's best, notably Cabernet Sauvignons that can stand comparison with many of the chateau wines of Bordeaux, sound Pinot Noirs and good Pinot Chardonnays, interesting wines from the Chenin Blanc (here often called, though wrongly, the White Pinot) and many others of the better varieties. Even on lesser and semi-generic wines such as Claret, Burgundy, Chablis and the like, an indication of Napa Valley origin is almost a guarantee of above average quality.

For Map, *see* CALIFORNIA.

NAPA GOLDEN CHASSELAS — Name sometimes given, though for no sensible reason, to the Palomino grape, in California; this of course is not a Chasselas at all, nor does it do particularly well in Napa.

NASCO — (Noss-co) — Superior white dessert wine from the island of Sardinia, produced near Cagliari.

NATURE — (Nah-tewr) — In French, a wine to which nothing has been added — i.e., in its natural state. Applied to Champagne (*see*) it is now practically synonymous with *brut*; until fairly recently, Champagne *Nature* meant still, or non-sparkling, Champagne; but this refreshing and charming dry wine must now legally be offered as *Vin Originaire de la Champagne Viticole* or as *Vin Nature de la Champagne*. Alas! the complications of modern life.

NATURWEIN — (Nah-*toor*-vine) — One of several terms which, on a German wine label, guarantee that the wine was made *without* the addition of sugar, before or during fermentation. All of the finer German wines are so made, including all estate-bottlings. Synonymous with *Naturwein* are the words: *natur, echt, rein, naturrein, ungezuckerter;* but wines carrying any of the following designations must also be natural, unsugared, even if the word *Naturwein* does not appear: *Original-Abfüllung, Kellerabfüllung, Kellerabzug, Schlossabzug, Wachstum, Creszenz, Gewächs, Cabinet* or *Kabinett, Fass No., Fuder No., edel, Spätlese, Auslese.*

NEBBIOLO — (Neb-be-*o*-lo) — The outstanding red wine grape of Italy, one of the world's best. Its name comes from *nebbia* (fog), for it ripens best and gives its finest wine in districts where there is a good deal of morning fog during September, notably the regions of Piedmont and northern Lombardy. Here it produces such splendid wines as Barolo, Barbaresco, Gattinara, Ghemme, Lessona, and the admirable Valtellina of Sondrio (*see* all of these); in less celebrated vineyard zones it nevertheless gives a very creditable red wine, this usually sold simply as Nebbiolo, and unfortunately sometimes sparkling. A shy bearer, at its best on steep hillsides, it yields full-bodied, sturdy wines, fairly high in alcohol and almost always requiring a good deal of age; when mature, these have real distinction and great class.

NEBUCHADNEZZAR — Name, variously spelled, given to a giant Champagne bottle, holding as much as twenty ordinary bottles, or 1⅔ cases. Unwieldy and ridiculous when full, it makes a conversation piece when empty.

NEDERBURG — An important South African vineyard, at Klein Drakenstein, near Paarl. *See* South Africa.

NEGRAR — (Nay-*grar*) — Small town in the very heart of the Valpolicella Country (*see*), produces some of that district's finest wine.

NEGRARA — (Nay-*grar*-ra) — Superior Italian red wine grape, used in Valpolicella and Bardolino (*see*).

NEGUS — Old English tipple, often taken as a nightcap, made of Port, lemon, nutmeg and sometimes sugar and hot water, served warm.

NÉNIN, Château — (*Nay*-nan) — One of the largest 1st Growth vineyards of Pomerol. Some 10,000 cases a year of excellent Claret, fruity, generous and soft.

NERVEUX — (Nair-*vuh*) — French wine taster's term, applied to wines that are especially well-knit and well-balanced, with both character and breed.

NEUCHÂTEL — (*Nuh-shat-tel*) — Perhaps the best known, although a long way from the best, white wine of Switzerland. It is produced by some 2,000 acres of vineyard along the northern shore of Lake Neuchâtel, less than twenty miles from the French border; its grape is the Chasselas, here called the Fendant, and it is a small, fresh, pale white wine, agreeable and inexpensive, as indeed it should be. Usually bottled when less than six months old, it is often *pétillant*, or slightly sparkling, in Switzerland, though not when prepared for export. A little red wine is also produced — *see* Cortaillod.

NEUMAGEN — (*Noy*-mahg-gen) — Proudly claiming to be the oldest wine town in Germany, perhaps with some justification, since all sorts of Roman relics have been unearthed nearby, Neumagen is a pleasant little Mittel-Mosel village, between Trittenheim and Dhron. Its wines, while hardly of first rank, are fresh, light and charming, notable for their bouquet. The best vineyards include: Rosengärtchen, Engelgrube, Laudamusberg, Leienberg.

NEUSTADT — (*Noy*-shtat) — Substantial and prosperous little city in the German Palatinate; it produces no wines of much consequence but is an important center of the trade.

NEW YORK STATE — Although second only to California in total wine production, New York's vineyard districts are neither numerous nor impressively large. Table grapes are grown in the Chautauqua area, west of Buffalo on Lake Erie, and to a diminishing extent in the Hudson Valley, but no wine of much consequence comes from either zone, and what really remains, therefore, are the Finger Lakes (*see*), especially Keuka and Canandaigua. Because of climate and other problems, most of the European vinifera vines cannot be grown commercially in New York, and New York State wines, if unblended, come therefore from the native varieties such as Delaware, Catawba, Elvira, Ives, Concord (*see* all of these), or from recently developed hybrids.

NIAGARA — White Eastern grape, sometimes used for wine in the Finger Lakes district; what is sold under this name is usually a rather sweet, golden table wine, without much character.

NIAGARA PENINSULA — Part of Canada (*see*) lying between Lakes Erie and Ontario. The climate, tempered by the lakes, is favorable for grape growing, and most Canadian wine is produced in this area.

NIEDERHÄUSEN — (*Nee*-der-*hoy*-zen) — One of the best wine-producing towns of Germany's Nahe Valley. Superior vineyards include Hermannshöhle, Hermannsberg, Pfingstweide, etc.

NIEDERMENNIG — (*Nee*-der-*men*-nig) — Little vineyard town of the Saar Valley, in Germany's Moselle district. Quite fine wines, though only in good years; Euchariusberg, Sonnenberg, Herrenberg are the best *Lagen*.

NIEDERWALLUF — (*Nee*-der-*vahl*-luf) — Wine-producing town in the Rheingau. *See* Walluf.

NIERSTEIN — (*Neer*-shtein) — One of the very great names in German wine, and easily the foremost wine town of Rheinhessen: first in celebrity, first by far in vineyard acreage, and first in quality as well. Its 1,300 acres of vines overlook the Rhine south of Mainz, and produce in favorable years up to a half million gallons of wine, most of it of good quality, a little of it, superb. The best is made from the Riesling grape and so states on its label; the finer vineyard sites, or *Lagen*, are: Rehbach, Hipping, Glöck, Auflangen, Flachenhahl, Kehr, Orbel, Kranzberg, Pettental, Oelberg, Heiligenbaum, Spiegelberg, Fuchsloch, Hölle, *Gutes* Domtal, etc., and a vineyard name is of capital importance on a bottle of Niersteiner — through an odd quirk of German wine law, practically any wine of Rheinhessen can be sold as Niersteiner, or Niersteiner Domtal (this last not being considered a vineyard name). To buy Niersteiner or Niersteiner Domtal is therefore to buy the equivalent of just Liebfraumilch; Niersteiner, plus the name of a top vineyard, especially if called Riesling and estate-bottled, is a noble wine indeed, ripe and racy and fine. Sylvaners from these better *Lagen* are also outstanding, although somewhat softer and with less breed.

NOAH — Biblical patriarch, ship-builder, friend of animals, mariner, and finally wine-grower for the last three and a half centuries of his life. He is supposed to have found water insupportable as a beverage after the Flood — "it tasted of sinners . . .
"Because all things corrupt therein
Both man and beast, were drowned for sin."
On account of this, and for his undoubted piety, he was vouchsafed the vine, and generations have risen up to be thankful to him.
ALSO, a green, native, Eastern grape, widely planted by despairing growers in Europe at the time of the phylloxera. The quality of the wine it gives would have been enough to discourage Noah himself.

NOBLE — Word used, with considerable justification, of certain grape varieties, certain vineyards and certain wines that seem to possess an inherent and permanent superiority over their fellows and their neighbors. All men may be created equal, but all vines are not, nor all hillsides. A noble variety is one capable of giving outstanding wine under proper conditions, and better-than-average wine wherever planted, within reason. A noble vineyard yields wine of some distinction, even in poor years. A noble wine is one that will be recognized as remarkable, even by a novice.

NOILLY PRAT — (*Nwah*-ye-Prah) — Perhaps the best known brand of French Vermouth.

NORHEIM — Important wine-producing town in the Nahe Valley, Germany. Best *Lagen* include Kafels, Hinterfels, Kirschheck.

NORTH COAST COUNTIES — Name given, for lack of a shorter and better one, to California's one truly distinguished district of fine wine, of which the center is San Francisco Bay. Not all the counties in question touch the Pacific, but they share, in general, the cool, coastal climate, and although the area has never been legally defined, it is generally considered to include, from north to south, the following counties: *Mendocino, Sonoma, Napa,* Solano, Contra Costa, *Alameda* (Livermore), San Mateo, *Santa Clara,* Santa Cruz, *San Benito,* Monterey. Only those in italics are of any real importance today as far as wine production is concerned.

For Map, *see* CALIFORNIA.

NOSE — Wine taster's term for bouquet or aroma; this is a neutral sort of word (like taste) and there is no connotation of superior quality.

NOSTRANO — (No-*strah*-no) — Name given by the peasant wine-producers of Italian Switzerland (round Locarno and Lugano in the Ticino, or Canton of Tessin) to the European vinifera vine, and the wine it gives, as compared with what is called Americano (*see*). Literally, it means "ours," and is used in this special sense in parts of northern Italy as well. Most Nostrano wine is made from a variety known as the Bondola, but there are increasingly important plantings in the Ticino of Merlot, Nebbiolo, Freisa and other better red wine grapes.

NOVITIATE OF LOS GATOS — Jesuit Seminary at Los Gatos, on the western edge of the Santa Clara Valley, California; admirably situated hillside vineyards form a good part of its endowment, and wines are made under the supervision of the Jesuit fathers, most of the actual work being done by Jesuit brothers, and novices, or students. A large part of the production is altar wine, available only to the clergy, but some table wines of good quality are sold to the general public under both varietal and generic names, as well as two unusual specialties in the way of dessert wines, a Black Muscat and a Muscat Frontignan.

NUITS — (Nwee) — *See* Côte de Nuits; also Nuits-Saint-Georges, below.

236

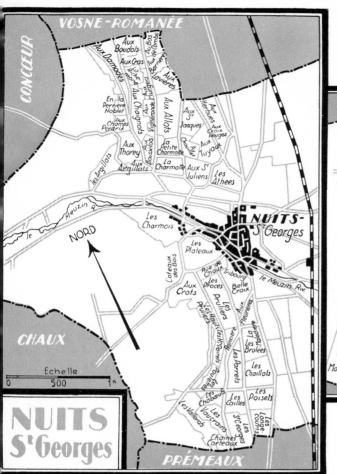

NUITS-SAINT-GEORGES — (Nwee San Shorsh) — Celebrated Burgundian town on the Côte de Nuits, to which it has given its name. An insignificant amount of white wine is produced (*see* Perrière), but the admirable reds, while rarely of the very topmost class, are typical and great Burgundies, generous, soft, well-balanced; in certain years those from the less good *climats* (usually sold at Nuits-Saint-Georges, without a vineyard name) often have a characteristic earthy flavor, or *goût de terroir*. The adjoining village of Prémeaux is considered part of Nuits, as far as its wines are concerned. The best vineyards of the two *communes* include the following: Les Saint-Georges, Les Pruliers, Les Cailles, Les Vaucrains, Les Boudots, Clos des Corvées, Les Porrets,

237

Clos des Argilières, Les Perdrix, Château Gris, Clos de Thorey, Les Richemones, Les Murgers, Clos de la Maréchale, Clos Arlot, etc. The terms "Nuits" and "Nuits-Saint-Georges," followed by a vineyard name, mean precisely the same thing and are interchangeable.

NUTTY — Having a flavor and aroma reminiscent of walnuts or, especially, hazel-nuts. Most often applied to Sherries.

OAK — The one wood used for barrels, casks, butts, pipes, puncheons and the like (much less commonly for vats, tanks, *cuves* and such larger cooperage) in which wine can almost be counted on to develop and improve; chestnut and redwood are acceptable substitutes, but more neutral and far less good, especially for red wines. All of the fine red wines of the world and most fortified wines owe part of their quality to the oak in which they have been stored. In California, and also in Spain, this is most often white oak from Tennessee, but nearly every wine-producing district has its special and cherished source of supply. New oak barrels are used every year by many of the leading Bordeaux and Burgundy producers in order to give added tannin and other less-easily defined qualities to the new wine. However, if kept too long in oak, new oak especially, these and all other table wines tend to become "withered" or "*sechés*" (*see*), and eventually "woody" or "oaky."

OBEREMMEL — (*O*-burr-*em*-m'l) – Little wine-producing village of the Saar, in Germany, adjoining Wiltingen. There are some 200 acres of vineyard, planted in Riesling grapes, and the wines in good and great vintage years are of extremely high quality, light, flowery, somewhat austere. The best *Lagen* include: Scharzberger (often so sold, without the name Oberemmel), and Oberemmeler Hütte, Altenberg, Karlsberg, Rosenberg, Agritiusberg, Raul, Eltzerberg. Also Falkenstein.

OBERINGELHEIM — (*O*-burr-*ing*-gel-*heim*) — *See* Ingelheim.

OBERNAI — (*O*-bair-nay) — Picturesque walled town in northern Alsace, southwest of Strasbourg; its wines are less good than those of nearby villages — Barr, Goxwiller, Mittelbergheim.

OCKFEN — (Awk-fen) — One of the very great white wine villages of the world, in the Saar Valley, near Wiltingen, in Germany. There are some 200 acres of Rieslings, planted on one incredibly steep, slate hillside: in favorable years such as 1953 and 1959 these produce white wines unsurpassed by those of any other German or French vineyard, and therefore in the world. Very light, almost steely, elegant, with a bouquet that can only be called incomparable, they are remarkable, and worth whatever they cost; in secondary years, they are hard and often green and acid. Best vineyard sites are Bockstein, Herrenberg, Geisberg, Oberherrenberg and Heppenstein. The leading estate, that of Adolf Rheinart Erben, has recently been sold; others include the State Domain, Gebert, Geltz, Max Keller.

OECHSLE — (Uhk-slay) — The usual German and Swiss equivalent of our Balling (see) as a measurement of the sugar content of must, or grape juice before fermentation, and as a fairly exact indication of the future alcoholic content of the resulting wine. The *"Grad Oechsle,"* divided by 8, gives this figure, but it is important to remember that this includes, quite often, the grape sugar, or sweetness, of an Auslese or Spätlese, which is never converted into alcohol and remains in the wine. Thus a great Auslese, of 120° Oechsle, would not end up as a dry wine of 15% alcohol, but as a sweet wine of perhaps 12%, or even less.

OEIL DE PERDRIX — (*Uh*-yuh Duh Pair-dree) — Literally, in French, "partridge-eye," used to describe the color of certain wines made from black grapes, most often Champagnes, which are in fact very light and pale *rosés*. The old term has its charm, and it means a sort of combination of very pale pink and bronze. Few wines have this color any more and almost none are so labeled.

OENOMEL — (Ee-no-mel) — Old-fashioned beverage made of grape juice and honey, fermented together. The author of these lines has never to his knowledge tasted it.

OESTERREICHER — (*Uhst*-ter-rike-ker) — Literally, in German, means the "Austrian" — a name often given to the Sylvaner (see) variety of grape in the Rheingau. Whether or not the Sylvaner is actually of Austrian origin is at least doubtful.

OESTRICH — (Uhst-rik) — With some 750 acres under vines, probably the largest wine-producing township in the Rheingau, directly overlooking the Rhine between Hattenheim and Winkel. Most of the vineyards are on fairly flat land and most of the wines are of second quality. Exceptions are those from the better vineyard sites, as: Oestricher Lenchen, Deez, Doosberg, Eiserberg, Klostergarten, etc. Wegeler Erben, Mühlens-Berna and the Pfarrgut are reliable producers.

OHIO — In pre-Civil War days and, in fact, until the first trans-continental railway was completed, Ohio was by far America's most important wine-producing state, and its wines were rated even more highly than those of the Finger Lakes district of New York. The earliest vineyards were planted by German settlers along the Ohio River, east and west of Cincinnati, where the steep hills overlooking the swift Ohio recalled the landscape of the Rhine, and inspired the most optimistic prophecies concerning the district's viticultural future. Mr. Nicholas Longworth was one of the first pioneers to establish an Ohio wine business national in scope; relying mostly on the Catawba grape, he had, by the 1850's, opened a New York sales agency and was selling his still and sparkling Catawba at prices quite comparable to those which French and German wines then commanded. Some of these wines actually received medals at fairs and expositions in Europe and were widely known.

Somewhat later, grapes began to be planted on a fairly large scale along the southern shore of Lake Erie, west of Cleveland, especially around Sandusky, and on the Lake Erie islands. The lake itself helped to protect the vines against spring and early fall frosts, and a substantial industry existed well into the present century and, in fact, until Prohibition. Although some vineyards are still in production, and Ohio still produces several million gallons of wine a year, its comparative importance in the field of wine has greatly declined; the best-known shipper, accounting for a major proportion of the total volume, is Meiers Wine Cellars at Silverton, Ohio, near Cincinnati. Most of the grapes are still grown near Sandusky and the once celebrated Ohio River vineyard slopes are almost entirely a matter of history today.

OFF — Perhaps the broadest and least specific term of disapprobation which can be applied to a wine. Basically, it means abnormal. An "Off Taste" is a taste which the wine should not have, for whatever reason and from whatever cause. It may be a fault that will soon correct itself, due, for example, to the fact that the wine has been shaken up; it may be a real and permanent flaw, like moldiness. "Off" should *not*, however, be used of a wine, however poor, which is simply coarse, or thin, or grapey (because made from a special variety of grape), or earthy. It means abnormal.

OIDIUM — Also called powdery mildew, a fungus, probably of American origin, which attacks the leaves, shoots and tendrils of the vine. It caused enormous damage in European vineyards when it first appeared there, in the mid-19th century, and is still troublesome, although it can now be controlled.

OLIVIER, Château — (O-leave-E-A) — Well-known and popular dry white Graves, a monopoly of the house of Eschenauer. Château Olivier is in the township of Léognan (*see*) and produces a small amount of red wine which also carries this name.

OLOROSO — (O-lo-*ro*-so) — One of the two basic types of Spanish Sherry, Fino being the other; literally, the word means "*que huele bien*," or "of agreeable odor," and an old, high quality Oloroso possesses in fact as intense, typical and recognizable a bouquet as any wine in the world. Darker in color than the Finos, ranging from dark gold to deep amber, fuller-bodied, generally higher in alcohol (18-21%), Oloroso Sherries are developed and matured without the flor yeasts which give the Finos their special character and quality, although nevertheless in *soleras*. Few are shipped in their natural bone-dry state, but are sweetened to please the public palate, and Olorosos can be anywhere from not-quite-dry to luscious and very sweet, as Cream Sherry and "East India." They are mostly properly classified as dessert wines or after-dinner wines, and are conventionally served at room temperature although some prefer them chilled.

ONCTUEUX — (Awnk-si-uh) — French word, of which the literal English translation is "unctuous"; the French sounds better when applied to wine. It is used exclusively to describe full-bodied wines that are quite sweet, soft, "fat," high in glycerine, and of good quality: the great Sauternes are prime examples.

OPORTO — Second city of Portugal, on the Douro River not far from its mouth: it has given its name to what is perhaps the most famous of all dessert wines, Port (*see*), which is produced in a delimited zone up the Douro Valley to the east. According to Portuguese law, all wines called Port must be shipped either from Oporto or from Vila Nova de Gaia, directly across the river. It is an attractive and picturesque old town, full of the "lodges" and warehouses of the great Port shippers, a great many of whom are English, as might be expected.

OPPENHEIM — (*O*-pen-heim) — Important wine-producing town, directly south of Nierstein, in Rheinhessen, Germany. Its 450 acres of vineyard (about one-third Rieslings, the rest Sylvaner and Müller-Thurgau) are mostly south of the village, on gently sloping soil that falls away toward Dienheim and the flat plain in the direction of Worms. The wines, although of good class, are well below the Niersteiners in quality, softer and with less breed. The better *Lagen* include: Kreuz, Sackträger, Herrenberg, Steig, Kröttenbrunnen, Goldberg, etc., and the best-known producer is the State Domain.

ORANGE — (O-rawnj) — Interesting old town of the lower Rhône Valley, north of Avignon. It was called *Arausio* in Roman days, and still has some exceedingly impressive ruins; its ruling family, the Princes of Orange, eventually became kings of Holland and then of England. It is today the center of an important wine-producing district, with Châteauneuf-du-Pape to its south, and Gigondas, Cairanne, Vacqueras, Rasteau, etc., off to the east and northeast.

ORDINAIRE — (Or-*dee*-nair) — French for common or ordinary. As applied to wine, one of unknown or unstated origin, sold simply as *vin rouge, vin blanc,* or *vin rosé* but of specified alcoholic content. It would be safe to say that fully half of all French wine consumed in France is so marketed.

ORDINARY — *See* Ordinaire. A rather loose term, in English, never legally defined, applied to cheap, common table wines.

ORGANOLEPTIC — Applied to the evaluation or judgment of wines, what can be determined or perceived by the senses (taste, smell and sight) rather than by physical or chemical analysis, in a laboratory. An expert's organoleptic examination will generally give a far better and more exact idea of a wine's marketability, quality and value than the tests of any laboratory technician, however competent.

ORIGINAL-ABFÜLLUNG — (O-*rig*-ee-*nahl-Ahb*-fue-lung) — Most widely used of several German terms meaning Estate-Bottling. Generally abbreviated to *Orig.-Abfg.*, it is a positive guarantee of authenticity, when followed by the producer's name, and almost never abused. Only *Naturwein* (unsugared, un-chaptalized) may be so labeled and all great German wines carry this designation, or one of its equivalents, on their labels.

ORLEANNAIS — (Or-lay-awn-nay) — Little wine-growing district, principally on the right bank of the Loire, west and therefore downstream from Orléans. Most of the vineyards, important and celebrated a century ago, have disappeared, and the great British expert, P. Morton Shand, has quoted a brief refrain that sounds today like their requiem:

> *"Orléans, Beaugency*
> *Nôtre-Dame-de-Cléry*
> *Vendôme! Vendôme!"*

Once planted in such *cépages nobles* as Pinot Noir, Chardonnay and Cabernet, most of the vineyards that remain are in Pinot Meunier today and some of them produce, especially round Beaugency, a fresh and very agreeable *vin rosé*, excellent as a *vin de pays*, but hardly deserving of wider fame. The rest is history and legend.

ORVIETO — (Or-vee-*ate*-toe) — Famous cathedral town in Umbria, Italy, and its popular, light white wine, occasionally *secco* (dry), more often *abboccato* (slightly sweet). It is shipped in squat little straw-covered *fiaschi* called *pulcianelle.* The Orvieto vineyards are like no others on earth: nine-tenths of the grapes, at least, come from what the Italians call *coltura promiscua,* vines that are interplanted with potatoes or "married" to trees, or strung over random pergolas or against walls or in cabbage patches — hardly what one would normally call vineyards at all. In the province of Terni (Orvieto's) there are some 3,500 acres of true vineyard, and over 125,000 of *coltura promiscua.* The wine, while hardly remarkable, is often, nevertheless, quite good.

OUVRÉE — (*Oo*-vray) — Old Burgundian measure of area, equal to about one-eighth of a journal, or .0428 hectare, or roughly one-tenth of an acre.

OXIDIZED — Said of a wine, especially a white wine, which has had too much contact with the air, has lost its freshness and perhaps darkened in color, and is on the way to becoming maderised *(see).* Such wines never recover, and should either be drunk immediately or thrown away.

P-Q

PAARL — (Parl) — River and town in Cape Province, South Africa; the Paarl Valley, directly west of Capetown, comprises one of the best Cape wine districts. *See* South Africa.

PACHERENC DU VIC-BILH — (Posch-a-rank do Veek-Beel) — Curious, fairly sweet white wine, somewhat comparable to that of Jurançon, produced north of Pau, in southwestern France. Its odd name comes from the local dialect, in which Pacherenc, or *pachet-en-renc,* means "pickets in rank," these vineyards having been the first in this part of France to be planted in the modern fashion, with the vines in regular rows and a picket, or prop, for each vine. Vic-Bilh is the name of a small, hilly district round the village of Portet, south of the Adour River.

PACHINO — (Pa-*key*-no) — A red wine, light purple in color, rather high in alcohol, almost always drunk young, produced (and largely consumed) in the province of Siracusa (Syracuse) in Sicily. Rarely if ever exported.

PADENGHE — (Pa-*deng*-gay) — Village near the southwestern shore of Lake Garda, in northern Italy; produces largely Chiaretto *(see)* plus a few red and *rosé* wines sold under its name.

PAILLE — (Pie) — French word meaning simply "straw"; a *vin de paille,* however, is a white wine made from grapes that have been allowed to dry and almost become raisins, on straw mats, occasionally

243

in the sun but more commonly indoors. The resulting wine is of course sweet, golden, usually quite high in alcohol. The most famous *vins de paille*, produced in extremely limited quantity, are those of Hermitage *(see)*, and the Jura *(see)*. See also *Passito*.

PALATINATE — (Pal-*lat*-teen-ate) — Major German wine-producing district, on the left bank of the Rhine, just north of Alsace *(see* Rheinpfalz).

PALESTINE — *See* Israel.

PALETTE — (Pah-*let*) — Red, *rosé* and white wine made not far from Aix-en-Provence, near Marseille, in southern France, where it enjoys a certain, hardly merited, local fame. There are only about 5,000 cases produced per year, but the name is an *Appellation Contrôlée*.

PALMER, Château — (Pahl-*mair*) — 3rd Classed Growth of Cantenac-Margaux. Outstanding Bordeaux vineyard which has consistently produced, since World War II, better wine than most of the 2nd Growths — in 1955, and again in 1961, among the very best of the Médoc. Some 10,000 cases a year of admirably balanced Claret, which to quote one French authority, is *"tendre, élégant et bouqueté."*

PALUS — (*Pal*-loo) — French word meaning originally "swamp" or "marsh," now applied in the Bordeaux Country to the areas of meadowland or reclaimed alluvial soil along the river banks. Little such land is planted to vineyard and most of the *palus* are specifically excluded from the delimited zones of *Appellations Contrôlées*. Vines on such soil are usually extremely productive but never yield wines of any quality.

PANIER À VENDANGE — (*Pan*-yea-ah Vawn-*dawnj*) — Wicker basket of any one of many shapes and sizes (usually a matter of local tradition) in which grapes are harvested and transported at vintage time.

PANIER-VERSEUR — (Pan-yea-Vair-sir) — *See* Cradle.

PAPE CLÉMENT, Château — (Pap-*Clay*-Mawn) — Excellent and ancient vineyard in the *commune* of Pessac, Graves, first planted in 1300 by Bertrand de Goth, Bishop of Bordeaux, who became Pope Clément V in 1305. Some 8,000 cases a year of fine red wine, one of the best of Graves.

PAPE, Le, Château — (Luh *Pahp*) — Excellent small vineyard of Léognan, in the Graves district of Bordeaux; it produces some 2,000 cases a year of fine red wine, which deserves to be better known, and a much smaller amount of even more remarkable white, hard to come by, but one of Bordeaux's best.

PARISH — In Great Britain (and in Louisiana), a township as well as an ecclesiastical division. Many English writers on wine correctly use "parish" as the equivalent of the French *commune;* this is not general American usage, however, and in the U.S., "parish" has the same meaning as the French, *paroisse*, whereas "township" means *commune*.

PARNAY — (Par-nay) — Village on the Loire, east (upstream) from Saumur; its red, white and *rosé* wines are of high quality, entitled to the appellation Saumur under which they are almost always sold. The most famous estate is the Château de Parnay, long the property of Monsieur Cristal, who, during the early years of this century, was among the most celebrated pioneers of modern viticulture in France.

PARSAC-SAINT-EMILION — (*Par*-sack-Sant-A-*me*-lee-awn) — One of the less distinguished of the secondary districts adjoining St. Emilion and entitled to the name in this combined form. Rather full wines that usually lack class; some 50- to 75,000 cases a year.

PASSÉ — (Pah-*say*) — French term, applied to a wine which is too old, past its prime, on the decline.

PASSE-TOUT-GRAINS — (Pahss-too-gran) — Red Burgundy wine, rarely from one of the better *communes,* made from Pinot Noir and Gamay grapes crushed together; it must now contain at least one-third of Pinot Noir. Labeled "Bourgogne-Passe-Tout-Grains," it is a rather common wine, generally inexpensive.

PASSITO — (Pass-*see*-toe) — An Italian wine made from grapes that have been partially dried or raisined, whether outdoors or under cover, generally a dessert wine, although such grapes are also used in the making of many Italian dry wines (*see* Governo). Most *Vin Santo (see)* is so made, as are many Moscato and Malvasia wines as well, such as Caluso *(see),* Enfer *(see),* etc.

PASTEUR, Louis (1822-1895) — Eminent French scientist, who first determined the true nature of the fermentation which produces wine, and the cause and cure of many of wine's maladies. He gave his name to the celebrated Institut Pasteur in Paris, to the process of pasteurization, and, as his considered opinion, "wine is the most hygienic and healthful of beverages."

PASTEURIZATION — Process of sterilizing wines and other liquids by heating them (usually to between 130° and 170° F.) so that the micro-organisms they contain are destroyed, rendering them stable. This of course cuts short the development and possibility of improvement of a superior wine, and fine wines are never pasteurized. There is nothing illegal or wrong about the pasteurization of common table or dessert wines, destined for early consumption.

PASTO — *See* Vino da Pasto, Vino de Pasto. In general, means a wine that can be drunk at table, with food, even when applied to Sherry.

PATRAS — One of the better known Greek wines, usually white and fortified; less often, an agreeable red or *rosé* wine from the province of Achaea, near Athens.

PATRIMONIO — (Pat-tree-*mo*-nee-o) — One of the best-known brands of Corsican wine, produced round St. Florent, on the northwest coast of the island, between Ile Rousse and Bastia. A red (sometimes labeled Cervione), a white and a *rosé* exist, all of good quality, the *rosé,* especially; all three are full-bodied and high in alcohol. They can occasionally be found (outside Corsica) in restaurants in Marseille and on the Riviera and even in Paris.

PAUILLAC — (Paw-yack) — Celebrated little town in the Haut-Médoc, perhaps the most remarkable wine-producing township in the world. Within its communal limits are produced a number of the very greatest red wines of France: Château Lâfite, Chateau Latour, Chateau Mouton-Rothschild, and many others of almost equal reputation and class, as Pichon-Longueville, Pichon-Longueville-Lalande, Lynch-Bages, Pontet-Canet, Batailley, etc., etc. All these, of course, carry the words *"Apellation Pauillac Contrôlée"* on their labels, and not much wine is sold simply as Pauillac. The wines of Pauillac, in good years, are "classic" Clarets in every sense of the word; full-bodied, long-lived, with great bouquet and a special, incomparable distinction — at their best they are beyond praise. An important and well-known co-operative cellar exists and sells one of its better wines as La Rose de Pauillac.

PAUL, Saint (d. 67 A.D.) — Apostle who wrote to his friend Timothy: "Drink no longer water, but use a little wine for thy stomach's sake and thine often infirmities."

PAVIE, Château — (Pa-*V*) — Large and well-known 1st Growth vineyard of St. Emilion. Some 15,000 cases a year of sound Claret, rarely remarkable but consistently good. Château Pavie-Macquin and Château Pavie-Decesse nearby produce wine of somewhat lesser quality.

PAYS — (Pay-*ee*) — Common, widely used French word, of which the original and basic meaning is "country"; *mon pays* can mean the village where one was born, a district, the city of Paris, France itself. Applied to wine, it has almost equally diverse meanings, about which almost all Frenchmen feel strongly but rarely agree. The term, however, does not appear on wine labels, except *very* rarely; colloquially, a *vin de pays* is a relatively little known, local wine, mostly consumed where made; the *vin du pays* is a specific wine of this sort produced in a specified district. Neither of these meanings has much legal standing and both terms are loosely used.

PÉCHARMANT — (*Pay*-char-mawn) — Fresh and attractive little red wine produced just outside Bergerac, in southwestern France. The grape varieties (Cabernet, Malbec, Merlot) are those of red Bordeaux, and in character Pécharmant is not unlike a lesser wine of the Médoc. Total production is about 10,000 cases a year.

PEDESCLAUX, Château — (*Ped*-ess-clo) — 5th Classed Growth of Pauillac, Haut-Médoc. Produces some 2,500 cases a year.

PEDICEL — Botanical name for the short stem which connects the individual grape with the bunch of which it is a part.

PEDRO XIMÉNEZ — (*Pay*-dro He-*may*-nays) — Spanish grape variety, widely grown in the Montilla, Málaga and Sherry districts. According

Echelle

0 1 2 3K

N
O E
S

St ESTÉPHE

GIRONDE Fl.

Ch. Rolland
Ch. Lafite-Rothschild
Ch. d'Anseillan
Ch. Latour du-Roch-Milon
Ch. Montgrand-Milon
Ch. Duhart-Milon
Ch. Lafleur-Milon
Ch. Mouton-Rothschild
Ch. Padarnac
Ch. Mouton d'Armailhac
Ch. Pibran
Ch. Pontet-Canet
Ch. Calvé-Croizet-Bages
Constant-Bages-Monpelou
Ch. Pedesclaux

PAUILLAC

Ch. Clerc-Milon-Mondon
Ch. Haut-Bages-Libéral
Ch. du Colombier Monpelou
Ch. Gd Puy-Ducasse
Ch. Lynch-Bages
Ch. Gd Puy-Lacosse
Ch. Bellevue-Cordeillan-Bages
Ch. Ht Bages Drouillet
Ch. Bellegrave
Ch. Pauillac
Ch. Lynch-Moussas
Ch. Fonbadet
Ch. Bellevue-St Lambert
Ch. Molecot
Ch. Pichon-Longueville-Comtesse de Lalande
Ch. Batailley
Ch. Pichon-Longueville
Ch. Latour
Ch. Batailley l'Aspic
Cru La Couronne

St JULIEN

St SAUVEUR

St LAURENT DE MÉDOC

PAUILLAC

to a highly unlikely story, it was brought to Spain in the 16th century by a German soldier, one Peter Siemens (whence its name), and is in fact the Riesling grape of the Rhine Valley. In Montilla *(see)* where it predominates, it gives a fine, dry wine, somewhat fuller-bodied and higher in natural alcohol than what the Palomino yields round Jerez, and often sold in its unfortified state as a 15-16% wine; in Málaga and the Sherry Country it is differently vinified — the grapes are laid out in the sun for two weeks or more and allowed to raisin, then fermented and fortified, so that the resulting wine is very sweet. Well-aged, this becomes what is usually called "P. X.," the best of all sweetening agents for Sherry, and the most expensive; it is sometimes drunk straight, practically as a liqueur.

247

PEDUNCLE — Botanical term for the stalk by which a bunch of grapes is attached to the vine.

PELURE D'OIGNON — (Pay-*loor Dawn*-yawn) — Literally, means "onion skin" in French; with respect to wine, the special russet-brown or tawny tinge which certain red wines acquire as they grow old. Also any light red or *rosé* which has this color.

PERELADA — (*Pair*-ray-*la*-tha) — Small wine-producing town on the Spanish side of the Pyrenees, inland from the Costa Brava and just north of Figueras. Its impressive castle is the property of Señor Mateu, formerly Mayor of Barcelona and more recently Spanish Ambassador to London; its wines include a very acceptable and popular *rosé*, a somewhat less good red and white, and a sparkling wine which was not long ago the subject of a celebrated legal controversy; shipped to London as "Spanish Champagne," its use of the name was challenged in the British courts by the French *Institut des Appellations d'Origine*, which eventually emerged victorious and thereby reconfirmed the exclusive right, under British law, of French Champagne producers to the name "Champagne."

PERFUME — Loosely used tasting term, which properly means fragrance or aroma (qualities which a young wine possesses and which come from the grape) rather than bouquet, which a wine acquires as it matures.

PERIGNON — *See* Dom Perignon.

PERLANT — (*Pair*-lawn) — French term, not legally defined but meaning a wine *very* slightly sparkling (less so than *crémant* or *pétillant*) and almost always naturally and accidentally and temporarily so. The German equivalent is *spritzig*.

PERLWEIN — (*Pairl*-vine) — In German, a slightly sparkling wine, one deliberately so vinified and made — *see pétillant*. Wines in this category have become very popular of late in Germany — they are fresh and agreeable and inexpensive, never outstanding.

PERNAND-VERGELESSES — (*Pair*-nawn Vair-juh-*less*) — Small village in Burgundy, just west, up a side valley, from Aloxe-Corton *(see)*. Its very finest wines, both red and white, do not carry the village name at all but are sold, quite legally and properly, as Corton, Corton-Charlemagne, and even Aloxe-Corton. What goes to market as Pernand-Vergelesses can nevertheless be very good (at least as good as most of what is labeled Aloxe-Corton or Savigny-les-Beaune) and has the advantage of being not very well-known and therefore inexpensive. One wholly remarkable red wine, not very far in quality from the best of Corton itself, and worth investigating wherever found, comes from a single *climat* in Pernand, called Ile des Vergelesses — this, estate-bottled by a good producer in a great vintage, is about the best value in the way of red Burgundy that exists today.

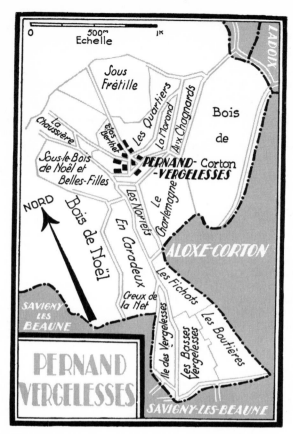

Map labels: 500ᵐ Echelle, LADOIX, Sous Frétille, Les Quartiers, La Morand, Aux Chagnards, Bois de, La Chaussière, Clos Berthet, Sous-le-Bois de Noël et Belles-Filles, PERNAND-VERGELESSES, Corton, NORD, Bois de Noël, Les Norrets, En Caradeux, Le Charlemagne, ALOXE-CORTON, Creux de la Net, Les Fichots, SAVIGNY LES BEAUNE, Ile des Vergelesses, Les Basses Vergelesses, Les Boutières, PERNAND VERGELESSES, SAVIGNY-LES-BEAUNE

PERRIÈRE — (Per-ry-*air*) — Name, presumably from the French, *pierre,* or stone, given to many stony vineyards, notably four in Burgundy: the Clos de la Perrière in Fixin *(see),* at the northern end of the Côte de Nuits, gives a red wine of real distinction and fine texture; the Perrière vineyard of Nuits-Saint-Georges yields one of the rare white wines of its district; the *climat* of Perrière (or Perrières) in Meursault is perhaps that little town's best and produces one of the finest full-bodied, dry white wines of France; Puligny-Montrachet Perrières fully deserves its rank as a *Premier Cru.*

PESSAC — (Pess-sac) — Celebrated wine-producing *commune* just west of Bordeaux, now practically a suburb. Its wines include the very finest of red Graves: Châteaux Haut-Brion, La Mission-Haut-Brion, Pape Clément, etc.

PÉTILLANT — (Pay-tee-yawn) — French term meaning slightly sparkling, or "crackling," as *frizzante* in Italian and *Perlwein* in German. By semi-official international accord, such wines may not have a pressure in

excess of two atmospheres (four atmospheres is the *minimum* for wine classified as sparkling, including Champagne) and most of the French ones such as Vouvray, where the term is most commonly used, have far less. Despite much that has been written on the subject, by people who should know better, this sparkle is hardly ever accidental or natural, but the planned result of special methods of vinification. Such wines are often agreeable and fresh and charming, and it is certainly absurd that they should be compelled to pay in the U.S., on account of this slight effervescence, a tenfold tax as compared with still wines. Because of this tax, few are ever imported.

PETIT — (Puh-*tee*) — Means "little" or "small" in French, and when applied to wine, is much more unfavorable than its English equivalent. A *petit vin* is a small wine, low in alcohol, deficient in body, of no real value or consequence. Petit Chablis (*see below*) is a rare, accidental exception.

PETIT CHABLIS — (Puh-*tee* Shab-lee) — Very agreeable, rather short-lived white wine, pale, dry and refreshing, made from the Chardonnay grape in certain parts of the Chablis district and in a few *communes* which directly adjoin it, where the soil is less chalky and the exposure less good. It was formerly called "*Bourgogne des Environs de Chablis*"; actually, it is, as its name indicates, a small Chablis, interesting only in good vintage years, an excellent lesser wine in its youth.

PETIT SYRAH — (Puh-*tee* See-rah) — Name given in California to a red wine grape which is presumed to be the Syrah (*see*) of the Rhône Valley in France. There are some 4,500 acres, mostly in Napa and Sonoma counties: it ranks seventh in total acreage among red wine grapes in the State. Its wine is never better than a satisfactory full-bodied *ordinaire*, deep-colored, rather common, with little in the way of true varietal character or bouquet, and after blending it usually ends up as something called "California Burgundy." Far more productive than the true Syrah of Hermitage, Châteauneuf-du-Pape and Côte Rôtie, with none of the distinguished qualities or even the faults of its supposed

French ancestor, it is probably not the Syrah at all, but a common variety called the Duriff, which was widely planted in the Rhône Valley a century ago but no longer grown in any French vineyard entitled to an *Appellation Contrôlée.*

PETIT VILLAGE, Château — (*Puh*-tee Vee-lahj) — One of the best vineyards of Pomerol, properly ranked as a *Premier Grand Cru.* Its wines are rather firm and slow to mature, but acquire with time great bouquet and distinction.

PETRUS, Château — (Pet-trewss) — Without question the best vineyard of Pomerol, now ranked (although unofficially, to be sure) on a par with the great 1st Growth Clarets of the Médoc, with Château Haut-Brion, Mouton-Rothschild and Cheval Blanc. Its production over the years has averaged in the neighborhood of 3,500 cases, but the figure has been substantially lower since the severe frosts during the winter of 1955-56. The wine is outstanding, soft and good even in mediocre years and, at its best, velvety, *gras,* admirably balanced, with great bouquet and breed. For label, *see* Page 388.

PEYRAGUEY — *See* Haut-Peyraguey and Lafaurie-Peyraguey.

PFALZ — (Pfahltz) — *See* Rheinpfalz.
For Map, *see* RHEINPFALZ.

pH — (P-H) — *See* acidity, real.

PHÉLAN-SÉGUR, Château — (*Fay*-lawn *Say*-gour) — Good *bourgeois* growth of St. Estèphe, Haut-Médoc.

PHYLLOXERA — (Fill-*lox*-er-ra) — An insect, or plant louse, which is, of all of the many enemies of the vine, perhaps the most devastating, whence its Latin name, *phylloxera vastatrix.* It apparently has always existed in the eastern part of the United States, but the native American vines are resistant to it, largely on account of their heavier and tougher roots. It was accidentally introduced into Europe, on vine cuttings brought over for experimental purposes, about 1860, and within two decades it destroyed, in France alone, some 2½ million acres of vineyard, and doubtless as wide an extent in other wine-producing countries, since the *vitis vinifera,* from which almost all the world's good wines are made, is almost fatally vulnerable to its attack. Countless remedies and preventive measures were proposed and attempted; none with any real degree of lasting success until native American vine stocks were brought over and the European vine grafted on these resistant roots. Many varieties of American vine, and innumerable crosses of these, have been planted, *vitis riparia, vitis rupestris, vitis berlandieri,* and many others, and practically all European wines now come from vines grafted on American roots. This is also the case in California, where the phylloxera crossed the Rockies and laid waste the vineyards in the 1880's. At the moment, the insect seems less dangerous, no longer existing in its winged, more infectious form, and a few bold California vintners have planted ungrafted *vinifera* vines, so far successfully, as at Almadén's Paicines vineyard.

There has been much discussion, pro and con, as to whether the great European wines are as good or have ever been as good, since made from the grapes of grafted vines, as they were before. This is the sort of question that will never find a proper and certain answer, and since pre-phylloxera wines hardly now exist, it is hardly worth arguing about.

PICHET — (Pee-shay) — French term for a small jug or pitcher of earthenware or wood, often used in restaurants for serving "open" wine at table.

PICHON-LONGUEVILLE, Château — (*Pee*-shawn-*Long*-uh-veel) — 2nd Classed Growth of Pauillac. One of the most consistent of the 2nd Growths and one of the best Clarets of Pauillac. The vineyard directly adjoins Château Latour, and is often referred to as "Pichon-Longueville-Baron," to distinguish it from Pichon-Longueville-Comtesse-de-Lalande; it yields some 8,000 cases of wine a year, round, fine, well-balanced, yet fairly full-bodied and long-lived.

PICHON-LONGUEVILLE-LALANDE, Château — (*Pee*-shawn-Long-uh-veel-La-*lawnd*) — 2nd Classed Growth of Pauillac. Just across the road from Pichon-Longueville and equally good, although its wine is of a quite different character and type, being lighter, with more fruit and finesse, due partly, no doubt, to a higher proportion of Merlot and therefore less Cabernet Sauvignon in the vineyard. There are some 10,000 cases a year of this "Pichon de la Comtesse."

PICKING BOXES — Instead of the picturesque wicker baskets generally used in Europe at vintage time, American growers more often use wooden boxes, or lugs: these can be stacked on trailers or dumped into gondolas for transportation to the winery.

PICPOUL — (Peek-pool) — Name given in the Armagnac Country to the Folle Blanche grape (*see*) which here, as in the Cognac district, gives a poor, thin, acid wine but an outstanding brandy. It is the only variety used in the best grades of Armagnac.

PIÈCE — (Pea-*ess*) — French for the oak barrel, roughly the equivalent of the *barrique* of the Bordeaux Country, in which the wines of Burgundy are ordinarily stored and aged. A *pièce* in the Côte d'Or contains 228 liters (60 gallons, or 25 cases of finished wine); in the Beaujolais, 215 liters (just under 56 gallons).

PIED — (Pea-*A*) — One of several French words for a single vine (*cep* and *souche* being two others). Ordinarily and alone, it of course means "foot," but in wine parlance one will often say that a given vineyard has "*3,000 pieds à l'hectare*," which means 3,000 vines per hectare, or some 1,200 to the acre.

PIEDMONT — (*Italian*, PIEMONTE — P-a-*mawn*-tay) — Most important wine-producing region of Italy, easily first in quality, usually second only to Apulia (*see*) in quantity, with an annual production of over 100 million gallons a year. Most of the vineyards are on the hills north and south of the wide, upper valley of the Po, in the Monferrato (*see*) especially. The most famous Piedmontese wines are red (Barolo, Barbaresco, Barbera, Freisa, Grignolino, etc.) but many good white table wines (Gavi, Cortese) are also produced, as well as most of the sparkling wines of Italy (Asti, etc.). Turin, the capital of Piedmont, is the principal center of the Italian Vermouth trade.

For Map, *see* ITALY.

PIERRE-À-FUSIL — (Pea-*air* ah *Foo*-zee) — French for gun-flint; when applied to wine, a special odor or flavor which recalls the smell of flint struck with steel. Often applied to the wines of Chablis. Flinty.

PIESPORT — (*Peas*-port) — One of the smallest yet deservedly one of the most famous wine-producing villages of Germany's Moselle Valley. Its 120 acres of steep, rocky vineyard, facing due south, produce wines which, at their best, have few equals — wonderfully delicate and fragrant, fruity, with an incomparable distinction all their own. These "Queens of the Moselle," as they have been called, of course carry the name of a specific vineyard, as Piesporter Goldtröpfchen, Taubengarten, Lay, Treppchen, Falkenberg, Gräfenberg, Güntherslay, etc., and are estate-bottled by their producers. On the other hand wines labeled simply Piesporter (or even Piesporter Goldtröpfchen *without* the words *Wachstum or Original-Abfüllung*) may and often do come from less celebrated townships nearby — Dhron, Neumagen, and even Longuich and Schweich. This practice, unfortunately, is "tolerated" under German wine law. (*See* GERMANY, Page 149.)

PINARD — (Pea-nahr) — French slang, especially soldiers' slang, for wine; most often inexpensive, red wine.

PINEAU DE LA LOIRE — (Pee-no duh la Lwahr) — Sometimes, though wrongly, written Pinot. Productive white grape of excellent quality, responsible for most of the best white wines of Touraine and Anjou, in France. Its proper name is Chenin Blanc (*see*), and botanically it is not related to the Pinot Noir, Pinot Blanc, Pinot Gris, etc. It is now quite extensively planted in the North Coast Counties of California, as Chenin Blanc, or often as "White Pinot," and gives fresh, fruity, agreeable wines with considerable bouquet; those that are deliberately made somewhat sweet are much less good. It is also, as in Saumur, an excellent grape for sparkling wines, and many of the best California Champagnes contain a good proportion of wine made from it.

PINEAU DES CHARENTES — (Pee-no day Shar-awnt) — Odd, sweet apéritif, which has achieved in recent years a certain popularity in France. It is actually a *mistelle* or *vin muté* — in other words, new wine in which the fermentation has been stopped by the addition of spirits; as such, it has much in common with white Port and with California Angelica (*see*), the difference being that in this case Cognac is used instead of high-proof brandy.

PINOT — (*Pee*-no) — Perhaps the most distinguished single family in the field of wine grapes, a name second to none in the Almanach de Gotha or Burke's Peerage of the vine. The Pinot Noir alone is responsible for all the great red Burgundies, from Pommard, Beaune and Corton, to Romanée Conti, Musigny and Chambertin. It also produces over 60% of all French Champagne. The white so-called Pinot Chardonnay or Chardonnay (*see*) is almost certainly not a true Pinot, although legally so in France; it is the other major grape of the Champagne Country, and the one variety grown, or even permitted, in Montrachet, Chablis, Pouilly-Fuissé. The Pinot Blanc is widely planted in lesser Burgundian vineyards, and another cousin, the Pinot Gris (also called the Ruländer and occasionally, though wrongly, the Tokay) yields excellent wine in Alsace and in Baden, and in northern Italy.

Transplanted to California, the Pinots preserve in general the distinguished characteristics of their French ancestors; they are shy-bearers, and their wines are more expensive than most, but the word Pinot on a California wine label is a pretty good assurance of superior quality. However, those labeled "White Pinot" are generally made from the Pineau de la Loire, or Chenin Blanc (*see*), which is not a true Pinot, and many of those named "Red Pinot" come from an inferior variety to which someone has given the advantageous name of "Pinot St. George."

In Italy, the Pinot Blanc gives an agreeable, dry white wine round Alba, in Piedmont, often sold as Pinot d'Alba and marketed in tall, slender green bottles; in Lombardy, in the neighborhood of Casteggio, both the Pinot Noir and Pinot Blanc are grown, mostly for sparkling wines; in the Tyrol there are small plantings of both, and especially of Pinot Gris, or Ruländer, which is one of the varieties used in Terlano (*see*).

PINOT CHARDONNAY — *See* Chardonnay.

PINOT GRIS — (*Pee*-no Gree) — An authentic cousin of the greater members of the Pinot family, sometimes called the Ruländer in Germany, the Auxerrois in certain parts of France and even (wrongly) the "Tokay" in Alsace. Its grapes are a sort of greyish-rose when ripe, and yield wines which are sometimes of considerable distinction, notably in Baden, Alsace, and northern Italy, but often somewhat flat, and lacking in acid.

PINOT MEUNIER — (*Pee*-no *Muhn*-yea) — Grape variety, probably a Pinot, but of an inferior strain. More productive than the true Pinot Noir, it is no longer legal in Burgundy but still "tolerated" in Champagne; it is the variety responsible for most of the Pinot Rosé of Alsace and for many pleasant *rosés* produced round Beaugency on the Loire. Its name comes from the fact that the underside of its leaves is powdery white, almost as if covered with flour, and the word *meunier* means "miller" in French. Grown to some extent in California, it generally passes there for Pinot Noir.

PINOT NOIR — (*Pee*-no Nwahr) — One of the very greatest of red wine grapes (*see* Pinot, above).

PIPE — Large barrel, customarily of oak and rather sharply tapered toward the ends, in which Port is stored in Portugal and in which it is often shipped. Its size may vary, but is usually 522 liters, or 138 U.S. (115 Imperial) gallons. The standard Madeira pipe is considerably smaller — 418 liters, or about 110 U.S. gallons.

PIQUANT — Wine taster's term (*pikant*, in German) used of a fresh, rather tart white wine, attractive and almost spicy.

PIQUÉ — (Pee-kay) — Said of a wine that has begun to go sour, with a trace of acetic acid in its make-up.

PIQUETTE — Derisive term applied to any poor, thin acid wine; correctly to something which is not legally wine at all, made of *marc*, or pomace or grape pressings, plus water and sugar — a sort of "second wine," often served free to cellar workers in Europe.

PLASTERING — The addition of calcium sulphate, or gypsum, to grapes before fermentation: this increases the total acidity and improves the color and clarity of the resulting wine. This is normal procedure in the making of Sherry and certain other wines and is, within specified limits, legal both in Spain and in America.

PLEIN — (Plan) — French for *full*. Applied to wines that are well-balanced, with good body and fairly high alcohol.

PODENSAC — (*Po*-dawn-sac) — Small town in the Graves district of France, producing rather sweet white wines. These are entitled to the appellation Cérons (*see*).

POINTE — (Pwant) — French for "punt" (an English word, although it will not be found in this sense in most dictionaries), meaning the depression or "push-up" in the bottom of most wine bottles, especially those used for Champagne. A bottle of sparkling wine *mise sur pointe* is one placed neck down, usually for ageing, stacked vertically with the cork of each bottle in the punt of the bottle below. It is thus, and *before* disgorging, that the finer Champagnes are aged, and it is only thus that they improve materially in bottle. This system of stacking for ageing is also sometimes called "*en masse*," and the term *mise sur pointe* is sometimes also used to mean the placing of bottles on "riddling racks" or "*pupitres*" for turning and shaking which precedes disgorging. See Champagne.

POINTE, Château La — (Pwant) — Important 1st Growth vineyard of Pomerol. Some 7,000 cases a year of very sturdy, full-bodied red wine.

POLCEVERA — (Paul-chay-*vair*-ra) — Rather good white table wine, often a little on the sweet side, produced near Genoa, Italy.

POLPENAZZE — (Paul-pen-*natz*-zay) — Village and small district near the southern end of Lake Garda (*see*), producing Chiaretto (*see*) and some rather agreeable, light red wines.

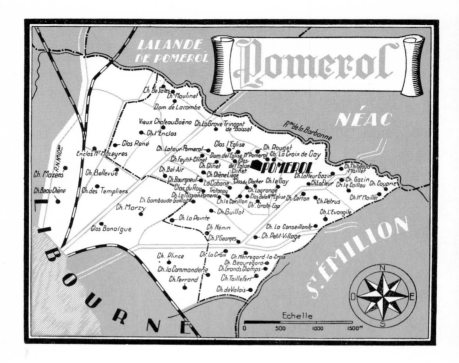

POMACE — (*Pum*-mess) — Mass of skins, seeds, stems, etc., left in the fermenting vat or wine-press after the wine or juice has been drawn off. *Marc*, in French.

POMEROL — (Paum-may-rawl) — One of the most interesting and attractive of all Clarets, produced only by some 1,500 acres of vineyard, mostly in a single township, the smallest of the famous districts into which the Bordeaux Country is divided, by tradition and by French law. Some twenty miles east of Bordeaux, it adjoins St. Emilion, runs up to the edge of the little city of Libourne, and its vines are planted on a high, gently rolling, rather gravelly plateau north of the Dordogne River.

In *average* quality the wines sold simply as "Pomerol" are perhaps the best district wines of Bordeaux; they have a winning and generous warmth, great depth of flavor, a color of dark lustrous crimson, and much of that peculiar velvety quality which the French call "*gras*." They mature more quickly than the Médocs, are less subtle, shorter-lived. The best chateau wines are of course much finer; they include Château Pétrus (almost in a class by itself), Château Certan and Vieux Château Certan, and Châteaux La Conseillante, Trotanoy, Petit Village, L'Evangile, Lafleur, Gazin, La Fleur-Pétrus, Nénin, La Pointe, Beauregard, L'Eglise Clinet, Latour-Pomerol, etc

256

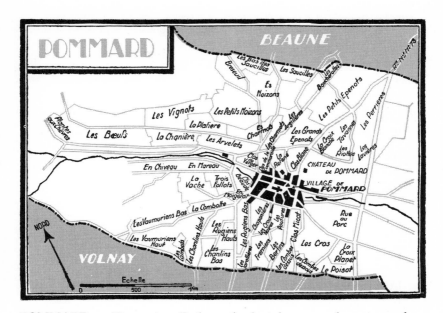

POMMARD — (*Po*-mar) — Perhaps the best known and most popular
of all red Burgundies, especially in English-speaking countries: three
times as much Pommard is shipped to the United States as red Burgundy
under any other single appellation. Only a fraction of this is of truly
superior quality; the name Pommard alone, unless followed by that of
one of the few truly outstanding vineyards of this little *commune*, is
anything but a hallmark of quality. The village is just south of Beaune,
and bounded in turn on the south by Volnay; its 846 acres of vines produce more wine (80- to 100,000 cases a year) than any other *commune*
of the Côte d'Or. Nevertheless, it is a long way from certain, despite
strict controls, that everything sold as "Pommard" is really genuine. The estate-bottled wines from outstanding vineyards, on the
other hand, are not only dependable but fine — soft, gracious, well-
balanced, not too deep in color, fruity and attractive, with considerable
breed. The best *climats* are Rugiens (which adjoins Volnay and gives a
rather full-bodied wine, with a wholly typical and rather agreeable, special *goût de terroir*); Épenots (also spelled Épeneaux) which adjoins
Beaune and is remarkable for its finesse and class; then Clos Blanc,
Arvelets, Chaponières, Pézerolles, Poutures, Chanlins Bas, Les Croix
Noires, La Platière, etc. (for a more complete list, *see* the Appendix).
All of these yield red wine exclusively, but there is an insignificant
amount of white produced, by a tiny vineyard known as the Coeur des
Dames. Two *cuvées* of the Hospices de Beaune, Dames de la Charité
and Billardet, carry the *Appellation Contrôlée* "Pommard" and bring
high prices.

257

PONTAC-MONPLAISIR, Château — (*Pawn*-tack-Mawn-play-*zeer*) — Good, small vineyard in Villenave d'Ornon, Graves. Red wine of sound quality and an even better white.

PONTET-CANET, Château — (*Pawn*-tay-*Can*-nay) — 5th Classed Growth of Pauillac. The largest classified vineyard of the Médoc (20,000 cases a year) and its popular red wine.

POOR — Used of a wine that has not much to it. Not necessarily bad. Mediocre and uninteresting.

PORT — Certainly the most famous of all dessert wines; originally and properly a sweet, heavily fortified wine from a delimited district in the upper Duoro Valley of northern Portugal. In most countries no other wine may be sold as "Port," and even in the United States the name is to some extent protected — the domestic product must be labeled American Port, New York State Port, or California Port. California, incidentally, produces nearly ten times as much "Port" as Portugal, but only a tiny fraction of this vast output is at all comparable, in character and quality, to the Portuguese original.

However, both in Portugal and in this country, Port is a wine which owes its sweetness to the high sugar content of the grapes from which it is made. These, crushed, are put to ferment, but at some carefully determined half-way point in their fermentation the juice is drawn off into casks or tanks which contain a predetermined amount of high-proof grape brandy. This, of course, immediately arrests the fermentation, and the result is a wine of 19 to 21 percent alcohol by volume, still quite sweet, the raw material of Port. What it becomes thereafter depends, to a large extent, on the quality of the grapes from which it was made, their variety and their vineyard, and on the cellar care which the crude new wine receives.

Port has been made in this way in Portugal, though of course vastly less well than now, since about 1450, and has been well-known and popular in northern Europe, in England especially, for nearly three centuries. It has never, except in its cheap, inferior, domestic version, acquired much acceptance in the United States.

Various types of Port are now made in Portugal, and they vary widely. The most expensive are VINTAGE PORTS. These are selected lots of wines of exceptionally good years, unblended, bottled young (more often in London than in Oporto). They require anywhere from fifteen to fifty years to reach their peak, throw a heavy sediment or film or crust in the bottle, have to be decanted with great care, and at their best are of quite extraordinary quality. They are regarded with a respect approaching reverence by their British devotees. Good recent vintages include 1960, 1955, 1950, 1947, 1945, 1942, 1935, 1934, 1927, 1924. Only the older are considered by connoisseurs as ready to drink.

More generally available and interesting is something called "Crusted Port" or "Port of Vintage Character." This is a blended wine, bottled early, and it, too, throws a heavy sediment.

Most of the Port shipped to the United States, however, (some 60,000 cases a year) is aged in wood and ready to drink when shipped. One, properly called RUBY PORT, is fairly young, fruity, attractive, although its quality depends entirely on its shipper and its price. TAWNY PORT has spent more time in oak, thus acquiring a lighter color and a brownish tinge. It is softer, rounder, more mature and usually, quite properly, more expensive. There exists, in addition, WHITE PORT, considerably less esteemed by experts, made precisely as the red is made but from white grapes, principally the Rabigato, Malvasia, Gouveio, etc. The leading red wine varieties include the Touriga, Bastardo, Tinta Francisca, Tinta Carvalha, Tinta Madeira, Mourisco, Tinta Cão, etc.

As the result of recent plantings of Tinta Madeira and Tinta Cão grapes, a limited amount of quite good Port is being produced in California, and the word Tinta usually appears on its label. But according to American wine laws and regulations, "Port" may be made anywhere, out of any grapes, including native Eastern varieties, or even table grapes, raisin grapes, or culls. It may be well and properly aged in oak, or it may, and often does, go to the consumer when under six months old. There is no guide to quality other than the rather untrustworthy one of price, and the producer's name or brand.

PORTUGAL — When it comes to wine, most people tend to think of Portugal in terms of Port, yet hardly two percent of Portuguese wine is Port, and more than half of this is exported. What the Portuguese themselves prefer, and consume in happy abundance, is table wine. About as large and as populous as Ohio, Portugal produces four times as much table wine as California and drinks over three times as much table wine as the United States, some 25 gallons per capita per year.

Most of this, of course, is simply *consumo,* or *vin ordinaire,* agreeable enough, and cheap. The reds are on the whole more deeply colored and slightly higher in alcohol than their French or California counterparts; the whites are rather coarse and common, as might be expected at this latitude; some of the *rosés* are refreshing and good.

A great deal of progress has been made in methods of vinification and cellar care over the past decades, and a number of superior Portuguese table wines are beginning to find a place in the world market, especially in England and to some extent in the United States. While they can hardly be called distinguished, these are often very agreeable, and good values. Several are sold simply under a brand name (as Lancer's, Mateus, etc.) without any precise indication of origin; others, and increasingly, carry a geographical appellation strictly defined by the Portuguese government.

The more important of these are, 1. what is known as *Vinho Verde* (literally, "green wine," but "green" only in the sense that it is young and fresh and lively), from northern Portugal, red, white, and *rosé;* 2. *Dão,* from a small mountainous district south of the Douro Valley, once again red, white, and *rosé;* 3. *Colares,* a fine, light red wine made from the Ramisco grape, planted in sandy coastal vineyards west of Lisbon; 4. *Bucelas,* rather sweet, white table wine made just north of Lisbon.

In addition to these, Portugal produces one of the most famous muscat wines of Europe, the golden *Moscatel de Setubal,* which is almost a liqueur. And of course Port and Madeira, to round out a truly unique range of great fortified wines.

POSSET — A cold-weather drink made of hot milk, curdled with wine or with beer, sweetened and spiced.

POT — (Po) — Small, very heavy bottle, holding 46 centilitres or about one U.S. pint, in which young "open" Beaujolais is often served, in and around Lyon; in color and shape it is like a slenderer version of the bottle used for Sauternes. The so-called "pots" shipped in recent years to the United States are neither of the same contents nor the same form.

POUGET, Château — (Poo-shay) — 4th Classed Growth of Cantenac-Margaux. Very small production of red wine.

POUILLY FUISSÉ — (*Poo*-ye *Fwee*-say) — Excellent dry white wine made from the Chardonnay grape in four small *communes,* or townships, just west of Macon, in southern Burgundy. Pouilly itself is not a township, but is officially ranked as a hamlet (*hameau*) in the *commune* of Fuissé; the others are Solutré (*see*), Chaintré and Vergisson. The average annual production is not far from 400,000 gallons, much of it consumed in Lyon and Paris when still young, the best, usually estate-bottled, is a dry, green-gold, racy, fruity wine, with exceptionally good balance and fine bouquet — perhaps not a great wine but very nearly one, somewhere between Meursault and Chablis in character. Most Pouilly-Fuissés are now bottled before they are a year old, and they do not improve past the age of three. *See* also Pouilly-Loché and Pouilly-Vinzelles.

POUILLY FUMÉ — (*Poo*-ye *Few*-may) — Also POUILLY-BLANC-FUMÉ, the terms being interchangeable. Excellent white wine, generally dry though sometimes with a trace of sweetness in great years, produced round the village of Pouilly-sur-Loire (*see*). Made entirely from the Sauvignon Blanc (or Blanc-Fumé grape), pale, racy, fruity, usually bottled when less than a year old, it has acquired in the last ten years a great and well merited popularity. The total production, often radically reduced by spring frosts, rarely exceeds 100,000 gallons a year.

POUILLY-LOCHÉ — (*Poo*-ye *Lo*-shay) — Dry white wine, fresh, pale and attractive, made from the Chardonnay grape in the village of Loché, which adjoins but is not legally part of the Pouilly-Fuissé production zone. *See* Pouilly-Vinzelles.

POUILLY-SUR-LOIRE — (*Poo*-ye sewer Lwahr) — Small town on the Loire River, not far from Nevers, in central France. The wine-producing district of which it is the center includes the adjoining *communes* of Les Loges, St. Andelain and Tracy; there are approximately a thousand acres of vineyard, about two-thirds planted to the common Chasselas grape (*see*) and one-third to the admirable Sauvignon Blanc, here known as the Blanc-Fumé (*see*). The Pouilly vineyards therefore produce two

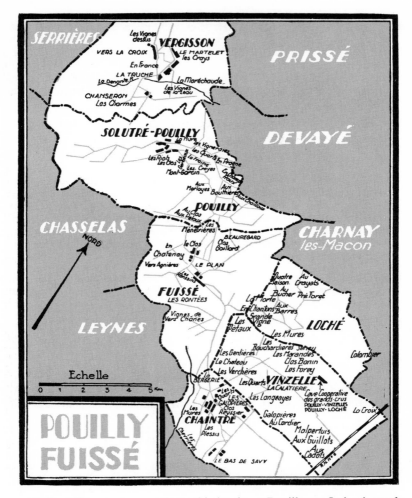

entirely different wines — that sold simply as Pouilly-sur-Loire is made
from the Chasselas; at best it is a fresh, agreeable carafe wine, short-
lived, without much character or distinction. For the vastly superior
wine made from the Sauvignon Blanc, *see* Pouilly-Fumé.

POUILLY-VINZELLES — (*Poo*-ye Van-*zell*) — Excellent dry white wine
made from the Chardonnay grape in the village of Vinzelles, near
Macon. Like Loché, Vinzelles directly adjoins the Pouilly-Fuissé district,
and its wines, while possibly a little lighter and shorter-lived, are very
like the Pouilly-Fuissés, and better than some. They are among the best
values in the way of white Burgundies shipped out of France.
    For Map, *see* POUILLY-FUISSÉ.

261

POUJEAUX — (Poo-show) — High gravelly plateau in the center of the Haut-Médoc, mostly inside the communal limits of Moulis (*see*). Many of the wines here produced have a special character and taste; they are mostly *bourgeois* growths, and the word Poujeaux is often part of their name, as Château Poujeaux-Theil (*see*), Poujeaux-Marly, Gressier-Grand-Poujeaux, Dutruch-Grand-Poujeaux, Lestage-Darquier-Grand Poujeaux, etc.

POURRITURE NOBLE — (*Poo*-ree-tew'r *No*-b'l) — See Botrytis.

POWERFUL — High in alcohol and/or assertive in aroma and flavor. A wine of definite character.

PRÉCOCE — (Pray-*cawss*) — French term meaning precocious, or early maturing, applied both to grape varieties and to wines. Most grape varieties grown in cool, northern districts are *précoces*, for otherwise they would not ripen, and their number includes almost all of the very best. On the other hand, a *vin précoce*, one soon ready and gaining little if aged, is, however agreeable and charming, rarely much more than that, and hardly ever great.

PREIGNAC — (*Prayn*-yac) — One of the five *communes* of the Sauternes district in France. Its best vineyards include Château Suduiraut, Château de Malle, etc.

PRÉMEAUX — (Pray-mo) — Village in Burgundy, directly adjoining Nuits-Saint-Georges on the south; its admirable red wines are legally entitled to the appellation Nuits-Saint-Georges, and are always so sold, usually plus the name of a vineyard. Several of these *climats* yield wines fully equal to the best of Nuits itself, as the Clos des Corvées, Les Perdrix, Les Argillières, and, of a slightly lower rank, the Clos des Forêts, Les Didiers, Clos Arlots, Clos de la Maréchale, etc. (*See* map page 237)

PREMIÈRES CÔTES DE BORDEAUX — (*Prem*-me-yea *Coat* duh Bordoe) — Major division of the Bordeaux wine country, consisting of the hilly right bank of the Garonne River between Bordeaux itself and Langon, 30 miles to the southeast. Thus the vineyards face those of Graves, Cérons, Barsac and Sauternes, across the verdant and lovely river valley; they produce some 3 million gallons of white wine, and about one-third as much red, per year. The latter is generally one of the pleasantest and soundest of inexpensive red Bordeaux; the white ranges from slightly *moelleux* to very sweet indeed, although there have been recent efforts, as in Entre-Deux-Mers, to produce dryer wines. Cadillac and Langoiran are perhaps the two of the best known *communes*; two others, Loupiac and Sainte-Croix-du-Mont (*see*) are geographically part of the Premières Côtes, but have individual *Appellations Contrôlées* of their own.

PRESS — Instrument of many diverse forms used since time immemorial to extract juice from grapes, either before fermentation (white wine) or after (red wine).

262

PREUSES — (Pruh-z) — One of the best of the seven *Grand Cru* vineyards of Chablis; its wines, often rather hard when young, develop slowly and generally acquire a very special and attractive bouquet and flavor reminiscent of hazel-nuts (*noisettes*).

PRIEURÉ-LICHINE, Château — (Pree-oo-ray Lee-sheen) — 4th Classed Growth of Cantenac-Margaux, formerly called Le Prieuré or Cantenac-Prieuré.

PRIMATIVO — (Preem-ma-*tee*-vo) — Remarkable red blending wine produced south of Bari, in the "heel" of Italy, usually shipped and consumed almost as soon as made. The vintage comes early in this hot country, and some Primativo, blended, of course, with older wine, is often being sold and drunk by the 15th of September of the year it is made. The best of it comes from the appropriately named town of Gioia, from the Troja grape, and has about 14% alcohol.

PRIORATO — (Pre-o-*rah*-toe) — Sweet, full-bodied, red dessert wine, usually fortified, produced round Tarragona on the Mediterranean Coast of Spain. It is often used in *sangría* (*see*) and other wine punches popular in Spain in summer.

PROOF — System of measuring and expressing alcoholic content; there are two scales. According to that used in the U.S., proof is the double of alcoholic content by volume at 60° F.; an 86 proof brandy, for example, will contain 43% alcohol by volume, and a 100 proof bonded whiskey 50% alcohol. In Great Britain, proof spirit contains 57.1% alcohol by volume; liquids containing less are said to be "under proof," and those containing more, "over proof."

PROSECCO — (Pro-*sake*-ko) — The sweeter of two excellent white wines (the other is called Verdiso, and they are both made from the Verdiso grape) from the town of Conegliano (*see*) north of Venice, Italy. There are several sparkling and semi-sparkling types as well, all with the same, rather striking and special bouquet.

PROTESTANT EPISCOPAL CHURCH — U.S. church, inheritor of the doctrine of the Church of England, which became an independent body within the Anglican communion in 1789, and whose House of Bishops, in Chicago on October 26, 1886, resolved that: "In the judgment of the House of Bishops the use of the unfermented juice of the grape, as the lawful and proper wine of the Holy Eucharist, is unwarranted by the example of our Lord, and an unauthorized departure from the custom of the Catholic Church."

PROVENCE — (Pro-*vawnss*) — Historically and traditionally, an ancient province of France where a separate language, Provençal, by no means just a dialect or patois, was and still is, to some extent, spoken; Aix-en-Provence was its capital, and it was considered to include the modern *départements* of Basses-Alpes, Vaucluse, Bouches-du-Rhône, Var and part of the Drôme; it became part of France in 1487. As far as wine is concerned, its modern meaning has been somewhat differently defined:

Vaucluse, Basses-Alpes and Drôme are outside the limits of viticultural Provence whereas some vineyards in the *département* of Alpes Maritîmes are now entitled to the appellation Côtes de Provence (*see*) although they were not part of France until 1860.

PRUNING — Complex agricultural science, which has been the concern of vineyardists and vine-dressers since the time of Noah, by which vines are cut back (in almost all cases during their dormant season) so as to form and train them systematically with some specific end in view. This end may be increased production, higher quality, a longer life for the vine itself, or any combination of these and many other desired results; literally thousands of books have been written on the subject over a period of more than twenty centuries. A capsule condensation of them is impossible and has no place in a volume of this sort.

From the wine-drinker's point of view there are perhaps a few generalizations that may be helpful:

1. Within definite limits, imposed by soil, climate, rainfall (and/or irrigation), almost any grape variety can be pruned so as to produce twice or even five times its minimum.

2. Again within limits, the commoner grape varieties do not yield markedly better wine when pruned to produce less per acre — a wine made from Carignan grapes by a man who harvests three tons per acre is NOT worth twice as much as a wine from his neighbor who gets six tons per acre.

3. The few wine grape varieties which can properly be described as "great" (perhaps a dozen, surely less than twenty) *always* give better wine if severely pruned so as to give their minimum crop, *providing* they are planted in districts suited to them.

4. There are many intermediate varieties (Sylvaner, Gamay, Merlot, Grenache) yielding wines best drunk young, which gain nothing and even lose quality if their production is too restricted.

PUGLIA — (*Pool*-ya) — Important wine-producing province in southern Italy. See Apulia.

PUISSEGUIN-SAINT-EMILION — (*Pweece*-gahn-Sant-A-*me*-lee-awn) — Secondary red wine district in the Bordeaux Country, adjoining St. Emilion (*see*) on the west, and entitled to the name in this combined form. Sturdy, full-bodied wines, not too expensive and often good values in the way of Claret. There are over a half million gallons a year.

PULCIANELLA — (Pool-chan-*nel*-la) — The small, squat, straw-covered bottle, or *fiasco*, of a special shape, in which the wines of Orvieto (*see*) are shipped.

PULIGNY-MONTRACHET — (*Poo*-lean-ye-Mawn-rash-*shay*) — Village of the Côte de Beaune, in Burgundy; together with the adjoining village of Chassagne-Montrachet, it produces what are generally and correctly regarded as the finest dry white wines of France. The most celebrated vineyards include Montrachet (about half in Chassagne), Chevalier-Montrachet (all in Puligny), Batard-Montrachet (nearly half in Chas-

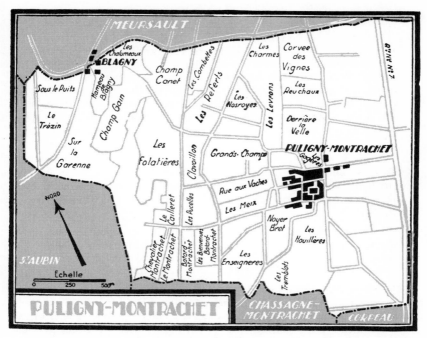

sange), Bienvenue-Batard-Montrachet (all in Puligny) and Criots-Batard Montrachet (all in Chassagne). *See* all of these, which are all sold under the vineyard name alone, with no mention of Puligny or Chassagne. Admirable wines, but of a somewhat less exalted class, are: Puligny Montrachet Les Combettes, Les Perrières, Champ Canet, La Truffière, Les Chalumeaux, Les Pucelles, Clos du Meix, Referts, Les Charmes, Les Folatières, Clavoillon, Cailleret, La Garenne, Hameau de Blagny, etc. There are just over 200 acres under vines, all Chardonnay, except for a small parcel of Pinot Noir, and the annual production is not far from 100,000 gallons. Even the lesser wines of Puligny have great breed and class and would rank as extraordinary in any other district.

PULP — The fleshy and juicy part of the grape.

PULPIT — A literal translation of the French, *pupitre*, applied in the Champagne Country to the two-sided perforated racks, hinged at the top and spread apart at the bottom so as to form a shape like the letter A, in which the bottles are placed during their "shaking" or "riddling" and clarification. *See* Champagne.

PUNCHEON — Cask of about 600 liters or 160 U.S. gallons, widely used in California wineries. This is roughly the amount of table wine that one can expect to get from a ton of grapes.

PUNT — The "push-up" or "kick-up" in the bottom of a wine or Champagne bottle.

PUTTONYOS — (Poo-tawn-*yawsh*) — Baskets or hods used during the grape harvest in the Tokay district of Hungary. When a good vintage year permits the making of the superior grade of wine called *Aszu* (the equivalent of a German Auslese), the overripe grapes are picked separately, and a varying number of *puttonyos* of these are added to each cask of normal wine. The number is usually stated on the wine's label, as *"Aszu 2 puttonyos," "Aszu 5 puttonyos,"* etc. Naturally, the more *puttonyos,* the sweeter, fuller-bodied and more expensive the wine.

QUART — One-fourth of a gallon: .946 liters in the U.S., 1.139 liters in Great Britain. In French, pronounced *caar*, it again means one-fourth: ¼ liter of open wine, or a quarter-bottle, or "split" of Champagne.

QUARTS DE CHAUME — (Car duh Shome) — Celebrated vineyard of the Coteaux du Layon (*see*), in the province of Anjou, France. Consisting of 120 acres of Chenin Blanc vines, with an incomparable southern exposure, it produces some of the finest and most expensive of the rich, golden, fruity wines for which Anjou is above all famous.

QUATOURZE — (Kah-tourz) — Red, white and *rosé* wine produced round the town of Narbonne, in southern France, not far from Carcassonne and the Spanish border. Made from the common grape varieties of the Midi, it is a fairly good *ordinaire*, but hardly deserves either its local fame or the V.D.Q.S. seal which it is allowed to carry.

QUEUE — (Kuh) — Old French measure of capacity or volume, said to come from the Latin term *culeus*. Until quite recently the wines at the Hospices de Beaune auctions were sold by *Queues* (although invariably lodged in *pièces*, or *demi-queues*) and the Burgundian *queue* is therefore 456 liters; the exact meaning of the word still varies from one French province to another, and a *queue* can be anywhere from 216 to 894 liters. We may well be thankful for the metric system.

QUINCY — (Can-see) — A pleasant, spicy, dry white wine from the village of this name, on the River Cher, not far from Bourges, in central France. Considered a wine of the Loire Valley (the Cher being a tributary of the Loire), made entirely from the Sauvignon Blanc grape, Quincy is not unlike a very dry Sancerre or Pouilly-Blanc-Fumé. There are some 400 acres of vineyard, and about 100,000 gallons of wine in overall per year.

QUINTA — (Keen-ta) — Portuguese term for a vineyard estate, including vines and buildings, more or less the equivalent of Château, *Domaine, Tenuta, Weingut*, etc.

R - S

RABAUD-PROMIS, Château — (Rab-bo-Pro-me) — 1st Classed Growth of Bommes, Sauternes. Fine, full-bodied wines, in general quite sweet. For nearly two decades, ending in 1952, Rabaud-Promis and Rabaud-Sigalas formed a single property, known as Château Rabaud.

RABAUD-SIGALAS, Château — (Rab-bo-See-gal-ahs) — 1st Classed Growth of Bommes, Sauternes. *See* above.

RABELAIS, François — (Rahb-a-lay) — Celebrated French writer, born near Chinon in the Loire Valley *circa* 1490, who wrote of wine and the joys of wine-drinking with an enthusiasm and eloquence rarely equaled. A collection of quotations from him on the subject would fill pages. In Gargantua I, he says, "There is not a corner nor burrow in all my body where this wine doth not ferret out my thirst."

RABLAY — (Rahb-lay) — One of the best wine-producing *communes* of the Coteaux du Layon (*see*), in Anjou. Sweet white wines of very high quality.

RABOSO — (Rob-*bo*-so) — Interesting and unusual red wine, produced from the grape of the same name in the province of Treviso, north of Venice. Extremely high in acid, it requires some ageing; low in alcohol, a pale, brilliant ruby in color, with a remarkable bouquet, it is, when mature, an extremely pleasant summer wine.

RACKING — The drawing off of clear young wine from one vat or cask or barrel to another, leaving the lees and sediment behind. This operation, essential in wine-making, is called *soutirage* in French, *Abstich* in

German, *travaso* in Italian, and normally involves the loss of 2% or 3% of the wine's volume. All well-made wines are racked at least twice and some of them four times before bottling.

RAINWATER — Odd name given to one of the lightest and palest of Madeiras. In the early 19th century, at least according to tradition, a gentleman and connoisseur of Savannah, Georgia, by the name of Habisham, developed a special and secret method of clarifying and handling his family Madeiras, shipped in cask by clipper ships from Funchal, so as to render them not only excellent but uniquely light-bodied and pale. They soon became famous at "Rainwater Madeiras" and their originator no less famous as "Rainwater Habisham." The word, long since in the public domain, is now used by many Madeira shippers.

RANCIO — (*Rawn*-see-o) — Special flavor that certain wines, fortified wines especially, acquire as they are aged in wood, akin to maderization but in this case desirable. Madeira itself, like Tawny Port and some Marsala, has this characteristic taste, but it is perhaps most pronounced in the apéritif wines of southern France, such as Banyuls.

RANDERSACKER — (*Rahn*-der-sock-er) — One of the better wine-producing villages of the Main valley, in Franconia, Germany; after Würzburg itself, the most important of all. Its wines are of course shipped in *Bocksbeutel,* the traditional flagon of this part of Germany, and the finer vineyards include Randersackerer Pfülben, Hohbug, Teufelskeller, Spielberg, etc.

RASTEAU — (Rass-toe) — Sweet, amber, fortified wine, somewhat on the order of a light, white Port, produced in the lower Rhône Valley, northeast of Avignon. Usually about 15% alcohol, occasionally higher.

RAUENTHAL — (*Rau*-en-tahl) — Small village of the Rheingau, set back in the Taunus hills behind Eltville. Its better vineyards (Baiken, Gehrn, Wieshell, Wülfen, Rothenberg, Herberg, etc.) constitute about the most valuable agricultural land per acre in Germany and, in the opinion of many experts, produce the most distinguished of all Rhine wines. These are especially notable for their "spiciness," fruit and breed, and in good vintages they are truly incomparable. Leading producers include the State Domain, Graf Eltz, Freiherr Langwerth von Simmern and the Winzerverein.

RAUSAN-SÉGLA, Château — (*Row*-sawn-*Seg*-la) — Generally considered the best vineyard, after Château Margaux itself, in the *commune* of Margaux; one of the most consistent and distinguished of the 2nd Classed Growths. Some 6,000 cases a year of red wine, *bouqueté* and fine.

RAUZAN-GASSIES, Château — (Row-sawn-Gas-see) — 2nd Classed Growth of Margaux. Perhaps a shade less outstanding than Rausan-Ségla but a good 2nd Growth. About 5,000 cases a year of suave, delicate Claret.

RAVAT — French hybridizer whose experiments in crossing native American and *vinifera* vines resulted in some of the best of these hybrids or, as they are called in France, *producteurs-directs*. These carry his name, as Ravat 262, which gives a light, fruity red wine, somewhat comparable to a Beaujolais, and Ravat 6, a superior white-wine grape.

RAVELLO — (Rahv-*vel*-lo) — Memorably beautiful little town, back of Amalfi and not far from Naples, in southern Italy. Its upland vine-yards produce a small amount of white and especially *rosé* wine, of good but not remarkable quality; a good deal of this is exported, much of it consumed, no doubt, by those who find it a nostalgic reminder of hours or days spent in this enchanting little place.

RAYNE-VIGNEAU, Château — (Rain-Veen-yo) — 1st Classed Growth of Bommes, Sauternes. One of the most remarkable of the great Sau-ternes vineyards; golden, sweet wines of extraordinary breed, power and depth of flavor.

RECIOTO — (Ray-*chawt*-toe) — Celebrated "special" wine of the Valpolicella Country, near Verona, in northern Italy. Made from partially raisined grapes, it is, when not sparkling, a remarkably fruity, highly perfumed, sweet red wine, on the order of an exceedingly light Port. When, which is unfortunately far more often, it is *frizzante,* or slightly sparkling, it remains a remarkable wine in its class, but one not likely to appeal to a confirmed wine drinker, accustomed to dry wines.

REFOSCO — (Ray-*fawce*-co) — Red wine grape of mediocre quality from northeastern Italy, considered by some experts to be probably the Mondeuse *(see)* under a different name. Transplanted to California, notably to the Napa Valley, it somehow became known as Crabb's Black Burgundy. In California, as in Italy, the wine is quite ordinary.

REGIONAL — Wine that takes its name from a district or region rather than from a specific town or vineyard, generally inexpensive and gen-erally a blend. Wines labeled "Anjou," "Médoc," "Côte de Beaune," for example, are regional wines.

REIMS — (Ranss) — Famous cathedral city east of Paris; with Épernay, one of the two major centers of the Champagne trade. Underground, it is an anthill of galleries and vaults and workrooms, cut in the white, underlying chalk, in which the Champagne is stored and aged and processed; these proved an invaluable refuge and shelter during the dark days of World War I.

REINHARTSHAUSEN, Schloss — (*Rhine*-harts-*how*-zen) — Celebrated German wine-producing estate in the heart of the Rheingau, between Erbach and Hattenheim, with some seventy-four acres of vineyard, belonging to the late Kaiser's collateral descendants. The labels of this estate carry the designation, "Orig.-Abfg. Prinz Friedrich von Prüssen" and come in three colors: the less expensive grades, crimson; the middle grades, brilliant, almost electric blue; and the Cabinet wines,

white with a narrow red border. Although the castle (never very impos-
ing or attractive) has now been converted into a hotel, the wines are as
distinguished as ever and among the Rhine's best. They come from important holdings in Erbacher Markobrunn, Brühl, Rheinhell, Siegelsberg, Steinmorgen, Gemark, and in Hattenheimer Willborn, Hassel,
Honigberg, etc.

REMUAGE — (Ray-moo-aj) — One of the essential operations in
Champagne making: the shaking and turning of the bottles in their
racks or *pupitres,* by which the sediment is brought down against the
cork, prior to disgorging. This is called *Rütteln* in German, and sometimes "riddling" in California. For all of this, *see* Champagne.

RESERVE — (Ray-*zerv*) — Word often found on commercial wine labels. It has no legal or real meaning, except what the producer or
shipper sees fit to give it.

REUILLY — (Ruh-yee) — Dry white wine, good but increasingly hard
to come by, produced not far from Quincy *(see)* near the Cher river in
the upper Loire basin, in France, from the Sauvignon Blanc grape. The
vineyards, often grievously damaged by spring frosts, are being gradually abandoned, and it is quite possible that Reuilly will cease to exist
within our lifetime.

RHEIMS — *See* Reims.

RHEINGAU — (*Rhine*-gow) — In the opinion of many experts, the
greatest white wine district in the world. It covers the foothills of the
Taunus range, west of Wiesbaden and more or less opposite Mainz, in
Germany, and overlooks an extraordinary reach of the Rhine which
here, on its way north from Switzerland to the North Sea, makes a great
bend and runs slightly south of west for over twenty miles. The vineyards, therefore, strung along the right or generally east bank of the
river, have here the most ideal exposure, nearly due south, and they
benefit from the warmth of the reflected sunshine off the Rhine. Legally,
the wines of Hochheim, east of the Rheingau proper, and overlooking
the Main, are Rheingau wines, as are also those of Assmannshausen
and Lorch, on the steep slopes of the Rhine gorge on to the north.
  The Rheingau's total production is extremely small by international
standards and amounts only to some 2½ million gallons a year, a good
part of which is drunk locally. There are about 5,000 acres under vines,
well over 70% of them Rieslings, and this variety predominates wherever good Rheingau wine is made. The cheapest wines are generally
sugared, to bring their alcoholic content up to the desired minimum,
and these carry just the name of a village on their label, as Rüdesheimer,
Johannisberger, Hochheimer, etc.; of course, all the better ones bear
the name of a specific vineyard, and are estate-bottled *(see)*. Assmannshausen produces a few red wines of fair quality and there exist random
plantings of red grapes elsewhere, but apart from these all the Rheingau
wines are white.

Rothenberg
Mäuerchen

Schloss Johannisberg
Klaus
Hölle
Erntebringer

Gräfenberg
Wasserrose

Baiken
Gehrn
Wieshell

RHEIN GAU

RAUENTHAL
STEINBERG KIEDRICH
HALLGARTEN
VOLLRADS
JOHANNISBERG
GEISEN
HEIM
WINKEL
OESTRICH

MARTINSTHAL
WIESBADEN
ELTVILLE
WALLUF
ERBACH
HATTENHEIM
HOCHHEIM

MAINZ

RÜDESHEIM
HESSEN
BINGEN
RHEIN

Sonnenberg
Langenstück

Domdechaney
Kirchenstück
Stein
Daubhaus

Berg Rottland
Berg Bronnen
Berg Lay
Berg Schlossberg
Klosterkiesel

Hasensprung
Jesuitengarten

Mannberg
Wisselbrunnen
Nussbrunnen

Marcobrunn
Siegelsberg
Steinmorgen

THE RHEINGAU

Most of them follow the usual German system of wine nomenclature
— a town name plus a *Lagename*, or vineyard name, as Rüdesheimer
Bischofsberg, Johannisberger Klaus, Rauenthaler Wieshell, Hochheimer
Domdechaney. A few vineyard names, however, are so famous that they
stand alone: Schloss Johannisberger, Schloss Vollrads, Steinberger, etc.
In addition, wines of superior quality often carry such designations as
Kabinett, Spätlese, Auslese (*see* all of these); estate-bottling is indicated
by the producer's name, plus some term such as *Original-Abfüllung,
Schlossabzug, Keller-Abfüllung.*

Few, if any, of the world's great vineyard districts can compare with
the Rheingau when it comes to the *average* quality of their wines. There
is nevertheless an astonishingly wide variation between the Rheingaus
of a poor vintage and those of a great year; and even among the wines
of any given harvest. Some sound and authentic bottles can be sold in
America for as little as $2, while others may cost $10 or more and be
well worth it. The most expensive of all, the Auslesen, Beerenauslesen
and Trockenbeerenauslesen, are generally quite sweet, and are truly
dessert wines, comparable to the finer French Sauternes, though much
lower in alcohol. Those of lesser rank are for the most part fairly but

271

not austerely dry, exceedingly fruity, with a characteristic and memorable bouquet, and rarely contain much over 11% of alcohol by volume. The "big" wines of great vintages are long-lived and rather slow to develop — best, perhaps when from four to ten years old; the smaller, lighter and dryer ones are usually in bottle by their first birthday and quite ready to drink a year or so later.

Between Hochheim on the east and Rüdesheim on the west (and not including Lorch and Assmannshausen) there are fourteen wine-producing villages, nine strung along the river and five set back in the hills; nine or ten of the fourteen are world famous, and all are listed in their proper alphabetical place in this volume. *See*, therefore, **Hochheim, *Walluf, **Eltville, ***Rauenthal, **Kiedrich, ***Erbach, ***Hattenheim, *Oestrich, **Hallgarten, ***Winkel, ***Johannisberg, **Geisenheim and ***Rüdesheim. Also Schloss Eltz, Schloss Reinhartshausen, Steinberg, Schloss Vollrads and Schloss Johannisberg.

RHEINHESSEN — (Rhine-hess-sen) — *See* Hessia.

RHEINPFALZ — (*Rhine*-pfahltz) — One of Germany's four major wine districts, in most years first in production, with some 35,000 acres under vines, and an average annual yield of better than 15 million gallons. This has been true since medieval days; the Pfalz, or Palatinate, then was known as the "Wine Cellar of the Holy Roman Empire," *propter vini copiam,* on account of the abundance of its wines. Actually both of its current names come from the Latin: Pfalz is a corruption of *Palast,* or palace, and Palatinate, after the "Palatine" Hill, one of Rome's seven, where the Roman emperors built their palaces, and from which the word "palace" stems. Before long, the person charged with the care of the emperor's palaces acquired the title of *comes palatinus,* or Count Palatine, and the title survived in Germany.

The present district is bounded on the east by the Rhine, on the south and west by Alsace-Lorraine, and on the north by Rheinhessen. The vineyards extend along the lower slopes of a chain of hills called the Haardt, a sort of lesser northern prolongation of the Alsatian Vosges, and over a good portion of the fertile plain that extends eastward toward the Rhine, opposite Mannheim, Karlsruhe and Baden-Baden. Most of all this produces nothing more than very common white and red table wine, with the white predominating by a wide margin.

Such wines as are fit for bottling and for export come almost exclusively from a small central section known as the Mittel-Haardt, between Neustadt and Bad Dürkheim. There is a good deal of ordinary red wine, made mostly from the so-called Portugieser grape, and a great deal more white, that worthy of note made mostly from the Riesling and some from the Sylvaner.

Four especially favored villages produce wine of top class: from north to south, Wachenheim, Forst, Deidesheim and Ruppertsberg (*see* these), but Bad Dürkheim, Kallstadt, Leistadt and Königsbach can all be ranked not too far behind.

The wines have a special character of their own: the lesser ones a

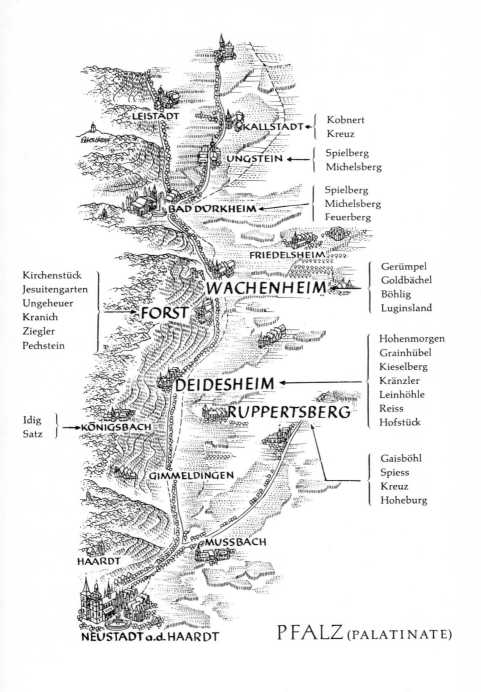

KALLSTADT → { Kobnert
Kreuz

UNGSTEIN → { Spielberg
Michelsberg

BAD DÜRKHEIM → { Spielberg
Michelsberg
Feuerberg

FRIEDELSHEIM

Kirchenstück
Jesuitengarten
Ungeheuer
Kranich
Ziegler
Pechstein

WACHENHEIM → { Gerümpel
Goldbächel
Böhlig
Luginsland

FORST

DEIDESHEIM → { Hohenmorgen
Grainhübel
Kieselberg
Kränzler
Leinhöhle
Reiss
Hofstück

RUPPERTSBERG

Idig
Satz } → KÖNIGSBACH

Gaisböhl
Spiess
Kreuz
Hoheburg

GIMMELDINGEN

MUSSBACH

HAARDT

NEUSTADT a.d. HAARDT

PFALZ (PALATINATE)

Bodengeschmack, or taste of heavy soil; but the Rieslings from the better vineyards are truly of the highest quality — fine, fuller-bodied than the Rheingaus but hardly inferior to them. They have considerable bouquet and breed and go better than most other German wines with food. The Beerenauslesen, etc., of great vintages are much sought after, and bring astronomic prices.

RHENISH — Old English term for wines of the Rhine, now largely replaced by "Hock" in Great Britain, and by "Rhine Wine" in the United States.

RHINE WINE — Properly and sensibly, a wine from the Rhine Valley. Unfortunately, under American law, almost any white wine under 14% alcohol may be so labeled, no matter where made or out of what sort of grapes. Those who wish to find some sort of an American equivalent of a German Rhine wine should look to Johannisberg Riesling and Sylvaner from California, or even (although they are vastly different in flavor) the better varietal wines from the Finger Lakes district of New York State. For fuller information about the German original, *see* Rheingau, Hessia, Rheinpfalz and Germany.

RHÔNE — (Rone) — One of the great rivers of Western Europe, rising in Switzerland, traversing Lake Geneva, emptying into the Mediterranean west of Marseille. Vines are grown along its banks throughout a large part of its whole length and a great variety of different wines are produced — those of the Valais, the Vaud, Lavaux, and what is called La Côte, in Switzerland; Seyssel, between Geneva and Lyon; and all those known as Rhône wines, or Côtes-du-Rhône *(see),* between Lyon and the Mediterranean. These include Côte Rôtie, Condrieu, Château-Grillet, Crozes, Hermitage, Cornas, St. Péray, Gigondas, Châteauneuf-du-Pape, Tavel, Lirac, etc. *(see* all of these).

  ALSO, a French *département,* that of the Beaujolais Country and the city of Lyon.

RIBEAUVILLÉ — (Ree-*bo*-vee-lay) — Important Alsatian vineyard town in the *département* of Haut-Rhin. White wines of exceptional quality.

RICEYS — (Re-*say*) — Curious, almost forgotten little corner along the southern edge of the French Champagne Country, in the *département* of Aube, adjoining Burgundy. Its vineyards, planted mostly to Pinot Noir but with some Gamay, yield about a thousand cases a year of a fresh, often quite pleasant, short-lived, non-sparkling *vin rosé,* called Rosé des Riceys. It is something of a collector's item but of no great class.

RICHEBOURG — (*Reesh*-bourg) — One of the very great red-wine vineyards of Burgundy, just over 19 acres, in the township of Vosne-Romanée. It is bounded on the south by Romanée-Conti and La Romanée, and on the east by Romanée Saint-Vivant; its wine (some 2,000 cases a year) is generally somewhat sturdier and fuller, with deeper color, than that of its illustrious neighbors — it is the "biggest"

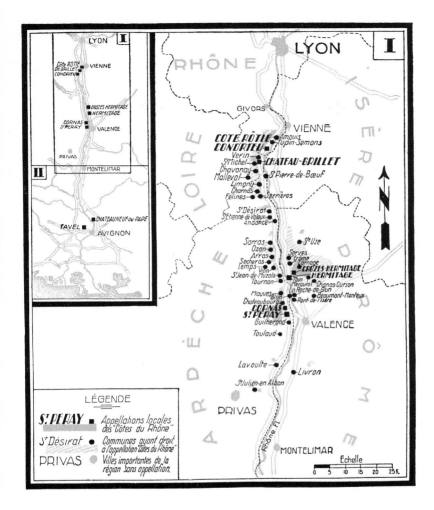

wine of Vosne-Romanée. Until quite recently, a portion of it was still planted to old, non-grafted vines, as in the pre-phylloxera period, and was considered to give an even finer wine. A major part of Richebourg belongs to the Domaine de la Romanée Conti (*see*).

RICHELIEU, Armand, Cardinal de — (1585-1642) — French cardinal and statesman, who asked: "If God forbade drinking would He have made wine so good?"

RIESLING — (*Reece*-ling) — One of the very greatest of white wine grapes, apparently a native of the Rhine Valley; it has been grown there

275

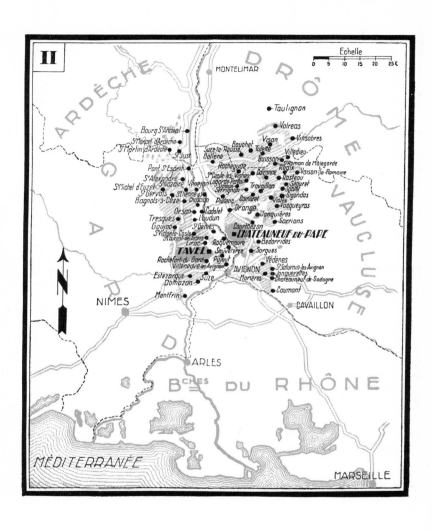

II

Echelle
0 5 10 15 20 25 K.

MONTÉLIMAR

ARDÈCHE
DRÔME
GARD
VAUCLUSE
B^ches DU RHÔNE
MÉDITERRANÉE

• Taulignan
• Valréas
• Visan   • Vinsobres
Bourg St Andéol •
St Marcel d'Ardèche •   Bouchet
St Martin d'Ardèche •   Suze-la-Rousse • Tulette
                    Bollène •   Buisson •   Villedieu
                    St Just •   St Roman de Malegarde •
          Rochegude •   Roaix •
Pont St Esprit •   Cairanne •   Vaison-la-Romaine •
St Alexandre •   Ste Cécile-les-Vignes •
St Michel d'Euzet • St Nazaire • Lagarde-Paréol •   Rasteau •
              Véneton • Sérignan •   Travaillan •   Séguret •
St Gervais •   St Étienne •   Sablet • Gigondas •
Bagnols-s-Cèze •   Chusclan •   Camaret •   Violès •
              Orsan • Codolet •   Piolenc • Orange •   Vacqueyras •
Tresques •   Laudun •   Jonquières •   Sarrians •
Gaujac •   St Genies •
St Victor-la-Coste •   Courthézon •
        St Laurent-des-Arbres •   CHÂTEAUNEUF-DU-PAPE •
                    Lirac •   Roquemaure •   Bédarrides •
TAVEL •   Sauveterre •   Sorgues •
Rochefort-du-Gard •   Pujaut •   Vedènes •
        Villeneuve-les-Avignon •   St Saturnin-les-Avignon •
                            AVIGNON   Jonquerettes •
Estézargue •   Suze •   Montières •   Châteauneuf-de-Gadagne •
    Domazan •
        Montfrin •   Caumont •

NÎMES   CAVAILLON

ARLES

MARSEILLE

since Roman days at least, and no acceptable evidence exists to show that it originated elsewhere. Stories to the effect that it is identical with the Sercial of Madeira and the Pedro Ximénez of Spain are unworthy of credence; in modern times it has been transplanted into many other countries, and has almost always yielded superior wine, in Chile and in California, in Austria and Switzerland and Italy. It gives its best and wholly remarkable wine where it is not asked to produce too much, in cool districts, and on slaty or stony soil.

Thus it is the one variety cultivated in all of the more distinguished Moselle vineyards, and in all the best of the Rheingau; it is widely planted in Rheinhessen and the Rheinpfalz, and immeasurably outdistances all its rivals in quality, if not always in acreage. Its wine is the best of Alsace; it does well in Austria and Switzerland and in the Italian Tyrol. The Chilean "Rieslings" (some of which may well be made from the more productive Sylvaner), shipped in flagons, or Bocksbeutel, are by far the most widely accepted South American wines in the United States.

In California (and even in New York State) there has been a good deal of confusion, some of it a long way from accidental, with respect to the variety and its name. Here the true variety is known as the "White Riesling" or "Johannisberg Riesling," but wines may be labeled "Riesling" if made from the Chauché Gris ("Grey Riesling") or the Sylvaner ("Franken Riesling"), or the "Emerald Riesling" (a modern hybrid), or even the "Missouri Riesling" (a native American vine, probably the Elvira). The same sort of loose popularization has taken place in Europe, and we have crosses such as the "Main Riesling" and vines such as the "*Wälschriesling*" which have no possible proper right to the name.

In California the true Riesling grape, without the benefit of *pourriture noble* yet grown farther south and under sunnier skies, gives a fine dry white wine of good bouquet and considerable distinction. It is almost always labeled "Johannisberg Riesling."

RIEUSSEC, Château — (*Rhee*-oo-sec) — 1st Classed Growth of Fargues, Sauternes. Rather full-bodied, deep-colored Sauternes, in general less sweet but more obvious and less fine than most of the other 1st Growths.

RILLY-LA-MONTAGNE — (*Ree*-ye-*La*-Mawn-*tahn*) — Secondary wine-producing village of the French Champagne Country, on the Montagne de Reims.

RIOJA — (Ree-o-ha) — The most important and by all odds the best table wine district of Spain. It takes its name from the Rio Oja, a small tributary of the River Ebro, which it joins on the edge of the Basque Country, near Pamplona, not very far from the western Pyrenees and the French border. This is high, cold, upland country, and the bare hills north and south of the valley are often white with snow as late as April; the average altitude of the vineyards is well over 1,500 feet. The wines are therefore anything but fiery and full-bodied (although they have often been called both by writers unfamiliar with them) and on the whole are lighter, lower in alcohol and dryer than those of Bordeaux, to which they bear a certain superficial resemblance.

Federico Paternina

"GRAN RESERVA"

Red Rioja Table Wine

VINTAGE 1955

Ollauri

(RIOJA)

Contents: 3/4 Quart
Alcohol by Volume 12%

R.E. 329   PRODUCT OF SPAIN

This kinship (much more marked in the red wines than in the white) is not altogether accidental; when the phylloxera (*see*) arrived and began to devastate the Bordeaux vineyards in the 1880's, several hundred French families from Bordeaux moved south into the still uninfected Ebro valley, and settled in Haro and Logroño, still today the main centers of the Rioja wine trade; they brought with them their Bordeaux methods and their Bordeaux skill. Both, in the light of what we now know about wine production, could stand a little refurbishing, especially as far as white wines are concerned, for Riojas are presently made, operation for operation, almost precisely as Bordeaux wines were made eighty years ago — aged three to five years in oak, and the whites rather liberally sulphured. There is no *pourriture noble* (*see*) in this high arid zone, and therefore no legitimate Rioja counterpart of Sauternes. The dry white wines tend to be dull, neutral and somewhat common; the reds are often quite outstanding and, considering their quality, remarkably inexpensive.

The principal white grapes are the Viura, Maturana, Calgraño and Turrantés (*"ni la comas ni la des — que par vino buena es"* or "don't eat it or give it away — it's good for wine").

Most of the red grape varieties, too, are Spanish; none of them are among those properly classified as "noble"; they include the Garnacha (Grenache), Graciano, Mazuela and Tempranillo. Yet, with a very low yield per acre, what they give is surprisingly good: rather light, fine-textured red wines, with a faint earthy flavor and a good deal of breed.

The Rioja district has been officially delimited and there is an excellent, well-staffed government viticultural station in Haro. There are unfortunately no specific vineyard appellations (although many wines are sold under names that appear to be, as "Viña X," etc.) and one has to rely on producers' names, or brands. Vintage years should be generally disregarded and are loosely used. Most producers offer a range of red

278

wines, from *Clarete* (usually the youngest, lightest and cheapest) to *Gran Reserva, Imperial*, and the like, which are always older and generally quite fine. The more reliable shippers include the Marqués de Riscal, the Marqués de Murrieta, Federico Paternina, the Bodegas Bilbainas, the Bodegas Franco-Españolas, La Rioja Alta, etc. The main wine producing towns, apart from Haro, are Elciego, Fuenmayor, Cenicero and Ollauri.

RIPAILLE — (Ree-*pie*) — Lesser white wine of the Haute Savoie *département* of France, made from Chasselas grapes near Thonon-les-Bains on Lake Geneva, rarely exported and of no great quality.

RIPE — Wine taster's term and high praise. Applied to a wine that has fruit, no trace of greenness or harshness, generally a white wine that is not bone dry although not necessarily sweet. Sometimes also means a wine ready to drink.

RIQUEWIHR — (Reek-veer) — One of the best wine-producing villages of Alsace and one of the most picturesque of France, its medieval walls and towers and gateways still intact and its narrow streets lined with fine old half-timbered houses. Some ten miles northwest of Colmar, it is set in the vineyard-covered foothills of the Vosges; its Rieslings are particularly famous.

RIVERO — (Ree-*vair*-ro) — Spanish wine district, in the province of Galicia, along the Portuguese border. Most of the *Vinos de Rivero*, for such is their legal name, are red-purple, very fruity, with a pronounced and highly special flavor which is not likely to appeal to everyone. A fortified sweet wine called Tostado del Rivero is produced in the same district.

RIVESALTES — (Reev-sahlt) — Town north of Perpignan in the French *département* of Pyrénées Orientales. It has given its name to a district comprising over a dozen townships and producing some 5 million gallons a year of fortified dessert wine, about a third of it called Muscat de Rivesaltes, and the rest, principally from Grenache and Malvoisie grapes, sold simply as Rivesaltes or Rivesaltes Rancio. It legally must contain a minimum of 15% alcohol by volume, and is somewhat comparable to Banyuls (*see*), although generally less fine.

ROANNAIS — (*Ro*-an-nay) — Roanne is a little city west of Lyon in central France, round which are produced a number of pleasant red *vins de pays*, fresh, light, early-maturing, made mostly from the Gamay grape, and sold as Côtes Roannaises or Vins de Renaison. They are entitled to the V.D.Q.S. seal, but few if any are exported.

ROBUST — Wine taster's term. Sound, sturdy, full-bodied, not necessarily fine.

ROCHE AUX MOINES, La — (Rawsh-oh-Mwahn) — One of the best vineyards of Savennières (*see*), which produces some of the most distinguished of the great sweet white wines of Anjou.

279

ROCHECORBON — (Rawsh-cor-bawn) — One of the more important villages of the Vouvray district, just east of Tours, in France.

ROCHEFORT-SUR-LOIRE — (*Rowsh*-for-sewer-*Lwar*) — Little town on the Loire, just west of Angers, responsible for some of the very finest white Anjou wines. These, made from the Chenin Blanc grape, rarely carry the town name except as the address of the producer, and are marketed either as Coteaux du Layon (a regional appellation) or as Quarts de Chaume (*see*).

ROCHET, Château — (Ro-shay) — 4th Classed Growth of St. Estèphe, Haut-Médoc. Some 5,000 cases a year of a soft, rather light Claret.

ROMANÈCHE-THORINS — (Ro-man-*esh-Tor*-ran) — Town on the eastern edge of the Beaujolais district, but not the name of a wine. Its vineyards form part of Moulin-à-Vent (*see*) and their wines are marketed under this appellation.

ROMANÉE, La — (La *Ro*-ma-*nay*) — Tiny vineyard, barely two acres in extent, producing one of the rarest of red Burgundies. It is in the township of Vosne-Romanée, directly above and west of Romanée-Conti, and its production is rarely much over 300 cases; in recent years it has not often given wines of outstanding quality.

ROMANÉE-CONTI — (*Ro*-ma-*nay Cawn*-tee) — Perhaps the most celebrated of all red Burgundies, traditionally the *ne plus ultra* of red wine, often, especially in pre-war years, fully worthy of its extraordinary reputation. The vineyard is of roughly 4⅓ acres and its average production is about 700 cases, although less than 100 in 1945; previously in old, ungrafted vines (Pinot Noir, needless to say), it was replanted in 1946 and is now producing, from vines grafted on American rootstocks, wines increasingly close in quality to what it yielded before. It takes its name from the Prince de Conti, its owner from 1760 to 1795, and was acquired in 1869 by M. Duvault-Blochet, the leading vineyard-owner of Burgundy of that day, and great-grandfather of one of the present proprietors, M. de Villaine. It now forms part of the Domaine de la Romanée-Conti, the most famous single estate of the Côte d'Or; this comprises Romanée-Conti and La Tâche (*see*), both in their entirety, a large part of Richebourg, and important holdings in Échézeaux and Grands Échézeaux. All of these, *grands seigneurs* in every sense of the term, are vinified and bottled in the estate cellars and have what might be called a certain family resemblance — believed, by certain experts, attributable to some secret of vinification. Romanée-Conti commands the highest price of any of these, and, in most years, the highest price of any red Burgundy. It is a great rarity and a very great wine.

For Map, *see* VOSNE.

ROMANÉE SAINT-VIVANT — (*Ro*-man-*nay* San-Vee-*vawn*) — Admirable Burgundian vineyard, directly adjoining Romanée-Conti and Richebourg, in the township of Vosne-Romanée. It takes its name from the Priory of Saint-Vivant, having been conveyed as a gift to the monks of this priory (some three miles west of Vosne) by the Duchess of Burgundy in 1232; it remained their property until the French Revolution. Twenty-three acres in extent, divided among several owners, its maximum legal yield is some 2,800 cases, although in practice rarely half of that. One of the finest of all red Burgundies, full, soft, with great bouquet, it has the incomparable distinction of the Romanées, and there are few if any better wines in France.

ROMER, Château — (Ro-mer) — 2nd Classed Growth of Fargues, Sauternes. Small production of good, rather sweet wine.

RONDINELLA — (Rawn-dee-*nel*-la) — Italian red wine grape of secondary importance, planted to a small extent in the vineyards of Valpolicella and elsewhere.

RONSARD, Pierre de — (Rawn-saar) — Eminent French lyric poet who celebrated the delights of his native Loire Valley, the wines occasionally, but even more the countryside and its lovely girls, in some of the most charming verses ever written.

ROSATO — (Roas-*sah*-toe) — Simply means *rosé* in Italian. Pink wine, of course, can be made anywhere. Italy's best, and they are not very numerous, come from Lake Garda (*see*), and from the Trentino and Alto Adige (*see*). They include Chiaretto and Chiarello, Lagrein Rosato, Marzemino d'Isera (*see* all of these) and Rosato d'Avio, from the lower end of Trentino. There are others, less fine, from the Chianti Country and even from Ravello, near Naples.

ROSÉ — (Ro-*zay*) — French word for pink, when applied to wine, now pretty much part of the English language, and used in almost every country where wine is produced or drunk. A true *vin rosé* is by no means a blend of red and white wines, but a special product, usually made from black grapes alone, and owing its color to the fact that it was neither fermented entirely with the grape skins (like all red wines), nor entirely without (like all white wines). *Rosés* of some sort are produced in almost all wine-growing countries, the best of them from the Grenache, Pinot Noir, Cabernet Franc, Gamay, and several Italian grape varieties: they should be served chilled and drunk young. Several excellent *rosés* are now being made in California, above all from the Grenache grape; the best French come from Tavel (*see*), Marsannay (*see*), the Loire Valley, the Beaujolais, northern Alsace, and Provence.

ROSÉ DE BEARN — (*Ro*-zay duh Bay-*arn*) — Pink or *rosé* wine of fair quality produced (from a number of different grapes) in the *département* of Basses-Pyrénées, near Pau. It carries the V.D.Q.S. seal (*see*).

ROSETTE — (Ro-*set*) — Rather agreeable white wine, not entirely dry, made north of Bergerac in the *département* of the Dordogne. It comes largely from the Semillon grape, plus some Sauvignon Blanc and Muscadelle; production amounts to some 75,000 gallons a year.

ROSSARA — (Roas-*sahr*-ra) — Italian red wine grape of superior quality, grown in the vineyards of Bardolino (*see*) and elsewhere.

ROSSO — (*Ross*-so) — Simply means red in Italian, and a *vino rosso* is a red wine, any red wine. The term in recent years has been given a somewhat different meaning in California, and now indicates a red table wine that is not altogether dry; there are many such in Italy, but all of the finest Italian red wines are without any trace of sweetness, and would therefore hardly qualify as *vini rossi* in California.

ROTTEN EGG FLAVOR — This is the definite, unmistakable odor of hydrogen sulphide or, as experts prefer to call it, metallic sulphur. It is entirely harmless, extremely disagreeable, inexcusable in wine and fortunately very infrequent. It is the result of bad cellar work and carelessness.

ROUGET, Château — (Roo-shay) — 1st Growth vineyard of Pomerol, producing some 5,000 cases a year.

ROUNDED — Well-balanced, without a major defect, complete. Could never be said of a poor wine but does not necessarily mean either fine or great.

ROUSSANNE — (Roo-*sahn*) — White wine grape widely cultivated in the Rhône Valley, also called the Roussette, giving, notably at Hermitage and St. Péray, a full-bodied white wine of rather pronounced character and considerable distinction.

ROUSSELET — (*Roos*-lay) — Pleasant dry white wine, produced in the old province of Béarn, near Pau, mostly from the Rousselet grape. It is entitled to and generally carries the V.D.Q.S. seal (*see*).

ROUSSETTE — (Roo-*set*) — Another name for the Roussanne grape (*see*). In the higher and cooler upper valley of the Rhône, between Lyon and Geneva, and in the hilly *département* of Haute Savoie, where it is generally called Roussette rather than Roussanne, it yields a number of

fresh, fragrant, extremely agreeable white wines, some made sparkling (*see* Seyssel), some still. A few of these are sold under the varietal name, as Roussette de Savoie.

ROUSSILLON — Old French province which originally comprised the modern *département* of Pyrénées Orientales, plus part of the Aude, on the Mediterranean coast, along the Spanish border. Its principal town is Perpignan. In total gallonage this is one of the major wine-producing regions of Europe, with a vast amount of *vin ordinaire,* a few somewhat better table wines (*see* Corbières), and more than three-quarters of the fortified wines of France. Roussillon, however, is not a wine name, except in the combined form, "Grand Roussillon" (*see*), which is one of the five *Appellations Contrôlées* of this district. Banyuls (*see*) is the most important of these; the others (Rivesaltes, Côtes d'Agly, Maury, and Côtes de Haut-Roussillon) are all listed elsewhere in this volume.

ROXHEIM — (Rawks-heim) — One of the better wine-producing towns of the Nahe district, in Germany.

RUCHOTTES — (Roosh-*shawt*) — Burgundian vineyard name, probably derived from *ruche,* or beehive, on account of the sweetness of the grapes there grown or the special bouquet and flavor, recalling that of honey, of the wine. The Ruchottes vineyard in Chassagne-Montrachet (*see*) produces one of the very finest white wines of France; Ruchottes-Chambertin (*see*) is ranked as a *Grand Cru.*

RUCHOTTES-CHAMBERTIN — (Roosh-*shawt Shawm*-bair-tan) — Little 8-acre plot, ranked as a *Grand Cru* of Burgundy and one of Chambertin's distinguished neighbors. Directly above and behind Mazis-Chambertin (*see*), it produces a fine red wine, one of the best of its famous township.

RÜDESHEIM — (*Rue*-dess-heim) — Picturesque and celebrated little town of the Rheingau, in Germany, directly facing across the wide, swift Rhine, Bingen (*see*) and the mouth of the Nahe. It is a major tourist center, and its two main streets, squeezed in between the river and the steep vineyards behind, are crowded all summer long, and no less so in the autumn, the vintage-festival season. There are countless cafés and *Weinstuben*, and a substantial part of the wine that its 650 acres of Riesling vines produce, is beyond question promptly and happily consumed within a few hundred yards of where it is made.

As wines, the better Rüdesheimers are nevertheless outstanding, in poor or fair years often the best of the whole Rheingau, full-bodied and distinguished, although in great years they are sometimes too heavy and too high in alcohol. Their good qualities, like their faults, can be attributed to the steepness of the rocky terraced vineyards, which are gravely affected by drought in dry, hot summers, especially those west of the town itself, on what is called the Rüdesheimer Berg. These carry the word *Berg* as part of their appellation, and names to look for on Rüdesheimer labels are Rüdesheimer Berg Rottland, Berg Roseneck, Berg Bronnen, Berg Lay, Berg Hellpfad, Berg Schlossberg, Berg Zollhaus, Berg Kronest, but also (not from the Berg) Rüdesheimer Klosterkiesel, Wilgert, Hinterhaus, Bischofsberg, etc. Top producers include Espenschied, Graf von Schönborn, Ritter zu Groensteyn, the State Domain, etc.

Also a small vineyard town of no great consequence or distinction in the Nahe Valley whose wines are often confused by the unwary with those of the great Rheingau slope described above. If properly labeled, these should carry the designation "Nahe," whereas those of the authentic Rüdesheim will be marked "Rheingau." Rüdesheimer Rosengarten is a wine of the Nahe.

RUEDA — (Rue-*eh*-dah) — One of the good, less-known white wines of northern Spain, produced between Valladolid and Zamora, in the Valley of the Duero.

RUFINA — (Rue-*fee*-na) — Town and small district in Italy's Chianti Country, in the valley of the river Sieve, some twenty miles northeast of Florence. Its wines are now sold, almost invariably, simply as Chianti (*see*) and are among the best of those not entitled to the *classico* designation, full-bodied, deep-colored, with fine bouquet.

RUFFINO — (Rue-*fee*-no) — Well-known brand of non-*classico* Chianti, produced and shipped by the firm of this name at Pontassieve, up the Arno from Florence.

RULLY — (*Roo*-ye) — Small town in Burgundy, just south of the southern end of the Côte d'Or, and therefore belonging to the Côte Chalonnaise; known in the wine trade for its production of Sparkling Burgundy (*see*). Over three-quarters of the wine actually grown in the *commune*, however, is white, and from the Chardonnay grape, fresh, dry, fruity and very palatable: the red comes from the Pinot Noir, but rarely carries the appellation Rully.

RUPPERTSBERG — (Roop-perts-bairg) — One of the four best wine-producing towns of the Palatinate, or Pfalz, in Germany. In average quality, its wines are perhaps slightly less distinguished than those of

Forst and Deidesheim (only 20% of its 420 acres of vineyard are planted to Riesling grapes, the rest mostly to Sylvaner) but they are nevertheless remarkable — full-bodied, ripe, fairly high in alcohol; the finest of them, from celebrated growers, are great wines in every sense of the word. They come from such vineyards as Gaisböhl, Spiess, Kreuz, Nussbien, Reiterpfad, Hofstück, Hoheburg, etc., and are estate-bottled by Bassermann-Jordan, Bürklin-Wolf, von Buhl, and a few others.

RUSSIAN RIVER — Like many California rivers, a not too impressive stream, which nevertheless includes Mendocino County and the northern half of Sonoma County in its basin. It runs north-south for most of its course, then cuts abruptly west through the redwood groves of the West Coast range, to the Pacific, some fifty miles north of San Francisco.

RUST — (Roost) — Rather sweet white wine from the province of Burgenland, in Austria.

RUWER — (Roo-ver) — Small tributary of the Moselle, which it joins some four miles east of Trier, looking much more like a trout stream than a famous river. Its wines are legally Moselles, and carry the regional designation "Mosel-Saar-Ruwer" on their labels; the best of them are among the greatest of all German wines, very close in quality and also in character to those of the Saar. There are only about 500 acres of vineyard in the whole valley, all Rieslings, planted on preposterously steep, black-slate, south-facing hillsides. Two estates, each dominating a tiny village, are internationally known; Eitelsbacher Karthäuserhofberg, which belongs to the Rautenstrauch family, and Maximin-Grünhauser, which is the fief of the Von Schuberts. But very good, somewhat lighter and lesser wines are made in Kasel (or Casel) further upstream, by a number of growers. *See* Eitelsbach, Maximin-Grünhaus, Kasel.

SAAR — (Sahr) — Small river in Germany, a tributary of the Moselle which it joins at Conz, just west of Trier. It rises in the Saar Basin, famous for its heavy industry; then, farther downstream, near the frontier of France and Luxembourg, runs through a steep valley no less famous for its wines. Legally these are Moselles, and carry the designation Mosel-Saar-Ruwer on their labels; they nevertheless have a special character of their own, being austere, almost "steely," very pale, low in alcohol, remarkable for their bouquet. Made from the Riesling grape in one of the coldest wine-growing areas of the world, they are tart and green in all except good vintage years, and are often converted into *Sekt,* or sparkling wine, but in years such as '59, '64 and '66 they are altogether extraordinary, fully the equals of any other white wines on earth. The most celebrated vineyard is the Scharzhofberg (*see*), and the leading wine-producing towns are, in about this order of quality: Wiltingen, Ockfen, Ayl, Kanzem (or Canzem), Oberemmel, Wawern, Niedermennig, Serrig, Filzen, Saarburg.

For Map, *see* MOSELLE.

SAARBURG — (Sahr-boorg) — Picturesque little town on the Saar, in Germany, not far from the French border. Most of its pale, tart white wines end up as *Sekt*, or Sparkling Moselle, and only in rare, especially good years do they, as still wines, achieve any real quality.

SABLES-SAINT-EMILION — (*Sahb*-ul-Sant-A-*me*-lee-awn) — Small district of red wine, directly adjoining St. Emilion (*see*) on the west. The word *sable*, in French, means "sand" — the sandy and alluvial soil of this little area, on the flat plain running down to the Dordogne River, practically in the town of Libourne, yields no great wines at all, but a few that are fruity, early-maturing, short-lived, highly agreeable. Château Martinet is perhaps the best.

SACCHAROMYCES — The yeasts of wine fermentation.

SACK — Term used in Elizabethan England (also "Sherris Sack") to mean Sherry; literally, the verb *sacar* in Spanish means (among other things) "to transfer from one place or country to another," and a *Vino de Saca* then meant, and now means, a wine destined for export. "Dry Sack," however, is a brand of Sherry, a good quality Amoroso, put out by the house of Williams & Humbert.

SACRAMENTAL WINE — Mass wine or altar wine, made in accordance with the regulations of the Roman Catholic Church, as defined by Canon Law, authorized for use in the ceremony of the mass.

SAGGIAVINO — (Sadj-ja-*vee*-no) — Italian for a *pipette* or "wine-thief," used for taking samples from a barrel.

SAINT AMOUR — (Sant Ah-mour) — Northernmost of the important wine-producing *communes* of the Beaujolais, and officially ranked as one of the nine best; it is directly northeast of Juliénas, and its full name is Saint-Amour-Bellevue (it should not, of course, be confused with the town of St. Amour, off east in the *département* of the Jura). Its wine is popular, perhaps partially on account of its romantic name, but on the whole it deserves its rank and its fame: it is a fruity, tender red wine, soon ready.

SAINT AUBIN — (Sant-toe-ban) — Wine-producing village of no great importance, back of Puligny-Montrachet and Chassagne-Montrachet, in Burgundy. Most of its better wines are sold as Côte-de-Beaune Villages (*see*) or as Bourgogne-Aligoté.

SAINT DENIS — *See* Clos St. Denis.

SAINT-EMILION — (Sant A-*me*-lee-awn) — Ancient and wonderfully picturesque little town, rich in ruins and medieval buildings, set on the edge of an escarpment overlooking the green Dordogne Valley, some twenty miles east of Bordeaux. It was already famous for its wines in the 4th century, and, with 16,000 acres of vines, its district produces more superior wine today than any other division of the Bordeaux Country. Most of the best vineyards are in the township of St. Emilion itself, but seven adjoining *communes* are also entitled to the appellation,

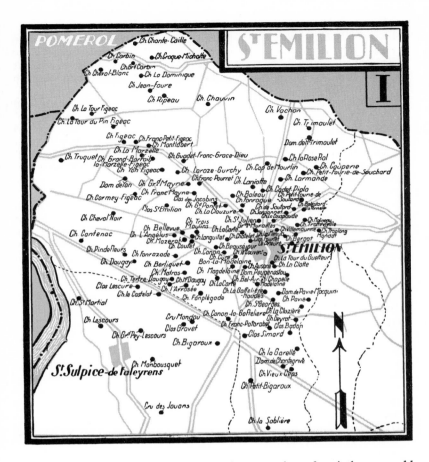

and five more areas, or *communes*, plus a portion of a sixth, may add
the words St. Emilion to their own name on wine labels, as Lussac-St.
Emilion, etc. The finest wines come either from the steep, chalky slopes
of the escarpment itself (*vins des côtes*), or from the high, gravelly
plateau behind (*vins des graves*, or Graves-St. Emilion); among the
former, Châteaux Ausone, Bélair, Magdelaine, Canon, Clos Fourtet,
Beauséjour, La Gafflière-Naudes are perhaps the most famous, with at
least 30 or 40 others deserving almost equal rank; of the latter, Château
Cheval Blanc is easily first, with Châteaux Figeac, Croque-Michotte,
Corbin, etc., not too far behind.

District wines labeled "St. Emilion" often come from the seven adjoining, less distinguished townships, (Saint-Christophe-des-Bardes, Saint-
Étienne-de-Lisse, Saint-Hippolyte, Saint-Laurent-des-Combes, Saint-Pey-
d'Armens, Saint-Sulpice-de-Faleyrens and Vignonet), but even these
have a relatively high average quality — they are sturdy, warm, gener-

ous, wholly agreeable Clarets, pleasing even when young, and attractive even when not "great"; they have been called "the Burgundies of the Bordeaux Country." The great chateaux-bottlings are, of course, of a far higher class and are by no means inferior to the great Médocs, although their character is quite different.

Wines from the secondary, nearby townships have less breed, and occasionally a *goût de terroir*, or taste of heavy soil, but they are generally inexpensive and often good values. The six appellations involved are as follows, and they rank in about this order of quality: SAINT-GEORGES-SAINT-EMILION, MONTAGNE-SAINT-EMILION, LUSSAC-SAINT EMILION, PUISSEGUIN-SAINT-EMILION, PARSAC-SAINT-EMILION, SABLES-SAINT-EMILION. A little white wine is produced, but is not entitled to any of these names.

ALSO, name given to the Ugni Blanc or Trebbiano variety of grape in the Cognac Country of France. Here, known as the St. Emilion, it has almost entirely replaced the somewhat finer Folle Blanche in the making of wine for distillation — it is productive, and yields exactly what is required: a wine low in alcohol and very high in acid. It apparently reached Cognac by way of St. Emilion where, although white, it was planted to some extent in the red-wine vineyards: late maturing, picked when not yet ripe, its grapes supplied a welcome additional acidity to the Cabernets and Merlots in great years.

SAINT-ESTÈPHE — (Sant Eas-*teff*) — Northernmost of the major wine-producing townships of the Haut-Médoc, directly adjoining Pauillac. Its best wines (Châteaux Cos d'Estournel, Calon-Ségur, Montrose, etc.) are sturdy, full-bodied, generous and attractive; they have perhaps less finesse and breed than comparable Clarets from Margaux, St. Julien and Pauillac, but a sort of forthright, lusty charm instead, which renders them most agreeable. There are many excellent lesser vineyards, *crus bourgeois* and the like, and regional wines labeled "St. Estèphe" are generally good values, although occasionally a bit on the heavy side, and sometimes slightly earthy.

SAINT-GEORGES, Château — (Sant-Shortj) — The largest vineyard and on the whole the best of the little district known as Saint-Georges-Saint-Emilion (*see*). Its average annual production is not far from 30,000 cases, a figure unsurpassed and indeed unequaled by any other chateau in the Bordeaux Country. In quality it is both dependable and good.

SAINT-GEORGES-SAINT-EMILION — (Sant-*Shorj*-Sant-A-*me*-lee-awn) — One of the best of the secondary *communes* adjoining St. Emilion (*see*), entitled to the name in this combined form. A number of its wines are decidedly superior to most of what is ordinarily sold under the more highly rated appellation St. Emilion. The better Châteaux include: Saint-Georges, Saint-Georges-Macquin, Samion, Jacquet, Tourteau, etc.

SAINT-JOSEPH — (San Sho-*zef*) — A Rhône wine, generally red although a little white and *rosé* is also made and legally entitled to the name, produced opposite Hermitage, on the right or west bank of the Rhône. Its quality is by no means outstanding.

SAINT-JULIEN — (Sant-*Shoe*-lee-an) — Township in the very center and heart of the Haut-Médoc. Its wines include none of the very highest rank, but practically no poor ones either, and when sold simply as "St. Julien," they are almost invariably the most expensive of the Bordeaux regionals. Sometimes called the perfect Claret for Claret-lovers, St. Julien is a little fuller than Margaux, generally has more finesse and bouquet than St. Estèphe, matures sooner than Pauillac. The more famous Châteaux include: Léoville-Poyferré, Léoville-Barton, Léoville-Las-Cases, Gruaud-Larose, Ducru-Beaucaillou, Beychevelle, Talbot, etc. *See* map on following page.

SAINT-LAURENT — (Sant-Low-rawn) — Township in the Haut-Médoc, west of St. Julien. There are three Châteaux officially classed in 1855; Château La Tour-Carnet (4th), Château Belgrave and Château Camensac (both 5ths).

SAINT-MACAIRE — (Sant-Mac-*care*) — See Côtes-de-Bordeaux.

ST. NICOLAS DE BOURGUEIL — (San *Ni*-ko-la duh Boor-*guh*-ee) — Superior red wine made from the Cabernet Franc grape in the province of Touraine, France. *See* Bourgueil.

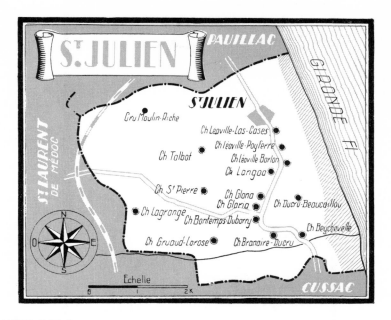

SAINT PÉRAY — (San Pay-ray) — White wine of the Rhône Valley, more often than not made sparkling by the Champagne process, produced round the village of this name, opposite Valence, on the right or west bank of the Rhône. Coming from the same grapes as white Hermitage, the Roussanne (or Roussette) and Marsanne, it is more golden in color and fuller-bodied than Champagne, but with quite definite, special character — certainly one of the better *vins mousseux* of France. As a still wine, it is a little lighter than white Hermitage, and less fine.

SAINT-PIERRE-BONTEMPS, Château — (Sant-Pea-*air*-*Bawn*-tawn) — Good 4th Classed Growth of St. Julien, producing a sound, well-balanced Claret especially popular in Belgium and in England. It has recently been reunited with its twin and neighbor, Château Saint-Pierre-Sevaistre, and the property's total output, under the two labels, is in the neighborhood of 10,000 cases a year.

SAINT-PIERRE-SEVAISTRE, Château — (Sant-P-*air*-Sev-*ace*-tr) — 4th Classed Growth of St. Julien. *See* Saint-Pierre-Bontemps.

SAINT-POURÇAIN — (Sant Poor-san) — Curious and rather rare red and *rosé* wine, made from the Gamay grape in central France. It is produced along the Sioule and Allier rivers, both tributaries of the Loire, and is considered a Loire wine.

SAINT ROMAIN — (San Ro-*mahn*) — Picturesque wine-producing village back of Meursault, in Burgundy. Its red and white wines, of secondary quality, are usually sold simply as "Bourgogne." *See* Arrière-Côtes.

SAINT SAPHORIN — (Sant *Saf*-fo-ran) — One of the best white wines of Switzerland, dry and pale, made from the Fendant or Chasselas grape on the northern shore of Lake Geneva, east of Lausanne.

SAINTE-CROIX-DU-MONT — (Sant-Crwa-do-Mawn) — Fruity, golden, full-bodied, extremely sweet white Bordeaux wine, high in alcohol (over 13%), rather comparable to Sauternes but heavier and less fine. The hilly and picturesque little district from which it comes lies some twenty miles southeast of Bordeaux, and faces Sauternes and Barsac across the green and fertile Garonne Valley. Total production amounts to about 150,000 cases a year, and the better known Châteaux include: Lamarque, Loubens, de Tastes, Grand Peyrot, Coulac, etc. (*See* Premières Côtes de Bordeaux.)

SAINTE-FOY-BORDEAUX — (Sant-Fwah-Bor-doe) — Small Bordeaux wine district, geographically part of Entre-Deux-Mers (*see*) but quite properly considered a separate entity by French wine law. Its white wines are passably good, semi-sweet, generally inexpensive, somewhat like Monbazillac produced nearby, although the latter is not, of course, a Bordeaux wine. A small amount of inconsequential red wine is also produced and legally entitled to the name.

SAINTE ROSELINE, Château — (Sant Ro-zay-*leen*) — Popular and pleasant *rosé* wine from Provence. The name is that of a single vineyard property in the village of Les Arcs, near Draguignan, not of a town or district.

SALINA — (Sah-*lean*-nah) — One of the Lipari Islands off the north coast of Sicily; source of most of the well-known Malvasia di Lipari (*see*).

SAMPIGNY-LES-MARANGES — (*Sam*-peen-ye lay Mar-ronj) — Village at the southern end of the Côte d'Or, in Burgundy. Produces an insignificant amount of passable red wine.

SAN BENITO — County and wine-producing district in California, properly considered one of the "North Coast Counties," although not actually on the Pacific. It lies directly east or inland from Monterey Bay, and the vineyards on the steep hillsides and in the high valleys of its southern half are among the best and coolest of the state. Its total acreage of superior wine grapes has increased substantially in the past few years (largely as a result of Almadén's new plantings at Paicines) and the relative importance of these is certain to increase as housing developments and subdivisions surround and finally overwhelm what were, only a few years ago, some of the best vineyards of the Livermore and Santa Clara valleys. More than half of San Benito's vines are choice French and German varieties — Chardonnay, Pinot Noir, Cabernet, Gewürztraminer, etc. — *planted on their own roots and ungrafted*. This bold experiment seems so far entirely successful, and the predictions of the late, great Professor Bioletti, who foresaw a remarkable viticultural future for San Benito County, seem likely to be fulfilled. Most of the vineyards are in the high country south of the town of Hollister and of San Juan Bautista, which was one of the original Spanish missions, just over a hundred miles due south of San Francisco.

For Map, see CALIFORNIA.

291

SANCERRE — (Sawn-sair) — Picturesque hill town, overlooking the up-per Loire, in central France; its white wine, pale, fresh, with consider-able breed and an engaging fruitiness and bouquet, greatly resembling the nearby Pouilly-Fumé (*see*) and made from the same grape, the Sauvignon Blanc. Perhaps on the whole even shorter-lived than Pouilly-Fumé and sooner ready, Sancerre is a great favorite in Paris restaurants and at its best is certainly one of the most agreeable of the lesser white wines of France. The best of it comes, not from the township of San-cerre, but from surrounding villages, of which Amigny, Bué, Champtin, Chavignol, Reigny, and Verdigny are especially noteworthy; the total production varies greatly from year to year, but the average is not far from 200,000 gallons. A little excellent *rosé* is produced in the district from the Pinot Noir, and some experts consider it the best *rosé* of France.

SANDUSKY — Town on Lake Erie between Cleveland and Toledo. Formerly a center of Ohio wine production, thanks to the vineyards nearby and on the Lake Erie islands.

SAN FRANCISCO BAY — Center of California's fine wine district; its arms and estuaries extend far back into the interior, and since it is tidal, and connected with the cool Pacific by the Golden Gate, its waters act as a sort of gigantic air-conditioning unit for a whole vast country. Thus, it is an odd fact that one can leave the Bay, and travel east, or northeast, or even due north, and find a progressively warmer climate for as much as fifty or a hundred miles. It is thanks to this that Napa, Sonoma, Santa Clara and the other "North Coast Counties" can produce far better wine than vineyards at a comparable latitude (about that of Sicily) abroad.

SAN GIOVETO — (San Jo-*vay*-toe) — Excellent Italian red wine grape, often called the San Giovese, the dominant variety in the Chianti Country and throughout the whole region of Tuscany. In other districts, Italy's Adriatic provinces, for example, it gives a good but shorter-lived and less distinguished wine. There have been random plantings of it in California, but few if any California Chiantis are made, even partially, from the San Gioveto.

SANGRIA — (Sahn-*gree*-ah) — Refreshing sort of wine punch, popular in Spain in warm weather. Its usual ingredients are red wine, lemon juice, sugar, water or soda water, sometimes plus berries or sliced fruit and various flavorings.

SANGUE DI GUIDA — (*Sahng*-gway dee *Jew*-dah) — Sturdy red wine produced south of Pavia, in the Lombardy region of Italy. The name means "Blood of Judas."

SANKT MARTIN — (Sankt Mar*teen*) — Secondary wine-producing village in the Pfalz, or German Palatinate. Rather heavy, common white wines.

SANKT NIKOLAUS HOSPITAL — (Sankt Nee-ko-*laus* Hos-pi-*tahl*) — Famous charity hospital and home for the aged at Cues, directly across from Bernkastel, on the Moselle. A good part of its endowment consists of vineyards in Graach, Bernkastel, Brauneberg, Lieser, etc.; the wines, generally of high quality, are estate-bottled and are sold at auction. A number of these, from plots bequeathed by Cardinal Cusanus, one of the founders, carry the words "Cardinal-Cusanus-Stiftswein."

SANSEVERO — (Sahn-say-*vair*-ro) — Good quality white wine, pale, fresh, dry, produced north of Foggia, in southern Italy.

SANTA CLARA — Valley and county at the southern end of San Francisco Bay, taking its name from the old Spanish mission in what is now the town of Santa Clara, near San José. Until not long ago, most of the valley floor was planted in walnuts and prune orchards, and many of the foothills to the east and west were covered with vineyards. As a result of the recent, astonishing increase in population in this part of California, most of these are tending to disappear, and housing developments are taking their place. A number of leading producers (notably Almadén and Paul Masson) have been forced to plant new vineyards in less populous districts further south, and others have simply ceased to exist. There remains the Novitiate of Los Gatos (a Catholic school), San Martin (with a plant in San José and vines near Gilroy), a small portion of the original Almadén vineyard, and a few others of less consequence; at the present rate, Santa Clara's great and well-deserved reputation as a fine wine-producing county will soon be a matter of history.

For Map, *see* CALIFORNIA.

SANTA CRUZ — One of California's "North Coast Counties," although never very important as far as wine was concerned; it lies along the Pacific, some fifty to eighty miles south of San Francisco, and directly west of Santa Clara. It is considerably more famous today for its redwood groves and summer resorts than for its vineyards, only a few of which are still in production. Hallcrest, near Felton, is perhaps the best.

SANTA GIUSTINA — (*Sahn*-ta Juice-*tee*-na) — Fragrant and attractive light red wine, produced in the outskirts of Bolzano *(see)* in the Italian Tyrol.

SANTA MADDALENA — (*Sahn*-ta Mahd-da-*lay*-na) — About the best red wine of the Italian Tyrol, fresh, soft, fruity, appetizing, rather light in color but with adequate body and good balance. It is produced on the northeastern edge of the town of Bolzano, principally from the Schiava grape *(see),* and is quite as well known and fully as popular in Switzerland and Austria as in Italy itself.

SANTENAY — (*Sawn't*-nay) — Southernmost village of the Côte d'Or, in Burgundy. Some very acceptable dry white wines are made from the Chardonnay grape, and others (less good) from the Pinot Blanc; the reds are better. These resemble somewhat the red wines of Chassagne-Montrachet nearby, being rather full and soft, yet with a good deal of tannin and occasionally an earthy taste, or *goût de terroir.* Not too expensive, they are often excellent values. The best vineyard is Gravières.

SAÔNE — (Sone) — French river, a major tributary of the Rhône which it joins at Lyon *(see)*, draining the Côte d'Or, the Maconnais and the Beaujolais. The Maconnais district is in the *département* of Saône-et-Loire.

SARDINIA — (*Italian* SARDEGNA — Sar-*dane*-ya) — Large island off the west coast of Italy, producing some 10 million gallons of wine a year, most of it quite ordinary table wine, rather high in alcohol (*see* Campidano, Vernaccia). There are a few liqueur or dessert wines of exceptional quality: Monica and Giró, both red, somewhat comparable to Port; Nasco, Moscato di Cagliari, Malvasia di Bosa (*see* all of these).

SARMENT — (Sahr-mawn) — French for "cane," the mature shoot of a vine, such as those that bear fruit and are pruned during the dormant season.

SASSELLA — (Sah-*sell*-la) — One of the best wines of Valtellina (*see*), made from the Nebbiolo grape in northern Lombardy.

SAUMUR — (*So*-muhr) — Major wine-producing area along the south or left bank of the Loire River, in France, technically part of the province of Anjou although most of its wines resemble rather more those of the adjoining province of Touraine. Saumur itself is an attractive river town, with an old chateau and a famed cavalry school; the best vineyards are south and southeast of the town, and the total production of the delimited zone is not far from 2 million gallons. Considerably more than half of this is white wine, made from the Chenin Blanc grape; the rest is *vin rosé* and red wine, both of better-than-average quality and both made from the Cabernet Franc. The more productive and inferior grape varieties are hardly grown at all and no wine from them is entitled to the appellations Saumur or Coteaux-de-Saumur. A very substantial amount of sparkling wine is made, both of the above grape varieties being used, and is sold in France and to the export trade as Sparkling Saumur, or Saumur Mousseux. The still white wines are generally dryer than those from the western part of Anjou, yet with a trace of sweetness; the best of them come from the villages of Montsoreau, Brézé, Bizay, Parnay, St. Cyr, Dampierre, Turquant, Varrains, Epieds and Saix; they improve greatly in bottle and are surprisingly long-lived. The *rosés* are made entirely from the Cabernet Franc grape, and are often too pale, being almost white wines to the eye as well as to the palate, though of good quality; the reds, also from the Cabernet Franc, are somewhat more uneven, but those of good vintage years can be surprisingly fine, somewhere between a Médoc and a Chinon in character, especially those from the village of Champigny.

SAUTERNES — (Saw-tairn) — Originally and properly the name of a little French village, set down in a district of vine-covered hillsides some thirty miles south of Bordeaux. The officially delimited Sauternes zone comprises five townships, Preignac, Bommes, Fargues, Barsac and Sauternes itself, and the total annual production hardly exceeds 300,000

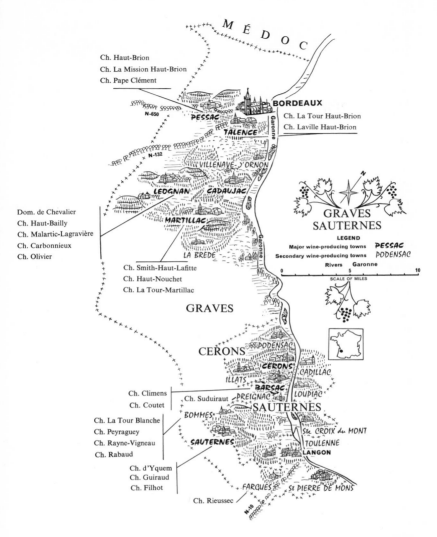

Ch. Haut-Brion
Ch. La Mission Haut-Brion
Ch. Pape Clément

MÉDOC

BORDEAUX
N-650
PESSAC
Ch. La Tour Haut-Brion
Ch. Laville Haut-Brion
TALENCE

N-132

VILLENAVE-D'ORNON

LEOGNAN   **CADAUJAC**

Dom. de Chevalier
Ch. Haut-Bailly
Ch. Malartic-Lagravière
Ch. Carbonnieux
Ch. Olivier

MARTILLAC

LA BRÈDE

Ch. Smith-Haut-Lafitte
Ch. Haut-Nouchet
Ch. La Tour-Martillac

GRAVES SAUTERNES

LEGEND
Major wine-producing towns   **PESSAC**
Secondary wine-producing towns   *PODENSAC*
Rivers   Garonne
0   5   10
SCALE OF MILES

GRAVES

CERONS   *PODENSAC*

CERONS   *CADILLAC*
ILLATS
BARSAC   *LOUPIAC*

Ch. Climens
Ch. Coutet

Ch. Suduiraut   *PREIGNAC*
SAUTERNES
BOMMES

Ch. La Tour Blanche
Ch. Peyraguey
Ch. Rayne-Vigneau
Ch. Rabaud

Ste CROIX du MONT

SAUTERNES   *TOULENNE*
LANGON

Ch. d'Yquem
Ch. Guiraud
Ch. Filhot

FARGUES   *St PIERRE DE MONS*
Ch. Rieussec
N-10

cases; no wine of other origin may legally be sold as Sauternes in France or in most other countries, the United States being, of course, an exception.

True Sauternes (note the final *s,* even in the singular) is a rich, golden wine, high in alcohol (often over 14%) and decidedly sweet; there is no such thing as a "Dry Sauternes" from France. The finest Sauternes are all sold under the names of specific chateaux, and are chateau-bottled; the leading vineyards include Château d'Yquem

295

(a true *grand seigneur*, and in a class apart), then Châteaux La Tour-Blanche, Lafaurie-Peyraguey, Haut-Peyraguey, Rayne-Vigneau, Suduiraut, Coutet, Climens, Guiraud, Rieussec, Rabaud-Sigalas, Rabaud-Promis, etc. The grapes grown are the Semillon and Sauvignon Blanc, plus a small amount of Muscadelle; these are picked late, in a series of harvestings, when they are not only ripe but over-ripe, and when their juice has been further concentrated by the action of a beneficient mold, the so-called *"Pourriture noble," botrytis cinerea.* As a result, Sauternes are among the sweetest of all *natural* wines, and should properly be described as natural dessert wines. At their best they are quite extraordinary, velvety and almost creamy despite their strength, remarkable for their fruit, their breed and their bouquet. The term Haut-Sauternes is a trade designation, generally applied to Sauternes that are particularly sweet, but it has no official meaning, and legally any wine that can be called Sauternes may also be sold as Haut-Sauternes.

In California and generally in the United States, the name "Sauterne" (without the final "s") has practically become a synonym for white table wine. Legally, it can be made from any and all varieties of grapes, grown no matter where; it is usually dry, and bears little or no resemblance to the French original; it must, however, carry an indication of its American origin in easily readable type on its front label. Many less scrupulous American producers bottle the same wine under the names "Chablis" and "Sauterne," which practice, of course, would be unthinkable and highly illegal in France. The nearest American equivalents of French Sauternes are considerably dryer than the French and are usually sold, not under this *passepartout* name, but as Semillon or Sauvignon Blanc, after the grapes out of which they are made. There are a few American sweet Sauternes, but these are made by a process altogether different from that prevailing in the true Sauternes Country of France.

SAVENNIÈRES — (Sav-ven-yair) — Attractive little village some ten miles southwest of Angers, producing the finest white wines of the Coteaux de la Loire *(see)* in Anjou, France. The two most famous vineyards are the Coulée-de-Serrant (10 acres) and the Roche aux Moines (about sixty acres); other leading estates include Bécherelle, Château d'Epiré, Château de Chamboureau, Château de Savennières, etc.

SAUVIGNON or SAUVIGNON BLANC — (*So*-veen-yawn) — Splendid white wine grape, perhaps surpassed in quality, among the world's known varieties, only by the Chardonnay and the true Riesling. In the Bordeaux Country, it is the leading variety of Graves and, with the Semillon, of Sauternes. Again in France, in the upper Loire Valley, where it is also known as the Blanc-Fumé, it yields such charming, fruity and racy wines as Pouilly-Fumé, Sancerre and Quincy. Finally, in the North Coast Counties of California, especially in Livermore and San Benito, it gives a somewhat fuller-bodied wine, but with the same unmistakable distinction and bouquet and flavor.

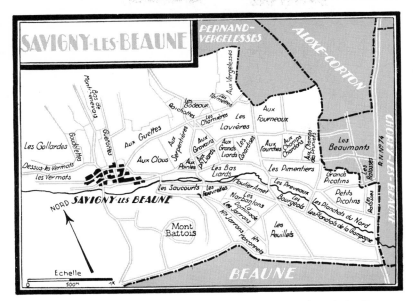

SAVIGNY-LÈS-BEAUNE — (*Sav*-veen-ye lay *Ɓone*) — Little Burgundian town, set down in a fold of the Côte northwest of Beaune; also its wines, about 95% of which are red. These are light, fresh and what the French call "*tendre*" (supple, fruity and early-maturing); according to an inscription over the cellar door of the Château de Savigny, they are also "nourishing, theological and *morbifuges*." In overall production, Savigny, with nearly 900 acres under vines, is one of the most important *communes* of the Côte d'Or; its best vineyards are Vergelesses, Marconnets, Dominode, Jarrons and Lavières. Never great but generally not too expensive, almost always agreeable and often delicate and fine, the Savignys, both red and white, are among the best and most dependable of the lesser Burgundies.

SAVOIE — (Sah-vwa) — District comprising the modern *départements* of Savoie and Haute-Savoie, south of Lake Geneva and bounded on the east by Italy. Most of the wines are of purely local interest, but Crépy and Seyssel (*see*) are perhaps exceptions.

SAVUTO — (Sah-*voo*-toe) — Good red wine of Calabria in southern Italy.

SCHARLACHBERG — (Shar-*loch*-bairg) — Literally, "scarlet hill" (although its soil is actually dull brick-red in color), the best-known vineyard slope of Bingen (*see*), directly opposite Rüdesheim, on the Rhine. It dominates the confluence of the Nahe and the Rhine and its wines, after those of Nierstein and Nackenheim, are among the best of Hessia; many of the finer *Lagen* are in the adjoining townships of Bingen-Büdesheim and Bingen-Kempten, and cannot be seen from the Rhine, since they face south.

297

SCHARZBERG — (Shartz-bairg) — Not to be confused with Scharzhofberg, which it adjoins, a good but hardly outstanding vineyard partly in Wiltingen and partly in Oberemmel on the Saar (*see*), in Germany. Rather tart, hard white wines, of good quality only in great vintage years.

SCHARZHOFBERG — (Shartz-hawf-bairg) — One of the very greatest white wine vineyards of the world, consisting of less than thirty acres of Riesling vines, planted on an exceedingly steep, slate hillside, in Wiltingen, on the Saar, in Germany. The Scharzhof is an old manor house that has belonged for several generations to the Egon Muller family; most of the vines are the property of Egon Muller himself, but his cousin, A. J. Koch, also owns a portion, as does the endowment of the Cathedral of Trier (the wines from this last being sold as Dom Scharzhofberger). The wine is called simply Scharzhofberger, without mention of Wiltingen, the village, and few wine names and few labels are accorded such unhesitating respect by wine-lovers in all countries; this is no more than fair for there are few wines as remarkable as a Scharzhofberger of a year like '53, or '59, and even the secondary years such as 1961 and 1962, yield a fine wine of surprising distinction; light, but with great depth of flavor, austere and yet fragrant and flowery, fresh and yet satisfying, the great Scharzhofbergers are not far from perfection.

SCHAUMWEIN — (*Showm*-vine) — General German term for sparkling wine. Legally, it may be made either by the Champagne process, or by the Charmat method of bulk fermentation; it must have a minimum pressure of 4 atmospheres; in addition, it must be made from European grape varieties (*vitis vinifera*) exclusively, rather than from American varieties or from hybrids.

SCHIAVA — (Ski-*ah*-va) — Interesting and excellent red wine grape, widely grown in the Italian Tyrol and to some extent along the western shore of Lake Garda; one of the rare fine wine grapes which is a good table grape as well. Generally trained on high pergolas, it gives wines that are rather light in color, low in tannin, fresh, fragrant, early-maturing — *see* Lago di Caldaro, Küchelberger, Santa Maddalena. Three sub-varieties of Schiava exist; the best, with the lowest yield and smallest berries, is the Schiava *gentile* (Kleinvernatch, in the local dialect); somewhat more productive is the Schiavone, or Schiava *meranese*; the Schiava *grigia* is third in importance, though all three are often grown in the same vineyard, at Santa Maddalena, for example.

SCHILLERWEIN — (Shil-ler-vine) — Mediocre pink wine, made in the German province of Württemberg, usually from red grapes and white planted in the same vineyard in haphazard fashion and harvested together. Its name has nothing to do with the poet Schiller, but comes from the German verb *schillern*, which means "shimmer." Rarely exported.

SCHLOSS — (Sh-lawss) — Literally means "castle," in German. When used of vineyards and wine, it is the equivalent of the French, *château*, and means the entire property, its buildings, its vineyard, and its wine. There are many combined forms, as Schlossberg, or "castle-hill," the name of many vineyards, in Rüdesheim, Zeltingen, etc.; also *Schlossabzug*, which means castle- or chateau-bottling, etc.

SCHLOSS BÖCKELHEIM — (Shlawss *Bick*-kel-heim) — Perhaps the best vineyard of the Nahe Valley, upstream and southwest of Kreuznach, owned by the German State. White wines of excellent quality.

SCHLOSS JOHANNISBERG — *See* Johannisberg, Schloss.

SCHLOSS REINHARTSHAUSEN — *See* Reinhartshausen, Schloss.

SCHLOSS VOLLRADS — *See* Vollrads, Schloss.

SCHLOSSBERG — (*Shlawss*-bairg) — Literally, "castle-hill" in German; as such it is a fairly common vineyard name, and has survived in many cases when the "castle" in question is in ruins or no longer exists. Thus, we have Zeltinger Schlossberg, Bernkasteler Schlossberg, and Lieserer Schlossberg on the Moselle, Saarburger Schlossberg on the Saar, Rüdesheimer Berg Schlossberg on the Rhine, etc., etc.

SCHOPPENWEIN — (*Showp*-pen-vine) — German term for *vin de carafe*, or even *vin ordinaire*, of modest but not necessarily poor quality.

SCUPPERNONG — One of the Muscadine grapes (*see*), originally wild, now cultivated to some extent in the Carolinas. It belongs to the subgenus *Rotundifolia* and wine has been made from its grapes since early Colonial days. It is not, however, a proper wine grape and the result, even with the addition of sugar, etc. is rarely better than poor.

SEC — (Seck) — French word for dry, i.e., with respect to wine, the opposite of sweet (although *un pays sec* is a dry country, and *un temps sec* is dry weather). Even the special wine-usage of the word has its complications and exceptions: Champagne *(see)* labeled "Sec" is anything but dry, and not far from the sweetest of the grades regularly marketed. The British statesman Canning is supposed once to have said, "Sir, the man who says he likes dry Champagne, lies." In any case, sweet Champagne has been considered unfashionable for well over a century, and even those who prefer it seem to accept it more readily when it comes to them disguised as its opposite. Non-sparkling French wines have not followed this pattern and, with them, *sec* still retains its original and proper meaning.

SECCO — *(Say-*co) — Italian word meaning dry; when applied to wine, the opposite of *abboccato* or *amabile (see).*

SECHÉ — (Sesh-shay) — French wine-taster's term applied to wines that have lost, often through over-long storage in barrel, their freshness and fruit. Literally, "dried," although "withered" is perhaps a more accurate translation.

SEDIMENT — The deposit, or precipitate of crystals and other solids which most wines tend to throw as they are aged in bottle: it is as natural a part of an old wine as the peel is part of an orange or the shell part of an egg. It should *never* be confused with cloudiness or haziness or lack of clarity, all of which are grave faults, and often indicate that a wine is not fit to drink. *Sediment,* on the contrary, *is not a defect in any sense;* it is a sign of bottle-age, and a fine red wine that claims to be old and has no sediment may well be regarded with suspicion. In the case of white wines, sediment usually takes the form of colorless crystals of cream of tartar, which is the base of baking-powder: these are tasteless and harmless and will often disappear if the wine is shaken and then left for a week or so in a warm room; if white and powdery rather than colorless, some pectins and albumens from the grape are probably also present. Red wine sediment is more copious and more complex, and sometimes forms a mask or crust over the inside of the bottle; it is composed of tannins, pigments and minute quantities of the mineral salts normally present in wine. In any case, sediment should settle fairly rapidly if the bottle is disturbed and should simply be left in the bottle when the clear wine is poured off. Certain very full-bodied red wines (Hermitage and Barolo, for example, in a great vintage) throw so heavy a sediment that they must often be decanted and rebottled, after two or three years' cellar-ageing, before they are shipped.

SEEDLING — Almost all vines are propagated from cuttings which are planted in a nursery and take root. A seedling, on the other hand, comes directly from a grape seed, and except under controlled conditions, its precise ancestry can hardly be known. All hybrids, accidental or otherwise, are seedlings, and all new varieties as well.

SEEWEINE — *(Say-*vine-nuh) — Name given to a collection of rather unimportant wines produced along the northern or German shore of

Lake Constance (*Bodensee,* in German). These include several whites made from the Ruländer, or Pinot Gris, round the towns of Meersburg and Hagnau, plus one oddity, an extremely pale *rosé,* almost a *blanc de noirs,* from the Pinot Noir, and locally famous as *Weissherbst.*

SEIBEL — (Si-bel) — One of the better-known French hybridizers — a number of whose phylloxera-resistant crosses have proven successful both in Europe and the United States. (*See* Hybrid.)

SEKT — (Sekt) — General broad German term for sparkling wine, whether made by the Champagne process or merely carbonated. By international accord the name Champagne, in Germany, is restricted to the French product.

SELLE, Château de — (Sell) — Well-known *rosé* and white wine of Provence, and the vineyard from which it comes, at Taradeau, near Draguignan.

SEMILLON — (*Say*-me-yawn) — Excellent white wine grape, widely grown in southwestern France and planted to some extent in California. It gives its best results when interplanted with or vinified with another variety, especially the Sauvignon Blanc, as in Sauternes and Graves. Alone, its wine has definite character and considerable class, but is often too low in acid, lacks freshness and fruit, as frequently in the case of Montravel *(see)* and Monbazillac *(see),* in France, and occasionally in California. On the whole, the best Semillon wines are those that have at least a trace of sweetness; bone dry, they can be slightly bitter, especially if produced in a warm district.

SERCIAL — (*Sair*-see-al) — An important and excellent white grape variety, producing what are, on the whole, the best dry wines of the island of Madeira. (*See*)

SERPETTE — (Sair-pet) — French name for a special pruning knife with a sharp, hooked tip, used for light pruning and for picking grapes at vintage time.

SERRIG — (Sair-rik) — One of the highest and coldest villages of Germany's Saar valley. Its 250 acres of vineyard yield a few wines of fine quality, but only in exceptionally good years; most of their production, very tart, pale, and low in alcohol, is used for sparkling wine, or *Sekt.*

SERVING — So much pretentious etiquette, not to say ritual, has come to surround the service of wine, that many eager potential wine-drinkers become frightened and discouraged at the start. Most of this is sheer abracadabra and nonsense: rules *do* exist, but it is safe to say that any person of taste would discover these for himself in the course of a month of daily wine-drinking. The real rules are based on common sense, anyway. Thus, the host is served first — principally so that he can sniff or taste the wine and be sure that it is good before it is offered to his guests. Thus, white wines and *vins rosés* are chilled — for the sufficient reason that ninety-nine people out of a hundred find them more refreshing and agreeable when so served. Thus, red wine is traditionally served with red meat — because most people find that the two complement one another. Thus, sweet wines, even as strawberry short-cake and chocolate pudding, belong at the end of a meal, not the beginning.

When several wines are served at a meal, which is not often, these days, the problem is possibly a little more complicated, but here, too, common sense can teach us. A less good wine should precede a better one; a lighter wine should precede a heavier one; a dryer wine should precede a sweeter one. When a meal includes both fish and meat, the fish (with dry white wine) precedes the meat (presumably with red), and so on.

Additional information on this subject will be found elsewhere in this volume; see, especially, Decant, Glasses, Temperature, and the Table of Wine-and-Food Affinities in the Appendix.

SET — Vineyardist's term for the crop in prospect once the vine's flowering is over and the grape berries have begun to form.

SÈVRE-ET-MAINE — (Sevr-A-Main) — District southeast of Nantes in lower Brittany, in which most Muscadet *(see)* is produced. This is legally entitled to the name "Muscadet de Sèvre et Maine" to differentiate it from the perhaps less good "Muscadet des Coteaux de la Loire," produced farther east, on the Loire hillsides.

SEYSSEL — (Say-*sell*) — Interesting white wine, pale, fresh, light, very dry, produced round the little town of this name on the Rhône River, east (upstream) from Lyon. A large part of the very limited production is made into *mousseux,* and Seyssel *Mousseux* is one of the very best sparkling wines of France, surpassed, perhaps, only by Champagne.

SHAKING — One of the essential steps (*remuage,* in French) in the making of sparkling wine by the Champagne process *(see).* The bottles, on special racks, are shaken and turned daily so as to work the sediment down against the cork, prior to disgorging.

SHERMAT — Short for "sherry material" — the young fortified wine destined to be converted (by any one of several methods) into California sherry.

SHERRY — Originally and correctly, a pale gold or amber-colored, fortified wine from a specific, delimited district in southern Spain, round the little city of Jerez de la Frontera, between Seville and Cadiz. It takes its name from Jerez (which is pronounced, approximately, *Haireth* in Spanish) and the word "Sherry" is an anglicized version of this name; it is written Xérès in French. At its best, Sherry is beyond question the finest apéritif wine in the world, deservedly the most famous; and, when prepared for market in a different fashion, it can be an admirable dessert wine as well.

Wines called "sherry" have been produced in other countries, especially Australia, South Africa and the United States, for well over a hundred years. A small percentage of these, made, blended and aged as Sherry is in Spain, have made remarkable progress in the past two decades and are surprisingly good today. But California alone produces nearly four times as much "sherry" as Spain, and only the vaguest sort of regulations cover its origin, its manufacture and its ageing. Most of it is made from raisin or table grapes, then "baked" at a high temperature to give it its special flavor, sweetened with grape concentrate, fortified with high-proof brandy, and sold when less than a year old. It is popular only because it contains a minimum of 20% of alcohol (which is more than it should), and because it is cheap.

The original Sherry vineyards, which have hardly changed in extent or in average annual yield in the past hundred years, lie mostly north, west and southwest of the town of Jerez, out of sight of the main road and main railway line from Seville; they can only be reached by dusty cart tracks across the rolling, arid, generally treeless and empty countryside. The best districts, or *pagos* (the names of which almost *never* appear on Sherry labels) are Macharnudo, Carrascal, Aniña and Balbaina; a few others, no less distinguished, produce Manzanilla (*see*) and are farther west, near Sanlúcar de Barrameda and the Atlantic; commoner wines come from vineyards to the south, overlooking the Bay of Cadiz, and from certain "approved" villages between Seville and Huelva.

The geographical location of the districts, as far as the quality of their wine is concerned, is less important than the precise type of soil on which the vines are grown. The best and least productive is what is known as *albariza* — a hard white chalk very like that prevailing in the vineyards of Chablis and Champagne: this gives wine of exceptional bouquet and great finesse; *barro* (literally, clay) is browner in color, more fertile, and yields larger crops of generally fuller-bodied wine; finally, *arena* (literally, sand) gives the highest gallonage of all per acre, but on the whole wines of less substance and character.

The leading grape variety by far is the Palomino, or Listan, especially in the chalky *albariza* areas whence come the best Finos and Amontillados, but a half dozen others are also quite extensively planted — the Albillo, Perruno, Mantuo Castellano, Mantuo de Pila, Beba and Mollar. The Pedro Ximénez (*see*) is also exceedingly important although not widely grown; its grapes are usually sun-dried before crushing and give an admirable, sweet, heavy wine, used in blending.

The *vendimia*, or grape harvest, normally takes place in the Sherry Country early in September and is eminently worth seeing — there are numerous *fiestas* and the whole operation is both surprisingly primitive and very picturesque. The grapes are brought to the press-houses on donkey-back, sorted by hand and set out on straw mats to dry for a few hours in the sun; they are then placed in *lagares*, or press troughs, and "trodden out" by special workers wearing cleated boots. Once the first, free-run juice is drawn off, the pomace, or *marc*, is stacked, wound round with bands of esparto grass, and pressed. The juice, called *mosto*, is of course only the raw material for Sherry, and the finished wine owes most of its character and a good deal of its quality to the various treatments it receives once in barrel. Even before they are trodden and pressed, the grapes are liberally sprinkled with chalk or gypsum — the *albariza* soil on which the best of them are grown — and this quite legal addition of calcium sulphate tends to improve both the acidity and the clarity of the wine. For Sherry, like Champagne, Port, Madeira and many others, is basically a "made" rather than a natural wine, far more easily controlled, imitated and even duplicated than, let us say, Montrachet or Scharzhofberger. For example, it could not even exist in its present form, or be called Sherry, without the addition of high proof grape brandy to bring it up from its natural strength of 13-14% of alcohol by volume to the 17-20% which it usually measures when shipped.

Yet many writers on the subject, including several who should know better, have chosen to speak of Sherry-making as if some mystery or deep secret, some accident or vagary of nature were involved. This is, to say the least, an injustice to the makers of Sherry, who are highly skilled professionals and know very well what they are about. Like schoolteachers and horse breeders and gardeners and many other people the world over, they are sometimes disappointed, sometimes surprised and delighted by the evolution of their charges. But rarely, and not even often. Being excellent showmen, they have long since learned that their visitors and guests greatly enjoy deciphering certain cabalistic signs inscribed in chalk on the heads of their oak casks (called *raya, palma, palo cortado,* etc.); these are really abbreviated tasting notes — indications of type and quality — and in Jerez they are chalked up for all to see, rather than discreetly noted down in private cellar books, as in Germany and France.

From the time fermentation begins, which is almost as soon as the grapes are crushed, until the final, blended, finished wine is ready for bottling, Sherry spends its entire life in 150-gallon casks or "butts" of American white oak, and it cannot be properly matured or aged in any other way. By December following the vintage, the newly fermented wine is clear and ready for tasting; at this stage it is invariably pale straw in color, and bone dry. Added sweetness and darker color both come later, and neither is in any degree accidental.

The taster's first task, in which the eye and nose are if anything more important than the palate, is to determine into which of two general, broad categories, each new wine falls. Those that are notably clean and light, with fine bouquet and some *flor* yeast on their surface, are destined to become Finos and Amontillados; they are drawn off into fresh barrels, fortified to about 15½%, and put away in the *criaderas,* or "nurseries" reserved for young Sherries of this type. Fuller-bodied, heavier wines, with less bouquet and no *flor* yeast, are fortified to 17-18%, sent to their separate *criaderas,* and will eventually emerge as Olorosos.

This *flor,* or "film yeast," which has the scientific name of *mycoderma vini,* is apparently indigenous only to the Sherry Country and the Château-Chalon district of the French Jura. It is essential in the making of fine dry Sherry and almost all of the recent improvement in the California product dates from its introduction there. In appearance, it is at first a sort of white film, becoming a thin, pebbly white crust on the wine's surface; it has an odd, rather agreeable, appetizing odor, which has been compared to the smell of fresh warm bread, and wines on which it has worked have and retain an altogether special character and flavor. Meanwhile wines under *flor* yeast, unlike all others of comparable alcoholic strength, will not spoil or turn to vinegar if exposed to the air, and the butts in a Sherry *bodega* are kept only about three-quarters full.

Once the young Sherries have completed their preliminary development in their *criaderas* (a year, or two, or more) they are graded once again and begin to find their way into the top tier of their appropriate *solera*. And the *solera* (*see*) is another factor without which fine Sherry, as we know it, could not exist.

In its simplest form, a *solera* is a collection of butts or barrels, arranged so as to form three or more sets or stages or tiers (usually, but not necessarily, superimposed) in which wines of the same type but of different ages are fractionally and progressively blended as they mature. The word is related to the Spanish *suelo,* which means floor or base, and the final stage of the *solera,* from which wines are drawn for bottling or further blending, is invariably the lowest, and on the ground. As a rule, not more than half, and in most cases less than a third, of the wine in this oldest bottom tier is ever withdrawn in any single year, and it is immediately replaced by wine from the next highest or next oldest stage, and so on, back to the *criadera.* Thus the final wine of a *solera* may really consist of small fractions of wines of from anywhere from six or seven to a hundred different vintages. There is therefore no such thing as a vintage *solera,* and in practice there is no such thing as a vintage Sherry. And since Sherry usually deteriorates rather than improves in bottle, there is no real reason for one's existence.

With age, in oak, Sherries have a tendency to become very slightly darker in color, noticeably dryer, and (unlike almost all other wines) higher in alcohol. Manzanillas and Finos of 15½% have been known to reach 21% after fifty or more years in cask; they acquire at the same time an intensity of flavor that makes them almost undrinkable — yet magnificent and priceless as blending wines.

The Sherries of commerce are almost never wines drawn from the final stage of any single *solera*: they are blends of these blends, "improved" perhaps by the addition of a small amount of precious old reserve, given softness and sweetness and more color in various ways (most of them legitimate but a few less so).

The sweetening and coloring agents used by reputable houses are called, appropriately enough, *vino dulce* and *vino de color.* Occasionally a single wine will fulfill both functions, but this is rather the exception than the rule.

By all odds the best *dulce* is what is known as "P.X." after the Pedro Ximénez grape from which it is made; when well-aged, this can be one of the most valuable of nectars — the finest Olorosos and Cream Sherries could hardly be produced without it. In point of fact it is what the

305

French would call a *vin de paille* and the Italians a *passito* — pressed from grapes that have been dried in the sun until they are almost raisins, fermented, fortified, then aged for long years in oak. Much less good is what is called *mosto apagado,* sweet grape juice in which fermentation has been impeded by the prompt addition of high-proof brandy: this, too, requires ageing if it is to lose its original harsh and spiritous character.

When it comes to color, Spanish *catadores,* or tasters, divide Sherries into six categories — *muy palido,* very pale, like Manzanilla and most Fino; *palido,* the usual shade of the Amontillado; *ambar,* or amber, as most "medium" Sherries; *oro,* or gold, for the dryer Olorosos; *oscuro,* dark, for the sweeter, luscious Olorosos, or "Creams"; *muy oscuro* for what the English, who drink most of it, call "brown Sherry." There are of course many subtle gradations within each category, and most of the less pale wines have received some addition of *vino de color.* Of this, there exist two sorts, both being essences or concentrates of grape juice, reduced very slowly, by boiling, to a fraction of their original volume — *sancocho,* to one-third, and *arrope,* to one-fifth (literally, the "quintessence"). Both acquire some caramel flavor as well as their almost mahogany color in the process.

Wines heavily dosed with *vino de color* are often called Pajarete or Paxarete (after a district in which they were once largely made); a great deal of such stuff is shipped to the United States as "blending Sherry" and used by distillers in coloring their whiskey.

Since Sherry, in fact and almost by definition, is a blended wine, and more often than not a blend of blends, and since tastes and preferences and personal budgets vary widely, it follows that there are always at least as many Sherries of any given type as there are blenders. Some of the larger houses, with immense stocks, produce the widest possible range of wines, in type, quality and price; others have only a few specialties and nevertheless seem to do very well. Nearly three hundred firms or individuals own *bodegas* in Jerez; thirty or forty maintain offices or agencies in London; a good many English companies bring Sherry in bulk from Spain, blend and bottle and re-export it under their own labels. Some Sherry is still shipped in butts (as most was, prior to Prohibition) and bottled in the United States. All, with practically no exceptions, carry a general designation of type, and a brand name. The best Sherry to buy, therefore, is the wine that appeals to one's personal taste, and that one can afford.

Sherry does not deteriorate as rapidly as table wine, once opened, but "goes off" nevertheless — the dryer sorts quite obviously within a day or two, the others a little more slowly. Most dry Sherries (some experts would say *all* Sherries) are best served chilled. All are better served in tulip-shaped glasses of at least 6 oz. capacity, half filled. A proper minimum drink of Sherry is at least 3 oz.

Much additional information on the subject will be found elsewhere in this volume, under such headings as *California, Manzanilla, Montilla, Amontillado, Amoroso, East India, Fino, Flor, Oloroso, Pedro Ximénez, Sanlúcar de Barrameda, etc.*

306

SHOT BERRIES — Small, seedless berries often found in a bunch of otherwise normal wine grapes. These are usually the result of incomplete pollenization and are called *millerands* in French.

SICILY — (Italian SICILIA, See-*chee*-lee-ah) — Largest island of the Mediterranean, about the size of Maryland, produces some 90 million gallons of wine a year. With a few exceptions (the red and especially the white wines of Etna, Corvo di Casteldaccia, etc.) the table wines are rather common, and are consumed currently and locally. Marsala *(see)* is of course Italy's leading fortified wine, amber, 17-19% alcohol, somewhat comparable to Sherry. There are also a number of Sicilian dessert wines of more than local fame — these, described in their proper place in this volume include: Moscato di Siracusa, Zucco, Malvasia di Lipari, Moscato di Pantelleria, Albanello, etc.

SICK — A sick wine is a bad wine, almost always cloudy, usually with a bouquet which is odd, unfamiliar and unpleasant, a flavor which is definitely "off." Fortunately, very few such wines ever reach the consumer.

SIFONE — (See-*fo*-nay) — Grape juice reduced to about one-third of its original volume, almost to the consistency of syrup. Used as a sweetening agent in Marsala *(see)*.

SILKY — Wine-taster's term, applied to wines that are notably smooth and fine-textured.

SILLERY — (*See*-yair-ree, generally *Sil*-ler-ree in English) — Village in the Champagne Country, southeast of Reims. Its wines, once famous in both France and England, are no longer highly regarded, and the name has almost ceased to exist as an appellation, since Verzenay (*see*) — once considered part of the Sillery zone — produces a much superior wine.

SION — (*See*-awn) — Interesting and picturesque little town, capital of the Swiss Canton of Valais, set down in the high, rocky, narrow, upper valley of the Rhône, not far from its source, in southern Switzerland. The wines made round Sion include the excellent red Dole *(see)* and red and white Ermitage, the white Johannisberg (legally so labeled, although often made from the Sylvaner grape) and a number of superior grades of Fendant, or Chasselas, notably those of Uvrier, Clavoz, Mont d'Or.

SKIN — The peel or outer covering of the grape; in some English-speaking countries, skins are more commonly called "hulls" or "husks."

SMALL — Wine-taster's term, applied to a wine of not much consequence, not much distinction, let alone body or power — possibly very agreeable all the same. Many "ordinary" wines are small, but there are plenty of us who would prefer them to great wines as a daily diet, as we might prefer good simple cooking to *la grande cuisine*.

SMITH-HAUT-LAFITTE, Château — (Smeet-O-La-feet) — Excellent, slow-maturing, long-lived red Graves, produced in the commune of Martillac. There are some 5,000 cases a year.

SOAPY — Wine-taster's term used of wines that are disagreeably flat, low in acid, and unappetizing.

SOAVE — (*Swa*-vay) — Excellent dry white wine, among Italy's best, produced just east of Verona, on the southernmost foothills of the Alps. The predominant grape varieties are the Garganega and Trebbiano, plus a little Riesling; the vines are trained high, pergola-fashion, six or seven feet above the ground. In addition to the extremely picturesque little town of Soave itself, the neighboring village of Monforte is considered part of the Soave zone, and a very large part of their local production is crushed by the local cooperative cellar, or Cantina Sociale, one of Italy's most important and best equipped. Shipped in tall, green bottles, like the wines of Alsace, Soave is pale straw in color, light, clean and fresh on the palate, dry without being acid — a most agreeable wine, in short, though hardly a great one. It matures early and should be drunk before it is three years old.

SOFT — Wine-taster's term, a generally favorable adjective, although not always so. A soft wine is one neither harsh nor green, although possibly mild and dull. All wines should have some softness — if they have too much they may be flat or even common.

SOLERA — (So-*lehr*-ah) — System by which certain fortified wines, Spanish Sherries above all, are matured and progressively blended; the object is, year after year, to produce wines of perfectly consistent quality that run perfectly true to type. Expert cellar-masters, given a proper range of young wines to work with, can achieve this result to a surprising degree.

The operation of a *solera* has been described in considerable detail under the heading Sherry (*see*). In recent years a number of the more conscientious California producers have set up *soleras,* following the Spanish pattern, and some of these (the ones at Almadén, for example, which contain over a million gallons of wine) are impressively large, even by Spanish standards. It is thanks to such installations and to the introduction of film yeast, or *flor* (*see*) that the finer American Sherries are now able to compete, in quality, with many of the imported.

A very similar system is now rather widely used in the maturing and blending of superior Port.

SOLUTRÉ — (*So*-loo-tray) — One of the four *communes* of the Pouilly-Fuissé district *(see),* producing somewhat lighter and more delicate wines than the others. The "Rock of Solutré," an extraordinary butte rising directly behind the village, is a famous landmark, visible for miles, and appears on many Pouilly-Fuissé labels.

SOMMELIER — (So-mel-yea) — French term for wine waiter. In French restaurants, the sommelier is usually in charge of some bottling and cellar work as well, and, when serving, wears a traditional uniform, with a chain, cellar keys, a tasting cup, and sometimes an apron.

SONDRIO — (*Sawn*-dree-o) — Town in northern Italy, only some dozen airline miles from the Swiss border, center of production of the red wine of Valtellina *(see)*

SONOMA — One of the most important wine-producing counties of northern California, and on the whole one of the best. It lies north of San Francisco; its southern edge is on tidewater and overlooks San Francisco Bay. The nearby town of Sonoma owes its origin to the northernmost of the twenty-one Spanish missions established by Franciscan monks north of what is now the Mexican border between 1769 and 1823; it was they who brought the vine and viticulture to California. Commercial vineyards were planted near Sonoma before the Civil War, and among the best known was Buena Vista, which belonged to Colonel (or Count) Haraszthy *(see),* who has not unfairly been called the father of the California wine industry.

Like many California counties, Sonoma is almost a little world in itself and has an astonishingly wide diversity of climates and soils and countryside. The interior, from San Francisco Bay and the town of Sonoma northward to Santa Rosa and Guerneville, is as cool as Burgundy in France, and admirably adapted to wine-growing; on the west, the Coast Range, covered with giant redwoods, along the bleak beaches of the cold Pacific, is not wine country at all, far too cold and too humid for the vine; farther north, in the Russian River Valley, from Healdsburg to Asti and beyond, there are thousands of acres of rolling hills and vineyards, as productive and as warm, as those of central Italy. These, largely planted to common, red wine varieties such as the Carignan, Petit Syrah, Mataro and Grenache, and of course the Zinfandel, give a more-than-respectable *vin ordinaire*, much better than that of the French Midi. The whites, from this northern, warmer part of the coun·y, are far less good than the reds.

For Map, *see* CALIFORNIA.

SORNI — (*Sore*-nee) — Extremely pleasant red wine of the Italian Trentino *(see)*; light, soft, well-balanced, made round the village of this name, largely from the Schiava grape, plus some Merlot and Teroldego.

SOUCHE — (Soo-sh) — French word (*see* also *Cep*) for a grape-stock, or vine.

SOUND — Wine-taster's term, used of a wine which is, as the French say, *franc de goût*, clean-tasting, well-constituted, without defects or abnormal qualities.

SOUPLE — (Soo-pl) — Literally, French for "supple," although more properly used of wine than its English equivalent. It means a wine not too high in tannin or acid, smooth, agreeable, ready to drink.

SOUR — In the realm of wine, the opposite of Sweet is *Dry*, not Sour, and a wine with too much natural acidity is Tart or Acid, never Sour. A sour wine is one well on its way to becoming vinegar, spoiled, and not fit to drink.

SOUTH AFRICA — Vines have been grown and wine made in South Africa since early Dutch colonial days, and one of the most famous vineyards, Groot Constantia (*see*) was planted in 1684. There are now some 40 million gallons produced annually, a great deal of it shipped to England, and although South African wines have never wholly regained the high reputation which they enjoyed (even in France) in the 19th Century, many of them are good and well-made today, by any standards. This is particularly true of the "Sherries," many of them made by the *flor* process, and solera blended. The leading vineyard areas are all fairly close to Cape Town, between French Hoek and Wellington, in the Paarl Valley, in the Stellenbosch district, and round Wynberg, near Constantia itself. It is interesting to note that these are at almost precisely the same Latitude South as the best vineyards of Chile and Australia.

SOUTH AMERICA — The vine, being a creature of the Temperate Zones, is truly at home only in the southern and cooler third of this vast continent, and apart from a few vineyards in Peru (all planted at surprisingly high altitudes), wine is only produced well south of the Tropic of Capricorn — in Argentina, Chile, Uruguay, and in the southernmost provinces of Brazil. South America nevertheless produces and consumes more than twice as much wine as North America, almost all of it table wine, imports only an infinitesimal amount, and, apart from Chile, exports practically none at all. Argentina is by a wide margin the largest producer, Chile easily the best. *See* these.

SOUTIRAGE — (Soo-tee-rahj) — French word for "racking" (*see*), the process of drawing off wine from one tank or barrel to another, leaving the sediment or lees behind.

SPAIN — Accurate statistics are hard to come by, but Spain, almost certainly, has the largest extent of vineyards of any country in the world, over 3½ million acres in all. Due to the prevailingly arid climate, the average yield per acre is far lower than in France or Italy (let alone California) and the total production of Spanish wine is only about one-third that of France or Italy — it amounts, nevertheless, to the very respectable figure of some 500 million gallons a year.

Only about 2% of this is Sherry, and Sherry, although easily the most famous, is no more the typical wine of Spain than Champagne is the typical wine of France. Most Spaniards have never tasted it, and over 90% of Spain's wine is common table wine, consumed currently and locally and never bottled.

Travelers in Spain will find such wine available everywhere: it varies widely in quality, but quite often is surprisingly good and it is always inexpensive.

Supposedly of a higher class, yet almost invariably disappointing, are many elaborately labeled local wines which are not exported and not likely to be: higher in alcohol and with more pronounced character than the others of their district, these rarely have any of the freshness and charm of French *vins de pays*.

On the other hand, the very best Spanish table wines, above all those of the Rioja (*see*) and to a lesser degree those of Valdepeñas (plus rare exceptions from other provinces), can be quite extraordinary, and remarkably good values, no less in the United States than in Spain.

Except in a few of the better-known districts, wine-making methods are archaic or even primitive in most of Spain and it is a tribute to the producers' care and honesty and their respect for sound tradition that the wines turn out as well as they do, for few can fairly be called bad. Many, if better vinified, would find a ready market abroad, such as the dry white wines of Rueda, in Old Castile; the reds of Toro, not far from Salamanca; and the *rosés* of Yecla, in the uplands west of Alicante. Yet a great deal of heavy-bodied, deep-colored, blending wine is also produced, especially in Aragón and in the province of Valencia, and shipped in bulk to France and Switzerland to add some substance and higher alcohol to lighter and paler red wines.

The best table wines of Spain, especially the best reds, are by a wide margin those of the Rioja district (*see*), in the high valley of the Ebro, west of Logroño and not far from the French border. The finer of these are exceptionally good by any standards, and surprisingly close to the great Bordeaux in quality. In a distinctly lower category come the rather pale, somewhat common red wines of Valdepeñas (*see*), from south of Madrid, and in a still lower class the reds of Alicante; some reds and whites from round Barcelona (Panadés, Alella, Perelada, etc.); and the reds, whites and *rosés* of the Miño Valley, along the Portuguese frontier.

A little Spanish sparkling wine is produced, the best of it quite passable but on the sweet side; it is often labelled "Xampán (pronounced *Champagne*), and comes from the Panadés district, southwest of Barcelona.

It is above all in the somewhat special field of apéritif wines that Spain excels, and indeed she has hardly any rival, since the gradual decline of Madeira (both in quality and in public favor) over the past century. Those who are familiar only with a few of the popular, standard brands of Sherry have no idea of the range and variety of wines that make up the Sherry family, and of course Manzanilla (*see*) and Montilla (*see*) are in their limited categories hardly less interesting.

The once famous Spanish dessert wines — Málaga, Tarragona, and the golden Malvasia of Sitges — have almost no commercial importance today, but they are still fine wines in their no-longer-fashionable class.

In a world of rising wine prices and improved technology, Spanish table wines should look forward to a bright future. Sherry, Manzanilla and Montilla will continue to be appreciated and ever more widely known by wine-lovers and true connoisseurs everywhere.

SPANNA — (*Spahn*-na) — Another name for the Nebbiolo grape (*see*).

SPARKLING BURGUNDY — Burgundy wine made sparkling or *mousseux* (*see*) by any one of several methods; generally red, although some *rosé* and some white are produced. Long popular in the United States and to a lesser degree in England, it is hardly ever drunk in France except by tourists, and does not even appear on the wine lists of most of the better French restaurants. The finer grades of still Burgundy are never used in its manufacture; it is a wine regarded with amused contempt by most real wine-lovers, and by all experts. American Sparkling Burgundy, whether produced in California or in New York State, is substantially as good as that made in France.

SPÄTLESE — (*Shpate*-lay-zuh) — German wine term, which literally means "late picking" or "late harvest." On a label it indicates a superior natural (i.e., unsugared) wine, made from grapes picked after the main, normal vintage is over. Such grapes of course tend to be somewhat riper than the average, and a Spätlese is therefore fuller-bodied, riper and generally a trace sweeter than other wines of the same vineyard and year; it also usually costs from 30% to 50% more. The German plural is *Spätlesen.*

SPICY — Said of a wine with a pronounced and special aroma or taste, piquant but natural, properly its own and on the whole agreeable. Gewürztraminer is an obvious example, but there are many others.

SPIRITUEUX — (*Speer*-ee-tyuh) — French word which, as a noun, means "spirits"; applied to wine, as an adjective, it means high in alcohol.

SPRAYING — The treating of vines with liquid insecticides or fungicides, under pressure. An essential and laborious part of the vine-grower's summer work in all countries.

SPUMANTE — (Spoo-*mahn*-tay) — Italian word which means foaming or sparkling; as applied to wine, a wine that is truly sparkling, as contrasted with one that is *frizzante* (*see*), or only slightly and briefly so. Spumanti are made in various ways, that called *Gran Spumante* usually by the French Champagne process of fermentation in bottle, most of the others by fermentation in bulk, the "*cuve close*" or "*Charmat*" method.

STABILIZING — The various treatments (including refrigeration and, in extreme cases, even pasteurization) to which many wines are subjected in order to enable them to resist, as far as possible, heat, cold and exposure to light, without losing their clarity and balance.

STAKE — Light post or picket, either of wood or metal, used to support a vine or, in some instances, the wire on which the vine is trained.

STALKY — *See* Stemmy.

STEELY — Extremely hard, and even tart, without being harsh or green. Austere, possibly remarkable, but unprepossessing.

STEINBERG — (Shtein-bairg) — Celebrated, historic 62-acre vineyard in the heart of Germany's Rheingau district. It was created and the wall around it was constructed in the 12th century by monks of the same Cistercian Order as those responsible for its sister domain, the Clos de Vougeot, in Burgundy; and the same remarkable man, St. Bernard de Clairvaux, oversaw the creation of both. Together with the adjoining monastery, Kloster Eberbach, the vineyard was taken over by the German state, and is now part of the *Staatsweingut.* It stretches over the

rolling hills directly behind Hattenheim, and its wines are sold as Steinberger, or Steinberger Kabinett, or Steinberger Spätlese Kabinett, or Auslese, Trockenbeerenauslese, etc. Between these various grades and classes, all *Naturweine* and all estate-bottled, there are of course enormous differences, even in any given year. All of them have, nevertheless, certain family characteristics — full body, authority, great class, power and depth of flavor sometimes at the expense of subtlety; forthrightness sometimes at the expense of charm. They are less good in very dry years than the Marcobrunners, and less attractive in poor years than the riper and fruitier Rüdesheimers; at their best they are simply incomparable.

STEINWEIN — (Shtein-vine) — Name sometimes (and wrongly) given to German *Frankenweine* as a whole — those, in other words, shipped in the traditional *Bocksbeutel*. Properly, however, a Steinwein is one from the town of Würzburg (*see*), grown on its steep slopes overlooking the Main river, and made from Riesling or Sylvaner grapes. The finer Steinweins are dry, full-bodied, well-balanced, of outstanding quality.

STEMMER — Machine, called an *égrappoir* in French, for separating the newly picked grapes from their stems, prior to fermentation.

STEMMY — Harsh, green, disagreeable flavor which wines sometimes acquire if fermented with the stems, or stalks. (French, *goût de rafle*.)

STILL — Non-sparkling. If a new wine, one that has finished its fermentation; if an older wine, one that contains no perceptible amount of CO_2, or carbon dioxide.

STURDY — Wine-taster's term, perhaps a little less favorable than robust.

SÜFFIG — (*Sue*-fig) — German wine-taster's word, applied to wines that are light, fresh, palatable, easy to drink.

SUAU, Château — (Su-O) — 2nd Classed Growth of Barsac. There is another and much larger vineyard with precisely the same name in the village of Capian, Côtes-de-Bordeaux (*see*).

SUDUIRAUT, Château de — (*Sood*-we-row) — 1st Classed Growth of Preignac, Sauternes. Splendid chateau and famous vineyard in the Sauternais, which, after passing through two decades of decline and neglect, is once more producing rich, full-bodied, rather sweet wines worthy of its great name.

SUGARING — French, *chaptalisation*; the adding of sugar (but not water) to must, or fermenting wine, its object being to bring the final alcoholic degree of the wine up to a normal level. It is forbidden in some countries, authorized in others, often abused. *See* also Amelioration, Gallisation.

SUGARS — As far as wine is concerned, these are most simply defined as the elements in must or grape juice that can be converted into alcohol through the action of yeast — *fermentable sugars*, in other words. But also normally present in grape juice and most wine are minute amounts of *non-fermentable sugars*, such as pentose; *reducing sugar* is the total of both, determined chemically. *Residual sugar* is the sugar remaining in a wine, for whatever reason, after fermentation.

SULPHITING — The adding of sulphur, in the form of sulphurous acid, sulphur dioxide or sulphites, to grape juice or to wine, with the object of delaying or preventing fermentation. This is common practice in modern wineries: the must, once sterilized, is later re-inoculated with a special chosen yeast culture. But when the same process is used to "hold" the sweetness of a light, partially fermented wine, the result, unless great care is exercised, can be most unfortunate — a wine that literally reeks of sulphur, like many cheap Liebfraumilchs and white Bordeaux. *See* Sulphur, below.

SULPHUR — Element properly and widely used in many phases of grape-growing and wine-making. Dusted or sprayed on the vines, it is an efficient safeguard against many of the diseases, funguses and pests to which grapes are subject; in the cellar, it is a standard sterilizing agent for casks, barrels, etc. But (*see* Sulphiting) it is often used, and often too freely used, to keep a poorly balanced white wine from oxidizing, or to "hold" a certain amount of sweetness in a wine which would otherwise continue fermentation and be completely dry. There is nothing objectionable about this practice, providing the sulphur is not too apparent in the finished wine. To a wine-taster, the presence of even a limited amount of sulphur usually makes itself known by a slight prickling in the nose, and an odd, faintly "pasty" impression on the tip of the tongue.

SULPHURING — *See* Sulphiting, above. Sulphuring, a quite different process, involves the sterilizing of casks or barrels in the cellar and the treatment of vines in the field. Vineyards are regularly dusted with flowers of sulphur to prevent oidium and mildew during the growing season; sulphur wicks are frequently burned in empty casks to eliminate harmful bacteria.

SWEET — Sweetness in a table wine, or a fortified wine for that matter, may be wholly natural or partly natural or not natural at all. In a fine French Sauternes or a Beerenauslese from the Rhineland, it comes from the grapes themselves, which have been allowed to hang on the vines until over-ripe (*see*, however, *Pourriture noble*) and is wholly natural; due to the difference in climate, no such natural sweet wines are produced, except experimentally, in the United States. In many other wines, sweetness also comes entirely from the grape, but remains in the wine because sulphur has been used or brandy added — the former being the case in cheap white Bordeaux and Liebfraumilch, the latter in Port, whether produced in Portugal or in California. Sherry and Marsala are sweet because of heavy, sweet wine or the equivalent of grape syrup added to them. Sweetness, in any case, is not necessarily a virtue, nor is it necessarily a fault; this depends entirely on the character of the wine.

SWITZERLAND — Despite her 30,000 acres of vineyards, Switzerland (half as large as Maine and no more populous than Massachusetts) imports far more wine than she produces and is, by a wide margin, the largest importer of wine among the nations of the world — the average annual total is about twice that of Great Britain and over six times that of the United States. Nearly 90% of this is inexpensive red table wine, shipped in bulk from Italy, Spain and, in much smaller volume, from France. In the way of white wine, Switzerland produces enough to satisfy her own national requirements and even to permit a certain amount of exportation. There are vineyards in over a dozen different cantons, but only four are of any real commercial importance: Vaud, consisting mostly of the northern shore of Lake Geneva; Valais, the upper valley of the Rhône, which here runs parallel to the Swiss-Italian border; Neuchâtel, its vines extending along the northern shore of the lake of that name, in northwestern Switzerland, not far from France; Tessin, or the Ticino, the Italian-speaking region round the lakes of Locarno and Lugano. Most of what the Tessin produces is common red table wine; a considerably better red, called Dole (*see*) is made in the Valais; practically all of the rest is white, and comes mostly from the Chasselas grape, here known as the Fendant — this is often the name under which the wine is sold. Some of the better growths, all listed elsewhere in this volume, are: Dézaley, St. Saphorin, Yvorne, Aigle, Sion and Neuchâtel. *See* also the cantons referred to above.

On the whole, Swiss wines are never great and few of them can even be called outstanding. But they are always well made, generally inexpensive, light, fresh and appetizing. Most of them are bottled when less than a year old.

SYLVANER — (Sil-*van*-ner) — Rather productive, superior white wine grape, probably of German or Austrian origin, widely planted in many

315

countries. In Germany, it is easily first in total acreage, although it gives a lighter, softer, shorter-lived wine than the more distinguished Riesling; in Alsace it is classed as a "noble" variety, an honor which it scarcely merits, since the wine it yields is really just an excellent *vin de carafe*, fresh, fruity and agreeable. It does well in Austria, and in the Italian Tyrol, especially round Bressanone, and there are some plantings in Switzerland, in California and in Chile. In the course of its travels it has acquired some odd pseudonyms: it is called the *Oesterreicher* (the "Austrian") in the Rheingau, the *Franken Traube* (or "Franconian grape") in the Rheinpfalz, and even the "Franken Riesling" in Franconia itself, where, for once, it approaches the true Riesling in quality. In Switzerland, it is sometimes known as the "Johannisberg," and it even calls itself, quite legally, the "Riesling" in California (*see*). It has been often successfully crossed with the true Riesling: the so-called *Mainriesling* and the popular Müller-Thurgau are two of the best-known offspring.

SYRAH — (See-rah) — Excellent red wine grape, the variety of red Hermitage (*see*) and one of those used in Châteauneuf-du-Pape. It gives a deep-colored, slow-maturing wine, high in tannin, with a distinctive and memorable bouquet. It is not the Petit Syrah widely grown in California, which is a far more productive and more ordinary grape, probably the Duriff (*see*).

SZEKSZARD — (Sex-ard) — Hungarian place name, and the red wine of this district.

T-U

TÂCHE, La — (La Tahsh) — One of the very great red Burgundies, produced by a small vineyard in the *commune* of Vosne-Romanée, entirely owned by the owners of Romanée-Conti (*see*) and a part of the domain which carries this name. In the days when wine regulations were less strict, its wines were sometimes labeled "La Tâche Romanée" and the late Christopher Morley gave this name to one of his books, *The Romany Stain*, but it is unlikely that Romanée had any connection with gypsies, as he fancied, and it is at least doubtful that Tâche, in this instance, means "stain." Before World War II, the vineyard consisted of about three and one-half acres, between Les Gaudichots and Les Malconsorts (*see* Vosne Romanée, and map); a new decree, during the German occupation in 1943, accorded to a major part of Les Gaudichots, the *appellation* La Tâche, and there are now about fifteen acres entitled to the name. This quadrupling of the vineyard's extent has of course increased its production, and 201 hectoliters (roughly 2,200 cases) were made in 1962. The wine has not much suffered (for Les Gaudichots was a very great vineyard) and is velvety, full-bodied, with quite extraordinary bouquet and depth of flavor.

For Map, *see* VOSNE.

TACHÉ — (Tah-*shay*) — Literally, "stained." Said of a white wine which has acquired a pinkish tinge, often accidentally, through having been put in a cask previously used for red wine.

TAIN L'HERMITAGE — (Tan *Lair*-me-taj) — Town on the Rhône south of Lyon, where the red and white wines of Hermitage (*see*) are produced.

317

TALBOT, Château — (Tal-bo) — Largest vineyard in the township of St. Julien, and one of the best equipped: a 4th Classed Growth, it produces some 15,000 cases a year of very sturdy, full-bodied Claret, deep-colored, rather slow to mature.

TALENCE — (Tal-lawnce) — Commune in the Graves district, now practically a suburb of Bordeaux. Housing projects have overrun most of its vineyards, and there are only two of any real importance that remain: Château La Tour-Haut-Brion, producing a good red wine, and Château Laville-Haut-Brion, one of the very finest of white Graves.

TANNIN — Technically, a group of organic compounds existing in the bark, wood, roots and stems of many plants; also in wine, red wine especially. To the taste, it is astringent and makes the mouth pucker, as almost always in the better young red Bordeaux wines of good years. It is particularly pronounced in wines that have not been *égrappés*, or separated from their stems before fermentation; some additional tannin is certainly picked up by wines stored in oak barrels, especially new oak barrels, and this often improves them greatly. Tannin forms part of the normal sediment that fine red wines throw as they grow older, and a mature wine has less tannin than a young wine. Some grape varieties are far higher in tannin than others, and these generally produce the wines which improve with age.

TANK — Large closed container used for wine fermentation (*see* also vat) or wine storage; if wood, usually in the form of an upright cylinder; if of stainless steel, often in the form of a globe; if of concrete, generally cubical.

TAP — To insert a spigot or faucet in the bunghole of a barrel or cask.

TAPPIT-HEN — Old Scottish term for an oversize drinking vessel, or a bottle holding as much as three normal wine bottles, or more.

TARRAGONA — (Tah-ra-*go*-na) — City and province south of Barcelona on the Mediterranean coast of Spain. A great deal of quite ordinary table wine is produced, and a few sweet fortified red wines of somewhat better class, usually known as Priorato in Spain itself, and called Tarragona, or even "Tarragona Port," when exported.

TARRY — Wine-taster's term (French, *goût de goudron*) used of certain very full-bodied red wines of great vintages; far from disagreeable, it is usually one of the characteristics of a fine red wine made from very ripe grapes.

TART — Said of a wine high, possibly even too high, in acid, but not necessarily either unpleasant or "green."

TARTAR — Tartaric acid is the principal acid of wine made from ripe grapes; some of this is invariably thrown off in the form of crystals of potassium bitartrate, or cream of tartar (German, *Weinstein*) as the wine is aged in cask, and sometimes also in bottle.

TASSE — (Tahss) — Common French word meaning cup. As far as wine is concerned, a small, shallow saucer, usually of silver with dimpled bottom and sides, in which young wines are tasted. It is part of a wine-waiter's equipment, plus a chain and keys.

TASTEVIN — (*Tat*-van) — Flat, shallow, silver wine-taster's cup widely used in Burgundy for sampling wines, especially young wines. It has given its name to the celebrated Burgundian confraternity of wine, the Confrérie du Tastevin, which has its headquarters in the old chateau of the Clos de Vougeot, and branches and chapters in many countries, including the United States.

TASTEVINAGE — (*Tat*-vee-*nahj*) — System of labeling certain Burgundy wines whereby, once approved by a committee of the Confrérie du Tastevin (*see*) and upon payment of a certain sum per bottle, these wines may carry a special, rather elaborate Tastevin label, on which the shipper's (not always the producer's) name also appears. Such wines are said to be *"Tastevinés."* This is an indication but by no means a guarantee of superior quality.

TASTING — Wine-tasting is both a very simple and an extremely complex art or science or skill: it may quite properly be described as any of these, or a combination of all three. There are two kinds of wine-tastings: one is intended to allow the consumer, whether a novice or a connoisseur, to taste a number of different wines and decide which he prefers and which he likes less well; his own palate is the final arbiter, and there is not, nor should there be, any appeal from his decision. A wine, for him, "is good if it tastes good."

The second sort of wine-tasting involves at least a certain amount of expert knowledge, and only those with wide experience and exceptional "taste memory" are capable of it. There exist quite definite standards as to what can be called quality or superiority in wine, and experts, tasting blind, will rarely vary in their ratings of any given wine, by more than four or five points out of 100. This is a far higher level of unanimity than music critics or art critics or literary critics ever achieve, yet taste and smell are in general the beggars among our five senses, for they have no accurate written language and no permanent record and no past.

Wine-tasters, however, have their own professional jargon, or cant, and although the terms they use often appear bizarre or pretentious or even ridiculous to those unfamiliar with them, they are certainly more precise than the language of music critics (a "lyric" tone, a "warm" voice) or that of painting ("vibrant," "sincere," "well-organized").

Professional wine-tasters do not drink the wines they taste: they examine them closely for color, either against a white tablecloth or a candle, or against the sky, tilting the glass in either case, to see if there is a trace of tell-tale brown or gold around the edge of the wine. They shake the wine or spin it in the glass, so as to bring out a maximum of bouquet, then sniff it carefully. They then sip it, wash it around in their mouths, and spit it out, breathing deeply, since the fact is that our nose, rather than our palate, is the best judge.

And then, in their notebooks, they give a fairly detailed verdict. Here are a few of the terms they use; all will be found in their alphabetical place in the encyclopedia, defined as accurately as seems possible:

Acid	Light
Astringent	Maderised (*Maderisé*)
Balanced	Metallic
Big	Mild
Bitter	Moldy
Body	Noble
Bouquet	Nutty
Brilliant	Off
Character	Ordinary
Clean	Perfume
Cloudy	Piquant
Coarse	Poor
Color	Powerful
Common	Ripe
Corky	Robust
Delicate	Rounded
Distinguished	Sick
Dry	Silky
Dull	Small
Earthy	Soapy
Elegant	Soft
Fine	Sound
Flat	Sour
Flinty	Spicy
Flowery	Steely
Fragrant	Stemmy
Fresh	Sturdy
Fruity	Sweet
Full	Tart
Great	Thin
Green	Withered
Harsh	Woody
Hazy	Yeasty
Heavy	Young

TAVEL — (Tah-*vel*) — The most famous *rosé* wine of France and probably one of the oldest, since it was said to have been a favorite of François I and was praised by the poet Ronsard. It is made, principally from the Grenache grape, plus a limited but important admixture of Cinsault (*see*) and some Clairette, Bourboulenc, Carignan, etc., round the village of this name, west and across the Rhône from Avignon. The soil in the limited production zone (recently and quite properly enlarged) is, on the whole, rocky, shallow and arid; the yield per acre is small, and the wine has, as a result, more flavor and bouquet and usually more alcohol (12½-14%) than other *rosés* of the Rhône Valley; its one close rival is Lirac (*see*) from a directly adjoining *commune*. The annual out-

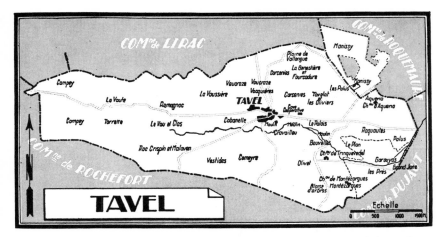

put is now not far from 400,000 gallons, well more than half from the large, modern, co-operative cellar. There are a good many smaller producers as well, and many of them estate-bottle.

Many writers on wine, most of them British, have contended that Tavel, is a unique exception among *rosés* and improves with age. This is anything but the opinion of the *vignerons* who themselves produce Tavel, who much prefer their wine when under two years old, and regard a five-year-old bottle as simply a curiosity. Vintage years on Tavel shipped to the United States should generally be distrusted; the youngest is probably the best.

TEINTURIER — Literally, in French, "dyer." Term applied to such comparatively rare grape varieties as have red or red-purple juice, rather than white. Some of these, for example the Salvador and Alicante Bouschet, are planted principally for this reason.

TEMPERANCE — Moderation, especially in the use of alcoholic beverages. Its meaning has been corrupted to signify total abstinence, as absurd an idea as that of a Temperate Zone completely without warmth. The evidence of centuries points overwhelmingly to the fact that true temperance is most general in countries where light table wines are the common, popular, daily beverage, and the testimony of most acute observers supports this view. Thus Pasteur called wine (by which he meant table wine) "the most healthful and hygienic of beverages." Adam Smith declared: "The cheapness of wine seems to be a cause, not of drunkenness but of sobriety." And Thomas Jefferson concluded: "No nation is drunken where wine is cheap and none sober where the dearness of wine substitutes ardent spirits as the common beverage."

TEMPERATURE — Wines, especially fine wines, are strikingly affected by the temperature at which they are served; a white wine too warm seems lifeless, flat and dull; a red wine too cold seems numbed, astrin-

321

gent, almost entirely lacking in bouquet. This is not a matter of etiquette but of fact, and anyone who cares to experiment can find it out for himself. Much of what has been written on the subject, particularly by Englishmen and Frenchmen, is entirely irrelevant to wine service in the far different climate of the United States. "Room temperature" in an English country house or a French chateau is not the room temperature of a New York apartment, or a New Orleans restaurant in summer. A wine that is best served "cool" in Europe may require considerable chilling to render it fresh and agreeable during July and August in America. Here are a few rules:

1. No wine should ever be served at over 70°, no matter what the temperature of the dining room.

2. Great red wines, particularly old ones, are at their best at 65° to 68°; if they warm up slightly while they are being served and drunk, this will help them rather than injure them.

3. Lesser red wines, the younger ones especially, should be served somewhat cooler, or even slightly chilled in warm weather. 60° is perhaps ideal, which means roughly the temperature of a good cellar.

4. Dry white wines and *vin rosés* should be well chilled, the finer ones and those low in alcohol (as Moselles) to about 55°; the others to 50°.

5. Sparkling wines and most sweet table wines (as Sauternes) should be iced. The great sweet German wines (*Beerenauslesen*, etc.), however, should not be brought to below 55°.

Needless to say, wines can be chilled just as well in an electric refrigerator as in an ice-bucket; the ice-bucket does have the important advantage of keeping the wine cool while it is being served; its principal disadvantage is that the wine in the neck of the bottle often is not chilled at all, and it is perfectly proper, although a little unorthodox, to put a bottle of white wine neck down in the ice bucket for a few minutes before it is served.

TENDRE — (*Tawn*-dr) — French wine-taster's term, literally "tender," applied to wines that are young, fresh, charming, light, easy to drink.

TENT — Old English term for a red wine from Spain, especially from Alicante. It probably derives from the Spanish *tinto* (*see*).

TENUTA VINICOLA — (Tay-*noo*-ta Vee-*nee*-co-la) — Italian term meaning a major vineyard estate — a "chateau" or "domaine" with its buildings and vineyards.

TERLANO — (Tair-*lahn*-no) — Most famous and one of the best white wines of the Italian Tyrol, produced round the village of this name in the narrow, deep, spectacular Adige Valley between Bolzano and Merano. Several different varieties of grape are grown in the vineyards — Riesling, Pinot *bianco*, Pinot *grigio*, plus a local variety called the Terlano, or Blatterle; the quality, and even character, of the wine often varies according to the variety which predominates, and it is rarely possible to determine this from the label. In general, Terlano is a soft, well-balanced, dry white wine, pale green-gold in color, not especially pronounced in bouquet and flavor, but delicate and pleasing. It is shipped in tall green bottles like the wines of Alsace.

TERMENO — (Tair-*may*-no) — Village just south of the Lago di Caldaro (*see*) in the Italian Tyrol; called Tramin in the days, before 1918, when this district was Austrian, and according to tradition, the original home of the Traminer grape.

TERNE — (Tairn) — French word meaning *dull* — specifically, when applied to wine, one that lacks brilliance of color, liveliness and character.

TEROLDEGO — (Tay-rawl-day-go) — Agreeable light red wine, fragrant and fresh, made from the grape of this name in the Italian Trentino (*see*), where it is practically the *vin du pays*. Production is centered round the twin towns of Mezzolombardo and Mezzocorona, northwest of Trento.

TERROIR — (Tear-wahr) — Soil or earth, used in a very special sense in French in connection with wine, as *goût de terroir*. Certain wines produced on heavy soil have a characteristic, unmistakable, almost indescribable, earthy flavor, somewhat unpleasant, common, persistent. This is a *goût de terroir*, and the German equivalent is *Bodenton* or *Bodengeschmack*. Superior wines rarely if ever have much of this, which, if once recognized, will not easily be forgotten.

TERTRE, Château du — (Shat-toe do *Tair*-tr) — 5th Classed Growth of Arsac, Haut-Médoc. Near the southern edge of the Médoc, produces some 10,000 cases a year of rather light, pleasant, fragrant Claret.

TERTRE-DAUGAY, Château — (*Tair*-tr-*Doe*-gay) — A 1st Growth of St. Emilion, good quality, rather small production.

TESSIN — (Tay-sahn) — Swiss canton. *See* Ticino.

THIEF — Pointed tube of glass or metal, sometimes called *chantepleure* (but more often *pipette*) in French, used for taking samples of wine through the bunghole of a barrel.

THIN — Applies to a wine deficient in alcohol and body; watery, poor.

THOUARCÉ — (Too-*ar*-say) — One of the best *communes* of the Coteaux du Layon (*see*), in Anjou. Sweet white wines of top quality.

TICINO — (Tee-chee-no) — Italian-speaking canton of Switzerland, south of the Alps, with some 4,500 acres of vineyard, producing, for the most part, rather common red wines. The best Ticino wine is called Merlot, (*see*) and is made from the Bordeaux grape of that name.

TIGNÉ — (Teen-yea) — Village not far from the Coteaux du Layon (*see*) in the Loire Valley, which, with adjoining *communes*, produces perhaps the best *rosé* wines of Anjou. The Château de Tigné and its adjoining property, the Clos du Moulin, are the principal vineyards.

TINAJA — (Teen-*ach*-ha) — Spanish word for the immense, earthenware amphoras in which the wines of Montilla (*see*) are fermented and first stored.

TINTA — (*Teen*-ta) — Name given in Portugal and in Madeira to a family of red wine grapes, all producing deep-colored, full-bodied red wine, mostly used for Port but some for red table wines such as Dão. They include the Tinto Cão, Tinta Madeira, Tinta Francisca, Tinta Miuda, Tinta Alvarelhão, Tinta Pinhiera, Tinta Carvalha, etc. There exist some plantings of the first two of these mentioned above in California, and they generally give the best California Port, often labeled "California Tinta Port."

TINTILLA — (Teen-*teel*-ya) — Sweet red wine produced in Spain, on the edge of the Sherry Country, especially near the town of Rota.

TINTILLO — (Teen-*teel*-yo) — In Spain, a red wine of little color, almost a dark *rosé*, like many of those of Valdepeñas.

TINTO — (*Teen*-toe) — In Spanish, a *vino tinto* is a red wine. The adjectives *rojo* and *negro* are also used, but more colloquially and less correctly.

TIPICO — (*Tee*-pee-co) — Italian equivalent of the French *Appellation Contrôlée:* a *vino tipico* is one defined by law as to origin, grape variety, etc.

TIRAGE — (Tee-*raj*) — French word meaning "drawing off," usually from cask into bottle. In the Champagne district (*see*), it means the first bottling of new still wine, plus the sugar syrup and yeast (*liqueur de tirage*) which will make it sparkle after a second fermentation in bottle.

TIREUSE — (Tee-*ruhz*) — In French, bottling machine, or a woman engaged in this work.

TISCHWEIN — (Tish-vine) — Literally, "table wine" in German, but usually applied only to light wines of no special quality or excellence, as *vin ordinaire*.

TOKAY — One of the most famous and, at its best, one of the finest white wines of the world. The best has never been cheap or easy to find, and this has been more than ever the case since World War II, now that the former royal, princely and even papal reserves are presumably consumed by deserving Commissars.

All true Tokay comes from a small district in the Carpathian Mountains of north-eastern Hungary called the Tokaj-Hegyalja, and the wine's name is spelled Tokaj in Hungarian. The principal grape variety is the Furmint, which has never been grown commercially elsewhere, and the total production, of all grades, amounts to about 2½ million gallons a year. What is exported is shipped in stubby, long-necked bottles of about 17 oz. (50 centiliter) capacity and the only exporter is the Hungarian Government.

The rarest and finest Tokay, which is truly more of an essence (*Eszencia*) or low-alcohol cordial than a wine, is comparable to a German *Trockenbeerenauslese*. The least expensive and commonest Tokay is a grade called *Szamorodni*, which can be anywhere from quite dry to fairly sweet, depending on the vintage, but is always rather high in alcohol, rarely under 13%.

Considerably better, more expensive and sweeter is what is called *Aszu*, the Hungarian equivalent of a German *Auslese*, which contains a certain fixed proportion of over-ripe grapes, shrunken by the *pourriture noble*, or *Edelfäule*. The quantity of such grapes used per cask in the making of the wine is usually stated on the label in terms of *puttonyos* (*see*), and the more *puttonyos*, the finer, sweeter and more expensive the *Aszu*.

All true Tokays have a wholly distinctive bouquet and flavor; even the lesser ones are often interesting and good values; the best (rarely found) are very great wines indeed.

ALSO, the name often given in Alsace to the Pinot Gris or Ruländer grape, and to wines made from it, although this grape is certainly not of Hungarian origin, is unrelated to the Furmint, and yields an entirely different wine.

ALSO, the name given to a California table grape, pink, thick-skinned, fleshy, which has no imaginable connection with the Furmint or with true Tokay wine. Wine made from this grape, never good, is legally entitled to the name "California Tokay."

TONNE — (Tawnn) — French for a large tank, cask, or tun, of indefinite size.

TONNEAU — (Tawn-*no*) — In general, in French, means practically the same thing as *tonne*; however, in the Bordeaux Country, it means quite specifically four *barriques* or 4 × 225 = 900 liters of wine; almost all Bordeaux wines, prior to bottling, are sold in terms of *tonneaux*, although casks of this size hardly exist and are not in general use. A *tonneau*, in trade practice, means 96 cases or 1,152 bottles of finished wine; usually the chateau-owner sells his wine either *frais compris jusqu'à la mise* (charges for racking, fining, filling, etc., up to the moment of chateau-bottling, included,) as do most of the most celebrated chateaux, or *sans frais*, which means that the buyer must stand the cost of this care, which amounts to ¾% per month, plus, generally, 3% or 6% for fining. In neither case are bottling charges included and these are usually set at not far from $2.50 per case, to cover the bottles, labels, cases, and the work involved.

TOPPING — The refilling of casks or barrels of young wine, usually carried out weekly, to be sure that there is no ullage, or air space between the wine and the bung. An essential part of good cellar work.

TOUL — (Tool) — French town in the province of Lorraine. A few very light and hardly more than passable *vins gris* are produced, largely from the Gamay and Pinot, on nearby slopes entitled to the appellation *Côtes de Toul*, and the V.D.Q. S. seal.

TOURAINE — (Tou-*rain*) — Old, extremely beautiful French province in the Loire Valley, consisting of the modern *départements* of Indre-et-Loire, Loir-et-Cher and Indre; its chief city is Tours, and it makes up most of what has come to be called the Chateau Country. Its production of *Appellation Contrôlée* wines amounts to somewhere between 4 and 6 million gallons a year, a little more than half of it white; the best known names, all listed in their alphabetical place in this volume, are Vouvray, Montlouis, (both white and both sometimes sparkling), Chinon, Bourgueil, Saint-Nicolas-de-Bourgueil (all three red). Lesser wines are marketed as Touraine-Amboise, Touraine-Azay-le-Rideau and Touraine-Mesland, and a great deal of light, pleasant red, white and *rosé* under the general, regional appellation of Touraine. The authorized grape varieties are, for white wine, principally the Chenin Blanc, plus the Sauvignon Blanc, the Pinot Gris and one called the "Arbois"; for red wines and *rosés*, the Cabernet Franc, the Malbec, the Pinot Meunier and the Groslot. Little of what is called "Touraine" is exported; most of it is drunk up, when still less than two years old, by the fortunate inhabitants of this "garden of France," and by thirsty tourists.

For Map, *see* LOIRE.

TOUR BLANCHE, Château La — (Tour Blawnsh) — Celebrated 1st Classed Growth vineyard of Bommes, Sauternes, owned by the French Government, and operated partly as a viticultural school. Its wines are generally a little less sweet and less high in alcohol than the other 1st Growth Sauternes, and are deservedly popular both in France and abroad.

TOUR-CARNET, Château La — (Tour-Car-nay) — 4th Classed Growth of St. Laurent, Haut-Médoc.

TOUR-DU-PIN-FIGEAC, Château La — (Tour-do-Pan-Fee-jack) — Excellent vineyard, directly adjoining Cheval Blanc in the Graves portion of St. Emilion. It is now divided into two separate properties, both producing very sturdy, full-bodied red wine.

TOUR-HAUT-BRION, Château La — (Tour-Oh-*Bree*-awn) — Small, good vineyard practically in the Bordeaux suburbs. Some 1,500 cases of superior red wine.

TRABEN-TRARBACH — (*Tra*-ben-*Trahr*-bach) — Twin towns on the Moselle, in Germany, downstream from Bernkastel and Wehlen but still part of that classic district of great white wine known as the Mittel-Mosel. Traben is on the left bank of the river, Trarbach on the right; between them, they have some 400 acres of vineyard, the best *Lagen* being Trarbacher Schlossberg, Huhnersberg, Ungsberg.

TRAMINER — (Tram-*me*-ner) (Tram-me-*nair*) — One of the better known white wine grapes of Alsace, the Rhine Valley, the Italian Tyrol and even California. Its name is believed to come from the village of Termeno (*see*) in the Tyrol. Grayish-pink in color when ripe, it has, both as a grape and as a wine, a rather special pronounced aroma all its own. Traminer wines are generally soft, rather low in acid, often with a trace of sweetness; the best of these are usually labeled *Gewürztraminer* (*see*).

TRAUBENSAFT — (Trow-ben-sahft) — German for grape juice, destined to be consumed in its unfermented state, usually white, not red.

TREBBIANO — (Treb-be-*ah*-no) — Good but not distinguished white wine grape, of major importance in Italy and to a lesser extent in southern France where, near Marseille, it yields the white wine of Cassis, and is known as the Ugni Blanc (*see*). This is also its name in California, and there is considerable acreage planted to it in the Livermore Valley. In Italy, it is the grape of White Chianti, of the white wine of Lugana (*see*) on Lake Garda, and it is one of the two principal grapes of Soave. Its wines, here and elsewhere, are generally pale gold in color, fairly full bodied, well balanced, often without very much in the way of real raciness or bouquet.

TRENTINO — (Tren-*tee*-no) — District north and east of Lake Garda, south of Bolzano, in northern Italy, forming the province of Trento, Austrian territory until 1918. As far as wine is concerned, it consists almost entirely of the deep, narrow valley of the Adige, and the lower slopes of the 7,000-foot peaks which form the valley walls. The annual production is nevertheless not far from 12 million gallons, most of it light red carafe wine of rather good quality, although there is some *vin rosé* and some white. Grape varieties include the Teroldego, the Schiava, the Marzemino, and others better known, such as Traminer, Pinot, Merlot, Trebbiano and even Lambrusco (*see* these). A good deal of sweet Vino Santo (*see*) is made; the best wines of the district (all described elsewhere in this volume) include those sold as Teroldego, Marzemino d'Isera, Sorni, Rosato d'Avio, Valdadige and Vallagarina, plus some that carry the varietal grape name.

TRIAGE — (Tree-ahj) — French word, practically synonymous with *épluchage*, meaning the sorting, or picking over, by hand, of grapes newly harvested, before crushing and fermentation, so as to eliminate the damaged or defective berries. This is standard practice in most wineries interested in the quality of what they make.

TRIE — (Tree) — French term for a special, expensive method of harvesting grapes, involving repeated partial pickings of only the very ripest bunches. The great natural dessert wines of Sauternes and the Rhine, and almost all others where *pourriture noble* (*see*) is involved, are made in this way.

TRIER — (*Tree*-er) — Principal city of Germany's Moselle Valley, not far from the border of Luxembourg. It was already an important town in Roman days, known as Augusta Trevirorum (whence Trèves, as it is still called in French) and its Roman monuments and ruins are still impressive. Many of the leading Moselle wine producers have their cellars in Trier: the Bischöfliches Priesterseminar, the Bischöfliches Konvikt, the Vereinigte Hospitien, the Friedrich Wilhelm Gymnasium, Von Kesselstatt, the Staatsweingut, etc., and the great semi-annual auctions at which most fine Moselles are sold take place there. The city itself has a few vineyards, though none of much consequence.

327

TRITTENHEIM — (*Trit*-ten-heim) — One of the good but hardly great wine-producing villages of Germany's Mittel-Mosel, with some 225 acres under vines. Its wines are light, engaging and attractive, soon ready; the best vineyard sites include, in about this order of excellence, Trittenheimer Laurentiusberg, Apotheke, Altärchen, Clemensberg, Sonnenberg.

TROCKEN — (*Trawk*-ken) — Literally means dry in German, but as a wine-taster's term it is distinctly less favorable than its English or its French equivalent, *sec*. Except with regard to sparkling wine, it can also mean "withered" (*see*) or *seché*, lacking in freshness and fruit.

TROCKENBEERENAUSLESE — (*Trawk*-ken-*beer*-en-*aus*-lay-zuh) — The highest, sweetest and most expensive of the numerous categories into which fine German wines are divided. Literally the word means a wine made from a selection (*Auslese*) of individually picked grapes (*Beeren*) which have been left on the vine until so ripe as to be practically dry (*trocken*) or raisined. Such grapes are harvested only in great years, and they yield an infinitesimal amount of very sweet, wholly remarkable, and fabulously expensive wine.

TROJA — (*Tro*-ya) — Extremely productive Italian red wine grape, giving a deep-colored, full-bodied, blending wine, rather high in alcohol; widely grown, especially in Apulia (*see*).

TROPLONG-MONDOT, Château — (*Tro*lawn-*Mawn*-doe) — 1st Growth of St. Emilion. Sturdy, full-bodied wine.

TROTANOY, Château — (*Tro*-tan-wah) — One of the best small vineyards of Pomerol. Some 2,000 cases a year of truly outstanding Claret.

TROTTEVIEILLE, Château — (*Trawt*-vee-A) — 1st Growth of St. Emilion. Wines remarkable for their finesse and breed.

TROUBLE — (*Troo*-bl) — French word, used of a wine which is hazy or cloudy, for whatever reason, not clear or brilliant.

TUILÉ — (Twee-lay) — French wine-taster's term, applied to red wines that have a brick-red or roof-tile tinge in their normal crimson, generally the mark of a wine that is already beginning to grow old, and will be short-lived.

TUN — A very large cask or tank or vat, used for wine storage.

TURSAN — (Toor-san) — Obscure French wine, red, white or *rosé*, produced not far from the Adour River in southwestern France, entitled to the V.D.Q.S. seal.

TUSCANY — (Italian TOSCANA — Toe-*skaahn*-na) — The region of Florence, including the Chianti Country, generally third or fourth in total production among the wine regions of Italy (after Apulia, Piedmont and sometimes Sicily) with an average of about 100 million gallons a year. Over 99% of this is table wine and practically all of it is red, a substantial part sold as Chianti (*see*). In addition to Chianti *classico*, which comes from a small, delimited district between Florence and Siena, many Tuscan wines once famous in their own right (Carmignano, Pomino, Rufina, etc.) are now usually marketed under this *passepartout* name, and have largely lost their identity, at least as far as foreign markets are concerned. Much very common wine is also shipped as Chianti, and little Tuscan wine under any other appellation. However, *see* Aleatico, Montepulciano, Vino Santo.

For Map, *see* ITALY.

TYROL — (*Teer*-roll) — Mountainous district, formerly part of Austria, now the Italian provinces of Trento and Bolzano (*see*), in which German is still largely spoken, and which produces many of the most agreeable and best red and white wines of northern Italy. *See* Alto Adige, Trentino.

For Map, *see* ITALY.

UERZIG — (Ert-zig) — Tiny village on the Mittel-Mosel with some 110 acres of steep, terraced vineyard. Its soil is mostly brick-red (rather than the prevailing black slate of the Moselle Valley) and the wines have a rather special character — a pronounced sprightliness and spiciness — in good years. The best vineyards are Würzgarten, Schwarzlay, Kranklay.

UGNI BLANC — (Oon-ye-Blawn) — Productive white wine grape, called the Trebbiano (*see*) in Italy and the St. Emilion in the Cognac Country, rather widely planted in southern France where the best wine it yields is that of Cassis (*see*). It is also grown in California's Livermore Valley, where, as in France and Italy, it gives a sound, well-balanced white wine, agreeable but without any great class.

ULLAGE — The empty space above the liquid in an incompletely filled wine cask: the amount that it lacks of being full. *Ouillage* is the French term that means the filling or "topping" of such casks; oddly enough, both words come from the Latin *ad oculum* — filling to the "eye" or bunghole of the cask.

UMBRIA — (Oom-bree-ah) — Region in central Italy, north of Rome and south of Florence, by no means a real vineyard country, yet producing nearly 20 million gallons a year of table wine. Its one wine of more than local fame is Orvieto (*see*).

USÉ — (Oo-zay) — French word meaning, literally, "worn out," and having not far from the same meaning when applied to wine: a tired wine, definitely past its prime and on the decline.

V-W

VACQUERAS — (Va-kay-ras) — Wine-producing town in the lower Rhône Valley northeast of Avignon. Usually a red wine, though some *rosé* is made. *See* Côtes-du-Rhone.

VALAIS — (*Val*-ay) — Swiss canton producing the best red wines of Switzerland and some of the more interesting and better whites. There are nearly 9,000 acres of vineyard strung along the rocky, enormously impressive, upper valley of the Rhône, here only some twenty airline miles from the Italian border but separated from Italy by the highest peaks of the Alps. The vines extend from near Martigny, (*see*) at the foot of Mont Blanc, past Sion, (*see*) Sierre and Visp, almost to Brig, at the northern end of the Simplon tunnel. Among the finer Valais wines are Dole (*see*), Ermitage, Johannisberg and numerous whites called Fendant after the grape variety out of which they are made.

VALDADIGE — (Vahl-*dad*-dee-jay) — The common, light red table wine of the Trentino (*see*) in Italy. Undistinguished, but usually fresh and pleasant.

VALDEPEÑAS — (Vahl-day-*pain*-yahss) — Name traditionally and loosely given (no longer correctly, however) to the whole vast production of white and red table wines of La Mancha, Don Quixote's country, a rolling upland plain south of Madrid. This is the common *vino corriente* of Spain and there are well over a million acres of vineyard (twice California's total) in production. Legally, this is now and henceforth to be called Vino Manchego or Vino de la Mancha.

The new appellation Valdepeñas is much more limiting, covering only about a million gallons a year, from five villages; of these, Valdepeñas itself, on the main highway south from Madrid to Andalucia, is by far the most important. The wines, furthermore, are supposed to undergo some ageing in oak, and the grape varieties are specified: Airén for white wines, Cencibel, said to be in fact the Tempranillo of the Rioja district, for the reds. It is accepted and common practice, however, to use at least 50% of white Airén in the making of red Valdepeñas, and the wine owes its light color and lack of tannin to this fact.

The white, on the whole, is less good than the red, rather golden and somewhat lacking in sprightliness and bouquet, a sound *ordinaire* which does not improve with keeping. The red, about 13% alcohol, has con-

330

siderably more fruit and charm, a color not much deeper than a dark rosé, a refreshing lightness and lack of astringency; it can well be served chilled and is best drunk young.

ALSO, a variety of red wine grape, certainly of Spanish origin, and perhaps the grape of Valdepeñas itself, of which nearly a thousand acres are planted in the warmer districts of California, where it gives a satisfactory, pleasant, undistinguished red wine.

VALLAGARINA — (*Vahl*-la-gar-*ree*-na) — Southern portion of the Trentino (*see*) in Italy. Its vineyards, along the Adige River, produce a good deal of agreeable, rather common, light red wine, and one or two specialties such as Marzemino d'Isera (*see*) that deserve a somewhat higher rating.

VALMUR — (Val-muir) — One of the seven Grand Cru vineyards of Chablis (*see*); may be labeled either Chablis *Grand Cru*-Valmur, or Chablis Valmur, *Grand Cru*.

VALPANTENA — (Vahl-pahn-*tay*-na) — One of the good lesser red wines of Verona, in Italy, produced just east of the Valpolicella district. It is not unlike Valpolicella, but with less bouquet and class.

VALPOLICELLA — (Vahl-po-lee-*chel*-la) — Admirable red wine, velvety, fragrant, fruity, rather light in alcohol and body but remarkable for its subtlety and breed, produced northwest of Verona, in northern Italy. There are five *comuni*, or townships, in the strictly delimited zone: Negrar, Fumane, Marano, San Pietro Incariano and Sant' Ambrogio; four grape varieties are grown, the Corvina, Molinara, Negrara and Rondinella. The lighter and lesser grades of Valpolicella are usually consumed as carafe wines (and there are no better such wines in the world) when about a year old; those of superior class (Valpolicella Superiore) are bottled after some 18 months in wood, and improve in bottle, but should generally be drunk before they are five years old.

VALTELLINA — (Vahl-tell-*leen*-na) — Vineyard district in northern Italy, near the Swiss border; its red wines, which are among Italy's best. The producing grape, known here as the Chiavennasca, is in reality none other than the famous Nebbiolo (*see*) of Piedmont, and here again it gives wines of remarkable firmness, body and class. The best of them come from five little hillside areas just east of the town of Sondrio, called, from west to east, Sassella, Grumello, Inferno, Grigioni and Fracia, the three first being generally considered the finest; in many instances their wines are sold simply under these vineyard names, with no mention of Valtellina at all. They are interesting and unusual wines, their deep crimson color tinged, one would almost say, with black; sturdy, well-knit, almost unattractively firm when young, they develop slowly and well in bottle, and are long-lived. The vineyards are no less extraordinary, for they are terraced along the lower slopes of a great, 12,000-foot mountain wall (the Swiss-Italian border) and face, across the narrow, slot-like valley of the Adda, mountains almost equally high, the *Alpi Orobie* of northern Lombardy.

VAR — (Varr) — French *département* on the Mediterranean between Marseille and Cannes. Produces, from scattered vineyards, most of them well back from the coast, a surprising amount of wine, much of it fairly good *rosé* and what is here called *blanc de blancs* (*see*), carafe wines both; the reds are pleasant but undistinguished. A few estates, the Domaine des Moulières, the Château de Selle, Ste. Roseline, etc. (*see*), bottle *rosé* wines of superior quality (*see* Côtes de Provence).

VARIETAL (as in "variety") WINE — A wine, in most cases one from California or New York State, which takes its name, not from a town or district, but from the variety of grapes out of which it is principally made. Varietal table wines include most of the best of the U.S., e.g., Cabernet Sauvignon, Pinot Noir, Johannisberg Riesling, Pinot Chardonnay, Grenache, Delaware, Elvira, etc., as distinguished from so-called "generic" wines such as California Claret, New York State Burgundy, etc. According to American law, a wine may only carry a varietal name if it is made at least 51% from the variety in question.

With a few exceptions, notably the wines of Alsace, Switzerland, Austria and the Italian Tyrol, European wines do not carry varietal names; this is due to the fact that the grape varieties grown and used in the fine wine districts abroad are specifically limited and designated, both by tradition and by law. Hence, varietal names for most fine European wines are implicit in the wines' *Appellation d'Origine* — its legally protected geographical name.

VAUCLUSE — (Vo-*cluze*) — French *département* in the lower Rhône Valley, a Papal enclave in the days of the Avignon Popes (1309-1377) and for long thereafter. Its wines include Châteauneuf-du-Pape (*see*), Gigondas, Rasteau, and many pleasant lesser wines, *rosés* and reds especially, often sold as *Côtes du Ventoux*, etc.

VAUD — (Vo) — Swiss canton, first in vineyard area (over 9,000 acres) in the Confederation: white wines almost exclusively, and these made almost exclusively from the Fendant or Chasselas grape. The more important vineyards extend along the northern shore of Lake Geneva, from Nyon to Lausanne (called La Côte) and from Lausanne on eastward to beyond Vevey (called Lavaux). The district called Chablais (*see*) is also in the Canton of Vaud, as are the Côtes de l'Orbe, near Neuchâtel.

VAUDÉSIR — (*Vo*-day-zeer) — One of the best of the seven *Grand Cru* vineyards of Chablis. Its wine is outstanding.

❡.D.Q.S., or VINS DELIMITES DE QUALITÉ SUPERIÉURE — (Van Day-*lee*-me-tay duh *Cahl*-lee-tay Soo-*pay*-ree-*err*) — Category of French wines, including many of truly superior quality, which are nevertheless not legally entitled to an *Appellation Contrôlée* (*see*). They are, however, strictly controlled by the French Government as to production zone, grape varieties and yield per acre. When shipped, their labels carry a special stamp with the initials V.D.Q.S. and the words "*Label de Garantie.*" The "*garantie*" in question is an official one and the stamp may only appear on wines produced in accordance with the Government's rules, wines, in addition which have been tasted and approved by a committee of impartial experts. There are over fifty such wines as of the present, all listed under their place-name in this volume, and also in the appendix. Some of the better-known ones are: Côtes du Luberon, Côtes de Provence, Costières du Gard, Minervois, Corbières, etc.

VELOUTÉ — (Vel-loo-tay) — Literally, in French, "velvety"; wine-tasters' term, applied to wines that are notably mature, mellow, fine-textured and soft, as *soyeux*, or "silky."

VELTLINER — (*Velt*-leen-ner) — Good quality white-wine grape, of importance principally in Austria, although it is grown to some extent in the Tyrol and in the cooler counties of California. Its wine somewhat resembles a Traminer, though with less pronounced bouquet and flavor.

VENDANGE — (Vawn-dawnj) — French for the grape harvest, or vintage, though *never* used of the "vintage" of a particular wine (*see millésime*). The equivalent terms are *vendemmia* (Ital.), *vendemia* (Sp.) and *Weinlese* (Ger.), and these too are applied to the harvest itself, not to the "year" which the wine may carry later on its label.

VENDEMIA — (Ven-*daim*-me-ah) — Spanish word meaning the grape harvest. Not, however, used in the sense of the word "vintage," nor meaning a specific year.

VENDEMMIA — (Ven-*daim*-me-ah) — Italian for grape harvest or vintage, not used of a particular year or vintage.

VENENCIA — (Ven-*nen*-see-ah) — Instrument used (like a *pipette* or "wine thief") in the Sherry and Manzanilla country to take samples of wine through the bunghole of a cask. In its simplest form, it is a strip of bamboo (*caña*) with one cylindrical section left intact at the lower end, so as to form a little cup. This cylindrical cup is now more often of silver, attached to a pliable whalebone rod, with a silver hook to serve as a handle at its upper end. An expert *bodeguero* in Jerez can use his *venencia* with extraordinary grace and skill.

VENETO — (*Vain*-nay-toe) — The region of Venice, fifth in wine production among Italian regions, some 80 million gallons a year. Much of this is quite ordinary but much, too, is good. Especially notable are the wines of Verona (*see*), Bardolino, Valpolicella, Soave; and those of the province of Treviso, (*see* Conegliano), but there are many others that belong in a somewhat lesser category: Raboso, Friularo, Colli Euganei, etc.

VENTE SUR SOUCHES — (Vawnt suhr Soosh) — In French, "sale on the vine" — commercial practice, which has unfortunately become widespread in the Bordeaux district in recent years, whereby the wine of a given vineyard is sold at a fixed price months before the vintage, and long before anything is known of the size of the crop or of its quality. This, which is of course pure speculation, has brought about higher prices and a regrettable tendency on the part of the Bordeaux trade to describe even the most mediocre vintages as "outstanding."

VENTOUX — (Vawn-*too*) — Name of a remarkable, isolated, 6,000-foot peak (Le Mont Ventoux literally means "The Windy Mountain," and it is well named) dominating a whole section of the lower Rhône Valley and the *département* of Vaucluse (*see*). Its lower slopes and the surrounding foothills are largely covered with vines and yield much excellent *vin rosé* (usually sold as Côtes-du-Ventoux), some very good red including Gigondas (*see*), a few white wines that are less interesting and even one sweet liqueur wine called Rasteau (*see*).

VERDELHO — (Vair-*del*-ho) — One of the best grape varieties of Madeira, producing an interesting, fortified wine, generally sold under this name — usually on the dry side and somewhat resembling Sercial, but with a special character of its own.

VERDICCHIO — (Vair-*dee*-key-o) — Superior Italian white wine grape; also its wine. *See* Castelli di Jesi.

VERDISO — (Vair-*dee-zo*) — Superior white wine grape and the interesting, dry white wine made from it, round the town of Conegliano (*see*), north of Venice in northern Italy. A sweeter still wine and some sparkling wines as well are made from the same grape in the same district, and called Prosecco (*see*). This has occasionally led to some confusion, since the word *secco*, in Italian, means "dry," whereas Prosecco is the sweeter of the two Verdiso wines.

VERDOT — (Vair-doe) — Superior red wine grape of the Bordeaux Country, grown generally in combination with the Cabernets, Merlot, Malbec, etc. It gives a full-bodied, deep-colored, slow-maturing wine, high in tannin.

VERGENNES — (Vair-*shenn*) — American grape variety, probably a Labrusca seedling, dating from Revolutionary days, named after the then Foreign Minister of France, Comte Charles de Vergennes, who, like Lafayette, was a staunch champion of the cause of American independence.

VERGISSON — (*Vair*-gee-sawn) — One of the four *commune*s producing Pouilly-Fuissé (*see*), perhaps the least important of the four.

VERJUS — (Vair-shuh) — Juice of unripe grapes, high in acid.

VERMENTINO — (Vair-men-*tee*-no) — Perhaps the best dry white wine of the Italian Riviera, fresh, pale, tart, excellent with seafood; that produced round Pietra Ligure is outstanding.

VERMOUTH (from the German *Wermut*, wormword) — A fortified white wine, flavored with various herbs, barks, seeds, spices, etc. The principal aromatic agent in vermouth consists of flowers of the shrub *Artemisia absinthium*, also known as wormwood; (the far more toxic leaves of the same plant are used in the making of Absinthe). Today, vermouth is used principally as an apéritif and as a cocktail ingredient. There are two main types: French and Italian. The French, pale in color, quite dry; the Italian, darker, usually with a base of muscat wine, quite sweet. French type vermouths are, nevertheless, made in Italy, and Italian type vermouths in France. Both are produced in many other countries, including Spain, Argentina and the United States, and are based on similar wines and the same aromatics, including *Artemisia* flowers, bitter orange peel, camomile, aloes, cardamon and anise. The better American vermouths are now substantially as good as the imported.

VERNACCIA — (Vair-*natch*-cha) — Unusual white wine of Sardinia, dry, rather aromatic, higher in alcohol (sometimes over 17%) than any other natural, unfortified wine in the world. It takes its name from the Vernaccia grape.

VERNATSCH — (Vair-*natch*) — Local name given to the Schiava grape (*see*) in the Italian Tyrol.

VERONA — (Vair-*ro*-na) — Charming little city in northern Italy, famous as the home of Romeo and Juliet, and, among wine-lovers, for the wines produced nearby, copiously and joyously consumed by the Veronese themselves, and now exported in increasing quantities. They include Soave, Valpolicella, Vanpantena, Bardolino, Chiarello (*see* all of these).

VERT — (Vair) — French wine-taster's term, applied to wines that are "green," or unripe, in the same sense as unripe fruit, disagreeably high in acid, and tart. In many cases this is a fault that will correct itself with time, and if the wine is otherwise well-balanced, it can be an indication (though by no means an assurance) of good future development and long life.

VERZENAY — (*Vair*-zuh-nay) — One of the best villages of the French Champagne Country, on the Montagne de Reims, rated 100% in the official classification. Its vineyards, much fought over in World War I, are planted to Pinot Noir exclusively. *See* Champagne.

VESTE — (Ves-tay) — Italian equivalent of the French word *robe* when applied to wine; a combination of color, clarity and brilliance — *una buona veste* is high praise.

VESUVIO — (Vay-*soo*-vee-o) — Wine, generally a dry, white wine, produced on the slopes of Mt. Vesuvius, near Naples.

VIDANGE — (Vee-dawnj) — Ullage. The empty space in an improperly filled cask of wine; more rarely, the air space under the cork of a bottled wine. If abnormally great, a danger signal in almost all cases.

VIEUX — (Vee-uh) — French word for "old" (the feminine is *vieille* — vee-yay), about as loosely used as in English.

335

VIEUX-CHÂTEAU CERTAN — (Vee-*yuh*-Shat-*toe*-*Sair*-tawn) — One of the very best vineyards of Pomerol, second perhaps only to Château Petrus. Some 4,000 cases a year of fine, sturdy, velvety Claret, consistently good, improving greatly in bottle.

VIF — (Veef) — French wine-taster's term, applied to a young wine that is fresh, light, agreeable; perhaps a little more tart than one called *tendre*, and a bit less tart than one called *vivace*.

VIGNE — (*Veen*-yuh) — In French, an individual vine, or, far more often, a small parcel of vineyard, one man's holding in a *climat* (*see*) or *vignoble* (*see*).

VIGNERON — (*Veen*-yair-rawn) — In French, a vineyardist, or winedresser, whether working for his own account or not.

VIGNOBLE — (*Veen*-yob'l) — In French, a vineyard area, or the vineyards of a district, generally sharing an appellation.

VILA NOVA DE GAIA — (Vee-la No-va day Guy-ya) — Town directly opposite Oporto on the Douro River, in Portugal. *See* Port.

VILLAFRANCA DEL PANADÉS — (*Veel*-ya *Frahn*-ca del Pahn ah-*daice*) — Important center of the wine trade, south of Barcelona, in Spain. Some very passable and surprisingly light white wines are made, a few less good reds, and what are on the whole the best sparkling wines of Spain, mostly fermented in bulk but a few by the authentic Champagne process.

VILLAUDRIC — (Veel-lo-dreek) — Inconsequential red and white wine produced round the town of this name in southwestern France. It has a right to the V.D.Q.S. seal.

VILLENAVE D'ORNON — (Veel-nav-*Dor*-nawn) — Wine-producing village in the Graves district of France. Its better Châteaux include: Couhins, Baret, Pontac-Monplaisir, etc.

VIN — French for wine, legally defined in France (as in the United States) as a beverage made through the partial or complete fermentation of the juice of fresh grapes. Thus, wines made from cherries and other fruits must be labeled "Cherry Wine," "Blackberry Wine," etc.

VIÑA — (*Veen*-ya) — Spanish word for "vineyard," often followed by a proper name.

VINAGRINHO — (Veen-ah-*green*-ho) — Portuguese term for the characteristic flavor of certain old Madeiras and old Ports, akin to *rancio* (*see*) largely the result of partial oxidation and a slight increase in volatile acidity.

VIN DE L'ANNÉE — (*Van* duh Lan-*nay*) — Literally, in French, "wine of the year," used to describe any wine, excellent or mediocre, which is less than a year old.

VIN BLANC — (Van Blawn) — French for white wine.

VIN DE CAFÉ — (*Van* duh Ca-*fé*) — An inexpensive, light-bodied red or *rosé* wine (occasionally but rarely a white wine), made to be consumed as a "bar wine" or *vin de comptoir* in France.

VIN CUIT — (Van Quee) — French wine taster's term, said of a wine which appears to have the aroma and taste of concentrate, or wine that has been heated before fermentation so as to reduce its volume and to increase its eventual alcoholic content and its body.

VINÉ — (*Vee*-nay) — French word meaning "fortified." Wines to which brandy or high-proof grape spirits have been added are *vins vinés*.

VINETTO — (Vee-*net*-toe) — Italian for a small wine, low in alcohol and light in body.

VINEUX — (Veen-uh) — French wine taster's term said of a wine which is obviously rather high in alcohol — perhaps too much so — and without much finesse. The German is *weinig*.

VINEYARD — A plantation of grape vines.

VINEYARD SITE — The rather clumsy English equivalent of the French word *climat*; the Spanish *pago*; and the German *Weinbergslagen*, meaning a specifically named plot of vines.

VIN FIN — (Van Fan) — Loosely used French term meaning, in general, a wine of superior quality; one made from superior grape varieties. Only in rare instances (*see* Côte de Nuits) has it a more specific definition according to French law.

VIN DE GARDE — (Van duh Gard) — French wine taster's term meaning a wine which will improve with keeping.

VIN GRIS — (Van Gree) — French term used to describe very pale *rosé* wines, especially those made from black grapes in eastern France, notably Lorraine and Alsace. Some of these are practically white, with an almost imperceptible pink or bronze tinge (*see* Lorraine).

VINHO — (*Veen*-ho) — General Portuguese term for wine.

VINHO GENEROSO — (*Veen*-ho Gen-air-*ro*-so) — Portuguese term reserved for certain fortified wines of superior quality and specific origin.

VINHO DE RAMO — (*Veen*-ho de *Rah*-mo) — Legal Portuguese name for the *consumo* (or table wine) from the Port district, which is sold unfortified for table use, rather than being made into Port.

VINHO DE TORNA VIAGEM — (*Veen*-ho de *Tor*-na Via-jem) — Old Portuguese term applied to wines which had been shipped in casks in sailing vessels to the East Indies and back, which supposedly greatly improved them. Certain Ports and Madeiras were so labeled and they were the Portuguese equivalent of "East India Sherries."

VINHO VERDE — (*Veen*-ho *Vair*-day) — Literally "green wine" in Portuguese. Odd name given to the sprightly, fresh, red, white and *rosé* wines (green only in the sense of being youthful — naturally not in color) produced in northern Portugal, not far from Spanish Galicia. Many of these are very pleasant, a few slightly sparkling, and some are now being exported to England and the United States.

VINICULTURE — General term covering whole science and business of the growing of wine grapes, the making of wine and the wine's ageing and preparation for market.

VINIFERA — (Vin-*nif*-fair-ah) — One, and by all odds the most important, of the 32 species which make up the genus *vitis*. Some 20 of these are native to the United States and 11 others native to Asia. *Vinifera*, "the wine bearer," apart from a few hybrids, is the one responsible for all of the wines of Europe, Africa, South America and California.

VINIFICATION — The making of wine from grapes, including its fermentation, treatment, ageing, etc. A very broad term which involves practically the whole process except what goes on in the vineyard.

VINILLO — (Vee-*neel*-yo) — Spanish equivalent of the French *Petit Vin*. A wine of light body, low alcoholic content, generally of poor quality.

VIN JAUNE — (Van Shone) — Odd, special wine produced in the Jura district of France, especially round Château Chalon (*see*) — not far in character from a very light Spanish Sherry.

VIN NATURE — (Van Nah-tewr) — A rather loosely used French wine term meaning, in general, a wine that has not been fortified or sweetened; in some cases, a Champagne which has received no *dosage* or sweetening.

VIN NON MOUSSEUX — (Van Non Moo-*suh*) — In French, simply means a non-sparkling wine, a still wine.

VIN NOUVEAU — (Van Noo-*vo*) — Properly applied, in French, it is any wine which has finished its fermentation and is less than a year old.

VIN D'UNE NUIT — (Van dune *Nwee*) — In French, a cheap, light red wine which has been left to ferment on its skins for twenty-four hours or less and which, therefore, has little color and tannin; for all practical purposes, identical with a *vin de café* (*see*).

VINO — (*Vee*-no) — The word for wine in Italian and Spanish.

VINO DA ARROSTO — (*Vee*-no da Ar-*ros*-toe) — Italian for a rather full-bodied red wine, one of better than average quality, properly served with red meat.

VINO CORRIENTE — (*Vee*-no Cor-ri-*en*-tay) — In Spanish, the equivalent of the French *vin ordinaire*; the young, inexpensive, relatively common wine, currently consumed by most Spaniards, often in carafe.

VINO DI LUSSO — (*Vee*-no dee *Loo*-so) — Italian wine term, literally "de luxe wine," a category which includes sparkling wines, fortified wines, etc.

VINO DE MESA — (*Vee*-no duh *May*-sa) — Spanish for table wine.

VINO DA PASTO — (*Vee*-no da *Pass*-toe) — In Italian, a table wine as distinguished from apéritif and dessert wines.

VIN ORDINAIRE — (Van Or-din-*naihr*) — *See* Ordinaire.

VINO ROSATO — *See* Rosato.

VINO ROSSO — *See* Rosso.

VINO SANTO — (*Vee*-no *Sahn*-toe), also **VIN SANTO**) – Italian white wine produced principally in Tuscany, but also, to some extent, in the Trentino (*see*), from grapes that have been allowed partially to raisin, either on the vine or indoors. Various grape varieties are used, most often the Trebbiano, and the resulting wine is of course golden in color, quite sweet, bottled generally after two or more years in cask (*see* Passito).

VINO DA TAGLIO — (*Vee*-no da *Tal*-yo) — Italian term for blending wine, usually one having certain special characteristics such as deep color, high alcohol, etc., used on account of these qualities to improve wines of lesser quality.

VINO TINTO — *See* Tinto.

VINO TIPICO — *See* Tipico.

VINO DE YEMA — (*Vee*-no duh *Yah*-ma) — In Spanish, a wine generally of superior quality, made of "free-run" juice or from grapes very lightly pressed.

VIN DE PAILLE — *See* Paille.

VIN DE PAYS — *See* Pays.

VIN DE PRESSE — (Van duh Press) — French for wine which is generally not the first "free-run" juice of the crushed grapes, but extracted by a wine press. The first *vin de presse* is usually blended with the "free-run" and gives it more substance, color and tannin, all of which it often lacks. Alone, *vin de presse* is likely to be somewhat harsh.

VIN DE PRIMEUR — (Van duh Pree-Muhr) — French term for a wine which matures early and is generally short-lived.

VIN ROSÉ — *See* Rosé.

VIN ROUGE — (Van Rouge) — Red wine, in French.

VIN SUR LIE — (Van Sewr Lee) — French and Swiss term for certain white wines which are drawn off for consumption or bottling before the final racking has taken place; in other words, while there is still some sediment or deposit in the cask. This is common practice in the Muscadet district of France, to an even greater extent in the Swiss vineyards along Lake Geneva. Such wines have a faint, rather agreeable, yeasty flavor, and an almost imperceptible sparkle.

VINTAGE — Word used in a confusing diversity of senses in English, often practically as a synonym for wine. Properly, however, the vintage is the annual grape harvest and the wine made from those grapes; to this extent, at least, every year is a vintage year and all wines are vintage wines unless they are blended — their vintage is the year they were produced. However, during the 19th century, it became common practice in a few wine-growing districts, notably the Port Country and Champagne, to blend all wines except those of unusually good years, and to allow only the latter to carry a date, or vintage; eventually, in the popular mind, in England and the United States, "vintage year" came to have the meaning of "good year," although it can have no possible such connotation except with regard to Champagne and Port. In Bordeaux, Burgundy, the Rhineland, etc., there are good vintages and bad (the latter, alas, all too frequent) but almost every wine carries its vintage on its label, and is therefore, by any sensible definition, a vintage wine, whether good or bad.

In most wine-producing countries, especially those fairly far north, there is a great difference in quality between the wines of one year and another; vintage years are important, and a reliable vintage chart can be very helpful. This is not so much the case in areas of less variable climate and more consistent sunshine, such as California and, to some extent, the lower Rhône Valley, Italy and Spain.

VIN DE TÊTE — (*Van* duh *Tet*) — Said in French of a wine of outstanding quality, the best of its sort; also, a "free-run" wine which has not received the addition of a *vin de presse*.

VINZELLES — (Van-*zell*) — Village in the French Maconnais district, not far from Pouilly. *See* Pouilly-Vinzelles.

VIOGNIER — (Vee-*on*-yea) — White grape of the Rhône Valley, in France, giving a wine of excellent quality and rather pronounced and special character. Sometimes spelled Vionnier, it is the variety of Château-Grillet and Condrieu (*see*) and is also used to some extent in the red Côte Rôtie.

VIRÉ — (*Vee*-ray) — Village north of Macon, in southern Burgundy. Its fresh, dry, fragrant white wines, made from the Chardonnay grape, are, with those of Clessé, among the best of the Maconnais. The outstanding vineyard is the Clos du Chapitre (*see*).

VISPERTERMINEN — (*Vis*-pair-tare-me-nen) — Small, Swiss vineyard in the Canton of Valais, the highest in altitude in Europe, being situated over 4,000 feet above sea level. Its wines, mostly red, are sometimes known as *Païen*, meaning "Pagan."

VITE ALBERATA — (*Vee*-tay Ahl-bear-*ra*-ta) — Vines trained on (or "married to") trees, in the Italian fashion; the tree, in such instances, is often called a *marito*, or husband.

VITICULTEUR — (Vee-tee-cuhl-*ter*) — In French, a vine grower, generally one who cultivated his own vineyard; *vigneron* (*see*) is nearly synonymous, but more often used of a skilled employee or share-cropper (*metayer*).

VITICULTURE — That branch of agriculture which involves the science and art of grape-growing; when this has to do with wine production, the proper word is viniculture (*see*).

VIVACE — (Vee-*vahss*) — French wine-taster's term, applied generally to young wines which are fresh, lively, often a bit tart, likely to keep well and improve.

VOEGTLINSHOFFEN — (Vukt-lins-hof-fen) — Alsatian vineyard town on the Vosges foothills south of Colmar, in the *département* of Haut-Rhin. Produces very light white wines of unusual finesse.

VOLLRADS, Schloss — (Vawl-rahdz) — The largest and one of the most famous vineyard estates of the Rheingau, back of the village of Winkel, and just east of Schloss Johannisberg. The castle itself, with a picturesque keep, or central tower, dating from 1355, is a splendid old manor house, and its 81 acres of vines produce an extremely wide range of estate-bottlings, all the way from the light, dry, modest *Original-Abfüllung* of secondary years to incomparable *Trockenbeerenauslesen* in great vintages. Wines considered unworthy of the *Schloss* label never are allowed to carry it, but those granted this diploma make up what is perhaps the most complicated hierarchy of classes, grades, labels and capsules in the whole, often complicated, world of wine. Before attempting to explain this, it may be well to say that Vollrads wines, with practically no exceptions, have to some degree a certain characteristic elegance, a fine bouquet, a pleasing lightness and fruit.

Of those permitted to bear the name of the owner (Graf Matuschka-Greiffenklau — who is a chess-player) and his coat-of-arms, the least

expensive are those that carry the words *Original-Abfüllung* and a green capsule; those with a green-capsule-with-silver-stripe are of slightly superior class, and if the stripe is gold, they are considered a shade better. On a higher level (a difference distinguishable by an expert, but by no means a giant step) are the three representatives of the red-capsule family — red, red-with-silver, red-with-gold.

We next move into what might be called "Officers' Quarters," and here once more we have the full range: two colors, three grades of each. But in this category the labels are marked, not *Original-Abfüllung,* but *Schlossabzug* — bottled by the Castle rather than the owner, although in fact, of course, both bottled both. Here, as before, we have green capsule and red capsule, and three sorts of each, with superiority indicated by silver and gold stripes, and in the same order.

When it comes to higher echelons, Schloss Vollrads does not use the word *Spätlese* on any of its labels (although wines have been known to be so marked by dishonest merchants) and the equivalent, here, is *Kabinett.* These wines now wear a blue capsule, once more divided into blue, blue-plus-silver and blue-plus-gold stripes. Then, of course, we have *Auslese, Beerenauslese, Trockenbeereanauslese, Bestes Fass,* in this ascending order. Almost all of these are superb, and worth whatever they cost.

It is to be regretted, certainly, that some simpler method of classification and quality identification cannot be found, for a collection of wines, however good, produced by just 81 acres in a good vintage.

VOLNAY — (Vawl-nay) — Justly celebrated village of the Côte de Beaune, in Burgundy, its vineyards bounded on the north by those of Pommard and on the south by Meursault's. The average quality of its red wines (the few whites are entitled to and carry the appellation Meursault) is extremely high, certainly above Pommard's, and the Volnays of good years are among the most prepossessing of all Burgundies, wonderfully soft and fine, *bouquetés*, with a special velvety quality, and great breed. The better vineyards include the Clos des Ducs, Caillerets, Champans, Chevret, Fremiets, Pousse d'Or (often, but less correctly, written Bousse d'Or), Clos des Chênes, etc.

VORLAUF —' (Vor-lauf) — Wine made from the first, gentle pressing of red grapes, usually a pale *rosé*. Name often given in Alsace to the light pink wine there made from the Pinot Noir and Pinot Meunier.

VOSGES — (Voj) — Mountain chain in eastern France, facing Germany's Black Forest across the wide, fertile plain of the Rhine Valley. The wines of Alsace (*see*) come from vineyards planted along the eastern slopes and foothills of the Vosges.

VOSNE-ROMANÉE — (Vone-*Ro*-ma-nay) — Perhaps the most remarkable wine-producing *commune* of all France, though its total production is comparatively small. Within its communal limits are grown some seven or eight truly incomparable red wines, the glories of Burgundy, known around the world: Romanée-Conti, Richebourg, La Tâche, La Romanée, all labeled simply with the vineyard name and no mention

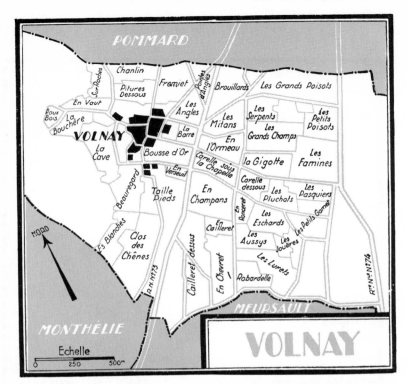

NOTE: What is certainly Volnay's best vineyard, the *Clos des Ducs,* was inexplicably left nameless on this old map. It consists of the blank section directly above and adjoining the village of Volnay, and is part of the estate of the present Marquis d'Angerville, whose father was largely responsible for the creation of *Appellations Contrôlées* in Burgundy.

of Vosne; then, having Vosne-Romanée as part of their name, Vosne-Romanée La Grande Rue, Les Malconsorts, Les Suchots, Les Beaux-Monts and many others. All of them (even the lesser wine sold simply as Vosne-Romanée) have certain characteristics in common: breed, elegance, exceptional balance, fine bouquet. *See* most of the vineyards listed above in their alphabetical place elsewhere in this volume.

See map on following page.

VOUGEOT — (Voo-sho) — Red Burgundy from a small plot of vines directly adjoining the Clos de Vougeot (*see*), but not entitled to this name. It is definitely of a lower grade than Clos de Vougeot itself, and often has a pronounced *goût de terroir*.

VOUVRAY — (Voo-vray) — The most famous white wine of Touraine, in the Loire Valley of France, and an old American favorite, perhaps due to the fact that AFHQ, in World War I, was set up in Tours, near-by. It is made entirely from the Chenin Blanc grape, and the legally

343

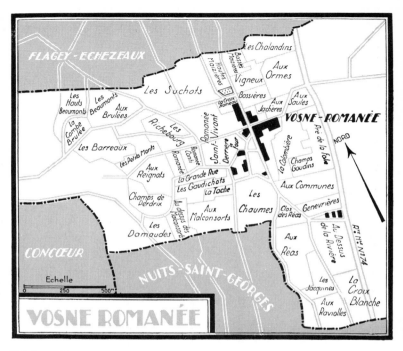

NODE

VOSNE ROMANÉE

NOTE: This old map fails to show one important change in appellations which became effective during World War II, whereby a large part of Les Gaudichots became part of La Tâche (*see*).

delimited zone of production consists of eight *communes:* Vouvray, Ste. Radegonde, Rochecorbon, Vernou, Noizay, Chançay, Reugny and Parçay-Meslay. A changeling among wines if there ever was one, Vouvray can be (depending on its vintage and its cellar treatment) a fruity, bone-dry wine, somewhat on the tart side; a rich, golden elixir, comparable to a great Sauternes or Rhine wine; a pale and appetizing wine with a slight sparkle (*pétillant*); an out-and-out sparkling wine, and one of the best of France. Despite much that has been said and written to the contrary, Vouvray does "travel"; it is also one of the longest-lived white wines of the world. Total production is in the neighborhood of three-quarters of a million gallons a year.

VULLY — (Voo-ye) — Wine producing district not far from Neuchâtel in the Swiss Canton of Vaud. White wines from the Fendant or Chasselas grapes.

WACHENHEIM — (*Vahk*-hen-heim) — One of the four best wine-producing towns of the German Rheinpfalz (*see*) or Palatinate. Its wines are a little lighter than those of Forst and Deidesheim nearby, but of the same noble class. There are some 840 acres of vineyard, about 25% of this in Riesling grapes, most of the rest in Sylvaner. Leading vineyards include: Wachenheimer Gerümpel, Böhlig, Rechbächel, Goldbächel, Luginsland and Langebächel. The leading producer is Dr. Bürklin-Wolf.

WACHSTUM — (*Vahk*-stoom) — German wine term meaning "growth," when followed by the name of a specific producer. Wines carrying this word on their labels must, according to German law, be *natur*, i.e., unsugared; but this is not a guarantee of Estate-Bottling.

WALDMEISTER — (*Vahld*-my-ster) — German name for the wild herb, woodruff (*asperula odorata*, of the madder family) which is the principal flavoring in what is known as May Wine, a popular sort of wine punch in Germany.

WALDRACH — (*Vahl*-drach) — Wine-producing village of secondary importance in the Ruwer Valley near Trier. Its best known vineyard is Schloss Marienlay.

WALLUF — (*Vahl*-luf) — The recently adopted name for the wines of what were previously two separate townships in the German Rheingau — Nieder-Walluf and Ober-Walluf. The best vineyards (87 acres in all) are: Wallufer Walkenberg, Mittelberg, Unterberg and Röderweg. The whites, mostly Rieslings, are of fine quality, but have a certain amount of "soil" taste, or *Bodenton*; there are also some reds made from the Pinot Noir. J. B. Becker is the leading producer.

WASHINGTON, State of — There exist two widely different climatic zones in Washington: that along the coast, including the Olympic peninsula and the Puget Sound region, which is relatively cool and humid, and that in the higher interior, with greater extremes of temperature and a long, hot arid summer. Side by side with the profusion of "berry wines," usually fortified and which might be more appropriately called light cordials, there is a small but growing production of fairly good, light table wines from irrigated vineyards in eastern Washington, notably in the Yakima Valley. Grape varieties include some Sylvaner, some true Riesling, Pinot Blanc, Pinot Noir, Carignan, and quite a few others, as well as some Eastern varieties such as Concord and Delaware. The western, or maritime, part of the state has many vineyards of Concords and related varieties, but produces no table wines of any real class.

WAWERN — (Vaa-vairn) — One of the good, lesser wine-producing vineyards of the Saar Valley in Germany. Some 70 acres of Rieslings — best vineyards are: Wawerner Herrenberg, Goldberg.

WEEPER — One of many terms employed to describe a wine bottle which has shown a tendency to leak or lose wine round its cork. This can be caused either by bad storage conditions or by an inferior cork. It is likely to result in a spoiled bottle.

345

WEHLEN — (*Vay*-len) — Little town on the Moselle, between Bernkastel and Zeltingen, now considered by most experts the best of that whole, small but renowned, wine district known as the Mittel-Mosel. A hundred years ago, or even fifty, this was not the case: Wehlen was ranked well below Brauneberg and Bernkastel, and hardly on a par with Graach, Zeltingen and Piesport. The change has been brought about largely through the efforts of a single numerous family called Prüm, whose wines consistently bring the highest prices at the great semiannual auctions in Trier, where the best Moselles are sold. The village is on the left (here the south) bank of the winding river, and faces the incredibly steep, high vineyard slope in the heart of which, painted on an almost perpendicular outcropping of slate, is the *Sonnenuhr*, or sundial, which has given its name to Wehlen's best wine. This, in good years, has few if indeed any equals: flowery, well-balanced, with an almost supernatural combination of delicacy and richness, it is perfection itself.

Leading vineyard sites include, beside Sonnenuhr, Lay, Klosterlay, Nonnenberg, Rosenberg, Abtei, etc.; a few of the finest wines come from vines planted along the communal border of Wehlen and Zeltingen, and are sometimes labeled Wehlener-Zeltinger, plus a vineyard name.

The most celebrated producers are Johann-Joseph Prüm, Sebastian Alois Prüm, Peter Prüm, Dr. Bergweiler (collaterally a Prüm), Dr. Weins Erben (also a Prüm connection), Hauth-Herpen, the St. Nikolaus Hospital, etc.

There are about 210 acres under vines.

WEIBEL — (Y-bel) — Important California wine producer, especially in the field of less expensive, sparkling wines. The winery is at Mission San Jose, Alameda County, southeast of San Francisco.

WEIN — (Vine) — German word for wine.

WEINBAUBESITZER — (Vine-bau-be-sitz-er) — In German, means a vineyard owner — more often than not a fairly prosperous one — who does not himself work in his own vineyard.

WEINBERG — (*Vine*-bairg) — In German, vineyard or vineyard property.

WEINGUT — (*Vine*-goot) — In German, a vineyard property, generally including the vines themselves, a winery, cellars, etc.

WEINSTRASSE — (*Vine*-shtrah-suh) — A road or itinerary which can be pleasantly and profitably followed by tourists in the German wine country. Usually these are marked and designated; Germany's best-known *Weinstrasse* extends through the Rheinpfalz from Kleinbockenheim west of Mannheim to Schweigen on the French frontier.

WEISSHERBST — (*Vice*-hairbst) — Literally in German "white harvest." As far as wine is concerned, a white wine made from black grapes or what the French would call a *blanc de noirs*. This is a specialty of the little villages strung along the northern shore of Lake Constance, which the Germans call the Bodensee. The best of them comes from the village of Meersburg, and is made from the Pinot Noir.

WENTE — (*Wen*-te) — Famous California wine-growing family whose vineyards have long produced some of America's finest white wines. Their first vines were planted near Livermore, in Alameda County, southeast of San Francisco, in 1883, and the business has remained a family enterprise ever since. A number of outstanding varietal wines are made, including Pinot Chardonnay, Pinot Blanc, Dry Semillon, Sauvignon Blanc, Grey Riesling, etc., plus a few that carry generic names such as Chablis and a certain number of less outstanding red and *rosé* wines, as well.

WESLEY, John (1703-1791) — British preacher and founder of Methodism who wrote in his Journal, September 9, 1771: "Wine is one of the noblest cordials in nature."

WHITE PINOT — California name for the white wine grape more properly called Chenin Blanc (*see*), or Pineau de la Loire (*see*).

WHITE RIESLING — See Riesling, Johannisberg Riesling.

WILTINGEN — (*Vil*-ting-en) — One of the most celebrated and best wine-producing towns of Germany, on the Saar River (*see*), southwest of Trier. Its 330 acres of vineyard are entirely planted in Rieslings and cover a few incredibly steep black-slate hillsides facing south. The best *Lagen* (or vineyard sites) include the incomparable Scharzhofberg (*see*) which many experts regard as the greatest white wine vineyard in the world, and, in addition, Wiltinger Braune Kupp, Rosenberg, Gottesfüss, Klosterberg, Braunfels and Kupp.

The wines from these, in poor years, are often so hard and austere as to be properly called "steely" and in very poor years many of them are sold to be blended and made into sparkling wine. In favorable and great years, however, the best Wiltingers are unsurpassed by any other white wines in Germany or in the world.

WINE — As legally defined in most countries, a beverage made from the partial or complete fermentation of the juice of fresh grapes.

WINE AND SODA — Pleasant summer drink consisting of ice, wine and soda in a tall glass. German wines, or comparable California wines (Riesling, Sylvaner, etc.) are perhaps best adapted for this purpose on account of their refreshing tartness. "Hock-and-soda" has been famous in England since the days of Byron. It goes without saying that no outstanding wine should be so drunk.

WINE INSTITUTE — A State-supported California organization whose purpose is the protection and advancement of the interests of California wine producers and the California wine trade.

WINERY — American name for an establishment where wine is made (as brewery, for beer, and distillery, for spirits).

WINE-MAKER — According to American usage, the person in charge of production in a winery.

WINE MERCHANT — Commonly, and according to the dictionaries, a person who deals in wine, generally as a retailer. Fifty or a hundred years ago, in most countries, this was regarded more as a profession than as a "trade"; "wine merchants" were expected to have a close, personal knowledge and appreciation of the goods they sold, and their status was not far from that of a trust officer in a bank — a person to whom one looked, with complete confidence, for accurate information and for sound advice. This is far from true today: hardly one retailer in fifty has tasted all the wines displayed on his shelves, and few of their clerks know as much about wine as do the customers they serve. This being the case, wine lovers who want something above the common average will do well to buy from those few special stores whose owners have made an effort to acquire the knowledge which their profession requires, and who may properly be described as "wine merchants." There are not too many of these in the United States, but their number, happily, seems to be increasing year by year.

WINE TASTER — Person, either professional or amateur, whose trained palate and specialized knowledge permit him to judge, evaluate and often identify wines organoleptically, or by tasting (*see*).

WINE WAITER — *See* Sommelier

WINKEL — (Vink-'l) — Small but important wine-producing town overlooking the Rhine in the heart of the German Rheingau, immediately west of Johannisberg. The word *Winkel* in German means "angle" (as well as "nook" or "quiet corner") and the "angle," looking very much like a carpenter's square, appears in the coat-of-arms of Winkel, and on the wine labels of several of its good producers.

Winkel's leading vineyard is *Schloss Vollrads* (*see*); others of the better vineyard sites or *Lagen* include: Winkeler Hasensprung, Kläuserweg, Jesuitengarten and Dachsberg.

WINO — The slang or colloquial term used, especially in California, to describe an alcoholic, generally of limited means, addicted to cheap, sweet, fortified wine.

WINTRICH — (Vint-rick) — One of the good, lesser wine towns of the Mittel-Mosel, in Germany, with about 200 acres of steep Riesling vineyards — better-known ones are: Wintricher Ohligsberg, Sonnseite, Grosser Herrgott and Geyerslay.

WINZER — (Vin-sir) — German for wine producer or wine grower, especially one who works in his own vineyard.

WINZERGENOSSENSCHAFT — (*Vince*-zer-gay-*nos*-sen-schahft) — An association or cooperative of wine producers in Germany.

WINZERVEREIN — (*Vince*-zer-ver-rine) — German wine producers' (usually peasant) cooperative or association.

WITHERED — Wine taster's term, probably the best English translation of the French *seché*. This is properly applied to a wine which has lost its freshness and fruit, either through too long storage in barrel, or through contact with the air, once uncorked.

WORMS — (Vormsz) — Historic little city on the Rhine near the southern edge of the province of Hessia. One of its Gothic churches, the Liebfrauenkirche, is surrounded by some twenty-six acres of vineyard called the Liebfrauenstift, which literally means the Church's endowment. It was this vineyard which gave its name to Liebfraumilch, and its wine (unfortunately never of very high quality) is sold as *Liebfrauenmilch* or *Liebfrauenstiftswein* today. Despite its fame, it is by no means in the same class as the better Hessian wines — Niersteiner, Nackenheimer, etc.

WOODY — Wine taster's term for a table wine, particularly one which has been stored too long in oak, and has acquired a woody aroma and flavor.

WÜRZBERG — (*Vurz*-bairg) — Less known vineyard in the village of Serrig on the Saar, in Germany; produces good wine only in exceptionally favorable years.

WÜRZBURG — (*Vurtz*-boorg) — The capital and principal town of the German province of Franconia (Franken); no less famous for its beer, Würzburger, than for its wine, also called Würzburger, produced on the rocky slopes overlooking the Main Valley nearby. This is the original home of Steinwein and the leading vineyard is called Würzburger Stein. There are 520 acres of vineyard in all, largely planted in either Sylvaner or Riesling, and apart from Würzburger Stein, the best *Lagen* or vineyard sites are Aussere Leiste, Innere Leiste, Neuberg, Abstleite, Harfe, Ständerbühl, Schalksberg and Steinmantel.

X-Y-Z

XÉRÈS — (Sair-ress) — Old name for the town of Jerez, or Jerez de la Frontera, in Spain, and for its wine, which we call Sherry. Still used in France, as *vin de Xérès*.

YEASTS — Unicellular microorganisms, some of which (*Saccharomyces ellipsoideus*) bring about fermentation in grape juice, through the agency of an enzyme, zymase (*see*), and turn it into wine; there exist many "selections" or "cultures" of these, some capable of working at lower temperatures than others, or having other advantages or disadvantages, and in most modern wineries the yeast cultures are chosen with great care. Other yeasts (*see* Flor) tend to give a Sherry flavor to wines inoculated with them, whether deliberately or accidentally; still others are responsible for various kinds of wine spoilage.

YEASTY — Wine taster's term, applied almost exclusively to young wines in barrel, which still have the odor of yeast or fermentation or lees. This is not a grave fault, and indeed some connoisseurs of Muscadet and of Swiss wines consider it a virtue and prefer their wines with this *goût de lie*; in any case, it will usually disappear as soon as the wine has been "racked" (transferred from one cask to another, leaving the sediment, or lees, behind). *See* Musty.

YIELD — As far as wine is concerned, usually the production of a given extent of vines, expressed in tons of grapes or gallons of wine per acre (*see* Hectolitre and Hectare for comparable terms in French). It is on this basis that the relative productivity of various grape varieties can be compared, and also that of different vineyards, although of course pruning, irrigation, etc., are all major factors. For a number of the very best French vineyards, the legal maximum is set at about two tons of grapes, or 320 gallons of wine per acre, and few of the finer, shy-bearing varieties ever give over four tons, or some 640 gallons, even when quality is not considered of primary importance. On the other hand, the common, more productive grapes often yield ten or more tons per acre, and far higher figures have been recorded. Needless to say, when yield increases in any such proportions, quality suffers. Yield per acre is one of the basic elements in any comparative rating or classification of superior vineyards and their wines.

YONNE — (Yawn) — Northernmost of the French *départements* that make up the old province of Burgundy. Its best known wine by far is Chablis (*see*), but there are a few others of fair quality, as Irancy (*see*).

YOUNG — So far as wine is concerned, this is not always a matter of months or years. A four-year-old Cabernet or Red Bordeaux is still young, and a six-year-old Vintage Port is still an infant. On the other hand, a three-year-old Muscadet or *vin rosé* or Sylvaner is already old. Correctly speaking, a young wine is one still not yet at its peak, still improving.

YQUEM, Château d' — (Dee-kem) — The incomparable *Grand Premier Cru* of Sauternes; the one wine, red or white, to be accorded this exalted rank in 1855, a higher classification even than the great Clarets. It is probably the most famous as well as the most valuable vineyard estate in the world, and its superb 15th century chateau dominates its vine-covered hillsides like a queen. For nearly two hundred years it has been the property of the Lur-Saluces family.

Over a century ago the Grand Duke Constantine of Russia (brother of the Czar) paid the then staggering price of 20,000 gold francs for four barrels of the 1847 vintage, and Yquem has been, ever since, one of the most consistently expensive of all wines; its vineyard, as might be expected, is one of those with the lowest yield per acre — an average of about 120 gallons, as compared with nearly three times as much for Château Lafite or Chambertin. There are some 200 acres under vines — Semillon, Sauvignon Blanc and a small amount of Muscadelle du Bordelais. The grapes are picked in successive *tries*, or harvestings, as the *pourriture noble*, or *botrytis* (*see*) reaches its peak, and the resulting wine is of course high in alcohol (13-16%), very sweet (with from 3% to 7% of unfermented sugar), luscious, almost creamy, with extraordinary fruit and breed.

The Château d'Yquems of great vintages are truly fabulous — the *ne plus ultra* of dessert wines, but even those of lesser years are remarkable, less overpowering, but with classic distinction and finesse.

Until quite recently, much of the wine produced at Yquem in "off" years, which failed to attain its normal degree of alcohol and sweetness,

was sold off in bulk without the chateau label, as "Bordeaux Supérieur." About as dry as a medium Graves, with considerable breed and bouquet, this obviously deserved a better fate, and a special name and label have now been created for it — Château Y. The letter Y, in French, is called *I-grec* and the wine's name is pronounced, therefore, Château *Ee-greck*. It is produced only in secondary vintages and is of course considerably cheaper than Yquem.

YVERDON — (E-vair-dawn) — Wine-producing town at the western end of Lake Neuchâtel, in Switzerland. White wines from the Fendant grape, none of outstanding quality.

YVORNE — (E-vorn) — One of the better white wines of Switzerland, made from the Fendant grape in the district known as the Chablais, southeast of Lake Geneva.

ZAHNACKER — (*Zahn*-ah-ker) — Celebrated Alsatian vineyard in the village of Ribeauvillé, Haut-Rhin.

ZELL — (Tsell) — Little vineyard town in the lower Moselle Valley, well outside the district of superior wine, presumably the original source of what has become internationally famous as Zeller Schwarze Katz. A common, nondescript, commercial Moselle blend (rarely, in fact, from Zell) this doubtless owes its popularity to its odd name and label: *Schwarze Katz* means "black cat," and the familiar cat is always present on the label.

ZELLENBERG — (Tsel-len-bairg) — Picturesque little village in Alsace, on the vine-covered Vosges foothills near Riquewihr. Good quality white wines.

ZELTINGEN — (Tsel-ting-gen) — One of the very great vineyard towns of the Mittel-Mosel, first in total production, and easily one of the eight or ten best in average quality. Its 470 acres of Riesling vines form part of the same high, incredibly steep, black-slate valley wall as those of Wehlen, Graach and Bernkastel, and have an admirable south-western exposure; its wines, with those of Brauneberg, are about the fullest-bodied of the fine Moselles. All of the best of them, of course, carry a specific vineyard name and are estate-bottled. Names to look for are Zeltinger Schlossberg, Sonnenuhr (or Sonnuhr), Himmelreich, Rotlay, Steinmauer, Kirchenpfad and Stephanslay, but there are many others.

ZINFANDEL — The most widely planted red wine grape (over 25,000 acres) of California. Fairly prolific, although less so than the Carignan, the Mataro, the Mission and even the Grenache, it gives far better red wine than these, and, in the cooler districts, at least, about as pleasant a *vin ordinaire* as one could ask for. It is definitely of the *Vitis Vinifera* family and therefore transplanted from Europe, and wine was being made from it round San Francisco in pre-Civil War days; despite much research, no one has ever been able to determine exactly where it came from in Europe, or its proper European name. It may well have been one of the tens of thousands of cuttings brought to California by Colonel Haraszthy (*see*); it is almost certainly *not* the Zierfandler (a lesser variety of Austria and southern Germany) despite the similarity of name.

Its wine, unlike that of almost all other "mass-production" grapes, has a definite, and easily recognizable, varietal character, bouquet and flavor, especially when from hillside vineyards in a cool district; it has a fine, bright ruby color, almost as much "fruit" as a French Beaujolais, and what has been called a "bramble" flavor, reminiscent of wild blackberries or dewberries. It gains little by ageing, and is best drunk young.

ZUCCO — (Zoo-co) — Famous Muscat wine of Sicily, produced near Palermo.

ZÜRICH — (Zur-rick) — Largest city of Switzerland. The canton of this name, at the turn of the century, had over 10,000 acres under vines; there are only some 1,700 today, the best of them southeast of the city, along the northern shore of the Zürichsee. There are both red wines and white, the former mostly from the Pinot Noir, here called the Klevner, the latter from the Rauschling (which should not be confused with the Riesling) and Müller-Thurgau (*see*). Some of them are of good quality, but they are almost all consumed locally.

ZWICKER — (*Zvick*-er) — Alsatian white wine, generally made from various grape varieties picked and crushed together: an inexpensive blend, in which the Chasselas usually predominates, though often with some Sylvaner. Bland and rather lacking in character, it is a passable carafe wine when young. *See*, however, Edelzwicker.

ZYMASE — The enzyme of yeast, which produces fermentation and thereby converts grape sugar into alcohol and carbon dioxide.

List of Maps

Appendices

APPENDIX 1

TOTAL WINE PRODUCTION AND WINE CONSUMPTION
OF THE PRINCIPAL WINE-PRODUCING
AND WINE-CONSUMING COUNTRIES

As reported to the Office International du Vin in Paris
by the various Governments involved

(Figures for 1963 where available, otherwise 1962)

COUNTRY	TOTAL[1] PRODUCTION in U.S. Gallons	TOTAL[2] CONSUMPTION in U.S. Gallons	PER[3] CAPITA in U.S. Gallons
France	1,928,771,250	1,458,544,500	30.3
Italy	1,826,212,500	1,395,602,250	27.1
Spain	677,906,250	502,490,625	16.3
Argentina	503,238,750	478,126,688	21.3
Portugal	404,433,750	244,711,688	24.5
Russia	230,737,500	324,187,500	1.4
U. S. A.	160,308,750	179,151,000	.9
West Germany	158,017,500	215,335,313	3.7
Roumania	144,742,500	164,587,500	7.3
Chile	128,358,750	104,737,500	13.5
Yugoslavia	134,925,000	118,852,125	6.2
Hungary	105,971,250	40,523,438	5.9
Bulgaria	103,372,500	33,491,063	4.2
Greece	100,065,000	81,246,375	9.8
South Africa	92,715,000	37,431,188	2.1
Brazil	49,875,000	38,902,500	.5
Austria	47,932,500	53,740,313	9.3
Australia	41,081,250	15,610,875	1.4
Switzerland	23,231,250	56,034,563	9.6
Uruguay	22,680,000	19,451,250	6.5
Canada	9,607,500	10,748,063	.6
Czechoslovakia	9,607,500	20,274,188	1.4
Israel	6,510,000	3,092,250	1.2
Luxembourg	3,360,000	3,566,063	10.8
Peru	1,968,750	2,693,250	.1
New Zealand	1,365,000	1,995,000	.8
Mexico	1,335,000	1,745,625	.04
Belgium	—	21,820,313	2.0
Denmark	—	3,840,375	.6
East Germany	—	16,209,375	1.0
Finland	—	2,618,438	.5
Great Britain	—	30,221,438	.7
Holland	—	9,825,375	.7
Ireland	—	1,147,125	.3
Lebanon	—	997,500	.3
Norway	—	1,396,500	.3
Sweden	—	8,154,563	1.0

[1] In most cases includes wines destined for distillation or for industrial use.
[2] In general, includes only wine consumed as wine, not as brandy, etc.
[3] In many instances does not include wines made by small growers for use at home.

As reported to the Office International du Vin in Paris
by the various Governments involved

COUNTRY	TOTAL IMPORTS[4] in U.S. Gallons	TOTAL EXPORTS[5] in U.S. Gallons
France	234,387,563	96,009,375
West Germany	106,483,125	5,062,313
Switzerland	39,077,063	149,625
Portuguese Colonies	34,363,875	—
Great Britain	30,648,188	—
Belgium-Luxembourg	25,137,000	1,820,438
Russia	19,650,750	—
East Germany	17,605,875	—
Free Ports (Former and present French Colonies)	16,458,750	—
United States	15,361,500	274,313
Czechoslovakia	11,047,313	—
Holland	10,249,313	174,563
Sweden	8,403,938	—
Austria	6,408,938	374,063
Poland	4,189,500	—
Canada	3,940,125	—
Denmark	3,441,375	—
Italy	1,795,500	65,535,750
Finland	1,571,063	—
Norway	1,346,625	—
Ireland	1,147,125	—
Hungary	1,147,125	17,680,688
Venezuela	548,625	—
New Zealand	274,313	—
Australia	174,563	2,269,313
Brazil	174,563	—
Japan	149,625	—
Mexico	124,688	—
South Africa	99,750	4,788,000
Algeria	—	206,981,250
Portugal	—	61,221,563
Spain	—	56,159,250
Morocco	—	36,633,188
Bulgaria	—	27,630,750
Tunisia	—	16,209,375
Greece	—	11,845,313
Yugoslavia	—	11,047,313
Roumania	—	10,573,500
Cyprus	—	3,915,188
Chile	—	1,546,125
Turkey	—	1,197,000
Egypt	—	448,875
Israel	—	399,000
Albania	—	199,500
Argentina	—	149,625

[4] Includes, in the case of France, wine imported from the former French Colonies in North Africa. In some instances, but not all, includes fruit wines, sake, etc.

[5] Includes in some cases but not all, fruit wines, etc.

COMMERCIALLY PRODUCED WINE ENTERING DISTRIBUTION CHANNELS
IN THE UNITED STATES, BY AREA WHERE PRODUCED
CALENDAR YEARS 1951 TO 1966

Year (Beginning January 1)	California[1]		Other States[2]		Total U.S. Produced[3]		Imported[4]		All Wine
	Quantity	Percent of Total	Quantity	Percent of Total	Quantity	Percent of Total	Quantity	Percent of Total	Quantity
	1	2	3	4	5	6	7	8	9
	1,000 GALLONS	PERCENT	1,000 GALLONS	PERCENT	1,000 GALLONS	PERCENT	1,000 GALLONS	PERCENT	1,000 GALLONS
1951	102,629	81.1	18,663	14.8	121,292	95.9	5,222	4.1	126,514
1952	116,005	84.3	16,243	11.8	132,248	96.1	5,372	3.9	137,620
1953	118,260	84.0	16,380	11.6	134,640	95.6	6,156	4.4	140,796
1954	116,843	82.2	18,911	13.3	135,754	95.5	6,402	4.5	142,156
1955	117,745	81.1	20,283	14.0	138,028	95.1	7,158	4.9	145,186
1956	123,984	82.6	18,236	12.2	142,220	94.8	7,819	5.2	150,039
1957	124,086	81.7	19,295	12.7	143,381	94.4	8,500	5.6	151,881
1958	122,247	79.1	23,338	15.1	145,585	94.1	9,048	5.9	154,633
1959	124,246	79.5	22,073	14.1	146,319	93.7	9,904	6.3	156,224
1960	129,092	79.0	23,524	14.4	152,616	93.4	10,736	6.6	163,352
1961	134,442	78.3	25,037	14.6	159,479	92.9	12,153	7.1	171,632
1962	127,371	75.8	26,670	15.9	154,041	91.6	14,041	8.4	168,082
1963	133,991	76.2	27,558	15.7	161,549	91.8	14,368	8.2	175,918
1964	143,123	77.1	26,946	14.5	170,069	91.6	15,556	8.4	185,625
1965	142,871	75.3	30,520	16.1	173,391	91.4	16,286	8.6	189,677
1966[5]	144,183	75.4	28,985	15.2	173,168	90.6	17,979	9.4	191,147

[1] Shipments of California wine to all markets less estimated shipments to foreign countries.
[2] Calculated by subtracting California wine (Column 1) from total U.S. Produced Wine (Column 5).
[3] Taxable withdrawals.
[4] Imports for consumption.
[5] Preliminary.

Sources: Prepared by Wine Institute from reports of the California State Board of Equalization; Internal Revenue Service, U.S. Treasury Department and Bureau of the Census, U.S. Department of Commerce.

UNITED STATES PRODUCED WINE ENTERING DISTRIBUTION
CHANNELS IN THE UNITED STATES, BY TYPE OF WINE
CALENDAR YEARS 1951 TO 1966[1]

Year (Beginning January 1)	Table		Dessert		Vermouth		Other Special Natural		Sparkling		All Wine
	Quantity	Percent of Total	Quantity	Percent of Total	Quantity	Percent of Total	Quantity	Percent of Total	Quantity	Percent of Total	Quantity
	1	2	3	4	5	6	7	8	9	10	11
	1,000 GALLONS	PERCENT	1,000 GALLONS	PERCENT	1,000 GALLONS	PERCENT	1,000 GALLONS	PERCENT	1,000 GALLONS	PERCENT	1,000 GALLONS
1951	33,474	27.6	83,738	69.0	2,698	2.2	230	0.2	1,151	0.9	121,292
1952	35,296	26.7	92,678	70.1	2,838	2.1	213	0.2	1,225	0.9	132,248
1953	37,228	27.7	92,673	68.8	3,102	2.3	238	0.2	1,399	1.0	134,640
1954	38,480	28.3	92,311	68.0	3,173	2.3	374	0.3	1,416	1.0	135,754
1955	39,203	28.4	93,692	67.9	3,304	2.4	123	0.1	1,705	1.2	138,028
1956	40,820	28.7	95,725	67.3	3,271	2.3	373	0.3	2,031	1.4	142,220
1957	40,800	28.5	93,697	65.3	3,519	2.5	3,128	2.2	2,238	1.6	143,381
1958	42,244	29.0	88,850	61.0	3,502	2.4	8,488	5.8	2,502	1.7	145,585
1959	43,172	29.5	86,448	59.1	3,706	2.5	9,932	6.8	3,061	2.1	146,319
1960	47,467	31.1	86,394	56.6	3,934	2.6	11,440	7.5	3,380	2.2	152,616
1961	50,718	31.8	87,922	55.1	4,266	2.7	12,889	8.1	3,684	2.3	159,479
1962	51,765	33.6	80,812	52.5	4,153	2.7	13,479	8.8	3,833	2.5	154,041
1963	56,141	34.8	83,749	51.8	4,275	2.6	13,155	8.1	4,229	2.6	161,549
1964	61,698	36.3	84,045	49.4	4,689	2.8	14,289	8.4	5,347	3.1	170,069
1965	65,118	37.6	81,649	47.1	4,846	2.8	15,529	9.0	6,250	3.6	173,391
1966[2]	68,219	39.4	77,133	44.5	4,862	2.8	15,556	9.0	7,397	4.3	173,168

[1] Taxable withdrawals.
[2] Preliminary.

Sources: Prepared by Wine Institute from reports of the Internal Revenue Service, U.S. Treasury Department.

IMPORTED WINE ENTERING DISTRIBUTION CHANNELS IN THE UNITED STATES, BY TYPE OF WINE, CALENDAR YEARS 1951 TO 1966[1][2]

Year (Beginning January 1)	Table		Dessert		Vermouth		Sparkling		All Wine
	Quantity	Percent of Total	Quantity	Percent of Total	Quantity	Percent of Total	Quantity	Percent of Total	Quantity
	1	2	3	4	5	6	7	8	9
	1,000 GALLONS	PERCENT	1,000 GALLONS	PERCENT	1,000 GALLONS	PERCENT	1,000 GALLONS	PERCENT	1,000 GALLONS
1951	2,259	43.3	775	14.8	1,545	29.6	643	12.3	5,222
1952	2,472	46.0	755	14.1	1,601	29.8	543	10.1	5,372
1953	2,893	47.0	881	14.3	1,779	28.9	604	9.8	6,156
1954	3,058	47.8	841	13.1	1,864	29.1	638	10.0	6,402
1955	3,455	48.3	924	12.9	2,092	29.2	687	9.6	7,158
1956	3,834	49.0	970	12.4	2,266	29.0	749	9.6	7,819
1957	4,265	50.2	1,071	12.6	2,390	28.1	773	9.1	8,500
1958	4,541	50.2	957	10.6	2,770	30.6	780	8.6	9,048
1959	5,171	52.2	977	9.9	2,897	29.3	860	8.7	9,904
1960	5,603	52.2	1,017	9.5	3,175	29.6	940	8.8	10,736
1961	6,715	55.3	1,107	9.1	3,368	27.7	964	7.9	12,153
1962	7,814	55.7	1,410	10.0	3,780	26.9	1,036	7.4	14,041
1963	8,000	55.7	1,441	10.0	3,905	27.2	1,023	7.1	14,368
1964	8,651	55.6	1,519	9.8	4,190	26.9	1,196	7.7	15,556
1965	8,950	55.0	1,585	9.7	4,315	26.5	1,436	8.8	16,286
1966	10,399	57.8	1,642	9.1	4,302	23.9	1,635	9.1	17,979

[1] Imports for consumption.

[2] Imported wines are not all reported by alcohol content category. All sake (rice wine) classified as table wine and all imported fruit wine classified as dessert wine.

Sources: Prepared by Wine Institute from reports of the Bureau of the Census, U.S. Department of Commerce.

IMPORTS OF WINE INTO THE UNITED STATES
BY TYPE OF WINE AND COUNTRY OF ORIGIN
CALENDAR YEAR 1966 [1][2]

Country of Origin	Table Quantity	Table Percent of Total	Dessert Quantity	Dessert Percent of Total	Vermouth Quantity	Vermouth Percent of Total	Sparkling Quantity	Sparkling Percent of Total	Total Quantity	Total Percent of Total
	1	2	3	4	5	6	7	8	9	10
	1,000 GALLONS	PERCENT	1,000 GALLONS	PERCENT	1,000 GALLONS	PERCENT	1,000 GALLONS	PERCENT	1,000 GALLONS	PERCENT
Italy	2,585	24.9	142	8.6	3,391	78.8	245	15.0	6,363	35.4
France	4,040	38.8	76	4.6	896	20.8	823	50.3	5,835	32.5
Spain	826	7.9	779	47.4	—	—	5	0.3	1,610	9.0
West Germany	1,399	13.5	4	0.2	2 [4]	[3]	48	2.9	1,454	8.1
Portugal	665	6.4	120	7.3	4	[3]	488	29.8	1,274	7.1
Denmark	3	[3]	352	21.4	1	[3]	—	—	355	2.0
Japan	211	2.0	38	2.3	—	—	4 [4]	[3]	249	1.4
Israel	201	1.9	12	0.7	1	[3]	8	0.5	222	1.2
Greece	138	1.3	16	1.0	—	—	—	—	154	0.9
Yugoslavia	86	0.8	9	0.5	4	[3]	4 [4]	[3]	96	0.5
Chile	72	0.7	—	—	—	—	—	—	72	0.4
Netherlands	28	0.3	12	0.7	—	—	8	0.5	47	0.3
Hungary	36	0.3	—	—	—	—	—	—	36	0.2
Madeira Islands	1	[3]	32	1.9	—	—	—	—	33	0.2
United Kingdom	7	0.1	7	0.4	9	0.2	5	0.3	28	0.2
Poland	1	[3]	26	1.6	—	—	—	—	27	0.2
Switzerland	23	0.2	—	—	—	—	4 [4]	[3]	23	0.1
Austria	21	0.2	—	—	—	—	—	—	21	0.1
Belgium	14	0.1	—	—	—	—	3	0.2	16	0.1
Czechoslovakia	—	—	15	0.9	—	—	—	—	15	0.1
Canada	12	0.1	—	—	—	—	—	—	12	0.1
Other Countries	31	0.3	4	0.2	2	[3]	1	0.1	38	0.2
Total	10,399	100.0	1,642	100.0	4,302	100.0	1,635	100.0	17,979	100.0

[1] Imports for consumption.

[2] Imported wines are not all reported by alcohol content category. All sake (rice wine) classified as table wine and all imported fruit wine classified as dessert wine.

[3] Less than .05 percent.

[4] Less than 500 gallons.

Sources: Prepared by Wine Institute from reports of the Bureau of the Census, U.S. Department of Commerce.

APPENDIX 2

CALIFORNIA

A TABLE OF VINEYARD TEMPERATURES

Vineyard temperatures are recorded in various countries in various ways: either for the seven-month cycle that extends from the first spring leaf to the latest harvest, or for the four months that generally elapse between the flowering of the vine and a normal vintage. For widely varying climates, the second system is thought by many European experts to give a fairer picture. Both, in any case, are based on a minimum daily temperature of 50° Fahrenheit (which the vine requires for its growth) and what follows is known as "heat summation." One takes, for example, the mean daily temperature for the month of June; if it happens to be 60°, there results a credit of 10° a day for June's 30 days, or 300 "degree days" for the month. A grand total of these monthly totals, whether for the seven months of April through October or for the four months, June-September, gives the temperature index. Here, based on the four-month cycle, are the figures for the great European districts and for California's best.

District   I — 62 - 65 daily average
District II — 65 - 68 daily average
District III — 68 - 70 daily average
District IV — 70 - 74 daily average
District V — 74 - 80 daily average

District	EUROPE	Heat Summation (over 50° F) June-July-Aug.-Sept.	Daily Average for these 4 months
I	Geisenheim (Rhine)	1495	62.3°
I	Trier (Moselle)	1525	62.5
I	Auxerre (Chablis)	1572	62.9
I	Châlons-sur-Marne (Champagne)	1644	63.5
II	Bordeaux (France)	1971	66.2
II	Beaune (Burgundy)	2002	66.4
III	Asti (Italian Piedmont)	2416	69.8
IV	Florence (Italy — Chianti)	2917	73.9
IV	Palermo (Sicily)	2936	74.0
V	Algiers (Algeria)	3600	79.5

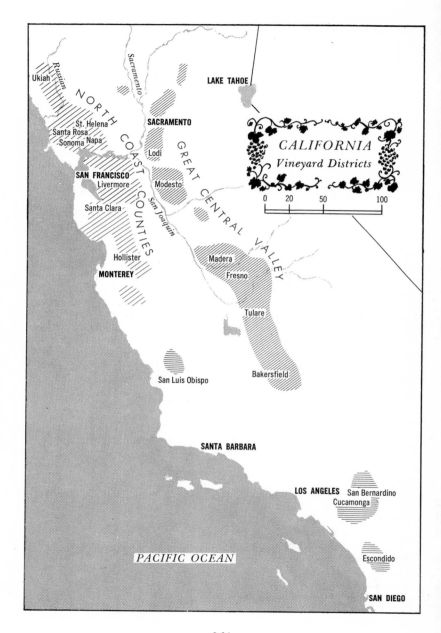

CALIFORNIA

I	Paicines (San Benito)	1601	62.6
I	Sonoma (Sonoma)	1682	63.8
I	Oakville (Napa)	1707	64.0
II	Hollister (San Benito)	1923	65.8
II	Los Gatos (Santa Clara)	2046	66.8
II	Healdsburg (Sonoma)	2164	67.7
III	St. Helena (Napa)	2214	68.1
III	Livermore (Alameda)	2305	68.9
III	Ukiah (Mendocino)	2360	69.3
III	Calistoga (Napa)	2419	70.0
IV	Lodi (San Joaquin Valley)	2499	70.5
V	Fresno (Central Valley)	3423	78.1
V	Bakersfield (Southern California)	3582	79.4

Vineyard Acreage (including both bearing and newly planted)
of Leading California Counties in 1966 as reported by the
California Department of Agriculture.

County	Raisin grapes acres	Table grapes acres	Wine grapes acres bearing 1966	Wine grapes total acreage 1966	Total 1966
Mendocino	10	—	4,700	5,700	5,710
Alameda	10	10	1,840	2,000	2,020
Contra Costa	10	40	1,400	1,400	1,450
Monterey	—	—	1,070	1,090	1,090
Napa	10	20	10,450	12,030	12,060
San Benito	—	—	2,240	4,300	4,300
San Luis Obispo	—	—	530	550	550
Santa Clara	120	110	2,940	3,030	3,260
Santa Cruz	—	10	90	90	100
Sonoma	—	10	11,560	12,730	12,740
Solano	—	—	—	720	720
Yolo	—	10	120	120	130
Fresno	149,380	12,360	11,090	12,610	174,350
Kern	21,910	11,660	4,990	5,990	39,560
Kings	3,380	10	720	720	4,110
Madera	27,490	500	5,540	7,210	35,200
Merced	8,590	660	6,160	7,960	17,210
San Joaquin	690	23,300	22,380	24,200	48,190
Stanislaus	8,260	410	10,180	11,070	19,740
Tulare	35,100	30,890	6,060	6,680	72,670
Amador	30	—	530	570	600
Placer	—	30	430	430	460
Riverside	5,670	4,830	1,270	1,300	11,800
San Bernardino	500	610	18,320	18,350	19,460
San Diego	450	500	510	510	1,460
Other Counties	90	80	170	330	500
STATE TOTAL	261,700	86,050	125,290	141,690	489,440

Grapes Crushed for Wine and Brandy Production, 1966
in the Leading California Districts as reported by the Wine Institute

District	Raisin grapes tons	Table grapes tons	Wine grapes tons	Total
Southern California Los Angeles, Riverside, San Bernardino, San Diego and Santa Barbara Counties	1,868	1,648	58,457	61,973
Southern San Joaquin Kern, San Luis Obispo and part of Tulare Counties	87,774	72,898	63,359	224,031
Central San Joaquin Fresno, Kings, Madera and part of Tulare Counties	521,376	89,253	152,378	763,007
Escalon — Modesto Stanislaus and part of San Joaquin Counties	34,831	31,471	142,076	208,378
Lodi — Sacramento Amador, Butte, El Dorado, Placer, Sacramento and part of San Joaquin Counties	14,900	101,816	75,406	192,122
North Coast — North Bay Marin, Mendocino, Napa, Solano and Sonoma Counties	158	12	96,677	96,847
North Coast — South Bay Alameda, Contra Costa, Monterey, San Benito, San Francisco, San Mateo, Santa Clara and Santa Cruz Counties	10,184	2,280	26,347	38,811
All Districts	671,091	299,378	614,700	1,585,169

The Ten Most Widely Planted Wine Grapes, by Varieties, by Counties
in Acres as reported bearing 1964, by the Calif. Department of Agriculture

County	Carignan	Zinfandel	Grenache	Alicante Bouchet	Mission	Palomino	Petit Syrah (Duriff)	Mataro	Burger	Colombard
Mendocino	2452	738	28	107	12	295	153	1	9	288
Alameda	69	245	—	14	1	15	57	43	57	49
Contra Costa	420	594	19	29	2	66	—	291	—	4
Monterey	—	15	—	—	—	—	—	—	—	—
Napa	811	955	17	223	—	330	1791	25	243	450
San Benito	70	147	152	—	13	58	9	16	30	—
San Luis Obispo	6	472	—	8	8	—	—	—	—	—
Santa Clara	476	425	131	54	116	167	236	144	—	125
Sonoma	1730	3950	21	485	26	736	1480	11	128	473
Sacramento	86	57	2	3	53	24	11	26	—	6
Solano	108	27	—	32	—	80	143	—	2	7
Fresno	1343	224	2353	2246	563	944	2	—	76	160
Kern	926	35	301	764	88	123	47	—	—	—
Kings	215	—	120	79	138	5	—	—	—	—
Madera	1715	81	1221	292	54	546	—	52	29	—
Merced	614	277	1194	173	670	556	—	4	—	452
San Joaquin	6892	6548	2836	2111	1527	774	299	20	558	43
Stanislaus	3936	271	2360	455	926	886	—	—	33	119
Tulare	903	27	209	774	85	739	272	—	547	5
Amador	39	411	—	1	111	9	—	—	—	—
Placer	33	223	16	19	76	10	—	247	—	—
Riverside	194	236	535	72	752	184	—	73	45	—
San Bernardino	795	5478	2138	1128	3161	1574	—	1680	652	—
San Diego	338	144	14	20	127	9	—	12	—	—
Total in California including less important counties	24198	22004	13701	9112	8581	8165	4506	2649	2413	2183

Other of the more common varieties, rather widely planted, include "Burgundy" (probably mostly Refosco and Mondeuse, but no Pinot Noir) 1076 acres; Feher Szagos (used for California Sherry in the Central Valley) 746 acres; Salvador (a hybrid, giving deep purple juice) 2250 acres; Grand Noir (another poor "Teinturier" used to give color to red wines that lack it) 444 acres; Green Hungarian (fair quality, origin unknown) 378 acres; Valdepeñas, (perhaps the common grape of central Spain) 1106 acres; etc. There are less than 10,000 acres of top quality wine grapes in California — see Tables, Pages 368-377.

Name of Grape Variety	Where Grown in Europe	Comments	Where Grown in California
Aleatico	Italy, notably the island of Elba.	Produces a sweet red dessert wine, on the order of a light Port, with pronounced Muscat flavor.	Warmer districts.
Alicante Bouschet	Midi district of France	A *"teinturier"* (which means "dyer") — one of the rare grapes with dark red juice, and grown largely for this reason. Common and coarse.	Practically everywhere.
Barbera	Northern Italy, especially Piedmont.	Gives a lusty, full-bodied, deep-colored wine, a bit astringent, lacking in delicacy and class; nevertheless with plenty of character, excellent with Italian food.	In Sonoma, Napa, and spottily in the warmer districts.
Cabernet Sauvignon	In all of the better Bordeaux vineyards, pre-dominates in the Médoc.	One of the two best red wine grapes of the world. Yields a superb, long-lived wine, of in-comparable balance and class.	In all of the better North Coast County vineyards.
Cabernet Franc	Widely in Bordeaux, especially St. Emilion and Pomerol. Also the Loire Val-ley — Chinon.	Slightly more productive; its wine is softer, rounder, sooner ready. Also called the Breton and Gros Bouchet (*not* Bouchet).	Hardly anywhere, unfortunately.
Carignan	Everywhere in the Midi dis-trict, in Algeria, widely in Spain.	One of the better mass pro-duction grapes; in some few districts gives sound, agreeable wine, never distinguished.	Practically everywhere.
Charbono	Uncertain; perhaps in French Savoie and Italian Piedmont.	Possibly a variety called Charbonneau or Douce Noire in Europe.	Napa.
Freisa	Italian Piedmont	Not an artistocrat but its wine has considerable character, some quality.	Sonoma and San Bernardino
Gamay	The grape so-called in Cali-fornia is *not* the Gamay of the Beaujolais Country.	?	Napa and other North Coast counties.

RED WINE GRAPES IN CALIFORNIA

Approximate Acreage in California	California Wine Type and How Usually Sold	Comments
150	So far, used in blends.	Could be interesting and deserves varietal status.
10,000	In the cheapest blends baptized "Burgundy" or "Claret."	Has no place in any respectable vineyard and should be eliminated.
200 +	Usually under its proper varietal name.	In Sonoma and Napa produces better wine on the whole than in Italy — perhaps California's outstanding "Italian type" wine.
2,500	Invariably as Cabernet or Cabernet Sauvignon.	America's best red wine, and a remarkably good one; those from the good North Coast County vineyards can hold their own against all but the very finest clarets of Bordeaux.
50 +	Generally blended with Cabernet Sauvignon, as in the Bordeaux Country.	Helps, softens and improves Cabernet Sauvignon; should be more widely planted and used.
29,000	Mostly just as "Burgundy" or "Claret" or "Red Wine"; rarely, when it comes from Sonoma or Napa, under its varietal name.	A Carignan from Sonoma is an excellent *ordinaire*, by no means to be despised. What comes from the warmer districts is pretty common but certainly at least as good as what the French Midi produces.
100 (?)	For no very good reason, under this undistinguished and unknown name.	Pretty common and coarse, even in the best vineyard districts.
50	So far, just in blends.	Will never be outstanding; nevertheless, a good, productive grape that should be more widely planted.
750	All too often as Gamay or Gamay Rosé.	An immensely productive grape giving a dull, rather common wine with no distinguishable Gamay character or flavor.

Name of Grape Variety	Where Grown in Europe	Comments	Where Grown in California
Gamay Beaujolais	The one red wine grape of the Beaujolais; also in lesser Burgundy vineyards; spottily elsewhere in France.	On the proper soil gives one of the most agreeable and justly popular wines of France — fruity, tender, early ready, sometimes distinguished; in other districts much less good.	Very spottily in San Benito, Napa, Santa Clara, etc.
Grenache	Almost everywhere in southern France and northern Spain.	An extraordinarily adaptable variety; depending on climate and soil, an admirable rosé (Tavel), good dessert wine (Banyuls), sound but undistinguished short-lived reds.	For rosé in the North Coast Counties; widely elsewhere for common table wine and Port.
Grignolino	Italian Piedmont.	Yields an interesting, often fine red wine, light in color, rather high in alcohol.	Mostly in San Bernardino and Sonoma.
Malbec	Bordeaux; also central France.	Also called the Cot, or Pressac; usually blended, gives a red wine of good color, excellent quality.	Experimentally.
Mataro	Widely in southern France and Spain.	Also called the Mourvèdre; just a common mass-production grape except in a few rare districts.	Widely in the warmer districts.
Merlot	Everywhere in Bordeaux, also in southern Switzerland and northern Italy.	**Usually blended with the Cabernet, at almost all of the great chateaux. Very high quality, yields a soft, fine, tender wine, soon ready.**	Hardly at all.
Mission	Unknown.	—	Very widely in the warmer districts.
Nebbiolo	Italian Piedmont.	Italy's greatest red wine variety — responsible for Barolo, Barbaresco, Gattinara, etc., etc.	Hardly at all.
Petit Syrah	?	This is almost certainly NOT the true and noble Petit Syrah of Hermitage, Côte Rôtie, etc., but a common Rhône Valley grape called the Duriff.	Extensively in Napa and Sonoma.

Approximate Acreage in California	California Wine Type and How Usually Sold	Comments
400	Now, increasingly, under its proper and proud name.	Gives remarkable wine in the North Coast Counties, often comparable to and even better than the Pinot Noir. Not very productive but tops in quality.
14,000	Mostly just as red wine, some as Port. That from the cooler coastal areas as perhaps California's finest *vin rosé*.	Yields one of the best of *rosés*, fresh, clean and fragrant when made in the cooler parts of California; also a rather ordinary red wine in the San Joaquin Valley, and better-than-average California Port.
50 (?)	Principally used for *rosé*, quite often under the varietal name.	Gives a far less good red wine than in Italy; the *rosé*, when properly vinified, has considerable character and is by no means bad.
25 (?)	With Cabernet, as in France.	Surely excellent. Deserves more attention.
2,500	Common red table wine — "Burgundy" or "Claret."	Less good on the whole than the Carignan; has little except its productivity to recommend it.
50 (?)	With Cabernet, as in France.	A judicious admixture would certainly improve all California Cabernets.
7,900	Largely in cheaper blends of Angelica and Port.	Despite its distinguished history (planted by the Franciscan Fathers; first *vinifera* grape in California), an extremely poor variety that has never produced good wine; deficient in color, it cannot even yield, alone, a passable California Port.
25 (?)	In blends or not at all.	Might or might not do well in the arid California climate. Certainly deserves a try.
4,400	Rarely under its varietal name; usually in the better grades of California "Burgundy."	Gives a deep-colored, sturdy wine, well-balanced and sound; while of no great class, certainly superior to the *vin ordinaire* of France and Italy.

371

Name of Grape Variety	Where Grown in Europe	Comments	Where Grown in California
Pinot Noir	The one and only great variety of Burgundy; also Champagne, Germany, spottily in Alsace and the Loire Valley.	Incomparable quality, very small yield. Ranks with the Cabernet Sauvignon for red wine but also gives superb *rosé*, excellent white wine, nearly ⅔ of all French Champagne.	Limited acreage in the North Coast Counties, esp. San Benito and Napa.
Pinot St. George	?	NOT a Pinot	North Coast Counties.
Refosco	Northern and central Italy.	Productive, undistinguished.	Warmer districts but spottily in Napa.
Ruby Cabernet	Nowhere.	—	Mostly experimentally.
San Gioveto	The Chianti Country and elsewhere in central Italy.	Also called the San Giovese; by far the most important variety for Chianti. In quality, fair to very good.	Hardly at all.
Salvador	Nowhere.	A hybrid and as such not permitted in any European wine that carries an appellation.	Extensively in the warmer districts.
Tinta Cao	Portugal.	One of the better grapes of the Port Country.	Experimentally.
Tinta Madeira	Portugal.	Another Port grape, quite productive.	Mostly in the warmer districts.
Trousseau	Jura district of France, also the Port Country of Portugal.	Called the Bastardo in Portugal, and widely grown; the red table wine which it gives in France has some character, is not remarkable.	Experimentally.
Valdepeñas	Central Spain.	Mass-production variety, big yield, quality no better than fair.	Warmer districts.
Zinfandel	Unknown.	Certainly a Vinifera grape of European origin but still not identified.	Everywhere. First in total acreage in California.

Approximate Acreage in California	California Wine Type and How Usually Sold	Comments
1700	Invariably under its varietal name.	Excellent, although not as outstanding in California as the Cabernet, nor as close, in character and bouquet, to its French counterpart; its wine is lighter, dryer, less velvety and less complex, with less depth of flavor than good, authentic French Burgundy. Nevertheless always, when genuine, a truly superior wine and fully as fine as any French Burgundy in the same price class.
250	Usually, and of course wrongly, as Red Pinot.	Yields a rather thin, characterless red wine, pleasant, a bit astringent.
275	Probably, most often, as "Burgundy" or in blends.	Before it was definitely identified was called Crabb's Black Burgundy in the Napa Valley. Sturdy, rather common red wine.
200 +	Usually under its varietal name. Sometimes as *rosé*.	A cross of Cabernet and Carignan, developed in California. Fair quality.
25 (?)	Supposedly in a few better California Chiantis.	Perhaps because differently vinified, seems to have little recognizable Chianti character.
2,200	Solely in blends, to give added color to Port and other red wines which would otherwise be too pale.	Has no possible value except as a coloring agent, or dye; can hardly be called a wine grape.
50 (?)	In some superior blends of Port.	Promising; deserves to be better known.
300 (?)	In the best California Port which is sometimes given the varietal name of Tinta.	Gives something enormously better than the run-of-the-mill California Port. Considerable fruit and bouquet.
50 (?)	Experimentally, in Port.	Seems less good in California than varieties listed above.
1500	In blends of less expensive red wine.	A sound, very productive variety giving a pleasant, if somewhat common, light table wine.
25,000	The best, from the North Coast Counties, as Zinfandel, or in light, agreeable blended wines labeled "Mountain Red," etc. Also widely in California Claret and even (much less successfully) in California Port.	An admirable, useful and productive grape, which yields, except in the warmest districts, about the most typical and best *vin ordinaire* of the United States — fruity, with a characteristic berry flavor, not too deeply colored, early ready and short-lived. In the irrigated San Joaquin Valley it does much less well.

WHITE WINE GRAPES IN CALIFORNIA

Name of Grape Variety	Where Grown in Europe	Comments	Where Grown in California
Aligoté	Burgundy.	Fair quality; permitted only in less famous vineyards.	Napa Valley.
Burger	Alsace and Germany.	Very productive; poor quality; no longer permitted in better vineyards.	Nearly everywhere.
Chasselas	Switzerland, Alsace, Germany, upper Loire Valley.	Also known as the *Fendant* or *Gutedel*; except in coolest districts, yields a dull, neutral wine.	Spottily in the North Coast Counties.
Chenin Blanc	Central Loire Valley — Vouvray, Saumur, Anjou.	Also called (correctly) *Pineau de la Loire*, and (incorrectly) *Pinot*. Productive, very good quality.	North Coast Counties.
Colombard	Cognac district.	Productive; gives a passable table wine, excellent brandy.	North Coast Counties and cooler Central Valley vineyards.
Emerald Riesling	Nowhere.	A variety developed in California.	North Coast Counties.
Folle Blanche	Cognac, Armagnac, lower Loire Valley, Midi, etc.	Productive; gives a fresh, tart wine, excellent brandy. Also known as *Piquepoul* and *Gros Plant*.	North Coast Counties.
Grey Riesling	Perhaps, under a different name, around Poitiers, in central France.	Not the true *Riesling* nor related to it. Perhaps the unimportant, mediocre *Chauché Gris*.	North Coast Counties.
White Muscat	Northern and central Italy, southern France.	Called the *Moscato di Canelli* or *Muscat de Frontignan*. Good quality.	North Coast Counties.
Palomino	Sherry district of Spain.	The principal grape used in Sherry.	Widely, but especially in the warmer districts.

374

WHITE WINE GRAPES IN CALIFORNIA

Approximate Acreage in California	California Wine Type and How Usually Sold	Comments
50	California Chablis.	Pleasant; not much character or class.
2,500	Used in cheaper, blended white wines, sold as California Chablis, Rhine, or Sauterne.	Yields a passable, neutral wine in cooler districts; elsewhere something both coarse and common. Immensely productive.
under 100	Blending wine.	Flat, watery, lacks acid. More properly classified as a good table grape.
400	Most often, these days, under its proper varietal name, though sometimes as *White Pinot,* or in Champagne.	Productive but excellent quality; pale, fresh, attractive wine with good bouquet; occasionally (and less successfully) somewhat sweet.
4,500	Most often as California Chablis, but increasingly in California Champagne.	Very productive. Its wine usually lacks distinction and has an underlying bitterness, pronounced flavor, but good acidity.
?	Sometimes so labeled, but often in wines called simply *Riesling.*	Productive, fairly good quality. Agreeable bouquet but no true *Riesling* character.
200	Occasionally marketed as *Folle Blanche;* more often, since its wine is fresh, light, tart and pale, used in the best California Chablis and Champagne.	Does better here than in France, though only in the cooler ditsricts. Deserves to be better known.
200 (?)	As *Grey Riesling.*	Now enjoys, especially in San Francisco, wide acceptance and favor which it in no way deserves, any more than the name of Riesling under which it masquerades. It is a bland, innocuous wine, pleasant enough but with no backbone or breed.
100 (?)	As *Muscat de Frontignan* or blended.	Gives something far different here from what it yields in Europe; a dry, rather interesting but not altogether pleasing wine, with characteristic Muscat flavor.
8,000	Almost entirely for Sherry. Used to be called the *Napa Golden Chasselas,* although it is not a *Chasselas,* and does better in warmer districts than in Napa.	For Sherry, no less outstanding in California than in Spain. Gives a poor, coarse, heavy table wine, and should never be used for this.

375

Name of Grape Variety	Where Grown in Europe	Comments	Where Grown in California
Pinot Blanc	Burgundy	Good quality but much less fine than the *Chardonnay*.	North Coast Counties.
Pinot Chardonnay	Burgundy, Chablis, Champagne.	Highest possible quality, small yield; perhaps not a *Pinot*.	North Coast Counties.
Riesling	Rhine, Moselle, Alsace, Austria, northern Italy.	Highest possible quality, small yield; sometimes confused with *Sylvaner* (*see*).	North Coast Counties.
Sauvignon Blanc	Graves and Sauternes, upper Loire Valley.	Very high quality, character, great class, small yield. Also called the *Blanc-Fumé*.	North Coast Counties and cooler Central Valley vineyards.
Sauvignon Vert	?	Not a *Sauvignon*.	North Coast Counties.
Semillon	Graves and Sauternes, Monbazillac.	Yields soft wines of very good quality.	North Coast Counties.
Sylvaner	Rhineland, Franconia, Alsace, northern Italy.	Productive, good quality. Sometimes wrongly called "*Franken Riesling.*"	North Coast Counties and cooler Central Valley vineyards.
Traminer	Alsace, northern Italy, Germany	Also called *Gewürztraminer*, fine quality, special flavor.	North Coast Counties.
Veltliner	Austria, northern Italy.	Very good quality.	North Coast Counties.
Ugni Blanc	Cognac district southern France, northern Italy, Chianti district.	Also called the *Trebbiano* and the *St. Emilion*. Productive, fair quality; good brandy.	North Coast Counties.

Approximate Acreage in California	California Wine Type and How Usually Sold	Comments
700	Invariably under its varietal name, since it is in great demand; occasionally, however, in the best California Champagne.	Gives better wine in California than in France; requires more bottle ageing than the Chardonnay but the end results of nearly equal quality. Fine bouquet, real distinction.
600	Only as Pinot Chardonay, save in the best California Champagne.	Highest quality, very small yield. Its wine is dryer, softer, lower in alcohol than in France, perhaps with less bouquet, but remarkable.
500	As *Johannisberg Riesling*, to distinguish it from *Grey Riesling* and also from *Sylvaner*, which can legally be labeled *Riesling* in California. Sometimes called *White Riesling*.	Highest quality, small yield. In California, its wine is dryer and yet less tart than the German Rhines and the Alsatians; less assertive and with less bouquet, yet of exceptional balance and class.
1,300	Usually under its varietal name; occasionally blended to give distinction to a California Dry Sauterne.	Maintains in California the character and high quality which it brings to the finest French dry Graves. At its best in the cooler areas, sometimes too pronounced in too warm a climate.
1,000	Happily, only in blends sold as cheaper California Chablis and Sauterne.	A small, harsh, bitter wine, no credit to the name of *Sauvignon*.
1,200	Most often as *Semillon*, but widely used in the very best California Sauterne, both dry and sweet.	Gives a dryer wine in the dry climate of California than in France; soft, definite varietal bouquet and flavor; very good but not top quality.
1,000	Usually as *Riesling,* its legal California name; sometimes as the best grade California Rhine wine; most properly, of course, as *Sylvaner*.	Quite productive, and very, very good. Its wine has more fruit than most in California; it is pale, fresh, light, with nice bouquet, early ready, short-lived.
250	Either as *Traminer* or *Gewürztraminer*, both names being legal and proper.	To a remarkable degree, in cooler districts, the wine develops in California the same extraordinary character and spicy bouquet that it has in Europe.
150	In the past, often as *Traminer,* which it much resembles; now always under its varietal name.	Does well in California, retains its spicy flavor and bouquet; should be more widely planted.
100 (?)	Almost always in blends.	Produces a very sound, well-balanced, neutral wine, good, but not much character and charm.

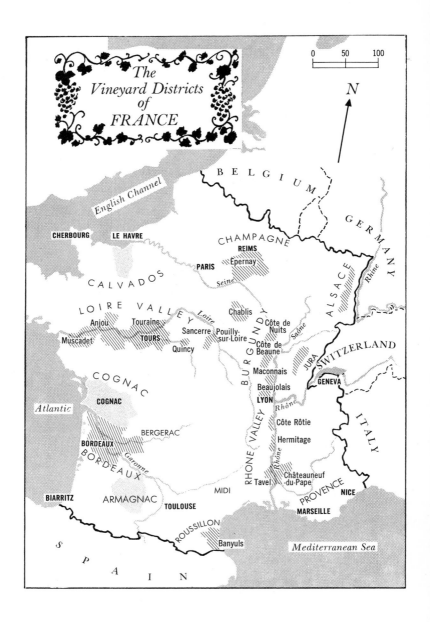

The
Vineyard Districts
of
FRANCE

0   50   100

N

BELGIUM

GERMANY

English Channel

CHERBOURG   LE HAVRE

CHAMPAGNE

REIMS

PARIS   Épernay

Seine

CALVADOS

ALSACE

Rhine

LOIRE VALLEY   Loire   Chablis   BURGUNDY   Côte de
Nuits

Anjou   Touraine   Sancerre   Pouilly-   Côte de
sur-Loire   Beaune

Muscadet   TOURS

Quincy

Saône

JURA   SWITZERLAND

Mâconnais

COGNAC   Beaujolais

GENEVA

COGNAC   LYON

Atlantic   Rhône   ITALY

Côte Rôtie

BERGERAC   Hermitage

BORDEAUX   RHONE VALLEY

BORDEAUX   Garonne   Rhône

BIARRITZ   Tavel   Châteauneuf
-du-Pape   PROVENCE   NICE

ARMAGNAC   MIDI

TOULOUSE   MARSEILLE

SPAIN   ROUSSILLON

Banyuls   Mediterranean Sea

APPENDIX 3

FRANCE

FRENCH WINE PRODUCTION IN 1966

(The following table originally appeared in *La Journée Vinicole Quotidien* and is here reproduced, adapted into English by special permission.)

Despite its apparent dullness, this table gives in fact an extraordinarily vivid and accurate picture of French wine production — of the difference between *grand vin* and *vin ordinaire,* of how and where and why both are grown in France. Please note, therefore:

1. The numbers in the extreme left-hand columns are the official French département numbers: this system even extends to the French equivalent of Zip Codes and even to car licence plates: a car from Paris (Seine) invariably has a licence number ending with 75; one from Bordeaux (Gironde) a number ending with 33, one from the Côte d'Or a number ending with 21, etc.

2. Vineyard owners are required by French law (strictly enforced) to report their total acreage of producing vineyard and their production in hectolitres. In 1966 there were 1,243,074 hectares (3,070,390 acres) of vineyard which yielded 60,934,937 hectolitres (8,104,342,000 bottles) of wine. This, one of the largest crops since World War II, amounted to 2,640 bottles per acre. The total vineyard acreage was almost the same in 1961, but produced only 46,714,754 hectolitres (6,213,062,000 bottles), or about 1,940 bottles per acre.

3. A total of 1,214,147 vineyard owners reported (which means that about one French family out of eight or nine was actively engaged in wine production). Comparing this with the total acreage, it is obvious that the average French vineyard owner has just over 2½ (actually 2.53) acres of producing vineyard. Only in ONE département, the Gironde (Bordeaux), is the average holding over five acres.

4. Out of 1,243,074 hectares (3,070,390 acres) of vineyard in production, less than one-fifth, 238,393 hectares (588,829 acres) produced wines entitled to an Appellation Contrôlée. This production amounted to 9,571,531 hectolitres (1,273,010,000 bottles) in all, or 2,160 bottles per acre, as compared with 2,640 bottles per acre for French wines as a whole, or 2,763 bottles per acre for non-Appellation Contrôlée wines.

5. It is interesting to note that 73% of the total production of wine in France in 1966 was either red or rosé and only 27% white, whereas 45% of Appellation Contrôlée wines was red or rosé and 55% white.

379

	Département	Number of Vineyard Owners Reporting	Total Acres of Vineyards in pro- duction	Acres of Vineyards Entitled to Appellation Contrôlée
1	Ain	17,334	8,971	126
2	Aisne	1,217	1,643	1,561
3	Allier	14,357	10,416	—
4	Alpes (Basses-)	5,382	6,160	—
5	Alpes (Hautes-)	3,162	3,769	—
6	Alpes-Maritimes	6,249	3,090	54
7	Ardèche	27,027	54,985	711
8	Ardennes	133	25	—
9	Ariège	5,948	4,352	—
10	Aube	4,844	5,002	3,707
11	Aude	44,239	278,611	7,052
12	Aveyron	16,787	15,230	—
13	Bouches-du-Rhône	20,402	66,991	395
14	Calvados	—	—	—
15	Cantal	401	138	—
16	Charente	27,545	82,444	—
17	Charente-Maritime	39,566	104,197	—
18	Cher	13,287	9,631	2,129
19	Corrèze	6,356	4,461	—
20	Corse (Corsica)	2,855	29,702	—
21	Côte d'Or	13,091	19,935	14,030
22	Côtes-du-Nord	—	—	—
23	Creuse	2	2	—
24	Dordogne	28,823	79,583	30,267
25	Doubs	1,280	410	—
26	Drôme	22,617	39,994	14,533
27	Eure	3	2	—
28	Eure-et-Loir	95	20	—
29	Finistère	—	—	—
30	Gard	41,979	216,002	12,948
31	Garonne (Haute-)	20,795	39,518	—
32	Gers	22,098	94,033	30
33	Gironde	41,856	272,728	186,920
34	Hérault	69,603	409,938	3,522
35	Ille-et-Vilaine	3	2	—
36	Indre	22,656	16,159	—
37	Indre-et-Loire	28,937	47,147	91
38	Isère	30,693	18,557	11,360
39	Jura	7,617	4,893	2
40	Landes	23,345	34,311	1,843
41	Loir-et-Cher	22,987	42,980	2,174
42	Loire	14,741	12,876	20
43	Loire (Haute-)	3,782	2,114	—
44	Loire-Atlantique	43,399	59,932	21,536
45	Loiret	7,568	5,009	—

Bottles of Appellation Contrôlée Wines Produced		Bottles of Wine Produced, including Appellation Contrôlée V.D.Q.S., and vin ordinaire		
White	Red or Rosé	White	Red and Rosé	Total
224,000	—	2,955,000	18,915,000	21,870,000
3,847,000	2,000	4,016,000	221,000	4,237,000
—	—	2,232,000	21,782,000	24,014,000
—	—	293,000	10,602,000	10,895,000
—	—	118,000	6,524,000	6,642,000
15,000	46,000	204,000	5,187,000	5,391,000
154,000	969,000	1,029,000	140,504,000	141,533,000
—	—	1,000	37,000	38,000
—	—	4,000	7,599,000	7,603,000
6,087,000	30,000	6,449,000	1,991,000	8,440,000
6,946,000	2,534,000	11,235,000	894,757,000	905,992,000
—	—	298,000	24,670,000	24,968,000
328,000	404,000	13,753,000	169,825,000	183,578,000
—	—	—	—	—
—	—	6,000	298,000	304,000
—	—	336,653,000	37,307,000	373,960,000
—	—	351,375,000	55,929,000	407,304,000
3,141,000	423,000	4,097,000	13,158,000	17,255,000
—	—	19,000	6,652,000	6,671,000
—	—	1,460,000	62,382,000	63,842,000
9,291,000	25,007,000	10,708,000	38,162,000	48,870,000
—	—	--	—	—
—	—	—	1,000	1,000
59,781,000	6,586,000	70,565,000	63,487,000	134,052,000
—	—	32,000	491,000	523,000
3,154,000	31,999,000	4,424,000	91,627,000	96,051,000
—	—	—	1,000	1,000
—	—	1,000	44,000	45,000
—	—	—	—	—
1,059,000	29,589,000	8,592,000	662,053,000	670,645,000
—	—	135,000	65,915,000	66,050,000
—	38,000	187,508,000	64,336,000	251,844,000
242,033,000	170,613,000	344,890,000	260,672,000	605,562,000
4,090,000	—	134,015,000	1,230,926,000	1,364,941,000
—	—	—	1,000	1,000
74,000	20,000	845,000	23,233,000	24,078,000
9,457,000	9,312,000	17,502,000	61,690,000	79,192,000'
—	1,000	3,775,000	40,884,000	44,659,000
1,845,000	1,655,000	2,484,000	6,404,000	8,888,000
—	—	65,529,000	21,935,000	87,464,000
2,404,000	2,920,000	37,869,000	69,309,000	107,178,000
15,000	8,000	269,000	24,108,000	24,377,000
—	—	59,000	3,539,000	3,598,000
22,424,000	204,000	60,803,000	50,506,000	111,309,000
—	—	295,000	10,883,000	11,178,000

Département	Number of Vineyard Owners Reporting	Total Acres of Vineyards in pro- duction	Acres of Vineyards Entitled to Appellation Contrôlée
46 Lot	12,442	23,408	—
47 Lot-et-Garonne	21,930	49,151	3,117
48 Lozère	1,896	931	—
49 Maine-et-Loire	28,837	63,165	38,354
50 Manche	—	—	—
51 Marne	14,227	33,325	33,165
52 Marne (Haute-)	2,987	911	—
53 Mayenne	38	10	—
54 Meurthe-et-Moselle	5,276	1,766	—
55 Meuse	1,040	477	—
56 Morbihan	52	32	—
57 Moselle	2,987	682	—
58 Nièvre	5,959	3,510	978
59 Nord	—	—	—
60 Oise	13	2	—
61 Orne	—	—	—
62 Pas-de-Calais	—	—	—
63 Puy-de-Dôme	19,145	12,352	—
64 Pyrénées (Basses-)	13,916	16,710	1,556
65 Pyrénées (Hautes-)	7,723	8,848	35
66 Pyrénées-Orientales	30,245	163,067	61,644
67 Rhin (Bas-)	21,757	12,602	8,319
68 Rhin (Haut-)	13,956	15,924	14,417
69 Rhône	19,879	46,589	37,816
70 Saône (Haute)	3,817	1,136	—
71 Saône-et-Loire	28,168	28,901	17,851
72 Sarthe	4,372	2,902	49
73 Savoie	14,200	7,931	—
74 Savoie (Haute-)	2,552	1,050	148
75 Seine	3	2	—
76 Seine-Maritime	1	—	—
77 Seine-et-Marne	924	198	12
78 Seine-et-Oise	621	106	—
79 Sèvres (Deux-)	19,818	15,158	1,667
80 Somme	—	—	—
81 Tarn	22,552	68,172	10,759
82 Tarn-et-Garonne	15,513	38,201	—
83 Var	32,172	148,501	588
84 Vaucluse	26,659	119,531	39,695
85 Vendée	47,862	33,582	57
86 Vienne	32,458	37,087	600
87 Vienne (Haute-)	1,036	440	—
88 Vosges	3,106	919	—
89 Yonne	8,947	7,148	2,991
Totals	1,214,147	3,070,390	588,829

Bottles of Appellation Contrôlée Wines Produced		Bottles of Wine Produced, including Appellation Contrôlée, V.D.Q.S., and vin ordinaire		
White	Red or Rosé	White	Red and Rosé	Total
—	—	389,000	37,454,000	37,843,000
6,975,000	270,000	23,326,000	74,198,000	97,524,000
—	—	—	1,753,000	1,753,000
28,182,000	46,631,000	34,720,000	90,593,000	125,313,000
82,498,000	359,000	86,528,000	754,000	87,282,000
—	—	21,000	1,444,000	1,465,000
—	—	1,000	10,000	11,000
—	—	9,000	3,104,000	3,113,000
—	—	5,000	611,000	616,000
—	—	21,000	24,000	45,000
—	—	104,000	1,381,000	1,485,000
1,028,000	—	1,219,000	4,466,000	5,685,000
—	—	—	—	—
—	—	—	2,000	2,000
—	—	—	—	—
—	—	561,000	24,877,000	25,438,000
1,778,000	334,000	7,958,000	15,960,000	23,918,000
13,000	72,000	2,446,000	8,442,000	10,888,000
65,587,000	12,575,000	75,392,000	231,826,000	307,218,000
34,889,000	194,000	44,729,000	2,075,000	46,804,000
51,167,000	459,000	53,413,000	2,160,000	55,573,000
84,000	110,167,000	429,000	138,401,000	138,830,000
—	—	18,000	1,480,000	1,498,000
23,295,000	30,075,000	25,129,000	56,242,000	81,371,000
34,000	8,000	470,000	4,156,000	4,626,000
—	—	9,013,000	16,852,000	25,865,000
336,000	—	1,109,000	1,756,000	2,865,000
—	—	—	2,000	2,000
—	—	—	—	—
33,000	—	43,000	319,000	362,000
—	—	5,000	222,000	227,000
1,076,000	2,044,000	2,234,000	25,062,000	27,296,000
—	—	—	—	—
17,710,000	—	47,790,000	111,636,000	159,426,000
—	—	577,000	66,136,000	66,713,000
49,000	706,000	17,389,000	376,200,000	393,589,000
1,703,000	85,430,000	37,023,000	244,997,000	282,020,000
90,000	—	7,986,000	47,914,000	55,900,000
761,000	153,000	21,713,000	37,193,000	58,906,000
—	—	11,000	541,000	552,000
—	—	—	1,193,000	1,193,000
7,096,000	420,000	8,548,000	7,533,000	16,081,000
700,753,000	572,257,000	2,196,826,000	5,907,516,000	8,104,342,000

PRODUCTION OF APPELLATION CONTRÔLÉE
WINES IN FRANCE, 1966 (IN TERMS OF BOTTLES)

(The following tables reproduced by permission from *La Journée Vinicole* give the official production in terms of bottles of all superior French wines in 1966. It should be kept in mind that 1966 was on the whole a very copious as well as a very good vintage and produced an above-average crop in almost all French districts.)

BURGUNDY AND BEAUJOLAIS

APPELLATION	White	Red & Rosé	Totals
Aloxe-Corton	9,000	678,000	687,000
Auxey-Duresses	167,000	306,000	473,000
Bâtard-Montrachet	48,000	–	48,000
Beaujolais	789,000	44,032,000	44,820,000
Beaujolais Supérieur	–	3,596,000	3,596,000
Beaujolais Villages	7,000	26,782,000	26,789,000
Beaune	53,000	1,770,000	1,824,000
Bienvenue-Bâtard-Montrachet	18,000	–	18,000
Blagny	12,000	17,000	30,000
Bonnes Mares	–	64,000	64,000
Bourgogne	1,713,000	8,156,000	9,869,000
Bourgogne Rosé Marsannay	–	286,000	286,000
Bourgogne Aligoté	8,139,000	–	8,139,000
Bourgogne Ordinaire	32,000	263,000	294,000
Bourgogne Grand Ordinaire	1,602,000	2,638,000	4,240,000
Bourgogne Passe-Tout-Grains	–	4,871,000	4,871,000
Bourgogne Hautes-Côtes de Beaune	6,000	415,000	421,000
Bourgogne, vin fin des Hautes Côtes de Nuits	6,000	32,000	39,000
Brouilly	–	5,577,000	5,577,000
Chablis	1,851,000	–	1,851,000
Chablis Grand Cru	252,000	–	252,000
Chablis Premier Cru	1,632,000	–	1,632,000
Chambertin	–	45,000	45,000
Chambertin Clos-de-Bèze	–	50,000	50,000
Chambolle-Musigny	–	657,000	657,000
Chapelle-Chambertin	–	18,000	18,000
Charmes-Chambertin	–	116,000	116,000
Chassagne-Montrachet	451,000	703,000	1,154,000
Cheilly-les-Maranges	1,000	35,000	36,000
Chenas	–	1,100,000	1,100,000
Chevalier-Montrachet	18,000	–	18,000
Chiroubles	–	1,564,000	1,564,000
Chorey-les-Beaune	1,000	402,000	403,000
Clos de la Roche	–	52,000	52,000
Clos Saint-Denis	–	22,000	22,000
Clos de Tart	–	17,000	17,000
Clos de Vougeot	–	215,000	215,000
Corton	5,000	412,000	417,000
Corton-Charlemagne	163,000	–	163,000
Côtes de Beaune	3,000	7,000	10,000

APPELLATION	White	Red & Rosé	Totals
Côtes de Beaune-Villages	—	605,000	605,000
Côtes de Brouilly	—	1,253,000	1,253,000
Criots-Bâtard-Montrachet	7,000	—	7,000
Dezizes-les-Maranges	—	21,000	21,000
Echézeaux	—	142,000	142,000
Fixin	—	95,000	95,000
Fleurie	—	3,629,000	3,629,000
Gevrey-Chambertin	—	1,491,000	1,491,000
Givry	36,000	275,000	311,000
Grands Echézeaux	—	37,000	37,000
Griotte-Chambertin	—	9,000	9,000
Julienas	—	2,531,000	2,531,000
Ladoix	6,000	249,000	255,000
La Tâche	—	28,000	28,000
Latricières-Chambertin	—	28,000	28,000
Mâcon	4,089,000	3,416,000	7,504,000
Mâcon Villages	5,723,000	666,000	6,389,000
Mâcon Supérieur	5,202,000	6,400,000	11,601,000
Mazis-Chambertin	—	31,000	31,000
Mazoyères-Chambertin	—	3,000	3,000
Mercurey	131,000	2,120,000	2,251,000
Meursault	1,680,000	83,000	1,763,000
Montagny	362,000	—	362,000
Monthélie	7,000	327,000	334,000
Montrachet	32,000	—	32,000
Morey-Saint-Denis	5,000	277,000	283,000
Morgon	—	3,836,000	3,836,000
Moulin-à-Vent	—	3,436,000	3,436,000
Musigny	1,000	43,000	44,000
Nuits or Nuits-Saint-Georges	9,000	1,271,000	1,279,000
Pernand-Vergelesses	33,000	288,000	321,000
Petit Chablis	693,000	—	693,000
Pommard	—	1,640,000	1,640,000
Pouilly-Fuissé	2,708,000	—	2,708,000
Pouilly-Fuissé Climats	392,000	—	392,000
Pouilly-Loché	88,000	—	88,000
Pouilly-Vinzelles	160,000	—	160,000
Puligny-Montrachet	814,000	32,000	846,000
Richebourg	—	37,000	37,000
Romanée, La	—	4,000	4,000
Romanée Conti	—	8,000	8,000
Romanée Saint-Vivant	—	35,000	35,000
Rosé des Riceys	—	14,000	14,000
Ruchottes-Chambertin	—	12,000	12,000
Rully	236,000	53,000	290,000
Saint-Amour	—	1,233,000	1,233,000
Saint-Aubin	130,000	146,000	277,000
Saint-Romain	138,000	47,000	185,000
Sampigny-les-Maranges	—	22,000	22,000
Santenay	24,000	1,156,000	1,179,000
Savigny-les-Beaune	65,000	1,251,000	1,316,000
Vins fins de la Côte de Nuits	—	757,000	757,000

APPELLATION	White	Red & Rosé	Totals
Volnay	—	1,077,000	1,077,000
Vosne-Romanée	—	728,000	728,000
Vougeot	6,000	62,000	68,000
Totals	39,755,000	145,802,000	185,557,000

BORDEAUX DISTRICT

APPELLATION	White	Red & Rosé	Totals
Barsac	2,321,000	—	2,321,000
Blaye or Blayais	30,848,000	51,000	30,899,000
Bordeaux	141,171,000	31,502,000	172,673,000
Bordeaux rosé	—	490,000	490,000
Bordeaux Côtes de Castillon	—	424,000	424,000
Bordeaux Supérieur	5,407,000	34,688,000	40,095,000
Bordeaux Clairet	—	208,000	208,000
Cérons	2,961,000	—	2,961,000
Côtes de Blaye	509,000	—	509,000
Côtes de Bordeaux Saint-Macaire	3,464,000	—	3,464,000
Côtes de Bourg, Bourg, Bourgeais	4,537,000	12,095,000	16,632,000
Côtes de Fronsac	—	3,090,000	3,090,000
Côtes de Canon-Fronsac	—	1,331,000	1,331,000
Entre-Deux-Mers	13,901,000	—	13,901,000
Graves	804,000	3,400,000	4,204,000
Graves Supérieur	7,066,000	—	7,066,000
Graves de Vayres	3,924,000	1,000	3,925,000
Haut Médoc	—	5,463,000	5,463,000
Lalande-de-Pomerol	—	2,703,000	2,703,000
Listrac	—	1,379,000	1,379,000
Loupiac	2,072,000	—	2,072,000
Lussac Saint-Émilion	—	3,523,000	3,523,000
Margaux	—	3,137,000	3,137,000
Médoc	—	6,988,000	6,988,000
Montagne Saint-Émilion	—	4,013,000	4,013,000
Moulis or Moulis-en-Médoc	—	861,000	861,000
Néac	—	1,000	1,000
Parsac Saint-Émilion	—	883,000	883,000
Pauillac	—	3,800,000	3,800,000
Pomerol	—	3,657,000	3,657,000
Premières Côtes de Blaye	137,000	5,133,000	5,269,000
Premières Côtes de Bordeaux	12,937,000	3,285,000	16,222,000
Puisseguin Saint-Émilion	—	2,682,000	2,682,000
Sables Saint-Émilion	—	748,000	748,000
Sainte-Croix-du-Mont	2,419,000	—	2,419,000
Saint-Émilion	—	26,230,000	26,230,000
Saint-Estèphe	—	5,014,000	5,014,000
Saint-Foy-Bordeaux	2,739,000	113,000	2,852,000
Saint-Georges Saint-Émilion	—	1,002,000	1,002,000
Saint-Julien	—	3,073,000	3,073,000
Sauternes	3,899,000	—	3,899,000
Totals	241,116,000	170,968,000	412,083,000

ALSACE

APPELLATION		White	Red & Rosé	Totals
Bas-Rhin Département		34,889,000	194,000	35,083,000
Haut-Rhin Département		51,167,000	459,000	51,626,000
	Totals	86,056,000	653,000	86,709,000

CHAMPAGNE

		White	Red & Rosé	Totals
Aisne		3,847,000	2,000	3,850,000
Aube		6,087,000	16,000	6,102,000
Marne		82,498,000	359,000	82,857,000
Seine-et-Marne		33,000	—	33,000
	Totals	92,465,000	377,000	92,842,000

JURA

		White	Red & Rosé	Totals
Arbois		774,000	1,448,000	2,222,000
Château-Châlon		59,000	—	59,000
Côtes du Jura		870,000	207,000	1,077,000
Etoile (l')		142,000	—	142,000
	Totals	1,845,000	1,655,000	3,500,000

LOIRE VALLEY

Anjou

	White	Red & Rosé	Totals
Anjou	10,523,000	495,000	11,018,000
Anjou Rosé	—	27,174,000	27,174,000
Anjou Rosé de Cabernet	—	19,856,000	19,856,000
Anjou Coteaux-de-la-Loire	450,000	—	450,000
Bonnezeaux	152,000	—	152,000
Coteaux de l'Aubance	257,000	—	257,000
Coteaux de l'Aubance Chaume	179,000	—	179,000
Coteaux du Layon	7,787,000	—	7,787,000
Quarts de Chaume	88,000	—	88,000
Saumur	9,411,000	111,000	9,522,000
Saumur Champigny	—	856,000	856,000
Cabernet de Saumur	—	507,000	507,000
Savennières	23,000	—	23,000

Muscadet

	White	Red & Rosé	Totals
Muscadet	1,995,000	—	1,995,000
Muscadet des Coteaux de la Loire	1,180,000	—	1,180,000
Muscadet de Sèvre et Maine	20,608,000	—	20,608,000

APPELLATION	White	Red & Rosé	Totals
Touraine			
Bourgueil	—	3,265,000	3,265,000
Chinon	21,000	2,389,000	2,410,000
Montlouis	1,175,000	—	1,175,000
Saint-Nicolas-de-Bourgueil	—	1,656,000	1,656,000
Touraine	3,967,000	4,284,000	8,251,000
Touraine Amboise	242,000	154,000	396,000
Touraine Azay-le-Rideau	62,000	—	62,000
Touraine Mesland	768,000	518,000	1,286,000
Vouvray	2,939,000	—	2,939,000
Vouvray Mousseux	2,688,000	—	2,688,000
Other Loire			
Coteaux du Loir	12,000	8,000	20,000
Jasnières	22,000	—	22,000
Ménétou-Salon	131,000	9,000	140,000
Pouilly, Blanc Fumé de	755,000	—	755,000
Pouilly-sur-Loire	273,000	—	273,000
Quincy	390,000	—	390,000
Reuilly	84,000	20,000	104,000
Sancerre	2,609,000	415,000	3,024,000
Totals	68,791,000	61,717,000	130,508,000

RHONE AND PROVENCE

	White	Red & Rosé	Totals
Bandol	49,000	706,000	755,000
Bellet	15,000	46,000	61,000
Cassis	317,000	313,000	630,000
Château-Grillet	3,000	—	3,000
Châteauneuf-du-Pape	138,000	9,980,000	10,118,000
Clairette de Bellegarde	714,000	—	714,000
Clairette de Die	2,645,000	—	2,645,000
Condrieu	19,000	—	19,000
Cornas	—	170,000	170,000
Côtes du Rhône	504,000	130,864,000	131,368,000
Côtes du Rhône Chusclan	—	1,397,000	1,397,000
Côtes du Rhône-Laudun	168,000	429,000	597,000
Côte Rôtie	—	334,000	334,000
Crépy	276,000	—	276,000
Crozes l'Hermitage	197,000	1,359,000	1,556,000
Hermitage	213,000	428,000	641,000
Lirac	7,000	756,000	763,000
Palette	11,000	91,000	102,000
Saint-Joseph	37,000	272,000	309,000
Saint-Péray	168,000	—	168,000
Seyssel	42,000	—	42,000
Seyssel mousseux	137,000	—	137,000
Tavel	—	2,241,000	2,241,000
Totals	5,660,000	149,386,000	155,046,000

ROUSSILLON AND RHONE
(DESSERT WINES)

APPELLATION	White	Red & Rosé	Totals
Banyuls	—	3,945,000	3,945,000
Banyuls Rancio (Grand Cru)	—	1,224,000	1,224,000
Côtes d'Agly	13,241,000	3,389,000	16,630,000
Côtes du Haut-Roussillon	24,009,000	125,000	24,134,000
Grand Roussillon	1,381,000	—	1,381,000
Maury	—	5,083,000	5,083,000
Muscat des Beaumes-de-Venise	366,000	—	366,000
Muscat de Frontignan	1,699,000	—	1,699,000
Muscat de Lunel	334,000	—	334,000
Muscat de Rivesaltes	10,401,000	1,000	10,402,000
Muscat de Saint-Jean-du-Minervois	70,000	—	70,000
Muscat de Mireval	166,000	—	166,000
Rasteau	918,000	—	918,000
Rivesaltes	21,183,000	—	21,183,000
Totals	73,768,000	13,767,000	87,535,000

SOUTHWESTERN FRANCE

	White	Red & Rosé	Totals
Bergerac	30,397,000	4,733,000	35,130,000
Bergerac Côte-de-Sausignac	444,000	—	444,000
Bergerac Côte-de-Sausignac rosé	—	1,057,000	1,057,000
Blanquette de Limoux	2,318,000	—	2,318,000
Clairette du Languedoc	1,822,000	—	1,822,000
Côtes de Bergerac	5,005,000	133,000	5,138,000
Côtes de Duras	8,380,000	384,000	8,764,000
Côtes de Montravel	1,869,000	—	1,869,000
Fitou	—	1,342,000	1,342,000
Gaillac	17,576,000	—	17,576,000
Gaillac Premières Côtes	134,000	—	134,000
Haut Montravel	1,129,000	—	1,129,000
Jurançon	1,707,000	—	1,707,000
Madiran	—	444,000	444,000
Monbazillac	11,209,000	—	11,209,000
Montravel	8,980,000	—	8,980,000
Pacherenc de Vic Bilh	83,000	—	83,000
Pécharmant	—	194,000	194,000
Rosette	178,000	—	178,000
Totals	91,231,000	8,287,000	99,518,000

BORDEAUX

THE OFFICIAL (1855) CLASSIFICATION OF
THE GREAT RED WINES OF BORDEAUX

This, except for the notations in parentheses, is the official list and the only authorized and proper one. However, wines marked (×) are no longer generally on the market or have practically ceased to exist as independent properties; those marked (+) are generally sold for a higher price than others in their class, and justifiably so; those marked (−), generally for a lower price. Thus, were a new classification to be made today, the châteaux marked (+) or (−) would probably be placed in a higher, or a lower, category.

It is interesting to note that, even within these categories, the wines are listed, not alphabetically, nor geographically by *commune,* but in their presumed order of merit. Thus, in 1855, Mouton Rothschild was ranked as the best of the "Seconds", Pontet-Canet as the best of the "Fifths", and so on.

All these châteaux are listed, with further details, in their proper alphabetical place in this volume.

THE MÉDOC

FIRST GROWTHS—PREMIERS CRUS

Vineyard	Commune	Cases Per Year
Château Lafite	Pauillac	17,300
Château Margaux	Margaux	15,400
Château Latour	Pauillac	17,300
Château Haut Brion	Pessac, Graves	20,800

SECOND GROWTHS—DEUXIÈMES CRUS

Château Mouton-Rothschild (++)	Pauillac	11,500
Château Rausan-Ségla	Margaux	10,500
Château Rauzan Gassies	Margaux	8,600
Château Léoville-Las-Cases	St. Julien	24,000
Château Léoville-Poyferré	St. Julien	21,000
Château Léoville-Barton	St. Julien	9,600
Château Durfort-Vivens	Margaux	8,600
Château Gruaud-Larose	St. Julien	19,200
Château Lascombes	Margaux	11,500
Château Brane-Cantenac	Cantenac-Margaux	24,000
Château Pichon-Longueville (Baron)	Pauillac	6,200
Château Pichon-Longueville-Lalande	Pauillac	14,400
Château Ducru-Beaucaillou	St. Julien	13,400
Château Cos d'Estournel	St. Estèphe	21,100
Château Montrose	St. Estèphe	12,500

THIRD GROWTHS—TROISIÈMES CRUS

Vineyard	Commune	Cases Per Year
Château Kirwan (−)	Cantenac-Margaux	7,700
Château d'Issan (−)	Cantenac-Margaux	5,800
Château Lagrange (−)	St. Julien	8,600
Château Langoa	St. Julien	4,800
Château Giscours	Labarde	25,000
Château Malescot-St. Exupéry (−)	Margaux	4,300
Château Cantenac-Brown	Cantenac-Margaux	5,800
Château Boyd-Cantenac	Margaux	5,800
Château Palmer (+)	Cantenac-Margaux	9,600
Château La Lagune (+)	Ludon	20,200
Château Desmirail (×)	Margaux	
Château Calon-Ségur (+)	St. Estèphe	17,300
Château Ferrière (×)	Margaux	
Château Marquis d'Alesme-Becker (−)	Margaux	1,900

FOURTH GROWTHS—QUATRIÈMES CRUS

Vineyard	Commune	Cases Per Year
Château St. Pierre-Sevaistre }	St. Julien }	1,900
Château St. Pierre-Bontemps }	St. Julien }	
Château Talbot (+)	St. Julien	19,200
Château Branaire-Ducru	St. Julien	10,600
Château Duhart-Milon	Pauillac	6,700
Château Pouget (−)	Cantenac-Margaux	1,450
Château La Tour-Carnet	St. Laurent	3,800
Château Rochet (−)	St. Estèphe	8,600
Château Beychevelle (+ +)	St. Julien	24,000
Château Le Prieuré (now called Prieuré-Lichine)	Cantenac-Margaux	6,200
Château Marquis de Terme	Margaux	7,700

FIFTH GROWTHS—CINQUIÈMES CRUS

Vineyard	Commune	Cases Per Year
Château Pontet-Canet (+)	Pauillac	29,000
Château Batailley	Pauillac	19,200
Château Haut-Batailley	Pauillac	5,800
Château Grand-Puy-Lacoste	Pauillac	7,700
Château Grand-Puy-Ducasse	Pauillac	3,400
Château Lynch-Bages (+)	Pauillac	17,300
Château Lynch-Moussas (−)	Pauillac	1,500
Château Dauzac (−)	Labarde	3,400
Château Mouton Baron Philippe (+) (called Château Mouton d'Armailhacq until 1956)	Pauillac	9,600
Château Le Tertre (−)	Arsac	4,300
Château Haut-Bages-Libéral (−)	Pauillac	6,700
Château Pédesclaux (−)	Pauillac	4,800
Château Belgrave	St. Laurent	11,500
Château Camensac	St. Laurent	5,800
Château Cos Labory	St. Estèphe	4,300
Château Clerc-Milon (−)	Pauillac	3,400
Château Croizet Bages (−)	Pauillac	8,600
Château Cantemerle (+)	Macau	5,800

NOTE: The seven Crus Exceptionnels have been marked with an asterisk (*),
and the Crus Bourgeois Supérieurs by an (s).

Château	Commune	Appellation (where different)
Abbé-Gorsse-de-Gorsse (s)	Margaux	
*Angludet	Cantenac	(Margaux)
Anseillan, d' (s)	Pauillac	
Anthonic	Moulis	
Arche, d'	Ludon	(Haut-Médoc)
Arsac, d' (s)	Arsac	(Haut-Médoc)
Barateau	Saint-Laurent	
Beaumont (s)	Cussac	(Haut-Médoc)
Beauséjour	Saint-Estèphe	
Beau Site (s)	Saint-Estèphe	
Bégorce-Zédé, la (s)	Soussans	(Margaux)
*Bel-Air Marquis d'Aligre	Margaux	
Bellegrave	Pauillac	
Bellevue-Saint-Lambert (s)	Pauillac	
Bel-Orme	St. Seurin-de-Cadourne	(Haut-Médoc)
Bibian (s)	Listrac	(Haut-Médoc)
Bontemps-Dubarry (s)	St. Julien	
Boscq, Le (s)	St. Estèphe	
Breuil, du	Cissac	(Haut-Médoc)
Cambon-La-Pelouse (s)	Macau	(Haut-Médoc)
Canteloup	St. Estèphe	
Capbern (s)	St. Estèphe	
Caronne-Sainte-Gemme	Saint-Laurent	(Haut-Médoc)
*Chasse-Spleen	Moulis	
Chesnaye, La (s)	Cussac	(Haut-Médoc)
Citran-Clauzel (s)	Avensan	(Haut-Médoc)
Clarke (s)	Listrac	(Haut-Médoc)
Closerie, La	Moulis	
Colombier-Monpelou (s)	Pauillac	
Constant-Bages-Monpelou (s)	Pauillac	
Constant-Trois-Moulins (s)	Macau	(Haut-Médoc)
Corconac	Saint-Laurent	(Haut-Médoc)
Coufran	St. Seurin-de-Cadourne	(Haut-Médoc)
*Couronne, La	Pauillac	
Coutelin-Merville	Saint-Estèphe	
Crock, Le (s)	Saint-Estèphe	
Daubos-Haut-Bages	Pauillac	
Dubignon-Talbot (s)	Margaux	
Duplessis	Moulis	
Duroc-Milon	Pauillac	
Dutruch-Grand-Poujeaux (s)	Moulis	

Château	Commune	Appellation
Egmont, d'	Ludon	(Haut-Médoc)
Fatin (s)	Saint-Estèphe	
Fellonneau	Macau	(Haut-Médoc)
Fonbadet (s)	Pauillac	
Fonpetite (s)	Saint-Estèphe	
Fonréaud (s)	Listrac	(Haut-Médoc)
Fontesteau	Saint-Sauveur	(Haut-Médoc)
Fourcas-Dupré (s)	Listrac	(Haut-Médoc)
Fourcas-Hostein (s)	Listrac	(Haut-Médoc)
Galan, du	Saint-Laurent	(Haut-Médoc)
Glana	Saint-Julien	
Gloria (s)	Saint-Julien	
Grand-Duroc-Milon	Pauillac	
Grand-St. Julien	Saint-Julien	
Gressier-Grand-Poujeaux (s)	Moulis	
Gurgue, La (s)	Margaux	
Hanteillan	Saint-Estèphe	
Haut-Bages-Averous	Pauillac	
Haut-Bages-Drouillet	Pauillac	
Haut-Marbuzet	Saint-Estèphe	
Haye, La (s)	Saint-Estèphe	
Houissant (s)	Saint-Estèphe	
Labégorce (s)	Margaux	
Ladouys	Saint-Estèphe	
Lafitte-Carcasset	Saint-Estèphe	
Lafon (s)	Listrac	(Haut-Médoc)
Labégorce-Zédé	Soussans	(Margaux)
Lamarque, de	Lamarque	(Haut-Médoc)
Lamothe de Bergeron	Cussac	(Haut-Médoc)
Lamouroux, de (s)	Margaux	
Lanessan (s)	Cussac	(Haut-Médoc)
Larrieu-Terrefort-Graves (s)	Macau	(Haut-Médoc)
Larrivaux	Cissac	(Haut-Médoc)
Lemoyne-Lafon-Rochet (s)	Ludon	(Haut-Médoc)
Lestage (s)	Listrac	(Haut-Médoc)
Lestage-Darquier-Grand-Poujeaux (s)	Moulis	
Liversan (s)	Saint-Sauveur	(Haut-Médoc)
Ludon-Pomiès-Agassac (s)	Ludon	(Haut-Médoc)
MacCarthy-Moula	Saint-Estèphe	
Malécot-Desse (s)	Pauillac	
Malecasse (s)	Lamarque	(Haut-Médoc)
Marbuzet (s)	Saint-Estèphe	
Martinens (s)	Cantenac	(Margaux)
Maucaillou	Moulis	
Maucamps (s)	Macau	(Haut-Médoc)
Médoc	Saint-Julien	
Meyney (s)	Saint-Estèphe	
Monbrison (s)	Arsac	(Haut-Médoc)
Montbrun	Cantenac	(Margaux)

Château	Commune	Appellation (where different)
Morin	Saint-Estèphe	
Moulin-à-Vent	Moulis	
Moulin-de-la-Rose	Saint-Julien	
*Moulin-Riche	Saint-Julien	
Moulis (s)	Moulis	
Nexon-Lemoyne (s)	Ludon	(Haut-Médoc)
Ormes, des	Saint-Julien	
Ormes-de-Pez, Les	Saint-Estèphe	
Paloumey (s)	Ludon	(Haut-Médoc)
Parempuyre, de (Cruse) (s)	Parempuyre	(Haut-Médoc)
Parempuyre, de (Durand-Dassier) (s)	Parempuyre	(Haut-Médoc)
Paveil-de-Luze (s)	Soussans	(Margaux)
Payrelebade, de	Listrac	(Haut-Médoc)
Peyrabon	Saint-Sauveur	(Haut-Médoc)
Pez, de	Saint-Estèphe	
Phélan-Ségur (s)	Saint-Estèphe	
Pibran	Pauillac	
Picard	Saint-Estèphe	
Pierre-Bibian (s)	Listrac	(Haut-Médoc)
Pomeys (s)	Moulis	
Pomiès-Agassac (s)	Ludon	(Haut-Médoc)
Pomys (s)	Saint-Estèphe	
Poujeaux-Marly (s)	Moulis	
*Poujeaux-Theil	Moulis	
Priban (s)	Macau	(Haut-Médoc)
Reverdi	Lamarque	(Haut-Médoc)
Roc, Le	Saint-Estèphe	
Rose-La-Biche (s)	Macau	(Haut-Médoc)
Rosemont (s)	Labarde	(Haut-Médoc)
Saransot-Dupré (s)	Listrac	(Haut-Médoc)
Ségur (s)	Parempuyre	(Haut-Médoc)
Ségur-Fillon (s)	Parempuyre	(Haut-Médoc)
Sémeillan (s)	Listrac	(Haut-Médoc)
Sénéjac	Le Pian	(Haut-Médoc)
Siran (s)	Labarde	(Haut-Médoc)
Testeron, de	Moulis	
Tour-de-Mons, La (s)	Soussans	(Margaux)
Tour-Milon, La	Pauillac	
Tour-Pibran, La	Pauillac	
Trois-Moulins, des (s)	Macau	(Haut-Médoc)
Tronquoy-Lalande (s)	Saint-Estèphe	
Verdignan	St. Seurin-de-Cadourne	(Haut-Médoc)
*Villegeorge	Avensan	(Haut-Médoc)

SAUTERNES AND BARSAC

GREAT FIRST GROWTH–GRAND PREMIER CRU

		Cases
Château d'Yquem	Sauternes	9,500

FIRST GROWTHS–PREMIERS CRUS

Château La Tour Blanche	Bommes	4,000
Château Lafaurie-Peyraguey	Bommes	3,500
Château Haut-Peyraguey	Bommes	1,500
Château de Rayne-Vigneau	Bommes	6,000
Château Suduiraut	Preignac	8,000
Château Coutet	Barsac	6,000
Château Climens	Barsac	4,500
Château Guiraud	Sauternes	8,000
Château Rieussec	Fargues	6,000
Château Rabaud-Promis	Bommes	7,000
Château Sigalas-Rabaud	Bommes	2,000

SECOND GROWTHS–DEUXIÈMES CRUS

Château Myrat	Barsac	3,000
Château Doisy-Daëne	Barsac	2,400
Château Doisy-Dubroca	Barsac	—
Château Doisy-Védrines	Barsac	3,100
Château D'Arche	Sauternes	1,000
Château Filhot	Sauternes	4,000
Château Broustet	Barsac	2,500
Château Nairac	Barsac	2,400
Château Caillou	Barsac	2,900
Château Suau	Barsac	1,400
Château de Malle	Preignac	2,800
Château Romer	Fargues	1,400
Château Lamothe	Sauternes	1,000

ST. EMILION

OFFICIAL CLASSIFICATION OF 1955

Since the wines of St. Emilion were not classified in 1855, it was decided exactly one hundred years later, in 1955, to establish a classification comparable to that of the Médoc, and a commission appointed by the *Institut National des Appellations d'Origine* carried out this difficult and thankless task.

It should be noted that Château Ausone and Château Cheval-Blanc are generally considered in a category apart, although they share the designation "First Great Growth" with ten other vineyards.

As in the Médoc, there exist many minor chateaux producing wines of excellent quality which are not included in this official classification.

		Cases
Château	Ausone	2,660
Château	Cheval-Blanc	7,720
Château	Beauséjour-Duffau	1,980
Château	Beauséjour-Fagouet	3,080
Château	Belair	3,860
Château	Canon	8,910
Château	Clos Fourtet	5,590
Château	Figeac	10,890
Château	La Gaffelière Naudes	7,920
Château	Magdelaine	4,760
Château	Pavie	13,330
Château	Trottevieille	4,030

GREAT GROWTHS—GRANDS CRUS

Château	L'Arrosée	
Château	L'Angelus	11,880
Château	Balestard-la-Tonnelle	3,650
Château	Bellevue	2,650
Château	Bergat	1,080
Château	Cadet Bon	1,610
Château	Cadet Piolat	8,550
Château	Canon-la-Gaffelière	14,060
Château	Cap de Mourlin	3,760
Château	Chapelle Madeleine	440
Château	Chatalet	
Château	Chauvin	3,900
Château	Corbin	5,770
Château	Corbin-Michotte	3,200
Château	Coutet	4,570
Château	Croque-Michotte	4,510
Château	Curé-Bon	1,490
Château	Fonplégade	7,540
Château	Fonroque	2,970
Château	Franc-Mayne	2,770
Château	Grand Barrail Lamarzelle Figeac	10,740
Château	Grand Corbin	6,420
Château	Grand Corbin Despagne	11,700
Château	Grand Mayne	6,290
Château	Grand Pontet	6,890
Château	Grandes Murailles	1,200
Château	Guadet Saint Julien	2,680
Clos des Jacobins		5,340
Château	Jean Faure	10,730
Château	La Carte	2,100
Château	La Clotte	1,800
Château	La Cluzière	750
Château	La Couspaude	2,050
Château	La Dominique	3,270

	Cases
Clos La Madeleine	940
Château Lamarzelle	2,820
Château Larcis Ducasse	5,940
Château Larmande	2,730
Château Laroze	4,460
Château Lasserre	2,480
Château La Tour du Pin Figeac	10,890
Château La Tour Figeac	8,120
Château Le Chatelet	990
Château Le Couvent	690
Château Le Prieuré	1,910
Château Mauvezin	1,390
Château Moulin-du-Cadet	2,480
Château Pavie-Decesse	2,970
Château Pavie-Macquin	5,090
Château Pavillon Cadet	1,210
Château Petit Faurie de Souchard	8,550
Château Petit Faurie de Soutard	3,420
Château Ripeau	
Château Saint Georges Côte Pavie	2,180
Clos Saint Martin	
Château Sansonnet	2,900
Château Soutard	9,800
Château Tertre-Daugay	8,980
Château Trimoulet	8,420
Château Trois-Moulins	1,640
Château Troplong-Mondot	13,200
Château Villemaurine	2,980
Château Yon-Figeac	7,370

GRAVES

The châteaux of the Graves District (neglected except for Château Haut-Brion in the classification of 1855) were officially rated by the Institut National des Appellations d'Origine in 1953, although rather superficially and incompletely and this classification was revised, although still inadequately, in 1959. A number of additional vineyards producing red wines or white or both certainly deserve a place in this list and some distinctions should certainly be drawn between the various qualities of wines which they produce. Here, nevertheless, is the official classification as it exists today.

CLASSIFIED RED WINES—CRUS CLASSÉS (ROUGES)

		Cases
Château Haut Brion	Pessac	19,200
Château La Mission-Haut-Brion	Pessac	7,680
Château Haut-Bailly	Léognan	5,760
Domaine de Chevalier	Léognan	2,590
Château Fieuzal	Léognan	4,500

Château Carbonnieux	Léognan	4,800
Château Malartic-Lagravière	Léognan	5,280
Château Latour-Martillac	Martillac	1,730
Château Latour-Haut-Brion	Talence	1,000
Château Smith-Haut-Lafitte	Martillac	4,610
Château Olivier	Léognan	480
Château Bouscaut	Cadaujac	4,800
Château Pape-Clement	Pessac	9,600

CLASSIFIED WHITE WINES—CRUS CLASSÉS (BLANCS)

Château Haut-Brion*	Pessac	960
Château Carbonnieux	Léognan	9,120
Domaine de Chevalier	Léognan	670
Château Couhins	Villenave d'Ornon	2,690
Château Latour-Martillac	Martillac	290
Château Malartic-Lagravière	Léognan	960
Château Olivier	Léognan	2,880
Château Bouscaut	Cadaujac	1,150
Château Laville-Haut-Brion	Talence	1,500

* Not classified for some unknown reason.

POMEROL

For Pomerol, directly adjoining St. Emilion, no official classification of vineyards has until now been authorized and/or published. The major châteaux are generally considered these:

FIRST GREAT GROWTH—GRAND PREMIER CRU

	Cases
Château Pétrus	2,800

FIRST GROWTHS—PREMIERS CRUS

Château Beauregard	4,000
Château Certan de May	1,000
Château Certan-Marzelle	1,400
Château Certan-Giraud	1,200
Château Clinet	4,500
Domaine de l'Église	1,800
Château l'Église Clinet	2,000
Clos l'Église	1,600
Château l'Evangile	4,000
Château Feytit-Clinet	1,400
Château Gazin	7,500
Château Gombaude Guillot	2,000
Château Guillot	2,000
Château La Conseillante	4,000

Château La Croix-de-Gay	2,400
Château Lafleur	1,400
Château La Fleur-Pétrus	2,800
Château La Grange	1,400
Château La Grave-Trigant-de-Boisset	2,380
Château La Pointe	6,500
Château Latour-Pomerol	2,500
Château Le Gay	2,400
Château Nenin	8,000
Château Petit-Village	4,000
Château Rouget	3,500
Château Trotanoy	2,300
Vieux Château Certan	5,600
Château La Vray-Croix-de-Gay	1,200

SECONDARY FIRST GROWTHS—DEUXIÈMES PREMIERS CRUS

	Cases
Château Bourgneuf	4,000
Domaine de Cantereau	500
Clos du Clocher	1,500
Château du Chene-Liège	—
Château l'Enclos	4,300
Château l'Enclos du Presbytère	—
Domaine de Tropchaud	—
Domaine de Haut-Pignon	—
Domaine Haut-Tropchaud	—
Château Gratte-Cap	3,540
Château Lacabane	5,460
Château Le Caillou	2,740
Château La Commanderie	2,550
Château La Croix	2,670
Château La Croix St. Georges	1,620
Château La Violette	1,250
Château Lafleur du Gazin	—
Château Mazeyres	4,860
Clos Beauregard	—
Château Pignon-de-Gay	1,000
Château Plince	2,700
Clos René	5,910
Château de Salles	19,800
Château Taillefer	9,440

BURGUNDY

The vineyards of Burgundy have never been, and cannot be, classified with anything like the precision and finality of the Bordeaux châteaux, where every major vineyard has a single owner and a single name. *(See* Burgundy, Domaine, Estate-Bottling). In Chablis and on the Côte d'Or, most of the named vineyards are divided among numerous different growers: some sixty producers, for example, own vines in the Clos de Vougeot which, therefore, in any given year, is not one wine but sixty different wines.

It' is, nevertheless, a mistake to imagine that the Côte d'Or vineyards have never been classified at all. An extremely careful survey and classification, no less official and no less thorough than the famous one of 1855 in Bordeaux, was published in 1861 by the *Comité d'Agriculture de l'Arrondissement de Beaune.* This eventually served as the basis of the Appellation Contrôlée regulations and, as a result, only the wines from certain specific *climats* or vineyards may legally be called Grands Crus, Premiers Crus, etc. From an overall standpoint, this old classification does have one major fault, since the Premiers Crus (or Premières Cuvées) of certain *communes,* such as Gevrey Chambertin and Vosne Romanée, are markedly superior to many Grands Crus (or Tétes de Cuvée) of lesser townships.

An attempt has been made to correct these injustices in the list which follows. Though by no means complete (there are 419 officially recognized *climats,* or vineyard names, on the Côte de Nuits, and over twice that many on the Côte de Beaune), it certainly includes almost all of those that one is likely to find on wine labels. The comparative ratings, while not official, are more or less those accepted by a majority of experts, although there will always be some differences of opinion.

WINES OF THE CÔTE D'OR
A. RED WINES

CÔTE DE NUITS Commune	Leading Vineyards	Acres Under Vines
Fixin 104 acres	*Les Hervelets*	9.4
	Clos du Chapitre	11.9
	Clos de la Perrière	11.9
	Les Arvelets	11.9
	Clos Napoléon	4.4
Gevrey-Chambertin 1,063 acres	CHAMBERTIN	32.1
	CLOS DE BÈZE	37.6
	LATRICIÉRES-CHAMBERTIN	17.3
	MAZIS-CHAMBERTIN	31.1
	CHARMES-CHAMBERTIN & ⎱ MAZOYÈRES-CHAMBERTIN ⎰	78.1
	GRIOTTE-CHAMBERTIN	13.6
	RUCHOTTES-CHAMBERTIN	7.7
	CHAPELLE-CHAMBERTIN	13.3
	CLOS SAINT JACQUES	6.4
	Combe aux Moines	
	Cazetiers	
	Varoilles	
	Fouchère	
	Etournelles	
	Clos Prieur	
	Lavaux	

400

Morey-Saint-Denis 256 acres	BONNES MARES	4.4
	(see below, Chambolle)	
	CLOS DE TART	37.8
	CLOS DE LA ROCHE	17.8
	Clos Saint-Denis	16.3
	Clos des Lambrays	
	Meix Rentiers	
	Clos Bussière	
Chambolle-Musigny 428 acres	MUSIGNY	26.4
	BONNES MARES	33.9
	LES AMOUREUSES	13.3
	Les Charmes	23.0
	Les Baudes	
	Combe d'Orveau	
	Les Cras	
	Derrière-la-Grange	
	Les Combottes	
	Les Sentiers	
Vougeot 154 acres	CLOS DE VOUGEOT	124.0
	Vougeot	
Flagey-Échézeaux 179 acres	GRANDS ÉCHÉZEAUX	22.5
	Echézeaux	74.1
Vosne-Romanée 414 acres	ROMANÉE-CONTI	4.4
	LA TÂCHE	14.8
	ROMANÉE SAINT-VIVANT	23.5
	RICHEBOURG	19.8
	LA GRANDE RUE	3.2
	LA ROMANÉE	2.0
	LES GAUDICHOTS	
	LES MALCONSORTS	14.7
	LES SUCHOTS	32.4
	LES BEAUX-MONTS	15.3
	Aux Brulées	
	Les Petits Monts	
	Aux Reignots	
	Clos des Réas	
Nuits Saint-Georges 928 acres	LES SAINT-GEORGES	18.5
(including Prémeaux)	LES CAILLES	9.4
	CLOS DES CORVÉES	18.3
	LES VAUCRAINS	14.8
	LES PRULIERS	17.5
	LES PORRETS	17.3
	CLOS DE THOREY	15.3
	LES BOUDOTS	15.8
	LES CRAS	7.7
	LES MURGERS	12.4
	LES RICHEMONES	5.4
	Les Didiers	6.9

	Perrière	9.9
	Les Perdrix	8.4
	Clos des Argilières	11.4
	Clos des Fôrets	16.6
	Clos Arlot	9.9
	Clos de la Maréchale	23.7
	Clos Saint-Marc	
	Château-Gris	

CÔTE DE BEAUNE

Aloxe-Corton 494 acres (including Ladoix and part of Pernand-Vergelesses)	CORTON BRESSANDES	42.0
	CORTON CLOS DU ROI	26.2
	CORTON	27.9
	CORTON RENARDES	37.1
	CORTON PERRIÈRES	26.9
	CORTON LES MARÉCHAUDES	16.6
	Corton Chaumes	11.1
	Corton Languettes	18.3
	Corton La Vigne-au-Saint	5.7
	Corton Les Meix	4.9
	Corton Les Pougets	24.7
	Corton Les Grèves	12.1
	Corton Les Fiètres	3.2
	Corton Les Paulands	6.7
	Les Chaillots	
	Les Fournieres	
	Les Volozières	

Pernand-Vergelesses 353 acres	*Ile des Vergelesses*	23.0

Savigny Les Beaune 935 acres	Vergelesses	42.0
	Lavières	
	Marconnets	
	Jarrons	
	Dominode	

Beaune 1,329 acres	GRÈVES	78.6
	FÈVES	10.6
	Bressandes	45.7
	Les Cent-Vignes	
	Les Cras	12.4
	Champimonts	41.0
	Marconnets	25.2
	Clos de la Mousse	8.4
	Clos des Mouches	61.5
	Les Avaux	33.1
	Aigrots	55.6
	Clos du Roi	34.3
	Les Toussaints	
	Les Theurons	
	Les Sizies	
	En l'Orme	
	A l'Écu	
	Pertuisots	

Pommard 839 acres	RUGIENS	14.6
	ÉPENOTS	25.7
	Clos Blanc	10.6
	Pézerolles	16.0
	Rugiens-Hauts	18.8
	Petits-Epenots	50.2
	Chaponières	8.2
	Chanlins-Bas	17.5
	Boucherottes	
	Platière	14.3
	Sausilles	9.4
	Jarollières	7.9
	Chanière	
	Charmots	
	Argillières	
	Fremiers	
	Bertins	
	Poutures	
	Arvelets	
	Croix-Noires	
	Clos de la Commaraine	
	Clos Micot	
	La Refene	
	Clos de Verger	
	Combes-Dessus	
Volnay 528 acres	CLOS DES DUCS	6.0
	CAILLERETS	35.6
	CHAMPANS	27.9
	Fremiets	16.1
	Chevret	15.1
	Santenots	19.8
	Les Angles	8.6
	Carelle-sous-la-Chapelle	9.4
	Bousse d'Or	4.9
	Verseuil	2.0
	Clos des Chenes	40.3
	Les Mitans	
	En l'Ormeau	
	Pointes-d'Angles	
	En Ronceret	
	La Barre	
Auxey 103.8 acres	Duresses	
Monthélie 231.0 acres	Les Champs Fulliots	
Chassagne-Montrachet 643.7 acres	*La Boudriotte*	44.2
	Clos St. Jean	35.6
	La Maltroie	
	Morgeot	
Santenay 619.5 acres	*Gravières*	72.6
	La Comme	
	Clos Tavannes	

403

Chambolle Musigny
  (*See* red wines)

Musigny Blanc

Vougeot (*See* red wines)

Clos Blanc de Vougeot

Nuits Saint-Georges
  (*See* red wines)

Perrière

Aloxe-Corton (*See* red wines)
  (including Pernand, Ladoix)

CORTON-CHARLEMAGNE

Corton
Corton Languettes
Corton Pougets

Beaune (*See* red wines)

Clos des Mouches

Auxey (*See* red wines)

Meursault 775.0 acres

PERRIÈRES	30.9
GENEVRIÈRES	34.6
Charmes	68.4
Poruzots	26.4
La Pièce-sous-le-Bois	28.0
Blagny	5.4
Dos d'Ane	20.3
Jennelotte	11.9
Santenots	7.2
Goutte d'Or	13.8
Bouchères	
Petures	
Cras	

Puligny-Montrachet 212.3 acres

MONTRACHET (part)	25.4
CHEVALIER MONTRACHET	17.6
BATARD-MONTRACHET	29.0
BIENVENUE-BATARD-	
MONTRACHET	5.7
COMBETTES	16.6
BLAGNY	10.6
CHALUMEAUX	17.3
FOLATIÈRES	8.4
CLAVOILLON	13.8
Pucelles	16.8
Cailleret	13.3
Champ-Canet	11.4
La Garenne	2.2
Les Referts	32.6
Sous-le-Puits	9.6
Levrons	1.5
Charmes	8.6
Truffière	
Meix	

Chassagne-Montrachet	MONTRACHET (part)	
(*See* red wines)	BATARD-MONTRACHET (part)	
	CRIOTS-BATARD-	
	MONTRACHET	4.0
	RUCHOTTES	7.5
	CAILLERET	15.0
	Morgeot	9.8

Santenay (*See* red wines)

CHABLIS

The vineyards of Chablis have been legally defined and delimited since 1938, and their wines divided into the following categories:

1. CHABLIS GRAND CRU. Only seven small vineyards are entitled to this, the highest ranking appellation; all seven are on the right bank of the Serein River, facing south and southwest, and six of the seven (all except Blanchots, which is in Fyé) are in the *commune* of Chablis proper. All produce wines of the highest class, but an expert might perhaps be disposed to list them in this order: *Vaudésir, Les Clos, Grenouilles, Valmur, Blanchots, Preuses* and *Bougros*. Their wines must be of at least 10½% alcohol by volume, and their production may not exceed an average of 312 gallons per acre. Only the Chardonnay grape may be grown.

2. CHABLIS PREMIER CRU. Wines coming from certain other specific vineyards, and usually carrying the vineyard name, and/or the important words *Premier Cru*. There are twenty-one such vineyards, in nine different townships, or *communes*, including Chablis itself; seven of the twenty-one are on the sunnier right bank of the Serein; all are planted to the Chardonnay grape exclusively, and their maximum legal average production is 354 gallons per acre, of wine with a minimum of 10% alcohol by volume. These, with their *commune* and their situation, are as follows, more or less in order of quality:

Vineyard	Commune	Bank of Serein
Monts de Milieu	Fyé and Fleys	Right
Montée de Tonnerre	Fyé and Fleys	Right
*Chapelot	Fyé and Fleys	Right
Fourneaux	Fleys	Right
*Vaulorent	Poinchy	Right
Vaucoupin	Chichée	Right
*Côte de Fontenay	Fontenay-près-Chablis	Right
Fourchaume	La Chapelle-Vaupelteigne	Right
*Les Fôrets	Chablis	Left
*Butteaux	Chablis	Left
Montmains	Chablis	Left
Vaillons	Chablis	Left
*Sechet	Chablis	Left
*Chatain	Chablis	Left

*Beugnon	Chablis	Left
Mélinots	Chablis	Left
Côte de Léchet	Milly	Left
*Les Lys	Chablis	Left
Beauroy	Poinchy	Left
*Troeme	Beines	Left
Vosgros	Chichée	Left
*Vogiros	Chichée	Left

*No longer an Appellation as of June 1967.

3. CHABLIS. Wines produced on certain delimited areas of chalky soil, from the Chardonnay grape, in twenty specific *communes*. Minimum alcohol, 10%; maximum average yield, 354 gallons. The *communes* are as follows: Chablis, Beines, Béru, Chemilly-sur-Serein, Chichée, Courgis, Fleys, Fontenay, Fyé, La Chapelle-Vaupelteigne, Ligny-le-Châtel, Lignorelles, Maligny, Milly, Poilly, Poinchy, Prehy, Rameau, Villy and Viviers.

4. PETIT CHABLIS. Lesser wines from the same twenty *communes,* also made from the Chardonnay grape. Minimum alcohol, 9½%.

BEAUJOLAIS

There are nine officially-ranked *crus,* or growths, which produce the best wine of the Beaujolais. Listed alphabetically, they are: Brouilly, Chenas, Chiroubles, Côte-de-Brouilly, Fleurie, Julienas, Morgon, Moulin-à-Vent, St. Amour.

Wines from the following thirty-five communes may legally be labelled "Beaujolais-Villages": Arbuissonnas, *Beaujeu,* Blacé, *Cercié, Chanes, La Chapelle-de-Guinchay, Charentay, Chenas, Chiroubles, Durette, Émeringes, Fleurie, Juillé, Julienas, Lancié,* Lantigné, *Leynes,* Montmélas-St. Sorlin, *Odénas,* Le Perréon, Pruzilly, *Quincié, Regnié,* Rivolet, *Romanèche-Thorins, St. Amour-Bellevue, St. Étienne-des-Oullières, St. Étienne-La-Varenne,* St. Julien-en-Montmélas, *St. Lager,* St. Symphorien-d'Ancelles, *St. Verand,* Salles, Vaux-en-Beaujolais, *Villié-Morgon.* The better are those printed in italics.

Maximum legal production of Beaujolais is roughly 540 gallons per acre, of Beaujolais Supérieur or Beaujolais Villages, 480 gallons per acre, of Beaujolais from one of the nine *crus,* 430 gallons per acre.

Total production in a good year like 1966 is in the neighborhood of twenty million gallons, divided more or less as follows:

Appelation	Bottles
Beaujolais	45,000,000
Beaujolais Supérieur	3,600,000
Beaujolais Villages	27,000,000
Brouilly	5,600,000
Chenas	1,100,000
Chiroubles	1,500,000
Côte-de-Brouilly	1,250,000
Fleurie	3,600,000
Julienas	2,500,000
Morgon	3,800,000
Moulin-à-Vent	3,400,000
St. Amour	1,250,000

VINS DÉLIMITÉS DE QUALITÉ SUPÉRIEURE

V.D.Q.S. Wines Listed by District and Type

R = Red   W = White   Ro = Rosé   S = Sparkling   D = Dessert

	Types	*Département*
MIDI		
Corbières	R W Ro	Aude
Corbières du Roussillon	R W Ro	Pyrénées-Orientales
Roussillon dels Aspres	R W Ro	Pyrénées-Orientales
Minervois	R W Ro D	Hérault
Costières du Gard	R W	Gard—Hérault
Coteaux de la Méjanelle	R W	Hérault
Saint-Saturnin	R Ro	Hérault
Montpeyroux	R W Ro	Hérault
Coteaux de Saint-Christol	R Ro	Hérault
Quatourze	R W Ro	Aude
La Clape	R W Ro	Aude
Saint-Drézery	R Ro	Hérault
Saint-Chinian	R Ro	Hérault
Faugères	R W Ro	Hérault
Cabriéres	Ro	Hérault
Coteaux de Vérargues	R Ro	Hérault
Pic-Saint-Loup	R W Ro	Hérault
Saint-Georges-d'Orques	R Ro	Hérault
Picpoul de Pinet	W	Hérault
PROVENCE		
Côtes de Provence	R W Ro	Var—Bouches-du-Rhône
RHONE		
Côtes du Ventoux	R W Ro	Vaucluse
Côtes du Lubéron	R W Ro	Vaucluse
Haut-Comtat	R Ro	Drôme
Chatillon-en-Diois	R W Ro	Drôme
Coteaux d'Aix en-Provence ⎱ Coteaux des Baux ⎰	R W Ro	Bouches-du-Rhône
Coteaux de Pierrevert	R W Ro	Basses-Alpes
LYONNAIS-CENTRE		
Vins du Lyonnais	R W Ro	Rhône
Vins de Renaison ⎱ Côte Roannaise ⎰	R Ro	Loire
Vins d'Auvergne ⎱ Côtes d'Auvergne ⎰	R W Ro	Puy-de-Dôme
LOIRE VALLEY		
Vins de l'Orléanais	R W Ro	Loiret
Mont près Chambord ⎱ Cour-Cheverny ⎰	W	Loir-et-Cher
Saint-Pourçain-sur-Sioule	R W Ro	Allier
Coteaux d'Ancenis	R W Ro	Loire-Atlantique

	Types	*Département*
MIDI		
Gros Plant du Pays Nantais	W	Loire-Atlantique
Côtes de Gien	R W Ro	Loiret; Cher
SAVOIE-BUGEY		
Vin de Savoie ⎫ Roussette de Savoie ⎬	R W Ro	Savoie; Haute-Savoie; Isère
Savoie Mousseux	S	Savoie; Haute-Savoie; Isère
Vins du Bugey ⎫ Roussette du Bugey ⎬	R W Ro	Ain
LORRAINE		
Moselle	R W	Moselle
Côtes de Toul	R W Ro	Meurthe-et-Moselle
SOUTHWEST		
Côtes de Fronton	R W Ro	Haute-Garonne; Tarn-et-Garonne
Côtes de Buzet	R W	Lot-et-Garonne
Côtes du Marmandais	R W	Lot-et-Garonne
Villaudric	R W	Haute-Garonne
Irouléguy	R W Ro	Basses-Pyrénées
Tursan	R W Ro	Landes, Gers
Lavilledieu	R W	Tarn-et-Garonne; Haute-Garonne
Béarn	R W Ro	Basses-Pyrénées; Hautes-Pyrénées; Gers
Cahors	R	Lot

APPENDIX 4

Gattungsnamen: Generic names in Germany

Gattungsname is the German for "generic" name. Under the new German law, however, the meaning of this term, with respect to German wines, has been so broadened as to greatly weaken and almost to destroy much of the sound foundation of German wine nomenclature. It should be stated at once, however, that the changed regulations do not affect, except in the most minor way, estate-bottled *Original-Abfüllung* wines nor even *verbesserte* or sugared wines bottled by their producers.

Briefly, it has always been recognized that certain wine designations, such as *vin rosé* and Sparkling Wine, are generic: they are non-geographical and descriptive. British law now regards Port and Champagne as non-generic, the property respectively of Portugal and France, whereas in the United States these and about a dozen other wine names may be used on the domestic product providing their American origin is clearly and prominently stated on the label.

Most of the major wine producing countries finally agreed, in Madrid and later and more explicitly in Lisbon, to accept and enforce the geographical exclusivity of one anothers' wine names, so that "Champagne" may no longer be produced in Germany, nor "Port" in France, nor "Chablis" or "Cognac" in Spain.

The new German laws have strictly adhered to these international agreements, but have accorded to their own shippers quite astonishing and disturbing liberties as far as German wines are concerned.

All village names, for example, have now become, within certain fixed limits, Gattungsnamen. A wine labeled Piesporter or Rüdesheimer need no longer come from Piesport or Rüdesheim, but from anywhere within nine *airline* miles of the village whose name it carries; the wine must be of "equal quality and value", but of this the shipper is the sole judge. It is therefore quite legal for a shipper to bottle Johannisberger and Rüdesheimer, or Bernkasteler and Zeltinger, out of the same tank.

Much worse, still, is the system of *Gattungslagenamen* (or "generic vineyard names") which has been set up. The use of these is governed by a mass of complex rules which no officialdom will be able to enforce and no consumer to understand. The net result is to reclassify, downgrade and place practically in the public domain, dozens of *Lagenamen* which wine-drinkers have thought applicable only to the wines of a specific given vineyard, so that henceforth they will have hardly any geographical meaning at all.

Certain *Lagen,* or vineyards, will have their names protected as before—those of which the boundaries are set down in the official land register (*Kataster*), and those which have acquired over the years a traditional or historic meaning (*Volkmundslagen*). But no indication of all this need appear on the label: the consumer must be his own policeman and his own guide.

Below is a partial list of what are now *Gattungslagen*. Unless estate-bottled, their wines need not come from the vineyard whose name they bear:

Saar

Niedermenniger Euchariusberg
Oberemmeler Scharzberg
Saarburger Schlossberg
Scharzberger
Wiltinger Scharzberg

Mosel

Bernkasteler Braunes
Graacher Braunes
Graacher Münzlay
Niederemmeler Michelsberg
Piesporter Michelsberg
Wehlener Münzlay
Wehlener Bickert
Uerziger Schwarzlay
Zeltinger Schwarzlay

Rheinhessen

Alsheimer Goldberg
Binger Rosengarten
Bodenheimer Hohberg
Dienheimer Goldberg
Nackenheimer Fritzenhöll
Niersteiner Fritzenhöll
Niersteiner Schnappenberg
Oppenheimer Goldberg
Oppenheimer Kröttenbrunnen

Rheingau

Eltviller Sandgrub

Eltviller Pellet
Eltviller Steinmächer
Eltviller Wagenkehr
Erbacher Pellet
Erbacher Kiesling
Geisenheimer Steinacker
Hallgartener Deutelsberg
Hallgartener Mehrhölchen
Hochheimer Daubhaus
Johannisberger Erntebringer
Kiedricher Sandgrub
Oestricher Deez
Rauenthaler Steinmächer
Rüdesheimer Häuserweg
Rüdesheimer Kiesel
Winkeler Erntebringer
Winkeler Oberberg

Rheinpfalz

Deidesheimer Grundpfad
Deidesheimer Neuberg
Deidesheimer Hofstück
Dürkheimer Feuerberg
Dürkheimer Spielberg
Dürkheimer Michelsberg
Forster Altenburg
Forster Hahnenböhl
Forster Langenböhl
Ruppertsberger Hofstück
Ruppertsberger Mühlweg
Wachenheimer Altenburg
Wachenheimer Neuberg

THE LEADING VINEYARDS OF GERMANY

VILLAGE	Best Known Vineyards in Each Village (Ranked approximately in this order)	VILLAGE	Best Known Vineyards In Each Village (Ranked approximately in this order)

(G)—*Gattungslage*— See page 409

MOSELLE

VILLAGE	Best Known Vineyards in Each Village	VILLAGE	Best Known Vineyards In Each Village
Trittenheim (225 acres)	Laurentiusberg Apotheke Altärchen Clemensberg Sonnenberg Olk Falkenberg Neuberg Sonnteil Weierbach	Kesten (100 acres)	Paulinshofberg
		Brauneberg (100 acres)	Juffer Falkenberg Hasenlaufer Kammer Sonnenuhr Lay
Neumagen (170 acres)	Rosengärtchen Leienberg Engelgrube Laudemusberg Kirchenstück Thierbach	Veldenz (100 acres)	Kirchberg
		Lieser (240 acres)	Niederberg Schlossberg
Dhron (180 acres)	Dhronhofberg Roterde Grosswingert Kandel Sangerei Hengelberg	Bernkastel (450 acres)	Doktor (or Doktor und Graben) Lay Badstube Schlossberg Pfalzgraben Rosenberg Schwanen Theurenkauf Steinkaul Bratenhöfchen Held Altenwald Pfaffenberg Kueser Weissenstein Kueser Kardinalsberg Braunes (G)
Piesport (120 acres)	Goldtröpfchen Treppchen Lay Taubengarten Güntherslay Gräfenberg Falkenberg Pichter Wehr Hohlweid Schubertslay Bildchen Michelsberg (G)		
		Graach (240 acres)	Josefshof Himmelreich Domprobst Stablay Abtsberg Goldwingert Lilienpfad Mönch Homberg Heiligenhaus Braunes (G) Münzlay (G)
Minheim (100 acres)	Rosenberg		
Wintrich (200 acres)	Ohligsberg Geyerslay Sonneseite Neuberg Grosser Herrgott Rosenberg Paulinshofberg		

(G)—*Gattungslage*— See page 409

MOSELLE (Cont'd.)

Wehlen (240 acres)	Sonnenuhr Nonnenberg Lay Rosenberg Klosterlay Abtei Feinter Wertspitz Bickert (G) Münzlay (G)	Traben-Trarbach (400 acres) Enkirch (320 acres)	Schlossberg Ungsberg Huhnersberg Königsberg Steffensberg Battereiberg Herrenberg Montenubel
Zeltingen (470 acres)	Schlossberg Sonnenuhr (or Sonnuhr) Himmelreich Rotlay Steinmauer Kirchenpfad Stephanslay Schwarzlay (G)	**•SAAR** Filzen (60 acres) Wawern (70 acres)	 Pulchen Urbelt Vogelberg Karlberg Herrenberg Goldberg
Erden (200 acres)	Treppchen Prälat Busslay Hödlay Herrenberg Kaufmannsberg Filiusberg Herzlay Kranklay	Kanzem (or Canzem) (100 acres)	Sonnenberg Berg Altenberg Wolfsberg Unterberg Horecker Kelterhaus
Uerzig (110 acres)	Würzgarten Lay Kranklay Schwarzlay (G)	Wiltingen (330 acres)	Scharzhofberg (or Wiltinger Scharzhofberg) Braune Kupp Gottesfüss
Kinheim (200 acres)	Hubertuslay Löwenberg Rosenberg		Rosenberg Klosterberg Braunfels Dohr
Cröv (or Kröv) (260 acres)	Niederberg Heislay Stephansberg Petersberg		Kupp Scharzberg (G)

(G)—Gattungslage — See page 409

SAAR (Cont'd.)

VILLAGE	Best Known Vineyards	VILLAGE	Best Known Vineyards
Oberemmel (200 acres)	Hütte Rosenberg Altenberg Agritiusberg Karlsberg Raul Eltzerberg Jesuittengarten Falkenstein Scharzberg (G)	Eitelsbach (75 acres)	Karthäuserhofberger Kronenberg Karthäuserhofberger Sang Karthäuserhofberger Burgberg Marienholz
Niedermennig (90 acres)	Sonnenberg Euchariusberg Herrenberg Zuckerberg	Kasel (or Casel) (240 acres)	Niesgen Taubenberg Steiniger Kohlenberg Kernagel Hitzlay Herrenberg Höcht
Ayl (110 acres)	Kupp Herrenberg Neuberg	Waldrach	Schloss Marienlay
Ockfen (200 acres)	Bockstein Geisberg Herrenberg Heppenstein Oberherrenburg	Avelsbach (120 acres)	Herrenberg Hammerstein Altenberg Rotlei

•RHEINGAU

Saarburg (100 acres)	Leyenkaul Mühlberg Rausch Schlossberg (G)	Hochheim (465 acres)	Domdechaney Kirchenstück Rauchloch Stein Hölle Daubhaus Raaber Stielweg Sommerheil Neuberg Wiener Gehitz Steinern Kreuz Beine Königen-Viktoria-Berg Hofmeister
Serrig	Heiligenborn Hindenburgslei Würzberg Marienberg Wingertscheck Kupp Schloss Saarfels		

•RUWER

Maximin Grünhaus (120 acres)	Herrenberg Bruderberg	Martinsthal (173 acres)	Langenberg Pfaffenberg Heiligenstock Geisberg Steinberg Wildsau

(G)—Gattungslage— See page 409

VILLAGE	Best Known Vineyards In Each Village (Ranked approximately in this order)	VILLAGE	Best Known Vineyards In Each Village (Ranked approximately in this order)
RHEINGAU (Cont'd.)			
Walluf (87 acres)	Walkenberg Unterberg Mittelberg Bildstock Steinritz Röderweg	Kiedrich (320 acres)	Gräfenberg Wasserrose Sandgrub Turmberg Heiligenstock Weihersberg Dippenerd Berg
Eltville (465 acres)	Sonnenberg Langenstück Klumbchen Mönchhanach Kalbspflicht Taubenberg Grauer Stein Sandgrub Weidenborn Freienborn Steinmacher Schlossberg Hahn Posten Albus Altebach Grimmen Setzling	Erbach (320 acres)	Markobrunn Siegelsberg Steinmorgen Brühl Honigberg Hohenrain Seelgass Rheinhell Michelmark Kahlig Brachhell Steinchen Hinterkirch Gemark Herrenberg Langenwingert Pellet Wormloch
Rauenthal (283 acres)	Baiken Gehrn Wülfen Rothenberg Herberg Wieshell Burggraben Maasborn Hilpitzberg Pfaffenberg Steinhaufen Siebenmorgen Langenstück Nonnenberg Kesselring Huhnerberg	Hattenheim (475 acres)	Steinberg Markobrunn Wisselbrunnen Engelmannsberg Hassel Willborn Hinterhausen Weiher Boden Pflänzer Gasserweg Stabel Kilb Dillmetz Klosterberg Bergweg Pfaffenberg Bitz Schützenhäuschen Boxberg Aliment Geiersberg Rothenberg

(G)—Gattungslage — See page 409

RHEINGAU (Cont'd.)

VILLAGE	Best Known Vineyards	VILLAGE	Best Known Vineyards
Oestrich (750 acres)	Lenchen Doosberg Deez Klostergarten Eiserberg Pfaffenberg Hölle Räucherberg Kerbesberg Klosterberg Magdalenengarten Rosengarten	Johannisberg (200 acres)	Schloss Johannisberg Schlossberg Klaus Sterzelpfad Kläuserpfad Hölle Kochsberg Kerzenstück Kahlenberg Hansenberg Vogelsang Weiher Mittelhölle Nonnhölle Unterhölle Steinhölle Goldatzel Schwarzenstein Erntebringer
Mittelheim (310 acres)	Oberberg Edelmann Neuberg Honigberg Stein Gottesthal Goldberg St. Nikolaus		
Hallgarten (370 acres)	Schönhell Mehrhölzchen Deutelsberg Hendelberg Rosengarten Würzgarten Jungfer Kirschenacker Deez	Geisenheim (485 acres)	Rothenberg Mäuerchen Katzenloch Lickerstein Kläuserweg Fuchsberg Fegfeuer Marienberg Mönchspfad Morschberg Altbaum Rosengarten Decker Hinkelstein Kreuzweg Kosakenberg Kirchgrube Kilsberg
Winkel (350 acres)	Schloss Vollrads Hasensprung Jesuitengarten Kläuserweg Honigberg Dachsberg Bienengarten Ansbach Klaus Oberberg		

(G)—Gattungslage — See page 409

RHEINGAU (Cont'd.)

VILLAGE	Best Known Vineyards	VILLAGE	Best Known Vineyards
Rüdesheim (650 acres)	Berg Rottland	Nackenheim (240 acres)	Rothenberg
	Berg Bronnen		Engelsberg
	Berg Roseneck		Stiel
	Berg Hellpfad		Fenchelberg
	Berg Lay		Rheinhahl
	Berg Schlossberg		Kapelle
	Berg Mühlstein		Spitzenberg
	Berg Zollhaus		Fritzenhöll (G)
	Bischofsberg		
	Klosterkiesel	Nierstein (1340 acres)	Rehbach
	Berg Burgweg		Auflangen
	Berg Stumpfenort		Hipping
	Berg Paares		Flächenhahl
	Hinterhaus		Glöck
	Berg Platz		Kehr
	Berg Dickerstein		Orbel
	Berg Kronest		Kranzberg
	Engerweg		Floss
	Wilgert		Streng
	Hasenlaufer		Pettental
	Berg Stoll		Oelberg
	Berg Eiseninger		Heiligenbaum
	Berg Ramstein		Brudersberg
	Berg Katerloch		Fuchsloch
	Linngrub		Gutes Domtal
	Häuserweg		Rohr
			Spiegelberg
Assmannshausen (180 acres)	Höllenberg		Hölle
	Hinterkirch		Kiliansberg
	Frankenthal		Fockenberg
			Schnappenberg (G)
Lorch (720 acres)	Pfaffenweis		
	Bodenthal	Oppenheim (450 acres)	Kreuz
	Krone		Sackträger
			Herrenberg
•HESSIA			Steig
			Reisekahr
Bodenheim (650 acres)	Hoch		Zuckerberg
	Kahlenberg		Daubhaus
	St. Alban		Schlossberg
	Silberberg		Herrenweiher
	Braunloch		Kehrweg
	Leidhecke		Goldberg (G)
	Westrum		Kröttenbrunnen (G)
	Kapelle		
	Bock		
	Sandkaut		
	Burgweg		
	Ebersberg		
	Mönchpfad		
	Rettberg		

(G)—Gattungslage — See page 409

VILLAGE	Best Known Vineyards In Each Village (Ranked approximately in this order)	VILLAGE	Best Known Vineyards In Each Village (Ranked approximately in this order)
HESSIA (Cont'd.)		Niederhäus	Hermannshöhle
			Hermannsberg
Dienheim	Guldenmorgen		Pfingstweide
(925 acres)	Kröttenbrunnen		Steyer
	Tafelstein		Rosenheck
	Rosswiese		Rossel
	Siliusbrunnen		Klamm
	Goldberg (G)		
		Norheim	Kafels
Bingen	Büdesheimer Scharlach-		Kirschheck
(720 acres)	berg		Götzenfels
	Büdesheimer Häusling		Hinterfels
	Büdesheimer Stein-		Dellchen
	kautsweg		
	Büdesheimer Schnack-	Roxheim	Huttenberg
	enberg		Hollenpfad
	Ohligberg		Birkenberg
	Mainzerweg		Muhlenberg
	Schlossberg		Neuenberg
	Eiselberg		
	Schwätzerchen	Rudesheim	Rosengarten
	Rochusberg		
	Kempter Rheinberg	Schloss	Kupfergrube
	Kempter Pfarrgarten	Böckelheimer	Kupferberg
	Kempter Kirchberg		Königsfels
	Rosengarten (G)		Königsberg
			In dem Felsen
•NAHE			Mühlberg
			Felsenberg
Bretzenheim	Vogelsang		Heimberg
	Schützenhöll		
		Winzerheim	Berg
Kreuznach	Hinkelstein		Rosenheck
	Kröttenpfuhl		Honigberg
	Kahlenberg		Schild
	Narrenkappe		
	Forst		
	Monchberg		
	Steinweg		
	St. Martin		
	Kronenberg		
	Mühlenberg		
	Brücken		
	Mollenbrunnen		
	Osterhölle		
	Brückes-treppchen		
Monzing	Gabelstück		
Münster	Pittersberg		
	Dautenpflänzer		
	Langenberg		

(G)—*Gattungslage*— See page 409

VILLAGE	Best Known Vineyards	VILLAGE	Best Known Vineyards
•PALATINATE (RHEINPFALZ)		Forst (495 acres)	Kirchenstück
Freinsheim (590 acres)	Gottesacker		Jesuitengarten
	Satzen		Ungeheuer
	Gross		Ziegler
	Oschelkopf		Kranich
			Freundstück
Kallstadt (720 acres)	Kobnert		Langenmorgen
	Kreuz		Langenacker
	Steinacker		Pechstein
	Nill		Mühlweg
	Kroenberg		Elster
	Annaberg		Hellholz
	Saumagen		Fleckinger
	Hort		Trift
			Walshöhle
Ungstein (650 acres)	Spielberg		Sechsmorgen
	Michelsberg		Gerling
	Herrenberg		Musenhang
	Roterd		Alser
			Pfeiffer
Bad Dürkheim (1900 acres)	Hochbenn		Boländer
	Schenkenböhl		Langenböhl (G)
	Fuchsmantel		Altenburg (G)
	Feuerberg (G)		Hahenböhl (G)
	Michelsberg (G)	Diedesheim (960 acres)	Hohenmorgen
	Spielberg (G)		Grainhübel
Wachenheim (840 acres)	Gerümpel		Kieselberg
	Goldbächel		Kränzler
	Böhlig		Leinhöhle
	Wolfsdarm		Rennpfad
	Bächel		Geheu
	Luginsland		Kalkofen
	Rechbächel		Grain
	Langebächel		Reiss
	Hägel		Mühle
	Dreispitz		Dopp
	Schenkenböhl		Herrgottsacker
	Altenburg (G)		Langenmorgen
			Forster Strasse
			Mäushöhle
			Hahenböhl
			Fleckinger
			Weinbach
			Hofstück (G)

(G)—Gattungslage— See page 409

VILLAGE	Best Known Vineyards In Each Village (Ranked approximately in this order)	VILLAGE	Best Known Vineyards In Each Village (Ranked approximately in this order)
PALATINATE *(Cont'd.)*			
Ruppertsberg (420 acres)	Gaisböhl Spiess Kreuz Nussbien Reiterpfad Hoheburg Foldschmied Achtmorgen Mandelacker Weisslich Kieselberg Linsenbusch Grund Hofstück (G)	Nordheim (310 acres)	Vögelein
		Randersacker (390 acres)	Pfülben Hohbug Teufelskeller Spielberg Marsberg
		Roedelsee (120 acres)	Kuchenmeister Schwanleite Schlossberg
Königsbach (325 acres)	Idig Satz Rolandsberg Harle Reiterpfad Bender Oelberg Weissmauer	Schloss Saaleck	Schlossberg
		Sommerach (170 acres)	Katzenkopf
		Veitshoechheim (115 acres)	Neuberg Abtsberg Fachtel Wölflein
•*FRANCONIA*		Volkach (85 acres)	Ratsherr
Castell (40 acres)	Schlossberg	Wuerzburg (520 acres)	Stein Aussere Leiste Innere Leiste Neuberg Abstleite Harfe Ständerbühl Schlaksberg Steinmantel
Escherndorf (195 acres)	Lump Eulengrube Hengstberg Kirchberg		
Frickenhausen (120 acres)	Kapellenberg	•*MITTEL-RHEIN*	
Homburg (40 acres)	Kallmuth		Oberdiebacher Fürstenberg Bacharacher Posten Cauber Blucherthal Bacharacher Wolfshohle Cauber Pfalzgrafenstein Steeger St. Jost Cauber Backofen Steeger Flur Steeger Mühlberg Oberweseler Oelsberg Oberweseler Rheinhell Bopparder Hamm
Hoerstein (60 acres)	Riesling-vom- Reuschberg		
Iphofen (310 acres)	Julius-Echter-Berg Kronsberg Kammer Burgweg Kalb		

(G)—Gattungslage — See page 409

APPENDIX 5

ITALIAN WINES

Since 1962 the Italian Government has embarked on a major and long-term program destined to bring under strict control all of the better and better known wines of Italy. These will eventually carry on their labels the words *Denominazione Controllata,* an equivalent of the *Appellation Controlée* of France, and be subject to no less rigorous supervision as far as their production, their authorized grape varieties and their authenticity are concerned. This is of course an immensely complicated, wholly praiseworthy, perhaps even too ambitious task. Yet considerable progress has already been made, a number of the implementing decrees have been issued, and labels are already beginning to carry (usually in green) the specific official designations.

Below is the list of such wines as proposed to the Common Market authorities. The list seems if anything almost too complete, and includes many wines never likely to be exported or even to be readily found outside of their limited production zone. Those of real importance will be found listed, either in their alphabetical place, or under the name of their region of origin (as Piedmont, Lombardy, Tuscany, etc.) or under that of the grape from which they are made (as Nebbiolo, Merlot, Moscato) in the alphabetical section of the Encyclopedia which precedes this Appendix. The list is that published by the *Office International de la Vigne et du Vin.*

PIEDMONT

Barolo
Barbera d'Asti
Barbaresco
Freisa di Chieri e d'Asti
Gattinara
Grignolino d'Asti

Brachetto d'Asti
Cortese dell' Alto Monferrato
Dolcetto delle Langhe e d'Ovada
Moscato d'Asti
Caluso Passito
Nebbiolo Piemontese

LIGURIA

Cinque terre
Coronata

Vermentino Ligure
Dolceacqua

LOMBARDY

Freccia Rossa di Casteggio
Moscato di Casteggio
Valtellina:
  a) Grumello
  b) Inferno
  c) Sassella
  d) Valgella
Lugana
Vini delGarda
Bianco Cortese dell'Oltrepo pavese
Barbera dell'Oltrepo pavese

Clastidium bianco di Casteggio
Clastidium rosso di Casteggio
Clastidium rosato di Casteggio
Riserva Oltrepo pavese rosso
Prosecco bianco dell'Oltrepo pavese
Sangue di Giuda rosso dell'Oltrepo pavese
Buttafuoco rosso dell'Oltre po pavese
Clastidium bianco Riserva di Casteggio
Oltrepo pavese
Riesling dell'Oltrepo pavese
Barbacarlo dell'Oltrepo pavese

420

ITALIAN WINES (Continued)

TRENTINO-ALTO ADIGE

Caldaro
Appiano
Termeno
Lago di Caldaro
Lagarino rosato
Santa Maddalena
Terlano
Meranese di Collina

Moscato Atesino
Termento aromatico
Colli Trentini
Marzemino trentino
Teroldego
Val d'Adige
Lagarino Rosato

VENETO

Soave
Bardolino
Valpolicella
Valpantena
Recioto Veronese
Bianco di Gambellara
Bianco e Rosso di Breganze
Bianco e Rosso dei Colli Berici

Bianco e Rosso dei Colli Euganei
Moscato di Arqua
Vino Veronese
Prosecco dei Colli Trevigiani
Colli Trevigiani
Merlot delle Venezie
Rosso dei Colli Veronesi

EMILIA-ROMAGNA

Lambrusco di Sorbara
Sangiovese di Romagna

Albana di Romagna

FRIULI-VENEZIA GIULIA

Bianco e rosso dei Colli Friulani
Bianco e rosso dei Colli Goriziani

TUSCANY

Chianti
Chianti classico
Chianti Colli Aretini
Chianti Colli Fiorentini
Chianti Colli Senesi
Chianti Colline Pisane
Chianti Montalbano
Chianti Rufina

Brunello di Montalcino
Vernaccia di San Gemignano
Monte-Carlo, bianco e rosso
Moscatello di Montalcino
Vin Santo toscano
Bianco dell'Elba
Aleatico di Porto Ferraio
Vin nobile di Montepulciano

MARCHE

Verdicchio dei Castelli di Jesi

Rosso Piceno

ITALIAN WINES (Continued)

UMBRIA

Orvieto

LAZIO

Vini dei Castelli Romani:
  a) Colli Albani
  b) Colli Lanuvini
  c) Colonna
  d) Frascati
  e) Marino
  f) Montecompatri
  g) Velletri

Est, est, est di Montefiascone
Cesanese del Piglio
Moscato di Terracina
Malvasia di Grottaferrata o Grottoferrata
Aleatico viterbese

ABRUZZI E MOLISE

Trebbiano di Abruzzo
Montepulciano di Abruzzo

Cerasuolo di Abruzzo

CAMPANIA

Capri
Lacrima Christi del Vesuvio
Gragnano
Falerno
Greco di Tufo
Fiano di Avellino

Ravello
Vesuvio
Conca
Taurasi
Solopaca

PUGLIE

Sansevero
Torre Giulia di Cerignola
Santo Stefano di Cerignola
Aleatico di Puglia
Moscato del Salento o Salento
Castel del Monte
Castel Acquaro
Malvasia di Brindisi

Primitivo di Manduria
Primitivo del Tarantino
Martinafranca
Squinzano
Barletta
Locorotondo
Moscato di Trani

BASILATA

Aglianico del Vulture
Malvasia di Lucania

Moscato di Lucania

ITALIAN WINES (Continued)

CALABRIA

Savuto
Ciro di Calabria
Greco di Gerace

Lagrima di Castrovillari
Moscato di Cosenza

SICILY

Corvo di Casteldaccia
Lo Zucco secco
Moscato Lo Zucco
Etna
Faro
Eloro
Mamertino

Frappato di Vittoria
Moscato di Noto
Moscato di Siracusa
Moscato di Pantelleria
Malvasia di Lipari
Bianco di Alcamo

SARDINIA

Giro di Sardegna
Monica de Sardegna
Nasco
Moscato del Campidano
Moscato di Tempio

Malvasia di Bosa
Vernaccia
Nuragus
Vermentino di Gallura
Oliena

APPENDIX 6

GENERAL

VINTAGE YEARS

I. CALIFORNIA

Superior wines, in California, vary in quality from one year to another, just as they do, to some degree, in all wine-producing lands. These differences, however, rarely follow any general and recognizable pattern, and are often the result of special, local conditions, and even sometimes due to the personal decisions of vineyard owners, such as when to start picking, which varieties to pick first, etc. Surprisingly enough (although *see* the table of vineyard temperatures on Page 355) grapes ripen somewhat later in the good wine districts of California than in France, have less sugar as well as less acid, and yield, from the same grape varieties, wines somewhat lower in alcohol. The average production per acre of such grapes is not far from the French and German average, although more consistent, so that there are, on the whole, fewer extremely bountiful harvests and fewer crop failures. In quality, too, the variations are less marked; a protracted period of humid or rainy weather in August or September is almost unheard of in California; no less so are those rare, exceptional summers with just enough rainfall and just enough sun to give the greatest wines of Burgundy, Bordeaux and the Rhineland.

It is primarily for this reason that many of the best wines of California never carry a vintage. It would be quite impossible to turn out anything reasonably accurate in the way of a California vintage chart. This fact has long been recognized by the best and most honorable California vintners. They market their Cabernets, Pinots, Rieslings and the rest, of succeeding vintages, at the same price, although they often hold back their finer lots of each year for later sale under some such designation as "Reserve."

In general, among California wines that carry a vintage, the youngest *vins rosés* are almost always to be preferred, and the same thing is almost true of white wines, which are not usually offered for sale until they are ready to drink, and are rarely as good when they are over three years old (with five years as an extreme limit) as they were before. They can be laid away as curiosities, but little is to be gained by keeping them, as wines.

With the one, notable exception of Cabernet Sauvignons, California red wines tend to follow the same pattern. Almost all of them are better, if properly stored, after a year or two; some Pinot Noirs after three years or four. The best Cabernets may and probably will improve for a decade or more, and remain good for another decade. This of course only holds true if cellar conditions are everything they should be.

Basically, a vintage on a bottle of California wine is in no sense an indication of quality, but merely a statement of age.

425

II. FRANCE

Ratings, 1 to 20, are based on the relative value and quality of the wines today, not on what they were when originally produced or first marketed. 18–20 = Very Great. 16–17 = Great. 15 = Very Good. 14 = Good. 12–13 = Fair. 11 = Poor. 10 and under = Very Poor. Where no ratings are given, the wines are either too old to be interesting or no longer on the market today.

RED BORDEAUX

1967. About once every decade, but now twice already in the Nineteen-Sixties, Bordeaux has the *gentillesse* to come up with a pair of vintage twins — very good or great years, back to back. Usually, in such cases, the first year gives the fuller bodied wine — some say because the vines are fatigued after a big vintage — and the second year's Clarets are lighter and shorter-lived, though possibly outstanding for their elegance and charm. 1952-53 followed this pattern, so did 1928-29 before the War, so, more recently, did '61-'62 (see below), and now we have 1966 and 1967.

With a few illustrious exceptions such as Château Mouton-Rothschild, the red Bordeaux of 1967 can hardly be called great, but there is no questioning the fact that they are very good. The crop was a large one, especially in the Médoc, and the wines are soft (the French might call them "tender"), early-maturing, very agreeable, without much staying power. The St. Emilions on the whole are somewhat better. Across the board, about 15/20.

1966 looks better and better with each passing month, and most of. us are having to revise upwards our already favorable opinions of its quality. The wines lack, perhaps, the power and authority of the '64s and '61s, but they make up in balance what they lack in weight, and almost without exception they are immensely pleasing. The regional wines and the lesser chateaux, surprisingly, are about ready to drink, less rough, less harsh, better-mannered and finer than the '64s, the most attractive such wines to reach the market in many a year. The great chateau-bottlings came forward last Fall; they may not last forever but are certainly good for the next ten years; they all have unusual bouquet, distinction and class and some may well prove extraordinary. Highly recommended, 18/20.

1965. One of the most dismal failures of the past decade. Many of the better chateaux bottled only a small fraction of their crop and the average level of quality is well below even that of 1963. 8/20.

1964. A great but extremely uneven year with some admirable high spots and some disappointing lows. Rain arrived during the picking season and those who had not finished their harvest were badly hurt. This was especially the case in the Médoc, where the wines range all the way from 13/20 to 18/20. St. Emilion was luckier, 17/20. Most of the wines are maturing very slowly, are still harsh, need time in bottle, will almost certainly end well. As a fair average, deserves 16/20 or a shade more.

1963. Disastrous in St. Emilion and Pomerol. Generally poor in the Médoc, although a few chateaux produced light, early-maturing, very agreeable Clarets. These are perfect for present consumption, and good values, if cheap. 11/20.

426

1962. Surprisingly (for the weather was miserable until late June), this proved to be both a copious year and an extremely good one, somewhat on the order of 1955. The wines on the whole are fruity, attractive, soft, with fine bouquet, readier and presently more agreeable than the 1961s. Undoubtedly they will improve further, but they are the best Clarets now generally available, perfect of their type, and good values. 16/20.

1961. This was an exceedingly great vintage in Bordeaux, one of the best of this century. The crop was a small one; the wines were expensive from the start and will get more so, but their quality can only be described as superb, unequalled since 1945. They are *just beginning* to be ready to drink and they may well outlast many of us, who are now their most fervent admirers. 20/20.

1960. Overshadowed, as was inevitable, by the highly publicized 1959s and the astonishing 1961s, the 1960s were well-balanced and agreeable Clarets from the very beginning and have always deserved more praise than they received. Those who appreciate the finesse and elegance of not-too-heavy red Bordeaux will find them admirable and surprisingly inexpensive. They should be drunk and enjoyed, not laid away. 14/20.

1959. A very great year, though hardly the "Year of the Century," as it was called. The wines, from the lesser ones to the best, had an immense early charm, and all too many of them were drunk before they had reached their peak, which, in a great many cases, is now. The better chateau-bottlings will continue to delight us for at least five or six years, the very finest have at least a decade or two to go, are extremely expensive, worth whatever price you pay for them. 16/20 to 19/20.

As far as older Clarets are concerned, here is the briefest sort of summary, applicable only to well-stored wines:

1958: Starting downhill. 1957: Hard, unprepossessing, may still come round. 1956: Gone, and no great loss. 1955: The best wines still wholly remarkable. A good gamble today but not much future. 1954: Too old, now best forgotten. 1953: When good, superb; a little risky. 1952: Has done less well than expected; dangerous. 1949: Holding well but often disappointing. 1947: For the moment, not what it should be; may and should recover. 1945: Extremely great when good.

Even older great vintages include '37, '34, '29, '28, '24, '21. Here there is so much variation from one bottle to the next that no intelligent evaluation is possible. It should be kept in mind that bottles of Claret over twenty years old are often recorked, and such recorking is usually an assurance of superior quality rather than the reverse.

WHITE BORDEAUX

1967. Thirty years ago, or a hundred and thirty years ago for that matter, Château d'Yquem sold for twice as much as Château Lafite on the Bordeaux market, or in London or in New York, and as it should today if actual cost of production were any criterion. But sweeter white wines are out of fashion these days, the Sauternes and all their fellow countrymen; the first growth Clarets bring twice the price of Yquem, the dryest possible white wines are all the vogue, and even the dry Graves are dryer; some producers have gone so far as to plant Cabernet grapes in Barsac and are attempting to make red wine, and even incorruptible Yquem has come out with a semi-dry white wine called "Château Y."

White Bordeaux is therefore, more than ever, a category of wines which deserves two vintage charts, not one. The weather which gives the great Sauternes (surely among the greatest white wines of the world, however rarely one may drink them) is not by any means always the weather that yields the best dry Graves, or the increasingly large number of white Bordeaux made in the same dry pattern. More and more dry white Bordeaux are made exclusively or mostly from the Sauvignon Blanc grape, and some carry the varietal name on their labels; they are not made from over-ripe grapes attacked by the *pourriture noble,* or "noble mould," as are all true Sauternes, and they taste more like the wines of Sancerre or Pouilly-Fumé than like the old-fashioned, golden, often over-sulphured, semi-dry Graves.

1967 was the first year since 1962 to produce outstanding wines in Sauternes, deserving perhaps 17/20, though it is a little early to judge, since the better ones will hardly be on the market before 1970. The dry wines, including Graves, are also very good, sprightly and fresh, perhaps 16/20.

1966. A very great vintage almost everywhere in Europe except, unfortunately, Sauternes, Barsac & Co., where 13/20 is almost too generous. Dry wines much better, though maybe not quite up to the '67s, full-bodied, well-balanced, will improve, say 15/20.

1965. Barely acceptable in a few dry wines. Poor. Under 10/20. Some sweet wines, if late harvested, better.

1964. Good but a bit heavy in the dryer wines. 14/20. Sweet wines disappointing, almost no *pourriture noble,* 12/20.

1963. Better than 1965. A few dry wines of considerable breed, finesse. 14/20. No good sweet wines, 10/20.

1962. A great year. Sauternes of truly *grande classe,* elegant, not too heavy, still extraordinarily inexpensive. 18/20. Most of the dry wines are growing old but they still rate 15/20.

1961. A very great vintage in Sauternes and Barsac, superb wines which will continue to improve for another decade at least, 19/20. Some rare dry wines still holding, 15/20.

1960. Now best forgotten. 10/20, perhaps.

1959. A great, classic year in Sauternes, and a great rarity today deserving at least 19/20. Never as good in dry wines and now to be avoided. 11/20.

Older white Bordeaux are only interesting in the rather restricted sector of Sauternes. 1953, '49, '45, '37, '29, '28, '21 were all superior. Graves older than the '61 are poor risks.

RED BURGUNDY

1967. For the space of nearly two decades, ending in 1962, those who follow vintage charts as others do the pennant races or the Dow-Jones averages found themselves faced with a series of phenomena as mysterious in their way as flying saucers. All of the odd-numbered years turned out to be great vintage years in red Burgundy; all of the even numbered, at best, were only fair, or poor. There seemed to be just enough exceptions (1951 and '52) to prove the game was honest, as a gambler might say. The more superstitious among us were delighted. Here, at last, was a sure thing. The sequence started in 1943 (that "best of the best forgotten" years of the German occupation) and continued on its merry way through 1945, 1947 and 1949. 1951-52 provided a break, but then the sequence got under way again, with '53, '55, '57, '59 (the first of the so-called "Vintages of the Century"), and then, in a final burst of glory, 1961. By then the "odds" were firmly in the saddle, and the "evens" could only boast, rather timidly, of 1952.

It is amusing to recall that a somewhat similar "run" of great years took place in Vintage Port some sixty years ago. On this occasion only leap years were involved (or American Presidential Election years if you prefer) and the sequence lasted from 1896 to 1912 or 1920.

Both eventually stopped, as such things do, even in Las Vegas and Monte Carlo. Since 1961, the "odds" in red Burgundy have given us only the dismal '63s, the cheerless '65s and, I am sorry to have to report, the better-but-not-much better wines of 1967.

Excellent in Beaujolais, very good on the Côtes-du-Rhône, good to remarkable in white Burgundy, 1967 was simply not red Burgundy's year. The Côte-de-Nuits are better than the Côte-de-Beaunes, and there are superior cuvées of both, but the September rains in 1967 came too soon and lasted too long for great wines to be anything but rare exceptions. Reluctantly, then, 13/20.

1966.   A wholly remarkable year. From the very beginning the wines had a special character and charm, an early sprightliness and fragrance and fruit which set them apart; in the past twelve months their development has surpassed our highest expectations — they are now more attractive and possibly even better than the '64s and are definitely headed for great things. They were all bottled in 1968, and the lighter ones are ready to drink six months or a year later, yet even these should have a life expectancy of seven or eight years. Perfect wines for the early 1970s. At least 18/20.

1965.   Just plain no good. Well under 10/20.

1964   was a very great vintage indeed, but its big sturdy wines have matured more slowly than was expected, and almost all of them will benefit greatly from another year or two or more in bottle. Laid away, they should prove worthy successors to the incomparable 1961s, even though the impatient French seem determined to drink them up immediately. 17/20.

1963.   Cross it off your list. With a few exceptions, under 10/20.

1962.   A vintage which has never received its just due of recognition. It appeared on the heels of 1961, its spectacularly excellent older brother; its weather was cold and rainy and utterly discouraging until the end of June; the vintners never expected very much of it and were pleased to find it good; few realized that it was not only good but great. Remember 1955? After a modest, unpublicized start, it began to make its way, and was finally acclaimed as perhaps the best year of its decade in Bordeaux, Champagne and Burgundy. The '62 red Burgundies are following the same path; they are unquestionably the best wines available for present drinking. 17/20.

1961. An exceedingly great year, perhaps the best in average quality since' World War II. The wines are firm, but so remarkably well-balanced that they never appear heavy; they have been slow to mature and they will obviously be long-lived. The crop was a very small one and the wines are expensive and increasingly hard to find, but it is difficult to see how they could be better. 19/20, and perhaps deserves the ultimate accolade of 20/20.

1960. Mediocre. No longer of any interest. Charitably, 10/20.

1959. This year was immediately christened the "Vintage of the Century" and perhaps properly so, although a number of other years since then have laid claim to the same title. But 1959 marked a sort of turning-point: its crop was the largest that had been recorded in several decades (although the total has twice been surpassed since then), and the last year in which fine Burgundies were inexpensive. The white wines were too heavy and untrustworthy from the start, but the reds, almost without exception, were delicious and charming and ready to drink almost at once. These have developed as expected. The very finest '59s are still sound — even superb; the others should be drunk promptly — they are beginning to go downhill. 13/20 to 17/20.

Ten years is about the average life span of a "modern" Burgundy — they were sturdier, more tannic, longer-lived if perhaps less pleasing when differently vinified before the last War — and although some '52s, '49s and '45s are still *grandes bouteilles,* they should be purchased only in small lots and from sure suppliers.

WHITE BURGUNDY

1967, even more in white Burgundy than in red, was a year of astonishing contradictions and inconsistencies in which the variations and small disasters of local weather played an unusual and predominant role.

Thus a large part of the Maconnais was struck by a devastating frost in May, and three-quarters of its expected crop destroyed; meanwhile Chablis, 200 miles further north, was untouched and happily produced what are probably its best wines since World War II.

A number of villages suffered grave damage from hail-storms in July, others from heavy rains just before the vintage in September, but there was no pattern in all this, and many vintners found themselves with empty cellars or poor wine at the end of the season, while their neighbors, a hillside or two away, rejoiced.

Thus the '67s will have to be bought with a maximum of discrimination and care: they are worth it, for the best of them are superb.

Chablis: — in quantity, a little below average; in quality, absolutely extraordinary, easily better than 1966, itself a very great year. The wines, the Grand Crus especially, have a wonderful finesse and balance, superb bouquet; they are all lightness and grace and it is hard to see how they could be any better than they are. 19/20, at least.

Pouilly-Fuissé and Maconnais: a pitifully small crop (frost + hail), high quality and priced accordingly. 18/20.

Côte d'Or: *extremely* uneven and, unless bought from a sure source, best avoided. A few skillful and lucky producers nevertheless came up with some very fine wines. All the way from 11/20 to 17/20.

1966. An extremely great vintage, quite in a class with 1962 and 1961, far better than 1964. The Chablis are excellent, perhaps softer and less sprightly than the '67s, but with their full share of breed and balance. The Pouilly-Fuissés and other Maconnais whites are the best now on the market, consistently pleasing and fine, just now approaching their peak. They deserve 17/20 or 18/20.

However, it is the great Côte d'Or whites that make the 1966 vintage so memorable. With the celebrated '61s and '62s now hard to find, and all but the best of them showing signs of age, the 1966 Meursaults, Pulignys, Chassagnes and Montrachets are completely in a class apart. They are great treasures. 19/20.

1965. Best in Chablis, where the light, pale, crisp, very dry wines will delight those knowing drinkers who like their Chablis with these, its traditional characteristics. 15/20. A few Maconnais wines are both inexpensive and good.

1964. Uneven, running the whole gamut from great to fair. No more than passable in Chablis and Pouilly; best on the Côte d'Or where the best producers (and only the best producers) made some fine, ripe, very full-bodied wines, better than the 1959s but with many of the same faults. Now 13/20 to 15/20.

1963. Interesting today only for its Grand Cru Chablis. These were hard, even a little tart, when first made, but they have begun to come round and blossom wonderfully; they will hold for at least another four or five years and many true connoisseurs of Chablis now find them the best wines of all for present drinking. 15/20.

1962. A very great vintage. Wines now at their peak but hard to find. 16/20.

1961. An equally great, perhaps longer-lived year. The best wines still improving and sensationally good. *Grande classe.* 19/20.
    Few white Burgundies live out a decade, and although rare still-excellent bottles of 1960, 1959, 1957, 1952 and even 1949 can occasionally be found (most often in the cellars of their producers), the moment has come, alas!, to bid these old friends an affectionate adieu.

BEAUJOLAIS

1967. It is important to remember, especially when buying wine in the United States, that there exist two entirely different kinds of Beaujolais. Both are good if genuine and unblended (which is by no means always the case) but if you are looking for one sort, you are certain to be surprised and very probably disappointed if you get the other.
    The first is the light, fragrant, delicious *vin du pays* of the country just northwest of Lyon, best served cool, or at cellar temperature, and best drunk young — which means, in France, from two to nine months old. It runs from 10 to about 11½% alcohol, it is usually served as open or carafe wine in bistros, it is one of the few red wines which make pleasant drinking between meals, and it is about as likely to improve with keeping as fresh lettuce. It is rarely as good in Paris as it is where made, and it is useless to expect it to be as good in New York or Chicago or San Francisco as it is in Paris. If this is what you want, or some close approximation of it, *never* buy a Beaujolais over 18 months old, with two years as the extreme limit, stick to the less expensive wines, though from the best source you know, and give your preference to wines that carry one of the following appellations: Beaujolais, Beaujolais Villages, Chiroubles, St. Amour, possibly Brouilly.
    The second sort of Beaujolais is what might be called a much more "serious" wine; it represents an attempt to make, in the Beaujolais Country and from the Gamay grape, something that is almost, in its lesser category, a *grand vin*. Wines of this sort *can* be exported without too much risk, they *do* improve in bottle; they need not be expensive but usually cost from $2.50 to $4 and are worth it

if carefully chosen; they have the fruit and flavor and much of the charm which is Beaujolais' hallmark, but they never have quite the appeal of their lighter and more light-hearted cousins. In ascending order of body and excellence and probable long life, here are their appellations (you are advised to buy estate-bottlings wherever possible): Beaujolais Villages (preferably with a vineyard name), Brouilly, Chenas, Côte-de-Brouilly, Morgon, Julienas, Fleurie, Moulin-à-Vent.

1967 produced admirable wines in both categories in the Beaujolais. The lesser, lighter wines, the simple Beaujolais and notably the Chiroubles, are fresher, spicier, more "Beaujolais" than any that have come along in years, and even the excellent, well-balanced 1966s seem a little pedestrian in comparison. But do not expect to drink the bigger '67s at once or very soon: the really good ones, which have not been "pushed" but allowed to follow their natural evolution, are wines of great class and we must wait for them another year or so. Do not expect them to be cheap, for the '67 crop was a small one, and the French are quite as aware of their exceptional quality as we are. 19/20.

1966. A copious and very great year. Had a new, young champion not emerged, they would still deserve the highest sort of rating, and many wine-drinkers may still prefer them. The lesser wines are a bit softer and rounder than the '67s, less firm but more agreeable than the '64s. The so-called *Grand Crus* have developed splendidly in bottle, and are and will remain for at least a year by far the best Beaujolais that can be had. 17/20.

1965. Happily, no longer around. 11/20.

1964. The lesser wines have long since been drunk up. The bigger ones will improve for at least half a decade. 16/20.

COTES DU RHONE

1967. Produced some extremely good, full-bodied, very promising red wines which deserve 15/20; the whites and the *rosés* much less successful, far below those of 1966 in quality, rate perhaps 12/20.

1966. Of outstanding quality everywhere, from Lyon all the way down to the sea. The red Hermitages are of rare excellence, probably early-maturing but fine; the Châteauneuf-du-Pape is about the best since 1961; even the whites have unusual freshness and breed, and the *rosés* are the best of this present decade. Across the board, at least 18/20.

1965. Much better than in the rest of France. The red Châteauneuf-du-Pape is fruity, on the light side, ready to drink. 14/20.

1964. Has somewhat disappointed us in its evolution: the big-bodied red wines remain rather hard, and are less agreeable than the '66s and '62s. 15/20. The whites and *rosés* are now over the hill.

1963. Best forgotten. Under 10/20.

1962. An extremely good year which, as in red Burgundy, has surprised and delighted us. Red wines about 16/20 or 17/20.

1961. A very great vintage in red wines; the few that can still be found are of top class. 18/20.

Older wines. Few are genuine, but a few of these few are incomparable. Look for estate-bottlings of 1957 and 1952. Note that many of these have to be decanted or at least recorked before they are shipped, since most have thrown considerable sediment. Do not, therefore, allow your suspicions to be aroused if you find a new cork in an old bottle: it is the wine, not the cork, that tells the story.

LOIRE VALLEY

1967. The wines of the Loire, for some odd incomprehensible reason, are usually to be found under the heading "Etcetera" on lists of French wine, as if they were just a sort of afterthought. Americans may be surprised therefore to learn that Frenchmen drink more Anjou wine than they do Beaujolais, and more bottles a year of wines of the Loire than of Burgundy and Beaujolais and Maconnais put together. Vouvray outsells Chablis in France by about two-to-one, Muscadet outsells all white Burgundies put together, and the production of a rather obscure red wine called Chinon is greater than that of the whole township of Margaux. Frenchmen are generally excellent judges of the value of what they buy (incidentally, they buy twice as much, per capita, in the way of American goods as Americans buy of French); furthermore, they can certainly be expected to know the comparative value of their own wines. And yet, there is not in the whole Loire Valley a single vineyard of as much as 250 acres under one ownership. These little individual holdings are, most of them, farther north than Duluth, as far north as Newfoundland, and obviously they give good wine only when the weather is at least fairly favorable. Vintage years are therefore very important.

1967 turned out to be a superb year almost everywhere on the Loire, the dry white wines (Sancerre, Pouilly-Fumé, Vouvray, Muscadet, etc.) and the *vins rosés* are perhaps the best of this decade, fine, fresh light wines with a special spiciness and elegance, 18/20; the sweeter whites of Anjou and the reds of Chinon, Bourgueil and Champigny also very good, though not quite up to the '64s and '61s. Say 16/20.

1966, too, was a very good year, though less so here than in Bordeaux and Burgundy. About 15/20.

1965. Very poor and now no longer available. Hardly 10/20.

1964 produced remarkable red wines, not only excellent but still improving, and sweet white wines of *grande classe*, at least 17/20. The dry whites and the *rosés* now too old.

1963. Poor and gone.

Loire wines, on the whole, are so agreeable when they are young that they rarely get a chance to demonstrate how good they can be when they are a bit older. Yet the sweeter white wines of Anjou, the best Quarts de Chaume, for example, and certain Vouvrays, are certainly the longest-lived white wines of France: a Chateau de Belle Rive 1937, to mention one, tasted in May 1968, showed no signs of debility or old age; it was better than any Sauternes or Montrachets of the same age and quite in the class with a Trockenbeerenauslese from the Rhine. Some red wines, too, made from the Cabernet grape and, properly stored, seem to last almost indefinitely. Collectors of great rarities should be on look-out for surviving bottles of 1961, 1959, 1947, 1937 which are worth about whatever they cost and yet are sometimes surprisingly inexpensive.

1967. In geography, in climate, and of course in grape varieties as well, the Alsatian wine country, which overlooks the Rhine, has much more in common with Germany than with the rest of France. Its fragrant Rieslings and spicy Traminers, in their tall slim bottles, are basically Rhine wines however indubitably French; vintage years, in Alsace, tend to follow the German rather than the French pattern.

As might be expected, therefore, 1967 was a somewhat uneven but quite extraordinary year, in total yield below average, with many of the lesser wines disappointing; the best are possibly the best Alsatians of this decade, finer and more elegant than the highly-touted '64s and '59s, lower in alcohol, with more bouquet and breed. They should not be drunk too soon, fully deserve 18/20.

1966, however, was an excellent vintage too, perhaps even better than '67 on the average, but without the same or comparable peaks of quality. Say 16/20, which may be too conservative.

1965. Very poor. Hardly 10/20.

1964. Big, overpowering, heady wines, without much distinction or finesse, more suited to a peasant kermesse than a gourmet dinner. 14/20.

1963. A very large crop; pleasant small wines when they were young, now gone. 11/20.

1962. Fair to good, going off. 12/20.

1961. Has held surprisingly well. The best Rieslings and Gerwürztraminers are the wines than an Alsatian producer would serve today to a discriminating friend. At least 14/20.

1960. Gone, and no loss. Under 10/20.

1959. Even the best are only curiosities by now. Too heavy to start with. With rare exceptions, not over 13/20.

CHAMPAGNE

A detailed vintage chart for Champagne cannot help being a little ridiculous: in five years out of ten the wine never even pretends to go to the consumer in an unblended state, and admittedly would be less good if it did; and what proportion of which vintage goes into a non-vintage Champagne is a well-kept trade secret.

It is certainly more sensible, therefore, to reserve comment on what might be called the "buried" years — those that disappeared into the non-vintage — and discuss only those that have been or are likely to be presented as *millésimes:* 1967, 1966, 1964, 1962, 1961, 1959, 1955 and 1952.

Although all Champagne drinkers should be aware of the fact by now, it may be just as well to say *once more* that although *the best Champagnes improve greatly with age in bottle, even for as much as fifteen years, when stored* sur pointe *or en masse, cork down, before disgorging, in the cellars where they are made, hardly any Champagne improves for more than a year or two once it has been disgorged and shipped. There presumably exist in Epernay and Reims small reserves of undisgorged 1952 wine of extraordinary freshness, coupled with maturity and rare quality, but the same 1952 wine, disgorged and shipped in 1955 or even 1960, is now over the hill. Whatever stories you may have been told, or however excellent your cellar, it is simply folly to buy Champagne to lay away, or to buy a Champagne over seven or eight years old unless you can be sure it has just been disgorged, and this is exceedingly unlikely.*

The whole Champagne business has changed beyond all recognition over the past two decades. Before World War I, and even World War II, the French exported not far from three-quarters of what they made; the total production has greatly increased, yet the French themselves now drink nearly three-quarters of it. What is made today is largely made for the French internal market, where it commands at least as high prices as we ourselves are prepared to pay. The French like their Champagne young, will rarely pay a premium for a vintage, particularly an older vintage, and whether we like it or not, apart from certain selected *cuvées* and special expensive bottlings (sometimes, but not always, worth what they cost), vintage Champagne may well, before long, be a thing of the past.

Meanwhile:

1967 and 1966.   Both surely outstanding. Legally, must be three years old before they are shipped. Buy and enjoy them as soon as they come on the market. At least 17/20.

1964.   Rather on the heavy side. 15/20.

1962 and 1961.   The best of what is now available. The '62s are lighter, finer, with more bouquet; the '61s better balanced and greater wines. 18/20.

1959.   Heavy, often dull. 14/20.

1955 and 1952.   Both very great years, originally over 18/20, now ?/20.

III.   GERMANY

RHINE AND MOSELLE

1967.   German wines, when they are very young, have the same sort of fresh, gay, joyous charm as very young children. They are still unruly, and sometimes sparkle when they are not expected to; they are still plump and roly-poly with their baby fat (or baby sweetness in the case of wine). One is tempted to say that they would be at their best with pablum or with porridge; they are sunny, lovable little fellows, never a bit sullen or ill-tempered or withdrawn, like young red Burgundies and young red Bordeaux. They seem to belong in a perpetual kindergarden (which, by the way, is a German word) and it is easy to suppose that they will never be as nice again, once they grow up.

Today it is apparently fashionable to treat all German wines in this way — rush them from press to glass-lined tank to bottling-line and shipping carton, rush them from dockside to retailer to customer to dinner-table, all in a space of months. Everything possible is done to preserve their youthfulness and prevent their becoming adults — storage in glass or plastic rather than the more costly and maturing oak, sulphur and sterile bottling instead of patience and time, a "just arrived" sale instead of a year or two in the wine-merchant's cellar. "Taste the wine we just bought," at the dinnertable, instead of, "here is a bottle we have been saving for a special occasion like today."

There are plenty of German wines, of course, which deserve nothing better than this, but the greatest German wines are quite certainly the greatest white wines in

435

the world. They merit and will overwhelmingly repay a little more patience and a little more care. Those who have only tasted them in their extreme youth can have no idea of their real excellence. Let us hope that when the 1967s arrive, they will be given a better chance to show themselves.

1967, on the Rhine, was a very great year, the best, without much question, since 1959, and deserves a rating of 18/20, possibly even 19/20. For the first time in nearly a decade there was a great deal of Edelfäule, that "noble mould" which gives to the best Auslesen, Beerenauslesen and Trockenbeerenauslesen, their unique elegance and almost overpowering fruit. Even the lesser '67s have much of the same spiciness and breed. No less in the Pfalz and Hessia than in the Rheingau, they are beauties and should be given time to develop their extraordinary bouquet.

On the Moselle, 1967 was a great year too, perhaps not quite up to '64, but in the same noble class. 16/20.

1966. Heavy rains in early October ruined what seemed destined to be a superlative vintage, and no Rhine wines of the very highest category were produced; on the other hand their average quality is superb, better even than in 1964; they are just beginning to develop and will certainly improve for at least five or six years. 17/20.

On the Moselle, a little less remarkable. Say 16/20.

1965. A copious year that produced good *verbesserte* wines, but almost no *Naturweine* at all; the former deserve 14/20, the latter, at best, 11/20.

1964. Excellent, rather full-bodied Rhine wines, now reaching their splendid peak of maturity. 16/20. Moselles and Saar wines of surpassing quality, the best since the incomparable '59s; fresh, sprightly, still improving, the finer Spätlesen and Auslesen rate 18/20 or possibly 19/20 and nothing that '66 or '67 can provide is likely to equal them.

1963. Fairly good but uneven. Exceptionally good *verbesserte* wines were made, especially on the Saar and Ruwer and in the Rheingau. 12/20.

1962. Mature, pleasant wines, dry, clean, appetizing; preferred by most Germans to the spectacular youngsters. 14/20.

1961. Another sound, good year featured today on a majority of German wine lists. 13/20.

1960. Poor. Now off the market. 8/20, if that.

1959. An exceedingly great and classic year, unsurpassed since the last war, comparable to 1921 in quality. The lesser wines are of course past their prime and no longer available; the best are at their peak. This is particularly true of the Saar, Ruwer, and certain select wines of the Mittel-Mosel, which fully merit 19/20.

There exist in a few connoisseurs' and many wine producers' cellars priceless bottles of older German wines, Auslesen, Beerenauslesen and Trokenbeerenauslesen for the most part. Many of these are quite astonishingly good, even some dating from before the First World War. Of course they are no longer commercially available.

IV.   ITALY

Vintage years, on most Italian wines, are not to be taken too seriously, and, as a matter of fact, few Italian wines improve materially in bottle, at least after the first year or two. The exceptions, all of them red, are mostly wines made from the Nebbiolo grape *(see)* in Lombardy and more especially Piedmont: Barolo, Barbaresco, Gattinara and Valtellina (Inferno, Sassella, Grumelio, etc.). For these, the best recent vintages are: 1967, 1966, 1964, 1962, 1961, 1958, 1957, 1956, 1955.

Valpolicella, one of the most delightful of wines, does not improve as much in bottle as many of its champions like to claim. Six or seven years is more or less its extreme life span, the best years for present consumption are 1964, 1966, 1967.

In *Classico* Chianti, notably the wines shipped in ordinary bottles rather than *fiaschi*, the outstanding years are, at present, 1966, 1964, 1962, 1961, with 1967 to follow.

V. SPAIN

Only in one small corner of Spain, which is, as almost might be expected, close to the French border, are wines produced which are more or less properly vintaged and which deserve this treatment. This is the Rioja district, about a hundred miles southwest of Biarritz and San Sebastian. All too little known, the Rioja produces some more than passable white wines, and some of the most remarkable red wines of Europe. The best of these can stand comparative tasting against the best of France, and a few of them, thirty years ago, used to bring as high prices in New York as Chateau Margaux.

Unfortunately, there is no organized system of chateau- or estate-bottling here in Spain; almost every producer buys grapes from his neighbors to supplement his own production, and often makes several quite different qualities of wine in any given vintage. The less noteworthy lots are aged and bottled and marketed normally, when four or five years old, whereas the more outstanding *cuvées* are given more time in wood plus a good many years in bottle, and emerge ten or fifteen or twenty years later, as "Reservas," often under a different label and at a higher price. The following recent vintages have given wines of exceptional quality (the last five, by now, are of course in the "Reserva" class): 1966, 1964, 1962, 1961, 1958, 1955, 1952, 1949, 1948, 1947.

When it comes to all other Spanish table wines, with the most rare exceptions, buy the most recent vintage: it will be the best.

VI. PORTUGAL

With the unique and splendid exception of Vintage Port, Portuguese wines hardly ever carry a vintage; when they do, this is much more in the nature of a not entirely dependable statement of age than any sort of indication of superior quality. It is one of the charms of Portuguese table wines — Vinho Verde, Dão, Collares, as well as the ever more popular rosés — that they do not take themselves too seriously.

Port, of course, is another matter, Vintage Port especially. In this case, the good years of the Nineteen-Sixties will probably be of more interest to our children than to ourselves, since the following great vintages should *only* be purchased for laying down: 1955, 1958, 1960, 1963.

The following are considered more or less ready. Those from before World War II are practically unprocurable. 1927, 1931, 1934, 1935, 1942, 1945, 1947, 1948, 1950, 1954.

APPENDIX 7

SERVING WINE

ABOUT WINE GLASSES

All good wines taste better in thin, stemmed, crystal glasses, preferably uncut, and as simple in design as possible. The color of the wine can be better judged when it is so served, and the wine seems to taste better in thin rather than heavy glass.

Shown below are eight glasses of American crystal designed by Frank Schoonmaker along the traditional lines that have been used by European glass producers for generations.

Any one of the three in the first series shown below could well serve as a single, all-purpose glass, or the first and third as a pair — the larger for red wine and the smaller for white.

| 10 oz. | 9 oz. | 8 oz. |
| Red wine | Single, all-purpose | White wine |

Other recommended shapes are as follows:

| 10½ oz. | 9 oz. | 6 oz. | 5 oz. | 7 oz. |
| For great red Burgundies | For Champagnes, sparkling wines | For Rhines, Moselles, Alsatian wines, etc. | For Sherry, Port, Madeira, etc. | For fine brandy, cordials, liqueurs |

Note: These glasses, of course, are not intended to be filled to the brim — no more than one-third to one-half full.

439

THE CLASSIC WINE-AND-FOOD AFFINITIES

A good many hundred million people drink wine daily, wherever wine is made, in the temperate zones of both hemispheres. This is mostly the inexpensive product of their own local vineyards, and as much a part of their ordinary diet as all the rest — meat, fish, vegetables, fruit and bread. Most wine-lovers and almost all true experts have a high regard for such *ordinaires,* and enjoy drinking them, always providing they are honest and well-made, which is often, but not always, the case. But such wines are staples, and apart from the general principle of moderation, they should be drunk exactly as one wishes to drink them: there are no rules. Most French and Italian peasants, lunching in the fields or vineyards, drink them straight from the bottle, and Spaniards, as often as not, out of *porrones,* or leather flasks. At home, they are sometimes served in tumblers, often diluted with water, or, in cafés, with soda water. They are generally, both red wines and white, chilled or at least cooled (in a well or a brook or a cellar) in hot weather; and, both red wines and white, served at the prevailing temperature at all other times. And this is as it should be.

Wines of superior class are another matter: they are ALWAYS the result of a special effort on the part of the producer, who has planted certain select varieties of vines on chosen hillsides where they yield less per acre, but better wine. Such producers are dedicated artisans, and in some instances true artists. It is with what they make that this volume is principally concerned.

At the risk of sounding arbitrary, or possibly even pompous, it can be said that these wines should be treated with the respect and care which the knowledge and skill and love which have gone into their production, fully merit and have copiously earned. No hard-and-fast rules govern their service, and what is given below is no more than the accumulated preferences of a good many generations of knowledgeable wine-drinkers. Much additional information will be found elsewhere in this Encyclopedia — *see* Glasses, Serving, Temperature, etc., etc.

440

WITH	SERVE	Temperature
Caviar	Champagne	Iced
Smoked salmon, olives, almonds, canapés, etc. as an apéritif	Dry Sherry, Montilla, Manzanilla, dry Madeira, Champagne	Well chilled
Oysters	Chablis, dry Graves, Muscadet, Pinot Blanc	Well chilled
Clams	Montilla, Manzanilla, dry Sherry, Pinot Blanc	Well chilled
Consommé or turtle soup	Madeira or medium Sherry, or no wine at all	Room temperature
Bisques, and other cream soups	Whatever white wine is to follow	Chilled
Heavy, vegetable soups, *pot-au-feu*, oxtail, etc.	Whatever red wine is to follow	Room temperature
Outdoor, cold buffet in summer	*Vin rosé*	Well chilled
Barbecue — chicken	*Vin rosé*, light, dry white wine	Well chilled
Barbecue — beef	Beaujolais, Zinfandel	Cool
Fish — poached, grilled or *meunière* — Crabs, lobsters	Light white Burgundy as Pouilly-Fuissé or dry Graves or Alsatian. Moselle — Soave. California Riesling	Chilled
More complex fish or shellfish dishes	Fuller white Burgundy, as Meursault. Graves; Rheingau wine.	Chilled
Cold fowl or cold meats	Gewürztraminer or California Pinot Chardonnay.	
Chicken or Turkey	*Either,* fuller white wine as above or, perhaps preferably, light red Bordeaux, California Cabernet	Chilled Room temperature
Roast Ham or Pork	Not too dry a white wine, *vin rosé*	Chilled
Veal, sweetbreads, etc.	Lighter red Bordeaux, Beaujolais, California Cabernet	Room temperature
Lamb	Fine red Bordeaux, California Cabernet	Room temperature
Beef, pheasant, etc.	St. Émilion or Pomerol — lighter red Burgundy, California Cabernet or Pinot Noir. Italian reds as Barbaresco, Barolo, Classico Chianti	Room temperature
Stews, pot roast, etc.	Beaujolais, Côtes-du Rhone, California Zinfandel or Gamay	Room temperature or cool
Stews, ragouts, prepared with wine	Full-flavored red wine — Burgundy, Rhône, California Pinot Noir	Room temperature
Game, as venison, wild duck, also steak	Burgundy, Hermitage, Chateauneuf-du-Pape, Pinot Noir, Barolo	Room temperature
Salad	No wine	
Cheese	Full-bodied red wine. Big Bordeaux, Burgundy, Rhône. Pinot Noir	Room temperature
Dessert — pastries Fruit, as pears	Sweet Sauternes, Anjou, Rhine Beerenauslesen, etc. Champagne	Well chilled
Walnuts, etc.	Port, sweet Madeira, sweet Sherry	Room temperature

GREAT OR EXCEPTIONAL WINES

Occasions may arise when one will wish to present to fellow wine enthusiasts rare bottles of wholly extraordinary quality, and it is often better in such cases to plan the menu around the wines, rather than vice versa.

Listed below are the dishes which are likely to enable wines of different categories to be shown at their best.

	Temperature	WITH
Dry Sherry of highest quality	50°	Slightly salted almonds and hazel nuts
Old dry Madeira	Room temp.	Terrapin, partly in honor of a great tradition
Old sweet Madeira	Room temp.	Alone or with walnuts after dinner
Dry white Bordeaux	50° — 55°	Sole with a sauce or Turbot *mousseline*
Grand Cru Chablis	55°	Oysters or cold fowl
Montrachet, Batard Montrachet, Corton Charlemagne, Meursault, etc.	55°	Special fish dish or lobster
Great vintage Médoc or red Graves	Room. temp.	Rack or leg of lamb, rare (no mint sauce, of course)
St. Émilion, Pomerol	Room. temp.	Steak, roast beef, pheasant, cheese
Great red Côte de Beaune Burgundy	60° — 68°	Guinea hen, pheasant, cheese
Great Côte de Nuits Burgundy	Room temp.	Beef, wild duck, cheese
Exceptional red Rhône wine	60° — 68°	Wild duck, woodcock, goat cheese
Champagne	Iced — 50° or less	Before or after a meal. All cold dishes
Great Sauternes, white Anjous of a great vintage	50°	Pastry or soufflé carefully chosen
Moselles of up to and including Auslese quality	55°	Trout *au bleu* or grilled Sole
Very finest Moselles of great years	60°	Alone, after a light dinner
Rhine wines of up to and including Spatlese quality	50° — 55°	Fish, chicken
Very finest Rhine Auslesen, Beerenauslesen, etc.	60°	Light pastry, soufflé, or alone after dinner
Old Barolo, Gattinara	Room temp.	Beef or game, cheese
Barbaresco, etc.	60° — 68°	Veal, cheese
Exceptional Chianti	60° — 68°	Beef or veal, cheese
Vintage Port	Room temp.	Alone or with walnuts after dinner

NOTE: Room Temperature is intended to mean 65° to 72°. No fine wine should be served at over 72° under any circumstances.

442